CORPORATE
SHOWCASE 6
PHOTOGRAPHY, ILLUSTRATION & GRAPHIC DESIGN

American Showcase, Inc.
New York

President and Publisher
Ira Shapiro

Vice President
Advertising Sales
Julia Martin

Vice-President
Operations
Wendl Kornfeld

Associate Publisher
Chris Curtis

Production Director
Kyla Kanz

Administration

Executive Assistant
Connie Grunwald
Controller
Ronald Durr
Accounting Assistant
Soraya Acosta

Marketing

Book Sales Manager
Ann Middlebrook
Promotion/Publicity Manager
Deborah Lovell
Book Sales/Shipping Coordinator
Joe Alvira

Advertising Sales

Sales Manager/Mail Service Manager
Lisa Wilker
Sales Representatives
New York
**John Bergstrom, Deborah Darr,
Barbara Preminger,
Wendy Saunders**
Rocky Mountain
Kate Hoffman
(303) 493-1492
West Coast
Bob Courtman
(213) 669-8021

Production

Production Manager
Stephanie Sherman
Production Coordinator
Katherine van Kessel
Grey Pages/Distribution Manager
Scott Holden
Traffic
Chuck Rosenow
Production Assistant
Stacey Dale Tappis

Published by
American Showcase, Inc.
724 Fifth Avenue, 10th Floor
New York, New York 10019
Telephone: (212) 245-0981
Telex: 880356 AMSHOW P

Corporate Showcase 6
0931144-46-9

ISSN 0742-9975

Book Design and Mechanical Production
Downey, Weeks & Toomey, Inc., NYC

Grey Pages Mechanical Production
The Mike Saltzman Group, NYC

Typesetting
**Ultra Typographic Service, Inc., NYC
Automatech Graphics Corporation, NYC**

Color Separation, Printing and Binding
Dai Nippon Printing Co. Ltd., Tokyo, Japan

Cover Credits

Cover Design: Downey Weeks & Toomey, Inc., NYC

Front Cover Photograph: Gabe Palmer

Title Page Illustration: David FeBland

U.S. Book Trade Distribution
Watson-Guptill Publications
1515 Broadway, New York, New York 10036
(212) 764-7300
Watson-Guptill ISBN: 8230-0951-3

For Sales Outside U.S.
Rotovision S.A.
10 Rue De L'Arquebuse
1211 Geneve 11, Switzerland
Telephone: (22) 212121
Telex: 421479 ROVI

CORPORATE
SHOWCASE 6
PHOTOGRAPHY, ILLUSTRATION & GRAPHIC DESIGN

Contents

Viewpoints

Graphic Arts Organizations

Grey Pages

Indexes

Alphabetical Listing
Illustrators, Photographers & Graphic Designers

SATISFY YOUR CREATIVE HUNGER

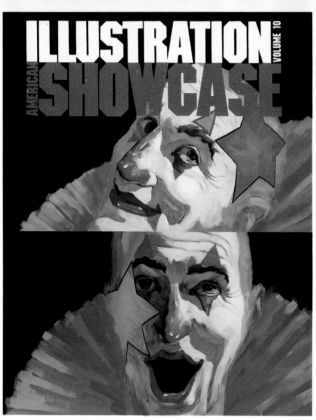

Feast Your Eyes on the Year's Best Illustration and Photography

Illustration

Do your writers, designers and photographers snarl at you? Are they ready to "kill all the lawyers" by the time a PR project is printed? If you see yourself here, maybe it's time for some new thinking...

When it comes to public relations and whether it's done in house or "out house," the argument is much like that of mothers working in versus outside the home. Each side has reasons why its approach is best, why the other guy's is not quite up to speed. I can't tell you how many times, for example, I've been met with that long, patronizing silence when I tell "annual report consultants" that we do everything but print in house; the pity (or is it disdain?) drips right through the telephone receiver.

I don't always care what "consultants" think, but I *do* care what top management thinks. And, frankly, what they think doesn't exactly give me those warm, cuddly feelings. Somewhere in the exclusive handbook of many corporations (some are wonderfully enlightened, of course, but let's be realistic) there must be a set of axioms for "handling" public relations. It must go something like this.

Axiom 1.

An outside PR consultant will do a better job than your in-house PR staff.

The consultant charges BIG BUCKS so it must be good, right? You and I may know that anyone can set himself (or herself) up as a public relations consultant, but do our top executives know that? Of course not. In the scheme of most corporations, the public relations function and its practitioners stand somewhat above housekeeping. It's difficult to show a direct bottom-line result so it's hard to prove its contribution to the organization.

Corporate officers need to *listen* to their PR people and take their advice as seriously as they do the advice of their lawyers and accountants. Their PR people are professionals, too; they keep up with trends in communication and design, and they know your company better than anyone on the outside. You hired them for their abilities and experience—get your money's worth.

Since outsiders are professionals, give them the time and attention necessary for them to produce a good product. Your in-house people don't need the same.

It's always amazing to me that top officers will take time (and lots of it) from their busy schedules to sit for photographs and be interviewed by outside writers. If they're dealing with in-house people, however, they're always in a big hurry to rush off. Is it any wonder when you get snapshots instead of portraits, or speeches and stories that don't accurately reflect your thinking?

Axiom 2.

Public relations, design and photography is something anyone can do (and do it better than your in-house staff). Never hesitate to second-guess them.

Do you "improve" on your lawyers' briefs and work? Do you "finesse" your accountants' numbers? Of course not. They're the experts and you trust them to do their jobs.

So why not accept the advice of your in-house PR people—after all, you're paying them to give you their best.

Let's be brutally honest—a lot of people cannot recognize technical quality in design and photography when they see it. And that's fine because it's not their job. But it *is* the job of your design and PR people.

When they recommend a particular photo or design format for a job such as the annual report, there's a lot more involved than meets *your* eye... sheer technical quality, composition, compatibility with format and theme as well as subject matter, compliance with safety requirements of situations portrayed and representational balance (do our photos show only middle-aged white males?).

Axiom 3.

A deadline's a deadline, except when you don't feel like meeting it.

Projects such as annual reports and other publications always come laden with deadlines that are essential if a project is ever to see the light of day. When press time is scheduled, it's like entering into a contract; if you don't uphold your end, the other party doesn't have to comply. And if we miss our press slot on, say, the annual report, the SEC could be breathing down *all* our necks.

Sure, we build in a little cushion in any production schedule but let's not get carried away. If the chairman gave you a deadline on a project, would you tell him (or her), "Gee, we haven't gotten it together yet, we need another week"? Of course not. Think of PR's printing deadlines in the same light.

Continued on page 28

Mark E. Alsop

324 Auburndale Avenue
Auburndale,
Massachusetts 02166
(617) 527-7862

Technical and Scientific
Illustration: specializing in full
color and three-point
perspective art

In-house CAD system

Member of the Graphic
Artists Guild

Clients include:

IBM/BTU Engineering
Lockheed
Honeywell
Epson
Millipore
Galileo Electro-Optics
Ortho Diagnostic Systems
Damon
Microsoft Press
Sail Magazine
High Technology Magazine
PC Tech Journal
Country Journal
The Boston Globe
Harvard Medical School

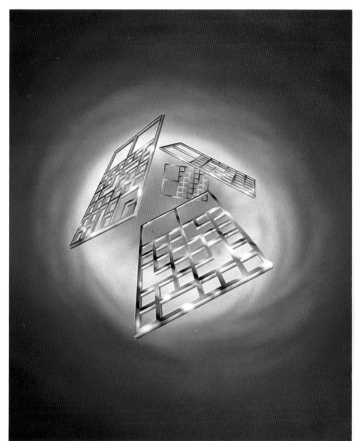

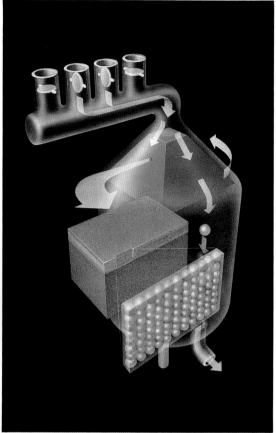

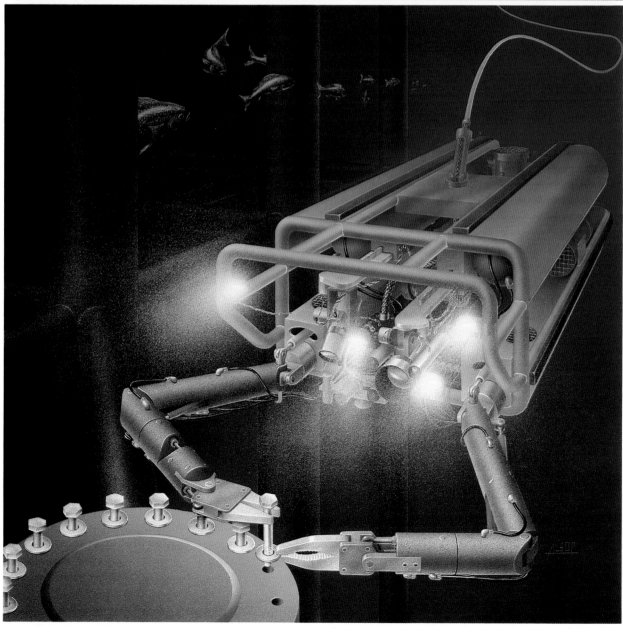

Ron Barrett

2112 Broadway
Room 402A
New York, New York 10023
(212) 874-1370

Represented in the
Southeast by:
Phelps & Jones
(404) 264-0264

Represented on the
West Coast by:
Funny Farm
(213) 204-6401

Represented elsewhere
in The Free World
by himself.

Represented for animation
by The Ink Tank
(212) 869-1630

Shown at right:
Sony Information Systems,
BMW, Sony Audio Products,
Chemical Bank.

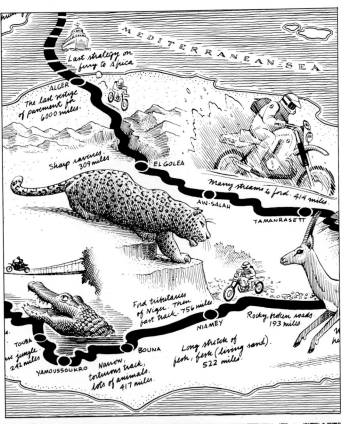

Andrea Baruffi
341 Hudson Terrace
Piermont, New York 10968
(914) 359-9542

Clare
Vanacore
Brooks

Represented by:
Lou Brooks Productions, Inc.

415 West 55th Street
New York, New York 10019
(212) 245-3632

Fine acrylic paintings and
illustrations of technological and
architectural landscapes.

Clients include:
Allied Chemical Company
Bell Atlantic
Commonwealth & Gas Co.
Eastern Gas & Fuel Association
First National Oil Brokers, Inc.
BF Goodrich
Peat, Marwick, Mitchell and Co.
Provident National Bank

Portfolio showing
available by appointment.

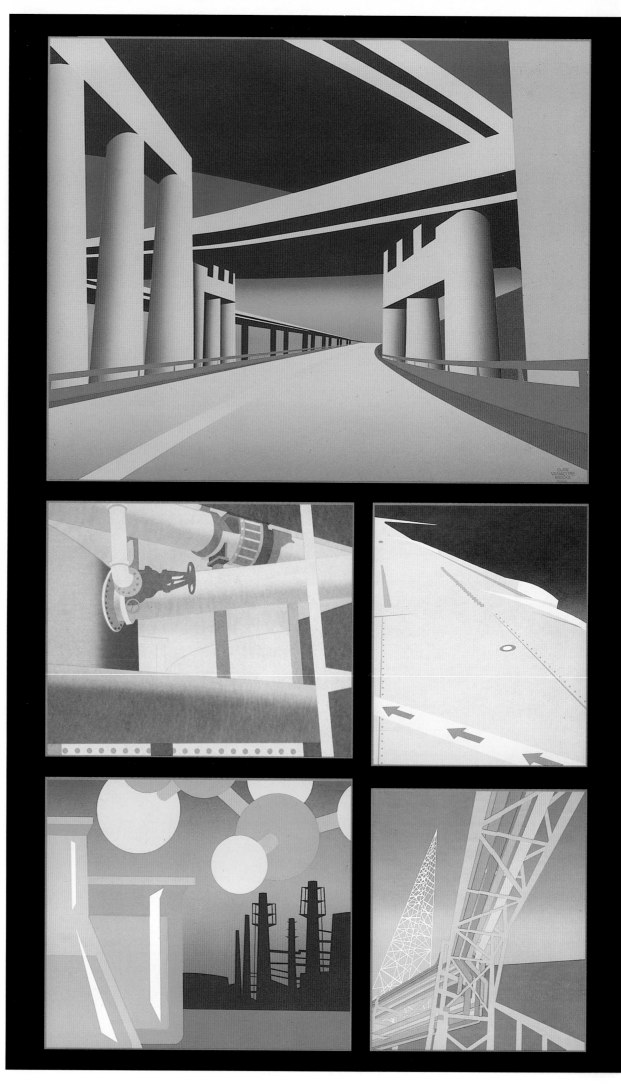

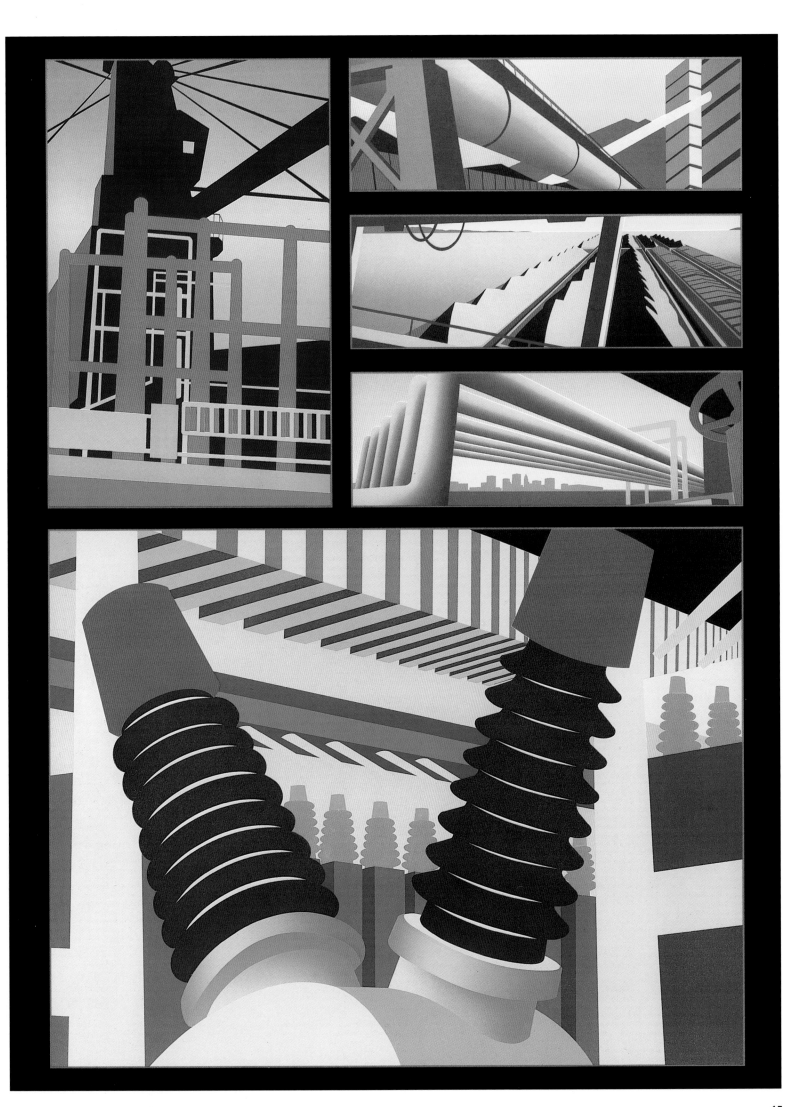

Coddbarrett Associates, Inc.

65 Ashburton Street
Providence, Rhode Island 02904
(401) 273-9898

Suite 209
230 Western Avenue
Boston, Massachusetts 02134
(617) 254-8878

Coddbarrett has been producing award winning 2D and 3D graphic illustrations, solid modeling and animation pieces for over five years. Coddbarrett sells and supports the same computer graphics systems used in production.

Major clients include:
Lotus Development Corporation, Shawmut Bank, WGBH, Dun and Bradstreet, Metropolitan Property and Liability Insurance

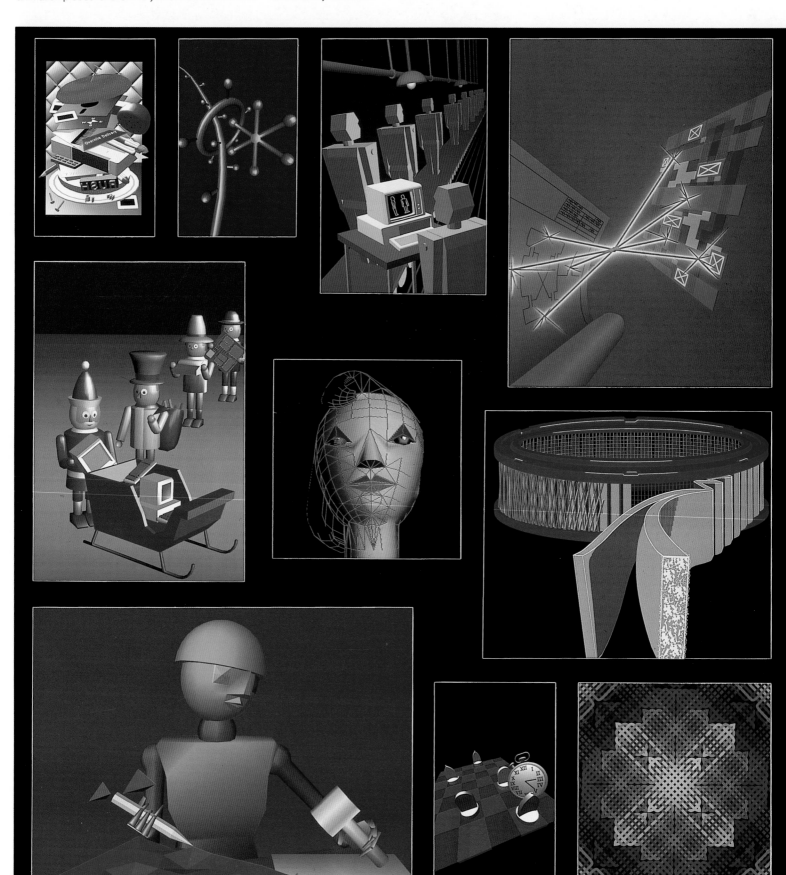

Frank Collyer

R.R. 1, Box 266
Stony Point, New York 10980
(914) 947-3050

Member Graphic Artists Guild

I can't solve any tax problems,
but if you need art with wit
and humor for the corporate
viewpoint, give me a call.
My pens, brushes and I have
a million miles of illustrative
experience, and we're just an
hour from Times Square!

Greg Couch

112 Willow Street #5A
Brooklyn, New York 11201
(718) 625-1298

Clients include:
Time Inc., Forbes, Fortune, Business Week, Ziff-Davis
Publishing, Industry Week, BBDO Direct, N.W. Ayer,
Chiat Day, DFS Dorland, Ogilvy Mather, Mobil Corp.,
Drexel Burnham Lambert, Toyota Motor Sales, DuPont,
Sandoz Pharmaceutical.

Member Graphic Artists Guild

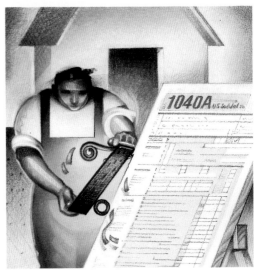

Walter Einsel

26 South Morningside Drive
Westport, Connecticut 06880
(203) 226-0709

Walter Einsel has been creating interesting three-dimensional graphic solutions for distinguished clients in exhibitions, TV commercials, annual reports, advertising and editorial.

A partial list of clients: ABC, Allied Van Lines, AT&T, The Bank of New York, Blue Cross, British Airways, CBS, Champion Papers, GE, General Foods, Gilbey's, Golf Digest, IBM, International Paper, Macy's, Medical Economics, Merrill-Lynch, NBC, Prudential, RCA, Readers Digest, Smithsonian, Tennis, U.S. National Parks Service, U.S. Postal Service. His work has received numerous awards from the AD Club of NY, AIGA, and the Society of Illustrators.

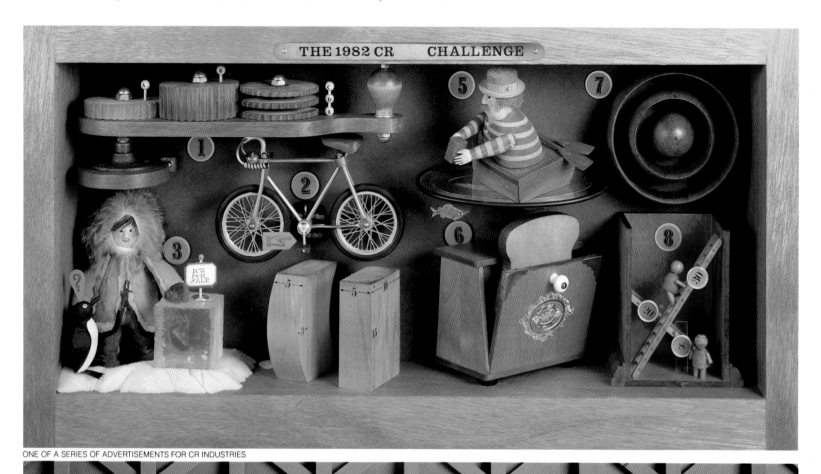

ONE OF A SERIES OF ADVERTISEMENTS FOR CR INDUSTRIES

FROM A BROCHURE FOR INTERNATIONAL PAPER

Richard Ely

Represented by
Erika Becker
150 West 55th Street
New York, New York 10019
(212) 757-8987

Richard Ely's portraits are in the permanent collections of the Smithsonian Institution; Metropolitan Museum of Art; Metropolitan Opera Guild; Museum of the City of New York; Lotos Club, New York; Museum of American Illustration, New York; Memorial Art Gallery at the University of Rochester.

Exhibiting during 1987 at the following Galleries:
LONDON   Fisher Fine Art Ltd.
NEW YORK   Gallery Josephine
PARIS   Galerie Colombier
TOKYO   Graphic-sha Gallery

Portfolio available on request.

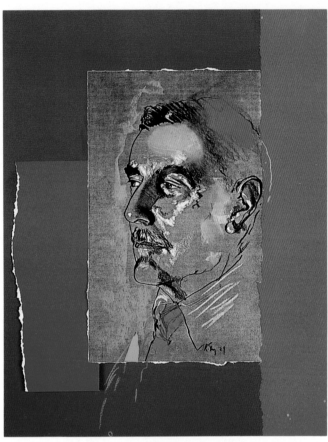

David Fe Bland

670 West End Avenue
New York, New York 10025
(212) 580-9299

Clients include:

ABC; American Express; AT&T; Avis; Avon Products; Bankers Trust; Benton & Bowles; Bloomingdales; CBS; California Federal Bank; Celanese; Chase Manhattan Bank; Dancer Fitzgerald Sample; Disneyland; Dutch Tourist Board; E. F. Hutton; Exxon; General Foods; Gimbels; Grey; HBO; IBM; Intercontinental Hotels; Izod; J. Walter Thompson; Lever Brothers; Macy's; Montgomery Ward; NBC; N. W. Ayer; New York Air; Ogilvy & Mather; People Express; Revlon; RCA; Sears Roebuck; Scali, McCabe Sloves; Sony; Texaco; T.V. Guide; TWA; Vista Hotels; Young & Rubicam.
© David Fe Bland 1987

Awards & Exhibitions.

Art Directors Annual
Art Direction Creativity
Graphis
Print
Advertising Techniques

Member Graphic Artists Guild

Jack Graber

Represented by:
Walter Supley, Jr.
the Creative Advantage
707 Union Street
Schenectady, New York 12305
(518) 370-0312

William Grant
4114 Highland Avenue
Brooklyn, New York 11224
(718) 996-3555

Jakesevic/Lamut

Nenad Jakesevic
Sonja Lamut

Represented by

Barbara Gordon
Associates

165 East 32nd Street
New York, New York 10016
(212) 686-3514

Artists also have a large selection of stock artwork
available.

Joyce Kitchell Illustration
2755 Eagle Street
San Diego, California 92103
(619) 291-1378

·JOYCE KITCHELL·

ILLUSTRATION
619·291·1378

Franck Levy

(212) 557-8256

Represented by Les Klein (212) 490-1460

1986 clients include:
Grey/IBM
McCann-Erickson/Coca-Cola
Jordan, Manning, Case, Taylor & McGrath/Hanes
Ogilvy & Mather/AT&T

Member of the Society of Illustrators

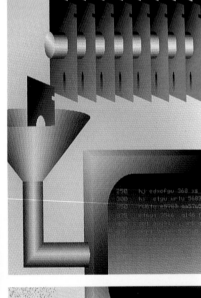
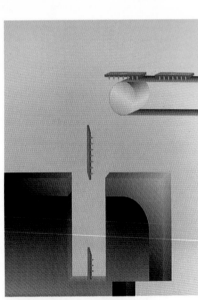
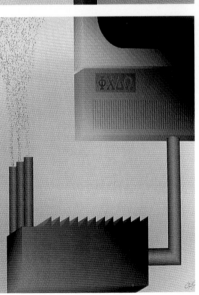
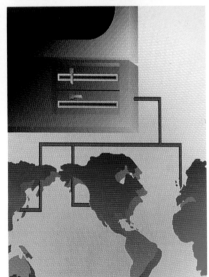

Michael McCurdy

145 Lake Buel Road
Great Barrington, Massachusetts 01230
(413) 528-5036 or (413) 528-2749

Wood engraving for distinctive illustration.

Partial client list:
Sara Lee Corporation, H.J. Heinz Company, Esquire, Personal Computing, Country Journal, Americana, Dodd, Mead & Company, Prentice-Hall, Inc., Little, Brown & Company, Houghton Mifflin Company, Sierra Club Books, Atlantic Monthly Press, Globe Pequot Press, University of Georgia Press, University of Ohio Press.

Best Illustrated Adult Trade Book, New England Book Show, 1986

One of Best Illustrated Children's Books, New York Times, 1986

Bronze Medal, Leipzig International Book Competition, 1983

Continued from page 10

Axiom 4.

Corporate pronouncements should be written for people with college-level reading skills—or—complex subjects deserve complex discussions.

You may understand your press releases when they're written by the attorneys but you have a distinct advantage. The typical reporter—and the typical reader—doesn't have the benefit of your inside knowledge. Chances are that the reporter will be calling your PR people—assuming he or she wasn't utterly turned off by your obscure message—for a real-world explanation.

Part of the PR department's job is taking complicated company issues and actions and making them understandable to the general public. You can't get a favorable reaction from people who don't understand your message.

Those of us who "do" PR for a living know that effective public relations practice includes a significant advisory role.

We know better than the attorneys the potential reaction—by the media and the public—to an event, announcement or suspicious silence; after all, we're the ones who talk with reporters and John and Jane Q. Public every day. Many of us also were on the other side as reporters at one time or another and got our share of laughs from poorly written or obscure releases.

While our efforts typically don't result in generating revenues, the advice we can offer *can* contribute to that sometimes-vague concept of goodwill that includes perceptions of honesty, integrity and fairness. In many cases, that's every bit as valuable as cold, hard cash!

We are part of the corporate team and we want to do our part to help meet our company's goals. And isn't that exactly what we *all* should be working toward.

Magda A. Ratajski
Vice President, Public Relations
Norfolk Southern Corporation
Norfolk, Virginia

Jacqui Morgan

315 East 58th Street
New York, New York 10022
(212) 421-0766

Watercolor

Represented in Germany by:
Meyer-Norten Group
089/986230

Clients include: Architectural
Digest, AT&T, Avon, American
Home Products, Booz Allen &
Hamilton, Burlington Mills,
Busch Gardens, Champion
Papers, Colgate Palmolive,
Eastern Airlines, Franklin Watts,
General Electric, General Foods,
Hilton Int'l, Holland American,
IBM, ITC, Irving Trust, Johnson
Wax, Macmillan, NBC, New York
Magazine, New York Times,
Pfiser, Playboy, Prentice-Hall,
Procter & Gamble, RCA, Sansui,
Scott Paper Co.

Works Exhibited in: Arras
Gallery, Linden Gallery, NYC,
Gallery 99, Fla., Smithsonian
Institute, Washington D.C.,
London, Munich, Tokyo, Warsaw.
Also seen in: Graphis, Print
Magazine, Gebrauchs Graphik,
American Artist, Society of
Illustrator's Annuals, Society of
Publication Designers & Art
Directors Annuals.

Listed in Who's Who in Graphic
Art. Winner of VI Warsaw Int'l
Poster Biennale. Author of
Watercolor for Illustration,
Watson-Guptill & *Wet-in-Wet*
watercolor instruction videos,
Twenty-Two Productions, NY.

Note: American Showcase
#8, 9, & 10.

Member Graphic Artists Guild

Donald Moss

DESIGN FOR SPORTS
232 Peaceable Street
Ridgefield, Connecticut 06877
(203) 438-5633

Life Member:
Society of Illustrators

Board Member:
National Art Museum of Sport

"SPORTS ARTIST OF THE YEAR"—U.S. Sports Academy
"Don Moss Goes First Class"—Charles Kuralt, CBS

"Moss has been asked to paint the country's finest ski runs...the most beautiful golf holes in America.... he accompanied Ted Hood to illustrate The America's Cup...portrayed NHL stars in action...the NFL had him design the Super Bowl poster and his painting of Don Shula graced the cover of Time."
—Parton Keese, N.Y. Times.

SEND FOR DFS BROCHURE/FINE ART PRINT OR POSTER.
"THE ART OF SPORTS"—SLIDE FILM, by appointment.

Donald Moss

DESIGN FOR SPORTS
232 Peaceable Street
Ridgefield, Connecticut 06877
(203) 438-5633

Clients include:

AT&T, American Bell
AMF, Head Ski & Tennis
Arnold Palmer Enterprises
Field Enterprises
Foote, Cone & Belding
Golf Digest
Lake Placid Olympic Comm.
Mercedes-Benz of N. America
National Broadcasting Co.
National Football League
Novo Laboratories
Olin Ski Company
Pepsico
Professional Golf Assn.
Roche Pharmaceutical, Inc.
Ski Magazine
SPORTS ILLUSTRATED
   (30 years-over 500 illustrations)
Sports Marketing Group
Stratton Corporation
Tennis Magazine
Travelers Insurance Co.
Unicover Corporation
Union Trust Company
United States Postal Service –
   (12 U.S. stamp designs)
United States Golf Assn.
The Winchell Company
World Championship Tennis

Books: (art included)

"Champions of American Sport"
"200 Years of Sport in America"
"200 Years of Illustration
   in America"
"Best of Sports Illustrated"
"Best of 18 Golf Holes
   in America"
"Magic and Other Realism"
"The North Light Collection"
"The Art of Watercolor"

Collections:

Baseball Hall of Fame
Basketball Hall of Fame
Football Hall of Fame
Golf House (U.S.G.A.)
National Art Museum of Sport
Society of Illustrators
Tennis Hall of Fame
U.S.A.F. Art Collection
U.S. Sports Academy

SPECIALIST IN SPORT LOGOS:

AMF/Head Ski Graphics
AMF/Head Tennis Graphics
Mercedes-Benz Grand
   Prix Logo
Mercedes Mile on Fifth
   Avenue Logo
National Art Museum of
   Sport Design
Olympics, 1980–Raccoon
   Symbol
U.S. Demo Ski Team Design
Stratton Mountain Corporate
   Identity

James Nazz

Constructed Illustration & Photography
159 2nd Avenue
New York, New York 10003
(212) 228-9713

Member Graphic Artists Guild

1. Wall Street Computer Review
2. Drug Topics
3. Photo District News
4. Long, Haymes & Carr/Pilot Life

1.

2.

3.

4.

Michael Ng

58-35 155 Street
Flushing, New York 11355
(718) 461-8264

Corporate and Advertising illustrations.
Black and white line work and watercolor.

Clients:
Saatchi and Saatchi Compton Inc., Grey Advertising,
Kalish and Rice Advertising, Ogilvy and Mather,
United Nations, IBM, CBS, Ziff Davis, Chase
Manhattan Bank, N.Y. Life Insurance, Scribner's Pub.
Co., Science Digest, New York Times.

Work appearing in Society of Illustrators 21 and
22 Annuals, American Showcase Volume 9.

Member of the Graphic Artists Guild

K. A. Orvidas
242 Yale Avenue
Kensington, California 94708
(415) 525-6626

Norman Rainock
Glen Allen, Virginia
(804) 264-8123

Memo to the young designers with great eyesight: You, too will someday awaken to find that glasses are needed for your typographical travels.

Ah, but you say you have perfect 20/20 vision and have no trouble proofing annual reports for hours? Glorious. Not to worry? Maybe you should.

As the editor of several annual reports and corporate publications designed for senior stockholders, it has been my painful duty to remind sharp-eyed designers that small type is a trial for those who must wear glasses in order to read the peerless prose of corporate America.

Think about it. What signal is sent by *small* type? Are we hiding something? Did the lawyers edit and reduce our copy to an obfuscatory size? And how can we communicate effectively if a reader has to struggle with out Helvetican hieroglyphics?

So designers, please heed my cry and keep your type sizes up! Make it big, I beg you, and make thousands of your formerly eyestrained readers happy with your typographical terpsichore.

Devere E. Logan
Director, Public Relations
Parker Hannifin Corporation
Cleveland, Ohio

Chris Spollen

Moonlight Press Studio
High Contrast Illustration
(718) 979-9695

Telex in studio (718) 979-8919

Clients:
Stanley Tool Company
International Paper
Bell South Company
Mutual Life Insurance
20th Century Fox
Chubb Group Insurance
Digital Computer Co.
Home Box Office
McCaffrey and McCall
MacLean Hunter Media, Inc.
Franklin Library
Consumer Report Magazine
Warner Brothers Pubs.
Benton & Bowles
Ziff-Davis
CBS Publishing
Medical Economics Company
Barron's
Popular Mechanics Magazine
Hayden Publishing Company
Datamation Magazine
Acute Care Medicine
Avis
Working Woman Magazine
Travel & Leisure Magazine
ABC
Milton Bradley Co.
Rodale Press
Glamour Magazine
Science 85 Magazine
Ogilvy & Mather Advertising
Sports Illustrated
Saatchi & Saatchi Compton
Atlantic Recording Corp.
Cline Davis & Mann
Western Union

Member:
Graphic Artists Guild
Society of Illustrators

A mini portfolio of samples sent
upon request:

To view more work:
American Showcase 8, 9 and 10;
Corporate Showcase 5;
Art Directors Index 12;
Black Book 1988
Outstanding American
  Illustrators Today.

PaineWebber gives billion dollar support to its municipal bond clients.

PaineWebber breaks new financial ground to build the Houston Convention Center.

Study the top performing underwriters of initial public offerings and two initials stand out.

Carol Wald

The Scarab Club
217 Farnsworth Avenue
Detroit, Michigan 48202
(313) 832-5805
(212) 737-4559

© Carol Wald

POSTERS
ANNUAL REPORTS
BROCHURES
ADVERTISING ILLUSTRATION
EDITORIAL ART

Carol Wald's illustration
portfolio has recently been
featured in the following
prestigious publications:

Ten page folio: Fortune Magazine
Ten page folio: Idea Magazine
Ten page folio: Communication Arts
Eight page folio: How Magazine
Four page folio: American Artist

Clients include:

Doral Saturnia Spa Resort
The Alfred, NYC.
NYNEX Business Systems
Estée Lauder
Lamb Weston
First Federal Savings & Loan
Hoechst – Roussel
Marshalk & Company
Young & Rubicam
Serino, Coyne & Nappi
Congregation of Marians
Seattle Symphony
Youngstown Symphony
Michigan Opera Theatre
Penthouse Enterprises
Reader's Digest International
13-30 Corporation
Nordstrom
U.S. Postal Service

Also: Forbes, Esquire, Venture,
Lears, P.C., Time, Business Week,
Connoisseur, GEO, Essence, U&lc,
Prevention, Modern Maturity,
Datamation, New York Times.

Shows & Awards: Art Director's
Annual, C.A. Annual, Print Regional,
Society of Publication Designers,
American Illustration.

THE NEW WEST SIDE STORY

WEST 61ST STREET· ACROSS FROM LINCOLN CENTER

CAROL WALD
ILLUSTRATOR

Ask me about alcohol withdrawal

IndexIllustrators

Photography

New York City

kawalerski

TED KAWALERSKI
(212) 242-0198

Stock Photography:
The Image Bank.

© Ted Kawalerski 1987.

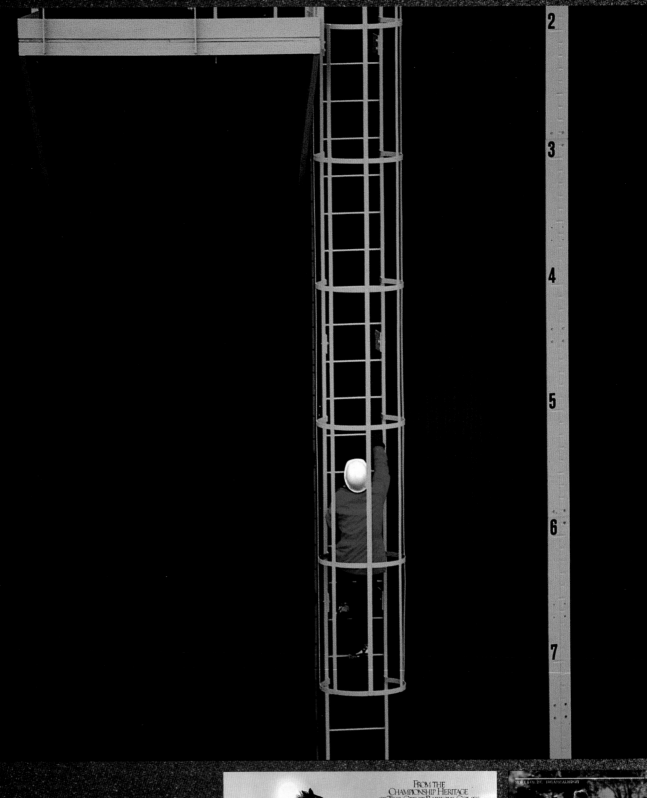

SHORTY
WILCOX

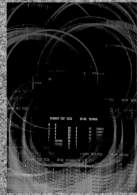

"GRAND SCALE PROJECTS DEMAND THE GRAND SCALE COMMITMENT OF AMERICAN OLEAN."

SHORTY WILCOX

c/o Al Forsyth
212-246-6367
303-453-2511

Also available Through
the Stock Collection

Doug Abdelnour

Represented by:

Bedford Photo-Graphic

The Playhouse
Route 22
P.O. Box 64
Bedford, New York 10506
(914) 234-3123

Architectural and Industrial Photography;
Exteriors, interiors, models, and panoramas

Locations: Anywhere

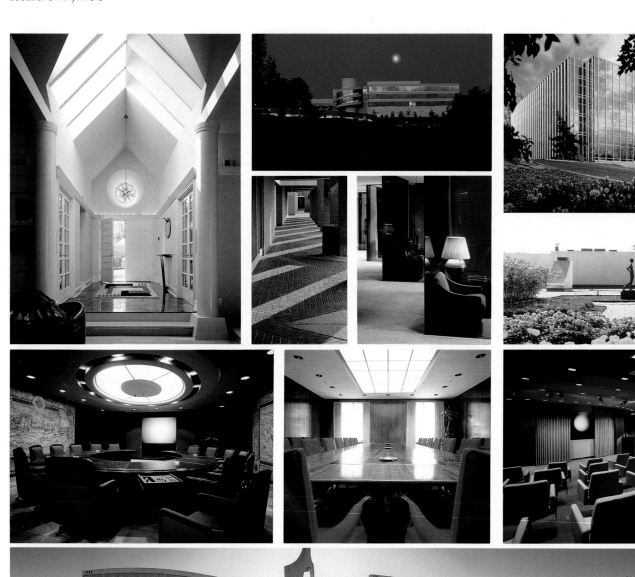

Jules Alexander

9 Belmont Avenue
Rye, New York 10580
(914) 967-8985

Location photography – a particular directorial ability in
the photography of people – for major magazines.
Client list and brochure available.

MIKE TYSON, GUS D AMATO FOR EASTMAN KODAK

Suppose you could have an expandable writing staff. It would automatically grow or shrink to keep pace with the workload, and it would always have the exact skills you needed, whether the project called for a knowledge of finance, aviation, medicine, or whatever. There is a way to have that flexibility and versatility: Learn the best ways to find and use freelance writers.

When should you bring in a professional writer? Basically, you need to enlist freelance talent when:

A monstrous project threatens to tie up your staff and disrupt your workflow.

Too many deadlines are coming at you too fast and a writing project requires more time.

You have landed a new account—a chemical manufacturer, for example—but you have no background in that field, and you need a professional writer who has the kind of expertise that you cannot supply in-house.

Because the freelancer is an outsider, he or she can bring a fresh outlook and a broad range of experience to focus on your project.

Finding the writer
Ask your colleagues to recommend writers. Whom did they use on projects similar to yours? Was the writer dependable? Did he or she meet deadlines? Was the writing imaginative or hackneyed? The freelance designers and photographers you know are also excellent sources of recommendations, because they work with freelance writers all the time.

Note bylines and much-read articles in local magazines and business journals. If you're looking for a writer with a specialty in a certain subject matter, scour the trade journals devoted to that field. Then call the editors and ask about writers whose work seems suitable.

There are also several directories available to help you find writers in a particular specialty or locale. One of the best is the annual *Directory of the American Society of Journalists and Authors* (ASJA), which lists more than 700 of the nation's leading nonfiction writers. Each listing is a mini-resume that gives publication credits, areas of expertise, and awards earned by the writer. Indexes by specialty and by geographic area are provided. The directory costs $50 from ASJA, 1501 Broadway, Suite 1907, New York, NY 10036.

ASJA also operates a writers referral service and will locate professionals throughout the U.S. and overseas to do any type of writing you need on practically any subject. There's a small fee of $25 for business clients, no fee for publishers for this service. Call Dorothy Beach at (212) 398-1934 for information.

Other helpful directories include *Freelancers of North America: 1984-1985 Marketplace,* which lists about 6,000 American and Canadian writers ($32.95 from Author Aid/Research Associates International, 340 E. 52nd St., New York, NY 10022); *Professional's Guide to Public Relations Services,* which includes writers along with many other useful services ($90 from Public Relations Publishing Co., 888 7th Ave., New York, NY 10106); *Working Press of the Nation,* Vol. 4, which lists 2,000 writers and photographers ($250 for the five-volume set from National Research Bureau, 424 North Third St., Burlington, IA 52601); and *Literary Market Place,* which is concerned primarily with book publishing, but has a section on magazines ($54.95 from R.R. Bowker Co., 205 E. 42nd St., New York, NY 10017).

After you've got the names of some likely writers:

Telephone them. Tell them about your project, and find out if they've done that type of work before, and if they can do it within your budget and time frame.

Ask them to bring or send you samples (clips) of their work. (An in-person interview is always best but not always possible.) Also ask for a brief resume or list of publication credits.

Read the samples carefully. Does the writer have a distinctive style that's evident in everything he or she does? If so, is it appropriate for your project? Or is the style varied to fit different projects and purposes? Is the writing clear, effective, convincing? Can the writer take a familiar idea and give it a certain freshness?

When you're sold on the person's writing ability, call one or two of the people they've worked for and ask about their dependability. Remember, it doesn't matter how good a piece of writing is if it comes in after the deadline.

Agree on the fee, by length of piece, research required, hourly, or on a project basis—to the satisfaction of both parties—before the writer starts work.

Using the writer
Get the writer involved early. The experienced writer can contribute valuable ideas and direction during the concept stage. After all, they've worked on many kinds of writing projects with many companies, firms, and publishers.

For projects involving design, get the writer and the artist together before anything is written. Let them work together so that text and design are complementary, so that the finished piece has a unified tone.

Give the writer what he or she needs. First of all, direction. What do you want to accomplish with this project? What audience are you trying to reach? What action do you want to elicit? Good writers will ask those questions.

Give the writer access to sources. Any background information you have on file and can easily supply will save the writer time and you money. Also, let the writer interview key people rather than getting all the information third-hand. Something always gets lost in the translation.

 Continued on page 54

Steve Altman

Altman Photography
79 Grand Street
Jersey City, New Jersey 07302
(201) 434-0022

"Corporate America's Storyteller"

Corporate Communications:
Annual Reports,
Brochures,
Illustration

Call Me Toll Free
1-800-543-8808
(In New Jersey, 201-434-0022)

Ovak Arslanian

344 West 14th Street
New York, New York 10014
(212) 255-1519

New York representative: Erika Koning
(212) 255-1519

Paris representative: FOVEA/Rose Marie Wheeler
75, Rue Bayen
75017 Paris – France
45.72.20.69/45.72.19.07

Location photography: advertising, architecture,
corporate/industrial, editorial. Stock available.

Clients include: Amstar Corp., Bear Stearns & Co.,
Dialogue Magazine, Discover, Du Pont Co., Equitable,
Fortune, Geo/France, Geo/Germany, High Tech
Magazine, IBM Corp., Loral Corp., Morgan Stanley/
Brooks Harvey, National Geographic Society,
Obayashi-Gumi, Occidental Land Research, Peabody
Int'l Corp., Prudential, Public Service Co. of New Mexico,
Scott Foresman, Smithsonian, Stern Magazine,
Union Pacific Corp., Whittle Comm., Zeckendorf Co.

Ovak Arslanian

344 West 14th Street
New York, New York 10014
(212) 255-1519

New York representative: Erika Koning
(212) 255-1519

Paris representative: FOVEA/Rose Marie Wheeler
75, Rue Bayen
75017 Paris – France
45.72.20.69/45.72.19.07

Location photography: advertising, architecture, corporate/industrial, editorial. Stock available.

Clients include: Amstar Corp., Bear Stearns & Co., Dialogue Magazine, Discover, Du Pont Co., Equitable, Fortune, Geo/France, Geo/Germany, High Tech Magazine, IBM Corp., Loral Corp., Morgan Stanley/ Brooks Harvey, National Geographic Society, Obayashi-Gumi, Occidental Land Research, Peabody Int'l Corp., Prudential, Public Service Co. of New Mexico, Scott Foresman, Smithsonian, Stern Magazine, Union Pacific Corp., Whittle Comm., Zeckendorf Co.

Joe Baker
35 Wooster Street
New York, New York 10013
(212) 925-6555

Business/Industrial Photography

Art Director: Frank Biondo
Agency: NW Ayer Inc.
Client: DuPont

Joseph Berger

121 Madison Avenue
New York, New York 10016
(212) 685-7191

Represented by Nancy Slome
(212) 685-8185

PEOPLE ON LOCATION

Recent clients include:
Alexander and Alexander
Commodore Computer
Dean Witter Reynolds
Hattori Corporation
McKinsey and Company

Forbes Magazine
Savvy Magazine
The Yacht Magazine

Ariel Peeri Design
G. M. Communications
Jim Johnston Advertising
Lord Geller Federico Einstein
McCaffrey and McCall
Warwick Advertising

Existing photography available.

Additional work may be seen in
Corporate Showcase 4 and 5.   © Joseph Berger 1986

WILLIAM DUNN. EXECUTIVE VICE PRESIDENT DOW JONES

D. RONALD DANIEL. MANAGING DIRECTOR McKINSEY AND COMPANY

LORD GELLER FEDERICO EINSTEIN ADVERTISING

JOE LaMARCA. RESTAURANTEUR FOR FAMILY COMPUTING

GAD ROMANN. ROMANN AND TANNENHOLTZ
ADVERTISING

CAROL NELSON. EXECUTIVE VICE PRESIDENT E.S. GORDON INC.

Continued from page 48

Keep the lines of communication open all during the writing process. Tell the writer to let you know of any problems, opportunities, or gaps in the research. Let the writer know immediately about any changes or additions to the project.

Allow room for creativity. If you dictate how the writer must express your message, you'll get what you ask for. But if you don't, you'll probably get something much better. "I put as few restrictions on people as possible," says Tom Voelker, who freelanced for five years before becoming chief copywriter at Bauerlein, Inc., in New Orleans. "On the other hand, I know what clients will accept, and I try to make that clear to the freelancer going in so they'll have the same sense."

Handle revisions with care. If the text needs minor revisions—a couple of words, a new title for a company official, etc.—many public relations people will handle the changes themselves. But if the revision is extensive, let the writer revise the piece, and thus maintain consistency in tone and style.

Generally, the negotiated price will include one revision by the writer—not a total rewrite because you've now changed your mind about what you wanted in the first place.

Be fair about rates and rights. It's hard to set a pricetag on creativity. One piece is not necessarily the same as another piece in terms of the time and difficulty involved in the writing. "We try to arrive at a reasonable rate and timetable for each assignment, based on the length of the written piece, the extent of the research required, the deadline, and the difficulty of the project," says Elena Sansalone, vice president of Hill and Knowlton, Inc.

Alan Caruba, a public relations consultant and writer based in New Jersey, suggests that a professional writer should be paid no less than $250 to $300 a day, and $500 a day is not uncommon. You're buying the years of experience, solid knowledge, and invaluable contacts the experienced writer brings to an assignment. Expect to pay $750 to $1,000 for a 1,500- to 2,000-word article or a minimum of $1,000 a month as a retainer for an established writer, says Caruba. Don't make your selection based on price alone, he warns. "It is always less expensive to get a good writer with good credentials."

In general, when you commission a writer to create a brochure, ad, speech, or other type of piece, you are buying all rights. The same is typically true for ghostwriting. However, an article that will bear the writer's byline usually—but not always—remains the writer's property. So make sure your contract states what rights you're buying.

Follow up with a letter of agreement that briefly outlines the scope of the project, fees, deadlines, and other limiting agreements.

Keep a good thing going. Every time a freelance writer does another project for you, they gain greater familiarity with your company and your product and can step in when needed with little orientation or explanation from you.

Maintain a good ongoing relationship with one or more writers whose work you like. Two key ways to do that are to pay promptly and to be honest about deadlines. Too often a writer burns the candle at both ends to meet an unrealistic deadline, only to learn later that the deadline was not real. And don't always wait until the last minute to give an assignment.

Nothing annoys a writer more than to deliver good work on time, then wait interminably for payment. Freelancers depend on those checks just as you depend on your paycheck. Pay promptly, and you'll inspire a great deal of loyalty.

Freelance writers are a creative resource. Use them to supplement your own resources and expand your capabilities at a fraction of what it would cost to add full-time employees to your staff.

Mary Elaine Lora, APR
Writer/Public Relations Consultant
New Orleans

Reprinted with permission from the April 1986 issue of the Public Relations Journal.

Charles Blecker

380 Bleecker Street
Suite 140
New York, New York 10014
(212) 242-8390

Specialist in location photography
for annual reports, advertising,
corporate/industrial, travel,
editorial and stock.

Stock available directly.

© Charles Blecker 1987

Alan Bolesta

11 Riverside Drive
New York, New York 10023
(212) 873-1932

Partial client list:
Allied Corporation, *American Photographer, Art Direction,* Audi, *Avenue,* Brown Brothers Harriman, *Business Week, Digital Review, Family Circle, Fleet Owner, Frequent Flyer,* GECC, Harper & Row, IBM, Macy's, Merrill Lynch, *Modern Photography, Money,* Peat Marwick, Penncentral, Schering Plough, S.D. Scott Printing, Sentry Insurance, *Signature,* Spectraphysics, *Studio Photography, Town & Country, Travel & Leisure.*

Alan Bolesta
11 Riverside Drive
New York, New York 10023
(212) 873-1932

Partial client list:
Allied Corporation, *American Photographer, Art Direction,* Audi, *Avenue,* Brown Brothers Harriman, *Business Week, Digital Review, Family Circle, Fleet Owner, Frequent Flyer,* GECC, Harper & Row, IBM, Macy's, Merrill Lynch, *Modern Photography, Money,* Peat Marwick, Penncentral, Schering Plough, S.D. Scott Printing, Sentry Insurance, *Signature,* Spectraphysics, *Studio Photography, Town & Country, Travel & Leisure.*

Steve Brady
207 East 30th Street
New York, New York 10016
(212) 213-6024

Location assignments for annual reports, brochures
and advertising.

Steve Brady

207 East 30th Street 3E
New York, New York 10016
(212) 213-6024

Location assignments for annual reports, brochures and advertising.

Steve Brady works in the fields of finance, industry, real estate, consumer, travel, energy and hi-tech. Recent clients include Gerald D. Hines Interests, Four Seasons Hotel, Conoco, Saga Corporation, Mitsubishi, NCAA, Xerox, Honeywell, New York Air, Hershey Hotels, Dow Chemical, Safeco, Prudential, Continental Airlines, US Steel, Shell Oil, N.Y.S.E., Celanese Corp., I.R.F.G. and Exxon.

His work has won recognition from Communication Arts, Print Magazine, N.Y.A.D.C., Graphis, AIGA and the Mead Annual Report Show. See additional work on pages 188 and 189.

For assignments, stock, color samples and a portfolio call (212) 213-6024 or (713) 660-6663.

Robert Buchanan

466 Lakeview Avenue
Valhalla, New York 10595
(914) 592-1204   (212) 627-8558

Photography demands technique and artistry. Robert Buchanan brings your most treasured ideas to light to enhance the concept of visual communication. As a fine commercial photographer, his sensitivity to details and commitment to follow-through has created a lasting relationship with clients.

Your creative ideas demand outstanding photography. Robert Buchanan is dedicated to craftsmanship and personal service. His career reflects a wide range of assignments in still life, fashion, food and product photography.

His clients include: Nestles, Boarshead, A & W, General Foods, Nabisco, IBM, Richardson/Vicks, Ledle, Texaco, Warner Lambert, Somerset Distillers, Airwick, Xerox.

Also see ASMP 5

(Located in Westchester, easily accessible to New York City and Connecticut)

Jonathan Clymer

146 West 29th Street
New York, New York 10001
(212) 714-9041

208 Undercliff Avenue
Edgewater, New Jersey 07020
(201) 941-2348

Corporate and industrial photography.
Studio and location.

Vincent Colabella

304 East 41st Street
New York, New York 10017
(212) 949-7456

Stephen Derr

420 West 45th Street
New York, New York 10036
(212) 246-5920

Corporate and advertising photography for clients
including: Allied Chemical, Biotechnology General,
Chase Manhattan Bank, Dillon Read, Federal Express,
First Boston, First Interstate Bank, Home Insurance,
IBM, MacGregor Sporting Goods, Merrill Lynch, Ryder
System, Shearson/American Express, Salomon
Brothers, Southern Bell, Subaru of America,
Sumitomo, United States Surgical.

Robert Essel

39 West 71st Street
New York, New York 10023
(212) 877-5228

Major Fortune 500 Companies include:
IBM, Exxon, Johnson & Johnson, RCA,
Martin Marietta and Celanese Corp.

My specialty is location work, worldwide.

Stock photography available directly or through
Manhattan Views.

Additional photography for viewing in Corporate
Showcase Volumes III, IV, and V.

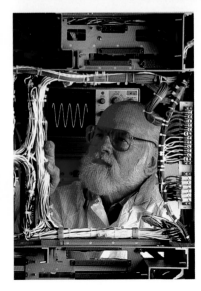

Esto
Photographics

222 Valley Place
Mamaroneck, New York 10543
(914) 698-4060

ESTO represents today's foremost architectural photographers: Peter Aaron, Wolfgang Hoyt, Dan Cornish, Peter Mauss, Jock Pottle and Max MacKenzie. Their work documents contemporary American design and is widely published in general circulation publications and the architecture press. The ESTO photographers are specially skilled in dealing with difficult lighting situations and location work. Among the recently photographed corporate installations are American Express, Conoco, HBO, Proctor and Gamble, IBM and Pepsico. ESTO will review your project and recommend the best available photographer for a documentation which combines journalistic clarity with a fine interpretation of light, space and function.

Robert I. Faulkner

52 Comstock Street
New Brunswick,
New Jersey 08901
(201) 828-6984

Specializing in photography of
architecture and interior design
Stock available. Portfolio upon
request.

Clients include:

I.M. Pei
Haines Lundberg Waehler
Swanke Hayden Connell
Edward Durrell Stone
Spector Group
Grad Partnership
Rothe-Johnson Associates
Barrett Ginsberg
Duffy Inc.
Johnson & Johnson
Prudential
Dun & Bradstreet
New Jersey Bell
Hilton Hotels
Purolator Courier
Revlon
North American Phillips
Carter Wallace
Pharmacia
Tishman Construction
Torcon Construction
Mahoney Troast
Sudler Construction
Trammell Crow
Lincoln Properties
Cushman Wakefield
Coldwell Banker
Bear & Sterns
Weichert Realty
Oliver Realty
Garibaldi Realty
Pace Advertising
Keyes Martin Advertising
Gillespie Advertising
Cherenson Group

Architectural Credits:

1. Minoru Yamasaki
2. Haines Lundberg Waehler
3. Haines Lundberg Waehler
4. Edward Durrell Stone
5. James R. Grieves
6. Swanke Hayden Connell

Scott Frances

175 5th Avenue
Suite #2401
New York, New York 10010
(212) 749-8026

1. Q.V. Restaurant, N.Y., N.Y.
2. Atlantic City Public Library, N.J.
3. Farnsworth House, Plano, Il.,
    for *House & Garden*
4. Metropolitan Museum of Art,
    N.Y., N.Y.
5. Metropolitan Museum of Art,
    N.Y., N.Y.

Partial Client List
Bromley-Jacobsen, Architects
Burson-Marsteller
Charles Morris Mount, Inc.
CBS Publications
Conde Naste Publications
Dorf Associates
Fairfax Advertising
The Glick Organization
The Gracie Mansion
    Conservancy
Grey Advertising/G.E.M.
Gruen Design
Hearst Magazines
House & Garden
Interior Design
Interior Facilities Assoc.
International Design Group
ICF
The Marketing Directors
Maurice Villency, Inc.
The Metropolitan Museum of Art
Newmark Advertising
Walker Group/CNI

1

2

3

4

5

Brett Froomer

39 East 12th Street
New York, New York 10003
(212) 533-3113

Represented by:
Susan Boyer
(212) 533-3113

Worldwide location
photography for corporate
annual reports, brochures
and advertising.

Stock photography available
through The Image Bank.

Garry Geer

Geer Photography
183 Saint Paul Street
Rochester, New York 14604
(212) 819-0808
(716) 232-2393

Specializing in corporate, editorial, and advertising
photography. Existing stock photography available
upon request.

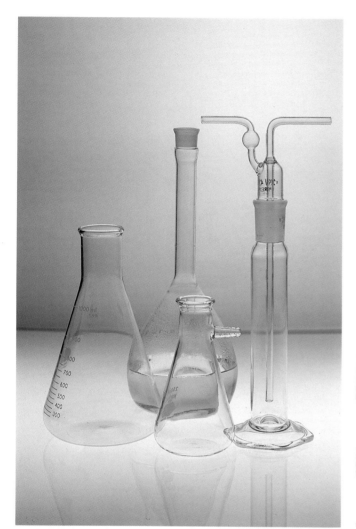

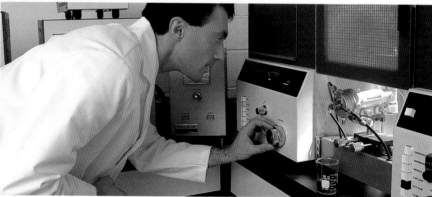

Gary Gladstone

The Gladstone Studio, Ltd.
237 East 20th Street
New York, New York 10003
(212) 777-7772

Corporate
Annual Reports
Capability Brochures
Institutional Illustration

Stock Photographs
The Image Bank

For your personal copy of Gary's printed portfolio "CORPORATE COLOR" please write on your company letterhead.

GRAPHIC ARTS ORGANIZATIONS

Arizona:

Phoenix Society of Visual Arts
P.O. Box 469
Phoenix, AZ 85001

California:

Advertising Club of Los Angeles
514 Shatto Pl., Rm. 328
Los Angeles, CA 90020
(213) 749-3537

Art Directors and Artists Club
2791 24th St.
Sacramento, CA 95818
(916) 731-8802

Book Club of California
312 Sutter St., Ste. 510
San Francisco, CA 94108
(415) 781-7532

Graphic Artists Guild of Los Angeles
849 S. Broadway
Los Angeles, CA 90014
(213) 622-0126

Los Angeles Advertising Women
5300 Laurel Canyon Blvd. #103
North Hollywood, CA 91607
(818) 762-4669

Los Angeles Chapter of the Graphic Artists Guild
5971 W. 3rd St.
Los Angeles, CA 90036
(213) 938-0009

San Francisco Society of Communicating Arts
Fort Mason
Building A
San Francisco, CA 94123
(415) 474-3156

Society of Illustrators of Los Angeles
1258 N. Highland Ave.
Los Angeles, CA 90038
(213) 469-8465

Society of Motion Pictures & TV Art Directors
14724 Ventura Blvd.
Sherman Oaks, CA
(818) 905-0599

Western Art Directors Club
P.O. Box 966
Palo Alto, CA 94302
(415) 321-4196

Women in Design
P.O. Box 2607
San Francisco, CA 94126
(415) 397-1748

Women's Graphic Center
The Woman's Building
1727 N. Spring St.
Los Angeles, CA 90012
(213) 222-5101

Colorado:

Art Directors Club of Denver
Suite 102
1550 S. Pearl Street
Denver, CO 80210

International Design Conference at Aspen
1000 N. 3rd
Aspen, CO 81612
(303) 925-2257

Connecticut:

Connecticut Art Directors Club
P.O. Box 1974
New Haven, CT 06521

District of Columbia:

American Advertising Federation
1400 K. St. N.W., Ste. 1000
Washington, DC 20005
(202) 898-0089

American Institute of Architects
1735 New York Avenue, N.W.
Washington, DC 20006
(202) 626-7300

Art Directors Club of Washington, DC
655 15th St., N.W.
Washington, DC 20005
(202) 347-5900

Federal Design Council
P.O. Box 7537
Washington, DC 20044

International Copyright Information Center, A.A.D.
1707 L Street, N.W.
Washington, DC 20036

NEA: Design Arts Program
1100 Pennsylvania Ave., N.W.
Washington, DC 20506
(202) 682-5437

Georgia:

Atlanta Art Papers, Inc.
P.O. Box 77348
Atlanta, GA 30357
(404) 885-1273

Graphics Artists Guild
3158 Maple Drive, N.E., Ste. 46
Atlanta, GGA 30305
(404) 262-8077

Illinois:

Institute of Business Designers
National
1155 Merchandise Mart
Chicago, IL 60654
(312) 467-1950

STA
233 East Ontario St.
Chicago, IL 60611
(312) 787-2018

Women in Design
2 N. Riverside Plaza
Chicago, IL 60606
(312) 648-1874

Kansas:

Wichita Art Directors Club
P.O. Box 562
Wichita, KS 67202

Maryland

Council of Communications Societies
P.O. Box 1074
Silver Springs, MD 20910

Massachusetts:

Art Directors Club of Boston
50 Commonwealth Ave.
Boston, MA 02116
(617) 536-8999

Center for Design of Industrial Schedules
221 Longwood Ave.
Boston, MA 02115
(617) 734-2163

Continued on page 76

Ken Haas, Inc.

15 Sheridan Square
New York, New York 10014
(212) 255-0707

Clients serviced include: AT&T; New York Telephone; Asarco; SCM; Peugeot; Dexter; Elscint; Chesebrough-Ponds; 3M; Penntech Paper; NBC; Stanadyne; Panasonic; Holiday Inns; St. Regis Paper; YMCA; Abraham & Strauss; Colgate-Palmolive; Harcourt, Brace, Jovanovich; CPC International; General Instrument; Hongkong Land; The Hongkong & Shanghai Bank; Oscar Mayer; Singer; Chris-Craft; Pinkerton's; Republic Bank of New York; Continental Illinois National Bank; Columbus Line; General

Electric; The Commonwealth Fund; Manufacturers Hanover Trust; Merrill Lynch; Dillon Read; The Henry Luce Foundation; Chicago Board Options Exchange; New York City Partnership; Cigna; Reuters; Sloan Kettering; IBM; Citicorp; Mass Transit Railway of Hong Kong; Harvard Medical School; E.F. Hutton; Pacific Telesis, Smithers Clinic of Roosevelt St. Luke Hospital.

Designers serviced include: Applebaum & Curtis; Beau Gardner; Bob Gill; Galen Harley; John Morning;

Arnold Saks; Reba Sochis; Henry Steiner; Marco DePlano; Anthony Russell; Graphic Expression; Burson Marsteller; Spence Glassberg; HBM/Creamer; Barton-Gillet; Becker Hockfield; Mayo-Infurna; Robert Miles Runyan, Sherin & Matejka.

Editorial credits include: Bicentennial cover of Newsweek, The New York Times Magazine, Fortune, People, Natural History, Americana, Outdoor Life, Oggi, Bunte.

FROM A BROCHURE FOR THE HARVARD MEDICAL SCHOOL, DESIGNED BY WILLIAM SHINN OF BARTON GILLET.

George Haling Productions: Industrial

NYC Photo District
(212) 736-6822

Energy
Esso-Rivista (Italy)
Exxon
Combustion Engineering
Conoco
Consolidated Natural Gas
PSE & G
Schlumberger Ltd.
Sun Company
Texaco

Transportation
American Airlines
Continental Airlines
Sabena
Seatrain

The Orient Express
TWA
United Airlines

Communications
ABC
CBS
IBM
ITT
Metromedia
NBC
New York Telephone
N.Y.C. Post Office
Perkin-Elmer
RCA
Sperry

Xerox
Blair Graphics
Inmont

**Forest Products/
Graphic Arts**
Champion International
Kimberly-Clark
Blair Graphics
Inmont
Sterling Roman Press

Editorial
Advertising Council
Camera Magazine
DU Magazine

Fortune Magazine
Ladies Home Journal
Lamp Magazine
LIFE Magazine
London Daily Telegraph
Money Magazine
Museum of Natural History
N.Y. Times Books
Réalités Magazine
Singer Corporation
Stern Magazine
Time-Life Books
United Fund

George Haling Productions: Corporate

NYC Photo District
(212) 736-6822

Photobases in New York and Europe.

Twenty-five years of excellence
Here and There.

Great stock of Now and Then.

Corporate/Financial
ADT
Alexander & Alexander
American Express
Carteret
Citco
Citibank (N.Y.)
Emery Financial Services
Hartford Group
Manhattan Life
Merrill-Lynch
Mitchell-Hutchins
Mortgage Bankers Assn.
Morgan-Stanley
Salomon Brothers

The Travelers

Industrial
Alcoa
Amerace
American Can
Blount
Celanese
Chrysler Corp.
Fasco
GAF
General Cable
General Electric
Hunt Chemical
IBM

Indian Head
Inmont
ITT
3M
Otis
Perkin-Elmer
PepsiCo
Singer
Sperry Rand
Thomas & Betts
Xerox

GRAPHIC ARTS ORGANIZATIONS

Continued from page 72

Graphic Artists Guild
P.O. Box 1454–GMF
Boston, MA 02205
(617) 451-5362

**Society of Environmental
Graphics Designers**
47 Third Street
Cambridge, MA 02141
(617) 577-8225

Michigan:

Creative Advertising Club of Detroit
c/o Rhoda Parkin
30400 Van Dyke
Warren, MI 48093

Minnesota:

**Minnesota Graphic Designers
Association**
P.O. Box 24272
Minneapolis, MN 55424

Missouri:

Advertising Center of Greater St. Louis
440 Mansion House Center
St. Louis, MO 63102
(314) 231-4185

Advertising Club of Kansas City
1 Ward Parkway Center, Ste. 102
Kansas City, MO 64112
(816) 753-4088

New Jersey:

Point-of-Purchase Advertising Institute
2 Executive Dr.
Fort Lee, NJ 07024
(201) 585-8400

New York:

The Advertising Club of New York
Roosevelt Hotel, Rm. 310
New York, NY 10017
(212) 697-0877

The Advertising Council, Inc.
825 Third Ave.
New York, NY 10022
(212) 758-0400

APA
Advertising Photographers of America, Inc.
45 E. 20th Street
New York, NY 10003
(212) 254-5500

**Advertising Typographers Association
of America, Inc.**
5 Penn Plaza, 12th Fl.
New York, NY 10001
(212) 594-0685

**Advertising Women of New York
Foundation, Inc.**
153 E. 57th St.
New York, NY 10022
(212) 593-1950

**American Association of Advertising
Agencies**
666 Third Ave.
New York, NY 10017
(212) 682-2500

American Booksellers Association, Inc.
122 E. 42nd St.
New York, NY 10168
(212) 867-9060

**The Public Relations Society
of America, Inc.**
845 Third Ave.
New York, NY 10022
(212) 826-1750

American Council for the Arts
570 Seventh Ave.
New York, NY 10018
(212) 354-6655

The American Institute of Graphic Arts
1059 Third Ave.
New York, NY 10021
(212) 752-0813

American Society of Interior Designers
National Headquarters
1430 Broadway
New York, NY 10018
(212) 944-9220

New York Chapter
950 Third Ave.
New York, NY 10022
(212) 421-8765

**American Society of Magazine
Photographers**
205 Lexington Ave.
New York, NY 10016
(212) 889-9144

Art Directors Club of New York
488 Madison Ave.
New York, NY 10022
(212) 838-8140

Association of American Publishers, Inc.
1 Park Ave.
New York, NY 10016
(212) 689-8920

Center for Arts Information
625 Broadway
New York, NY 10012
(212) 677-7548

The Children's Book Council, Inc.
67 Irving Place
New York, NY 10003
(212) 254-2666

CLIO
336 E. 59th St.
New York, NY 10022
(212) 593-1900

Foundation for the Community of Artists
280 Broadway, Ste. 412
New York, NY 10007
(212) 227-3770

Graphic Artists Guild
30 E. 20th St., Rm. 405
New York, NY 10003
(212) 777-7353

Guild of Book Workers
663 Fifth Ave.
New York, NY 10022
(212) 757-6454

Institute of Outdoor Advertising
342 Madison Ave.
New York, NY 10017
(212) 986-5920

**International Advertising
Association, Inc.**
475 Fifth Ave.
New York, NY 10017
(212) 684-1583

The One Club
251 E. 50th St.
New York, NY 10022
(212) 935-0121

**Printing Industries of Metropolitan
New York, Inc.**
5 Penn Plaza
New York, NY 10001
(212) 279-2100

Continued on page 82

Kent Hanson
147 Bleecker Street
New York, New York 10012
(212) 777-2399

Editorial, advertising, and corporate photography.
Portfolio available upon request.

Stock Photographs: DOT Picture Agency
(212) 684-3441
Telex 238198 TLXA UR

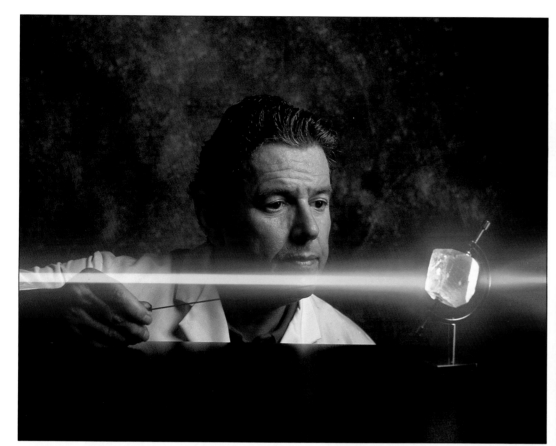

Ted Horowitz

465 West End Avenue
New York, New York 10024
(212) 595-0040

Specialist in worldwide corporate photography for the
Fortune 500.

Selected Stock Photography Available.

Ted Horowitz

465 West End Avenue
New York, New York 10024
(212) 595-0040

Specialist in worldwide corporate photography for the
Fortune 500.

Selected Stock Photography Available.

George Kamper

(212) 912-1595
(716) 454-7006

A working photographer with
the eye of a designer, solving
corporate and advertising visual
communications problems.
We bring ideas to our clients at
every phase of the project, and
deliver final chromes ready for
reproduction. Call for our portfolio.

Represented in Philadelphia by
Deborah Wolfe, Ltd.
(215) 232-6666

New, cool Cats. The Feline Phenomenon from Bausch & Lomb. 'Cat eye' design, high performance sun protection for men and women.

UNRETOUCHED PHOTO ILLUSTRATION BY BOB CONGE

Robert M. Knowles
2 Fordham Hill Oval
Bronx, New York 10468
(212) 367-4430

U.S. NAVY

FUJI AIRSHIP

U.S. NAVY

COVIDEA

DEAN WITTER REYNOLDS

GRAPHIC ARTS ORGANIZATIONS

Continued from page 76

Society of Illustrators
128 E. 63rd St.
New York, NY 10021
(212) 838-2560

Society of Photographers and Artists Representatives
1123 Broadway
New York, NY 10010
(212) 924-6023

Society of Publication Designers
25 W. 43rd St., Ste. 711
New York, NY
(212) 354-8585

Television Bureau of Advertising
485 Lexington Ave.
New York, NY 10017
(212) 661-8440

Type Directors Club of New York
545 W. 45th St.
New York, NY 10036
(212) 245-6300

U.S. Trademark Association
6 E. 45th St.
New York, NY 10017
(212) 986-5880

Volunteer Lawyers for the Arts
1560 Broadway, Ste. 711
New York, NY 10036
(212) 575-1150

Women in the Arts
325 Spring St.
New York, NY 10013
(212) 691-0988

Women in Design
P.O. Box 5315
FDR Station
New York, NY 10022

Ohio:

Advertising Club of Cincinnati
385 West Main St.
Batavia, OH 45103
(513) 732-9422

Cleveland Society of Communicating Arts
812 Huron Rd., S.E.
Cleveland, OH 44115
(216) 621-5139

Columbus Society of Communicating Arts
c/o Salvato & Coe
2015 West Fifth Ave.
Columbus, OH 43221
(614) 488-3131

Design Collective
D.F. Cooke
131 North High St.
Columbus, OH 43215
(614) 464-2883

Society of Communicating Arts
c/o Tailford Assoc.
1300 Indian Wood Circle
Maumee, OH 43537
(419) 891-0888

Pennsylvania:

Art Directors Club of Philadelphia
2017 Walnut St.
Philadelphia, PA 19103
(215) 569-3650

Tennessee:

Engraved Stationery Manufacturers Association
c/o Printing Industries Association of the South
1000 17th Ave. South
Nashville, TN 37212
(615) 327-4444

Texas:

Advertising Artists of Fort Worth
3424 Falcon Dr.
Fort Worth, TX 76119

Art Directors Club of Houston
2135 Bissonet
Houston, TX 77005
(713) 523-1019

Dallas Society of Visual Communication
3530 High Mesa Dr.
Dallas, TX 75234
(214) 241-2017

Print Production Association of Dallas/Fort Worth
P.O. Box 160605
Irving, TX 75016
(214) 871-2151

Virginia:

Industrial Designers Society of America
6802 Poplar Pl., Ste. 303
McLean, VA 22101
(703) 556-0919

Tidewater Society of Communicating Arts
P.O. Box 153
Norfolk, VA 23501

Washington:

Puget Sound Ad Federation
c/o Sylvia Fruichantie
Kraft Smith Advertising
200 1st West St.
Seattle, WA 98119
(206) 285-2222

Seattle Design Association
P.O. Box 1097
Main Office Station
Seattle, WA 98111
(206) 285-6725
(Formerly Seattle Women in Design)

Seattle Women in Advertising
219 First Avenue N., Ste. 300
Seattle, WA 98109
(206) 285-0919

Society of Professional Graphic Artists
c/o Steve Chin, Pres.
85 S. Washington Street, Ste. 204
Seattle, WA 98104

Wisconsin:

The Advertising Club
407 E. Michigan St.
Milwaukee, WI 53202
(414) 271-7351

Illustrators & Designers of Milwaukee
c/o Don Berg
207 E. Michigan
Milwaukee, WI 53202
(414) 276-7828

Whitney Lane

109 Somerstown Road
Ossining, New York 10562
(914) 762-5335

Representative: Betsy Heisey
(914) 762-5335

Stock photography available through The Image Bank.

I specialize in photography for Corporate
Communications and Advertising.

Not all my clients see things the same way:
AT&T, Avon, Ciba-Geigy, Dean Witter, Duracell,
Comstock Foods, IBM, Ingersoll-Rand,

Johnson & Johnson, Lederle, Olin, Osram, Pepsico,
Reader's Digest, Textron, Upjohn, and . . .

My studio (part of a 200-year-old farmhouse) is located
in Westchester, only a short distance from New York
City. Unique locations are everywhere.

You deserve photography as strong as your ideas. Call
for my portfolio. Also see: Corporate Showcase 3, 4
and 5. American Showcase 7 and ADIP 10.
All photos © Whitney Lane 1987.

SHELL CHEMICAL

NYACK: DAGLEY ASSOCIATES: DANA BRITTON

EXPERIMENTAL STOCK: LEGS THAT WON'T QUIT WHEN THE SUN GOES DOWN.

READER'S DIGEST: CAN COCAINE CONQUER AMERICA? NORMAN HOTZ AD

LEDERLE: CARRAFIELLO, DIEHL: CARON LEEDS AD

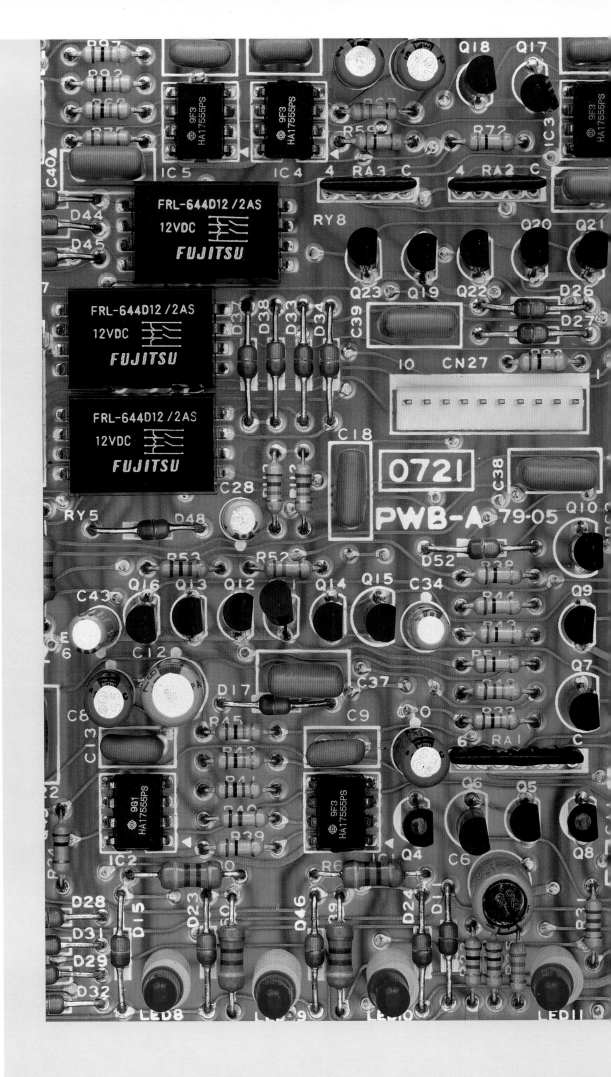

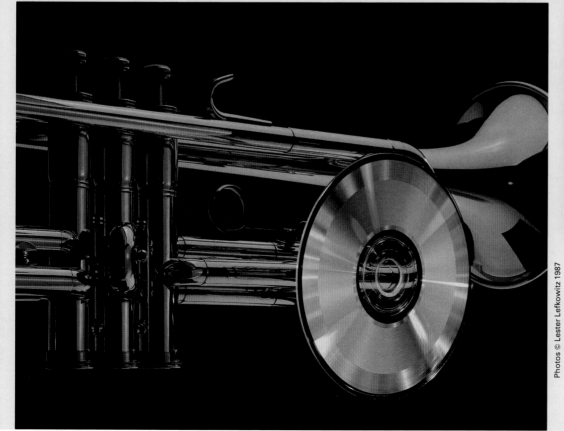

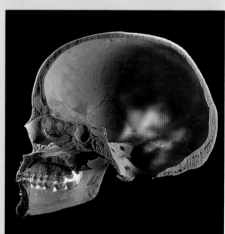

Photos © Lester Lefkowitz 1987

Lester Lefkowitz

Tech Photo, Inc.

*Photography
for Science
and Technology*

(212) 627-8088
(516) 751-5193

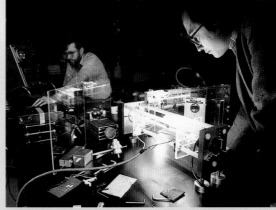

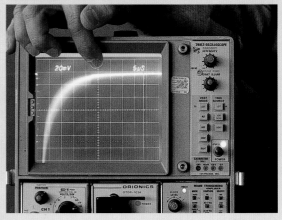

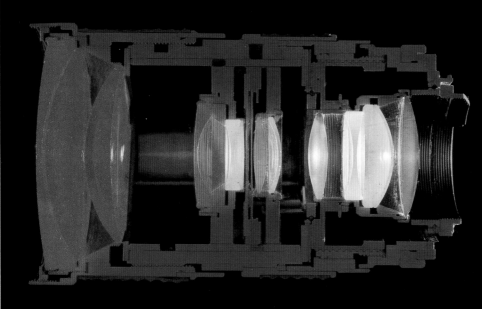

Lester Lefkowitz

Tech Photo, Inc.

*Photography
for Science
and Technology*

(212) 627-8088
(516) 751-5193

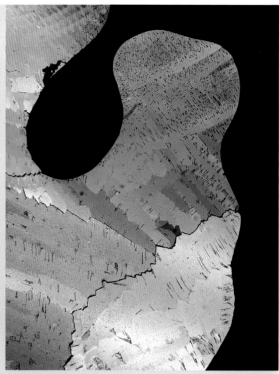

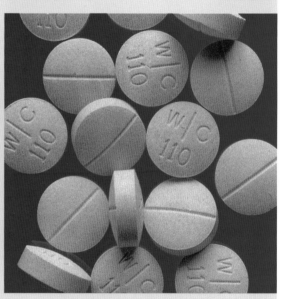

Lester Lefkowitz

Tech Photo, Inc.

*Photography
for Science
and Technology*

(212) 627-8088
(516) 751-5193

Peter Loppacher
Photography

56 Jane Street
New York, New York 10014
(212) 929-1322

Location specialist
Architecture and interiors
Corporate and real estate
Stock

Clients include:
American Express
Shearson-Lehman
Jones Lang Wootton
Sylvan Lawrence Company
Olympia and York
California Redwood Association
London and Leeds Corp.
Formica Corp.
First Boston Corp.

Mark Mac Laren

430 East 20th Street
New York, New York 10009
(212) 674-8615
(212) 674-0155

Landscapes and architecture
for corporate and advertising clients worldwide.

Extensive stock photography covering a wide variety
of subjects in 50 states, 24 countries and 7 continents.

For additional work, please see American Showcase 10.

The Two Worlds of Corporate Advertising

If you have ever felt you and your advertising agency are coming from two different worlds regarding corporate advertising, you are right.

Less than 2 percent of all advertising is corporate, so understandably agencies are staffed with people geared to product advertising. The fundamental differences between product advertising and corporate advertising can cause agency-client relations problems and result in poor corporate advertising from otherwise competent and creative ad people.

Unless your agency knows the special requirements of advertising that is part of a public relations or financial relations effort, it is apt to try to force corporate advertising into the more familiar formats of product advertising. Understanding the differences between the two can avoid a lot of client-agency headaches.

In four out of five large companies, corporate advertising is handled by the public relations or corporate communication department. Typically these staff people have backgrounds in journalism, English, the humanities and the social sciences. Their job experience prior to entering the corporate world probably includes editorial work or newspaper reporting. While this grounding prepares public relations practitioners to manage a corporation's news, public affairs and press relations, it is only marginally helpful in understanding advertising.

While some communication curricula today include a basic advertising course, it is frequently taught by professors with backgrounds in product advertising who are oriented to sales rather than public relations. To my knowledge no college or university offers a specific course in corporate advertising.

Ad agency staffers, on the other hand, usually have more varied backgrounds. The emphasis is on business and marketing for account contact personnel, while the writers have a wide range of backgrounds. It has long been recognized that creative freshness and originality in advertising can emerge from people with varied educational backgrounds. Today the agency emphasis is on writing for television, which demands a high level of idea generation but makes relatively modest demands on English language skills, and it's not unusual to find ad writers who can't write anything else.

It can be argued that the differences between advertising and public relations people are rooted in their psychological make-ups. Those with somewhat gentler personalities go in one direction, while more result-oriented people go in another. I will leave it to you to decide which is which. It is no wonder that at the seam where these two disciplines meet—corporate advertising—problems can erupt. However, these differences can also result in great creativity. It depends on whether the differences are understood and used to advantage, or whether they get out of hand and result in a breakdown in client-agency communication.

Let's examine the two worlds, but first let it be understood that I am not taking sides, nor am I saying that one discipline is right and the other wrong. They are just different.

Ads, not stories. Press releases are really written for two audiences: editors and the target public. The editor must be attracted by newsworthiness, story content and quality of writing. This has led to the sensible practice of putting all the basic information in the first paragraph and then enlarging on the story in waves, with the less essential details toward the end of the story.

That's a terrible way to write an ad. Ad copy should be of a piece, starting with an attention-getting headline. The copy should carry the reader from the thought in the headline through the essence of the message and end with a strong, memorable last line, or clincher.

Public relations people tend to think of ads as stories with perhaps a photograph or two. An ad should be thought of as a unit. The art director today in most good ad agencies has an equal role with the writer in originating the basic concept (headline and visual treatment taken as a whole). This "concept" approach makes maximum use of the freedom an advertiser has to employ all of that expensive white space to attract attention and involve the reader. The total effect should be a strong, memorable impression that may be achieved as much by style and taste as by content.

Continued on page 104

Abraham Menashe

Humanistic Photography
306 East 5th Street
New York, New York 10003
(212) 254-2754

Photography that focuses on our unique spirit;
communicating care, celebrating the environment,
portraying our pursuit for excellence. Photography
that highlights our humanity and contributes to a
better world.

Color or black and white, for Annual Reports,
Advertising, Illustration, and Editorial.

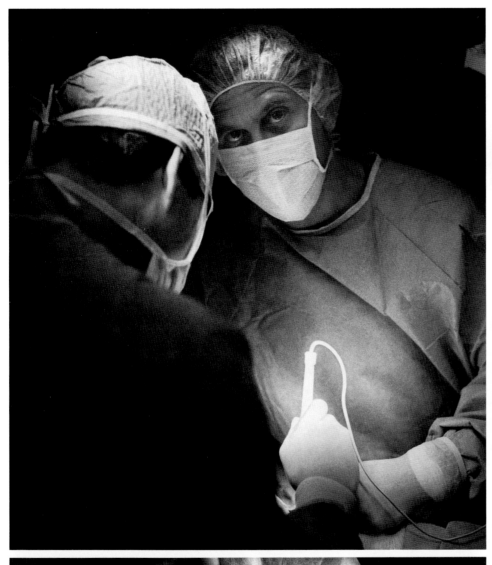

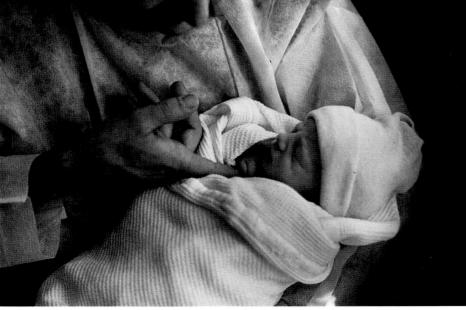

Donald L. Miller

295 Central Park West
New York, New York 10024
(212) 496-2830

Specializing in C.E.O's, Chairman, Presidents,
Directors, and top management

Donald L. Miller

295 Central Park West
New York, New York 10024
(212) 496-2830

Specializing in C.E.O's, Chairman, Presidents,
Directors, and top management

Thom O'Connor
Photography

74 Fifth Avenue
New York, New York 10011
(212) 620-0723

Corporate and Editorial
Photography

For clients including:

Allstate
Sears
E.F. Hutton
Merrill, Lynch
Touche Ross
Business Week
PC Magazine
The New York Times

Gabe Palmer

**Gabe Palmer's
Mug Shots™**

Fire Hill Farm
West Redding, Connecticut 06896
(203) 938-3246

Stock and corporate
photography on location and
in the studio

ASSIGNMENT:
Palmer/Kane
West Redding, Connecticut 06896
(203) 938-2514

STOCK:
The Stock Market
New York
(212) 684-7878

After Image
Los Angeles
(213) 480-1105

Masterfile
Toronto
(416) 977-7267

Imperial Press
Tokyo
81-3-585-2565

The Stock House
Hong Kong
852-5-H22-0486

Stock Photos
South Melbourne
61-3-699-7084

Ace Photo
London
011-44-1-629-0303

A.G.E. Fotostock
Barcelona
34-3-300-2552

Granata Press Service
Milan
022-282-7960

Sentrale Farbbild Agentur b.m.b.h.
Dusseldorf
011-49-211-574037

Zesa Hamburg
Hamburg

Esarl Sarbeild-Hgentur t.m.b.h.
Vienna
043-222-34-9208

Esarl France s.a.r.l.
Paris
033-142-74-5547

Key Color
Zurich
041-251-0676

Benelux Press
Voorburg
031-70-87-0681

Stock...

for people who need people.

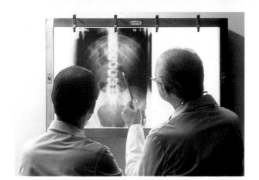

Alex Pietersen

29 Raynor Road
Morristown, New Jersey 07960
(201) 267-7003

Agencies

Deltakos (Div of J. Walter Thompson) • D'Arcy-MacManus Masius • Saatchi & Saatchi Compton Inc. • Wunderman, Ricotta & Kline • The J.N. Company • Rolf Werner Rosenthal Inc. (Div of Ogilvy & Mather) • Keyes Martin • Ogilvy & Mather Direct

Partial List of Clients

Eli Lilly • Upjohn Co • Squibb • Rousselle • Cordis • Neuromed • Centocor • Johnston Equipment Inc. • W.H. Freeman and Company Publishers • Silver Burdett & Ginn • Speedo • I.B.M. • Allied Chemical • Tobor Pictures Ltd. • AT&T

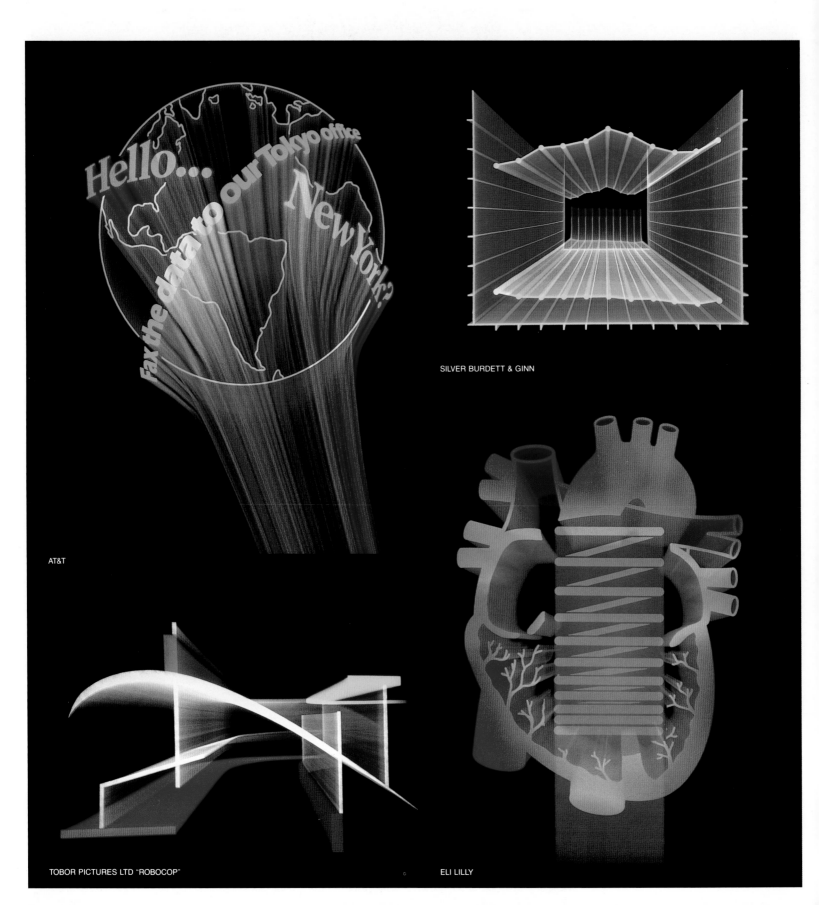

AT&T

SILVER BURDETT & GINN

TOBOR PICTURES LTD "ROBOCOP"

ELI LILLY

Bill Ray

350 Central Park West
New York, New York 10025

Represented by Marlys Ray
(212) 222-7680

© Bill Ray, 1987

For more of my work see pages
106-107 Corporate Showcase
3, Corporate Showcase 4,
American Showcase 9. Black
& while samples and portfolio
on request.

1. James C. Marlas, Chairman,
   CEO, Mickelberry Corp.

2. Walter J. O'Brien, Vice
   Chairman, J. Walter
   Thompson Group, Inc.

3. Don Johnston, Chairman,
   CEO, J. Walter Thompson
   Group, Inc.

4. Louis J. Forgione, Treasurer,
   General Re Corp.

5. James E. Burke, Chairman,
   CEO, Johnson & Johnson.

6. Frederick W. Smith,
   Chairman, CEO, Federal
   Express Corp.

7. Len Casillo, Designer,
   General Motors.

1.

2.

3.

4.

5.

6.

7.

Jon Riley

12 East 37th Street
New York, New York 10016
(212) 532-8326

1. AT&T
2. New Yorker Magazine
3. Coca-Cola
4. AT&T
5. AT&T
6. Property Capital Trust
7. AT&T

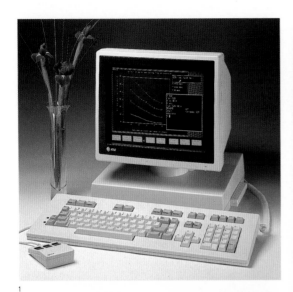

1

2

3

4

5

6

7

Jon Riley

12 East 37th Street
New York, New York 10016
(212) 532-8326

1. Bankers Trust Co.
2. Property Capital Trust
3. New York Life
4. Avon
5. Avon
6. Avon
7. Enro Shirt

1

4

5

6

2

3

7

Bob Sacha

370 Central Park West
New York, New York 10025
(212) 749-4128

Advertising, Annual Reports, Corporate, Editorial

Some clients:
Fallon McElligott Rice, Sony, AT&T, New York Stock
Exchange, Mellon Mortgage Trust, Shearson Lehman
Brothers, McGraw-Hill, Regis McKenna Inc., Forbes,
Fortune, National Geographic.

INTERNATIONAL PAPER

APPLE COMPUTER

Jed Share/Tokyo

Sunny Heights Seijo
2-8-8-102 Seijo
Tokyo, Setagaya-Ku. 157. Japan
Telephone 81-3-415-5475 or
Fax 81-3-470-0243

Winner of the two highest
awards for annual report
photography in Japan

Representative in the
United States:
Ursula G. Kreis
(212) 562-8931

代表　株式会社
エイダスインターナショナル
Tel: (03) 478-1715
Fax: (03) 470-0243

Peter Angelo Simon

568 Broadway Suite 701
New York, New York 10012
(212) 925-0890

We create images which convey the power, excitement and precision of high technology processes and concepts for corporate advertising, annual reports and graphic communications of all kinds.

Our clients have come to rely on our imagination, state of the art photography and grace under pressure.

We produce images for:

IBM, Bell Labs, AT&T, General Motors Corp., Panasonic, Medicus Intercon, Smithsonian, Omni, and many other corporations, agencies and designers large and small.

Wide range of stock photography available.

Portfolio available upon request.

For more images see: Corporate Showcases 2 & 5 and ASMP Books 1, 2, 3, & 5.

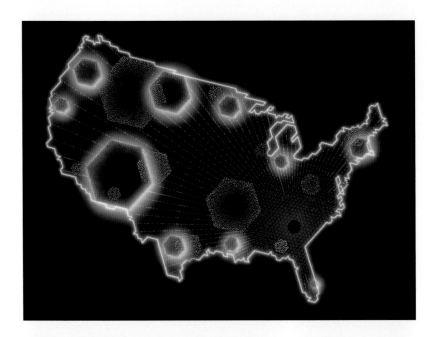

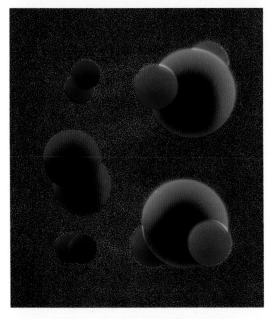

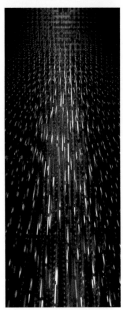

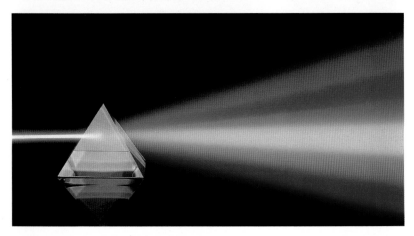

Kim Steele

640 Broadway
New York, New York 10012
(212) 777-7753

Top: Fortune Magazine cover
story on high tech future;
Here developing optical
coatings for lasers.

Left: C.E.O. of regional bank in
Florida for Peat Marwick

Right: Laser application in
plastic surgery for OMNI
Magazine

Representation: BLACK STAR

Continued from page 90

Watch your grammar. While poor grammar may turn an editor off, it may be exactly what is needed to concisely communicate a memorable advertising message. Agencies long ago began to ignore many grammatical niceties in the interest of conveying an idea. Remember that advertising does not normally attempt to set standards. Rather, it follows the current styles of speech and expression. Much as this may grate, that's the way it is, at least for product advertising.

However, in the case of corporate advertising, which may indeed be used to set or illustrate a company's standards, it is entirely appropriate to adhere to the rules of good grammar. Consider that two important publics for corporate advertising, the press and educators, are also the most likely to be offended and complain about bad grammar in ads. The language choice depends on how a company wishes to be perceived. It should be management's decision. If you decide to stay with good grammar, this point will probably need to be explained to each new creative team.

I like to tell copywriters that while most product advertising should use the language of the customer, corporate advertising has to use the language of management, which, presumably, is educated. In any event, most managements wish to appear so. This approach also makes it clear why corporate ads generally should not be frivolous or silly. If you think of corporate ads as the voice of management, you won't stray too far from the correct tone. Moreover, this approach should keep you from creating corporate ads that are too stuffy, although management frequently needs guidance to avoid that impression.

Don't shoot the rabbit with a cannon. The marketing background of most advertising people has accustomed them to think in terms of advertising effectiveness at any price. According to them, if the advertising is stimulating sales at an acceptable rate it matters little if some small portion of the audience is offended by the advertising.

Unfortunately, as public relations practitioners know, the first people to write complaint letters are usually executives' spouses, stockholders, and major customers. Further, most of the letters go to the chief executive officer and are bucked to the public relations department for answers that turneth away wrath.

Now, that dichotomy of interests sets the stage for a lot of standard dialogue between ad agency and corporate account. As the agency people see it, they have just outdone themselves with a new ad campaign that clearly will get everyone's attention. It makes exactly the right points and will probably be the most cost-efficient program they have ever come up with. The corporate communication director, on the other hand, sees the same campaign as perhaps accomplishing that goal with most of the target audience, but in a way that may tear up the landscape.

At this point communication directors must be careful or they may permanently cool the enthusiasm of the agency creative team. Don't leave them convinced that your company is not only stuffy, but that it doesn't care whether the ads are really productive and doesn't know a good ad from a bad one. You need a lot of tact as well as firmness, and a full explanation of the dynamics of what happens as a result of corporate advertising that offends perhaps the most important publics of all.

Watch the humor. Humor is a very good tool in product advertising. It is rarely used in corporate ads. Why? Because it frequently bombs. There is a difference between the sophisticated wit management may find acceptable in corporate ads and the quite appropriate street-level humor used in product advertising.

It should be pointed out here that advertising tone will vary greatly with the corporation. A style that may fit a new, aggressive company battling its way up may project a brashness and irreverence totally out of place for an established company that is a leader in its field. Recognizing the right tone is far easier for the corporation's director of communications than for the ad agency. Take this into account in indoctrination meetings.

Set advertising goals. Advertising people, as discussed earlier, are either born with or develop an internal compass that points them in the direction of sales. Corporate advertising has other, and sometimes a combination of, objectives.

These have to be spelled out very carefully from the beginning. It is not enough to say the ads are trying to sell the corporation. That may be understood by the ad agency, but it is not specific enough for a cost-effective corporate ad program. Try answering the question, "When this ad runs, what do we want to happen?" That is the explicit objective needed. Unfortunately, this kind of orientation is left out of the backgrounds of most public relations practitioners, although it is fundamental to marketing.

Continued on page 116

Jeanne Strongin

61 Irving Place
New York, New York 10003
(212) 473-3718

Assignment Photography/
Portraits in the studio and on
location/Editorial/Corporate/
Annual Report/Advertising/
Travel

See American Showcase
Volumes 6, 7, 9 and 10

Portfolio Available on Request

Photographs:
John Chiles, Texaco
David Boies, Cravath Swain
  & Moore
Karen Valenstein, E.F. Hutton

JEANNE STRONGIN   212 473-3718

Michel Tcherevkoff

873 Broadway
New York, New York 10003
(212) 228-0540

Represented by:

New York City—Fran Black (212) 580-4045
Philadelphia—Deborah Wolfe (215) 232-6666
Chicago—Joni Tuke (312) 787-6826

Call for Michel's mini-portfolio

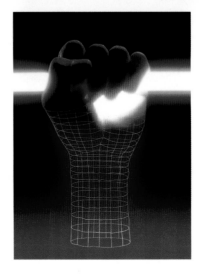

Peter Vadnai

180 Valley Road
Katonah, New York 10536
(914) 232-5328

Specializing in corporate assignments "on location."
Extensive "Fortune 500" client list.

Stock photographs: The Stock Market, New York

VADNAI

Joseph Patrick Vericker

60 East 42nd Street
Suite 411
New York, New York 10165
(212) 863-9801

PO Box 390
Bronx, New York 10465

111 Cedar Street
Fourth Floor
New Rochelle, New York 10801
(914) 632-2072

Corporate, Public Relations, Annual Report, Editorial, and Advertising.

Daniel Wagner

50 West 29th Street (12th floor)
New York, New York 10001
(212) 532-8255

Clients include:
AT&T, Coca-Cola Bottling Co., Forbes, Fortune, IBM,
Institutional Investor, Marcal Paper Products, Marschalk
Advertising, Mobil Oil, Money Magazine, Newsweek,
The New York Times, Ogilvy & Mather, Scientific
American, Seagrams, Time Inc., Warner Communications

Member ASMP   All Photos © Daniel Wagner 1987

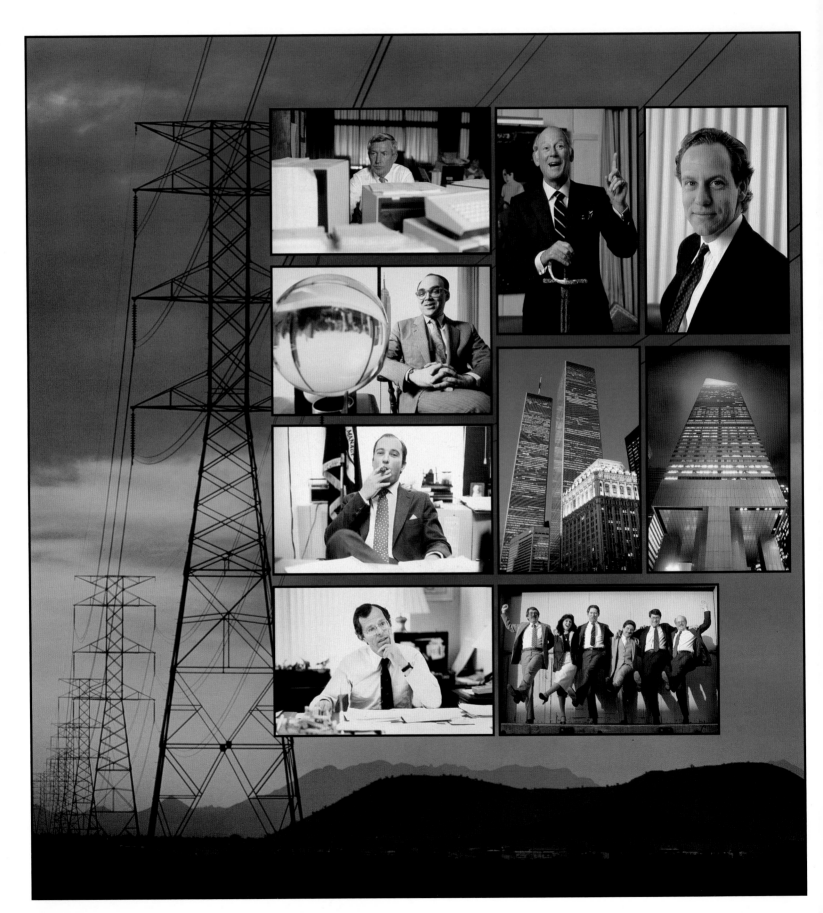

Tony Ward
Studio:
704 South 6th Street
Philadelphia, Pennsylvania 19147

Represented in New York by: Jerry Cornfeld
(212) 873-7119

Advertising and Corporate photography for Towers,
Perrin, Forster and Crosby, RCA, Smithkline Beckman,
Citibank, Shared Medical Systems, Turner Construction,
Dupont, Rohm & Haas, Jefferson Hospital of
Philadelphia, Cigna, The Money Store.

TONY WARD

Philadelphia, 215-238-1208 / New York, 212-873-7119

Steve Weinberg

47 East 19th Street
New York, New York 10003
(212) 254-9571

Los Angeles
(213) 281-1886

Worldwide location
photography for annual reports,
corporate/industrial,
advertising, editorial and travel.

Partial client list:
Chemical Bank
Playboy Enterprises
Pfizer Pharmaceuticals
KLM Airlines
The Entertainment Network
Successful Meetings Magazine
M.D. Publications
Nissan
Bridgestone
Hanover Properties
Newspaper Advertising Bureau
Jackson Communications

STEVE
WEINBERG

47 East 19th Street
New York, New York 10003
212/254-9571

Los Angeles
213/281-1886

Yoav

4523 Broadway
New York, New York 10040
(212) 942-8185

Represented by:
Phototake, The Creative Link
(Ask for Leila)
(212) 942-8185

For Phototake Ad
See also ASMP stock section page 3

NEW JERSEY BELL

MAYOR KOCH

CBS

TEL-AVIV UNIVERSITY

UNITED TECHNOLOGIES

Northeast

Connecticut
Massachusetts
New York
Pennsylvania
Rhode Island
West Virginia

Continued from page 104

An ad agency's success depends on preparing ads that get results, ads that make waves. Agencies take pride in campaigns whose success can be documented. The corporate communication director may want advertising that improves the company image, but, being experienced in sensitive corporate areas, many have a built-in objection to making waves. Well, face it: If you want to change the company's image you will have to make waves, albeit favorable ones. Establish the corporate direction early and precisely for your ad agency. Then stick to it.

Credibility. Some statements made in a press release are more believable when printed as part of a news story, with the implied endorsement of the publication. These same statements become absurd when made in an ad. As much as you pay for media space, one of the things you don't get is automatic believability. Credibility has to be designed into an ad. Practitioners know that one of the best ways to gain credibility with a reporter is to be candid. It's the same in advertising. Admit to a minor fault and readers will believe most of whatever else you tell them.

Dull is dull. It is amazing how often agencies are asked to write ads on subjects that are far too uninteresting to make it as news stories. "After all," goes the thinking, "as long as we are paying for the space why not tell the viewers or readers exactly what we want them to know?" Unfortunately, audiences have a great facility to tune out something that doesn't interest them. There are lots of advertising devices, like trick headlines, color and multiple-space units, that can help with marginally interesting subjects, but they are poor substitutes for a good story. Provide your agency with an adequate story budget. Let the creative people weave in the necessary message, but give them something interesting to weave it around.

Who, what, why, when and how, but especially where. Not even the most inexperienced brand manager would ask the ad agency to develop a campaign for a product without explaining its ingredients, what it is for, who uses it, how it differs from other products and what makes it better.

That same kind of information about the company is needed for corporate advertising. But you also need to provide the agency with one more thing: the corporate mission, or *where* the company is going. Too often this company description and direction is omitted from agency indoctrinations. Despite all the strategic planning that has been done in recent years, the basic corporate mission as it applies to communications is often overlooked.

This is the client's job. Corporate mission shouldn't be left to the agency to invent as it goes along. Sure, even without indoctrination the agency may come up with ads that seem to fit the general description of the corporation. But that isn't likely, and after two or three attempts the client will probably assume the agency doesn't know what it's doing. Too often, however, the fact is the client has never bothered to examine its basic product—the company.

Repeat, repeat, repeat. Any account executive or agency media person will tell you that you can run an ad three or four times before it begins to lose readership value. Most product advertisers recognize this, but the public relations and news orientation of corporate advertising clients makes it difficult for them to accept this fact. Well, just because you ran an ad once doesn't mean everybody saw it. Besides, repetition is a good thing. It makes good economic and marketing sense.

Staying healthy. Keep the agency-client relationship healthy with periodic checkups. Top management should conduct performance reviews to evaluate expectations versus delivery. It's a little awkward at first, but it's better than waiting till the problems become terminal. The Association of National Advertisers has a book on auditing client-agency relations, or call me—after all, I'm in the business.

Thomas F. Garbett
Corporate Advertising Consultant
Waterford, Connecticut

Reprinted with permission from the November 1984 issue of the Public Relations Journal.

Theodore Anderson
235 North Madison Street
Allentown, Pennsylvania 18102
(215) 437-6468

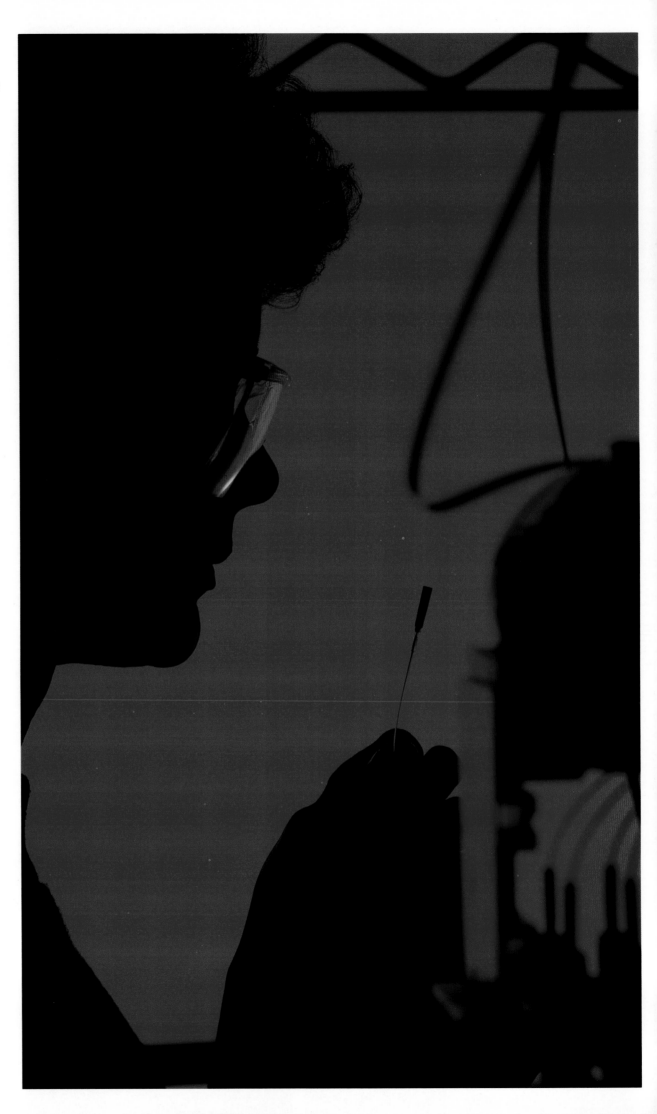

Theodore Anderson
235 North Madison Street
Allentown, Pennsylvania 18102
(215) 437-6468

Cavanaugh-On Location

P.O. Box 158
Buffalo, New York 14151
(716) 837-0697

Represented By:
Cheryl Sidel
(716) 833-8877

Location Photography
• Corporate
• Aerial
• A/V Multi-Image
• Stock

Problem solving-Miracle working...Not just getting a good shot in a difficult situation...But working on tight deadlines...Tighter budgets...Impossible logistics.. Endless details. I don't work on a project, I get immersed in a project...Forming a highly charged, creative "Master Mind" Team with the client, producer, art director and other production people. If your next project is important and the parameters crazy but you want it to be fun...call me.

1986 National Clients: Burger King, Chase Corp., Ford Motor, General Mills, ITT, NYNEX, Upjohn, Westwood Pharmaceuticals. 1986 Regional Clients: Brimms Mfg., Buffalo Telephone Co., Ellis Singer Group, Healy-Schutte & Co., Levy King & White, M&T Bank, Snyder Corp.

Member ASMP
AMI

John DeWaele
14 Almy Street
Lincoln, Rhode Island 02865
(401) 726-0084

Photography on location
Corporations and Advertising

JOHN DeWAELE

PHOTOGRAPHY ON LOCATION

401-726-0084

Barney Leonard Photography

518 Putnam Road
Merion, Pennsylvania 19066
(215) 664-2525

Corporate and Industrial Location Photography for annual reports, corporate publications, and multi-image presentations.

Barney Leonard
Photography
518 Putnam Road
Merion, Pennsylvania 19066
(215) 664-2525

Corporate and Industrial
Location Photography for
annual reports, corporate
publications, and multi-image
presentations.

Ed Malitsky

337 Summer Street
Boston, Massachusetts 02210
(617) 451-0655

On location for annual reports, corporate, industrial,
advertising and editorial assignments, stock.

Member: A.S.M.P.

Ralph Mercer

239 A Street
Boston, Massachusetts 02210
(617) 482-2942

Location and studio photography for corporate
advertising, annual report, and collateral usage.
Conceptual special effects photography is a specialty.

Clients include: Honeywell, DuPont, Motorola, Inc.,
Lotus Development Corp., New England Telephone
Co., InfoCom., and Teradyne.

HONEYWELL/A.D. RANDY SHERMAN

KLOSS VIDEO/A.D. JOHN KANE

TERADYNE/A.D. ROGER SAMETZ

CONCEPT AND PHOTOGRAPH BY MERCER

125

These three thoughts are directed to the photographers, illustrators and graphic designers represented in Corporate Showcase. In fact, they are also directed to those not represented here. They come with good wishes from a fellow communicator, someone who has been president of a public relations agency for thirty years.

None of us has very much time. This fact applies to those of us who work with words, work with visual images and work with both. I don't mean it the way you may think. I mean it in terms of the time we have to flag down the attention of our audience and then hold it long enough to transmit a message…and maybe even a feeling about the message.

People read fast, see fast and perceive fast today. They screen out what doesn't matter to them and decide in fractions of a second what might be interesting. This process leaves us with no alternative except to communicate in a full sense—that is, build a bridge directly from us to each individual in the target market. It is no longer useful to beam out a message and hope somebody notices—even when that message is beautifully drawn, superbly photographed or magnificently written. If it doesn't work on a one-on-one basis with very large numbers of people in the marketplace, it's not worth the trouble. It may be art (which has value with smaller audiences, even audiences of one), but it isn't commercial communication.

In public relations, we try to generate ideas that are sufficiently relevant to our audience, sufficiently different (even surprising) and sufficiently important to win attention in an instant. Quality, even artistry, is where we begin. We can't end there. The images in this book make it clear that you approach communications the same way.

Why do I raise this issue? Because it is one on which those of us who work primarily with words and those of us who work primarily with visual images can readily agree. After that, the coordination gets harder.

Everyone who has worked on an annual report or brochure or advertisement or publicity feature knows that word-oriented professionals tend to process data differently from image-oriented ones. I don't know whether the roots of this condition lie in the two hemispheres of our brains or in the ways we begin to perceive and think when we are growing up—or both. I do know that some of us communicate with our opposite numbers exceptionally well. Too many professionals don't. Result: The author doesn't get the kinds of photographs, illustrations or graphics he/she had in mind. Or the photographer, illustrator or designer finds that the writer missed the point.

There is no magic solution, but the twain can, in fact, meet—or come wonderfully close. We and our professional colleagues try to cross each other's perceptual frontiers on an organized basis. Those of us who write urge photographers, illustrators and designers with whom we work to read and discuss our annual reports, brochures, releases, speeches and other materials. Those of us who work with images, on the other hand, call on writers to look at our portfolios, to think about them and learn to understand their visual rationales and techniques.

The rewards are great: When we approach a communications project together, both of us ultimately experience the exhilaration of saying, "I see exactly what you mean." Each of us has crossed a difficult barrier. The big winner is the client.

News demands focus. Of course, you say. Again, it's meant differently from what you might think. We once retained a well reputed, local news photographer for an assignment in a small city in the South. The president of a client was coming to make a major address to the most important elected officials, corporate and union executives, civic leaders and clergymen in the region. We wanted the speech covered.

It was no ordinary speech. The president's New York based company had built a major manufacturing plant in this southern city a year before and had made no provisions for even a modest community relations effort. Predictably, local suspicions grew into open hostility, and soon bottles of paint remover were being hurled at company cars. It was to deal with this ugly situation that the company had retained one agency.

Continued on page 142

Mozo

MOZO Photo/Design
282 Shelton Road (Route 110)
Monroe, Connecticut 06468-2529
(203) 261-7400

Additional work can be seen in American Showcase
8/206, 9/193, 10/199 and Corporate Showcase 5/107.

Stock, reprints and portfolio available upon request.

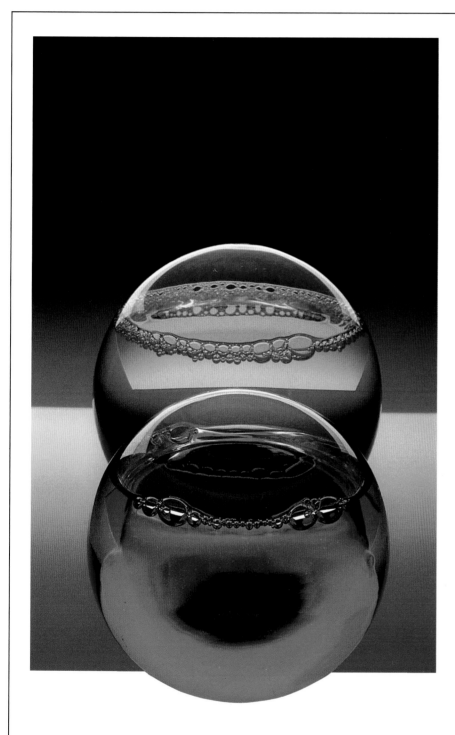

Seth Resnick

15 Sleeper Street #507
Boston, Massachusetts 02210
(617) 423-7475

Location

Corporate
Advertising
Editorial
Travel

Stock

Picture Group Inc.
(401) 273-5473

Seth Resnick

15 Sleeper Street #507
Boston, Massachusetts 02210
(617) 423-7475

Location

Corporate
Advertising
Editorial
Travel

Stock

Picture Group Inc.
(401) 273-5473

Jeffrey L. Rotman

14 Cottage Avenue
Somerville, Massachusetts 02144
(617) 666-0874

On-location photography around the world, specializing in underwater. Available for assignments.

Extensive underwater stock including coral reefs, divers, marine life, and shipwrecks.

Exotic foreign stock including:
snake charming (India)
hippo hunting (Africa)
belly dancing (Egypt)

cocaine manufacture (Bolivia)
mud wrestling (Turkey)

Editorial clients include Audubon, Discover, Figaro, Geo, Life, Minolta Mirror, National Geographic, Natural History, New York Times, Omni, Penthouse, People, Science Digest, Sierra Club, Smithsonian, Time, Travel & Leisure, U.S. News & World Report, and Zoom.

Bruce H. Schaeffer

631 North Pottstown Pike
Exton, Pennsylvania 19341
(215) 363-5230

I call my company Great Valley
Commercial Photography.
I work for some of the fastest
growing companies in the U.S.
located right here in my area.
I'd like to work for your
company. We also own our own
custom E-6 and C41 Lab.

Please call to see rest of the
portfolio.

Russ Schleipman

298A Columbus Avenue
Boston, Massachusetts 02116
(617) 267-1677

Advertising, Annual Report, Corporate, Editorial,
Industrial, Travel

Clients Include: AMCA International, Automatix,
Bausch & Lomb, Boston Five, Centocor, Chelsea,
Courier, Dennison, Digital, Dunkin' Donuts, Ernst &
Whinney, First NH Banks, Forbes, Fortune, Helix, Life,
M/A-COM, Money, New England Electric, New World
Bank, Outside, Polaroid, Raytheon, Repligen,
Rockresorts, Sail, Shawmut, Tech Ops

Frank Siteman
136 Pond Street
Winchester, Massachusetts 01890
(617) 729-3747

Clients include:
Anheuser-Busch, Inc.,
Fidelity Investments,
General Foods,
John Hancock,
M.I.T.
Polaroid Corporation,
S.D. Warren,
Wang Laboratories.

Capturing the Spirit of Human Endeavor for Annual Reports, Advertising, and Special Projects

Jamey Stillings

87 North Clinton Avenue
Fifth Floor
Rochester, New York 14604
716 232 5296

Represented by Pat Urban

ASMP
Languages: English, German, Spanish

Jamey Stillings
87 North Clinton Avenue
Fifth Floor
Rochester, New York 14604
(716) 232-5296

Represented By Pat Urban

ASMP
Languages: English, German,
Spanish

Dan Vecchio Photography

129 East Water Street
Syracuse, New York 13202
(315) 471-1064

Locations
Exteriors
Stock
Interiors

Client List:
AFL-CIO, American Heart Association, Carrier
Corporation, CitiBank Corporation, Eastman Kodak
Company, E.F. Hutton, General Electric Company,
IBM, Marine Midland Bank, Miller Brewing Company,
MONY, Niagara Mohawk Power Corporation,
Oberdorfer Pumps, Pyramid Companies, State of
New York.

For more of my work see Corporate Showcase 5,
page #174

Robert L. Wilson

CHIMERA INC.
P.O. Box 1742
Clarksburg, West Virginia 26302
(304) 623-5368

Baltimore, Maryland
(301) 727-3371

TELEX: 271195 EXEC UR

PHOTOGRAPHER
WRITER
CINEMATOGRAPHER

General Electric
Dresser Industries
Conoco Inc.
TIME

INTERNATIONAL ITINERARY
(Substantial cost savings.)

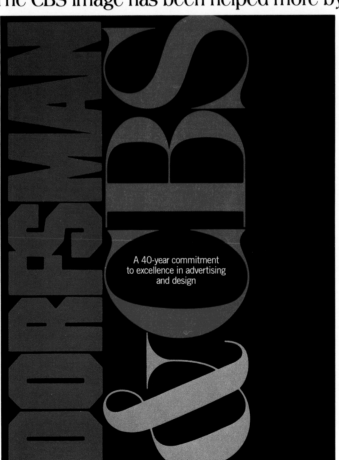

Mid-Atlantic

Maryland
Virginia
Washington, D.C.

Robert Bennett
819 Leigh Mill Road
Great Falls, Virginia 22066
(703) 759-4582

Mike Carpenter
5127 Harford Lane
Burke, Virginia 22015
(703) 978-2196

Location photography for the business world.

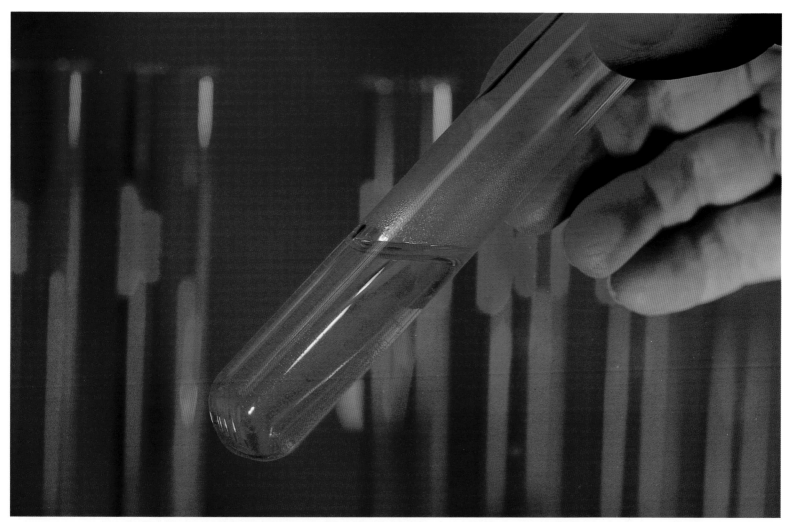

Continued from page 126

Now a year of unceasing effort had passed. We had arranged for the company to reach out to the people...and for the people to come and call. We had generated countless dialogues between company officials and local residents—from City Council members to tenant farmers. We had helped the company to perform as a model corporate citizen.

Finally, we felt the time had come to bring the president to town. A year ago he had been the subject of enmity. We were confident that he could now address the community and succeed.

He delivered the address, which built from a quiet review of the past to a stirring look into a future that the city and the company could share. He concluded. There was total silence. What did it mean? Then, suddenly, every member of the audience stood and cheered. The applause was like thunder.

I waited for the strobes to flash. They did not come. The applause peaked. Still no strobes. Then I saw our photographer. He was standing on a chair, cheering and applauding, caught up in the magic of the moment.

If you are represented by photographers in this book, you most likely know better. When it comes to news, your calling requires you to be in the heart of the action yet, in a curious way, removed. Please consider this tale a gentle reminder.

We can't guarantee published credit. Finally, on a practical note, a plea for understanding. When you sell photographs to a public relations agency for release to media, you can require that the agency credit you in its captions. You cannot require that the newspaper or magazine credit your picture because the agency can't. In most cases, media oblige. In some they don't. If you are unwilling to accept this reality, don't shoot for publicity use.

David S. Wachsman
President
David S. Wachsman Associates Inc.
Public Relations
New York City

Jarvis J. Grant

1650 Harvard Street N.W.
Suite #709
Washington, D.C. 20009
(202) 387-8584

For location and studio assignments in editorial/corporate photography. Available also for museum and gallery assignments of fine art object photography.

I have been a member on the creative teams of the following: Art Institute of Chicago, American Crafts Magazine, Artist Equity, Ceramics Monthly Magazine, Cocoran Gallery of Art, John Jay College of Criminal Justice, Howard University, The Menil Foundation, The Labor Agency of Metropolitan Washington, National Park Service, National Urban Coalition, National Urban League, Smithsonian Institution, Studio Museum in Harlem, Washington D.C. Dept. of Human Services, The Washington Review, and The Visions Foundation.

For photography that communicates ideas and motivates response give me a call. Portfolio upon request.

AWARDS:
D.C. Commission of the Arts and Humanities Photography Fellowship

J. GRANT

(202) 387-8584 • Washington, D.C.

Greg Pease

23 East 22nd Street
Baltimore, Maryland 21218
(301) 332-0583

Stock photography available
Studio Manager: Kelly Baumgartner

Also see:
American Showcase 4, 5, 6, 7, 8, 9, 10
Corporate Showcase 1, 4, 5

Greg Pease

23 East 22nd Street
Baltimore, Maryland 21218
(301) 332-0583

Stock photography available
Studio Manager: Kelly Baumgartner

Also see:
American Showcase 4, 5, 6, 7, 8, 9, 10
Corporate Showcase 1, 4, 5

Ross Stansfield

4938 D Eisenhower Avenue
Alexandria, Virginia 22304
(703) 370-5142

Studio and location

Clients include: Coca Cola, Marriot Corporation, The
Peau Corporation, Future Farmers of America, Fairfax
Hospital Association, N V Homes, Metropolitan Office
Furniture, The United States Air Force, The United Way,
The Washington Post, American Concrete Pressure
Pipe Association.

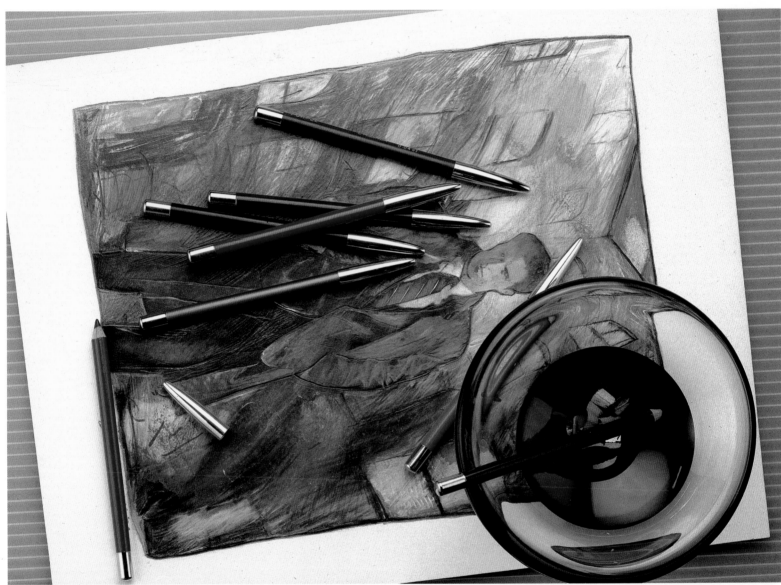

THE PEAU CORPORATION, ILLUSTRATION BY BRIAN McCALL

THE UNITED STATES AIR FORCE

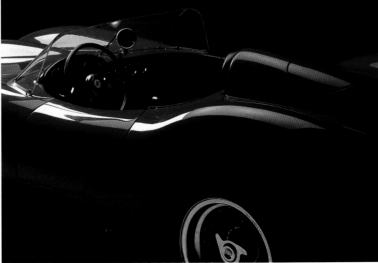

THE WASHINGTON POST

Southeast

Florida
Georgia
Louisiana
North Carolina
Tennessee

Henderson/Muir Photography

6005 Chapel Hill Road
Raleigh, North Carolina 27607
(919) 851-0458

New 7000 square-foot
studio now available.

See additional work in
American Showcase,
Volumes 8, 9, & 10.

Stock Representation through:
Woodfin Camp & Associates
(212) 750-1020 New York
(202) 638-5705 Washington

Clients include:
Ajinomoto, U.S.A.
Athol Vinyl Fabrics
Bald Head Island
Branch Banking & Trust
Collins & Aikman
Colorcraft Corporation
Data General
Domino's Pizza
General Electric
Hardees Food Systems
Harlon Properties Group
Harris Semi-Conductor
Hilton Hotels
IBM
ITT
Karastan Carpets
Liggett & Myers
Mallinckrodt
McDonalds
Mead CompuChem
Mitsubishi Semi-Conductor
NC Travel & Tourism
NC State Ports
Northern Telecom
Piedmont Airlines
Record Bar, Inc.
Research Triangle Foundation
Sheraton Hotels
The New York Times Magazine
Thurston Trucking Company
Time-Life Books
Union Carbide
U.S. Air
Wachovia Bank & Trust

Advertising,
Business Publications,
Annual Reports,
Corporate/Industrial,
Travel/Personalities

Represented by:
Faithe Benson
(919) 851-0458

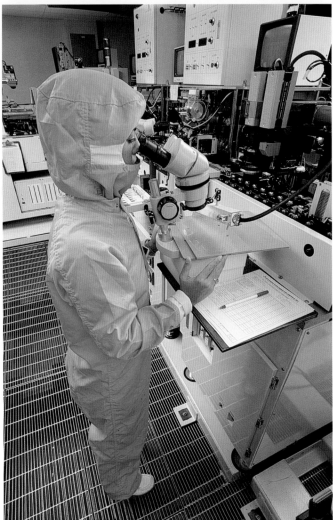

Jackson Hill

2032 Adams
New Orleans, Louisiana 70118
(504) 861-3000

Represented by:
Southern Lights Photography, Inc.
(504) 861-3000

Jackson shoots alligators sliding down the bayou, space ships blasting into the blue, corporate officers on parade, roughnecks wrestling pipe, bankers making deals, presidents campaigning, computers twinkling, fashion models slinking, redfish blackening, scientists cooking their witches' brew, ships slashing through ocean swells, surgeons laying open the human heart and anything else on location where you have to get it right the first time.

Tom Knibbs

4149 Northwest Fifth Avenue
Boca Raton, Florida 33432
(305) 338-6808

Represented in New York by;
Mark Ramon
(212) 473-6259

Specializing in architectural and interior design photography for more than 12 years in the Southeast. Well published in national and regional magazines including Architectural Digest, Better Homes & Gardens, Southern Accents, South Florida Home & Garden, Designer's Quarterly, Professional Builder, Builder, National Real Estate Investor, Design and Construction and Area Development, his work is welcomed by editors and art directors. Tom has helped earn professionals dozens of architectural and interior design awards in major competitions. Stock photography available through The Image Bank. Portfolio on request.

Tom Raymond

Route 6, Box 424C
Jonesborough, Tennessee 37659
(615) 753-9061

- Corporate
- Advertising
- Medical
- Editorial

Photography on location by a photographer who communicates well with people.
Member ASMP

Clients include:
Arcata Inc.
Bristol Memorial Hospital
Camara Inns
Charles B. Slack Inc.
First American Corporation
First Tennessee Bank
Fortune Magazine
Heritage Federal
Horizon Magazine
Hospital Corporation of America
The New York Times
Rodale Press
Tennessee Tourism Council
T L Enterprises
Ultrasport Magazine
13-30 Corporation

Stock Available Upon Request

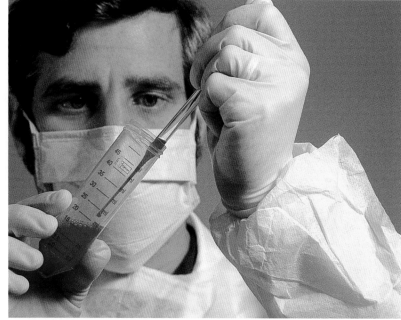

Ron Sherman

P.O. Box 28656
Atlanta, Georgia 30328
(404) 993-7197

Representative:
Bruce Wetta/WOODEN REPS
(404) 892-6303

Location photography for annual reports, advertising, corporate, industrial, editorial, travel and sports assignments.

Stock Photography available.
(404) 993-7197

Also see ads in Corporate Showcase Volume 3, Volume 4, Volume 5, American Showcase Volume 8 and Volume 10 and ASMP BOOK 1981, Book 2, Book 3 and Book 4.

Member ASMP, APA

© 1987 Ron Sherman

Design: Critt Graham & Associates

Midwest

Illinois
Indiana
Iowa
Michigan
Minnesota
Ohio

*Christopher***Kean**

Christopher Kean

Photography

624 W Adams St

Chicago IL 60606

Telephone

312 559 0880

*Christopher***Kean**

Christopher Kean

Photography

624 W Adams St

Chicago IL 60606

Telephone

312 559 0880

OLAUSEN

J udy Olausen, chosen one of ten best by Hasselblad,

has worked for Chermayeff & Geismar, Dayton Hudson, General Mills, Herman Miller, 3M, and Washington Post.

Her address is 213½ North Washington Avenue, Minneapolis, Minnesota 55401.

Telephone (612) 332-5009.

Paul Mellon, Mellon Bank

**Tony Armour
Photography**

1726 North Clybourn Avenue
Chicago, Illinois 60614
(312) 664-2256

Corporate Communications
Large Format
Interior & Exterior Locations
People & Product

Alex Atevich

325 North Hoyne Avenue
Chicago, Illinois 60612
(312) 942-1453

Location and studio photography for advertising,
annual reports, corporate communications, editorial
and travel.

Additional work can be seen in Corporate Showcase
#4 and #5.

Portfolio available on request.

Tom Berthiaume Studio

Tom Berthiaume Studio
1008 Nicollet Mall
Minneapolis, Minnesota 55403
(612) 338-1999

Specializing in the corporate portrait in studio and
on location. B/W and color.
Photographs by T. Berthiaume and M. Norberg.

Represented in Chicago by Vincent Kamin and
Associates.
(312) 787-8834

Represented in Minneapolis by Sandra Heinen.
(612) 332-3671

Wayne Cable

Cable Studios
2212 North Racine
Chicago, Illinois 60614
(312) 525-2240

Specializing in advertising, architectural, editorial and corporate photography. Limited edition cibachrome prints available as well as extensive stock photography.

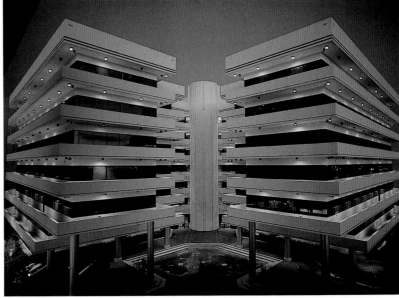

Kent Clawson

2530 West Wilson Avenue
Chicago, Illinois 60625
(312) 583-0001

Specializing in advertising, corporate, industrial, architectural and travel photography. Fluent in Spanish. Portfolio upon request.

Clients include:
Maytag, Swift, Metromail, Pemex, National Crane, Homart, Sandoz Pharmaceutical, Chief Industries, Harrod's, Sakowitz, Sheraton, Montgomery Ward, United Way, Commonwealth Electric, McDonald's, Domeq, Roux, Bankers Life, VISA, Best Western.

Rick Dieringer

19 West Court Street
Cincinnati, Ohio 45202
(513) 621-2544

A partial list of clients:
Procter & Gamble
Kroger
Hyatt Regency Hotels
Clarion Hotels
Harnischfeger Corp.
Microtie Inc.
Delta Queen Steamboat Co.
Formica Corp.
Springwater Sweets
Sheppard Chemical Co.
Emery Industries
Clippard Instrument
    Laboratory Inc.
Inc. Magazine
ChoiceCare.

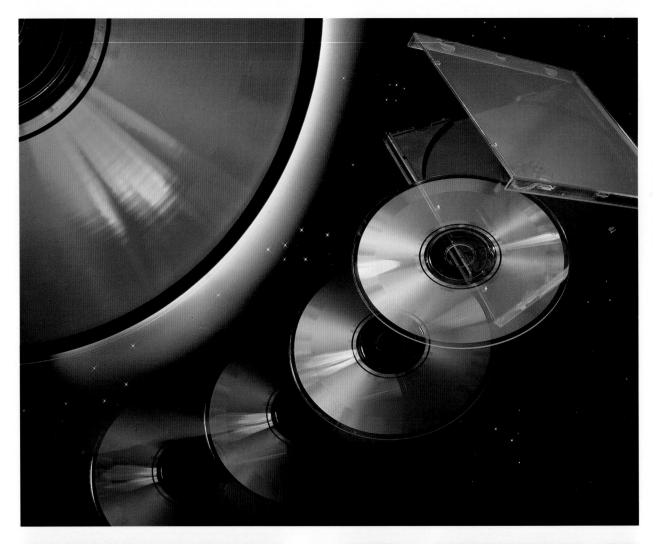

John Gilroy
Photography

2407 West Main Street
Kalamazoo, Michigan 49007
(616) 349-6805, (616) 381-8764

Images shown are from annual
report photography for The
Upjohn Company, magazine
cover photography for
Consumers Power Company
and annual report photography
for First Of America Bank
Corporation.

For more examples of work see
Corporate Showcase 4 and 5.

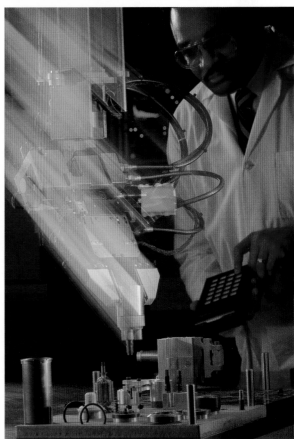

Industrial photographers who are fortunate enough to be assigned a corporate annual report job have a great responsibility to both themselves (if they would like to work for the client in the future) and the client. Today's photographers must be a great deal more than someone you call to provide beautiful photographs. They (if they are going to be successful) must also be accomplished salesmen and good communicators in general.

When meeting with the agency or the corporate public affairs people, you're given direction as to the theme of the shoot (hopefully), the type of shots they're looking for and the time frame. The time frame will usually be a few days shorter than you actually need to do a first class job and the theme will most likely change shortly after you finish the assignment.

The agency and corporate PR people, while supplying very good direction as to what they want to see in your shots, most likely know little more about the locations you'll be shooting than you do. They've probably never been to your assigned locations, and may not know much, if anything, about the specific operations there. There's also a very good chance that you'll find less than optimum conditions there (like dormant trees or mud two feet deep). The weather will probably also be working against you. After all, annual reports come out in the spring and it's only logical that the photography be done just prior to or shortly after deadline, which is, of course, the dead of winter.

To help cover yourself in these situations there are a few things you must do (this applies to both freelance and in-house photographers).

First of all, know your subject. Regardless of the subject, you should put together all the background information before the shoot. Then, upon arriving at the location, be it a drilling rig in the Chaco of Paraguay or a chemical plant in New York, you should acquaint yourself with the various areas and functions of the subject locations. After meeting your company contact, make sure you're assigned someone with extensive knowledge of the location and its operations to take you on a walk through. You don't just want a tour guide who tells you where you can't go and when to put your earplugs in.

Ask about everything. Most importantly, tape record the explanations and descriptions. Memories are short, especially if you're visiting several locations. Then, make sure you ID each shot as you go. The first question the art director will ask is, "What is that thing and what does it do?" If you can give at least a simple explanation and then leave a copy of the tape of your notes, you'll be appreciated as being much more than just another photographer.

Also, find out what the safety regulations are for the industry you're photographing. Preferably, have a safety officer with you during the shoot. If that's not possible, always be aware of possible violations. Whether the location is in the U.S. or not, U.S. regulations must be observed in the photos. The attorneys for the corporation are concerned only with U.S. safety regulations. If they have even the slightest question about your best shot, it won't be used. Better safe than sorry.

Although many would like you to believe differently, most corporations are very conscious of the area surrounding their locations. For that reason, if you're showing some of the surroundings you'll be expected to show that the facility exists in harmony with it. If

that's impossible, get the shot anyway. The facility comes first. Whether it's an ugly location (dormant trees and power lines always seem to be in strategic locations) or bad weather, if the facility looks great the other areas can always be retouched. Today, with the availability of computer retouching equipment, the lab can possibly bail you out on one of those shots. But don't think you can forget the surrounding areas. Computer retouching is very expensive and a cost the company likes to avoid. (For those of you who are about to throw this book across the room because I used the word computer, I must confess I am very high on computer technology and its photographic and publishing applications. You're all eventually going to have to work with it, like it or not. But, that's another story.)

Now that you know what you're shooting and what it does and everyone is dressed properly and the location is in harmony with the environment, shoot away. Get all those spectacular shots you envisioned in the walk through. But, also shoot documentation type shots. Shots that say, "Here's the facility, it looks good and it's doing its job."

This is mainly because corporate CEO's are usually much more conservative than the art director, and like it or not, that's how they usually want their corporation represented. Whether the shots they ultimately choose are the best is irrelevant. They do have the final say, and that's what's published.

You may not agree with their choices, but if you've brought back shots they like and can discuss the operation with them, but you'll be back again.

William D. Dykes
Manager Business Communications
Occidental Oil and Gas Corporation
Bakersfield, California

Sarah Hoskins
1206 Isabella
Wilmette, Illinois 60091
(312) 256-5724

Ingram
Photography

1000 West Monroe Street
Chicago, Illinois 60607
(312) 829-4652

Represented by
Ellen Marie Ingram

Copyright 1987 Russell Ingram

Clients Include:

Arthur Andersen & Company
Avis
CNA
Crain Communications
DDB Needham
Daniel J. Edelman, Inc.
First National Bank of Chicago
Ford Trucks
Hewitt Associates
ICG RR
IC Industries
Navistar
Sara Lee
Trane Corp.
Union Carbide
USG Corp.
Westinghouse

Ingram Photography
1000 West Monroe Street
Chicago, Illinois 60607
(312) 829-4652

Represented by
Ellen Marie Ingram

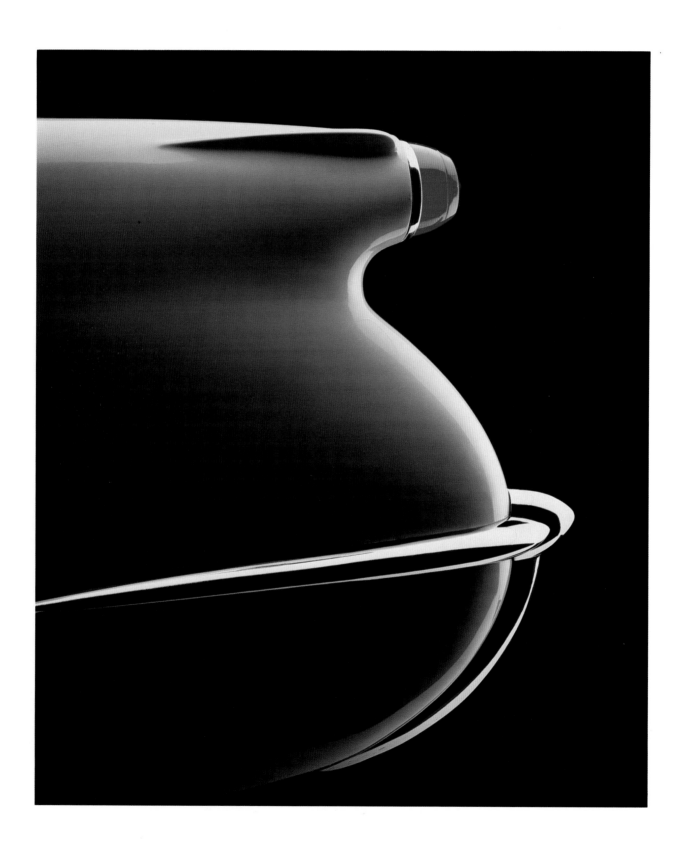

Phillip
MacMillan
James

2300 Hazelwood Avenue
Saint Paul, Minnesota 55109-2649
(612) 777-2303

Member ASMP

Client list includes:
Landor Associates
Vignelli Associates
AMFAC
Honeywell
CPT
Turner Construction
House Beautiful
Cargill
Stein Design
Anderson Windows
Ellerbe
Cold Spring Granite
Westinghouse Elevators
Time-Life Books
McGraw-Hill Publications
Embassy Suites Hotels
McDonald's
3M

David Joel Photography Inc.

1342 West Hood Avenue
Chicago, Illinois 60660
(312) 262-0794

Corporate
Industrial
Annual reports
Medical
Education

Specializing In Multiple Strobe-Light Applications
On Location

Partial client list:

Quaker Oats Co., Tribune Co., Borg Warner Corporation,
Ameritech Mobile, Arthur Andersen & Company,
CNA Financial Corporation, Beatrice Foods, United
Charities, Hill & Knowlton, Carnegie Council, Chicago
Pacific Corporation, Illinois Bell, Encyclopedia
Britannica, Burson Marsteller, Allstate Insurance,
Kraft Inc., Sara Lee Corporation

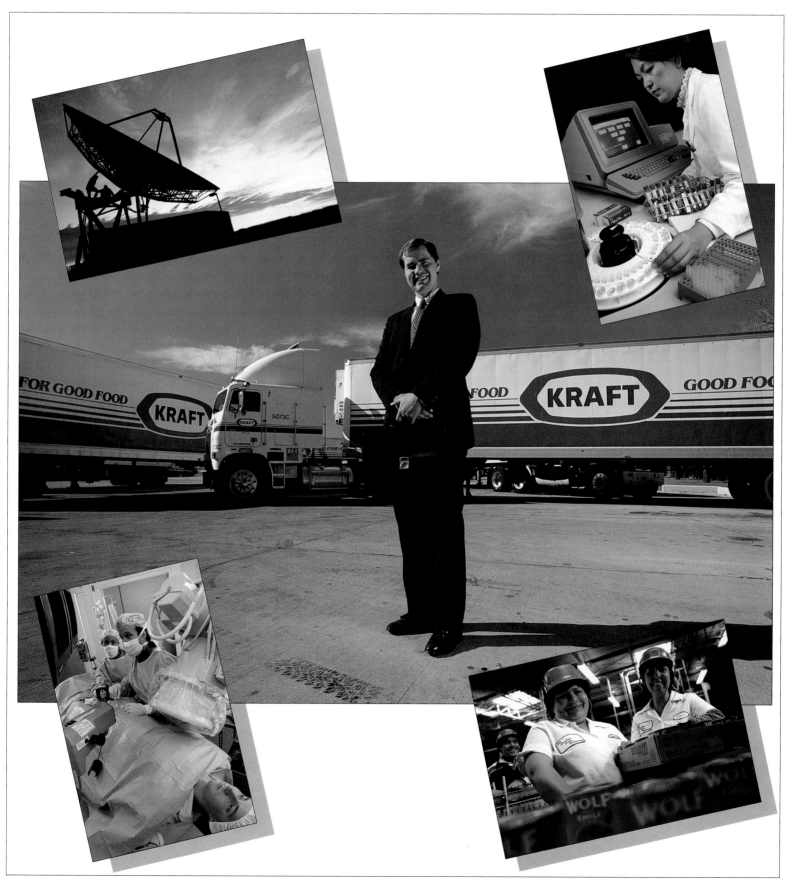

Kim Kauffman
Photography, Inc.

444 Lentz Court
Lansing, Michigan 48917
(517) 371-3036

Represented by Ed Bonnen
(517) 371-3086

Location and studio photography for portrait,
corporate, editorial, industrial, advertising & still life.

Located within an hour and a half from all major
population centers in Michigan.

See Corporate Showcase 5, p. 212.

Member ASMP

Photographs © Kim Kauffman 1986

David Kogan

1313 West Randolph Street
Chicago, Illinois 60607
(312) 243-1929

Location and studio photography for annual reports, corporate communications and advertising. Black & White and color.

Recent clients include:

American Airlines
Raven Industries
Illinois Bell Telephone
Budget Rent a Car
Sears
J. Walter Thompson
Frito Lay
Working Women Magazine
Foote Cone & Belding
Illinois Hospital Assoc.
Beltone Electronics
St. Charles Kitchens
Union Carbide
Leo Burnett
United States Information
   Agency
Architex International
Optibelt
etc.

Richard Mack

Richard Mack Photography, Ltd.
2119 Lincoln
Evanston, Illinois 60201
(312) 869-7794

Location and studio
photography for annual reports,
advertising, and corporate
communications.

A partial list of clients includes:

ABN/LaSalle Bank Corp.
Alcan Aluminum Corp.
AT&T
Bell & Howell Corp.
Dun & Bradstreet
Dresher, Inc.
FiatAllis Corp.
FirstChicago Corp.
Furnas Electric
General Numeric Corp.
Holiday Inn Corp.
IC Industries
Marriott Hotels
McDonald's Corp.
Merrill-Lynch
Metropolitan Life Insurance
Metropolitan Structures Corp.
A. O. Smith Corp.
Westinghouse Corp.
Willamette Industries

Richard Mack
PHOTOGRAPHY

3 1 2 / 8 6 9 - 7 7 9 4

Don O'Barski

The Image Works, Incorporated
17239 Parkside Avenue
South Holland, Illinois 60473
(312) 596-0606

Location photography for annual reports, advertising,
capability brochures, product literature, and audio-
visual presentations.

WANTED
Sages. Wits. Philosophers.
Problem-solvers. Boat-rockers.

We hope you've enjoyed reading the **VIEWPOINTS** in this issue. This popular feature is designed to enlighten as well as entertain as it provides unique insights on the current state of corporate communications.

We'd like to take this opportunity to invite you to share your own thoughts, opinions and methods with thousands of your colleagues worldwide.

The average **VIEWPOINT** is 1000 words but we'll consider longer (or shorter) pieces. Have the article titled, typed double-space, and be sure to include your own name, title, company and address. Contributors to the next volume will receive a copy of the book, a small gift, and our eternal gratitude. (Of course, we can't *guarantee* that your article will be published but we do promise to acknowledge and read every submission.)

Go ahead, write down all those things you've always wanted to get off your chest. Speak out to those photographers, illustrators, and designers you

hire…share confidences with your colleagues…tell off your boss. Do it while you're feeling outraged/satisfied/frustrated about the work you create. Do it *today* and mail it to:

Wendl Kornfeld, V.P.
American Showcase, Inc.
724 Fifth Avenue—10th Floor
New York, New York 10019

Thanks a lot. We're looking forward to hearing from you and hope to see you in **CORPORATE SHOWCASE VOLUME 7!**

Photo Images, Inc.

Brian Kaplan, C.P.P.
Phil Farber, C.P.P.
430 West Erie Street
Chicago, Illinois 60610
(312) 664-5953

Location & Studio Photography
for advertising, audio-visual,
annual reports and corporate
communications.

A partial list of clients includes.

American Airlines
American Hospital Publishing, Inc.
American Hospital Supply
Aumiller Youngquist Architects
Austin Knight Advertising
Barrel O' Fun Food Products
Bell & Howell
Belwith International, LTD
Bomido, Inc.
Chicago Magazine/WFMT
CIGNA Ind. Financial Services
Discover Corp.
Ethitek Pharmaceutical Co.
Fiocchi/Stopa & Associates
Forging Industry Association
General Foods Corp.
Grant Broadcasting Systems, Inc.
Harvey Weiss & Associates
Hunter Publishing Company
John Hancock Mutual Life Co.
Marshall Medical, Inc.
Meeting Media Enterprises, LTD
Motivation Media
National Easter Seal Society, Inc.
Norelco—Consumer Products
    Division
Nutra Sweet
OHM Electronics
Packaging Corporation of America
Ramada Hotels
Ray-O-Vac Corporation
Sanka Coffee
Schram Advertising, Inc.
Security Lighting Systems, Inc.
The Executive Technique
Westin Hotels

Member: Certified Prof. Photg.
of Illinois
P.P. of A.
A.P.P.I.
P.P.A.N.I.

Please call the studio to view a
more extensive portfolio:

See also:
Corporate Showcase 5
Chicago Talent Sourcebook 7
Northern Review—Midwest 86

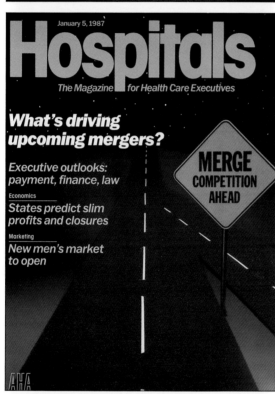

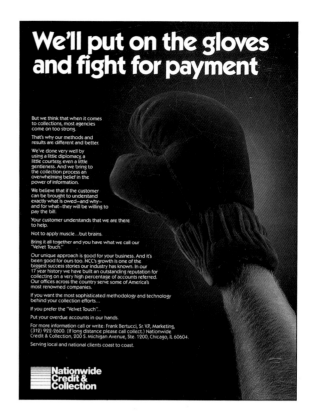

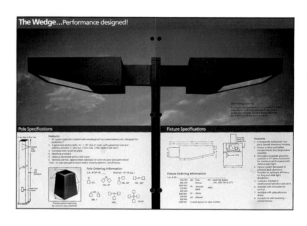

Pioneer Hi-Bred
International, Inc.

Curt Maas
5860 Merle Hay Road, Box 127
Johnston, Iowa 50131
(515) 270-3732

Location photography worldwide for corporate,
industrial, agricultural and editorial assignments.

© 1987 Curt Maas

Pioneer Hi-Bred
International, Inc.

Scott Sinklier
5860 Merle Hay Road, Box 127
Johnston, Iowa 50131
(515) 270-3732

Photography for annual reports, corporate
communications and advertising.

Harry J. Przekop, Jr.

332 South Cuyler Avenue
Oak Park, Illinois 60302
(312) 524-9743

Represented by Ellen Harmon.

Advertising and Corporate
Photography for People, Health
Care, Medicine and Science.

Stock Available: New York and
Chicago.

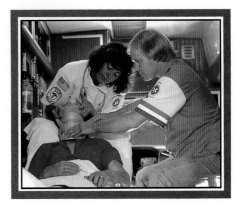

Przekop.
Pr ᶻe ᶜ ǩop?
Prěz·cŏp!

Andrew Sacks

20727 Scio Church Road
Chelsea (Detroit),
Michigan 48118
(313) 475-2310

Clients for displayed photos: (all shot on location, un-retouched)

Chip tester and library scene: Manufacturer's Bank, annual report.

Iacocca: American Library Association, poster.

Auto designer: Newsweek, editorial illustration.

Accident: Owens-Illinois, poster.

Stock photos of agriculture, industry, and regional scenes available both from my files and New York agency.

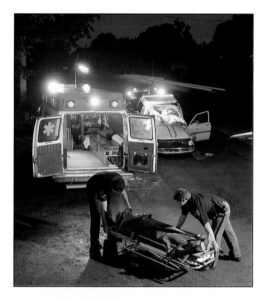
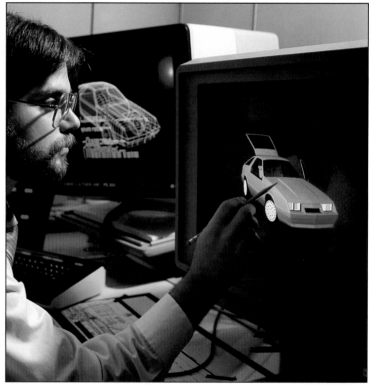

Terry Shapiro

1147 West Ohio Street
Chicago, Illinois 60622
(312) 226-3384
Call or write for additional color and B&W sample sheets

Location and studio photography for annual reports
and corporate advertising. Member APA, and ASMP.

A partial client list includes: Abbott Labs, Acco,
American Dental Association, American Hospital
Association, Jim Beam Distilling, William Blair &
Company, Borden, Robert Bosch, Brunswick
Corporation, Chemplex, Chicago City Ballet, Hewlett-
Packard, Illinois Tools Works (ITW), ITT Corporation,
Hughs Optical, Maremont Corporation, Parker-
Hannifin Corporation, G.D. Searle, Singer Controls,
Tenneco, Union 76, Upjohn, Wells Fargo Bank.

Art Shay

618 Indian Hill Road
Deerfield, Illinois 60015
(312) 945-4636

Chicago-based coverage for publications including Time, Life, Fortune, Sports Illustrated, Business Week, Forbes, Town & Country, Parade, North Shore, Chicago Tribune, Signature, People Magazine.

Annual reports, books, ads, brochures, slides for: Blue Cross, National Can, GM, Ford, Safety Kleen, ABC, NBC, CBS, Jewel, Amana, The Media Works, Campbell-Mithun, Motorola, Zenith, Baxter Labs, N.Y. Stock Exchange, Consumer's Power, Bally, Exchange National Bank, American National Bank, 1st National Bank Waukegan, Gateway Foundation, Contemporary Books, Ditto, O.M. Scott, A.O. Smith, Quill, Anixter.

Numerous Art Director Awards, one Life Picture of the Year, produced playwright, columnist, 1982 national senior racquetball champion.

Dick Spahr

1133 East 61st Street
Indianapolis, Indiana 46220
(317) 255-2400

Client list: Aero Mayflower, Agfa-Gevaert, B.F. Goodrich, Bloomhorst Story O'Hara Inc., Blue Cross Blue Shield, Boehringer Mannheim, Caldwell-Van Riper, DesignMark, Firestone, Garrison Jasper and Rose, Goodyear, Great Lakes Chemical, GTE, Hendrickson, Herring Design, Indiana National Bank, ITT, Kalmar Advertising, Merchants National Bank, Miller-Brooks, Ogilvy-Mather, Pizza Hut, Quinlan Keene Peck & McShay, Sony, Stewart-Winner, Temple-Inland, Uniden, Wavetek, Young & Laramore.

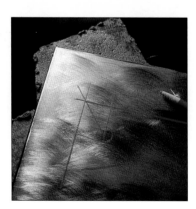

Mike Steinberg
**SHOOTS PEOPLE
AND PLACES**

633 Huron Road
Cleveland, Ohio 44115
(216) 589-9953

Represented by:
Rick Nicholson
(216) 398-1494

HESSELBART & MITTEN/WATT. INC. FOR UNIVERSITY HOSPITAL OF CLEVELAND

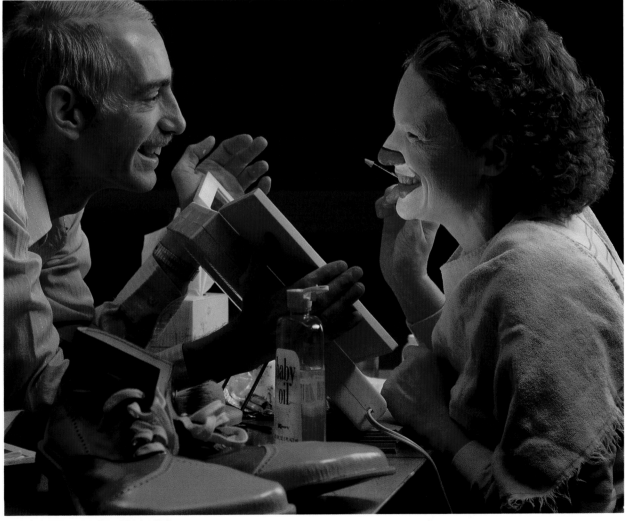

EDWARD HOWARD & COMPANY FOR OHIO BELL

ARCHIVE. IF YOU'RE WITHOUT IT,

YOU'RE NOT WITH IT.

Over 7,000 ad agency ADs, CDs and TV producers are with it.

Archive is the only magazine of its kind. No other publication shows you the newest, most innovative and successful print, television and poster advertising the way Archive does. Not just from the U.S, but around the world.

Advertising that's inspiring, stimulating, fresh and provocative. And you see it in a clear, visual format so you can quickly focus on your areas of interest.

You can get 6 idea-packed issues of Archive at an annual subscription price of $39.97. Call (212) 245-0981, or write:

ARCHIVE

c/o American Showcase,
724 Fifth Avenue,
New York, NY 10019.

Southwest

Oklahoma
Texas

Aker/Burnette Studio, Inc.

Joe C. Aker
Raymond V. Burnette III
4710 Lillian
Houston, Texas 77007
(713) 862-6343

Los Angeles
(213) 623-3054

Architectural interior, exterior, and model photography.
Model photocompositions and photography a speciality.
Portfolio available upon request.

ARCHITECTURAL MODEL PHOTOGRAPHY AND PHOTOCOMPOSITES

TRAMMELL CROW CO., MILWAUKEE

LINCOLN PROPERTY CO., DALLAS

LASALLE PARTNERS INC., CHICAGO

SKIDMORE, OWINGS & MERRILL, HOUSTON

ARCHITECTURAL PHOTOGRAPHY

THE FARB COMPANIES, HOUSTON

TRAMMELL CROW CO., DALLAS

TRAMMELL CROW CO., DALLAS

SKIDMORE, OWINGS & MERRILL, HOUSTON

MIKE DAMORE, ARCHITECT, HOUSTON

SIKES JENNINGS KELLY & BREWER, HOUSTON

G N ASSOCIATES, NEW YORK

LLOYD JONES FILLPOT & ASSOC., HOUSTON

Steve Brady
5250 Gulfton, Suite 2G
Houston Texas 77081
(713) 660-6663

Location assignments for annual reports, brochures
and advertising.

Steve Brady

5250 Gulfton, Suite 2G
Houston Texas 77081
(713) 660-6663

Location assignments for annual reports, brochures and advertising.

Steve Brady works in the fields of finance, industry, real estate, consumer, travel, energy and hi-tech. Recent clients include Gerald D. Hines Interests, Four Seasons Hotel, Conoco, Saga Corporation, Mitsubishi, NCAA, Xerox, Honeywell, New York Air, Hershey Hotels, Dow Chemical, Safeco, Prudential, Continental Airlines, US Steel, Shell Oil, N.Y.S.E., Celanese Corp., I.R.F.G. and Exxon.

His work has won recognition from Communication Arts, Print Magazine, N.Y.A.D.C., Graphis, AIGA and the Mead Annual Report Show. See additional work on pages 58 and 59.

For assignments, stock, color samples and a portfolio call (713) 660-6663 or (212) 213-6024.

J. Brousseau

Photographer* Dallas
(214) 638-1248

Also see us in Corporate
Showcase 4 and 5.

Stock photography available.

Jim Caldwell

2422 Quenby
Houston, Texas 77005
(713) 527-9121

Industrial, advertising, corporate and editorial
photography. Stock available.

Major clients include: AT&T, Coca-Cola Foods,
Coldwell Banker, Exxon U.S.A., Exxon Americas,
Houghton-Mifflin Publishers, Kentucky Fried Chicken,
Kingdom of Saudi Arabia, *Newsweek*, Owens-Corning
Fiberglas, Prudential Insurance, *Shell Oil News*,
Texas Children's Hospital, Texas Heart Institute,
Texas Monthly, Warner Amex Communications.

Photographs © 1985 Jim Caldwell

Eclipse

Jim Raker
2727 East 21st Street, Suite 600
Tulsa, Oklahoma 74114
(918) 747-1991 Studio
(918) 742-9526 Office
(312) 583-0001 Chicago

Specializing in corporate, industrial, advertising, annual report and travel photography. Location or studio work. Any format, anywhere. Extensive travel worldwide.

Partial client list:

Agrico, ARCO, Brunswick/Zebco, CBS, Citgo Petroleum, Coburn Optical, Eastman Kodak, Helicomb International, InterNorth, Invivo Research, Minolta, John Morrell, Mutual of Omaha, Rodenstock, Sears/Homart, Samson Resources, Shakey's Pizza, Sheraton, Smith Kline & French/Norden Labs, Telex Computers, United Way, Williams Brothers, Williams Companies.

Raymond Gendreau

415 North Bishop Avenue
Dallas, Texas 75208
(214) 760-1999

Represented by:
Elizabeth Simpson
(214) 943-9355

Location or studio photography for Advertising and
Corporate/Industrial Clients.

1986 Clients include:
American Way, Cadillac Fairview, The Dallas Morning
News, Halliburton, *High Technology*, Justin Boots,
MBank of Texas, Morrow Green, Nortek, Overhead Door,

The Richards Group, Sedco Industries, Singer Systems,
Southern Magazine, Stanley Korshak, *Success
Magazine*, Texas Monthly.

Stock photography available through studio

Mark Green

2406 Taft Street
Houston, Texas 77006
(713) 523-6146
Tlx #4997187 GREEN UI

Represented by Nancy Holland
(713) 975-7279

Corporate/Industrial.
Annual Report.
Advertising.
Travel.
Stock.

For more work see Corporate
Showcase Volumes 3, 4, & 5.
ASMP Silver Book 5.

All Photos © 1986 Mark Green.

Poster:
Product Introduction,
4 × 5 Professional Chrome

Client:
Polaroid Corporation
Cambridge, Mass.

Design:
Marie McGinley,
Polaroid Corporation Graphics

After 40 years of instant innovation
Polaroid introduces something *perfectly* conventional.

POLAROID
PROFESSIONAL
CHROME

The conventionally processed (E-6) 4 × 5″ transparency film
in easy-to-use Polaroid single-exposure packets.

Century Dev.

479%

F11

SHELL CHEM

LUKE AFB

Cover Shot

NORTH SEA

CONOCO

BKK

FLORENCE

SCOTLAND

PHOTO: MARK GREEN
713- 523-6146

New Delhi
84 - 3275P

Michael Ives

1000 Cornell Parkway
Suite #200
Oklahoma City, Oklahoma 73108
(405) 947-0606

Location and studio photography for advertising,
corporate, and editorial.

Member ASMP.

Steve Jennings
Jennings Photography
P.O. Box 33203
Tulsa, Oklahoma 74153
(918) 745-0836

Editorial Representation by:
PICTURE GROUP
(401) 273-5473

Client List:
AMOCO
AT&T
Cities Service
Estech
Ford Motor Co.
MAPCO
Miller Brewing
Newsweek
J.C. Penney
Philip Morris
Price-Waterhouse
Samson Resources
Southland Corp.
Southwestern Bell
Sun Company
Telex
Texaco
USA Today
Williams Companies

Louis Reens

4814 Sycamore
Dallas, Texas 75204
(214) 827-3388

Represented by:
Photocom, Inc.
Jeff Knipp
Melanie Spiegel
(214) 428-8781

Architecture, Interiors, and
Travel for advertising, corporate
and editorial assignments.

Refer to Corporate Showcase 4
(page 207) and 5 (page 246) to
see more photography by Louis
Reens, or call Photocom, Inc.
to review portfolio.

Donovan Reese

4801 Lemmon Avenue
Dallas, Texas 75219
(214) 526-5851

Location Photography for Advertising, Annual Report,
Architectural, Corporate, Industrial & Travel Clients.
Worldwide . . . or beyond.

Stock Available. Full Format Studio. Portfolio upon
request.

Additional Images: Corp. Showcase 5, p. 247
Adweek/ADI 11, p. 294

Ron Scott

1000 Jackson Boulevard
Houston, Texas 77006
(713) 529-5868

Whether in exotic locations or on elaborate sets Ron Scott shoots for the best. It may look like just plain fun or no work at all but there is always a lot more than meets the eye behind one of Ron's photos. "The picture may be just a girl on the beach but it has to be the right beach, the right girl and the right bathing suit. A good stylist and location scout help but I usually wind up scouting and selecting the final location, doing the casting and buying the bathing suit to get it all just right."

The photo may be for a high flying client but the work is all on the ground. "Real airplanes are too valuable hauling around passengers to be grounded for a week to do a photo shoot, so we use a set. The seats and other furnishings, like carpet and curtains, are authentic and always in short supply. But with carefully chosen angles, selective lighting and a great cast of characters we can make a better picture with four seats and a fiberglass backdrop than we could aboard the real thing."

Some clients for whom Ron has done his best: American Express, Arco Petroleum, Avis, British Caledonian Airways, Carter Hawley Hale Stores, GATX, Georgia-Pacific, Harte-Hanks Publications, Hewlett-Packard, *High Technology Magazine*, Holiday Inn, Honda America, IBM, Kodak, Malone & Hyde, Marriott, Memorex, Mobile, Monsanto, National Gypsum, Northrup, Perkin-Elmer, *Personal Computing Magazine*, Polaroid, Southern Pacific Railway, Standard Brands, Stauffer Chemical, Texaco, TRW, US West, Westinghouse.

© 1987 Ron Scott, Member ASMP.

Ron Scott

1000 Jackson Boulevard
Houston, Texas 77006
(713) 529-5868

Cowboys or computers, Ron Scott shoots Texas. "Texas is a natural for many subjects, some of them quite obvious like cowboys and ranching. But Texas is also an ideal location for many other photos as well, especially during the winter months when we have our best weather. We have many cool clear days followed by spectacular sunsets and the grass stays green well into January. The great thing too about Texas is the people, ready to help out with a location or an unusual prop. We rarely have to pay fees to shoot anywhere and locations like the ship channel docks or either of the airports are easy to arrange and hassle free."

Texas is the home for many of Ron's clients as well, but it is more than just home for him. "When I leave Texas I don't leave it behind. I find that an open and friendly approach often gets me things and into places that a more hostile and abrupt one won't. Having grown up in Texas I've learned a way of doing things that gets the job done, yet doesn't leave the other guy feeling like he's been stepped on. I'd like to say it is something I worked long and hard to perfect, but the truth is that it's a natural byproduct of where I live."

Some of Ron's clients that call Texas home are: American Rice, Anderson-Clayton, Astroworld/Six Flags, Brown & Root, Cameron Iron, Coca-Cola Foods, Compaq Computer, Continental Airlines, Cooper Industries, CRS Architects, Datapoint, Dresser, Exxon, Eyetech, First City Banks, Gerald D. Hines Interests, Hycel, Igloo, Intermedics, Lomas & Nettleton, Minute Maid, Pier 1, Sakowitz, Shell, Southwest Airlines, Steak & Ale, Texas Instruments, *Texas Monthly Magazine*, U.S. Homes, Wide-Lite, Zapata.

© 1987 Ron Scott. Member ASMP.

Micheal Simpson

415 North Bishop Avenue
Dallas, Texas 75208
(214) 943-9347

Represented by:
Elizabeth Simpson
(214) 943-9355

Studio and location photography for Advertising and Corporate/Industrial Clients.

1986 Clients include:
American Airlines, A-R-A, Bell Atlantic, Bonneau Eyewear, CitiCorp, Chemical Bank, Dr. Pepper, Esco, E-Systems, Frito Lay, Genstar, MTech, Northern Telecom, Otis Engineering, Poser Business Forms, Prudential Insurance, Seismic Engineering, Texas Book Company.

Magazine Clients:
American Way, Dallas Magazine, Meeting Manager, Modern Office Technologies, Omni, Private Clubs, Texas Business.

Portfolio Upon Request.

Stock photography available through the studio or contact F.P.G. International, New York.

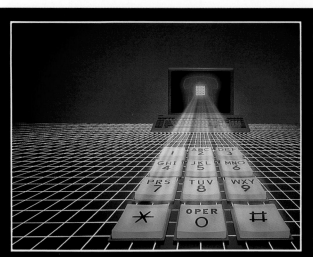
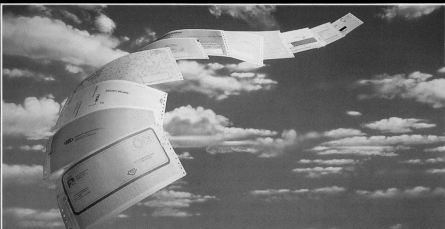

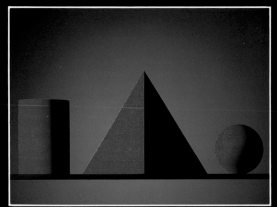

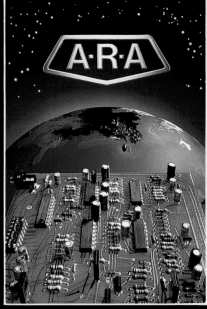
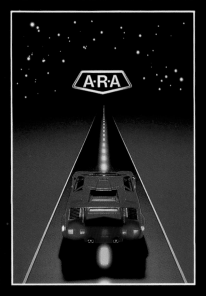
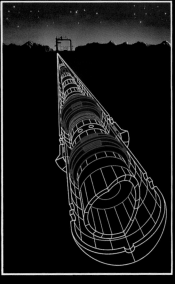
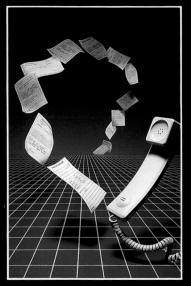

Bob Werre

2437 Bartlett Street
Houston, Texas 77098
(713) 529-4841

Distinctive Images for Business
Studio or Location

Clients include:
Dow Chemical
Exxon U.S.A.
Exxon Chemical
Dresser Atlas
Texaco
Texaco Chemical
Gulf Oil
Dupont
Dowell Schlumberger
Schlumberger
United Energy Resources
Smith International
Hydril
Hughes
Igloo Corporation
Browning Ferris Industries
Cooper Industries
I.B.M.
Mitsubishi
Metier Systems
Cryolife
Intermedics
Hines Industrial
Friendswood Development
First City Bank
Canadian Imperial Bank of
    Commerce
Houston Post
L.D. Brinkman
Coca Cola Foods
Sysco
General Homes
Gemcraft Homes
Weekley Homes

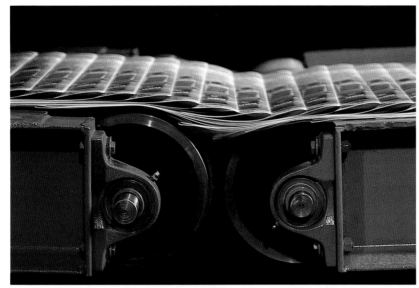

Les Wollam

5215 Goodwin Avenue
Dallas, Texas 75206
(214) 760-7721

Environmental portraiture: from the people outstanding in their fields to a man standing out in his field. For additional portraiture see Corp. Showcase Vol. 4, page 217. Additional images in Corp. Showcase Vol. 1, 2 & 5.

Recent clients include: American Airlines, Business Week, Central and South West Corp., Diamond Shamrock, Electrospace, Fortune, HiTeck Marketing, IBM, NY Times, Occidental Chemical, Southwestern Energy Co., Summit Energy, Texas Utilities, Triton Energy, and Wachovia Bank & Trust Co.

Rocky Mountain

Colorado
Montana
Utah

Jim Cambon

Denver, Colorado
(303) 571-4555
Fort Collins, Colorado
(303) 221-4545

Our Clients include:
Aetna Life & Casualty, Bob Coonts Graphic Design, ESAB North America, First Interstate Banks, Hewlett-Packard, Kodak, Kraft, M.W. Kellogg Company, Platte River Power Authority, Sam Cooper Graphic Design, Valiant Products Corporation, Viadent Inc., Water-Pik

See also Corporate Showcase 4 & 5
© 1987 Jim Cambon

Location photography for corporate use requires special techniques to record a blend of reality and illusion. My special techniques include extensive preparation, careful communication, attention to detail, and relentless editing of relaity. This editing relies on composition, timing and use of light.

"Perfection is attained, not when there is nothing left to add; but when there is nothing left to take away."
Antoine de Saint Exupery

The black and white photo above shows the existing reality. The color photo to the left shows the result of blending existing reality and illusion by editing extraneous detail with composition and lighting.

If the reality of your facility could use some editing, call me — I'll show you why less is more.

Jim Johnson

Photographer & Pilot
16231 East Princeton Circle
Denver, Colorado 80013
(303) 680-0522

Location and studio photography
Corporate communications
Advertising
Industrial
Aerial

Patricia Barry Levy

Denver, Colorado
(303) 458-6692

Clients include Brown and Caldwell Engineers, Clarion Hotels, Colorado Housing Finance Authority, Colorado National Bank, Consumer Health Services, City and County of Denver, Gates Rubber Company, National Farmers Union Insurance Companies, Rocky Mountain Bankcard System, Tele-Communications, U.S. West.

Periodicals include Changing Times, Forbes, Inc., Sylvia Porter's Personal Finance, U.S. News and World Report.

Additional work in ASMP Book 5.

Kent Miles
Photography

25 South 300 East
Salt Lake City, Utah 84111
(801) 364-5755

P.O. Box 7071
Beverly Hills, Ca. 90212
(213) 274-2553

The West and the World.
Corporate
Editorial
Commercial
Multi-Image
Documentary
Portraiture

Extensive travel experience with
a strong people oriented
portfolio.

Call or write for samples.

Partial client list:
Benchmark, Inc.
Bonneville Media Productions
Crown Union
Evans Communications, Inc.
First Interstate Bank
Holy Cross Hospital
Intermountain Health Care
Kimball Travel Consultants
Lewis, Gilman & Kynett, Inc
Mormon Church
Oral History Institute
University of Utah
Utah Travel Council
Utah Winter Games
   Organizing Committee
Yellow Freight

Stock Available

Member ASMP

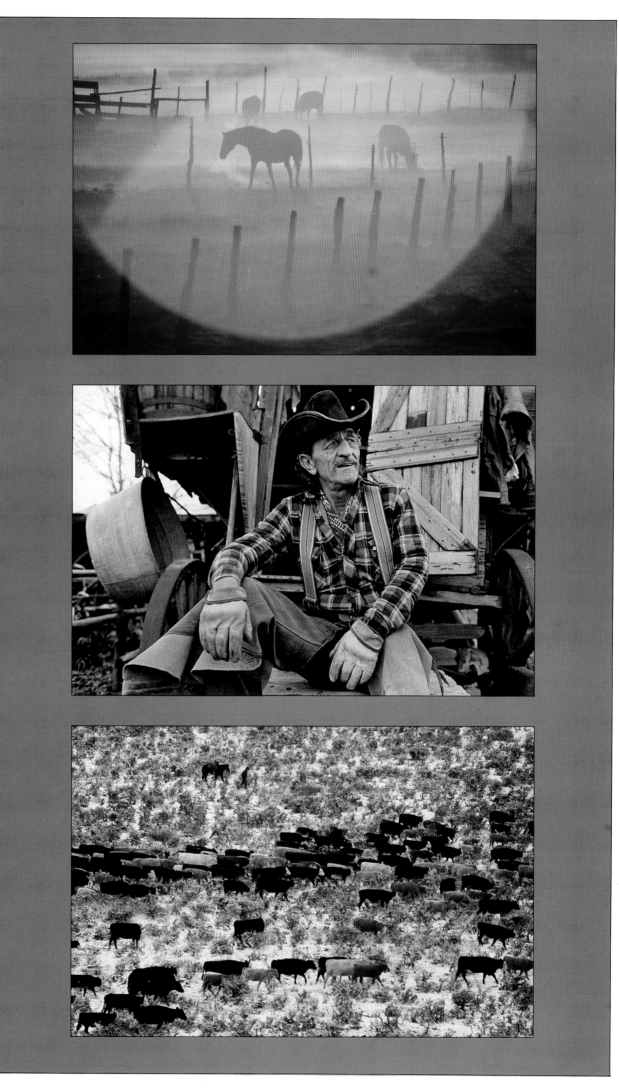

David Scott Smith
1437 Avenue E
Billings, Montana 59102
(406) 259-5656

Corporate and editorial location photography.

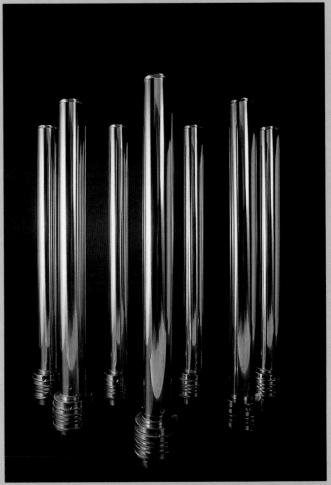

Doug Stearns

1738 Wynkoop Street
Denver, Colorado 80202
(303) 296-1133

Providing photographic solutions
for corporate communications
and advertising. On location or
in the studio.

Portfolio available upon request.
Also see page 265 of Corporate
Showcase #5.

Clients include:
AT&T Information Systems
Boeing Computers
Boettcher & Company
Burson-Marsteller, NY
Central Bank of Denver
CH2M Hill
Color Tile
Daniels and Associates
Desks, Inc.
Empire Savings
Ethan Allen Furniture
First Interstate Bank
First Wyoming Bancorporation
Gates Energy Products
General American Insurance
Guaranty National Corporation
Hensel Phelps Construction
Integrated Resources, Inc.
IntraWest Bank
Masonite Corporation
Nordica Ski Boots
Owens-Corning Fiberglass
Pearle Vision
Prudential Insurance Company
Rocky Mountain News
Safeco Insurance Company
Samsonite Corporation
Scientific Software, Inc.
Selz, Seabolt & Associates
Taco Bell
Talley Corporation
Trammell Crow Company
United Banks of Colorado
Vari L Company
Wickliff & Company
Writer Corporation

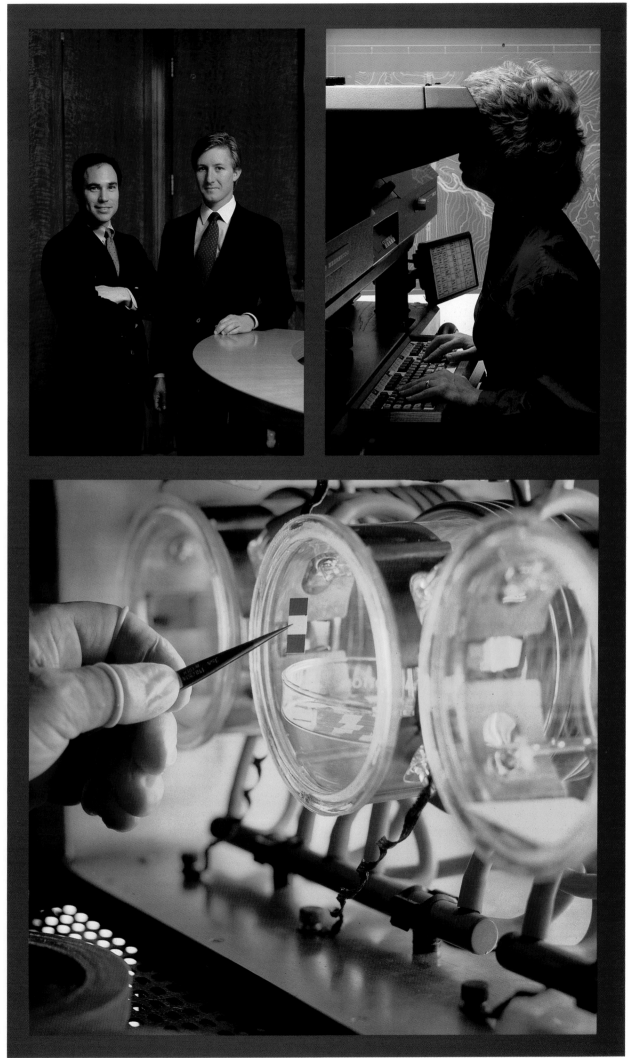

Stearns

David X. Tejada

1553 Platte Street, Suite 205
Denver, Colorado 80202
(303) 458-1220

Represented by:

Christine Goodman

(303) 298-7085

Specializing in location photography for corporate annual reports, brochures, and advertising clients. Black and white portfolio available upon request.

Clients include:
AMI, Inc.
Anheuser Busch
AT&T
Energy Systems
Integrated Resources, Inc.
Marriott Hotels
MCI Communications
Mountain Bell
Omnibankcorp
Prudential-Bache
Ramada Hotels
Security Pacific Mortgage Corp.
Trusthouse Forte Hotels
The United Way

West Coast

**California
Nevada
Washington**

Karen Anderson Photography

1170 North Western Avenue
Los Angeles, California 90029
(213) 461-9100

Corporate and Advertising.
Location and Studio.
Photographic Illustration.
Annual Reports.
Capability Brochures.

Member: APA

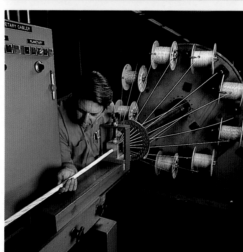

214

Frank Baker

15031 Parkway Loop Suite B
Tustin, California 92680
Orange County
(714) 259-1462

Specializing in business
photography for corporate and
industrial communications.

Clients include:

Allergan Pharmaceutical
American Hospital Supply
AST Research
Avery International
Beatrice
California Avocado Commission
Carl Karcher Enterprises
CMS
Doelz Network
Elco
GTE
Taco Bell
Toshiba
TRW
Winchells

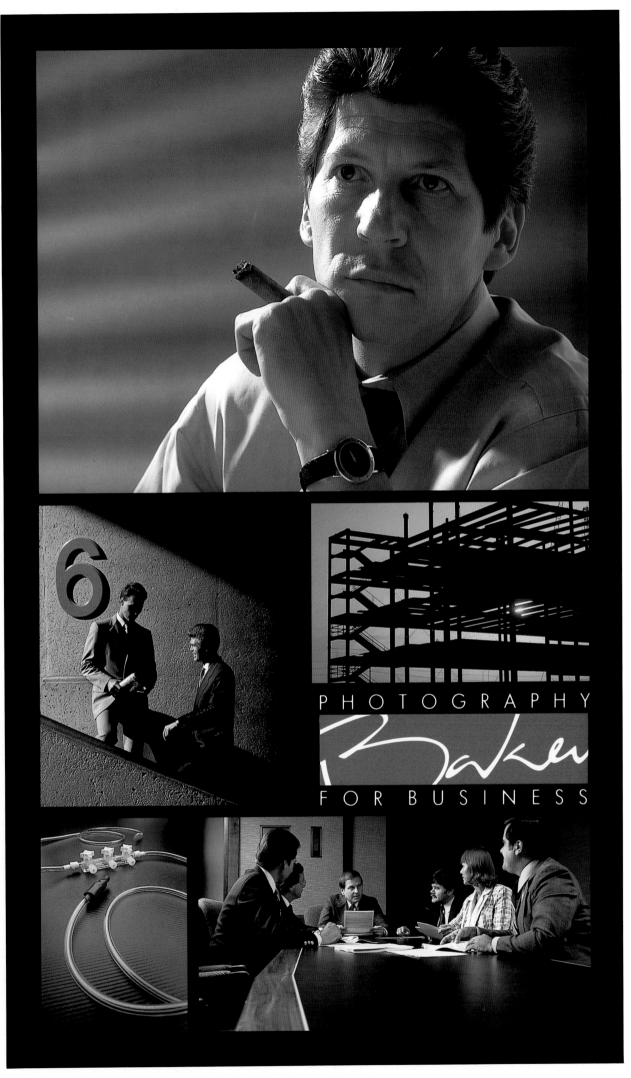

PHOTOGRAPHY
FOR BUSINESS

Kevin Burke

1015 North Cahuenga Boulevard
Los Angeles, California 90038
(213) 467-0266

Full range of Corporate Photography in California and
Nationwide for Annual Reports, Facility/Capability
Brochures, Advertising, and Executives. Location
and Studio.

Recent projects for the following clients:
American Protection Industries, Ameron, Bank of America,
California Biotechnology, Daniels Manufacturing Co.,
David Orgell Inc., EIL Instruments, Empex Corporation,
Garrett Corporation, GTE, Jet America, Norris
Industries, NuMed, Security Pacific Bank, Smith
International, Southern California Edison, Sunkist,
Toshiba, Unocal, W.R. Grace Co.

For other samples please see Corporate Showcase 3
and 5 or call for portfolio.

Burman & Steinheimer

2648 Fifth Avenue
Sacramento, California 95818
(916) 457-1908

Photographers: Shirley Burman and
Richard Steinheimer

Location photography in the West for corporate and editorial clients.

We serve major transportation companies and their suppliers, as well as public utilities, construction and technical companies. We are well known for the documentation of historic restorations as well as new construction.

Clients include: Advanced Micro Devices, AMTRAK, Apple Computer, Lawrence Bender & Associates, Bo-Tree Productions, Burlington Northern Railroad, California State Railroad Museum, Chicago and NorthWestern Railroad, Delphian Corporation, Golden West Books, Hewlett Packard Associates, Intel Corporation, The Railway and Locomotive Historical Society, Nevada State Railroad Museum, Sacramento Housing and Redevelopment Agency, Schuller, Foote, McElwee and Roche, Southern Pacific Transportation Company, Trains Magazine and Westways Magazine.

(Below) Steve Ellis, Southern Pacific Transportation Co., from the exhibition, "Winter's Professionals."
© Richard Steinheimer.

Hank de Lespinasse

Hank de Lespinasse Studios, Inc.
2300 East Patrick Lane #21
Las Vegas, Nevada 89119
(702) 798-6693
(702) 361-6628

Stock: The Image Bank

For additional work see:
American Showcase 3, page 238
ASMP Book 1, page 408
ADIP 6, page 95
Black Book '77, page 182
Black Book '78, page W26
or call for samples

1. American Airlines (poster)
2. Ad: John Farrell, Colonna, Farrell: Design Associates, for Smothers Brothers Wines.
3. Stephen Wynn, Chairman of Golden Nugget Inc., for Newsweek

Recent clients include: Gatx Leasing, Yugo America, Ethel M Chocolates, Cetlin Design, Hughes Aviation Services, Biomedical Information Corp., Meetings & Conventions, Time, Newsweek, Drug Topics, ABC, Business Week, Cahners Publishing, Home Entertainment, HP Publishing, Mohawk Rubber Co., Moser White Design, Redman Homes, Inc., Wico Corp., Tropicana Hotel, Trends in Brick.

© Hank de Lespinasse 1987

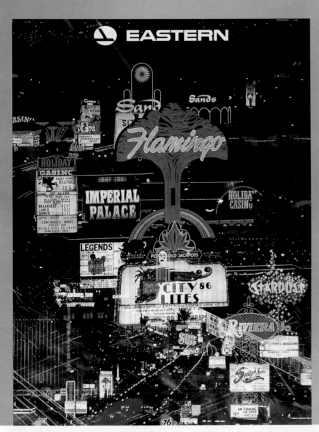

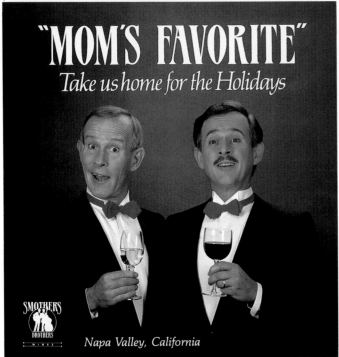

Kim
Andrew
Frazier

San Francisco, California

Distinctive Photography
P.O. Box 6132
Hayward, California 94540
(415) 889-7050

Photographic illustrations for
corporate communications and
advertising. Specializing in
people and products on
location.

Portfolio and stock index
available upon request.

Van W. Frazier

2770 South Maryland Parkway
Las Vegas, Nevada 89109
(702) 735-1165

Specializing in Portraiture of Chief Executive Officers, Directors and top level management. Individuals and groups, in studio or on location.

Clients include:
Caesar's Palace, Showboat Hotel, Boyd Group, City of Las Vegas, Osmonds, U.S. Senator Harry Reid, First Interstate Bank, Southern Utah State College, Boy Scouts of America, Palace Station Casino, Allstate Insurance, Duvall Network, Nevada Beverage, Silver State Disposal, Nevada Federal Credit Union.

Jeff Hunter

4626½ Hollywood Boulevard
Los Angeles, California 90027
(213) 669-0468

Corporate, Advertising, Industrial,
Editorial and Travel Photography.

Clients Include:
Pepsi-Co
Hilton Hotels
Best Western Hotels
Trust House Forte Hotels
Mexican Ministry of Tourism
Money Magazine

Woman's Day Magazine
Clairol
Great Western Financial Systems
Far East National Bank
Fries Entertainment Corp.
Nature Made Vitamins
Master Builders
Yamaha International
Ethan Allen Furniture
Sea World
The Image Bank

Urban Pacific Development Corp.
Tejon Ranch Corp.
Knoll International
Beneficial Standard Life Ins.
FINA
South Coast Medical Center
West Covina Medical Center
L.A. Herald Examiner
L.A. County Fair

Stock Photography Available: The Image Bank

For More Samples, See:
American Showcase, Vol. 8
Corporate Showcase, Vol. 4
American Showcase, Vol. 10
New York Art Directors Club, 61st Annual

The Annual Shoot-Out

The annual report is the most important publication a public company produces. The challenge facing most companies and many public relations practitioners is how to make this document one that stands out from all the others in the marketplace.

Over the years, a range of specialists has emerged to help corporations produce the most outstanding annual report possible, among them the annual-report photographer.

A photographer who specializes in annual reports knows which photographic metaphors are overused and can help identify new ways to present the company's message. Says annual-report photographer Bill Rivelli, "People have become much more sophisticated in their visual outlook because we are all bombarded with visual imagery through television, advertising, and the numerous corporate publications that are produced today. To produce an annual report that makes a statement about a company, a photographer must look beyond putting together objects in a room. Photographers need to use their visual understanding of the environment to capture with a camera the graphic relationships between objects, color, and light to make meaningful statements about what a company stands for or is striving to achieve."

While photography is a very versatile medium, readily manipulated with filters and lenses to turn ordinary views into extraordinary vistas, photography is still perceived as a medium that presents reality. Illustration is often seen as the best medium to present concepts and ideas. Before you decide whether illustration or photography works best for your report, it is important to think carefully about what the report's theme is. The decision should be based on the intrinsic qualities of each medium. Photography's strongest asset is that it can be utilized to capture any scene on film, conveying a sense that what one is seeing is real.

Explaining why he chose photography for an annual report one year and illustration another, Brian Martin, vice president, corporate communications, American Can Company, says, "In 1985, we wanted to use our logo to illustrate the presence of American Can in different business sectors. The thrust of the annual report was to take a symbolic approach showing our logo symbol among other symbols. To use photography, we would have had to create a real setting and place the American Can 'A' in it. Since this would never happen naturally, we felt the photograph would have a 'set-up' feel to it. Instead, we commissioned a painter to do a series of paintings showing the logo with symbols from our three business areas.

"In 1984, on the other hand, the theme of the report was 'A Stake in our Future'. There, photography was crucial because we wanted to capture the spirit of the people who share in the success of a great company— our customers, investors, employees, and community members."

Photography can have a major impact on whether a company's key audiences—analysts following the industry, current and potential investors, and the business media—see its message.

But if photography is to have an impact, it has to be different. Hackneyed images, such as key executives in board rooms or in their offices, silhouetted product shots dispersed through pages with financial figures, or mundane plant shots, will not present an image of a company creatively meeting challenges.

Using photography creatively does not mean being gimmicky. It does mean relying on the photographer's eye and the camera's flexibility to present a new way of looking at a company's product, its manufacturing facility, or its senior executives. It means being daring enough to try something new. It means, for example, allowing the photographer to use special techniques to manipulate light and shape to produce an abstract photograph of a product or instrument used in a manufacturing facility.

For photography to be creative, the photographer should participate in the creative process that goes into producing the annual report. Choose photographers early, and let them help to define how photography can best make an impact.

Choosing the right photographer is critical. Within the field of annual-report photography, there are sub-specialties—photographers recognized for their ability to manipulate light and color, others known for photographing people. In addition, there are photographers in related areas that should be considered. For example, if a company decides to use portraits of senior executives as the theme of an annual report, consider a photographer recognized by the art world as a great portraitist. If a company creates fashion products, a top fashion photographer could bring a different touch to an annual report. If color and light abstractions fit into a theme, a photographer known for bold advertising photographs could be considered. It is also useful to look into the editorial, advertising, and art world to see if there is a photographer who is currently creating images that will enhance a report.

While using dynamic photography can make a strong statement about a company, using unimaginative photography will also carry a message, one that you might not intend. In a time when so many companies are utilizing sophisticated techniques, it is critical to find the right photographer who will work with the annual-report creative team and use a camera to capture a company and its message in a different way—enticing analysts, business reporters, and other members of the target audience to spend more than a few seconds with a company's most important publication of the year.

Amy Binder
Executive Vice President
Ruder Finn & Rotman

Reprinted with permission from the October 1986 issue of the Public Relations Journal.

Larry Keenan

421 Bryant Street
San Francisco, California 94107
(415) 495-6474

Advertising, annual reports,
corporate/industrial, travel,
conceptual and special effects
photography. International
experience, numerous awards.
Stock photography library.

CLIENTS:
Activision
Ampex
Apple Computers
Bank of America
Blue Cross
Broderbund
CBS Records
Clorox
Del Monte
Electronic Arts
Genentech
General Instrument
Hewlett-Packard
Levi-Strauss
Lorimar Productions
Microsoft
NorthStar Computers
Omni Magazine
PacBell
Syntex Labs
Tandem Computers

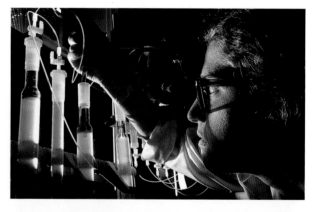

Jim McCrary

211 South La Brea Avenue
Los Angeles, California 90036

Represented by: David L. Zaitz
(213) 936-5115

Jim enjoys turning ordinary subjects into extraordinary images. His twenty years of experience with location and studio photography in 8 × 10 to 35mm formats enables him to handle any assignment in the advertising, annual report, corporate/industrial and executive portrait fields.

Affability and ability to work to tight layouts or to execute his original ideas within short time frames explain Jim's high percentage of repeat business.

Rockwell International, GTE Sprint, Panavision, Litton Industries, Getty Oil, Universal Pictures, Kaiser Chemical, Walt Disney Studios, Celestron (telescopes), Alpine/Luxman, Union Oil, Roland (keyboards), Tokina (lenses), American Pharmaseal, Martin Marietta.

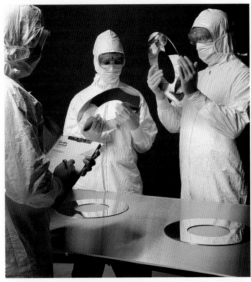

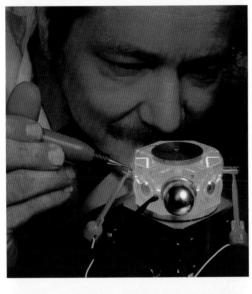

Glenn Otto

10625 Magnolia Boulevard
North Hollywood, California 91601
(818) 762-5724

Location and studio photography for advertising, annual reports, corporate communications, audio visual, architecture, and travel assignments.

For: American Magnetics, ATI/Deseret Medical, Cadillac, California Bankers Association, Calmat, Chesebrough Pond's/Ragu Foods, Chevron USA, Deutsch Metal Components, Domino's Pizza, Harada Industry of America, Hexcel, Hughes Offshore. Kenwood Electronics, Komatsu Fork Lift USA, Laker Airlines, Lear Siegler, Litton, Metromedia, Pennzoil, Stehlin Research Foundation, Thermador, U.S. Leisure/Muskin.

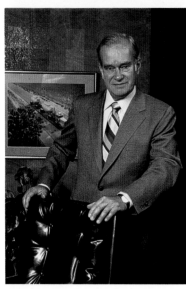

Teri Sandis[...]
Lightra, Inc

1545 North Wilcox Ave[...]
Hollywood, California [...]
(213) 461-3529

Food photography for [...]

Clients include:
Van de Kamp's
Nissin Foods
Las Palmas
Early California Foods
Sanyo, Inc.
Sunset Magazine & B[...]
Martha White Co.

CHICKEN à l'ORANGE with
Almond Rice • 270 Calories

CHEESE CANNELLONI with
Tomato Sauce • 270 Calories

TURKEY DIJON—with Zucchin[i]
& Carrots • 280 Calories

FILET OF FISH DIVAN
270 Calories

©1987 Stouffer Foods Corporation

*FOOD PHOTOGRAPHY [...]

David Powers

17 Brosnan
San Francisco, California 94103
(415) 864-7974

Location and studio
photography for annual reports
and corporate communications,
and magazines.

Clients include:
Banana Republic
Barton-Gillet
Bricker/Evans
Coherent
Crown Zellerbach
Gillian Craig Associates
Gould, Inc.
Image Magazine
Kaiser Foundation Health Plan
Lighthouse Media
Mark Anderson Design
Nagel Design Group
Pacific Bell
Pacific Medical Center
PC World Magazine
Rolm Corporation
Russell Leong Design
Stanford Medical Center
Utah International
Wells Fargo Bank
Wheeler Advertising and Design.

Member APA

Stock Photography available:
STOCK BOSTON, (617) 266-2300

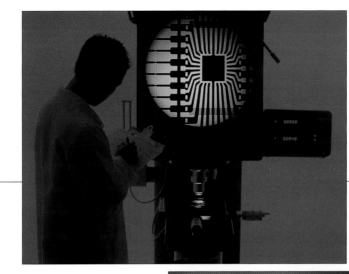

Bob Rowa

PROGRESSIVE I
209 Los Banos A
Walnut Creek (Sa
California 94598
(415) 930-8687

Photography and
multi-image prod
for corporate con

Clients include:
The Concord Pav
Embarcadero Ce
 (Photo-Synthes
Ford of Canada
Formica Corpora
IBM
Marriott Corporat
Northern Telecor
Pacific Bell
Pacific Gas and I
Saga Corporatio
Southern Califorr
Subaru (Flying C
Travel and Leisur
The Wyatt Comp
Xerox Corporatic

Los Angeles Rep
Phillip Shuey
(818) 994-1479

Stephen Simpson, Inc.

701 Kettner Boulevard #124
San Diego, California 92101
(619) 239-6638

Primary clients are large developers, high-tech companies and medical and financial institutions. Studio or location, all formats, all films.

Extensive stock from the above as well as all regions of the West and SouthWest.

You have to be versatile and flexible to succeed in a small market. Give me a call. I'll be happy to send a package of work.

See also Corporate Showcase 2, 3, 4 and 5.

Doug Wilson

Location Photography
10133 NE 113th Place
Kirkland, Washington 98033
(Seattle)
(206) 822-8604

There's something special about being on location at first light or the end of the day, when the light is magic, it's worth the long days, the lack of sleep, the waiting.

These are the special moments I seek to capture for my clients on assignment or adding to my selection of fine stock images.

New York Representation
Ben Chapnick
Sal Catalano
Black Star
450 Park Avenue South
New York, New York 10016
(212) 679-3288

Seattle (stock)
West Stock
1-800-821-9600
(206) 621-1611

Salt Lake City (stock)
The Stock Solution
(801) 569-1155

Denver (stock)
Stock Imagery
(303) 592-1091

Canada (stock)
Image Finders
(604) 688-3818

Member ASMP

WHO WAS HERB LUBALIN?

THE FACE BEHIND THE FACES.

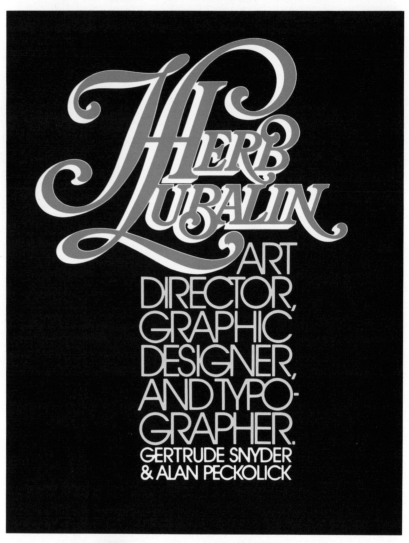

He was a skinny, colorblind, left-handed artist, known to friends and colleagues as a deafeningly silent man. But through his typography-based and editorial designs, he created bold new forms for communication and changed the dimensions of advertising and graphics.

Herb Lubalin is the definitive book about the typographic impresario and design master of our time. It is illustrated with more than 360 extraordinary examples of Lubalin's award-winning work, including: ■ Logos and Letterheads ■ Editorial and Book Design ■ Packaging ■ Advertising and Sales Promotion ■ Annual Reports ■ Best of *U&lc*, and more.

"The magnitude of Herb Lubalin's achievements will be felt for a long time to come....I think he was probably the greatest graphic designer ever."
—Lou Dorfsman, Vice President, Creative Director, Advertising and Design, CBS Inc.

184 pages, Color throughout, 9" x 11⅞" Clothbound, Retail Value: $39.95

SPECIAL OFFER
Send for your copy of **Herb Lubalin** today and pay only $35.00.* Postage and handling are FREE within the U.S. and Canada. To order, **call 212-245-0981** and charge your AMEX, Visa or Mastercard. Or send your check or money order to:
AMERICAN SHOWCASE, INC.
724 Fifth Avenue, New York, NY 10019
*New York residents, please add appropriate sales tax.

Stock

Phoebe Dunn

20 Silvermine Road
New Canaan, Connecticut 06840
(203) 966-9791

Phoebe Dunn is internationally recognized for capturing the magic world of babies and children with imagination, sensitivity and versatility. Natural light and locations a specialty.

Experience in advertising, magazine illustrations, packages, annual reports, illustrations for 15 children's books, promotional material, calendars.

Clients include: Reader's Digest, Campbell Soup, Chesebrough-Ponds, Eastman Kodak, Boehringer-Ingelheim, General Foods, Gerber, Hasselblad, J&J, Kimberly-Clark, Eli Lilly, P&G, Union Carbide, 3M Company, Parents, Women's Day, Random House, Hallmark, Argus.

See also American Showcase, Volumes 3-6.

Direct sale of stock images available through the studio.

Original Hasselblad transparencies of babies, children, family relationships, retired and nature design also available through Al Forsythe at DPI. (212) 627-4060.

David Muench

David Muench
Photography, Inc.
P.O. Box 30500
Santa Barbara, California 93130
(805) 967-4488

A Collection of Stock Photography.

Focusing on the American Landscape...East...West...North... and South. The wild beauty and presence of mountain, desert, coast, prairie, water, texture and sky...the elements.

Specializing in the mysterious moods, natural rhythms, unusual lighting, and spacial forms. Over 25 large format books exhibit this original photography on the American landscape. Photographs are made primarily on large format 4 × 5 films.

Available for advertising, annual reports, books, editorial, calendar, poster and brochures.

Photography is in both color and black and white.

DAVID MUENCH

235

Photri (Photo Research International) Jack Novak

505 West Windsor Avenue
P.O. Box 971
Alexandria, Virginia 22313
(703) 836-4439 Telex 89-9167

Other phone locations:
New York (212) 926-0682
Chicago (312) 726-0433
Atlanta (404) 588-9609
Dallas (214) 641-6049
Los Angeles (213) 622-4220

A super stock library with input from ASMP photographers in many countries. We are the stock photo agency for SPACE, AEROSPACE, the MILITARY & WASHINGTON, D.C. All other subjects available including photo-research.

Graphic Design

**DAVID BRIER
DESIGN WORKS, INC.**
51 PROSPECT TERRACE
E. RUTHERFORD, N.J. 07073
201·896·8476

U *nder the direction of multi-award winning, highly acclaimed designer David Brier, this design office produces consistently appropriate and unique solutions for corporations, agencies, and publishers.*

Thru his astute sense of Design & Art Direction, David Brier has satisfied ABC-TV, Grey Advertising, HBO, NBC-TV, The New York City Opera, The New York Times Magazine, Revlon, 13.30 Corporation, Time/ Life, Watson-Guptill, Whittle Communications, and many others.

The capabilities of David Brier Design Works, Inc. covers every area of communications including promotion, packaging, alphabet design, logotype development, publication design and more. Call or write for further information or samples.

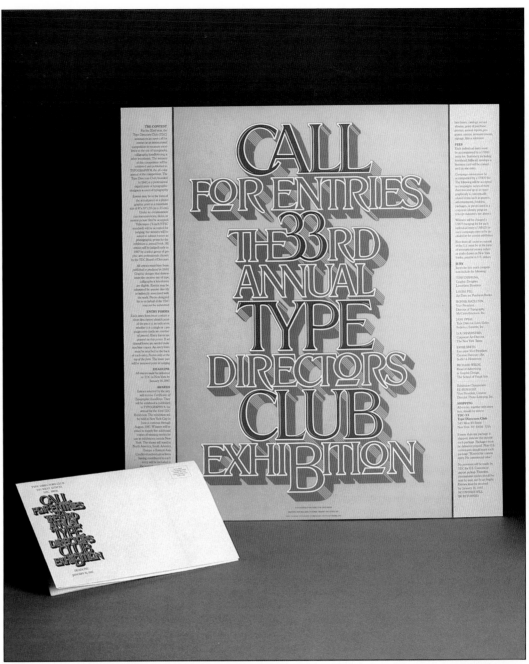

*For the 33rd year, the Type Directors Club had its call for entries. Brier designed and conceived of this **POSTER** being a display of fine typography itself that would inspire a high return for the Club.*

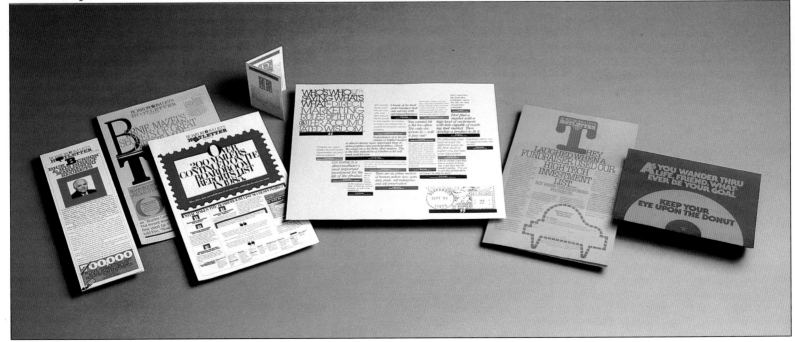

*Boardroom Lists, Inc. is the very adventurous and highly successful list management arm of Boardroom Reports. Offering what is known as their **PROMOTIONAL NEWSLETTER**, Brier has the task every month of creating a visual treat to house the expert copywriting that goes into this award-winning result producing campaign.*

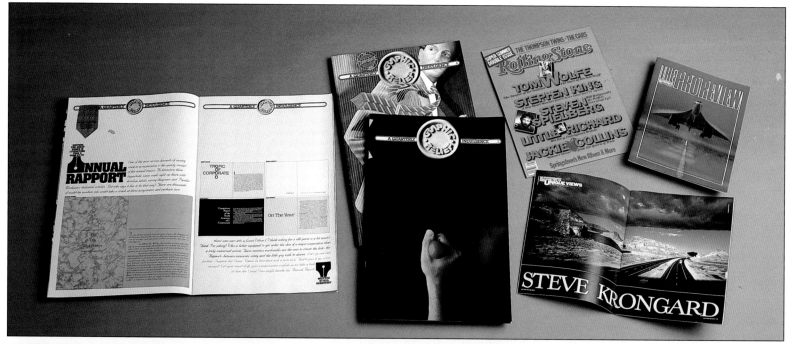

*EDITORIAL DESIGN requires sensitivity and experience whether a cover or a complete redesign. As shown above, **GRAPHIC RELIEF** and **PRO REVIEW** showcase a complete editorial format while **ROLLING STONE** displays a special cover design for their year-end double issue each proving themselves highly successful in the marketplace.*

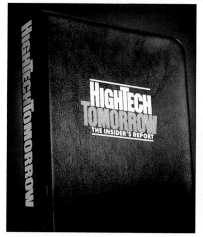

*For a newsletter, Brier did this **BINDER & LOGO** for subscribers to refer to.*

*Rich and classy **PACKAGING** had to be developed including the naming of this new granola product for Glenn Foods.*

*A **LOGOTYPE** was developed for WNYC's radio show reflecting its enthusiasm.*

*For Bianca Graphics, a N.Y. printer, Brier not only designed and conceived the **AD CAMPAIGN** but wrote all copy as well. Having exceeded all sales expectations, discussions for a second campaign are underway.*

"Kids America, our children's radio program, required a logo appropriate for children and adults alike. The logo David Brier designed not only accomplished our corporate goals but also brought a wit and whimsey that, one for one, affects every person that sees it. With his design knowledge, your company image, like ours, can also come out of the closet."
Keith Talbot, Producer
KIDS AMERICA, WNYC Radio

■

"As someone extremely impressed with your work for other publications, I was quite excited to have you design our August cover. And I was not disappointed.
"I have worked with many designers over the years, and I would have to place you at the top in terms of creative talent and professionalism."
Michael Scheibach, Editor
MAGAZINE DESIGN & PRODUCTION

■

"The ability to understand, and translate into a coherent and compelling graphic form, the usual garbled instructions from an art director (in this case, me!) is what sets the true professional apart. David Brier is one of them."
Derek W. Ungless, Art Director
ROLLING STONE

**DAVID BRIER
DESIGN WORKS, INC.**
51 PROSPECT TERRACE
E. RUTHERFORD, N.J. 07073
201·896·8476

Brogren/Kelly & Associates

3113 E. Third Ave., Suite 220
Denver, Colorado 80206
(303) 399-3851

Graphic Design, Illustration & Advertising

A successful, award-winning graphic design firm that is nationally recognized for its Corporate Design capabilities.

Our marketing approach to problem-solving produces creative solutions that meet both large and small client's needs with the same quality results.

Corporate Identity design services include Brandname Development, Trademark Design, Package Design, Logo & Logotype Design, Stationery Packages, Signage and Complete Identification Systems.

Brandname Development
Tofruzen Tofu Frozen Dessert

Complete Identification Systems
Saint Francis Healthcare System

Package Design
Manelli Shoes, Div. of Associated Shoe

Crow Publications

Manelli Shoes

Polar Storm Windows

First Dakota Home S&L

US Recycling Corp.

Shannon Golf Books

HC Copeland & Associates

The Fluorocarbon Corp.

Colorado School of Mines

Trademarks and Logos

Trademark & Signage
Que Pasta Itilian Restaurants

Product Brochures
Citicorp Retail Services/Radio Shack, AMI Healthcare Systems

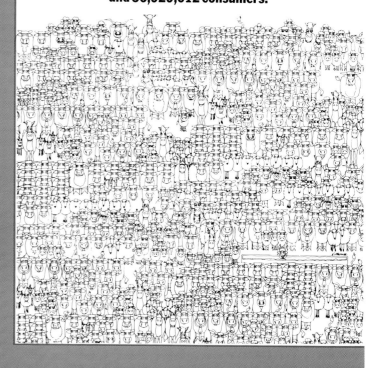
Publication Design
Colorado Junior Symphony Guild

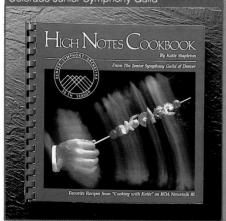

Capabilities Brochures
Van Gilder Insurance Corporation

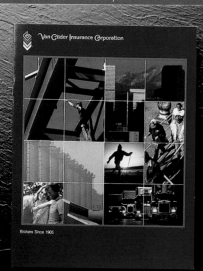

Graphic Design and Illustration services include Annual Reports, Product Brochures, Technical Bulletins, Catalogs, Capabilities Brochures, Publications, Advertising, Audio-Visual and Display.

Clients include:
AMI Healthcare Systems
Beaumont Properties, Inc.
Citicorp Retail Services
Colorado Hospital Assn.
Colorado School of Mines
Eclipse Productions
Grubb & Ellis
Hendricks & Howard
 Development Co.
Home Mechanix Magazine
LC Fulenwider, Inc.
Lincoln Property Co., Inc.
Saint Francis Healthcare
 System
The Linpro Company
Trammell Crow Company
Tri-State Generation &
 Transmission
United Business Publications
US Ski Team
Van Gilder Insurance Corp.

Annual Reports
Griffin Petroleum, Colorado Hospital Assn., Tri-State Generation & Trans.

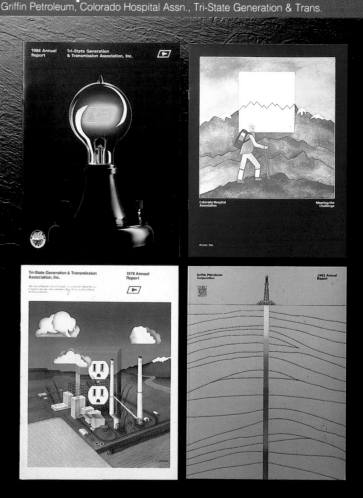

Brogren/Kelly & Associates
303/399-3851
Graphic Design, Illustration & Advertising 3113 E. Third Ave., Suite 220, Denver, CO 80206

Designed To Print, Inc.
130 West 25th Street
New York, NY 10001
(212) 924-2090

Creative problem solving
that answers corporate
marketing objectives

Packaging
Corporate Identity
Sales Promotion
Corporate Communications
Posters

BIO-MEDICAL

The philosophy *"Paper is part of the picture"* was created for Strathmore Paper Company by Will Bradley in the late 1800's and is still used as a part of their corporate advertising campaign. Bradley, a true pioneer of graphic design, believed that through the combination of typography visual images and the color and textures of paper, a message could be sent to the reader with a stronger, more impressive impact. Designing the first promotional piece for Strathmore was a welcome challenge for Bradley. *"I became so intrigued with the printing possibilities of these new Strathmore papers, their pleasing color and tints, that I enthusiastically agreed to undertake the commission—a decision for which I shall always feel thankful."* Bradley's work can be seen as part of the permanent collection of the Metropolitan Museum of Art in New York City.

Clients Include:
Nestlé Foods Corporation
Johanna Farms, Inc.
HBO/Cannon Video
Columbia Pictures Int'l.
Tri-Star Pictures, Inc.
Bio-Medical, Ltd. (Japan)
Pressman Toy Co.
Lindenmeyr Paper Co.
Larami Corp.

Downney, Weeks & Toomey

Corporate Identity & Marketing Communications Design

519 Eighth Avenue, New York, NY 10018   Telephone 212 564 8260
London Affiliate: Duffin/Foxell/Weeks, 70 High Street, Teddington Middlesex TW11 8JE   Telephone 01 943.2238

Annual Reports   **Environmental Design**   **Catalogs**   **Sales Promotion**   **Product Announcements**

Downey, Weeks & Toomey

Corporate Identity & Marketing Communications Design

519 Eighth Avenue, New York, NY 10018   Telephone 212 564 8260
London Affiliate: Duffin/Foxell/Weeks, 70 High Street, Teddington Middlesex TW11 8JE   Telephone 01 943.2238

Direct Mail/Response   **Packaging**   **Posters**   **Corporate Magazines**   **Logo Development**

OMNI International Hotel

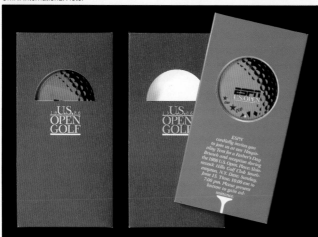

ESPN

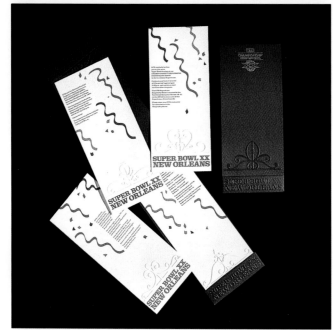

GTE

MSG/Madison Square Garden Network

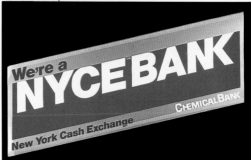

Chemical Bank

Television Enterprise Network

HBO

U.S. Sprint

Glazer and Kalayjian, Inc.
Communications Design Group

301 East 45th Street
New York, NY 10017

212·687·3099

Design, Copywriting and Production of:

Advertising, Marketing Programs, Brochures, Calendars,
Annual Reports, Posters, Logos and Symbols,
Identity Programs, Sales Kits, Publications, Audio Visual
Presentations, Exhibition Graphics

Beneficial Insurance Group

Young Presidents' Organization

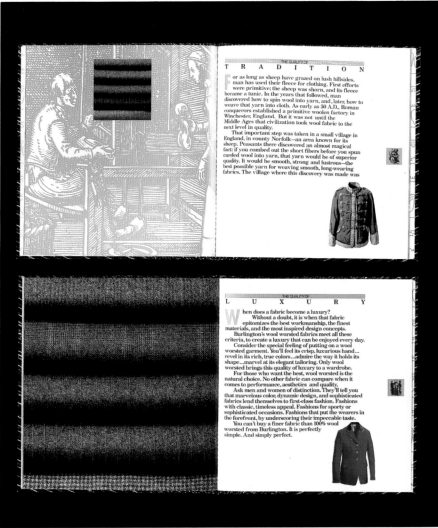

Burlington Industries

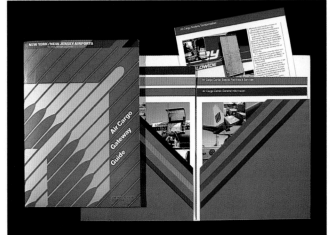

The Port Authority of New York/New Jersey

Sony

Panasonic Battery Division
Package and Product Design
Panasonic Industrial Company

Saab 9000 Radio
Control Panel Layout
Saab Scania

McGraw Hill French and Spanish Book Covers
Webster Division
McGraw Hill

Lady Stetson Bottles
Coty Division
Pfizer, Inc.

Product Design
Packaging Design
Graphic Design
Marketing

Group Four Design offers a comprehensive "Program Approach" to optimize New Product Development, Package Innovation and Niche Market opportunities.

Please contact: Group Four Design
Marketing Department
Avon, CT 06001
203 678-1570

Jem Packaging
Hasbro, Inc.

Royal Product Design
Package Design
Royal Consumer Business Products

Ross Culbert Holland & Lavery

Well-designed maps and charts are a synthesis of beauty, intelligence and utility.

Within RCH&L's general area of expertise — marketing and communications design — we find the specialty of chart and map design particularly challenging. Even though most projects may not be as far-reaching as Pioneer 10 Spacecraft's hull engraving or as enduring as Lascaux's cave wall inscriptions, the process of design is the same.

We create a context for the project by analysing the audience, media and desired impact. Then we work with your raw numerical data, schematic diagrams or rough sketches to develop a visual concept within that context. We draw from our large inventory of styles—ranging from highly technical to

"Data processing is such an abstract concept. RCH&L managed to translate our data into concrete visuals. They developed our whole graphic identity into a world-class design system."

PAM HELWIG-DAVIES
VICE PRESIDENT OF SALES AND MARKETING
NOBLE LOWNDES INTERNATIONAL

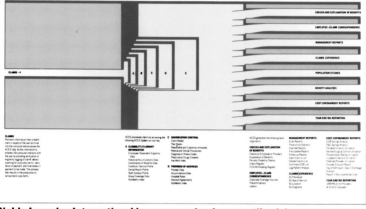

Noble Lowndes International is a health benefits data processor. We designed this chart stressing their simple, versatile claims system to help them gain the confidence of potential clients.

"The pyramid chart was incredible— so effective it served as *the* standard illustration for the divestiture. It was on the wall of every Bell office in America and abroad."

RICK WILBINS
DISTRICT MANAGER
EXECUTIVE COMMUNICATIONS, AT&T

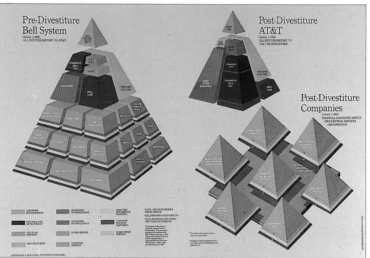

Prior to the divestiture, AT&T asked us to design a chart that would show its employees the new corporate structure. We chose the corporate pyramid, a classic symbol of endurance, as the basis for our thinking. It was honored by the American Institute of Graphic Arts for its design.

The bar chart above and the divestiture chart at the left were both designed for AT&T's *Bell Magazine*.

"RCH&L designed everything for *Peanut* from logo to rate card. They're full of fun, spunky ideas *and* good sense. Nothing mundane ever comes from them."

LEANNA LANDSMANN
VICE PRESIDENT
HARCOURT BRACE JOVANOVICH

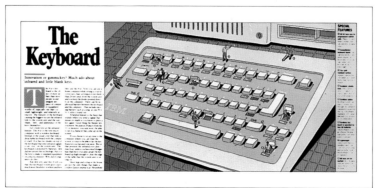

Peanut Magazine's audience was home computer users from age 8 to 80. We put people on the keyboard to add a playful, non-technical feeling.

Familiar, pictorial imagery such as computers (above, *Time* Magazine) and coins (above, Hearst Publications) works well in magazines.

informative yet whimsical—to use the appropriate language for the visual story that needs to be told, the message that needs to be conveyed.

Prior to starting a project, we draft a proposal which we review together. We discuss objectives, responsibilities, fees and expenses, and terms and conditions. The proposal is mutually agreed upon before we proceed with the project.

Our capabilities include concept and creative direction, design, copywriting, photography, illustration, marketing, production and fabrication. Projects include promotion, advertising, corporate communications, publishing, packaging and product design.

When you think of charts and maps, think of RCH&L. And since we often design our maps and charts as part of a larger project, we would be pleased to show you the rest of our portfolio as well.

**Our design offices are at
15 West Twentieth Street
New York, New York 10011
212-206-0044**

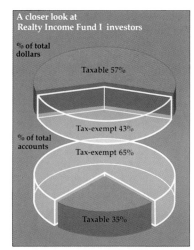

A closer look at Realty Income Fund I investors

% of total dollars

Taxable 57%

Tax-exempt 43%

% of total accounts

Tax-exempt 65%

Taxable 35%

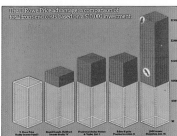

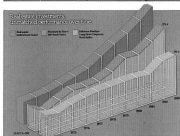

This series of charts, which we have developed over several years for T. Rowe Price through McCaffrey McCall, recently won an award from the AIGA.

"RCH&L really knows how to work well with an ad agency. They're flexible and *great* with deadlines. And they're right on target with their design concepts."

LYNDA DECKER
ART DIRECTOR
McCAFFREY McCALL ADVERTISING

Buy a good-neighbor policy.
Invest in your community the United Way.

How do you get employees involved in charity? First, you get their attention. This eye-catching poster for Merrill Lynch shows that the United Way has locations hard at work throughout the area. The companion piece zooms in on their local community activities, stressing their attention to people.

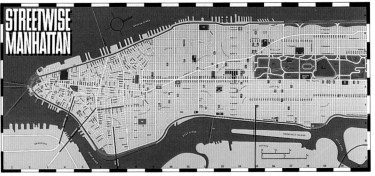

STREETWISE MANHATTAN

Award-winning, best-selling *Streetwise Manhattan* became the prototype for an entire line of maps sold across the U.S. It was designed to appeal equally to both male and female audiences.

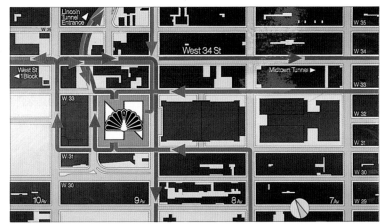

The architecture firm of Kohn Pederson Fox commissioned us to develop a series of seven maps for an unusu- ally elaborate site planning presentation. Here, we showed the merits of the vehicular access to the site.

VEGETATION

This looks like a classic topographic map but has a hidden image. Can you see the dog's head?

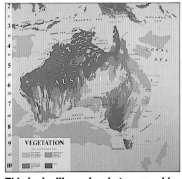

"We value their input—their opinions are consistently fresh, intelligent and accurate—just the ticket when you're too close to the big picture."

MARK STRAUSS
ASSOCIATE PARTNER
KOHN PEDERSON FOX, P.C.

Free fertilizer for ideas.

One of the first steps in developing your advertising campaign is finding out what's being done in the same area —food, automobile, travel, cosmetics, or whatever.

You don't want to do something that's been done, or worse yet, that's being done.

And, unless you know what's being done, it's very difficult to stand out.

So you need to know what's going on. Both in the US, and internationally.

And you need to know on a continuing basis.

The ways to get this kind of information are either expensive or inefficient, or both. Clipping services charge a lot, don't organize the stuff very well, and generally don't edit out the chaff.

So someone in your company winds up getting a pile of tearsheets with no rhyme or reason to them.

That's not worth much.

Archive solves the problem.

Archive magazine is the solution to this state of affairs.

Archive is an internationally famous advertising magazine which is edited by the equally internationally famous Walter Lurzer, of West Germany.

When you subscribe to Archive, you get an in-depth overview of what's happening in, say, the fashion or liquor industry, *all over the world.*

The material is organized by category, is easy to read, and easy to understand. A careful study of Archive will reap big dividends for anyone involved in the creation, selling, or commissioning of advertising.

That means you.

For only $35 a year (less than the price of a lunch, and a discount off the cover price) you can get Archive com-

ing to you every two months.

One copy free.

To introduce you to Archive, we'll send you one copy free for the asking. At the same time, we'll enter an Archive subscription in your name at the special rate of $35.00 for 5 more issues (6 in all). That's a savings of 22% off the cover price.

If, for any reason, you are not completely satisfied, simply return the bill marked "cancel" and owe nothing. The first issue is yours to keep with our compliments.

For fast subscription service, call (212) 245-0981. Or write, Archive, c/o American Showcase, 724 Fifth Avenue, New York, NY 10019.

IndexPhotographers & Graphic Designers

Continued on next page.

IndexPhotographers & Graphic Designers

Continued from previous page.

Phone Listings & Addresses of Representatives, Visual Artists & Suppliers

Contents

Regions

New York City

Northeast
- Connecticut
- Delaware
- Maine
- Maryland
- Massachusetts
- New Hampshire
- New Jersey
- New York State
- Pennsylvania
- Rhode Island
- Vermont
- Washington, D.C.
- West Virginia

Southeast
- Alabama
- Florida
- Georgia
- Kentucky
- Louisiana
- Mississippi
- North Carolina
- South Carolina
- Tennessee
- Virginia

Midwest
- Illinois
- Indiana
- Iowa
- Kansas
- Michigan
- Minnesota
- Missouri
- Nebraska
- North Dakota
- Ohio
- South Dakota
- Wisconsin

Southwest
- Arizona
- Arkansas
- New Mexico
- Oklahoma
- Texas

Rocky Mountain
- Colorado
- Idaho
- Montana
- Utah
- Wyoming

West Coast
- Alaska
- British Columbia
- California
- Hawaii
- Nevada
- Oregon
- Washington

Grey Pages

Representatives

Legend
A = Animator
AV = Audio Visual
C = Cartoonist
D = Director
F = Film
G = Graphic Designer
H & MU = Hair & Make-up
I = Illustrator
L = Lettering
M = Music
P = Photographer
R = Retoucher
TV = Television

New York City

A

Abbey, Ken & Assoc/421 Seventh Ave, New York, NY 212-758-5259
David Greenberg, (P), Hal Oringer, (P), Ted Pobiner, (P), A J Sandone, (P)
Adams, Ray/22 W 38th St, New York, NY 212-719-5514
Adler, Phil/35 W 38th St, New York, NY 212-354-0456
Walter Auster, (P)
Altamore, Bob/237 W 54th St 4th Fl, New York, NY 212-977-4300
Cailor/Resnick, (P)
American Artists/353 W 53rd St #1W, New York, NY 212-682-2462
Don Almquist, (I), Joyce Ballantyne, (I), Keith Batcheller, (I), Frank Bolle, (I), Dan Bridy, (I), Rick Brown, (I), Bob Byrd, (I), Rob Cage, (I), Gary Ciccarelli, (I), Hank Connelly, (I), Jim Deigan, (I), Norm Doherty, (I), Alfred D'Ortenzio, (I), Lane DuPont, (I), Russell Farrell, (I), John Freas, (P), George Gaadt, (I), Jackie Geyer, (I), Michael Goodwin, (I), John Hamagami, (I), Karel Havileck, (I), Doug Henry, (I), John Holm, (I), Chris Hopkins, (I), Todd Kat, (I), Richard Kriegler, (I), Diane LaRoja, (I), Kaaren Lewis, (I), Ed Lindlof, (I), Jerry LoFaro, (I), Ron Mahoney, (I), Julia Manya, (I), Mick McGinty, (I), Steve Miller, (I), Richard Nelsen, (I), Jim Owens, (I), George Poladian, (I), Tony Randazzo, (I), Ed Renfro, (I), Paul Rogers, (I), Mike Ruland, (I), Jan Sawka, (I), Todd Schorr, (I), Victor Scocozza, (I), Joe Scrofani, (I), Mary Sherman, (I), Vince Streano, (I), Rudy Tesa, (I), Ron Wolin, (I), Jonathan Wright, (I), Andy Zito, (I), Craig Zuckerman, (I)
Anthony, Ed/133 W 19th St 3rd Fl, New York, NY 212-924-7770
Anton, Jerry/107 E 38th St #5A, New York, NY 212-679-4562
Bobbye Cochran, (I), Abe Echevarria, (I), Norman Green, (I), Aaron Rezny, (P), Bob Ziering, (I)
Aparo, Vincent/65 W 68th St, New York, NY 212-877-5439
Charles Baum, (P)
Arnold, Peter Inc/1181 Broadway 4th Fl, New York, NY 212-840-6928
Fred Bavendam, (P), Bob Evans, (P), Jacques Jangoux, (P), Manfred Kage, (P), Stephen Krasemann, (P), Hans Pfletschinger, (P), David Scharf, (P), Erika Stone, (P), Bruno Zehnder, (P)
The Art Farm/420 Lexington Ave, New York, NY 212-688-4555
Dick Carroll, (I), Sururi Gumen, (I), Bob Lubbers, (I), Dick Naugler, (I), Linda Pascual, (I), Scott Pike, (I), Bob Walker, (I), Kong Wu, (I), Bill Zdinak, (I)
Artco/24 W 57th St #605, New York, NY 212-489-8777
Ed Acuna, (I), Peter Caras, (I), Jeff Cornell, (I), Bob Dacey, (I), Beau & Alan Daniels, (I), Ron DeFelice, (I), Christine Fromentine, (I), Enid Hatton, (I), Rick Mcullom, (I), Joseph Milioto, (I), Jim Sharpe, (I), Rick Tulka, (I), Sally Vitsky, (I)
Artists Associates/211 E 51st St #5F, New York, NY 212-755-1365
Norman Adams, (I), Don Braupigam, (I), Michael Deas, (I), Mark English, (I), Alex Gnidziejko, (I), Robert Heindel, (I), Steve Karchin, (I), Dick Krepel, (I), Skip Liepky, (I), Fred Otnes, (I), Daniel Schwartz, (I)
Arton Associates/216 E 45th St, New York, NY 212-661-0850
Paul Giovanopoulis, (I), Jacob Knight, (I), Carveth Kramer, (I), Michelle Laporte, (I), Karen Laurence, (I)
Asciutto Art Reps/19 E 48th St 3rd Fl, New York, NY 212-838-0050
Anthony Accardo, (I), Alex Bloch, (I), Olivia Cole, (I), Kitty Diamantis, (I), Simon Galkin, (I), Donald Gates, (I), Meryl Henderson, (I), Taylor Jones, (I), Paul Lackner, (I), Sally Marshall Larrain, (I), Goran Lindgren, (I), Loreta Lustig, (I), Tod Mason, (I), Sal Murdocca, (I), Jan Pyk, (I), Donna Ward, (I), Fred Winkowski, (I)
Ash, Michael/5 W 19th St, New York, NY 212-741-0015
Azzara, Louise/131 E 17th St, New York, NY 212-674-8114

B

Backer, Vic/30 W 26th St, New York, NY 212-620-0944
Badin, Andy/835 Third Ave 4th Fl, New York, NY 212-986-8833
Jeff Feinen, (I), Brian Kossoff, (P), Michael Kozmiuk, (I), Robert S Levy, (I), Harry Pincus, (I)
Bahm, Darwin/6 Jane St, New York, NY 212-989-7074
Julian Allen, (I), Joan Landis, (I), Rick Meyerowitz, (I), Arno Sternglass, (I), Sketch Pad Studio, (I), John Thompson, (I), Robert Weaver, (I)
Baker, Valerie/152 W 25th St 12th Fl, New York, NY 212-807-9754
Barboza, Ken Assoc/853 Broadway #1603, New York, NY 212-505-8635
Pinder Hughes, (P)
Barclay, R Francis/5 W 19th St, New York, NY 212-255-3440
Bauchner, Susan/134 Beaumont St, Brooklyn, NY 718-648-5345
Jacques Charlas, (P)
Becker, Erica/150 W 55th St, New York, NY 212-757-7987
Richard Ely, (I), Esther Larson, (I)
Becker, Noel/150 W 55th St, New York, NY 212-757-8987
Howard Tangye, (P), Sy Vinopoll, (P)
Beilin, Frank/405 E 56th St, New York, NY 212-751-3074
Benedict, Brinker (Ms)/165 E 89th St, New York, NY 212-534-1845
Bernstein & Andriulli/60 E 42nd St #505, New York, NY 212-682-1490
Richard Anderson, (I), Tony Antonios, (I), Per Arnoldi, (I), Graphic Assoc, (I), Garin Baker, (I), Garie Blackwell, (I), Airstream, (I), Melinda Bordelon, (I), Rick Brown, (I), Everett Davidson, (I), Cathy Deeter, (I), Griesbach/Martucci, (I), Victor Gadino, (I), Joe Genova, (I), Marika Hahn, (I), Veronika Hart, (I), Catherine Huerta, (I), Cathy Johnson, (I), David McCall Johnston, (I), Kid Kane, (I), Mary Ann Lasher, (I), Bette Levine, (I), Todd Lockwood, (I), Michael Molkenthin, (P), Bill Morse, (I), Frank Moscati, (P), Simpson/Flint, (P), Craig Nelson, (I), Joe Salina, (I), Marla Shega, (I), Chuck Slack, (I), Peter Stallard, (I), Murray Tinkelman, (I), Clay Turner, (I), Chuck Wilkinson, (I), Paul Wollman, (I), James B. Wood, (P)
Bishop, Lynn/134 E 24th St, New York, NY 212-254-5737
Irene Stern, (P)
Black Silver & Lord/415 Madison Ave, New York, NY 212-580-4045
Gloria Baker, (P), Kip Brundage, (P), Norm Clasen, (P), Fred Mullane, (P), Michel Tcherevkoff, (P), Roger Tully, (P)
Black Star/450 Park Ave S, New York, NY 212-679-3288
John W. Alexanders, (P), Nancy Rica Schiff, (P), Kim Steele, (P), Arnold Zann, (P)
Blum, Felice S/79 W 12th St, New York, NY 212-929-2166
Boghosian, Marty/1123 Broadway #412, New York, NY 212-242-1251
James Salzano, (P)
Booth, Tom Inc/425 W 23rd St #17A, New York, NY 212-243-2750
William Garrett, (P), Joshua Greene, (P), Bob Hiemstra, (I), Richard Holiman, (I), Patrick Russell, (P), Geoff Spear, (P), Michael Tighe, (P), Alexander Vethers, (I)
Brackman, Henrietta/415 E 52nd St, New York, NY 212-753-6483
Brackman, Selma/251 Park Ave S, New York, NY 212-777-4210
Brennan, Dan/32 E 38th St, New York, NY 212-889-6555
Tom Biondo, (P), Knut Bry, (P), Francois Deconnick, (P), Renato Grignaschi, (P), Bob Krieger, (P), Michel Momy, (P)
Brindle, Carolyn/203 E 89th St #3D, New York, NY 212-534-4177
Brody, Sam/230 E 44th St #2F, New York, NY 212-758-0640
Robert Butler, (P), Linda Clenney, (I), Fred Hilliard, (I), Gary Kufner, (P), Stanford Smilow, (P), Steen Svenson, (P), Rudi Tesa, (P)
Brown Ink Assoc/267 Fifth Ave #1004, New York, NY 212-686-5576
Deborah Albena, (I), Paulette Bogan, (I), Bob Brown, (I), Lisa Campbell, (I), Virginia Curtin, (I), Darrel Kanyok, (I), Richard Kushner, (I), Kurt Merkel, (I), John Reiner, (I), Christine Roose, (I), Jody Silver, (I), Conrad Weiss, (I)
Brown, Bob/267 Fifth Ave #706, New York, NY 212-686-5576
Brown, Doug/17 E 45th St #1009, New York, NY 212-980-4971
Abe Seltzer, (P), Andrew Unangst, (P)
Browne, Pema Ltd/185 E 85th St, New York, NY 212-369-1925
George Angelini, (I), Robert Barrett, (I), Joe Burleson, (I), Peter Catalanotto, (I), Robert C Howe, (I), Ron Jones, (I), Kathy Krantz, (I), David Plourde, (I), Karen Pritchett, (I), John Rush, (I), John Sandford, (I), Alice deKok, (I)
Bruck, J S/157 W 57th St, New York, NY 212-247-1130
Richard Anderson, (I), Eva Cellini, (I), Joseph Cellini, (I), Michael Dudash, (I), Tom Freeman, (I), Donald Hedlin, (I), Jim Mathewuse, (I), Richard Newton, (I), Victoria Vebell, (I), Gary Watson, (I)
Bruck, Nancy/315 E 69th St #2B, New York, NY 212-288-6023
Gary Feinstein, (P), Pamela Patrick, (I)

Representatives
Continued

Please send us your additions and updates.

Bruml, Kathy/262 West End Ave, New York, NY — 212-874-5659
　Charles Folds, (P), Michael Skott, (P)
Byrnes, Charles/5 E 19th St #303, New York, NY — 212-473-3366
　Steve Steigman, (P)

C
Cafiano, Charles/140 Fifth Ave, New York, NY — 212-777-7654
　Kenro Izu, (P)
Cahill, Joe/135 E 50th St, New York, NY — 212-751-0529
　Shig Ikeda, (P), Brad Miller, (P), Howard Sochurek, (P)
Camera 5 Inc/6 W 20th St, New York, NY — 212-989-2004
　Bob Bishop, (P), Peter Calvin, (P), Karin Epstein, (P), Curt
　Gunther, (P), Boyd Hagen, (P), Ralph Lewin, (P), Michael
　Marks, (P), Ralph Pabst, (P), Neal Preston, (P), Ken Regan, (P),
　Bob Sherman, (P), Ben Weaver, (P), Bob Wiley, (P)
Camp, Woodfin & Assoc/415 Madison Ave, New York, NY — 212-750-1020
　Robert Azzi, (P), Kip Brundage, (P)
Canter, Theresa/1483 First Ave #5G, New York, NY — 212-734-1352
　Denes Petoe, (P)
Caputo, Elise & Assoc/305 Madison #1805, New York, NY — 212-949-2440
　Ric Cohn, (P), Joe Toto, (F)
Carleo, Teresa/1328 Broadway PH, New York, NY — 212-244-5515
　Steve Chenn, (P)
Carmel/69 Mercer St, New York, NY — 212-925-6216
　Guy Powers, (P)
Carp, Stan/11 E 48th St, New York, NY — 212-759-8880
　Nick Samardge, (P), Allen Vogel, (P)
Casey, Judy/200 W 54th St #3C, New York, NY — 212-757-6144
　Michael Doster, (I), Torkil Gudnason, (P), Michael O Brien, (P),
　Taolo Roversi, (P)
Casey, Marge/245 E 63rd St, New York, NY — 212-486-9575
　Peter Bosch, (P), Thomas Hooper, (P), John Manno, (P)
Cedeno, Lucy/10 W 18th St, New York, NY — 212-255-9212
Celnick, Manny/36 E 12th St, New York, NY — 212-473-4455
　Edward Selnick, (P)
Chie/15 E 11th St #2M, New York, NY — 212-243-2353
Chislovsky, Carol/853 Broadway, New York, NY — 212-677-9100
　Randal Birkey, (I), Alex Bostic, (I), Russell Cobane, (I), Bob
　Cooper, (I), Ignacio Gomez, (I), Ken Graning, (I), John Gray, (I),
　Michael Haynes, (I), Hubert, (I), Tim Herman, (I), William
　Hosner, (I), Jim Hunt, (I), Joe Lapinski, (I), Felix Marich, (I), Joe
　Ovies, (I), Vincent Petragnani, (I), Chuck Schmidt, (I), Sandra
　Shap, (I), Danny Smythe, (I), Randy South, (I), Nighthawk
　Studios, (I), Bob Thomas, (I)
Cohen, Bruce/54 W 16th St, New York, NY — 212-620-7839
Collignon, Daniele/200 W 15th St, New York, NY — 212-243-4209
　Bob Aiese, (I), Dan Cosgrove, (I), Bill Frampton, (I), David
　Gambale, (I), Mel Greifinger, (I), Richard Hughes, (P), Mike
　Lester, (I), Dennis Mukai, (I), Fran Oelbaum, (I), Cindy Pardy,
　(I), Alex Tiani, (I), Vicki Yiannias, (I), Varlet-Martinelli, (I)
Conlon, Jean/461 Broome St, New York, NY — 212-966-9897
　Elizabeth Brady, (I), Kenro Izu, (P), Holly Shapiro, (S), Nana
　Watanabe, (P)
Conroy, Chris/124 E 24th St, New York, NY — 212-598-9766
　Howard Alt, (P), David Kennedy, (P)
Crawford, Janice/340 E 93rd St #9I, New York, NY — 212-722-4964
Creative Freelancers/62 W 45th St, New York, NY — 212-398-9540
　Harold Brooks, (I), Howard Darden, (I), Claudia Fouse, (I),
　Rosanne Percivalle, (I)
Creative Talent/62 LeRoy St, New York, NY — 212-243-7869
　Marshall Cetlin, (I), Alan Henderson, (I), Guy Smalley, (I)
Crecco, Michael/342 Madison Ave, New York, NY — 212-682-5663
Cullom, Ellen/55 E 9th St, New York, NY — 212-777-1749

D
Dagrosa, Terry/374 Eighth Ave 2nd Fl, New York, NY — 212-645-4082
　Rod Cook, (P)
Davies, Nora/370 E 76th St #C103, New York, NY — 212-628-6657
DeBacker, Clo/29 E 19th St, New York, NY — 212-420-1276
　Bob Kiss, (P)
Dedell, Jacqueline/58 W 15th St 6th Fl, New York, NY — 212-741-2539
　Teresa Fasolino, (I), Chermayeff and Geismar, (I), Ivan Powell,
　(I), Barry Root, (I), Richard Williams, (I), Henry Wolf, (P)
Des Verges, Diana/73 Fifth Ave, New York, NY — 212-691-8674

Deverin, Daniele/226 E 53rd St, New York, NY — 212-755-4945
　Paul Blakey, (I), Greg Couch, (I), Mort Drucker, (I), David
　Johnson, (I), Lazlo Kubinyi, (I), Charles Shields, (I), Jeff Smith,
　(I), Don Weller, (I)
DeVito, Kitty/43 E 30th St 14th Fl, New York, NY — 212-889-9670
　Bart DeVito, (P)
DeVlieger, Mary/2109 Broadway, New York, NY — 212-903-4321
DeWan, Michael/250 Cabrini Blvd #2E, New York, NY — 212-927-9458
　Nancy Bundt, (P), Don Sparks, (P)
Dewey, Frank & Assoc/420 Lexington Ave, New York, NY — 212-986-1249
Dickinson, Alexis/175 Fifth Ave #1112, New York, NY — 212-473-8020
　Richard Dunkley, (P), Paul Hoffman, (P)
Dorman, Paul/419 E 57th St, New York, NY — 212-826-6737
　Studio DGM, (P)
Drexler, Sharon/451 Westminster Rd, Brooklyn, NY — 718-284-4779
　Les Katz, (I)
Droske, Diane/300 E 40th St #19R, New York, NY — 212-867-2383
　Tom Hollyman, (P), Nancy LeVine, (P), Tobey Sanford, (P)
DuBane, J J/130 W 17th St, New York, NY — 212-696-0274

EF
Eagles, Betsy/130 W 57th St, New York, NY — 212-582-1501
　Ron Nicolaysen, (P), Lance Steadler, (P)
Edlitz, Ann/230 E 79th St #14F, New York, NY — 212-744-7945
Ellis, Mirjana/176 Westminster Rd, Brooklyn, NY — 718-282-6449
　Ray Ellis, (P)
Eng, Barbara/110 E 23rd St, New York, NY — 212-254-8334
Englert, Tim/305 W 84th St #313, New York, NY — 212-496-2074
Everly, Bart/156 Fifth Ave #327, New York, NY — 212-924-1510
Eyre, Susan/292 Marlboro Rd, Brooklyn, NY — 718-282-5034
　Robert Phillips, (P)
Feldman, Robert/358 W 18th St, New York, NY — 212-741-7254
　Alen MacWeeney, (P), Terry Niefield, (P)
Fischer, Bob/135 E 54th St, New York, NY — 212-755-2131
　James Moore, (P)
Fishback, Lee/350 W 21st St, New York, NY — 212-929-2951
Flesher, Lex/7 E 14th St #903, New York, NY — 212-255-4863
Folickman, Gail/399 E 72nd St, New York, NY — 212-879-1508
Foster, Peter/870 UN Plaza, New York, NY — 212-593-0793
　Charles Tracey, (P)
Friess, Susan/36 W 20th St, New York, NY — 212-675-3021
　Richard Goldman, (P)
Friscia, Salmon/20 W 10th St, New York, NY — 212-228-4134
Furst, Franz/420 E 55th St, New York, NY — 212-684-0492
　Greg Pease, (P)

G
Gargagliano, Tony/216 E 45th St, New York, NY — 212-661-0850
Gaynin, Gail/241 Central Park West, New York, NY — 212-255-3040
　Terry Clough, (P)
Gebbia, Doreen/156 Fifth Ave, New York, NY — 212-807-0588
Gelb, Elizabeth/856 West End Ave, New York, NY — 212-222-1215
Geng, Maud/, New York, NY — 212-513-1557
　Caroline Alterio, (I), Peter Barger, (I), Vicki Smith, (I)
Ginsberg, Michael/339 E 58th St, New York, NY — 212-628-2379
Giraldi, Tina/54 W 39th St, New York, NY — 212-840-8225
Godfrey, Dennis/95 Horatio St #203, New York, NY — 212-807-0840
　Jeffrey Adams, (I), Daryl Cagle, (I), Joel Nakamura, (I), Karen
　Payne, (I), Morgan Pickard, (I), Wendy Popp, (I), Greg
　Ragland, (I), Lane Smith, (I)
Goldman, David/18 E 17th St, New York, NY — 212-807-6627
　Norm Bendell, (I), Jay Brenner, (P), Jim Kingston, (I), Joe
　Marvullo, (P)
Goldmann, Howard/309 Fifth Ave #506, New York, NY — 212-481-0911
Goldsmith, Randi/56 W 84th St #1R, New York, NY — 212-580-1143
Goldstein, Michael L/107 W 69th St, New York, NY — 212-874-6933
　Carla Bauer, (I), Fred Schulze, (P)
Gomberg, Susan/145 E 22nd St, New York, NY — 212-473-8747
　Julius Ciss, (I), Michael Conway, (I), Robert Dale, (I), Jeff Faria,
　(I), Richard Fried, (P), Allen Garns, (I), Ron Lieberman, (I),
　Janeart Limited, (P), Dan McGowan, (I), Enzo Messi & Urs
　Schmidt, (I), Kathy S Schorr, (I), James Tughan, (I)
Goodman, Barbara L/50 W 34th St, New York, NY — 212-594-9209
Goodwin, Phyllis A/10 E 81st St, New York, NY — 212-570-6021

Carl Furuta, (P), Cosimo, (P), Karen Leeds, (P)

GORDON, BARBARA ASSOC/165 E 32ND ST, NEW YORK, NY (P 24) 212-686-3514
Ron Barry, (I), Linda Benson, (I), Judith Cheng, (I), Bob Clarke, (I), Keita Colton, (I), James Dietz, (I), Glenn Harrington, (I), Robert Hunt, (I), Nenad Jakesevic, (I), Jackie Jasper, (I), Sonja Lamut, (I), April Lawton, (I), Andrew Nitzberg, (I), Sharleen Pederson, (I), Jas Szygiel, (I), Jackie Vaux, (I)

Gordon, Fran/1654 E 13th St #5A, Brooklyn, NY 718-339-4277
Gotham Art Agency/25 Tudor Pl, New York, NY 212-286-9786
Green, Anita/160 E 26th St, New York, NY 212-674-4788
Alan Dolgins, (P), Stuart Peltz, (P)
Grien, Anita/155 E 38th St, New York, NY 212-697-6170
Dolores Bego, (I), Fanny M Berry, (I), Hal Just, (I), Jerry McDaniel, (I), Don Morrison, (I), Marina Neyman-Levikova, (I), Alan Reingold, (I), Ellen Rixford, (I), Bill Wilkinson, (I), Mangal, (I)
Griffith, Valerie/10 Sheridan Square, New York, NY 212-675-2089
Groves, Michael/220 E 57th St #18D, New York, NY 212-532-2074
Ulf Skogsbergh, (P)

H Hainy, Barry/82 Jane St, New York, NY 212-929-4313
Hajjar, Rene/220 Park Ave S, New York, NY 212-777-5361
Chris Jones, (P)
Hankins + Tegenborg Ltd/60 E 42nd St #428, New York, NY 212-867-8092
Peter Attard, (I), Ralph Brillhart, (I), George Bush, (I), Jamie Cavaliere, (I), John Cernak, (I), Jim Cherry, (I), Mac Conner, (I), David Cook, (I), John Dawson, (I), Guy Deel, (I), Ron DiScensa, (I), John Dismukes, (I), John Ennis, (I), George Fernandez, (I), David Gaadt, (I), Sergio Giovine, (I), James Griffin, (I), Tom Hall, (I), Ray Harvey, (I), Edwin Herder, (I), Michael Herring, (I), Kevin Hulsey, (I), Miro, (I), Aleta Jenks, (I), Rick Johnson, (I), Uldis Klavins, (I), Richard Lauter, (I), Cliff Miller, (I), Wendell Minor, (I), Greg Olanoff, (I), Walter Rane, (I), Robert Sabin, (I), Harry Schaare, (I), Bill Schmidt, (I), Dan Sneberger, (I), Frank Steiner, (I), Ludmilla Strugatsky, (I), Robert Travers, (I), Bob Trondsen, (I), Victor Valla, (I), Jeff Walker, (I)
Hansen, Wendy/126 Madison Ave, New York, NY 212-684-7139
Minh, (P)
Hare, Fran/126 W 23rd St, New York, NY 212-794-0043
Peter B Kaplan, (P)
Harmon, Rod/254 W 51st St, New York, NY 212-245-8935
Brian Hennessey, (P), Al Rubin, (P), David Spagnolo, (P)
Henry, John/237 E 31st St, New York, NY 212-686-6883
Gregory Cannon, (P), Rosemary Howard, (P)
Herron, Pat/829 Park Ave, New York, NY 212-753-0462
Larry Dale Gordon, (P), Malcolm Kirk, (P)
Heyl, Fran/230 Park Ave #2525, New York, NY 212-581-6470
Phillip Harrington, (P)
Hoeye, Michael/120 W 70th St, New York, NY 212-362-9546
Lilo Raymond, (P), Richie Williamson, (P)
Holmberg, Irmeli/280 Madison Ave #1402, New York, NY 212-775-1810
Vincent Amicosante, (I), Rainbow Grinder, (I), Walter Gurbo, (I), Mitchell Hyatt, (I), Sharmen Liao, (I), John Martinez, (I), Barbara Maslen, (I), Lu Matthews, (I), Bill Nelson, (I), Debbie Pinkney, (I), Bob Radigan, (I), Bill Rieser, (I), Nicholas Wilton, (I)
Holt, Rita/280 Madison Ave, New York, NY 212-683-2002
Hovde, Nob/829 Park Ave, New York, NY 212-753-0462
Malcolm Kirk, (P), J Frederick Smith, (P)
Hurewitz, Gary/5 E 19th St #303, New York, NY 212-473-3366
Howard Berman, (P), Steve Bronstein, (P), Earl Culberson, (P), Steve Steigman, (D)
Husak, John/568 Broadway #405, New York, NY 212-226-8110
Frank Marchese, (G), William Sloan, (I)

IJ Iglesias, Jose/1123 Broadway #714, New York, NY 212-929-7962
Stan Fellerman, (P), Sven Lindman, (I), Akio Matsuyoshi, (I), George Ruentiz, (I)
Jacobsen, Vi/333 Park Ave S 2nd Fl, New York, NY 212-677-3770
Jedell, Joan/370 E 76th St, New York, NY 212-861-7861
Johnson, Bud & Evelyne/201 E 28th St, New York, NY 212-532-0928
Kathy Allert, (I), Betty de Araujo, (I), Irene Astrahan, (I), Rowan

Barnes-Murphy, (I), Cathy Beylon, (I), Lisa Bonforte, (I), Carolyn Bracken, (I), Jane Chambliss-Rigie, (I), Roberta Collier, (I), Frank Daniel, (I), Larry Daste, (I), Ted Enik, (I), Carolyn Ewing, (I), Bill Finewood, (I), Robert Gunn, (I), Yukio Kondo, (I), Mei-ku-Huang, (I), Tom LaPadula, (I), Bruce Lemerise, (I), Turi MacCombie, (I), Dee Malan, (I), Brookie Maxwell, (I), Darcy May, (I), Eileen McKeating, (I), Steven Petruccio, (I), Mitch Rigie, (I), Christopher Santoro, (I), Stan Skardinski, (I), Barbara Steadman, (I), Pat Stewart, (I), Tom Tierney, (I), Tricia Zimic, (I)

Joseph Mindlin & Mulvey/1457 Broadway #1001, New York, NY 212-840-8223
Joseph Dawes, (I), John Dyess, (I), Paula Goodman, (I), Mark Hannon, (I), Tad Krumeich, (I), Mike McCreanor, (I), Justin Novak, (I), Frederick Porter, (I), Tom Powers, (I), Herb Reed, (I), John Rice, (I), Sally Scheadler, (I)

K Kahn, Harvey Assoc Inc/50 E 50th St, New York, NY 212-752-8490
Alan Cober, (I), Bernard Fuchs, (I), Nicholas Gaetano, (I), Gerald Gersten, (I), Wilson McLean, (I), Bob Peak, (I), Isadore Seltzer, (I), Norman Walker, (I)
Kane, Barney & Friends/18 E 16th St 2nd Fl, New York, NY 212-206-0322
Margaret Brown, (P), Jack DeGraffenried, (I), Joe Denaro, (I), Michael Farina, (I), Nat Giorgio, (I), William Harrison, (I), Steve Hochman, (I), Steven Keyes, (I), Harvey Kurtzman, (I), Bob Lapsley, (I), Peter Lloyd, (I), Ted Lodigensky, (I), Rich Mahon, (I), Robert Melendez, (I), Doug Rosenthal, (I), Sue Rother, (I), Gary Ruddell, (I), Joseph Sellars, (I), Bill Thomson, (I), Glen Tunstull, (I), Larry Winborg, (I), Jenny Yip, (I)
Kane, Odette/119 W 23rd St, New York, NY 212-807-8730
Charles Seesselberg, (P)
Kaplan, Holly/35 W 36th St, New York, NY 212-563-2730
Bruno, (P)
Kaufman, Hillery/206 Lincoln Pl, Brooklyn, NY 718-230-3348
Kauss, Jean-Gabriel/122 E 42nd St #3103, New York, NY 212-370-4300
Guy Fery, (I), Jesse Gerstein, (P), Francois Halard, (P), Jacques Malignon, (P), Mike Noome, (I)
Keating, Peggy/30 Horatio St, New York, NY 212-691-4654
Bob Parker, (I), Frank Paulin, (I), Suzanne Peck, (I), Fritz Varady, (I), Carol Vennell, (I), Norma Welliver, (I)
Keiserman/Kandel/108 E 31st St, New York, NY 212-686-1042
Nicholas Baratta, (P), Vincent Ricucci, (P), Steve Young, (P)
Kenney, John Assoc/251 W 30th St 16th Fl, New York, NY 212-279-1515
Gary Hanlon, (P), Elizabeth Heyert, (P), David Stetson, (P)
Kestner, V G/427 E 77th St #4C, New York, NY 212-535-4144
Kim/209 E 25th St, New York, NY 212-679-5628
Kimche, Tania/470 W 23rd St, New York, NY 212-242-6367
Richard Goldberg, (I), Rafal Olbinski, (I), Miriam Schottland, (I), E T Steadman, (I)
Kirchoff-Wohlberg Inc/866 UN Plaza #4014, New York, NY 212-644-2020
Angela Adams, (I), Bob Barner, (I), Esther Baron, (I), Brian Cody, (I), Gwen Connelly, (I), Floyd Cooper, (I), Betsy Day, (I), Lois Ehlert, (I), Al Fiorentino, (I), Frank Fretz, (I), Jon Friedman, (I), Jeremy Guitar, (I), Konrad Hack, (I), Ron Himler, (I), Rosekrans Hoffman, (I), Kathleen Howell, (I), Susan Jaekel, (I), Chris Kalle, (I), Mark Kelley, (I), Christa Kieffer, (I), Dora Leder, (I), Tom Leonard, (I), Susan Lexa, (I), Don Madden, (I), Jane McCreary, (I), Lyle Miller, (I), Carol Nicklaus, (I), Sharon O'Neil, (I), Ed Parker, (I), Jim Pearson, (I), Charles Robinson, (I), Bronwen Ross, (I), Arvis Stewart, (I), Pat Traub, (I), Lou Vaccaro, (I), Joe Veno, (I), John Wallner, (I), Alexandra Wallner, (I), Arieh Zeldich, (I)
Klein, Leslie D/104 E 40th St, New York, NY 212-490-1460
Eric Meola, (P), Digital Productions, (P)
Klimt, Bill & Maurine/15 W 72nd St, New York, NY 212-799-2231
Wil Cormier, (I), Jamie DeJesus, (I), Jacques Devaud, (I), Doug Gray, (I), Paul Henry, (I), Steven Huston, (I), Ken Joudrey, (I), Pinturov, (I), Frank Morris, (I), Alan Neider, (I), Gary Penca, (I), Bill Purdom, (I), Mark Skolsky, (I)
Kopel, Shelly & Assoc/51 E 42nd St #716, New York, NY 212-986-3282
Bliss Brothers, (I), Penny Carter, (I), Tom Christopher, (I), Marcus Hamilton, (I), Jim Manos, (I), Meryl Rosner, (I)
Korman, Alison/240 E 76th St, New York, NY 212-686-0525

David Bishop, (P), Susan Kravis, (I)
Kramer, Joan & Assoc/720 Fifth Ave, New York, NY — 212-567-5545
  David Cornwell, (P), Clark Dunbar, (P), John Lawlor, (P),
  James McLoughlin, (P), Frank Moscati, (P), Jeff Perkell, (P),
  John Russell, (P), Glen Steiner, (P), Simpson/Flint, (P), Ken
  Whitmore, (P), Edward Young, (P)
Kreis, Ursula G/63 Adrian Ave, Bronx, NY — 212-562-8931
  Stephen Green-Armytage, (P), John T. Hill, (P), Bruce
  Pendleton, (P), Jed Share, (P)
Krongard, Paula/210 Fifth Ave #301, New York, NY — 212-683-1020
  Bill White, (P)

L Lada, Joe/330 E 19th St, New York, NY — 212-254-0253
  George Hausman, (P)
Lafayette-Nelson & Assoc/64 W 15th St, New York, NY — 212-989-7059
Lamont, Mary/200 W 20th St, New York, NY — 212-242-1087
  Jim Marchese, (P)
Lander/Osborn/333 E 30th St, New York, NY — 212-679-1358
  Francois Cloteaux, (I), Catherine Deeter, (I), Phil Franke, (I),
  Mel Furukawa, (I), Cathy Culp Heck, (I), Saul Lambert, (I),
  Frank Riley, (I), Barron Storey, (I)
Lane Talent Inc/104 Fifth Ave, New York, NY — 212-861-7225
Larkin, Mary/308 E 59th St, New York, NY — 212-308-7744
  Lynn St John, (P)
Lavaty, Frank & Jeff/50 E 50th St #5, New York, NY — 212-355-0910
  John Berkey, (I), Jim Butcher, (I), Don Daily, (I), Bernard
  D'Andrea, (I), Michael Davis, (I), Roland DesCombes, (I),
  Christine Duke, (I), Bruce Emmett, (I), Gervasio Gallardo, (I),
  Tim Hildebrandt, (I), Martin Hoffman, (I), Stan Hunter, (I), Chet
  Jezierski, (I), Mort Kunstler, (I), Paul Lehr, (I), Lemuel Line, (I),
  Robert LoGrippo, (I), Darrel Millsap, (I), Carlos Ochagavia, (I)
Lee, Alan/33 E 22nd St #5D, New York, NY — 212-673-2484
  Werner Kappes, (I), Peter Vaeth, (P)
Leff, Jerry/420 Lexington Ave #2738, New York, NY — 212-697-8525
  Franco Accornero, (I), Ken Barr, (I), Tom Beecham, (I),
  Semyon Bilmes, (I), Mike Bryan, (I), Ron DiCianni, (I), Norm
  Eastman, (I), Bryant Eastman, (I), Charles Gehm, (I), Penelope
  Gottlieb, (I), Gary Lang, (I), Ron Lesser, (I), Dennis Magdich,
  (I), Frank Marciuliano, (I), Michael Nicastre, (I), Rosanne
  Nicotra, (I), Rick Ormond, (I), John Parsons, (I), Dazzeland
  Studios, (I), James Woodend, (I)
Legrand, Jean Yves & Assoc/41 W 84th St #4, New York, NY — 212-724-5981
  Jim Cherry, (I), Holly Hollington, (I), Barry McKinley, (P), Peter
  Sato, (I), Jack Ward, (P)
Leone, Mindy/381 Park Ave S #710, New York, NY — 212-696-5674
  Bill Kouirinis, (P)
Leonian, Edith/220 E 23rd St, New York, NY — 212-989-7670
  Philip Leonian, (P)
Lerman, Gary/113 E 31st St #4D, New York, NY — 212-683-5777
  Paul Barton, (P), John Bechtold, (P), Jan Cobb, (P)
Levitt, Lee/43 W 16th St #16, New York, NY — 212-206-7257
Levy, Leila/4523 Broadway #7G, New York, NY — 212-942-8185
  Yoav Levy, (P)
Lewin, Betsy/152 Willoughby Ave, Brooklyn, NY — 718-622-3882
  Ted Lewin, (I)
LGI/241 W 36th St 7th Fl, New York, NY — 212-736-4602
Lindgren, Pat/41 Union Sq W #1228, New York, NY — 212-929-5590
  Barbara Banthein, (I), Tom Bloom, (I), Regan Dunnick, (I),
  Charles White III, (I), Audrey Lavine, (I)
Locke, John Studios Inc/15 E 76th St, New York, NY — 212-288-8010
  John Cayea, (I), John Clift, (I), Oscar DeMejo, (I), Jean-Pierre
  Desclozeaux, (I), Blair Drawson, (I), James Endicott, (I),
  Richard Erdoes, (I), Jean Michel Folon, (I), Michael Foreman,
  (I), Andre Francois, (I), George Giusti, (I), Edward Gorey, (I),
  Peter Lippman, (I), Sam Maitin, (I), Richard Oden, (I), William
  Bryan Park, (I), Colette Portal, (I), Fernando Puigrosado, (I),
  Hans-Georg Rauch, (I), Ronald Searle, (I), Tim, (I), Roland
  Topor, (I)
Longobardi, Gerard/5 W 19th St, New York, NY — 212-255-3440
Loshe, Diane/10 W 18th St, New York, NY — 212-691-9920
Lott, Peter & George/60 E 42nd St #411, New York, NY — 212-687-4185
  Juan Barberis, (I), Ted Chambers, (I). Tony Cove, (I), Jim

Dickerson, (I), David Halpern, (I), Ed Kurtzman, (I), Marie
  Peppard, (I), Steen Svenson, (P)
Lynch, Alan/635 Madison Ave 6th Fl, New York, NY — 212-688-1832
  Stephen Hall, (I), Jim Warren, (I)

M Madris, Stephen/445 E 77th St, New York, NY — 212-744-6668
  Gary Perweiler, (P)
Manasse, Michele/1960 Broadway #2E, New York, NY — 212-873-3797
  Suzanne H Sullivan, (I)
Mandell, Ilene/61 E 86th St, New York, NY — 212-860-3148
Mann, Ken/20 W 46th St, New York, NY — 212-944-2853
  Rebecca Blake, (P), Hashi, (P), Dicran Studio, (P)
Marchesano, Frank/35 W 36th St, New York, NY — 212-563-2730
Marek & Assoc Inc/160 Fifth Ave, New York, NY — 212-924-6760
Marie, Diana Rose/38 E 19th St, New York, NY — 212-477-5107
Marino, Frank/35 W 36th St, New York, NY — 212-563-2730
  Bruno Benvenuti, (P)
Mariucci, Marie A/32 W 39th St, New York, NY — 212-944-9590
Mars/Barracca/156 Fifth Ave #1222, New York, NY — 212-645-6772
  Andrea Baruffi, (I), Robert Evans, (I), Rick Fischer, (I), Yan
  Nascimbene, (I), Larry Noble, (I), Donna Ruff, (I), JC Suares, (I)
Marshall, Mel/40 W 77th St, New York, NY — 212-877-3921
Mason, Kathy/101 W 18th St 4th Fl, New York, NY — 212-675-3809
  Don Mason, (P)
Mathias, Cindy/7 E 14th St, New York, NY — 212-741-3191
  Vittorio Sartor, (I)
Mattelson, Judy — 212-684-2974
  Karen Kluglein, (I), Marvin Mattelson, (I), Gary Viskupic, (I)
Mautner, Jane/85 Fourth Ave, New York, NY — 212-777-9024
  Kozlowski, (P)
Mayo, Vicki/425 E 86th St, New York, NY — 212-722-7228
McVey, Meg/54 W 84th St # 2F, New York, NY — 212-362-3739
Meixler, Harriet/36 W 37th St, New York, NY — 212-868-0078
  Susanne Buckler, (P)
Mendelsohn, Richard/353 W 53rd St #1W, New York, NY — 212-682-2462
Mendola, Joseph/420 Lexington Ave #2911, New York, NY — 212-986-5680
  Paul Alexander, (I), Robert Berran, (I), Dan Brown, (I), Jim
  Campbell, (I), Carl Cassler, (I), Joe Csatari, (I), Kenneth Dewey,
  (I), Jim Dye, (I), John Eggert, (I), Jon Ellis, (I), Peter Fiore, (I),
  Antonio Gabriele, (I), Tom Gala, (I), Hector Garrido, (I), Mark
  Gerber, (I), Ted Giavis, (I), Dale Gustafson, (I), Chuck Hamrick,
  (I), Attila Hejja, (I), Dave Henderson, (I), Mitchell Hooks, (I),
  Joel Iskowitz, (I), Bob Jones, (I), Dave Kilmer, (I), Michael
  Koester, (I), Richard Leech, (I), Dennis Luzak, (I), Dennis Lyall,
  (I), Jeffrey Mangiat, (I), Goeffrey McCormack, (I), Ann Meisel,
  (I), Roger Metcalf, (I), Ted Michner, (I), Mike Mikos, (I),
  Jonathon Milne, (I), Barry Morgen, (I), Wally Neibart, (I), Chris
  Notarile, (I), Phil Roberts, (I), Rob Sauber, (I), David
  Schleinkofer, (I), Mark Schuler, (I), Mike Smollin, (I), Kip
  Soldwedel, (I), John Solie, (I), George Sottung, (I), Joel
  Spector, (I), Cliff Spohn, (I), Paul Tankersley, (I), Jeffrey
  Terreson, (I), Thierry Thompson, (I), Mark Watts, (I), Alan
  Welkis, (I), Ben Wohlberg, (I)
Metz, Bernard/43 E 19th St, New York, NY — 212-254-4996
Michalski, Ben/118 E 28th St, New York, NY — 212-683-4025
Miller, Susan/1641 Third Ave #29A, New York, NY — 212-905-8400
Mintz, Les/111 Wooster St #PH C, New York, NY — 212-925-0491
  Bernard Bonhomme, (I), Robert Burger, (I), Hovik Dilakian, (I),
  Amy Hill, (I), George Masi, (I), Kirsten Soderlind, (I), Kurt Vargo,
  (I), Dennis Ziemienski, (I)
Monomakhoff, Kathleen/304 E 20th St #7B, New York, NY — 212-807-7703
Moretz, Eileen P/141 Wooster St, New York, NY — 212-254-3766
  Charles Moretz, (P), Jeff Morgan, (P)
Morgan, Vicki Assoc/194 Third Ave, New York, NY — 212-475-0440
  John Alcorn, (I), Stephen Alcorn, (I), Willardson + Assoc, (I),
  Ray Cruz, (I), Sabina Fascione, (I), Vivienne Flesher, (I), Kathy
  & Joe Heiner, (I), Tim Lewis, (I), Emanuel Schongut, (I), Nancy
  Stahl, (I), Bruce Wolfe, (I), Wendy Wray, (I), Brian Zick, (I)
Morse, Lauren/78 Fifth Ave, New York, NY — 212-807-1551
  Alan Zenreich, (P)
Mosel, Sue/310 E 46th St, New York, NY — 212-599-1806
  Gerard Gentil, (P), Stan Shaffer, (P)

Representatives
Continued

Please send us your additions and updates.

Moskowitz, Marion/342 Madison Ave #469, New York, NY   212-719-9879
   Diane Teske Harris, (I), Arnie Levin, (I), Geoffrey Moss, (I)
Moss, Eileen/333 E 49th St #3J, New York, NY   212-980-8061
   Bill Cigliano, (I), Tom Curry, (I), Mike Davis, (I), Dennis Gottlieb,
   (I), Robert Pizzo, (I), Scott Pollack, (I)
Moss, Susan/29 W 38th St, New York, NY   212-354-8024
   Louis Mervar, (P)
Muth, John/37 W 26th St, New York, NY   212-532-3479
   Pat Hill, (P)

NO
Napaer, Michele/349 W Broadway, New York, NY   212-219-0325
   Michael Abramson, (P)
Neail, Pamela R Assoc/27 Bleecker St, New York, NY   212-673-1600
   Sean Daly, (I), Dennis DiVincenzo, (I), Barbara Goodrich, (I),
   Thea Kliros, (I), Tony Mascio, (I), Cary McKiver, (I), Ryuji Otani,
   (I), Brenda Pepper, (I), Janet Recchia, (I), Linda Richards, (I),
   Gail Severance, (I), Alex Vosk, (I), Pat Zadnik, (I)
Newborn, Milton/135 E 54th St, New York, NY   212-421-0050
   Braldt Bralds, (I), Carol Gillot, (I), Robert Giusti, (I), Dick Hess,
   (I), Mark Hess, (I), Victor Juhasz, (I), Simms Taback, (I), David
   Wilcox, (I)
O'Rourke-Page Assoc/219 E 69th St #11G, New York, NY   212-772-0346
   Jonathan Exley, (P), Honolulu Crtv Grp, (P), Sam Haskins, (P),
   Robert Kligge, (P), Rob Van Petten, (P), Lincoln Potter, (P), Jim
   Raycroft, (P), Smith/Garner, (P), Eric Schweikardt, (P), William
   Sumner, (P), John Thornton, (P), John Zimmerman, (P)
Oye, Eva/307 E 44th St, New York, NY   212-286-9103

PQ
Palmer-Smith, Glenn Assoc/160 Fifth Ave, New York, NY 212-807-1855
   James Moore, (P), Charles Nesbitt, (P)
Pelaez, Jose/568 Broadway #103, New York, NY   212-925-5149
Penny & Stermer Group/48 W 21st St 9th Fl, New York, NY   212-243-4412
   Bob Alcorn, (I), Manos Angelakis, (I), Ron Becker, (I), Jane
   Clark, (I), Julian Graddon, (I), Rich Grote, (I), Michael
   Hostovich, (I), Michael Kanarek, (I), Andy Lackow, (I), Julia
   Noonan, (I), Deborah Bazzel Pogue, (I), Steve Shub, (I), Gary
   Smith, (I), Page Wood, (I)
Peretti, Linda/420 Lexington Ave, New York, NY   212-687-7392
   Ken Tannenbaum, (P)
Peters, Barbara/One Fifth Ave, New York, NY   212-777-6384
   Jacques Dirand, (P), Lizzie Himmel, (P)
Petersen, Victoria/16 W 71st St, New York, NY   212-799-7021
Phyllis/38 E 19th St 8th Fl, New York, NY   212-475-3798
   John Weir, (P)
Pritchett, Tom/330 W 4th St, New York, NY   212-688-1080
   Steve Durke, (I), George Parrish Jr, (I), George Kanelous, (I),
   Mike Robins, (I), Terry Ryan, (I)
Puhalski, Ron & Assoc/1133 Broadway #221, New York, NY   212-242-2860
   Michael Vernaglie, (I), Gregory Voth, (I)
Pushpin Assoc/215 Park Ave S, New York, NY   212-674-8080
   Istvan Banyai, (I), Lou Beach, (I), Christopher Blumrich, (I),
   Seymour Chwast, (I), Bob Crawford, (I), Jose Cruz, (I), Hiro
   Kimura, (I), Elizabeth Koda-Callan, (I), Richard McNeel, (I),
   Sarah Moon, (P), Roy Pendleton, (I), Stanislaw Zagorski, (I)
Quercia, Mat/78 Irving Pl, New York, NY   212-477-4491

R
Rapp, Gerald & Cullen Inc/108 E 35th St #1C, New York, NY   212-889-3337
   Michael Brown, (I), Lon Busch, (I), Ken Dallison, (I), Jack
   Davis, (I), Bill Delvin, (I), Bob Deschamps, (I), Ray Domingo, (I),
   Ginnie Hoffman, (I), Lionel Kalish, (I), Sharon Knettell, (I), Lee
   Lorenz, (I), Allan Mardon, (I), Elwyn Mehlman, (I), Marie
   Michal, (I), Alex Murawski, (I), Lou Myers, (I), Gary Overacre,
   (I), Jerry Pinkney, (I), Charles Santori, (I), Bob Tanenbaum, (I),
   Michael Witte, (I), Barry Zaid, (I)
Ray, Marlys/350 Central Pk W, New York, NY   212-222-7680
   Bill Ray, (P)
Reese, Kay Assoc/175 Fifth Ave #1304, New York, NY   212-598-4848
   Jonathan Atkin, (P), Lee Balterman, (P), Gerry Cranham, (P),
   Ashvin Gatha, (P), Lowell Georgia, (P), Peter Gullers, (P), Arno
   Hammacher, (P), Jay Leviton, (P), George Long, (P), George
   Love, (P), Jon Love, (P), Lynn Pelham, (P), Richard Saunders,
   (P), Milkie Studio, (P), T Tanuma, (P), Peter Treiber, (P)

Reid, Pamela/66 Crosby St, New York, NY   212-832-7589
   Madeleine Cofano, (H), Thierry des Fontaines, (P), Laura
   Mercier, (M) Bob Recine, (H), Bert Stern, (P), Mane/Christiane,
   (S), Franck Thiery, (P)
Renard, Madeline/501 Fifth Ave #1407, New York, NY   212-490-2450
   Guy Billout, (I), Steve Bjorkman, (I), Chas Wm Bush, (P), John
   Collier, (I), Etienne Delessert, (I), Bart Forbes, (I), Audra Geras,
   (I), Tim Girvin, (I), Lamb & Hall, (P), Miles Hardiman, (I),
   Personality Inc, (I), John Martin, (I), Richard Newton, (I), Al
   Pisano, (I), Robert Rodriguez, (I), Javier Romero, (I), Michael
   Schwab, (I), Jozef Sumichrast, (I), Kim Whitesides, (I)
Rep Rep/211 Thompson St, New York, NY   212-475-5911
   Rob Fraser, (P), Rosemary Howard, (P), Marcus Tullis, (P)
Ridgeway, Karen/330 W 42nd St #3200NE, New York, NY   212-714-0147
   Scott Bricher, (I), Marilyn Jones, (I), David Rickerd, (I), Ron
   Ridgeway, (I), Gordon Swenarton, (I)
Riley, Edward T Inc/81 Greene St, New York, NY   212-925-3053
   Elliot Banfield, (I), Quentin Blake, (I), Zevi Blum, (I), CESC, (I),
   William Bramhall, (I), Chris DeMarest, (I), Paul Degen, (I),
   (I), David Gothard, (I), Carolyn Gowdy, (I), Paul
   Hogarth, (I), Edward Koren, (I), Pierre Le-Tan, (I), Joseph
   Mathieu, (I), Sara Midda, (I), Robert A Parker, (I), Jim
   Parkinson, (L), Cheryl Peterson, (I), J J Sempe, (I), Brenda
   Shahinian, (I), Philippe Weisbecker, (I)
Rindner, Barbara/216 E 45th St, New York, NY   212-661-0850
Rivelli, Cynthia/303 Park Ave S, New York, NY   212-254-0990
Roman, Helen Assoc/140 West End Ave #9H, New York, NY   212-874-7074
Rosenberg, Arlene/200 E 16th St, New York, NY   212-289-7701
Rudoff, Stan/271 Madison Ave, New York, NY   212-679-8780
   David Hamilton, (P), Gideon Lewin, (P)

S
S I International/43 East 19th St, New York, NY   212-254-4996
   Bob Bass, (I), Karen Baumann, (I), Stephen Berger, (I), Jack
   Brusca, (I), Ernie Colon, (I), Richard Corben, (I), Richard
   Courtney, (I), Allen Davis, (I), Robert DeMichiell, (I), Walt
   DeRijk, (I), Robert Fine, (I), Devis Grebu, (I), Enric, (I),
   Sanjulian, (I), Susi Kilgore, (I), Gaetano Liberatore, (I), Sergio
   Martinez, (I), Vince Perez, (I), Martin Rigo, (I), Doug Rosenthal,
   (I), Artie Ruiz, (I), Paul Tatore, (I), Bodhi Wind, (I), Kathy
   Wyatt, (I)
Sacramone & Valentine/302 W 12th St, New York, NY   212-929-0487
   Stephen Ladner, (P), Tohru Nakamura, (P), John Pilgreen, (P),
   Robin Saidman, (P), Gianni Spinazzola, (P)
Samuels, Rosemary/200 W 20th St, New York, NY   212-477-3567
Sander, Vicki/48 Gramercy Park North #3B, New York, NY   212-674-8161
   Ed Gallucci, (P), George Menda, (P)
Sandler, Cathy/470 W 24th St #5E, New York, NY   212-242-9087
   Aaron Rapoport, (P)
Scharak, Lisa/401 E 58th St #B-4, New York, NY   212-460-8067
Schecter Group, Ron Long/212 E 49th St, New York, NY   212-752-4400
Schickler, Paul/135 E 50th St, New York, NY   212-355-1044
Schochat, Kevin R/221 W 21st St #1D, New York, NY   212-243-6229
   Chuck Carlton, (P), Douglass Grimmett, (G), Bill Kramer, (P)
Schon, Herb/1240 Lexington Ave, New York, NY   212-737-2945
Schub, Peter & Robert Bear/37 Beekman Pl, New York, NY   212-246-0679
   Robert Freson, (P), Alexander Lieberman, (P), Irving Penn, (P),
   Rico Puhlmann, (P), Snowdon, (P), Albert Watson, (P)
Seigel, Fran/515 Madison Ave 22nd Fl, New York, NY   212-486-9644
   Leslie Cabarga, (I), Cheryl Cooper, (I), Kinuko Craft, (I), Peter
   Cross, (I), Joe English, (I), Earl Keleny, (I)
Shamilzadeh, Sol/1155 Broadway 3rd Fl, New York, NY   212-532-1977
   Ryszard Horowitz, (P), The Strobe Studio, (P)
Shapiro, Elaine/369 Lexington Ave, New York, NY   212-867-8220
Sharlowe Assoc/275 Madison Ave, New York, NY   212-683-2822
   Claus Eggers, (P), Nesti Mendoza, (P)
Sheer, Doug/29 John St, New York, NY   212-732-4216
   Karen Kent, (P)
Shepherd, Judith/186 E 64th St, New York, NY   212-838-3214
   Barry Seidman, (P)
Siegel, Tema/461 Park Ave S 4th Fl, New York, NY   212-696-4680
Sigman, Joan/336 E 54th St, New York, NY   212-832-7980
   Robert Goldstrom, (I), John H Howard, (I), Jeff Seaver, (I),

James Tennison, (I)

Simon, Debra/164 W 21st St, New York, NY — 212-505-5234
Uli Rose, (P)
Simoneau, Christine/PO Box 12541, New York, NY — 212-696-2085
Sims, Jennifer/1150 Fifth Ave, New York, NY — 212-860-3005
Clint Clemens, (P), Robert Latorre, (P)
Sjolin, Robert Nils/117 W 13th St, New York, NY — 212-242-7238
Richard Brummett, (P)
Slocum, Linda/15 W 24th St 11th Fl, New York, NY — 212-243-0649
Slome, Nancy/121 Madison Ave, New York, NY — 212-685-8185
Joe Berger, (P), Dennis Galante, (P)
Smith, Emily/30 E 21st St, New York, NY — 212-674-8383
Smith, Piper/484 W 43rd St #8R, New York, NY — 212-594-7756
Bradley Clark, (I), Michele Laporte, (I), Richard Mantel, (I)
Smith, Rita Assoc/1407 Broadway, New York, NY — 212-730-0065
Solomon, Richard/121 Madison Ave, New York, NY — 212-683-1362
*Rick Brown, (I), Ray-Mel Cornelius, (I), Jack E. Davis, (I), Gary
Kelley, (I), Elizabeth Koda-Callan, (I), David Palladini, (I), C F
Payne, (I), Rodica Prato, (I), Ian Ross, (I), Douglas Smith, (I),
John Svoboda, (I), Shelley Thornton, (I)*
Sonneville, Dane/PO Box 20415 Greeley Sta, New York, NY — 212-603-9530
*Leland Bobbe, (P), Jim Kinstrey, (I), John Pemberton, (P),
Jamie Phillips, (P), Bob Shein, (I), Bill Truran, (P)*
Stein, Jonathan & Assoc/353 E 77th St, New York, NY — 212-517-3648
*Mitch Epstein, (P), Burt Glinn, (P), Ernst Haas, (P), Nathaniel
Lieberman, (P), Alex McLean, (P), Gregory Murphey, (P), Joel
Sternfeld, (P), Jeffrey Zaruba, (P)*
Steiner, Susan/130 E 18th St, New York, NY — 212-673-4704
Stevens, Norma/1075 Park Ave, New York, NY — 212-427-7235
Richard Avedon, (P)
Stockland, Bill/17 E 45th St, New York, NY — 212-972-4747
*Joel Baldwin, (P), Walter Iooss, (P), Eric Meola, (P), Michael
Pruzan, (P)*
Stogo, Donald/310 E 46th St, New York, NY — 212-490-1034
*Tom Grill, (P), John Lawlor, (P), Tom McCarthy, (P), Peter
Vaeth, (P)*
Stringer, Raymond/123 W 44th St #8F, New York, NY — 212-840-2891
Ajin, (I)
Susse, Ed/56 W 22nd St 5th Fl, New York, NY — 212-243-1126
Karl Zapp, (P)

T Taborda, Carlos/344 E 85th St #1E, New York, NY — 212-734-1903
Tanenbaum, Dennis/286 Fifth Ave 4th Fl, New York, NY — 212-279-2838
Taylor, Nancy/153 E 57th St, New York, NY — 212-223-0744
Therese, Jane/6 W 20th St, New York, NY — 212-675-8067
Nancy & David Brown, (P)
Thomas, Brenda & Assoc/127 W 79th St, New York, NY — 212-873-7236
Tise, Katherine/200 E 78th St, New York, NY — 212-570-9069
*Raphael Boguslav, (I), John Burgoyne, (I), Bunny Carter, (I),
Roberts & Van Heusen, (I), Judy Pelikan, (I), Cathleen
Toelke, (I)*
Townsend, Kris/18 E 18th St, New York, NY — 212-243-2484
David W Hamilton, (P)
Tralongo, Katrin/144 W 27th St, New York, NY — 212-255-1976
Mickey Kaufman, (P)

U V Umlas, Barbara/131 E 93rd St, New York, NY — 212-534-4008
Hunter Freeman, (P)
Van Arnam, Lewis/154 W 57th St, New York, NY — 212-541-4787
Paul Amato, (P), Mike Reinhardt, (P)
Van Orden, Yvonne/119 W 57th St, New York, NY — 212-265-1223
Joe Schneider, (P)
Vance, Joy/515 Broadway #2B, New York, NY — 212-219-0808
Al Satterwhite, (P)
VisualWorks Inc/545 W 45th St, New York, NY — 212-489-1717
Vollbracht, Michelle/225 E 11th St, New York, NY — 212-475-8718
Walter Wick, (P)
Von Schreiber, Barbara/315 Central Pk West, New York, NY — 212-873-6594
Jean Pagliuso, (P), Hiro, (P), Neal Slavin, (P)

W Y Z Ward, Wendy/200 Madison Ave #2402, New York, NY — 212-684-0590
Wasserman, Ted/310 Madison Ave, New York, NY — 212-867-5360

Watterson, Libby/350 E 30th St, New York, NY — 212-696-1461
Karen Leeds, (P)
Wayne, Philip/66 Madison Ave #9C, New York, NY — 212-696-5215
Roberto Brosan, (P)
Webb, Thomasina/350 W 24th St, New York, NY — 212-620-7832
Weissberg, Elyse/299 Pearl St #5E, New York, NY — 212-406-2566
Jack Reznicki, (P), Bill Smith, (P)
Wheeler, Paul/50 W 29th St #11W, New York, NY — 212-696-9832
*John Dominis, (P), Greg Edwards, (P), Foto Shuttle Japan, (P),
Seth Joel, (P), John McGrail, (P), Joe McNally, (P), Michael
Melford, (P), Aaron Rapoport, (P), Steven Smith, (P), Peter
Tenzer, (P), Leroy Woodson, (P)*
Williamson, Jack/1414 Ave of the Americas, New York, NY — 212-832-2343
DiFranza Williamson, (P)
Yellen, Bert & Assoc/575 Madison Ave, New York, NY — 212-605-0555
Bill Connors, (P), Joe Francki, (P), Gordon Munro, (P)
Youngs, Maralee/318 E 39th St, New York, NY — 212-679-8124
Zanetti, Lucy/139 Fifth Ave, New York, NY — 212-473-4999
Zitsman, Cookie/30 Magaw Pl #3A, New York, NY — 212-928-6228
*Kathy Abrams, (I), Calvin Redmond, (P), Ken Rosenberg, (P),
Ricardo Salas, (P)*
Zlotnick, Jenny/14 Prince St, New York, NY — 212-431-7680

Northeast

A B Ackermann, Marjorie/2112 Goodwin Lane, North Wales, — 215-646-1745
PA *H Mark Weidman, (P)*
Air Noveau Inc/3 Coventry Dr, Freehold, NJ — 201-308-0500
The Art Source/444 Bedford Rd, Pleasantville, NY — 914-747-2220
*James Barkley, (I), Karen Baumann, (I), Paul Birling, (I), Vince
Caputo, (I), Betsy Feeney, (I), Steve Haefele, (I), Robert Lee, (I),
Harry Rosenbaum, (I), Jonathan Rosenbaum, (I)*
Artco/227 Godfrey Rd, Weston, CT — 203-222-8777
*Ed Acuna, (I), Peter Caras, (I), Jeff Cornell, (I), Bob Dacey, (I),
Beau & Alan Daniels, (I), Ron DeFelice, (I), Christine
Fromentine, (I), Enid Hatton, (I), Rick Mcullom, (I), Joseph
Milioto, (I), Jim Sharpe, (I), Rick Tulka, (I), Sally Vitsky, (I)*
Artifacts Agency/368 Grove St, Glenrock, NJ — 201-445-3635
Artists International/7 Dublin Hill Dr, Greenwich, CT — 203-869-8010
Bancroft, Carol & Friends/185 Goodhill Rd, Weston, CT — 203-226-7674
*Bill & Judy Anderson, (I), Cal & Mary Bausman, (I), Wendy
Biggins, (I), Jim Cummins, (I), Susan Dodge, (I), Andrea
Eberbach, (I), Marla Frazee, (I), Bob Giuliani, (I), Fred Harsh,
(I), Ann Iosa, (I), Laurie Jordan, (I), Bryan Jowers, (I), Barbara
Lanza, (I), Mila Lazarevich, (I), Karen Loccisano, (I), Jimmy
Longacre, (I), Al Lorenz, (I), Laura Lydecker, (I), Stephen
Marchesi, (I), John Mardon, (I), Bob Masheris, (I), Elizabeth
Miles, (I), Yoshi Miyake, (I), Nancy Munger, (I), Rodney Pate,
(I), Cathy Pavia, (I), Ondre Pettingill, (I), Jackie Rogers, (I), Gail
Roth, (I), Miriam Schottland, (I), Blanche Sims, (I), Charles
Varner, (I), John Weecks, (I), Linda Boehm Weller, (I), Ann
Wilson, (I), Chuck Wimmer, (I), Debby Young, (I)*
Beckelman, Barbara/251 Greenwood Ave, Bethel, CT — 203-797-8188
Birenbaum, Molly/7 Williamsburg Dr, Cheshire, CT — 203-272-9253
*Alice Coxe, (I), W E Duke, (I), Sean Kernan, (P), Joanne
Schmaltz, (P), Paul Selwyn, (I), Bill Thomson, (I)*
Black Silver & Lord/66 Union St, Belfast, ME — 207-338-1113
*Gloria Baker, (P), Kip Brundage, (P), Norm Clasen, (P), Fred
Mullane, (P), Michel Tcherevkoff, (P), Roger Tully, (P)*
Breza, Susan/105 Prospect Ave, Langhorne, PA — 215-752-7216
*Nessa Becker, (I), Ray Dallasta, (I), Sandi Glass, (I), Polly
Lewis, (I), Tony Mascio, (I)*
Brown, Jill/911 State St, Lancaster, PA — 717-393-0918
brt Photo Illustration, (P)

C D Camp, Woodfin Inc/925 1/2 F St NW, Washington, DC — 202-638-5705
Colucci, Lou/128 Broadway #106, Patterson, NJ — 201-881-7618
Creative Advantage Inc/707 Union St, Schenectady, NY — 518-370-0312
Richard Siciliano, (P)
D'Angelo, Victoria/309 Madison Ave, Reading, PA — 215-921-8430
Andy D'Angelo, (P)

DeBren, Alan/355 Pearl St, Burlington, VT — 802-864-5916
  John Goodman, (P)
Donaldson, Selina/37 Hemlock, Arlington, MA — 617-646-1687

E G H
Ella/229 Berkeley #52, Boston, MA — 617-266-3858
  Norman Adams, (P), Bente Adler, (I), Wilbur Bullock, (I), Rob Cline, (I), Jack Crompton, (I), Anna Davidian, (I), Sharon Drinkwine, (I), Anatoly Dverin, (I), Scott Gordley, (I), Eaton & Iwen, (I), Roger Leyonmark, (I), Janet Mager, (I), Bruce Sanders, (I), Ron Toelke, (I)
ESTO PHOTOGRAPHICS/222 VALLEY PL, MAMARONECK, NY (P 65) — **914-698-4060**
  Peter Aaron, (P), Dan Cornish, (P), Wolfgang Hoyt, (P), Max Mackenzie, (P), Peter Mauss, (P), Jock Pottle, (P)
Geng, Maud/116 Commonwealth Ave, Boston, MA — 617-236-1920
  Caroline Alterio, (I), Peter Barger, (I), Vicki Smith, (I)
Giandomenico, Terry (Ms)/13 Fern Ave, Collingswood, NJ — 609-854-2222
  Bob Giandomenico, (P)
Gidley, Fenton/43 Tokeneke Rd, Darien, CT — 212-772-0846
Goldstein, Gwen/91 Hundred Rd, Wellesley Hills, MA — 617-235-8658
  Michael Blaser, (I), Steve Fuller, (I), Lane Gregory, (I), Terry Presnall, (I), Susan Spellman, (I), Gary Torisi, (I), Joe Veno, (I)
Haas, Ken/PO Box 86, Oley, PA — 215-987-3711
  Peter Leach, (P), Ken Ravel, (I), Michael Schroeder, (I), Emilie Snyder, (I)
Hone, Claire/2130 Arch Street, Philadelphia, PA — 215-568-5434
Hopkins, Nanette/PO Box 323, Haverford, PA — 215-431-3240
  Rick Davis, (P)
Hubbell, Marian/99 East Elm St, Greenwich, CT — 203-629-9629

K L
Kaltenbach, Faith/PO Box 317, Lititz, PA — 717-626-0296
  Grant Heilman, (P)
Kanefield, Andrew/14 North Gate, West Newton, MA — 617-965-3557
  Christopher Cunningham, (P), Peter Jones, (P), Bob O'Shaughnessy, (P), Lewis Portnoy, (P)
Kasak, Harriet/458 Newton Trpk, Weston, CT — 203-454-4687
Kurlansky, Sharon/192 Southville Rd, Southborough, MA — 617-872-4549
  Steve Alexander, (I), Charles Freeman, (I), Judy Gailen, (I), John Gamache, (I), Susan Hanson, (I), Peter Harris, (I), Terry Van Heusen, (I), Geoffrey Hodgkinson, (I), Mark Kelly, (I), Dorthea Sierra, (I), Colleen, (I)
Labonty, Deborah/PO Box 7446, Lancaster, PA — 717-872-8198
  Tim Schoon, (P)
Lipman, Deborah/506 Windsor Dr, Framingham, MA — 617-451-6528
  Mark Fisher, (I), Richard A. Goldberg, (I), James Hanlon, (I), Richard M. Joachim, (I), Armen Kojoyian, (I), Carol LaCourse, (I), Katherine Mahoney, (I)

M O
Mattelson Assoc/37 Cary Rd, Great Neck, NY — 212-684-2974
  Karen Kluglein, (I), Marvin Mattelson, (I), Gary Viskupic, (I)
McNamara, Paula B/182 Broad St, Wethersfield, CT — 203-563-6159
  Jack McConnell, (P)
Metzger, Rick/186 South St, Boston, MA — 617-426-2290
  Steve Grohe, (P)
Montreal Crtv Consrtm/1155 Dorchester W #1520, Montreal H3B 2J6, QU — 514-875-5426
Morgan, Wendy/5 Logan Hill Rd, Northport, NY — 516-757-5609
  Scott Gordley, (I), ParaShoot, (P), Fred Labitzke, (I), Don Landwehrle, (P), Preston Lyon, (P), Al Margolis, (I), David Rankin, (I), Fred Schrier, (I), Art Szabo, (P), David Wilder, (P)
Oreman, Linda/15 Atkinson St, Rochester, NY — 716-232-1585
  Nick Angello, (I), Jim & Phil Bliss, (I), Roger DeMuth, (I), Jeff Feinen, (I), Bill Finewood, (I), Doug Gray, (I), Stephen Moscowitz, (I), Vicki Wehrman, (I)

P R
Palulian, Joanne/18 McKinley St, Rowayton, CT — 203-866-3734
  Scott Barrows, (I), M John English, (I), David Lesh, (I), Kirk Moldoff, (I), Dickran Palulian, (I), Walt Spitzmiller, (I)
Publishers Graphics/251 Greenwood Ave, Bethel, CT — 203-797-8188
  Paul Harvey, (I)
Putscher, Tony/2303 Green St, Philadelphia, PA — 215-569-8890
Radxevich Standke/15 Intervale Terr, Reading, MA — 617-944-3166

Christian Delbert, (P)
Reese-Gibson, Jean/4 Puritan Rd, N Beverly, MA — 617-927-5006
Riley, Catherine/45 Circle Dr, Hastings On Hudson, NY — 914-478-4377
  Jon Riley, (P)
Robbins, David Group/256 Arch Rd, Avon, CT — 203-673-6530
  Mike Eagle, (I)
Rubenstein, Len/One Winthrop Sq, Boston, MA — 617-482-0660
  Jim Conaty, (P)

S T
Satterthwaite, Victoria/115 Arch St, Philadelphia, PA — 215-925-4233
  Michael Furman, (P)
Sequis Ltd/PO Box 398, Stevenson, MD — 301-583-9177
  Jeremy Green, (P)
Shulman, Carol/6182 Chinquapin Pkwy, Baltimore, MD — 301-323-8645
Smith, Russell/65 Washington St, S Norwalk, CT — 203-866-8871
  Gordon Smith, (P)
Smith, Wayne R/145 South St Penthouse, Boston, MA — 617-426-7262
  Robert Brooks, (I), John Holt, (I), Ben Luce, (I), Ed Porzio, (I)
Snyder, Diane/3 Underwood Rd, Wyncote, PA — 215-572-1192
  Craig Bakley, (I), Gordon Kibbee, (I), Michael McNelly, (I), Verlin Miller, (I), Shelly Roseman, (P), Lee Wojnar, (P)
Spencer, Sandy/700 S 10th St, Philadelphia, PA — 215-238-1208
  Anthony Ward, (P)
Spiak, Al/35 Monroe Ave, Dumont, NJ — 201-387-9395
Stemrich, J David/612 N 12th St, Allentown, PA — 215-776-0825
  Mark Bray, (I), Kevin Bubbenmoyer, (P), Bob Hahn, (P), Montieth Studio, (P)
Stevens, Rick/925 Penn Ave #404, Pittsburgh, PA — 412-765-3565
Stoller, Erica/222 Valley Pl, Mamaroneck, NY — 914-698-4060
Sweeny, Susan/425 Fairfield Ave, Stamford, CT
Ternay, Louise/119 Birch Ave, Bala Cynwyd, PA — 215-667-8626
  Vince Cuccinotta, (I), Don Everhart, (I), Greg Purdon, (I), Peter Sasten, (G), Bill Ternay, (I), Victor Valla, (I)

U V W Z
Unicorn/1148 Parsippany Blvd, Parsippany, NJ — 201-334-0353
  Greg Hildebrandt, (I)
Valen Assocs/PO Box 8, Westport, CT — 203-227-7806
  Chas Adams, (I), George Booth, (C), Whitney Darrow, (C), Eldon Dedini, (I), Joe Farris, (C), William Hamilton, (C), Stan Hunt, (C), Anatol Kovarsky, (C), Henry Martin, (C), Warren Miller, (I), Frank Modell, (C), Mischa Richter, (C), Charles Saxon, (C), Jim Stevenson, (C), Henry Syverson, (C), Bob Weber, (C), Rowland Wilson, (I), Gahan Wilson, (I), Bill Woodman, (I), Bill Ziegler, (I)
Waterman, Laurie/130 South 17th St, Philadelphia, PA — 215-988-0390
Wayne, Lynn/99 Wilson Ave, Windsor, CT — 203-522-3143
Wigon, Leslie/191 Plymouth Dr, Scarsdale, NY — 914-472-9459
Wolfe, Deborah Ltd/731 North 24th St, Philadelphia, PA — 215-232-6666
  Steve Cusano, (I), Harry Davis, (I), Jeff FitzMaurice, (I), Robin Hotchkiss, (I), Ron Lehew, (I), Bill Margerin, (I), Bob Schenker, (I), Jas Szygiel, (I), Charles Weckler, (P), Frank Williams, (I)
Worrall, Dave/125 S 18th St, Philadelphia, PA — 215-567-2881
  Weaver Lilley, (P)
Worthington, Diane/372 Marlborough St, Boston, MA — 617-247-2847
  Kurt Stier, (P)
Zellner, Robin/54 Applecross Cir, Chalfont, PA — 215-822-8258
  Charles Callahan, (P)

Southeast
A B C
Ad Artist SE/1424 N Tryon, Charlotte, NC — 704-372-6007
Aldridge, Donna/755 Virginia Ave, Atlanta, GA — 404-872-7980
  Chris Lewis, (I)
And Associates/573 Hill St, Athens, GA — 404-353-8479
  Dan McClure, (P), Dennis O'Kain, (P), Elaine H Rabon, (I), Drake White, (P)
Babcock, Nancy/1496 N Morningside Dr NE, Atlanta, GA — 404-876-0117
Beck, Susanne/2721 Cherokee Rd, Birmingham, AL — 205-871-6632
  Charles Beck, (P)
Burnett, Yolanda/559 Dutch Vall Rd, Atlanta, GA — 404-873-5858
  Jim Copland, (P), Charlie Lathem, (P)

Representatives

Continued

Please send us your additions and updates.

Couch, Tom/1164 Briarcliff Rd NE #2, Atlanta, GA — 404-872-5774
  Granberry/Anderson Studio, (P)

FGH

Fink, Duncan/437 S Tryon St, Charlotte, NC — 704-377-4217
  Ron Chapple, (P), Mitchell Kearney, (P)
Forbes, Pat/11459 Waterview Cluster, Reston, VA — 703-437-7042
  Kay Chenush, (P)
Grubbs/Bate & Assoc/1151 W Peachtree St NW, Atlanta, GA — 404-892-6303
  Image Electronic, (I), Stefan Findal, (P), Mike Hodges, (I),
  Johnna Hogenkamp, (I), David Marks, (I), Theo Rudnak, (I),
  Joe Saffold, (I), Michael West, (P), Bruce Young, (I)
Hathcox, Julia/5730 Arlington Blvd, Arlington, VA — 703-845-5831
  David Hathcox, (P)

JKL

Jett & Assoc/PO Box 70285, Louisville, KY — 502-634-4911
Jourdan, Carolyn/520 Brickell Key Dr #1417, Miami, FL — 305-372-9425
Judge, Marie/9452 SW 77th Ave, Miami, Fl — 305-595-1700
Kohler, Chris/1105 Peachtree St, Atlanta, GA — 404-876-0315
Linden, Tamara/919 Lenox Hill Ct, Atlanta, GA — 404-262-1209
  Tom Fleck, (I), Joe Ovies, (I), Charles Passarelli, (I), Larry
  Tople, (I)

MPS

McGee, Linda/1816 Briarwood Ind Ct, Atlanta, GA — 404-633-1286
McLean Represents/401 W Peachtree St NW #1720,
Atlanta, GA — 404-881-6627
  Joe Isom, (I), Jack Jones, (I), Martin Pate, (I), Steve Spetseris,
  (I), Warren Weber, (I)
Phelps, Catherine/3210 Peachtree Rd NE, Atlanta, GA — 404-264-0264
  Tom McCarthy, (P), Tommy Thompson, (P), Bill Weems, (P)
Pollard, Kiki/848 Greenwood Ave NE, Atlanta, GA — 404-875-1363
  Betsy Alexander, (G), John Findley, (I), Dennis Guthrie, (I),
  James Soukup, (I), Mark Stanton, (I)
Prentice, Nancy/315-A Pharr Rd, Atlanta, GA — 404-266-9707
Propst, Sheryle/PO Box 1583, Norcross, GA — 404-263-9296
  Fred Gerlich, (P), Herring & Klem, (I), Reggie Stanton, (I)
Silva, Naomi/100 Colony Sq #200, Atlanta, GA — 404-892-8314
  Daryl Cagle, (C), Stefan Findel, (P), Kevin Hamilton, (I), Rob
  Horn, (L), Mike Moore, (I), Christy Sheets Mull, (I), Alan Patton,
  (I), Gary Penca, (I), Don Sparks, (P), John Yates, (G)
Sumpter, Will/1106 W Peachtree St #106, Atlanta, GA — 404-874-2014

TUW

Torres, Martha/927 Third St, New Orleans, LA — 504-895-6570
Uter, Bonnie & Assoc/573 Hill St, Athens, GA — 404-353-8479
  Dan McClure, (P), Dennis O'Kain, (P), Elaine Rabon, (I), Drake
  White, (P)
Wells, Susan/5134 Timber Trail, Atlanta, GA — 404-255-1430
  Paul Blakey, (I), Jim Caraway, (I), Don Loehle, (I), Richard
  Loehle, (I), Randall McKissick, (I), Monte Varah, (I),
  Beth White, (I)
Wexler, Marsha Brown/6108 Franklin Pk Rd, McLean, VA — 703-241-1776
Williams, Phillip/1106 W Peachtree St #201, Atlanta, GA — 404-873-2287
  Jamie Cook, (P), Chipp Jamison, (P), Rick Lovell, (I), Kenvin
  Lyman, (G), Bill Mayer, (I), David McKelvey, (I), John
  Robinette, (I)

Midwest

AB

Andoniadis, Nina/900 Mark Ln #302, Wheeling, IL — 312-253-7488
Art Staff Inc/1200 Penobscot Bldg, Detroit, MI — 313-963-8240
Ball, John/203 N Wabash, Chicago, IL — 312-332-6041
Bartels, Ceci Assoc/111 Jefferson Rd, St Louis, MO — 314-961-1670
  Eric Dinyer, (I), Shannon Kriegshauser, (I), Don Kueker, (I),
  Greg MacNair, (I), Jean Probert, (I), Terry Sirrell, (I), Terry
  Speer, (I)
Berk, Ida/1350 N La Salle, Chicago, IL — 312-944-1339
Birdwell, Steven/208 W Kinzie St, Chicago, IL — 312-467-1430
Bonnen, Ed/913 Beach, Lansing, MI — 517-371-3086
Bradley, Francie/7630 N Euclid, Gladstone, MO — 816-436-7130
Brenna, Allen/Southgate Plaza #515, Minneapolis, MN — 612-835-1831
Brenner, Harriet/660 W Grand Ave, Chicago, IL — 312-243-2730
  Dick Krueger, (P)

Brooks, Douglas/1230 W Washington Blvd, Chicago, IL — 312-226-4060
  VanKirk Photo, (P)
Buermann, Jeri/321 N 22nd St, St Louis, MO — 314-231-8690
Bussler, Tom/19 E Pearson #410, Chicago, IL — 312-944-3837
  Sid Evans, (P)

CD

Carr, Ken/4715 N Ronald St, Harwood Heights, IL — 312-867-5445
Christell, Jim & Assoc/307 N Michigan Ave #1008, Chicago, IL — 312-236-2396
  Michel Ditlove, (P), Ron Harris, (P)
Coleman, Woody/490 Rockside Rd, Cleveland, OH — 216-621-1771
  Stuart Daniels, (I), Vladimir Kordic, (I), John Letostak, (I), Ernest
  Norcia, (I), Bob Novack, (I), Ezra Tucker, (I)
Commercial Images Group/15339 Center St, Harvey, IL — 312-333-1047
Daguanno, Donna/211 E Ohio #621, Chicago, IL — 312-644-0172
  Chris Hawker, (P)
Demunnik, Jack/2138 N Hudson #206, Chicago, IL — 312-883-7262
DeWalt & Assoc/210 E Michigan St #203, Milwaukee, WI — 414-276-7990
  Tom Fritz, (P), Don Glassford, (I), Mary Gordon, (G), Dennis
  Matz, (I), Tom Redman, (I)
Dodge, Tim/2412 E Stratford Ct, Milwaukee, WI — 414-964-9558
  Barbara Ericksen, (I), Jeff Hangartner, (I), Ken Hanson, (G),
  Paul Henning, (P), Tom Kwas, (P), Dave Vander Veen, (P)
Dolby, Karen/215 W Ohio, Chicago, IL — 312-321-1770

EFG

Emerich Studios/300 W 19th Terrace, Kansas City, MO — 816-474-8888
Erdos, Kitty/210 W Chicago, Chicago, IL — 312-787-4976
Feldman, Kenneth/30 E Huron, Chicago, IL — 312-337-0447
Fiat, Randi/612 N Michigan, Chicago, IL — 312-784-2343
Fleming, Laird Tyler/1 Memorial Dr, St Louis, MO — 314-982-1700
  Willardson + Assoc, (P), John Bilecky, (P)
Fried, Monica/1546 N Orleans, Chicago, IL — 312-642-8715
Frost, Brent & Laumer, Dick/4037 Queen Ave S, Minneapolis, MN — 612-922-3440
Green Gotfried & Assoc/29 E Ohio, Chicago, IL — 312-661-0024

H

Hanson, Jim/540 N Lake Shore Dr, Chicago, IL — 312-527-1114
  Bob Bender, (P), Richard Fegley, (P), Bob Gelberg, (P), Rob
  Johns, (P), Rick Mitchell, (P), Barry O'Rourke, (P), John Payne,
  (P), Al Satterwhite, (P)
Harlib, Joel/405 N Wabash #3203, Chicago, IL — 312-329-1370
  Bob August, (I), Nick Backes, (I), John Casado, (I), Lawrence
  Duke, (P), Peter Elliott, (P), Marty Evans, (P), Randy Glass, (I),
  Karel Havlicek, (I), Barbara Higgins-Bond, (I), DeWitt Jones,
  (P), Richard Leech, (I), Tim Lewis, (I), Peter Lloyd, (I), Bret
  Lopez, (P), David McMacken, (I), Joe Ovies, (I), Fred Prepera,
  (I), Matthew Rolston, (P), Todd Shorr, (I), Jay Silverman, (P),
  Robert Tyrrell, (I), Bill Vann, (I), Ron Villani, (I), Allan Weitz, (P),
  Kim Whitesides, (I), Bruce Wolfe, (I), Bob Ziering, (I)
Hartig, Michael/3620 Pacific, Omaha, NE — 402-345-2164
Heinen, Sandy/219 N 2nd St #409, Minneapolis, MN — 612-332-3671
Higgens Hegner Genovese Inc/510 N Dearborn St, Chicago, IL — 312-644-1882
Hogan, Myrna & Assoc/333 N Michigan, Chicago, IL — 312-372-1616
  Terry Heffernan, (P)
Hoke, Wayne & Assoc/17 N Elizabeth St, Chicago, IL — 312-666-0175
Horton, Nancy/939 Sanborn, Palatine, IL — 312-934-8966
Hull, Scott Assoc/20 Lynnray Circle, Dayton, OH — 513-433-8383
  Mark Braught, (I), Tracy Britt, (I), Greg Deart, (F), David Groff,
  (I), Julie Hodde, (I), Greg LaFever, (I), John Maggard, (I), Larry
  Martin, (I), Ted Pitts, (I), David Sheldon, (I), Don Vanderbeek,
  (I), Lee Woolery, (I)

JKL

Jenkins, John/1147 W Ohio #403, Chicago, IL — 312-243-6580
Jeske, Kurt/612 S Clinton, Chicago, IL — 312-922-9200
Jordano, Charles/2623 Rhodes, Troy, MI — 313-528-0593
Kamin, Vince & Assoc/111 E Chestnut, Chicago, IL — 312-787-8834
  Tom Berthiaume, (P), Dave Jordano, (P), Ron Lieberman, (I),
  Mary Anne Shea, (I), Roy Volkman, (P)
Kapes, Jack/233 E Wacker Dr #1412, Chicago, IL — 312-565-0566
  Stuart Block, (P), John Cahoon, (P), Jerry Friedman, (P), Carl
  Furuta, (P), Klaus Lucka, (P), Dan Romano, (I), Nicolas
  Sidjakov, (G)
Kezelis, Elena/215 W Illinois, Chicago, IL — 312-644-7108

Representatives

Continued

Please send us your additions and updates.

Kleber, Gordon/125 W Hubbard, Chicago, IL	312-661-1362
Koralik, Connie/26 E Huron, Chicago, IL	312-944-5680
Glenn Gustafson, (I), Robert Keeling, (P), Kazu, (P)	
Lakehomer & Assoc/405 N Wabash #1402, Chicago, IL	312-644-1766
Tim Schultz, (P)	
Lasko, Pat/452 N Halsted, Chicago, IL	312-243-6696
Ralph King, (P)	
Levey, Rebecca/405 N Wabash, Chicago, IL	312-329-9040
Linzer, Jeff/4001 Forest Rd, Minneapolis, MN	612-926-4390
Lonier, Terry/215 W Ohio #5W, Chicago, IL	312-527-1880
Lukmann, Geri/314 W Institute Pl, Chicago, IL	312-787-1774
Brent Carpenter, (P), Steve Nozicka, (P)	

MN

McMasters, Deborah/157 W Ontario, Chicago, IL	312-943-9007
Richard Foster, (P)	
McNamara Associates/1250 Stephenson Hwy, Troy, MI	313-583-9200
Max Alterruse, (I), Gary Ciccarelli, (I), Garry Colby, (I), Hank Kolodziej, (I), Chuck Passarelli, (I), Tony Randazzo, (I), Gary Richardson, (I), Dick Scullin, (I), Don Wieland, (I)	
McNaughton, Toni/233 E Wacker #2904, Chicago, IL	312-938-2148
Pam Haller, (P), Rodica Prato, (I), James B. Wood, (P)	
Miller Services/45 Charles St E, Toronto M4Y 1S6, ON	416-925-4323
Miller, Richard/743 N Dearborn, Chicago, IL	312-280-2288
Paul Barton, (P), Morton Beebe, (P), Rebecca Blake, (P), Chris Butler, (I), Geoffrey Clifford, (P), Marc Hauser, (P), Richard High, (C), Bob Krogle, (I), Jim Krogle, (I), Robert Sacco, (P)	
Mohlman, Jeanette/114 W Illinois, Chicago, IL	312-321-1570
Mohlo, David/ Werremeyer Inc/12837 Flushing Meadow Dr, St Louis, MO	314-966-3770
Moore, Amanda/1752 N Mohawk, Chicago, IL	312-337-0880
Peter Sagara, (P)	
Moore, Connie/1540 N North Park, Chicago, IL	312-787-4422
Richard Shirley, (I)	
Morawski & Assoc/1550 E Nine Mile Rd, Ferndale, MI	313-543-9440
Moshier & Maloney/535 N Michigan, Chicago, IL	312-943-1668
Nicolette Anastas, (I), Dave Wilson & Assoc, (I), Steve Carr, (P), Dan Clyne, (I), Ron DiCianni, (I), David Gaadt, (I), John Hamagami, (I), Rick Johnson, (I), Bill Kastan, (I), Ed Lindlof, (I), Dennis Luzak, (I), Colleen Quinn, (I), Paul Ristau, (I), Stephen Rybka, (I), Skidmore-Sahratian, (I), Al Stine, (I), Jim Trusilo, (I), John Youssi, (I)	
Murphy, Sally/70 W Hubbard, Chicago, IL	312-346-0720
Nagan, Rita/1514 NE Jefferson St, Minneapolis, MN	612-788-7923
Nelson, Sandy/315 W Walton, Chicago, IL	312-266-8029
Newman, Richard/1866 N Burling, Chicago, IL	312-266-2513
Nicholson, Richard B/2310 Denison Ave, Cleveland, OH	216-398-1494
Martin Reuben, (P), Mike Steinberg, (P), Al Teufer, (P), J David Wilder, (P)	
Nicolini, Sandra/230 N Michigan #523, Chicago, IL	312-346-1648
Elizabeth Ernst, (P), Tom Petroff, (P)	

OP

O'Brien-Stieber/203 N Wabash #1600, Chicago, IL	312-726-9690
O'Farrel, Eileen/311 Good Ave, Des Plaines, IL	312-297-5447
O'Grady Advertising Arts/333 North Michigan Ave #2200, Chicago, IL	312-726-9833
O'Neill, Mary/17006 Woodbury Ave, Cleveland, OH	216-252-6238
Osler, Spike/2616 Industrial Row, Troy, MI	313-280-0640
Mark Coppos, (P), Madison Ford, (P), Rob Gage, (P), Rick Kasmier, (P), Jim Secreto, (P)	
Peterson, Vicki/535 N Michigan Ave #2802, Chicago, IL	312-467-0780
Charlie Gold, (P), Elyse Lewin, (P), Howard Menken, (P), Robert Stevens, (P), Charlie Westerman, (P)	
Phase II/155 N Michigan Ave, Chicago, IL	312-565-0030
Bill Cigliano, (I), Michael Elins, (I), David Krainik, (I), Kathy Petrauskas, (I), Mark Sauck, (I), Richard Taylor, (I)	
Photo Services Owens-Corning/Fiberglass Towers, Toledo, OH	419-248-8041
Jay Langlois, (P), Joe Sharp, (P)	
Platzer, Karen & Assoc/535 N Michigan Ave, Chicago, IL	312-467-1981
Larry Banner, (P), Michael Caporale, (P), Ray Cioni, (I)	
Pool, Linda/6905 E 102nd St, Kansas City, MO	816-761-7314
Michael Radencich, (P)	

Potts, Carolyn/3 E Ontario #25, Chicago, IL	312-935-1707
Barbara Bersell, (P), John Craig, (I), Alan Dolgins, (P), Gregory Murphey, (P), Fred Nelson, (I), Joe Ovies, (I), Kulp Productions, (P), Leslie Wolf, (I)	
Potts, Vicki/139 N Wabash, Chicago, IL	312-726-5678
Mitchell Einhorn, (P), Mercer Engelhard, (P), David Gerhardt, (P), Kathy Sanders, (P)	
Pride, Max/401 W Superior, Chicago, IL	312-664-5392

RS

Rabin, Bill & Assoc/666 N Lake Shore Dr, Chicago, IL	312-944-6655
John Alcorn, (I), Joel Baldwin, (P), Joe Baraban, (P), Roger Beerworth, (I), Guy Billout, (I), Howard Bjornson, (P), Thomas Blackshear, (I), R O Blechman, (I), Charles William Bush, (P), JoAnn Carney, (P), John Collier, (I), Jackie Geyer, (I), Paul Giovanopoulos, (I), Tim Girvin, (G), Robert Giusti, (I), Kunio Hagio, (I), Lamb & Hall, (P), Mark Hess, (I), Richard Hess, (I), Walter Ioss, (P), Art Kane, (P), Rudi Legname, (P), Daniel Maffia, (I), Jay Maisel, (P), Dan Malinowski, (P), Jim Matusik, (P), Eric Meola, (P), Eugene Mihaesco, (I), Richard Noble, (P), Robert Rodriguez, (I), Reynold Ruffins, (I), Michael Shwab, (I), Ed Sorel, (I), George Stavrinos, (I), Simms Taback, (I), Ezra Tucker, (I), Pete Turner, (P), David Wilcox, (I)	
Ray, Rodney/405 N Wabash #3106, Chicago, IL	312-472-6550
Scarff, Signe/22 W Erie, Chicago, IL	312-266-8352
Larry Kolze, (P)	
Sell, Dan/233 E Wacker, Chicago, IL	312-565-2701
Alvin Blick, (I), Paul Bond, (I), Wayne Carey, (I), Justin Carroll, (I), Bobbye Cochran, (I), Wil Cormier, (I), Bill Ersland, (I), Rick Farrell, (I), Dick Flood, (I), Bill Harrison, (I), Dave LaFleur, (I), Gregory Manchess, (I), Bill Mayer, (I), Frank Morris, (I), Tim Raglin, (I), Ian Ross, (I), Mark Schuler, (I), R J Shay, (I), Jay Songero, (I), Dale Verzaal, (I), Jay, (I), Fran Vuksanovich, (I), Phil Wendy, (I), John Zielinski, (I)	
Shulman, Salo/215 W Ohio, Chicago, IL	312-337-3245
Stan Stansfield, (P)	
Sims, Mel/233 E Wacker Dr #4304, Chicago, IL	312-938-8937
Britt Collins, (I)	
Sinclair, Valerie/77 Florence St #301, Toronto M6K 1P4, ON	416-588-1527
John Martin, (P), James Toogan, (I)	
Skillicorn, Roy/233 E Wacker #29031, Chicago, IL	312-856-1626
Wickart Brothers, (I), Tom Curry, (I), David Scanlon, (I)	
Snowberger, Ann/3312 W Belle Plaine, Chicago, IL	312-463-3590
Tim Bieber, (P)	

T

Timon, Clay & Assoc Inc/540 N Lake Shore Dr, Chicago, IL	312-527-1114
Bob Bender, (P), Michael Fletcher, (P), Larry Dale Gordon, (P), Don Klumpp, (P), Chuck Kuhn, (P), Barry O'Rourke, (P), Al Satterwhite, (P), Michael Slaughter, (P)	
Trembeth, Rich/30 E Huron #4904, Chicago, IL	312-727-1096
Trinko, Genny/126 W Kinzie St, Chicago, IL	312-222-9242
Cam Chapman, (P)	
Trott, David/32588 Dequiendre, Warren, MI	313-978-8932
Tuke, Joni/368 W Huron, Chicago, IL	312-787-6826
Jay Ahrend, (P), David Beck, (I), Dan Blanchette, (I), Ken Goldammer, (I), Chris Hopkins, (I), Susan Kindst, (P), Brian Otto, (I), John Welzenbach, (P), Ken Westphal, (I)	

VWZ

Virnig, Janet/3308 Girard Ave S, Minneapolis, MN	612-822-6444
Wainman, Rick & Assoc/166 E Superior #212, Chicago, IL	312-337-3960
Warner, Rebecca/230 W Huron, Chicago, IL	312-951-0880
Yunker, Kit/ Allchin, Scott/1335 N Wells St, Chicago, IL	312-321-0655
Zann, Sheila/502 N Grove, Oak Park, IL	312-386-2864
Arnold Zann, (P)	

Southwest

AB

Art Rep Inc/2801 W Lemmon #305, Dallas, TX	214-521-5156
Tom Bailey, (I), Lee Lee Brazeal, (I), Ellis Chappell, (I), Dean St Clair, (I), Tom Curry, (I), M John English, (I), Tom Evans, (I), Tim Girvin, (I), Bill Harrison, (I), Jim Jacobs, (I), Kent Kirkley, (P), Gary McCoy, (P), Genevieve Meek, (I), Frank Morris, (I),	

Representatives

Continued

Please send us your additions and updates.

Michael Schwab, (I), Andrew Vracin, (P), Kim Whitesides, (I),
Terry Widener, (I)

Assid, Carol/122 Parkhouse, Dallas, TX	214-748-3765
Booster, Barbara/4001 Bryn Mawr, Dallas, TX	214-373-4284
Boston, Belinda/PO Box 821095, Dallas, TX	214-821-3042
Kenneth Huey, (I)	
Bozeman, Debbie/PO Box 140152, Dallas, TX	214-526-3317

C D

Callahan, Joe/330 E Mitchell, Phoenix, AZ	602-248-0777

Tom Gerczynski, (P), Mike Gushock, (I), Jon Kleber, (I),
Howard Post, (I), Dan Ruiz, (I), Mark Sharpls, (I), Dan
Vermillion, (P), Balfour Walker, (P)

Campbell, Patty/2610 Catherine, Dallas, TX	214-946-6597
Douglas Doering, (P)	
Cobb & Friend/2811 McKinney #224, Dallas, TX	214-855-0055

Kent Barker, (P), Greg Bates, (I), Cathie Bleck, (I), Margaret K
Cheatham, (I), Michael Johnson, (P), David Kampa, (I), Geof
Kern, (I), Rick Kroninger, (P), Mercedes McDonald, (I),
Michael McGar, (I), Dennis Murphy, (P), R Kenton Nelson, (I),
Steve Pietzsch, (I), Tom Ryan, (P), James N Smith, (I), James
Tennison, (I), Michele Warner, (I), Ken Westphal, (I), Kent
Barker, (P), Greg Bates, (I), Cathie Bleck, (I), Margaret K
Cheatham, (I), Michael Johnson, (P), David Kampa, (I), Geof
Kern, (I), Rick Kroninger, (P), Mercedes McDonald, (I),
Michael McGar, (I), Dennis Murphy, (P), R Kenton Nelson, (I),
Steve Pietzsch, (I), Tom Ryan, (P), James N Smith, (I), James
Tennison, (I), Michele Warner, (I), Ken Westphal, (I)

Crowder, Bob/4404 Main St, Dallas, TX	214-823-9000
Barry Kaplan, (P), Moses Olmoz, (P), Al Rubin, (P)	
DiOrio, Diana/1819 Augusta Ct #148, Houston, TX	713-266-9390

John Collier, (I), Ray Mel Cornelius, (I), Regan Dunnick, (I),
Larry Keith, (I), Bahid Marinfar, (I), Dennis Mukai, (I), Thom
Ricks, (I)

E F H

Edwards, Nancy/2121 Regency Dr, Irving, TX	214-438-4114
Freeman, Sandra/3030 McKinney #1706, Dallas, TX	214-871-1956
Fuller, Alyson/5610 Maple Ave, Dallas, TX	214-688-1855
Hamilton, Chris/3900 Lemmon, Dallas, TX	214-526-2050
Holland, Nancy/1669 S Voss #590, Houston, TX	713-975-7279

L M N P

Lynch, Larry/3527 Oak Lawn Ave #145, Dallas, TX	214-521-6169
Morton Beebe, (P), Robert Latorre, (P), Richard Wahlstrom, (P)	
McCann, Liz/3000 Carlisle #206, Dallas, TX	214-630-7756

Bill Crumpt, (P), Michael Doret, (I), Ben James, (I), Phil
Kretchmar, (P), James B. Wood, (P)

Noble, Peter/8344 East RL Thornton #300, Dallas, TX	214-328-6676
Photocom Inc/1707 S Ervay, Dallas, TX	214-428-8781
Louis Reens, (P)	
Production Services/1711 Hazard, Houston, TX	713-529-7916

George Craig, (P), C Bryan Jones, (P), Thaine Manske, (P)

S W

Spiegal, Melanie/2412 Converse, Dallas, TX	214-428-8781

Robb Debenport, (P), Jeff Haynie, (I), Louis Reens, (P), Michael
Steirnagle, (I), Kelly Stribling, (I), Richard Wahlstrom, (P)

Washington, Dick/914 Westmoreland, San Antonio, TX	512-342-2009
Whalen, Judy/5551 Vanderbilt, Dallas, TX	214-630-8977
Willard, Paul Assoc/815 North First Ave #3, Phoenix, AZ	602-257-0097

Kevin Cruff, (P), Matthew Foster, (I), Rick Gayle, (P), Rick
Kirkman, (I), Kevin MacPherson, (I), Curtis Parker, (I), Nancy
Pendleton, (I), Bob Peters, (I), Roy & Peggy Roberts, (I), Norma
Samuelson, (I), Wayne Watford, (I), Jean Wong, (I)

Rocky Mountain

F G

Foremark Studios/PO Box 10346, Reno, NV	702-786-3150
Garrett, Ann/1100 Acoma, Denver, CO	303-893-1199
Goodman, Christine/1836 Blake St #201, Denver, CO	303-298-7085
Bill Koropp, (P), David X Tejada, (P), Geoffrey Wheeler, (P)	

K N

Kelly, Rob/3113 E 3rd St #220, Denver, CO	303-399-3851
Pat Fujisaki, (I), Ron Sauter, (I)	

No Coast Graphics/2629 18th St, Denver, CO	303-458-7086

John Cuneo, (I), Cindy Enright, (I), Tom Nikosey, (I), Chris F
Payne, (I), Jim Salvati, (I), Mike Steirnagle, (I)

R S

Roberts, Hallie/16 W 13th Ave, Denver, CO	303-534-7267
Ryan, Patti/550 E 12th Ave #910, Denver, CO	303-832-9214
Bob Fader, (P)	
Sperling, Alice/1050 Corona #307, Denver, CO	303-832-4686
Synchrony/655 Broadway #800, Denver, CO	303-825-7513

West Coast

A B

Aline, France/1076 S Ogden Dr, Los Angeles, CA	213-933-2500

Guy Billout, (I), Thomas Blackshear, (I), Steve Hulen, (P),
Michael Lamotte, (P), Bret Lopez, (P), Manuel Nunez, (I),
Michael Schwab, (I), Veronica Sim, (P), Peggy Sirota, (P), Bob
Stevens, (P), Ezra Tucker, (I), Kim Whitesides, (I), Bruce
Wolfe, (I), Bob Zoell, (I)

Arnold, Wendy/4620 Coldwater Cnyn, Studio City, CA	818-762-8850
Ayerst, Deborah/828 Mission St, San Francisco, CA	415-974-1755
Baker, Kolea/1822 N E Ravenna Rd, Seattle, WA	206-443-0326
George Abe, (I), Don Baker, (I)	
Becker, Roxanne/521 State St, Glendale, CA	818-243-6400
Braun, Kathy/75 Water St, San Francisco, CA	415-543-7377

Arnold & Assoc, (F), Sandra Belce, (L), Tandy Belew, (G),
Michael Bull, (I), Anka, (I), Eldon Doty, (I), Boyington Film, (F),
Jim Fulp, (I), Stephen Osborn, (I), Jim Parkinson, (L), Allan
Rosenberg, (P), Diane Tyler, (M)

Brenneman, Cindy/1856 Elba Cir, Costa Mesa, CA	714-641-9700
Brooks/6632 Santa Monica Blvd, Los Angeles, CA	213-463-8844
Mike Chesser, (P)	
Brown, Dianne/732 N Highland, Los Angeles, CA	213-464-2775
David LeBon, (P), Bill Werts, (P)	
Burlingham, Tricia/10355 Ashton Ave, Los Angeles, CA	213-271-3982
Bob Stevens, (P)	
Busacca, Mary/130 Buena Vista, Mill Valley, CA	415-381-9047

Bob August, (I), Mark Busacca, (I), Ignacio Gomez, (I), Paul
Hoffman, (P), Alton Kelley, (I), Rich Mahon, (I), Joe Murray, (C),
Tom Nikosey, (I)

Bybee, Gerald/1811 Folsom St, San Francisco, CA	415-863-6346

C

Caplan, Deborah/654 Cloverdale Ave #204, Los Angeles, CA	213-935-8248
Carroll, J J/PO Box 3881, Manhattan Beach, CA	213-318-1066
Fred Nelson, (I)	
Church, Spencer/425 Randolph Ave, Seattle, WA	206-324-1199

John Fretz, (I), Terry Heffernan, (P), Mits Katayama, (I), Ann
Marra, (G), Scott McDougall, (I), Dale Nordell, (I), Marilyn
Nordell, (I), Rusty Platz, (I), Ted Rand, (I), Diane
Solvang-Angell, (I), Dugald Stermer, (I), West Stock, (S), Craig
Walden, (I), Dale Windham, (P)

Collier, Jan/166 South Park, San Francisco, CA	415-552-4252

Barbara Banthien, (I), Bunny Carter, (I), Chuck Eckart, (I), Cris
Hammond, (I), Robert Hunt, (I), Kathy O'Brien, (I), Bernard
Phillips, (P), Gretchen Schields, (I), Robert Steele, (I)

Cook, Warren/PO Box 2159, Laguna Hills, CA	714-770-4619
Kathleen Norris Cook, (P)	
Cormany, Paul/11607 Clover Ave, Los Angeles, CA	213-828-9653

Mark Busacca, (I), Bryant Eastman, (I), Dave Eichenberger, (I),
Bob Gleason, (I), Lamb & Hall, (P), Jim Heimann, (I), Bob
Krogle, (I), Gary Norman, (I), Ed Scarisbrick, (I), Stan Watts, (I),
Dick Wilson, (I), Andy Zito, (I)

Cornell, Kathleen/1046 N Orange Dr, Los Angeles, CA	213-462-5622

Nancy Duell, (I), Miles Hardiman, (I), Masami, (I), Daniel
McGowan, (I), Jan Oswald, (P), Bonnie Timmons, (I)

Courtney & Natale/8800 Venice, Los Angeles, CA	213-202-0344

Douglas Bevans, (I), Bart Doe, (I), Diane Teske Harris, (I), Matt
Mahurin, (I), Paul Maxon, (P), Linda Medina, (I), Judy Reed,
(I), Jeff Scales, (P), Chuck Schmidt, (I)

Crosse, Annie/10642 Vanora Dr, Sunland, CA	818-352-5173

Wendy Lagerstrom, (I), Henri Parmentier, (I), Ted Sizemore, (I),
Terry Smith, (I)

Representatives
Continued

Please send us your additions and updates.

DEF

Dicker, Debbie/765 Clementina St, San Francisco, CA   415-621-0687
Keith Ovregaard, (P)

Donnellan, Scott/112 Pine Pl #2, Santa Cruz, CA   408-425-1750

Drayton, Sheryl/5018 Dumont Pl, Woodland Hills, CA   818-347-2227

Dryden, Lorna/2104 Holly Dr, Los Angeles, CA   213-461-4805

DuCane, Alex/8350 Marmont Ln, Los Angeles, CA   213-654-3534

Dubow, Chuck/7461 Beverly Blvd #405, Los Angeles, CA   213-938-5177
Terry Anderson, (I), Rick Ellescas, (I), Marc Ericksen, (I), Roger Hubbard, (I), Richard Ikkanda, (I), Paul Kratter, (I), Mike Rogers, (I), Larry Salk, (I)

Egbert, Lydia/190 Cervantes Blvd #7, San Francisco, CA   415-921-2415

Epstein, Rhoni & Assoc/3814 Franklin Ave, Los Angeles, CA   213-663-2388

Ericson, William/1024 Mission St, South Pasadena, CA   213-461-4969

Faia, Michele/387 Brookmere Dr, San Jose, CA   408-281-2590

Feliciano, Terrianne/16782 Red Hill #B, Irvine, CA   714-250-3377

Fenton, Paul/1680 Vine St #819, Hollywood, CA   213-463-5596

Ferguson, Lynnda/6439 Cleon, N Hollywood, CA   818-761-3636

Finlayson & Assoc/1448 Portia St, Los Angeles, CA   213-481-0228

Fisher, Susan/22 Marinero Cir #37, Tiburon, CA   415-435-6198

Fleming, Laird Tyler/407 1/2 Shirley Pl, Beverly Hills, CA   213-552-4626
Willardson + Assoc, (P), John Bilecky, (P)

Fletcher, Lois/28956 West Lake Vista Dr, Agoura, CA   818-707-1010
Earl Miller, (P)

Fox & Clark/8350 Melrose Ave #201, Los Angeles, CA   213-653-6484

Franco, Evelyn/1164 S La Brea, Los Angeles, CA   213-937-3345
Steve McMahon, (P)

G

Gale, Gary/3539 Jennings St, San Diego, CA   619-222-6563

Gardner, Jean/4121 Wilshire Blvd #311, Los Angeles, CA   213-384-2615

Garvin, Bob/1100 Glendon Ave #732, Los Angeles, CA   213-279-1539

George, Nancy/360 1/2 N Mansfield Ave, Los Angeles, CA   213-935-4696
Brent Bear, (P), Sid Bingham, (I), Justin Carroll, (I), Randy Chewning, (I), Bruce Dean, (I), Steve Hendricks, (I), Hank Hinton, (I), Gary Hoover, (I), Richard Kriegler, (I), Larry Lake, (I), Gary Lund, (I), Rob Sprattler, (I), Bruce Wilson, (P), Jeannie Winston, (I)

Gilbert, Sam/410 Sheridan, Palo Alto, CA   415-325-2102

Glick, Ivy/350 Townsend St #421, San Francisco, CA   415-543-6056
David Bishop, (P), Jim Blakeley, (P), Don Dudley, (I), Mike Steirnagle, (I)

Goldman, Caren/4521 Cleveland Ave, San Diego, CA   619-298-4043

Graham, Corey/2 Harbor Point #501, Mill Valley, CA   415-383-1134

Gray, Pam/1912 Hermosa Ave #F, Hermosa Beach, CA   213-374-3606

Group West Inc/5455 Wilshire Blvd #1212, Los Angeles, CA   213-937-4472
Neil Boyle, (I), Nixon Galloway, (I), Frank Germain, (I), Roger Hammond, (I), Fred Hatzer, (I), Ron McKee, (I), Norman Merritt, (I), Bill Robles, (I), Ren Wicks, (I)

H

Hackett, Pat/2030 First Ave #201, Seattle, WA   206-623-9459
Bill Cannon, (P), Steve Coppin, (I), Larry Duke, (I), Bill Evans, (I), Norman Hathaway, (I), Ed Hauser, (I), Gary Jacobsen, (I), Larry Lubeck, (P), Bill Mayer, (I), Mike Schumacher, (I), John C Smith, (I), John Terence Turner, (P)

Haigh, Nancy/90 Natoma St, San Francisco, CA   415-391-1646

Halcomb, Mark/1259-A Folsom, San Francisco, CA   415-861-8877

Hall, Marni & Assoc/620 N Citrus Ave, Los Angeles, CA   213-934-9420

Hart, Vikki/780 Bryant St, San Francisco, CA   415-495-4278
G K Hart, (P), Kevin Hulsey, (I), Aleta Jenks, (I), Tom Kamifuji, (I), Heather King, (I), Julie Tsuchiya, (I), Jonathan Wright, (I)

Hauser, Barbara/PO Box 1443, San Francisco, CA   415-339-1885

Hedge, Joanne/2433 28th St #O, Santa Monica, CA   213-874-1661
Delana Bettoli, (I), Chris Dellorco, (I), Ignacio Gomez, (I), Bette Levine, (I), Kenvin Lyman, (I), Rick McCollum, (I), David McMacken, (I), Dennis Mukai, (I), Vida Pavesich, (I), William Rieser, (I), Jim Salvati, (I), Joe Saputo, (I), Julie Tsuchiya, (I)

Heimberg, Nancy/351 1/2 N Sycamore Ave, Los Angeles, CA   213-933-8660

Hillman, Betsy/2230 Francisco #106, San Francisco, CA   415-563-2243
Chuck Bowden, (I), Tim Boxell, (I), Hiro Kimura, (I), John Marriott, (P), HKM Productions, (P), Greg Spalenka, (I), Joe Spencer, (I), Jeremy Thornton, (I), Jackson Vereen, (P)

Hjul, Diana/8696 Crescent Dr, Los Angeles, CA   213-654-9513

Neal Brisker, (P), John Reed Forsman, (P), Jim Greenberg, (P)

Hodges, Jeanette/12401 Bellwood, Los Alamitos, CA   213-431-4343
Ken Hodges, (I)

Hughes, April & Assoc/1350 California St #302, San Francisco, CA   415-441-4602
Romeo Bongrazio, (I), Steve Fukuda, (P), Kelly Hume, (L), David Jensen, (I), Paul Matsuda, (P), Bill Park, (I), Sue Rother, (I), Barton Stabler, (I), Diana Thewlis, (I), David Uhl, (I)

Hunt, Joann/3435 Army St #206, San Francisco, CA   415-821-9879

Hyatt, Nadine/PO Box 2455, San Francisco, CA   415-543-8944
Jeanette Adams, (I), Rebecca Archey, (I), Charles Bush, (P), Frank Cowan, (P), Marty Evans, (P), Gerry Gersten, (I), John Hyatt, (I), Bret Lopez, (P), Tom McClure, (I), Jan Schockner, (L), Victor Stabin, (I), Liz Wheaton, (I)

JK

Jorgensen, Donna/609 Summit Ave, Seattle, WA   206-284-5080
Alice Brickner, (I), Frank Denman, (P), Fred Hilliard, (I), Richard Kehl, (I), Doug Keith, (I), David Lund, (I), Robert Peckham, (I), Tim Stevenson, (I)

Kahn, Patrick/309 N Sycamore Ave, Los Angeles, CA   213-935-0071

Karpe, Michele/4328 Ben Ave, Studio City, CA   818-763-9686

Kersz, Valerie/183 N Martel Ave #220, Los Angeles, CA   818-763-9686

Kirsch, Melanie/825 1/2 Sweetzer Ave, Los Angeles, CA   213-651-3706
Bob August, (I), Kevin Hulsey, (I), Todd Smith, (P), Jeff Wack, (I)

Knable, Ellen/PO Box 67725, Los Angeles, CA   213-855-8855
Charles Bush, (P), Stan Caplan, (P), Mark Coppos, (P), David Erramouspe, (I), Joe Heiner, (I), Kathy Heiner, (I), John Hyatt, (I), Rudi Legname, (P), Vigon/Nahas/Vigon, (I), Robert Rodriguez, (I), Jonathan Wright, (I), Brian Zick, (I)

Koeffler, Ann/1555 Greenwich #9, San Francisco, CA   415-885-2714
Randy Berrett, (I), Karl Edwards, (I), Bob Hickson, (I), Paul Kratter, (I), Kevin O'Shea, (I), Michael Pearce, (I), Stephen Peringer, (I), Ken Rosenberg, (I), Chris Shorten, (P), Sarn Suvityasiri, (I)

Kovac, Elka/1609 Greenfield Ave, Los Angeles, CA   213-473-6316

L

Lanier, Kate/633 W 6th St, Los Angeles, CA   213-935-9343

Laycock, Louise/8800 Venice Blvd, Los Angeles, CA   213-204-6401

Lee & Lou/1548 18th St #101, Santa Monica, CA   213-828-2259
Rob Gage, (P), Bob Grigg, (P), Richard Leech, (I)

Lilie, Jim/251 Kearny St #511, San Francisco, CA   415-441-4384
Lou Beach, (I), Alan Dolgins, (P), David Fischer, (P), Patricia Mahoney, (I), Masami Miyamoto, (I), Larry Noble, (I), Robert Rodriguez, (I), Dugald Stermer, (I), Ezra Tucker, (I), Stan Watts, (I), Dennis Ziemienski, (I)

Linville, Betty/6546 Hollywood Blvd #220, Los Angeles, CA   213-467-4455
Douglass Hyun, (P)

Lippert, Tom/1100 Glendon #732, Los Angeles, CA   213-279-1539

London, Valerie/9756 Charleville Blvd, Beverly Hills, CA   213-277-8090

Luna, Tony/45 E Walnut St, Pasadena, CA   213-681-3130

MN

MK Communications/2737 Polk St #2, San Francisco, CA   415-775-5110
Mike Godfrey, (I), Robert Holmes, (P), Jim Sadlon, (P), Max Seabaugh, (I)

MacKenzie, Stewart/515 Diamond St, San Francisco, CA   415-626-4542

Macias, Lori/16846 Armstead, Granada Hills, CA   818-368-2237

Magestic, Michael/23316 Burbank Blvd, Woodland Hills, CA   818-703-8348

Malone, Sara/26 Medway Rd #6, San Rafael, CA   415-459-6435

Marie, Rita & Friends/6376 W 5th St, Los Angeles, CA   213-934-3395
David Beck, (I), Chris Consani, (I), Mort Drucker, (I), Jim Endicott, (I), Marla Frazee, (I), Gary Pierazzi, (I), Robert Pryor, (I), Paul Rogers, (I), Gary Ruddell, (I), Dick Sakahara, (I), Danny Smyhte, (I), Greg Wray, (I)

Martha Productions/1830 S Robertson Blvd #203, Los Angeles, CA   213-204-1771
Bob Brugger, (I), Jacques Devaud, (I), Stan Evenson, (I), Tracy Garner, (I), John Hamagami, (I), William Harrison, (I), Arthur Hill, (I), Catherine Leary, (I), Ed Lindlof, (I), Rudy Obrero, (I), Cathy Pavia, (I), Wayne Watford, (I)

Mastrogeorge, Robin/11020 Ventura Blvd Box 294, Studio City, CA   818-954-8748

Representatives

Continued

Please send us your additions and updates.

May, William & Assoc/PO Box 781, Malibu, CA — 213-457-1380
McBain, Morgan/650 San Juan Ave, Venice, CA — 213-392-9341
   Joann Daley, (I), Ron Derhacopian, (P), John Taylor Dismukes,
   (I), Scott Ernster, (I), Bob McMahon, (I), Greg Moraes, (I)
McBride, Elizabeth/70 Broadway, San Francisco, CA — 415-863-0655
   Keith Criss, (I), Robert Holmes, (P), Patricia Pearson, (I), Bill
   Sanchez, (I), Earl Thollander, (I), Tom Vano, (P)
McCargar, Lucy/652 Bair Isl Rd, Redwood City, CA — 415-363-2130
   Tim Mitoma, (I), Dennis Nolan, (I), Mary Ross, (I)
McKenzie, Dianne/125 King St, San Francisco, CA — 415-541-9051
   Victor Budnik, (P)
Melrose, Penny/1333 Lawrence Expwy #150, Santa Clara, CA — 408-737-9494
Michaels, Martha/3279 Kifer Rd, Santa Clara, CA — 408-735-8443
Mix, Eva/4985 S Santa Rosa Ave, Santa Ana, CA — 707-584-1608
Mizejewski, Max/942 Shearwater St, Ontario, CA — 714-947-8585
Moniz, Karletta/250 Newhall Ave, San Francisco, CA — 415-821-6358
Morgan-Friedman/PO Box 19608-329, Irvine, CA — 714-551-6445
Morris, Leslie/1062 Rengstorff Ave, Mountain View, CA — 415-966-8301
   Paul Olsen, (I)
Newman & Franks/2956 Nicada Dr, Los Angeles, CA — 213-470-0140
   Tim Huhn, (I)

OP

Ogden, Robin/8126 Blackburn Ave, Los Angeles, CA — 213-858-0946
   Karen Bell, (I), Joe Crabtree, (I), Jan Evans, (I), Steve Gray, (I),
   Gerry Hampton, (I), Lou LaRose, (I), Jim Miller, (P), Julie
   Perron, (I), John Puchalski, (I), Ken Rosenberg, (I), Corey
   Wolfe, (I)
Ostan-Prentice/Ostan/13802 Northwest Passage #203,
   Marina Del Rey, CA — 213-305-7143
Padgett, Donna/13520 Terrace Pl, Whittier, CA — 213-945-7801
Parrish, Dave/Photopia/PO Box 2309, San Francisco, CA — 415-441-5611
Parsons, Ralph/1232 Folsom St, San Francisco, CA — 415-339-1885
Partners Reps/12813 Milbank St, Studio City, CA — 818-995-6883
Pate, Randy/The Source/3848 Ventura Canyon Ave, Sherman
   Oaks, CA — 818-985-8181
Peek, Pamela/1964 N Rodney Dr #201, Los Angeles, CA — 213-660-1596
Phillips, Ellen/1717 Mason St #2, San Francisco, CA — 415-928-6336
Pierceall, Kelly/25260 Piuma Rd, Malibu, CA — 213-559-4327
Piscopo, Maria/2038 Calvert Ave, Costa Mesa, CA — 714-556-8133
   Adrienne Warren, (P)
Pohl, Jacqueline/2947 Jackson St, San Francisco, CA — 415-563-8616
Pribble, Laurie/911 Victoria Dr, Arcadia, CA — 818-574-0288
Publication Arts Network/717 Market St, San Francisco, CA — 415-777-5988

RS

Reece, Sandra/2565 Canyon Dr, Los Angeles, CA — 213-465-7576
   Ken Chernus, (P), Ralph Pleasant, (P), David Zanzinger, (P)
Rosen, Michael/870 N El Centro Ave #6, Los Angeles, CA — 213-462-5726
Rosenthal, Elise/3443 Wade St, Los Angeles, CA — 213-306-6878
   Saul Bernstein, (I), Chris Butler, (I), Alan Daniels, (I), Alan
   Hashimoto, (I), James Henry, (I), Jim McKiernan, (I), Kenton
   Nelson, (I), Peter Palombi, (I), Tom Pansini, (I), Kim Passey, (I),
   Bill Robles, (I), Tom Tomita, (I), Larry Winborg, (I)
Salisbury, Sharon/116 W Blithedale, Mill Valley, CA — 415-495-4665
   Keith Batcheller, (I), Craig Calsbeck, (I), Jim Endicott, (I), Bob
   Graham, (I), Bo Hylen, (P), Larry Keenan, (P), Bette Levine, (I),
   Dave McMacken, (I), Robert Mizono, (P), Vida Pavesich, (I)
Salzman, Richard W/1352 Hornblend St, San Diego, CA — 619-272-8147
   Tony Baker, (I), Ruben DeAnda, (I), Manuel Garcia, (I), Jason
   Harlem, (P), Denise Hilton-Putnam, (I), Bernie Lansky, (C),
   Gordon Menzie, (P), Dave Mollering, (I), Imagery That Moves,
   (G), Dianne O'Quinn-Burke, (I), Everett Peck, (I), Nono Remos,
   (R), Terry Smith, (I), Debra Stine, (I), Walter Stuart, (I),
   Jonathan Wright, (I), Daniels, (I)
Sandler, Neil/3443 Wade St, Los Angeles, CA — 213-306-6878
Scott, Alexis/940 N Highland Ave, Los Angeles, CA — 213-856-0008
Scott, Freda/244 Ninth St, San Francisco, CA — 415-621-2992
   Sherry Bringham, (I), David Campbell, (P), John Hersey, (I),
   Gayle Kabaker, (I), Jeff Leedy, (F), Francis Livingston, (I), Alan
   Mazzetti, (I), Diane Padys, (P), Susan Schelling, (P), Judy
   Unger, (I)
Scroggy, David/2124 Froude St, San Diego, CA — 619-222-2476
   Ed Abrams, (I), Jodell D Abrams, (I), Joe Chiado, (I), Rick

   Geary, (I), John Pound, (I), Hal Scroggy, (I), Debbie Tilley, (I)
Shaffer, Barry/PO Box 480888, Los Angeles, CA — 213-939-2527
Shigekuni, Cindy/PO Box 2336, Beverly Hills, CA — 213-838-8811
Slobodian, Barbara/745 N Alta Vista Blvd, Hollywood, CA — 213-935-6668
   Bob Greisen, (I), David Kaiser, (I), Tom O'Brien, (P), Forest
   Sigwart, (I), Scott Slobodian, (P)
Sobol, Lynne/4302 Melrose Ave, Los Angeles, CA — 213-665-5141
   Frank Marquez, (I), Arthur Montes de Oca, (P)
Stefanski, Janice/2022 Jones St, San Francisco, CA — 415-928-0457
   Adrian Day, (I), Michael Jay, (P), Barbara Kelley, (I), Steven
   Lyons, (I), George Olson, (P), Katherine Salentine, (I), Rolf
   Sieffe, (P), Cliff Spohn, (I)
Steinberg, John/11731 Crescenta, Los Angeles, CA — 213-471-0232
   Jay Ahrent, (P), John Alvin, (I), Bo Gehring & Associates, (I),
   Beau Daniels, (I), Alan Daniels, (I), Precision Illustration, (I),
   David Kimble, (I), Reid Miles, (P), Richard Moore, (P), Larry
   Noble, (I), Frank Page, (I), Mark Stehrenberger, (I), Ed Wexler,
   (I)
Stern & Assoc/1083 Clay St #101, San Francisco, CA — 415-434-1010
Stivers, Robert/101 Scholz Plz PH 21, Newport Beach, CA — 714-645-9070
Studio Artists Inc/638 S Van Ness Ave, Los Angeles, CA — 213-382-6281
   Chuck Coppock, (I), George Francuch, (I), Bill Franks, (I),
   Duane Gordon, (I), Larry Willett, (I)
Sullivan, Diane/3727 Buchanan St, San Francisco, CA — 415-563-8884
   Lawrence Duke, (P)
Sullivan, Martha/2395 Paradise Dr, Tiburon, CA — 415-435-4181
   Patricia Brabant, (P)
Sweet, Ron/716 Montgomery St, San Francisco, CA — 415-433-1222
   Charles East, (D), Randy Glass, (I), John Hamagami, (I), Bob
   Haydock, (I), Gregg Keeling, (I), Richard Leech, (I), Will
   Nelson, (I), Walter Swarthout, (P), Jack Unruh, (I), Don Weller,
   (I), Bruce Wolfe, (I), James B Wood, (P)

TV

Tabke, Tim/35-23 Ryder St, Santa Clara, CA — 408-733-5855
Taggard, Jim/PO 4064 Pioneer Square Station, Seattle, WA — 206-547-0807
   Sjef's-Photographie, (P)
Thomsen, Dale/40 Gold St, San Francisco, CA — 415-434-0380
Thornby, Kirk/1039 S Fairfax Ave, Los Angeles, CA — 213-933-9883
Todd, Deborah/259 Clara St, San Francisco, CA — 415-495-3556
Tomson, Jerry/1050 N Wilcox Ave, Hollywood, CA — 213-469-6316
   Robert Grigg, (P)
Tos, Debbie/7306 W 82nd St, Los Angeles, CA — 213-410-0402
   Carl Furuta, (P)
Tranter, Susan/23011 Moulton Pky #E-9, Lauguna Hills, CA — 714-770-1680
Trimpe, Susan/2717 Western Ave, Seattle, WA — 206-728-1300
   Don Baker, (I), Wendy Edelson, (I), Stephen Peringer, (I)
Turnbull, Gerry/9348 Santa Monica Blvd #101, Beverly Hills,
   CA — 213-659-1737
Vandamme, Mary/1242 Francisco #1, San Francisco, CA — 415-771-0494
   John Blaustein, (P), John Collier, (I), Robert Giusti, (I), Joe and
   Kathy Heiner, (I), Alan Krosnick, (P), Kenvin Lyman, (I), Dennis
   Mukai, (I), Bill Rieser, (I), Ed Scarisbrick, (I), Michael Schwab,
   (I), Charles Shields, (I), Rick Strauss, (P), Carol Wald, (I), Kim
   Whitesides, (I)

WY

Wagoner, Jae/200 Westminster Ave #A, Venice, CA — 213-392-4877
   Tim Alt, (I), Michael Backus, (I), Roger Beerworth, (I), Stephen
   Durke, (I), Steve Jones, (I), Lee MacLeod, (I), Craig Nelson, (I),
   Robert Tanenbaum, (I), Don Weller, (I)
Wiegand, Chris/7106 Waring Ave, Los Angeles, CA — 213-931-5942
Winston, Bonnie/228 S Beverly Dr #210, Beverly Hills, CA — 213-275-2858
   David Andrade, (I), Garry Brod, (P), Robert Ferrone, (P), Kiko
   Ricotti, (P), Rob White, (P)
Youmans, Jill/1021 1/2 N La Brea, Los Angeles, CA — 213-469-8624
   Dan Cooper, (I), Jeff George, (I), Brian Leng, (P), Jeff Leung,
   (I), Christine Nasser, (I), Joyce Patti, (I), Bill Salada, (I)
Young, Jill/Compendium Inc/945 Front St #206, San
   Francisco, CA — 415-392-0542
   Judy Clifford, (I), Armondo Diaz, (P), Celeste Ericsson, (I),
   Marilee Heyer, (I), Rae Huestis, (G), Mary Jew, (G), Bonnie
   Matza, (G), Barbara Muhlhauser, (G), Martin Schweitzer, (G),
   Donna Mae Shaver, (P), Cecily Starin, (I), Sarn Suvityasiri, (I),

REPRESENTATIVES

Ed Taber, (I), Carlotta Tormey, (I)

Z Zank, Elen/262 Donahue St, Sausalito, CA 415-332-3739
Chip Carroon, (P)
Zimmerman, Delores H/9135 Hazen Dr, Beverly Hills, CA 213-273-2642

Illustrators

New York City

A

Abraham, Daniel E/425 Fifth Ave	718-499-4006
Abrams, Kathie/41 Union Square W #1001	212-741-1333
Accardo, Anthony/19 E 48th St 3rd Fl	212-838-0050
Accornero, Franco/620 Broadway	212-674-0068
Acuna, Ed/24 W 57th St #605	212-489-8777
Adams, Angela/866 UN Plaza #4014	212-644-2020
Adams, Jeanette/261 Broadway	212-732-3878
Adams, Jeffrey/95 Horatio St	212-807-0840
Aiese, Bob/925 E 14th St	718-253-2367
Airstream/ Pam Wall/60 E 42nd St #505	212-682-1490
Airstream/ Pat Bailey/60 E 42nd St #505	212-682-1490
Ajhar, Brian/321 E 12th St #30	212-254-0694
Albahae, Andrea/2364 Brigham St 1st Fl	718-934-7004
Alcorn, John/194 Third Ave	212-475-0440
Alcorn, Stephen/194 Third Ave	212-475-0440
Allaux, Jean Francois/21 W 86th St	212-873-8404
Alleman, Annie/324 Pearl St	212-732-4492
Allen, Julian/31 Walker St	212-925-6550
Allen, Terry/291 Carroll St	718-624-1210
Allert, Kathy/201 E 28th St	212-532-0928
Aloisio, Richard/145 E 16th St	212-473-5635
Alpert, Alan/405 E 54th St	212-741-1631
Alpert, Olive/9511 Shore Rd	718-833-3092
Alves, Harold/381 Park Ave S 11th Fl	212-684-6984
Anderson, Mark/301 W 37th St 5th Fl	212-674-3831
Angelakis, Manos/48 W 21st St 9th Fl	212-243-4412
Angelo, Peter/328 W 46th St #1R	212-246-1243
Angerame, Diane/57-30 254th St	718-428-7794
Antonios, Tony/60 E 42nd St #505	212-682-1490
Apelmann, Morton/30 W 32nd St	212-564-8258
Arcelle, Joan/430 W 24th St	212-924-1865
Aristovulos, Nick/16 E 30th St	212-725-2454
Arnold, Robert/149 W 14th St	212-989-7049
Arnoldi, Per/60 E 42nd St #505	212-682-1490
Assel, Steven/472 Myrtle Ave	718-789-1725
Astrahan, Irene/201 E 28th St	212-532-0928
Azzopardi, Frank/1039 Victory Blvd	718-273-4343

B

Bacall, Aaron/204 Arlene St	718-494-0711
Backhaus, R B/280 West End Ave	212-877-4792
Baker, Garin/35 W 92nd St #7A	212-865-1975
Baker, Nancy/423 Atlantic Ave #3L	718-462-1847
Baldus, Fred/29 Jones St	212-620-0423
Baldwin, Read/230 Fifth Ave #200	212-481-7311
Ballantyne, Joyce/353 W 53rd St #1W	212-682-2462
Banfield, Elliot/81 Greene St	212-925-3053
Barancik, Cathy/140 Grand St	212-226-2329
Barberis, Juan C/60 E 42nd St	212-687-4185
Barner, Bob/866 UN Plaza #4014	212-644-2020
Barnes, Michele/111 Sullivan St #3B	212-219-9269
Barnes-Murphy, Rowan/201 E 28th St	212-532-0928
Baron, Esther/866 UN Plaza #4014	212-644-2020
Barr, Ken/420 Lexingron Ave #2738	212-697-8525
Barrera, Alberto/463 West St #1017D	212-645-2544
BARRETT, RON/2112 BROADWAY #402A (P 12)	**212-874-1370**
Barry, Ron/165 E 32nd St	212-686-3514
Bartalos, Michael/81 Second Ave #3	212-254-5858
Bartoloni, Gary/203 W 98th St #6E	212-749-4498
Bass, Bob/43 E 19th St	212-254-4996
Bauer, Carla Studio/156 Fifth Ave #1100	212-807-8305
Bauman, Jill/PO Box 152	718-631-3160
Baumann, Karen/43 E 19th St	212-688-1080
Beach, Lou/215 Park Ave S	212-674-8080
Becker, Ron/265 E 78th St	212-535-8052
Beckhardt, Karen/137 E 26th St #B4	212-889-6437
Beecham, Tom/420 Lexington Ave #2738	212-697-8525
Bego, Dolores/155 E 38th St	212-697-6170
Beiman, Nancy/14 Horatio St #12A	212-675-5595
Bellaire & Inoue Visual Comm/323 Park Ave S	212-473-8330

Bellows, Amelia/125 Fifth Ave #206	212-777-7012
Ben-Ami, Doron/808 Union St	718-638-6675
Bendell, Norm/18 E 17th St 3rd Fl	212-807-6627
Benson, Linda/165 E 32nd St	212-686-3514
Berger, Stephen/43 E 19th St	212-254-4996
Berkey, John/50 E 50th St	212-355-0910
Berran, Robert/420 Lexington Ave #2911	212-986-5680
Berry, Fanny Mellet/155 E 38th St	212-697-6170
Beylon, Cathy/201 E 28th St	212-532-0928
Biggert, Joseph/155 W 81st St #6A	212-580-7955
Billout, Guy/222 W 15th St	212-255-2022
Bilmes, Semyon/15-69 Ocean Ave #3J	718-338-4268
Bittman, Monika/709 Carroll St	718-622-2061
Bjorkman, Steve/501 Fifth Ave #1407	212-490-2450
Blackwell, Garie/60 E 42nd St #505	212-682-1490
Blake, Marty/24 Jane St #5B	212-929-4440
Blake, Quentin/81 Greene St	212-925-3053
Blakey, Paul/226 E 53rd St	212-755-4945
Blasutta, Mary Lynn/41 E 22nd St #4A	212-777-2944
Bloch, Alex/19 E 48th St 3rd Fl	212-838-0050
Bloom, Tom/235 E 84th St #17	212-628-6861
Blum, Zevi/81 Greene St	212-925-3053
Blume, George/350 E 89th St	212-502-3976
Blumrich, Christoph/215 Park Ave S	212-674-8080
Bochner, Nurit/28 Tompkins Pl	718-596-3476
Boguslav, Raphael/200 E 78th St	212-570-9069
Bonanno, Paul/54-11 69th Ln	718-565-5542
Bonforte, Lisa/201 E 28th St	212-532-0928
Bonhomme, Bernard/111 Wooster St #PH C	212-925-0491
Bordelon, Melinda/60 E 42nd St #505	212-682-1490
Bostic, Alex/853 Broadway	212-677-9100
Botas, Juan/207 E 32nd St	212-420-5984
Boyd, Harvey/24 Fifth Ave	212-475-5235
Boyd, Kris/318 E 89th St #1D	212-876-4361
Bozzo, Frank/400 E 85th St #5J	212-535-9182
Bracken, Carolyn/201 E 28th St	212-532-0928
Bralds, Braldt/135 E 54th St	212-421-0050
Bramhall, William/81 Greene St	212-925-3053
Brandt, Joan/15 Gramercy Park S	212-473-7874
Brayman, Kari/333 W 55th St	212-582-6137
Breakey, John/42-52 Layton #1H	718-507-6467
Breinberg, Aaron/1123 Broadway	212-243-4929
Bricher, Scott/330 W 42nd St #3200NE	212-714-0147
Brickner, Alice/4720 Grosvenor Ave	212-549-5909
Brillhart, Ralph/60 E 42nd St #428	212-867-8092
Broderson, Charles/873 Broadway #612	212-925-9392
Brofsky, Miriam/186 Riverside Dr	212-595-8094
Brooks, Andrea/99 Bank St #3G	212-924-3085
BROOKS, CLARE VANACORE/415 W 55TH ST (P 14,15)	**212-245-3632**
Brooks, Hal/20 W 87th St	212-595-5980
Brooks, Lou/415 W 55th St	212-245-3632
Brothers, Barry/1922 E 18th St	718-336-7540
Brown, Bradford/4103 Lowerre Pl	212-231-8223
Brown, Dan/420 Lexington Ave	212-986-5680
Brown, Donald/129 E 29th St	212-532-1705
Brown, Judith Gwyn/522 E 85th St	212-288-1599
Brown, Peter D/235 E 22nd St #16R	212-684-7080
Brundage, Cheryl/314 Washington Ave	718-789-6392
Brusca, Jack/43 E 19th St	212-254-4996
Bryan, Diana/200 E 16th St #1D	212-475-7927
Bryan, Mike/420 Lexington Ave #2738	212-697-8525
Bryant, Rick J/18 W 37th St #301	212-594-6718
Bucalo, Ron/870 W 181st St #35	212-928-7857
Buchanan, Yvonne/411 14th St	718-965-3021
Buehler, Mark/418 Atlantic Ave	718-797-3689
Burger, Robert/111 Wooster St #PH C	212-925-0491
Burgoyne, John/200 E 78th St	212-570-9069
Bush, George/60 E 42nd St #428	212-867-8092
Bushman, Lynne/186 Franklin St	212-925-4701
Byskiniewicz, Maryika/75-23 113th St #4F	718-261-5883

Illustrators

Continued

Please send us your additions and updates.

C

Cain, David/200 W 20th St #607	212-691-5783
Campbell, Jim/420 Lexington Ave #2911	212-986-5680
Cantarella, Virginia Hoyt/107 Sterling Pl	718-622-2061
Carbone, Kye/241 Union St	718-802-9143
Carr, Noell/30 E 14th St	212-675-1015
Carter, Bunny/200 E 78th St	212-570-9069
Carter, Penny/51 E 42nd St #716	212-986-3282
Casale, Paul/5304 11th Ave	718-633-7909
Cassler, Carl/420 Lexington Ave #2911	212-986-5680
Cavaliere, Jamie/60 E 42nd St #428	212-867-8092
Celsi, David/91 E 3rd St #2B	212-475-1325
Ceribello, Jim/11 W Cedar View Ave	718-317-5972
Cesc/81 Greene St	212-925-3053
Cetlin, Marshall/62 LeRoy St	212-243-7869
Chambless-Rigie, Jane/201 E 28th St	212-532-0928
Charmatz, Bill/25 W 68th St	212-595-3907
Cheng, Judith/88-57 195th St	718-465-5598
Chermayeff, Ivan/58 W 15th St	212-741-2539
Chernishov, Anatoly/3967 Sedgwick Ave #20F	212-884-8122
Chester, Harry/501 Madison Ave	212-752-0570
Chironna, Ronald/135 Sturges St	718-720-6142
Chow, Tad/179 Bay 35th St	718-946-8519
Christopher, Tom/51 E 42nd St #716	212-986-3282
Chwast, Jacqueline/490 West End Ave	212-873-5033
Chwast, Seymour/215 Park Ave S	212-674-8080
Ciardiello, Joe/2182 Clove Rd	718-727-4757
Ciccarielli, Gary/353 W 53rd St #1W	212-682-2462
Ciesiel, Christine G/101 MacDougal St	212-982-9461
Cieslawski, Steven/321 86th St #H-1	718-748-8746
Ciss, Julius/145 E 22nd St	212-473-8747
Clark, Jane/48 W 21st St 9th Fl	212-243-4412
Clarke, Robert/159 W 53rd St	212-581-4045
Cloteaux, Francois/333 E 30th St	212-679-1358
Cody, Brian/866 UN Plaza #4014	212-644-2020
Cole, Olivia/19 E 48th St 3rd Fl	212-838-0050
Collier, Roberta/201 E 28th St	212-532-0928
Colon, Ernie/43 E 19th St	212-254-4996
Colton, Keita/165 E 32nd St	212-686-3514
Connelly, Gwen/866 UN Plaza #4014	212-644-2020
Conner, Mona/1 Montgomery Pl #8	718-636-1527
Continuity Graphics Assoc'd Inc/62 W 45th St	212-869-4170
Conway, Michael/316 E 93rd St #23	212-369-0019
Cook, David/60 E 42nd St #428	212-867-8092
Cooper, Cheryl/515 Madison Ave	212-486-9644
Cooper, Floyd/866 UN Plaza #4014	212-644-2020
Cooperstein, Sam/677 West End Ave	212-864-4064
Corben, Richard/43 E 19th St	212-254-4996
Cormier, Wil/15 W 72nd St	212-799-2231
Cornell, Jeff/24 W 57th St #605	212-489-8777
Cornell, Laura/118 E 93rd St #1A	212-534-0596
Corvi, Donna/568 Broadway #604	212-925-9622
COUCH, GREG/112 WILLOW ST #5A (P 18)	**718-625-1298**
Coulson, David/32 Thompson St #1	212-431-5468
Courtney, Richard/43 E 19th St	212-254-4996
Cove, Tony/60 E 42nd St	212-687-4185
Crawford, Margery/237 E 31st St	212-686-6883
Crawford, Robert/340 E 93rd St #9I	212-722-4964
Crawford, Ronald/354 22nd St #6	718-768-6194
Creed, Cora/651 Vanderbilt St	718-633-7753
Crews, Donald/653 Carroll St	718-636-5773
Crosthwaite, Royd/50 E 50th St #5	212-355-0910
Cruse, Howard/88-11 34th Ave #5D	718-639-4951
Cruz, Jose/215 Park Ave S	212-674-8080
Cruz, Ray/194 Third Ave	212-475-0440
Csatari, Joe/420 Lexington Ave #2911	212-986-5680
Cuevos, Stillerman, Plotkin/230 E 44th St	212-661-7149
Cummings, Coco/95 Grand St #1	212-925-8747
Cummings, Pat/28 Tiffany Pl	718-834-8584
Cunningham, Jean/177 Waverly Pl #4F	212-675-1731
Cunningham, Robert M/177 Waverly Pl #4F	212-675-1731
Cusack, Margaret/124 Hoyt St	718-237-0145
Cushwa, Tom/303 Park Ave S #511	212-228-2615

D

D'Andrea, Bernard/50 E 50th St #5	212-355-0910
D'Andrea, Domenick/50 E 50th St #5	212-355-0910
D'Onofrio, Alice/866 UN Plaza #4014	212-644-2020
D'Ortenzio, Alfred/353 W 53rd St #1W	212-682-2462
Dacey, Bob/24 W 57th St #605	212-489-8777
Dalaney, Jack/184 Thompson St	212-777-7713
Dale, Robert/1573 York Ave	212-535-2505
Dallison, Ken/108 E 35th St #1	212-889-3337
Daly, Sean/85 South St	212-668-0031
Daniel, Frank/201 E 28th St	212-532-0928
Daniels, Alan/24 W 57th St #605	212-489-8777
Daniels, Beau/24 W 57th St #605	212-489-8777
Daniels, Sid/12 E 22nd St #11B	212-673-6520
Darden, Howard/62 W 45th St	212-398-9540
Darrer, Tony/515 E 79th St	212-628-0708
Daste, Larry/201 E 28th St	212-532-0928
Davidson, Everett/60 E 42nd St #505	212-682-1490
Davis, Allen/141-10 25th Rd #3A	718-463-0966
Davis, Nelle/20 E 17th St 4th Fl	212-807-7737
Davis, Paul/14 E 4th St	212-460-9644
Dawson, John/60 E 42nd St #428	212-867-8092
Day, Betsy/866 UN Plaza #4014	212-644-2020
DeAraujo, Betty/201 E 28th St	212-532-0928
Deas, Michael/39 Sidney Pl	718-852-5630
Deel, Guy/60 E 42nd St #428	212-867-8092
Deeter, Catherine/333 E 30th St	212-679-1358
Degen, Paul/81 Greene St	212-925-3053
DeGraffenried, Jack/18 E 16th St	212-206-0322
Deibler, Gordon/1 Wrld Trade Ctr #8817	212-323-8022
DeJesus, Jamie/15 W 72nd St	212-799-2231
Del Rosso, Richard/303 W 42nd St #312	212-974-1059
DeLattre, Georgette/100 Central Park South	212-247-6850
DeMarest, Chris/81 Greene St	212-925-3053
DeMichiell, Robert/43 E 19th St	212-254-4996
Denaro, Joseph/18 E 16th St	212-206-0322
DeRijk, Walt/43 E 19th St	212-254-4996
Deschamps, Bob/108 E 35th St #1	212-889-3337
DesCombes, Roland/50 E 50th St #5	212-355-0910
DeSeve, Peter/461 W 21st St #3	212-627-5533
Devlin, Bill/108 E 35th St #1	212-889-3337
Dewey, Kenneth F/226 E 53rd St	212-755-4945
Diamantis, Kitty/19 E 48th St 3rd Fl	212-838-0050
Diamond Art Studio/11 E 36th St	212-685-6622
Diamond, Ruth/95 Horatio St #521	212-683-4351
DiCianni, Ron/420 Lexington Ave	212-697-8525
DiComo Comp Art/12 W 27th St	212-689-8670
Dietz, Jim/165 E 32nd St	212-686-3514
Dilakian, Hovik/111 Wooster St #PH C	212-925-0491
Dinnerstein, Harvey/933 President St	718-783-6879
Dircks, David/141 Ridge St #6	212-982-5534
Dittrich, Dennis/42 W 72nd St #12B	212-595-9773
DiVincenzo, Dennis/27 Bleecker St	212-673-1600
Dodds, Glenn/392 Central Park West #9M	212-679-3630
Domingo, Ray/108 E 35th St #1	212-889-3337
Donner, Carroll/830 Broadway 10th Fl	212-254-0069
Doret, Michael/12 E 14th St	212-929-1688
Doret/ Smith Studios/12 E 14th St	212-929-1688
Drovetto, Richard/355 E 72nd St	212-861-0927
Drucker, Mort/226 E 53rd St	212-755-4945
Duarte, Mary Young/350 First Ave #9E	212-674-4513
Dubanevich, Arlene/866 UN Plaza #4014	212-644-2020
Dudash, Michael/157 W 57th St	212-247-1130
Dudzinski, Andrzej/52 E 81st St	212-628-6959
Duerk, Chris/259 E 33rd St #3	212-683-7729
Duke, Randy/235 E 149th St	212-292-1226
Dyess, John/1457 Broadway #1001	212-840-8223

E

Eagle, Cameron/170 E 3rd St #4J	212-777-6054
Eastman, Norm & Bryant/420 Lexington Ave #2738	212-697-8525
Eggert, John/420 Lexington Ave #2911	212-986-5680

Egielski, Richard/463 West St	212-255-9328
Ehlert, Lois/866 UN Plaza #4014	212-644-2020
Eisner, Gil/310 W 86th St #11A	212-595-2023
Ellis, Dean/30 E 20th St	212-254-7590
Elmer, Richard/504 E 11th St	212-598-4024
ELY, RICHARD/150 W 55TH ST (P 20)	**212-757-8987**
Emerson, Carmela/217-11 54th Ave	718-224-4251
Emmett, Bruce/285 Park Pl	718-636-5263
Endewelt, Jack/50 Riverside Dr	212-877-0575
Enik, Ted/82 Jane St #4A	212-620-5972
Ennis, John/308 W 73rd St #3B	212-496-7215
Enric/43 E 19th St	212-688-1080
Ensor, Barbara/90 Fulton St	212-619-6103
Erickson, Mary Anne (Shea)/154 Eighth Ave #4	212-929-7964
Ettlinger, Doris/73 Leonard St	212-226-0331
Eutemy, Loring/51 Fifth Ave	212-741-0140
Evcimen, Al/305 Lexington Ave #6D	212-889-2995
Ewing, Carolyn/201 E 28th St	212-532-0928

F

Fabara, Carlos/5033 65th Pl	718-565-2874
Familton, Herb/59 W 10th St #1D	212-254-2943
Farina, Michael/18 E 16th St 2nd Fl	212-206-0322
Farmakis, Andreas/835 Third Ave	212-758-5280
Farrell, Marybeth/423 Amsterdam Ave #2D	212-799-7486
Fascione, Sabina/194 Third Ave	212-475-0440
Fasolino, Teresa/58 W 15th St	212-741-2539
Faulkner, Matt/435 Clinton St #4	718-858-1724
Faust, Clifford/322 W 57th St #42P	212-581-9461
FEBLAND, DAVID/670 WEST END AVE (P 21)	**212-580-9299**
Fernandes, Stanislaw/35 E 12th St	212-533-2648
Fertig, Howard/75-15 210th St	718-468-3627
Fichera, Maryanne/12 W 27th St	212-689-8670
Filippucci, Sandra/270 Park Ave S #9B	212-477-8732
Fine, Robert/43 E 19th St	212-254-4996
Finewood, Bill/201 E 28th St	212-532-0928
Fiore, Peter/11-22 130th St	718-358-9018
Fiorentino, Al/866 UN Plaza #4014	212-644-2020
Fischer, Rick/156 Fifth Ave #1222	212-645-6772
Fitzgerald, Frank/PO Box 6113	212-722-6793
Flaherty, David/534 W 50th St #5A	212-765-7201
Flesher, Vivienne/194 Third Ave	212-475-0440
Forbes, Bart/501 Fifth Ave #1407	212-490-2450
Forrest, Sandra/315 Central Pk W #3N	212-580-8510
Foster, B Lynne/540 Ft Washington Ave #3D	212-781-1055
Foster, Stephen Design/244 Fifth Ave	212-532-0771
Fox, Barbara/301 W 53rd St	212-245-7564
Francis, Judy/110 W 96th St	212-866-7204
Fraser, Betty/240 Central Park South	212-247-1937
Freas, John/353 W 53rd St #1W	212-682-2462
Freelance Solutions/369 Lexington Ave 18th Fl	212-490-3334
Freeman, Irving/145 Fourth Ave #9K	212-674-6705
Freeman, Tom/157 W 57th St	212-247-1130
Freidman, Wendy/23 E 10th St	212-598-0393
Fretz, Frank/866 UN Plaza #4014	212-644-2020
Fricke, Warren/15 W 72nd St	212-799-2231
Fried, Janice/51 W 46th St #3B	212-398-0067
Friedman, Jon/866 UN Plaza #4014	212-644-2020
Friedman, Wendy/23 E 10th St #3G	212-598-0393
Froom, Georgia/62 W 39th St #803	212-944-0330
Funtastic Studios/506 W 42nd St	212-239-8245
Furukawa, Mel/116 Duane St	212-349-3225

G

Gabriele, Antonio J/420 Lexington Ave #2911	212-986-5680
Gadino, Victor/1601 Third Ave	212-534-7206
Gaetano, Nicholas/821 Broadway 6th Fl	212-674-5749
Gala, Tom/420 Lexington Ave #2911	212-986-5680
Gale, Cynthia/229 E 88th St	212-860-5429
Galkin, Simon/19 E 48th St 3rd Fl	212-838-0050
Gallardo, Gervasio/50 E 50th St	212-355-0910
Galub, Meg/405 W 57th St	212-757-3506
Gambale, David/200 W 15th St	212-243-4209
Gampert, John/PO Box 219	718-441-2321

Garner, David/175 W 87th St #26H	212-874-3147
Garrick, Jacqueline/333 E 75th St	212-628-1018
Garrido, Hector/420 Lexington Ave #2911	212-986-5680
Garrison, Barbara/12 E 87th St	212-348-6382
Gates, Donald/19 E 48th St 3rd Fl	212-838-0050
Gayler, Anne/320 E 86th St	212-734-7060
Gehm, Charles/420 Lexington Ave #2738	212-697-8525
Geller, Amy/11-15 45th Ave	718-786-5277
Gem Studio/420 Lexington Ave #220	212-687-3460
Genova, Joe/60 E 42nd St #505	212-682-1490
Gentile, John & Anthony/850 Seventh Ave #1006	212-757-1966
Geras, Audra/501 Fifth Ave #1407	212-490-2450
Gerber, Mark & Stephanie/159 Madison Ave #4H	212-684-7137
Gershinowitz, George/PO Box 204 Chelsea Sta	212-691-1376
Gersten, Gerry/1380 Riverside Dr	212-928-7957
Giavis, Ted/420 Lexington Ave #2911	212-986-5680
Giglio, Richard/299 W 12th St	212-675-7642
Gignilliat, Elaine/150 E 56th St	212-935-1943
Gillot, Carol/162 W 13th St	212-243-6448
Giorgio, Nate/18 E 16th St	212-206-0322
Giovanopoulos, Paul/216 E 45th St	212-661-0850
Gold, Marcy/200 E 28th St #2C	212-685-4974
Goldstrom, Robert/471 Fifth St	718-768-7367
Good Guys/596 Broadway #1216	212-226-8018
Goode, Harley/1 Prospect Pk SW	718-788-0989
Goodell, Jon/866 UN Plaza #4014	212-644-2020
Goodman, Paula/1457 Broadway #1001	212-840-8223
Goodrich, Carter/140 W 22nd St 7th Fl	212-243-3954
Gordon, Rebecca/201 W 16th St	212-989-5762
Gore, Elissa/583 W 215th St #A3	212-567-2161
Gornley, Peter/25 W 43rd St #711	212-221-5900
Gorton, Julia/85 South St #6N	212-825-0190
Gothard, David/81 Greene St	212-925-3053
Gottfried, Max/82-60 116th St #CC3	718-441-9868
Gottlieb, Penelope/420 Lexington Ave #2738	212-679-8525
Gourley, Robin/225 Lafayette St #407	212-431-8415
Gowdy, Carolyn/81 Greene St	212-925-3053
Graboff, Abner/25 E 21st St	212-460-9270
Grace, Alexa/70 University Pl	212-254-4424
Graddon, Julian/48 W 21st St 9th Fl	212-243-4412
Graham, Mariah/670 West End Ave	212-580-8061
Graham, Thomas/408 77th St #D4	718-680-2975
Grammer, June/126 E 24th St #3B	212-475-4745
GRANT, WILLIAM/4114 HIGHLAND AVE (P 23)	**718-996-3555**
Graphic Assoc/ Clay Turner/60 E 42nd St #505	212-682-1490
Graphic Assoc/ Ron Fleming/60 E 42nd St #505	212-682-1490
Grashow, David/81 Greene St	212-925-3053
Gray, Doug/15 W 72nd St	212-799-2231
Gray, John/264 Van Duzer St	718-447-6466
Gray, Susan/42 W 12th St #5	212-675-2243
Grebu, Devis/43 E 19th St	212-688-1080
Gregoretti, Rob/240-13 Hanford St	718-229-5647
Greifinger, Mel/200 W 15th St	212-243-4209
Greiner, Larry/63 E 7th St	212-982-2428
Greis, Gene/215 W 10th St	212-206-6392
Griesbach/Martucci/35 Sterling Pl	718-622-1831
Griffel, Barbara/23-45 Bell Blvd	718-631-1753
Griffin, James/60 E 42nd St #428	212-867-8092
Grimmett, Douglas/36 E 23rd St 7th Fl	212-777-1099
Grinko, Andy/125 Cedar St	212-732-5308
Gross, Mort/2 Park Ave #1804	212-686-4788
Grossman, Robert/19 Crosby St	212-925-1965
Guarnaccia, Steven/430 W 14th St #508	212-645-9610
Guitar, Jeremy/866 UN Plaza #4014	212-644-2020
Gumen, Murad/33-25 90th St #6K	718-478-7267
Gunn, Robert/201 E 28th St	212-532-0928
Gurbo, Walter/55 Hudson St #3A	212-775-1810
Gurney, John Steven/523 E 16th St	718-462-5073
Gusson, Steven/105 Bergen St	718-852-7791

H

Haas, Arie/62 W 45th St	212-382-1677
Hack, Konrad/866 UN Plaza #4014	212-644-2020

Illustrators

ILLUSTRATORS

Hahn, Marika/11 Riverside Dr	212-580-7896
Hall, Deborah Ann/105-28 65th Ave #6B	718-896-3152
Hall, Joan/155 Bank St #H954	212-243-6059
Hallgren, Gary/231 W 29th St #805	212-947-1054
Hamann, Brad/135 Prospect Pk W	718-768-7365
Hamrick, Chuck/420 Lexington Ave #2911	212-986-5680
Hannon, Mark/1457 Broadway #1001	212-840-8223
Harrington, Glenn/165 E 32nd St	212-686-3514
Harris, Diane Teske/342 Madison Ave #469	212-719-9879
Harrison, William/18 E 16th St	212-206-0322
Hart, Veronika/60 E 42nd St #505	212-682-1490
Harvey, Ray/60 E 42nd St #428	212-867-8062
Harwood, Laurel/1239 Broadway #1350	212-689-3515
Hays, Michael/43 Cheever Pl	718-852-2731
Heapps, Bill/2441 41st St	718-726-2193
Heck, Cathy/333 E 30th St	915-686-9343
Hedin, Donald/157 W 57th St	212-247-1130
Heindel, Robert/211 E 51st St	212-755-1365
Heiner, Joe & Kathy/194 Third Ave	212-475-0440
Heller, Karen/300 W 108th St	212-866-5879
Helman, Marc/425 W 46th St #4E	212-307-1281
Henderson, Alan/31 Jane St #10B	212-243-0693
Henderson, Meryl/19 E 48th St 3rd Fl	212-838-0050
Henry, Paul/15 W 72nd St	212-799-2231
Herbick, David/5 Montague Terrace	718-852-6450
Herder, Edwin/60 E 42nd St #428	212-867-8092
Hering, Al/277 Washington Ave #3E	718-789-7685
Herman, Rolla/462 Greenwich St	212-226-1510
Herman, Tim/853 Broadway	212-677-9100
Hernandez, Richard/144 Chambers St	212-732-3474
Herrmann, Hal/50 E 50th St	212-752-8490
Hewitt, Margaret/31 Ocean Pkwy #2C	718-436-2039
Hill, Amy/111 Wooster St #PH C	212-925-0491
Himler, Ron/866 UN Plaza #4014	212-644-2020
Hochman, Steve/504 Grand St #A62	212-460-9876
Hoffman, Ginnie/108 E 35th St #1	212-889-3337
Hoffman, Rosekrans/866 UN Plaza #4014	212-644-2020
Hofkin, Bonnie/204 W 80th St	212-787-6384
Hogarth, Paul/81 Greene St	212-925-3053
Holland, Brad/96 Greene St	212-226-3675
Holland, Gary/140 W 86th St #15A	212-877-9165
Holst, Joni/1519 81st St	212-661-9700
Hong, Min Jae/422 E 14th St #1B	212-674-4320
Hooks, Mitchell/321 E 83rd St	212-737-1853
Hortens, Walter/154 E 64th St	212-838-0014
Hosner, William/853 Broadway	212-677-9100
Hostovich, Michael/127 W 82nd St #9A	212-580-2175
Howard, John/336 E 54th St	212-832-7980
Howell, Kathleen/866 UN Plaza #4014	212-644-2020
Howland, Gary/140 W 86th St #15A	212-877-9165
Huang, Mei-ku/201 E 28th St	212-532-0928
The Hub/16 E 16th St 4th Fl	212-675-8500
Hubert, Laurent/216 E 45th St	212-661-0850
Huerta, Catherine/60 E 42nd St #505	212-682-1490
Huffman, Tom/130 W 47th St #6A	212-819-0211
Hughes, Mary Ellen/403 E 70th St	212-288-8375
Huling, Phil/33 E 22nd St #5F	212-673-0839
Hull, Cathy/236 E 36th St #102	212-683-8559
Hunt, Jim/853 Broadway	212-677-9100
Hunter, Stan/50 E 50th St	212-355-0910
Huston, Steven/15 W 72nd St	212-799-2231
Huttner & Hillman/137 E 25th St	212-532-6062

Idelson, Joyce/11 Riverside Dr	212-877-6161
Image Network Inc/645 West End Ave	212-877-2517
Incandescent Ink Inc/111 Wooster St #PH C	212-925-0491
Incisa, Monica/141 E 56th St	212-752-1554
The Ink Tank/2 W 47th St	212-869-1630
Inoue, Izumi/323 Park Ave S	212-473-8330
Iskowitz, Joel/420 Lexington Ave #2911	212-986-5680
Ivenbaum, Elliott/267 W 90th St	212-664-5656
Ivens, Rosalind/483 13th St	718-499-8285

J	
Jaben, Seth/54 W 21st St #62	212-242-3181
Jamieson, Doug/42-20 69th St	718-565-6034
Jampel, Judith/148 Columbus Ave	212-873-5234
Jasper, Jackie/165 E 32nd St	212-686-3514
Jeffers, Kathy/106 E 19th St 12th Fl	212-475-1756
Jetter, Frances/390 West End Ave	212-580-3720
Jezierski, Chet/50 E 50th St	212-355-0910
Jinks, John/690 Greenwich St #BD	212-675-2961
Jobe, Jody/875 W 181st St	212-795-4941
Johnson, David McCall/60 E 42nd St #505	212-682-1490
Johnson, Doug/45 E 19th St	212-260-1880
Johnson, Kristin/441 W 37th St	212-594-2343
Jones, Bob/420 Lexington Ave #2911	212-986-5680
Jones, Lauretta/315 E 5th St	212-777-3978
Jones, Randy/323 E 10th St	212-677-5387
Jones, Taylor/19 E 48th St 3rd Fl	212-838-0050
Joseph, Paula/16 W 16th St #9SN	212-242-6137
Joudrey, Ken/15 W 72nd St	212-799-2231
Just, Hal/155 E 38th St	212-697-6170

K	
Kagansky, Eugene/1610 43rd St #C11	718-633-2842
Kahn, Sandra/344 E 49th St #7A	212-759-0630
Kalish, Lionel/30 E 10th St	212-228-6587
Kallan, Elizabeth Kada/67 Irving Place	212-674-8080
Kalle, Chris/866 UN Plaza #4014	212-644-2020
Kanarek, Michael/48 W 21st St 9th Fl	212-243-4412
Kane, Harry/310 E 49th St	212-486-0180
Kantra, Michelle/40 W 27th St	212-684-6700
Kappes, Werner/33 E 22nd St #5D	212-673-2484
Karlin, Bernie/41 E 42nd St	212-687-7636
Karlin, Eugene/39-73 48th St	718-457-5086
Katsin, Nancy/17 E 31st St #4F	212-213-0709
Katz, Les/451 Westminster	718-284-4779
Kaufman, Curt/215 W 88th St	212-873-9841
Keleny, Earl/515 Madison Ave 22nd Fl	212-486-9644
Kelley, Barbara/555 10th St	718-788-2465
Kelley, Mark/866 UN Plaza #4014	212-644-2020
Kelly, Susannah/77 Perry St	212-206-8960
Kendrick, Dennis/99 Bank St #3G	212-924-3085
Kernan, Patrick/413 W 48th St	212-581-2069
Keyes, Steven/18 E 16th St	212-206-0322
Kibbee, Gordon/6 Jane St	212-989-7074
Kieffer, Christa/866 UN Plaza #4014	212-644-2020
Kilmer, David/420 Lexington Ave #2911	212-986-5680
Kimura, Hiro/262 W 24th St #2E	212-929-3266
Kingston, James/31 E 31st St	212-685-2520
Kirk, Daniel/85 South St #6N	212-825-0190
Klavins, Uldis/60 E 42nd St #428	212-867-8092
Klein, David G/257 Winsdor Pl	718-788-1818
Klein, Renee/291 Carroll St	718-624-1210
Kluglein, Karen/	212-684-2974
Knettell, Sharon/108 E 35th St #1	212-889-3337
Knight, Jacob/216 E 45th St	212-661-0850
Kojoyian, Armen/52 Clark St #5K	718-797-5179
Kondo, Yukio/201 E 28th St	212-532-0928
Koren, Edward/81 Greene St	212-925-3053
Kosarin, Linda/21 W 38th St 9th Fl	212-840-7676
Kotzky, Brian/132-42 Booth Memorial Ave	718-353-5480
Kovalcik, Terry/48 W 20th St	212-620-7772
Kramer, Carveth/216 E 45th St	212-661-0850
Kretschmann, Karin/323 W 75th St #1A	212-724-5001
Kronen, Jeff/231 Thompson St #22	212-475-3166
Krumeich, Tad/1457 Broadway #1001	212-840-8223
Kubinyi, Laszlo/226 E 53rd St	201-833-4428
Kuester, Bob/353 W 53rd St #1W	212-682-2462
Kukalis, Romas/420 Lexington Ave #2911	212-986-5680
Kunstler, Mort/50 E 50th St	212-355-0910
Kuper, Peter/250 W 99th St #9C	212-864-5729
Kurman, Miriam/422 Amsterdam #2A	212-580-1649
Kursar, Ray/1 Lincoln Plaza #43R	212-873-5605
Kurtzman, Edward/60 E 42nd St	212-687-4185

Please send us your additions and updates.

Kurtzman, Harvey/18 E 16th St 212-206-0322

L Lacey, Lucille/77-07 Jamaica Ave 718-296-1813
Lackow, Andy/1325 Third Ave 212-472-8898
Ladas, George/157 Prince St 212-673-2208
Lakeman, Steven/115 W 85th St 212-877-8888
Lambert, Saul/138 E 13th St 212-260-3684
LAMUT,SONJA & JAKESEVIC, NENAD/165 E 32ND ST (P 24) ... **212-686-3514**
Landis, Joan/6 Jane St 212-989-7074
Lang, Cecily/19 Jones St #21 212-206-1251
Lang, Gary/420 Lexington Ave #2738 212-697-8525
LaPadula, Tom/201 E 28th St 212-532-0928
Lapinski, Joe/853 Broadway 212-677-9100
Laporte, Michele/216 E 45th St 212-661-0850
Larrain, Sally Marshall/19 E 48th St 3rd Fl 212-838-0050
Lasher, Mary Ann/60 E 42nd St #505 212-682-1490
Laslo, Larry/179 E 71st St 212-737-2340
Laurence, Karen/216 E 45th St 212-661-0850
Lauter, Richard/60 E 42nd St #428 212-867-8092
Lawton, Nancy/601 W 113 St #9B 212-222-0210
Lazure, Catherine/593 Riverside Dr #6D 212-690-1867
Le-Tan, Pierre/81 Greene St 212-925-3053
Lebbad, James A/1133 Broadway #1229 212-645-5260
Leder, Dora/866 UN Plaza #4014 212-644-2020
Lehr, Paul/50 E 50th St #5 212-355-0910
Lemerise, Bruce/201 E 28th St 212-532-0928
Leonard, Richard/212 W 17th St #2B 212-243-6613
Leonard, Tom/866 UN Plaza #4014 212-644-2020
Lesser, Robert/412 E 11th St #3B 212-228-1371
Lesser, Ron/420 Lexington Ave #2738 212-697-8525
Lettick, Birney/121 E 35th St 212-532-0535
Levin, Arnie/342 Madison Ave #469 212-719-9879
Levine, Andy/25-91 38th St #2 718-956-8539
Levine, Bette/60 E 42nd St #505 212-682-1490
Levine, Rena/200 Bethel Loop #12G 718-642-7339
Levine, Ron/1 W 85th St #4D 212-787-7415
LEVY, FRANCK/305 E 40TH ST #5Y (P 26) **212-557-8256**
Lewin, Ted/152 Willoughby Ave 718-622-3882
Lewis, Howard B/140 W 22nd St 7th Fl 212-243-3954
Lewis, Tim/194 Third Ave 212-475-0440
Lexa, Susan/866 UN Plaza #4014 212-644-2020
Liao, Sharmen/280 Madison Ave #1402 212-775-1810
Liberatore, Gaetano/43 E 19th St 212-254-4996
Lieberman, Ron/109 W 28th St 212-947-0653
Lilly, Charles/56 W 82nd St #15 212-873-3608
Lindberg, Jeffery K/449 50th St 718-492-1114
Lindgren, Goran/19 E 48th St 3rd Fl 212-838-0050
Lindlof, Ed/353 W 53rd St #1W 212-682-2462
Line, Lemuel/50 E 50th St 212-355-0910
Lippman, Peter/410 Riverside Dr #134 212-865-1823
Little Apple Art/409 Sixth Ave 718-499-7045
Lloyd, Peter/18 E 16th St 212-206-0322
Lockwood, Todd/60 E 42nd St #505 212-682-1490
Lodigensky, Ted/18 E 16th St 212-206-0322
LoGrippo, Robert/50 E 50th St #5 212-355-0910
Lopez, Antonio/31 Union Square W #10A 212-924-2060
Lorenz, Lee/108 E 35th St #1C 212-889-3337
Lovitt, Anita/308 E 78th St 212-628-8171
Low, William/31 Ocean Pkwy #2C 718-436-2039
Lozner, Ruth/171 W 71st St #10C 212-799-2628
Luce, Ben/5 E 17th St 6th Fl 212-255-8193
Lulevitch, Tom/101 W 69th St #4D 212-362-3318
Lustig, Loretta/19 E 48th St 3rd Fl 212-838-0050
Lyall, Dennis/420 Lexington Ave #2911 212-986-5680

M MacCombie, Turi/201 E 28th St 212-532-0928
Mack, Stan/226 E 53rd St 212-755-4945
Maddalone, John/1123 Broadway #310 212-807-6087
Madden, Don/866 U N Plaza #4014 212-644-2020
Mahon, Rich/18 E 16th St 212-206-0322
Mahoney, Ron/353 W 53rd St #1W 212-682-2462
Maisner, Bernard/184 Second Ave #2A 212-475-5911

Maitz, Don/50 E 50th St #5 212-355-0910
Malan, Dee/201 E 28th St 212-532-0928
Malonis, Tina/34-44 71st St 718-565-8209
Mangal/155 E 38th St 212-697-6170
Mangiat, Jeffrey/420 Lexington Ave #2911 212-986-5680
Manos, Jim/51 E 42nd St #716 212-986-3282
Mantel, Richard/484 W 43rd St #8R 212-594-7759
Manyum, Wallop/37-40 60th St 718-476-1478
Marcellino, Fred Studio/432 Park Ave S #601 212-532-0150
Mardon, Allan/108 E 35th St #1C 212-889-3337
Margulies, Robert/561 Broadway #10B 212-219-9621
Marich, Felix/853 Broadway 212-677-9100
Marinelli, Robert/165 Bryant Ave 718-979-4018
Martin, Bruce Rough Riders/389 Ave of Americas 212-620-0539
Martin, John/501 Fifth Ave #1407 212-490-2450
Martinez, John/280 Madison Ave 212-775-1810
Martinez, Sergio/43 E 19th St 212-254-4996
Martinot, Claude/145 Second Ave #20 212-473-3137
Masi, George/111 Wooster St #PH C 212-925-0491
Maslen, Barbara/45 W 18th St 212-645-5325
Mason, Brick/349 E 14th St #3R 212-777-4297
Mason, Tod/19 E 48th St 3rd Fl 212-838-0050
Mathewuse, James/157 W 57th St 212-247-1130
Mathieu, Joseph/81 Greene St 212-925-3053
Matsuyoshi, Akio/165 Perry St #1B 212-242-7043
Mattelson, Marvin/ 212-684-2974
Maxwell, Brookie/53 Irving Pl 212-475-6909
May, Darcy/201 E 28th St 212-532-0928
Mazur, Ruby (Mr)/300 E 75th St #16K 212-734-2950
McAllister, Kevin/163-19 26th Ave 718-746-3998
McArthur, Dennis/170-44 130th Ave 212-559-0029
McCollum, Rick/24 W 57th St #605 212-489-8777
McConnell, Gerald/10 E 23rd St 212-505-0950
McCormack, Geoffrey/420 Lexington Ave #2911 212-986-5680
McCreanor, Mike/1457 Broadway #1001 212-840-8223
McCreary, Jane/866 UN Plaza #4014 212-644-2020
McDaniel, Jerry/155 E 38th St 212-697-6170
McKeating, Eileen/862 Union St #6H 718-638-0760
McKenzie, Crystal/20 E 20th St #502 212-598-4567
McKie, Roy/75 Perry 212-989-5186
McLean, Wilson/50 E 50th St 212-752-8490
McMullan, James/222 Park Ave S #10B 212-473-5083
McNeel, Richard/215 Park Ave S 212-674-8080
McPheeters, Neal/16 W 71st St 212-799-7021
Mead, Kimble Pendleton/125 Prospect Park West 718-768-3632
Mehlman, Elwyn/108 E 35th St #1 212-889-3337
Meisel, Ann/420 Lexington Ave #2911 212-986-5680
Meisel, Paul/90 Hudson St #5E 212-226-5463
Meisler, Meryl/553 8th St 718-499-9836
Melendez, Robert/18 E 16th St 2nd Fl 212-206-0322
Merrell, Patrick/48 W 20th St 212-620-7777
Messi, Enzo & Schmidt, Urs/145 E 22nd St 212-473-8747
Meyerowitz, Rick/68 Jane St 212-989-2446
Michaels, Bob/304 E 49 St 212-752-1185
Michal, Marie/108 E 35th St #1 212-889-3337
Michner, Ted/420 Lexington Ave #2911 212-986-5680
Midda, Sara/81 Greene St 212-925-3053
Mihaesco, Eugene/25 Tudor City Pl #1423 212-692-9271
Mikos, Mike/420 Lexington Ave #2911 212-986-5680
Milicic, Michael/587 Ft Washington Ave #10E 212-927-2353
Miller, Cliff/60 E 42nd St #428 212-867-8092
Miller, Lyle/866 UN Plaza #4014 212-644-2020
Millington, Hunter/49 W 11th St #14 212-645-8688
Milne, Jonathon/420 Lexington Ave 212-986-5680
Minor, Wendell/277 W 4th St 212-691-6925
Mitchell, Celia/30-25 Steinway St #1B 718-626-4095
Mitsuhashi, Yoko/43 E 29th St 212-683-7312
Miyamoto, Linda/PO Box 2310 718-596-4787
Montiel, David/115 W 16th St #211 212-989-7426
Moore, Brian/2938 Brighton 12th St, Brooklyn, NY ... 718-934-1581
Moraes, Greg/60 E 42nd St #428 212-867-8092
MORGAN, JACQUI/315 E 58TH ST (P 29) **212-421-0766**

Morgen, Barry/337 W 87th St #G	212-595-6835
Morris, Frank/15 W 72nd St	212-799-2231
Morrison, Don/155 E 38th St	212-697-6170
Morse, Bill/60 E 42nd St #505	212-682-1490
Moss, Geoffrey/315 E 68th St	212-472-9474
Murawski, Alex/108 E 35th St #1	212-889-3337
Murdocca, Sal/19 E 48th St 3rd Fl	212-838-0050
Myers, David L/228 Bleecker St #8	212-989-5260

N Najaka, Marlies/241 Central Park West — 212-580-0058

Nakai Sacco & Crowell/218 Madison Ave	212-213-5333
Nakamura, Joel/95 Horatio St	212-807-0840
Nascimbene, Yan/156 Fifth Ave #1222	212-645-6772
NAZZ, JAMES/159 SECOND ST #12 (P 32)	**212-228-9713**
Neff, Leland/506 Amsterdam Ave #61	212-724-1884
Nemirov, Meredith/110 Kent St	718-389-5972
Nessim, Barbara/63 Greene St	212-677-8888
Neubecker, Robert/395 Broadway #14C	212-219-8435
Neumann, Ann/444 Broome St	212-431-7141
Newton, Richard/501 Fifth Ave #1407	212-490-2450
Neyman-Levikova, Marina/155 E 38th St	212-697-6170
NG, MICHAEL/58-35 155TH ST (P 33)	**718-461-8264**
Nicastre, Michael/420 Lexington Ave #2738	212-697-8525
Nicholas, Jess/18 E 16th St	212-206-0322
Nicklaus, Carol/866 UN Plaza #4014	212-644-2020
Nicotra, Rosanne/611 Goethals Rd N	718-761-8621
Nitzburg, Andrew/165 E 32nd St	212-686-3514
Noftsinger, Pamela/600 W 111th St #6A	212-316-4241
Noonan, Julia/873 President St	718-622-9268
North, Russ/40 W 20th St #901	212-242-6300
Nosek, Laslo/440 West End Ave	212-362-7376
Nosz Studio Inc/440 West End Ave	212-362-7376
Notarile, Chris/420 Lexington Ave #2911	212-986-5680
Novak, Justin/1457 Broadway #1001	212-840-8223

O Oberheide, Heide/295 Washington Ave #5B — 718-622-7056

Ochagavia, Carlos/50 E 50th St	212-355-0910
Odom, Mel/252 W 76th St #B1	212-724-9320
Oelbaum, Fran/200 W 15th St	212-243-4209
Olanoff, Greg/60 E 42nd St #428	212-867-8092
Olbinski, Rafal/470 W 23rd St	212-242-6367
Olitsky, Eve/235 W 102nd St #12K	212-678-1045
Olsen, Mimi Vang/545 Hudson St	212-675-5410
Olson, Richard A/85 Grand St	212-925-1820
Orlin, Richard/2550 Olinville Ave	212-882-6177
Orloff, Denis/682 Carroll St #1	718-965-0385
Ormond, Rick/420 Lexington Ave #2738	212-697-8525
Osaka, Rick/14-22 30th Dr	718-956-0015

PQ Pace, Don/546 Pacific St — 718-797-3184

Panos, Joyce/29-05 159th St	718-939-7339
Pantuso, Mike/350 E 89th St	212-534-3511
Pappas, Joanne/532 5th St #3R	718-499-4429
Paragraphics/427 3rd St	718-965-2231
Pardy, Cindy/200 W 15th St	212-243-4209
Parker, Robert Andrew/81 Greene St	212-925-3053
Parsons, John/420 Lexington Ave #2738	212-697-8525
Paslavsky, Evan/510-7 Main St N	212-759-3985
Pasternak, Robert/114 W 27th St #55	212-675-0002
Paul, Tony/467 W 57th St	212-986-1840
Peak, Bob/50 E 50th St	212-752-8490
Pearson, Jim/866 UN Plaza #4014	212-644-2020
Pechanel, Vladimir/34-43 Crescent St #4C	718-729-3973
Pederson, Judy/96 Greene St	212-226-3675
Peele, Lynwood/344 W 88th St	212-799-3305
Pelavin, Daniel/46 Commerce St #4	212-929-2706
Pelikan, Judy/200 E 78th St	212-570-9069
Pendleton, Roy/215 Park Ave S	212-674-8080
Percivalle, Rosanne/430 W 14th St #510	212-243-6589
Perez, Vince/43 E 19th St	212-254-4996
Perini, Benny/88 Richmond St	718-622-4578
Personality Inc/501 Fifth Ave #1407	212-490-2450

Peterson, Cheryl/81 Greene St	212-925-3053
Peterson, Robin/411 West End Ave	212-724-3479
Petragnani, Vincent/853 Broadway	212-677-9100
Petruccio, Steven/201 E 28th St	212-532-0928
Pettingill, Ondre/245 Bennett Ave #7B	212-942-1993
Pierson, Mary Louise/310 W 56th St	212-315-3516
Pincus, Harry/160 Sixth Ave @ 210 Spring St	212-925-8071
Pinkney, Debbie/55 Hudson St #3A	212-775-1810
Pinturov/15 W 72nd St	212-799-2231
Piscopia, Joe/114 Beadel St	718-384-2206
Plastic Triangle/146 W 16th St #4B	718-875-9345
Podwill, Jerry/108 W 14th St	212-255-9464
Pogue, Deborah Bazzel/48 W 21st St 9th Fl	212-243-4412
Poladian, Girair/42 E 23rd St #6N	212-601-2520
Pollack, Scott/333 E 66th St	212-686-2528
Popp, Wendy/95 Horatio St #203	212-807-0840
Porter, Frederick/1457 Broadway #1001	212-840-8223
Powell, Ivan/58 W 15th St	212-741-2539
Powers, Christine/198 Berkeley Pl	718-783-1266
Powers, Tom/1457 Broadway #1001	212-840-8223
Prato, Rodica/154 W 57th St #123	212-683-1362
Purdom, Bill/780 Madison Ave #7A	212-988-4566
Pyk, Jan/19 E 48th St 3rd Fl	212-838-0050
Quartuccio, Dom/5 Tudor City Pl #2201	212-661-1173
Quon, Mike Design Office/568 Broadway #703	212-226-6024

R Racz, Michael/224 Ave B #23 — 212-477-0401

Radigan, Bob/280 Madison Ave #1402	212-775-1810
Ragland, Greg/258 Broadway #4E	212-513-7218
Raglin, Tim/138 W 74th St	212-873-0538
Rainbow Grinder/55 Hudson St #3A	212-775-1810
Rane, Walter/60 E 42nd St #428	212-867-8092
Realo, Perry A/155 E 2nd St #4B	212-254-5635
Reay, Richard/515 W 236th St	212-884-2317
Reddin, Paul/120 Windsor Pl	718-965-0647
Reed, Chris/14 E 4th St #817	212-677-7198
Reed, Herb/1457 Broadway #1001	212-840-8223
Reese, Ralph/6 W 20th St 2nd Fl	212-243-7362
Reim, Melanie/214 Riverside Dr #601	212-749-0177
Reingold, Alan/155 E 38th St	212-697-6170
Renfro, Ed/250 E 83rd St #4E	212-879-3823
Reott, Paul/51-10 Van Horn St	718-426-1928
Reynolds, Scott/308 W 30th St #9B	212-239-0009
Rice, John/1457 Broadway #1001	212-840-8223
Rich, Anna M/777 St Marks Ave	718-604-0121
Rich, Norman/2557 Marion Ave #3G	212-733-5140
Richards, Linda/128 E 91st St	212-673-1600
Ridgeway, Ron/330 W 42nd St #3200 NE	212-714-0130
Rigie, Mitch/201 E 28th St	212-532-0928
Rigo, Martin/43 E 19th St	212-254-4996
Risko, Robert/201 W 11th St	212-989-6987
Rixford, Ellen/308 W 97th St	212-865-5686
Roberts, Phil/420 Lexington Ave #2911	212-986-5680
Robinson, Charles/866 UN Plaza #4014	212-644-2020
Rodriguez, Robert/501 Fifth Ave #1407	212-490-2450
Rogers, Lilla/483 Henry St	718-624-6862
Roman, Barbara/48-53 205th St	718-229-6393
Romer, Dan/125 Prospect Park W	718-768-3632
Romero, Javier/54 W 21st St #1002	212-206-9175
Root, Barry/265 Riverside Dr #4F	212-927-8378
Roper, Bob/43-17 55th St	718-898-8591
Rosen, Terry/101 W 81st St #508	212-580-4784
Rosenblum, Richard/392 Fifth Ave	212-279-2068
Rosenthal, Doug/24 Fifth Ave	212-475-9422
Rosenthal, Marc/230 Clinton St	718-855-3071
Rosenzweiz, Myra/310 W 90th St	212-362-9871
Rosner, Meryl/51 E 42nd St #716	212-986-3282
Ross Culbert Holland & Lavery/15 W 20th St	212-206-0044
Ross, Barry/211 W 102nd St #5A	212-663-7386
Ross, Bronwen/866 UN Plaza #4014	212-644-2020
Ross, Ian/106 Lexington Ave #2	212-685-4178
Ross, Richard/204 W 20th St	212-675-8800

Illustrators

Continued

Please send us your additions and updates.

Roy, Frederick/205 W 14th St	212-255-0775
Rubel, Nicole/349 W 85th St #61	212-799-5855
Ruddell, Gary/18 E 16th St	212-206-0322
Rudenjack, Phyllis/245 E 72nd St	212-772-2813
Ruff, Donna/595 West End Ave	212-255-1635
Ruffins, Reynold/15 W 20th St 9th Fl	212-627-5220
Ruiz, Artie/43 E 19th St	212-254-4996
Russell, Billy D/483 Columbus Ave #2B	212-873-7975
Russell, Melissa/350 E 89th St	212-502-3976
Ryan, Terry/330 W 4th St	212-688-1080

S

Sabanosh, Michael/433 W 34th St #18B	212-947-8161
Sabin, Robert/60 E 42nd St #428	212-867-8092
Saffion, Lino/3159 37th St	718-721-4891
Saksa Art & Design/41 Union Sq W #1001	212-255-5539
Saldutti, Denise/463 West St #354H	212-255-9328
Salina, Joe/60 E 42nd St #505	212-682-1490
Samuels, Mark/25 Minetta Ln #4A	212-777-8580
Sanders, Jane/47-51 40th St #6D	718-786-3505
Sanjulian/43 E 19th St	212-688-1080
Santa-Donato, Paul/25 W 39th St	212-921-1550
Santoro, Christopher/201 E 28th St	212-532-0928
Sargent, Claudia K/15-38 126th St	718-461-8280
Saris, Anthony/103 E 86th St	212-831-6353
Sauber, Rob/420 Lexington #2911	212-986-5680
Sawka, Jan/353 W 53rd St #1W	212-682-2462
Schaare, Harry/60 E 42nd St #428	212-867-8092
Schaedler, Sally/1457 Broadway #1001	212-840-8223
Schaer, Miriam/522 E 5th St	212-673-4926
Schaller, Tom/2255 Broadway #303	212-362-5524
Scheld, Betsy/429 E 65th St #13	212-734-6226
Schimoler, Thomas/181 Baltic St #1	718-237-1586
Schmidt, Bill/60 E 42nd St #428	212-867-8092
Schmidt, Chuck/853 Broadway	212-677-9100
Schneegass, Martinu/35 Carmine #9	212-645-0836
Schongut, Emanuel/194 Third Ave	212-475-0440
Schottland, Miriam/470 W 23rd St	212-242-6367
Schreier, Joshua/466 Washington St	212-925-0472
Schuler, Mark/420 Lexington Ave #2911	212-986-5680
Schumer, Arlen/313 E Sixth St	212-254-8242
Schwarz, Jill Karla/80 N Moore St	212-227-2444
Scott, Bob/106 Lexington Ave #1	212-684-2409
Scrofani, Joe/353 W 53rd St #1W	212-682-2462
Seaver, Jeffrey/130 W 24th St #4B	212-741-2279
Segal, John/324 W 101st St	212-662-3278
Seltzer, Isadore/336 Central Park West	212-666-1561
Sempe, J J/81 Greene St	212-925-3053
Sentnor, Robert/3871 Sedgwick Ave	212-884-7048
Shafer, Ginger/113 Washington Pl	212-989-7697
Shahinian, Brenda/81 Greene St	212-925-3053
Shap, Sandra/853 Broadway	212-677-9100
Shea, Mary Anne/154 Eighth Ave #4	212-929-7964
Shega, Marla/60 E 42nd St #505	212-682-1490
Shenefield, Barbara/22 W 25th St	212-254-1946
Sherman, Mary/165 E 32nd St	212-686-3514
Sherman, Maurice/3855 Nautilus Ave	718-763-7455
Shields, Charles/226 E 53rd St	212-755-4945
Shohet, Marti/26 W 17th St 8th Fl	212-627-1299
Shub, Steve/48 W 21st St 9th Fl	212-243-4412
Siciliano, Gerald/261 Fourth Ave	718-636-4561
Siegel, Norm/333 E 49th St	212-980-8061
Silverman, Burt/324 W 71st St	212-799-3399
Singer, Alan D/70 Prospect Park W	718-768-6664
Singer, Paul Design/494 14th St	718-499-8172
Skardinski, Stan/201 E 28th St	212-532-0928
The Sketch Pad Studio/6 Jane St	212-989-7074
Skolsky, Mark/15 W 72nd St	212-799-2231
Skopp, Jeniffer/465 11th St	718-965-3754
Slack, Chuck/60 E 42nd St #505	212-682-1490
Slackman, Charles B/320 E 57th St	212-758-8233
Slavin, Fran/452 Myrtle Ave	718-403-9643
Sloan, William/568 Broadway #405	212-226-8110

Smalley, Guy/40 E 34th St #203	212-683-0339
Smith, Brett/353 W 53rd St #1W	212-682-2462
Smith, Gary/48 W 21st St 9th Fl	212-243-4412
Smith, Jeffrey/226 E 53rd St	212-755-4945
Smith, Joseph/159 John St #6	212-825-1475
Smith, Laura/12 E 14th St #4D	212-206-9162
Smith, Trudi/866 UN Plaza #4014	212-644-2020
Smith, Vicki/504 E 5th St #6C	212-475-1671
Smollin, Mike/420 Lexington Ave #2911	212-986-5680
Smythe, Danny/853 Broadway	212-677-9100
Sneberger, Dan/60 E 42nd St #428	212-867-8092
Soderlind, Kirsten/111 Wooster St # PH C	212-925-0491
Soldwedel, Kip/420 Lexington Ave #2911	212-986-5680
Solie, John/420 Lexington Ave #2911	212-986-5680
Solomon, Debra/536 W 111th St #55	212-662-5619
Soloski, Tommy/49 W 85th St #1D	212-787-7142
Sottung, George/420 Lexington Ave #2911	212-986-5680
Spacak, Peter/611 Broadway #610	212-505-6802
Spector, Joel/130 E 16th St	212-254-3527
SPOLLEN, CHRIS/362 CROMWELL AVE (P 37)	**718-979-9695**
Sposato, John/43 E 22nd St #2A	212-477-3909
Stabin, Victor/100 W 15th St #4I	212-243-7688
Stahl, Nancy/194 Third Ave	212-475-0440
Stallard, Peter/60 E 42nd St #505	212-682-1490
Stamaty, Mark Alan/118 MacDougal St	212-475-1626
Staples, Matthew/141 W 36th St 14th Fl	212-279-7935
Starace, Tom/2 Stuyvesant Oval	212-228-8674
Stavrinos, George/76 W 86th St #6D	212-724-1557
Steadman, Barbara/330 E 33rd St #10A	212-684-6326
Steadman, E T/470 W 23rd St	212-242-6367
Steiner, Frank/60 E 42nd St #428	212-867-8092
Stephens, Lynn/52 W 87th St #4A	212-787-6195
Sternglass, Arno/622 Greenwich St	212-675-5667
Sterrett, Jane/160 Fifth Ave #700	212-929-2566
Stewart, Arvis/866 UN Plaza #4014	212-644-2020
Stewart, Pat/201 E 28th St	212-352-0928
Stillerman, Robbie/230 E 44th St #2F	212-661-7149
Stillman, Susan/126 W 71st St #5A	212-724-5634
Stone, Gilbert/58 W 15th St	212-741-2539
Strachan, Bruce/224 E 11th St #24	718-383-1264
Streeter, Sabina/141 Wooster St	212-254-7436
Strimban, Robert/349 W 20th St	212-243-6965
Studio 23/6 W 20th St 2nd Fl	212-243-7362
Suares, J C/156 Fifth Ave #1222	212-645-6772
Sullivan, Suzanne Hughes/1960 Broadway #2E	212-873-3797
Sweny, Stephen/217 E 29th St #52	212-532-4072
Szabo, Gustav/440 West End Ave	212-362-7376
Szilagyi, Mary/410 Central Park West	212-666-7578
Szygiel, Jas/165 E 32nd St	212-686-3514

T

Taba, Eugene/1185 Sixth Ave 8th Fl	212-730-0101
Taback, Simms/38 E 21st St	212-674-8150
Taleporos, Plato/333 E 23rd St	212-689-3138
Tankersley, Paul/29 Bethune St	212-924-0015
Tauss, Mark/484 W 43rd St #40H	212-228-4662
Taylor, Doug/106 Lexington Ave	212-674-6346
Taylor, Katrina/216 E 45th St	212-661-0850
Tedesco, Michael/120 Boerum Pl #1E	718-596-4179
Ten, Arnie/446 62nd St	718-745-8477
Terreson, Jeffrey/420 Lexington Ave #2911	212-986-5680
Theakston, Greg/15 W 72nd St	212-799-2231
Thomas, Darby/197-19 99th Rd, Hollis, NY	718-465-4761
Thompson, Thierry/420 Lexington Ave #2911	212-986-5680
Thomson, Bill/18 E 16th St	212-206-0322
Thorpe, Peter/254 Park Ave S #6C	212-477-0131
Tierney, Tom/201 E 28th St	212-532-0928
Tocchet, Mark/1071 Arnow Ave	212-654-4667
Tod-Kat Studios/353 W 53rd St #1W	212-682-2462
Torpedo Studios/350 E 89th St	212-502-3976
Travers, Robert/60 E 42nd St #428	212-867-8092
Trondsen, Bob/60 E 42nd St #428	212-867-8092
Trossman, Michael/411 West End Ave #16D	212-799-6852

Illustrators

ILLUSTRATORS

Trull, John/1573 York Ave	212-535-5383
Tunstull, Glenn/47 State St	718-875-9356
Turk, Steve/100 Sullivan St #2F	212-226-4578

U V
Uram, Lauren/251 Washington Ave #2F	718-789-7717
Vaccaro, Lou/866 UN Plaza #4014	212-644-2020
Valla, Victor/60 E 42nd St #428	212-867-8092
Varlet-Martinelli/200 W 15th St	212-243-4209
Vaux, Jacquie Marie/165 E 32nd St	212-686-3514
Vebell, Victoria/157 W 57th St	212-247-1130
Vecchio, Carmine/200 E 27th St	212-683-2679
Velasquez, Eric/226 W 113th St	212-866-2209
Ventura, Dana/134 W 32nd St #602	212-244-4270
Vermont, Hillary/218 East 17th St	212-674-3845
Victor, Joan B/863 Park Ave #11E	212-988-2773
Vierheller, Shirley/485 Madison Ave	212-355-2323
Viskupic, Gary/	212-684-2974
Vitsky, Sally/24 W 57th St #605	212-489-8777
Viviano, Sam/25 W 13th St	212-242-1471
Vogt, Elaine/242 E 83rd St	212-988-6430
Vosk, Alex/521 E 82nd St #1A	212-737-2314
Voth, Gregory/231 W 20th St	212-807-9766

W
Wajdowicz, Jurek/1123 Broadway	212-807-8144
Waldman, Michael/506 W 42nd St #G4	212-239-8245
Walker, Jeff/60 E 42nd St #428	212-867-8092
Walker, John S/47 Jane St	212-242-3435
Waller, Charles/35 Bethune St PH C	212-989-5843
Wallner, Alexandra & John/866 UN Plaza #4014	212-644-2020
Wanamaker, Jo Ann/225 W 86th St	212-724-1786
Ward, Donna/19 E 48th St 3rd Fl	212-838-0050
Warhola, James/23-11 40th Ave	718-937-6467
Wasserman, Randi/28 W 11th St	212-254-0468
Wasson, Cameron/4 S Portland Ave #3	718-875-8277
Weaver, Robert/42 E 12th St	212-254-4289
Weiman, Jon/147 W 85th St #3F	212-787-3184
Weinstein, Maury/40 W 27th St 5th Fl	212-684-6700
Weisbecker, Philippe/21 W 86th St	212-580-3143
Weisser, Carl/38 Livingston St #33	718-834-0952
Weissman, Sam/2510 Fenton Ave	212-840-3300
Wells, Skip/244 W 10th St	212-242-5563
Whistl'n Dixie/25 W 39th St #902	212-764-5591
White, Richard A/250 Washington Ave	718-783-3244
Whitehead, Samuel B/206 Eighth Ave	718-965-2047
Whitehouse, Debora/1457 Broadway #1001	212-840-8223
Whitesides, Kim/501 Fifth Ave #1407	212-490-2450
Wiemann, Roy/PO Box 271/Prince St Sta	212-431-3793
Wilkinson, Bill/155 E 38th St	212-697-6170
Wilkinson, Chuck/60 E 42nd St #505	212-682-1490
Willardson + Assoc/194 Third Ave	212-475-0440
Williams, Elizabeth/349 E 82nd St	212-517-4593
Williams, Richard/58 W 15th St	212-741-2539
Wilshire, Mary/217 E 85th St #15W	212-570-4165
Wilson, Amanda/346 E 20th St	212-260-7567
Wilson, Deborah C/339 E 33rd St #1R	212-532-5205
Wilton, Nicholas/147 Sullivan St #2C	212-254-0571
Wind, Bodhi/43 E 19th St	212-254-4996
Winkowski, Fred/48 W 71st St	212-724-3136
Winters, Nina/20 W 77th St	212-877-3089
Wohlberg, Ben/43 Great Jones St	212-254-9663
Wolfe, Bruce/194 Third Ave	212-475-0440
Wolff, Punz/151 E 20th St #5G	212-254-5705
Wolfgang, Sherri/313 E 6th St	212-254-8242
Wollman, Paul/60 E 42nd St #505	212-682-1490
Wood, Page/48 W 21st St 9th Fl	212-243-4412
Woodend, James/420 Lexington Ave #2738	212-697-8525
Woodman, Jowill/334 W 49th St #5RW	212-765-8406
Wray, Wendy/194 Third Ave	212-475-0440
Wyatt, Kathy/43 E 19th St	212-254-4996
Wynne, Patricia/446 Central Pk West	212-865-1059

Y
Yalowitz, Paul/215 E 26th St #7	212-532-0859

Yankus, Marc/179 Prince St	212-228-6539
Yeldham, Ray/420 Lexington Ave #2911	212-986-5680
Yemi/605 E 11th St	212-627-1269
Yiannias, Vicki/200 W 15th St	212-243-4209
Yip, Jennie/6103 Twentieth Ave	718-236-0349
York, Judy/165 E 32nd St	212-686-3514
Yule, Susan Hunt/176 Elizabeth St	212-226-0439

Z
Zacharow, M Christopher/109 Waverly Pl #4R	212-460-5739
Zagorski, Stanislaw/142 E 35th St	212-532-2348
Zaid, Barry/108 E 35th St #1	212-889-3337
Zann, Nicky/155 W 68th St	212-724-5027
Zeldich, Arieh/866 UN Plaza #4014	212-644-2020
Zick, Brian/194 Third Ave	212-475-0440
Ziemienski, Dennis/55 Cheever Pl	718-643-7055
Ziering, Bob/151 W 74th St	212-873-0034
Zimic, Tricia/341 E 6th St #4A	212-598-4228
Zimmerman, Jerry/48 W 20th St 2nd Fl	212-620-7777
Zimmerman, Robert/254 Park Ave S #6C	212-477-0131
Zwarenstein, Alex/15 W 72nd St	212-799-2231

Northeast

A
Abel, Ray/18 Vassar Pl, Scarsdale, NY	914-725-1899
Adam Filippo & Moran/1206 Fifth Ave, Pittsburgh, PA	412-261-3720
Adams, Norman/229 Berkeley #52, Boston, MA	617-266-3858
Addams, Charles/PO Box 8, Westport, CT	203-227-7806
Adler, Bente/103 Broad St, Boston, MA	617-266-3858
Agans, Carol/3 Medford Ave, Mercerville, NJ	
Ahmed, Ghulan Hassan/5738 Edgepark Rd, Baltimore, MD	301-444-8246
Alcorn, Bob/434 South Main St, Heightstown, NJ	609-448-4448
Aldrich, Susan/PO Box 114, Northport, NY	516-261-6220
Alexander, Paul R/37 Pine Mountain Rd, Redding, CT	203-544-9293
Allanson, Bryan/275 W Clinton St, Dover, NJ	212-696-7403
ALSOP, MARK/324 AUBURNDALE AVE, AUBURNDALE, MA	
(P 11)	**617-527-7862**
Alterio, Caroline/116 Commonwealth Ave, Boston, MA	617-236-1920
Amicosante, Vincent/, , RI	617-241-7640
Ancas, Karen/7 Perkins Sq #11, Jamaica Plain, MA	617-522-2958
Anderson, Richard/490 Bleeker Ave, Mamaroneck, NY	914-381-2682
Annand, Jonathan/10 Manor Rd, Harrington Park, NJ	201-768-6072
Archambault, David/56 Arbor St, Hartford, CT	203-523-9876
Ashmead, Hal/39 Club House Dr, Woodbury, CT	203-263-3466
Avati, Jim/10 Highland Ave, Rumson, NJ	201-530-1480

B
Bailey, Brian/619 Bloomfield St #3, Hoboken, NJ	201-963-9643
Baker, Lori/33 Richdale Ave, Cambridge, MA	617-492-5689
Bakley, Craig/68 Madison Ave, Cherry Hill, NJ	609-428-6310
Ball, Harvey/340 Main St, Wooster, MA	617-752-9154
Bang, Molly Garrett/43 Drumlin Rd, Falmouth, MA	617-540-5174
Bangham, Richard/2006 Cascade Rd, Silver Spring, MD	301-649-4919
Banta, Susan/17 Magazine St, Cambridge, MA	617-876-8568
Barbagallo, Ron/36 E 35th St, Bayonne, NJ	201-437-2394
Barger, Peter/116 Commonwealth Ave, Boston, MA	617-513-1557
Barkley, James/25 Brook Manor, Pleasantville, NY	914-769-5207
Barrett, Tom/151 Tremont St #14R, Boston, MA	617-426-1918
BARUFFI, ANDREA/341 HUDSON TERRACE, PIERMONT, NY	
(P 13)	**914-359-9542**
Becker, N Neesa/241 Monroe St, Philadelphia, PA	215-925-5363
Beisel, Dan/4713 Ribble Ct, Ellicott City, MD	301-461-6377
Belser, Burkey/1818 N St NW #110, Washington, DC	202-775-0333
Bendis, Keith/275 Tanglewylde Rd, Lake Peekskill, NY	914-528-7378
Bennett, James/301 Willow Ave #1, Hoboken, NJ	201-963-1457
Benson, John D/2111-A Townhill Rd, Baltimore, MD	301-665-3395
Berlin, Frederic/220 Ferris Ave, White Plains, NY	914-946-1950
Berry, Sheila & Richard/803 E 5th St, South Boston, MA	617-269-1338
Biggins, Wendy/185 Goodhill Rd, Weston, CT	203-226-7674
Birling, Paul/444 Bedford Rd, Pleasantville, NY	914-747-2220
Birmingham, Lloyd P/Peekskill Hollow Rd, Putnam Valley, NY	914-528-3207
Blaser, Michael/91 Hundred Rd, Wellesley Hills, MA	617-235-8658
Bomzer Design Inc/66 Canal St, Boston, MA	617-227-5151

Illustrators
Continued

Please send us your additions and updates.

Bone, Fred/28 Farm Court, New Britain, CT	203-827-8418
Bono, Peter/59 Van Houten, Passaic, NJ	201-778-5489
Booth, Brenda/PO Box 596, Chappaqua, NY	914-238-5325
Booth, George/PO Box 8, Westport, CT	203-227-7806
Boston Illustration Co/371 Beacon St, Boston, MA	617-236-0350
Botsis, Peter/1239 University Ave, Rochester, NY	716-271-2140
Boynton, Lee A/7 Gladden Rd, Annapolis, MD	301-263-6336
Brautigan, Don/29 Cona Ct, Haledon, NJ	201-956-7710
Bray, Mark/RD 1/Huffs Church Rd, Alburtis, PA	215-845-3229
Breeden, Paul M/Sullivan Harbor Farm, Sullivan Harbor, ME	207-422-3007
Breiner, Joanne/11 Webster St, Medford, MA	617-354-8378
Bremer/Keifer Studio/21 Lake Dr, Enfield, CT	203-749-9680
Brewster, John/601 Riverside Ave, Westport, CT	203-226-4724
Brickman, Robin/32 Fort Hoosac Pl, Williamstown, MA	413-458-9853
Bridy, Dan Visuals Inc/119 First Ave, Pittsburgh, PA	412-288-9362
Brown, Michael D/932 Hungerford Dr #24, Rockville, MD	301-762-4474
Brown, Richard/3979 York Rd, Furlong, PA	212-683-1362
Bucella, Martin/72 Martinique Dr, Cheektowaga, NY	716-668-0040
Bullock, Wilbur/229 Berkeley #52, Boston, MA	617-266-3858
Burroughs, Miggs/PO Box 6, Westport, CT	203-227-9667
Burrows, Bill & Assoc/103 E Read St, Baltimore, MD	301-752-4615
Buschini, Maryanne/238 W Highland Ave, Philadelphia, PA	215-242-8517
Butcher, Jim/1357 E Macphail Rd, Bel Air, MD	301-879-6380
Buterbaugh, Richard/, ,	302-656-8809
Butterworth, Martin/700 Plaza Dr, Seacaucus, NJ	201-330-8080
Byrd, Robert/409 Warwick Rd, Haddonfield, NJ	609-428-9627

C
Cable, Jerry/29 Station Rd, Madison, NJ	201-966-0124
Cagle, Daryl/17 Forest Lawn Ave, Stamford, CT	203-359-3780
Callahan, Kevin/26 France St, Norwalk, CT	203-847-2046
Calleja, Bob/490 Elm Ave, Bogota, NJ	201-488-3028
Calver, Dave/271 Mulberry St, Rochester, NY	716-271-6208
Cantin, Charles/809 Cartier, Quebec G1R 2R8, QC	418-524-1931
Caporale, Wende L/Studio Hill Farm Rte 116, N Salem, NY	914-669-5653
Caputo, Vince/444 Bedford Rd, Pleasantville, NY	914-747-2220
Caras, Peter/227 Godfrey Rd, Weston, CT	203-222-8777
Carbone, Lou/286 Slyvan Rd, Bloomfield, NJ	201-338-8678
Cardella, Elaine/215 Clinton St, Hoboken, NJ	201-656-3244
Cardillo, James/49-D Village Green, Budd Lake, NJ	201-691-1530
Carlson, Frederick H/2335 Meadow Dr, Pittsburgh, PA	412-371-8951
Carson, Jim/11 Foch St, Cambridge, MA	617-661-3321
Cascio, Peter/98 Harding Rd, Glen Rock, NJ	201-445-3262
Casilla, Robert/36 Hamilton Ave, Yonkers, NY	914-963-8165
Catalano, Sal/114 Boyce Pl, Ridgewood, NJ	201-447-5318
Cayea, John/39 Lafayette St, Cornwall, NY	914-534-2942
Cellini, Eva & Joseph/415 Hillside Ave, Leonia, NJ	201-944-6519
Chadwick, Paul/, New Milford, CT	203-868-9261
Chandler, Jean/385 Oakwood Dr, Wyckoff, NJ	201-891-2381
Chandler, Karen/14 Andrew Pl, Locust Valley, NY	516-671-8562
Chen, Tony/241 Bixley Heath, Lynbrook, NY	516-596-9158
Chui, George/2250 Elliot St, Merrick, NY	516-223-8474
Cincotti, Gerald/371 Beacon St, Boston, MA	617-236-0456
Clark, Bradley/99 Mill St, Rhinebeck, NY	914-876-2615
Clark, Cynthia Watts/99 Mill St, Rhinebeck, NY	914-876-2615
Clark, Patricia C/6201 Benalder Dr, Bethesda, MD	301-229-2986
Clarke, Bob/55 Brook Rd, Pittsford, NY	716-248-8683
Cline, Rob/356 E Main St, Newark, DE	302-368-3757
Cober, Alan E/95 Croton Dam Rd, Ossining, NY	914-941-8696
CODDBARRETT ASSOC/65 ASHBURTON AVE,	
PROVIDENCE, RI (P 16)	**401-273-9898**
Cohen, Alan R/2828 N Howard St, Baltimore, MD	301-366-3855
Cohen, Dee/10407 Parkwood Dr, Kensington, MD	202-364-1118
Cohen, Susan D/208 Park Ave #3R, Hoboken, NJ	201-659-5472
COLLYER, FRANK/RR 1 BOX 266, STONY POINT, NY (P 17)	**914-947-3050**
Concept One/Gizmo/366 Oxford St, Rochester, NY	716-461-4240
Condon, Ken/42 Jefferson St, Cambridge, MA	617-492-4301
Conge, Bob/28 Harper St, Rochester, NY	716-473-0291
Console, Carmen/8 Gettysburg Dr, Voorhees, NJ	215-463-6110
Cook, Susan Anderson/675 Leone St, Woodbridge, NJ	201-750-0977
Cooper, Bob/311 Fern Dr, Atco Post Office, NJ	609-767-0967
Cooper, Steven/26 Lafayette St, Wakefield, MA	617-245-7528
Cornell, Jeff/58 Noyes Rd, Fairfield, CT	203-259-7715

Cosatt, Paulette/60 South St, Cresskill, NJ	201-568-1436
Costas, Laura/2707 Adams Mill Rd, Washington, DC	202-265-4499
Courtney, John Jr/4-19 Grunauer Pl, Fairlawn, NJ	201-797-8090
Cox, Birck/1305 E Chocolate Ave, Hershey, PA	717-533-1878
Craft, Kinuko/RFD #1 PO Box 167, Norfolk, CT	203-542-5018
Cramer, D L/10 Beechwood Dr, Wayne, NJ	201-628-8793
Crofut, Bob/8 New St, Ridgefield, CT	203-431-4304
Crompton, Jack/229 Berkeley #52, Boston, MA	617-266-3858
Cross, Peter/210 Cherry St, Katonah, NY	914-232-3975
Cusano, Steve/731 N 24th St, Philadelphia, PA	215-232-6666

D
Daily, Don/57 Academy Rd, Bala Cynwyd, PA	215-664-5729
Dally, Lyman M/166 Beachwood Rd, Parsippany, NJ	201-887-1338
Daly, Tom/47 E Edsel Ave, Palisades Park, NJ	201-943-1837
Darrow, Whitney/PO Box 8, Westport, CT	203-227-7806
Davidian, Anna/229 Berkeley #52, Boston, MA	617-266-3858
Davidson, Peter/144 Moody St, Waltham, MA	617-899-3239
Davis, Gary/1 Cedar Pl, Wakefield, MA	617-245-2628
Davis, Harry/731 N 24th St, Philadelphia, PA	215-232-6666
Davis, Michael/516 Orange St, New Haven, CT	203-773-0526
Dawes, Joseph/20 Church Ct, Closter, NJ	201-767-8127
Dean, Glenn/RD #2 Box 788, Sussex, NJ	201-827-7350
Dedini, Eldon/PO Box 8, Westport, CT	203-227-7806
DeKiefte, Kees/185 Goodhill Rd, Weston, CT	203-226-7674
Demarest, Robert/87 Highview Terr, Hawthorne, NJ	201-427-9639
Demers, Donald/PO Box 4009, Portsmouth, NH	207-439-1463
DeMuth, Roger Taze/2627 DeGroff Rd, Nunda, NY	716-468-2685
Dey, Lorraine/10 Highland Ave, Rumson, NJ	201-530-1480
Dion, Madge/320 Palmer Terrace, Mamaroneck, NY	212-730-0101
Dior, Jerry/9 Old Hickory Ln, Edison, NJ	201-561-6536
Dodge, Paul/731 N 24th St, Philadelphia, PA	215-232-6666
Dodge, Susan/6 W Main St, Middletown, DE	302-378-9657
Donnarumma, Dom/25 Stanwood Rd, New Hyde Park, NY	516-248-5113
Dorsey, Bob/107 H Hoopes Ave, Auburn, NY	315-255-2367
Drescher, Joan/23 Cedar, Hingham, MA	617-749-5179
Drinkwine, Sharon/229 Berkeley #52, Boston, MA	617-266-3858
Driver, Ray/5725-B Harpers Farm, Columbia, MD	301-596-6955
Duke, Christine/Maple Ave Box 471, Millbrook, NY	914-677-9510
Duke, W E Illustration/312 Westfield Rd, Holyoke, MA	413-536-8269
Dunne, Tom/16 Cherry St, Locust Valley, NY	516-676-3641
DuPont, Lane/6 Gorham Ave	203-222-1562
Dverin, Anatoly/229 Berkeley #52, Boston, MA	617-266-3858
Dykeman, James/14 Cherry Hill Cir, Ossining, NY	914-941-0821

E
Eagle, Mike/7 Captains Ln, Old Saybrook, CT	203-388-5654
Ebel, Alex/30 Newport Rd, Yonkers, NY	914-961-4058
Echevarria, Abe/Box 98 Anderson Rd, Sherman, CT	203-355-1254
Eckstein, Bob/107 Cherry Lane, Medford, NY	516-654-0291
Edens, John/2464 Turk Hill Rd, Victor, NY	716-425-3441
Eggleton, Bob/57 Eddy St #513, Providence, RI	401-831-5030
Ehrenfeld, Jane/39 Nieman Ave, Lynbrook, NY	516-599-6327
Einsel, Naiad/26 S Morningside Dr, Westport, CT	203-226-0709
EINSEL, WALTER/26 S MORNINGSIDE DR, WESTPORT, CT	
(P 19)	**203-226-0709**
Ellis, Jon/3204 Whitney Ct, Bensalem, PA	215-750-6180
English, M John/18 McKinley St, Rowayton, CT	203-866-3734
Enos, Randall/11 Court of Oaks, Westport, CT	203-227-4785
Epstein, Aaron/2015 Aspen Dr, Plainsboro, NJ	212-410-7169
Epstein, Len/720 Montgomery Ave, Narbeth, PA	215-664-4700
Epstein, Lorraine/Dows Ln, Irvington-on-Hudson, NY	914-591-7470
Eucalyptus Tree Studio/2220 N Charles St, Baltimore, MD	301-243-0211

F
Faria, Jeff/937 Garden St, Hoboken, NJ	201-656-3063
Farnsworth, Bill/PO Box 653, New Milford, CT	203-355-1649
Farris, Joe/PO Box 8, Westport, CT	203-227-7806
Feeney, Betsy/444 Bedford Rd, Pleasantville, NY	914-747-2220
Feinen, Jeff/4702 Sawmill Rd, Clarence, NY	716-759-8406
Fiedler, Joseph D/500 Sampsonia Way, Pittsburgh, PA	412-322-7245
Fisher, Mark/506 Windsor Dr, Framingham, MA	617-451-6528
Fitz-Maurice, Jeff/720 Crown St, Morrisville, PA	215-295-3266
Flat Tulip Studio/Rt 1 Box 146, Marietta, PA	717-426-1344
Flynn, Maura/8 George St, Manhasset, NY	516-627-6608

Illustrators

Continued

Please send us your additions and updates.

Ford, Pam/251 Greenwood Ave, Bethel, CT	203-797-8188
Forman, James/2 Central Pl, Lynbrook, NY	516-599-2046
Foster, Susan/3903 Rosemary St, Chevy Chase, MD	301-652-3848
Fox, Jerry/1480 Rt 46 #63-A, Parsippany, NJ	201-299-8368
Franke, Phil/10 Nehring Ave, Babylon Village, NY	516-661-5778
Frinta, Dagmar/ NY	518-861-6942
Fromentine, Christine/227 Godfrey Rd, Weston, CT	203-222-8777
Fuchs, Bernard/3 Tanglewood Ln, Westport, CT	203-227-4644
Fuller, Steve/7 Winding Brook Dr, Guilderland, NY	518-456-7496

G

Gaadt, George/888 Thorn, Sewickley, PA	412-741-5161
Garland, Michael/78 Columbia Ave, Hartsdale, NY	914-946-4536
Gay-Kassel, Doreen/7 S Lanning Ave, Hopewell, NJ	609-466-9457
Gebert, Warren/71 Sedgwick Ave, Yonkers, NY	914-968-5247
Geraci, Phillip/RFD, Marlborough, NH	603-847-9009
Gerlach, Cameron/2644 N Calvert St, Baltimore, MD	301-889-3093
Geyer, Jackie/107 6th St #207 Fulton Bldg, Pittsburgh, PA	412-261-1111
Giardina, Laura/12 Buckingham Ct, Pomona, NY	914-354-0871
Gist, Linda E/224 Madison Ave, Fort Washington, PA	215-643-3757
Giuliani, Alfred/10 Woodland Terrace, Lincroft, NJ	201-741-8756
Giusti, Robert/340 Long Mountain Rd, New Milford, CT	203-354-6539
Glanzman, Louis S/154 Handsome Ave, Sayville, NY	516-472-3320
Glasbergen, Randy J/PO Box 611, Sherburne, NY	607-674-9492
Glazer, Ted/28 West View Rd, Spring Valley, NY	914-354-1524
Glessner, Marc/24 Evergreen Rd, Somerset, NJ	201-249-5038
Gold, Al/266 Mill St, Elmwood Park, NJ	201-794-8786
Goldberg, Richard/368 Congress St 5th Fl, Boston, MA	617-338-6369
Goldinger, Andras/215 C St SE #310, Washington, DC	202-543-9029
Goldman, Marvin/RD 3 Gypsy Trail Rd, Carmel, NY	914-225-8611
Gordley, Scott/229 Berkeley #52, Boston, MA	617-266-3858
Goryl, John/128 Diamond St, Swoyersville, PA	717-961-3355
GRABER, JACK/707 UNION ST, SCHENECTADY, NY (P 22)	**518-370-0312**
Grashow, James/14 Diamond Hill Rd, W Redding, CT	203-938-9195
Green, Norman/11 Seventy Acres Rd, W Redding, CT	203-438-9909
Greene, Anne/34 Woodford St, Worcester, MA	617-752-2572
Gregory, Lane/91 Hundred Rd, Wellesley Hills, MA	617-235-8658
Grewe, Nilou/4 Wakeman Pl, Larchmont, NY	914-834-6820
Grote, Rich/21 Tyndale Rd, Hamilton Square, NJ	609-586-5896
Groyher, Jack/707 Union St, Schenectady, NY	518-370-0312
Gustafson, Dale/56 Fourbrooks Rd, Stamford, CT	203-322-5667
Gyson, Mitch/4412 Colmar Gardens Dr E, Baltimore, MD	301-243-3430

H

Haas, Gordon & Shelly/86 Prospect Ave, Montclair, NJ	201-746-0539
Haefele, Steve/2101 Crompond Rd, Peekskill, NY	914-736-0785
Haffner, Marilyn/185 Holworthy St, Cambridge, MA	617-354-0696
Hallman, Tom/38 S 17th St, Allentown, PA	215-776-1144
Hamilton, Laurie/5403 McArthur Blvd NW, Washington, DC	202-362-8041
Hamilton, William/81 Sand Rd, Ferrisburg, VT	802-877-6869
Handelsman, Bud/PO Box 8, Westport, CT	203-227-7806
Handville, Robert T/99 Woodland Dr, Pleasantville, NY	914-769-3582
Haney, William/16 River Road RD #3, Neshanic Station, NJ	201-369-3848
Harden, Laurie/RD 4/Box 31, Boonton Township, NJ	201-335-4578
Hardy, Neil O/2 Woods Grove, Westport, CT	203-226-4446
Harris, Ellen/125 Pleasant St #602, Brookline, MA	617-739-1867
Harris, Peter/37 Beech St, Wrenthem, MA	617-384-2470
Harsh, Fred/185 Goodhill Rd, Weston, CT	203-226-7674
Harsh, William/8 Euliata Terr, Brighton, MA	617-427-5182
Harvey, Paul/45 Fern Valley Rd, Weston, CT	203-226-5234
Hatton, Enid/46 Parkway, Fairfield, CT	203-259-3789
Hazelton, Betsey/106 Robbins Dr, Carlisle, MA	617-369-5309
Healy, Deborah/72 Watchung Ave, Upper Montclair, NJ	201-746-2549
Hearn, Diane Dawson/22 Spring St, Pauling, NY	914-855-1152
Hearn, Walter/22 Spring St, Pauling, NY	914-855-1152
Heath, R Mark/4338 Roland Springs Dr, Baltimore, MD	301-366-4633
Heimann, Steve/PO Box 406, Oradell, NJ	201-345-9132
Hejja, Attila/300 Edward St, Roslyn Heights, NY	516-621-8054
Henderson, Dave/7 Clover Ln, Verona, NJ	201-783-5791
Herrick, George W/120 Hillside Ave, Hartford, CT	203-527-1940
Herring, Michael/RD 1 Box 205A, Cold Spring, NY	914-265-9476
Hess, Mark/88 Quicks Lane, Katonah, NY	914-232-5870
Hess, Richard/Southover Farms RT 67, Roxbury, CT	203-354-2921
Heyck, Edith/92 Water St, Newburyport, MA	617-462-9027

Hildebrandt, Greg/1148 Parsippany Blvd, Parsippany, NJ	201-334-0353
Hildebrandt, Tim/10 Jackson Ave, Gladstone, NJ	201-234-2149
Hill, Michael/828 Park Ave, Baltimore, MD	301-728-8767
Hoffman, Martin/RD 2 Box 50, Worcester, MA	607-638-5472
Hoffman, Nancy/16 Ridge Dr, Berkeley Heights, NJ	201-665-2177
Hogan, Jamie/36 Green St, Jamaica Plain, MA	617-522-5503
Hokanson, Lars/PO Box 199, Hopeland, PA	717-733-9066
Howard, Bill/5301 New Hampshire Ave NW, Washington, DC	202-882-6253
Howell, Van/PO Box 2036, Setauket, NY	516-862-9450
Huehnergarth, John/196 Snowden Ln, Princeton, NJ	609-921-3211
Huelsman, Amy/24 S Calumet Ave, Hastings on Hudson, NY	914-478-0596
Huerta, Gerard/45 Corbin Dr, Darien, CT	203-656-0505
Hulsey, John/Rte 9D, Garrison, NY	914-424-3544
Hunt, Stan/PO Box 8, Westport, CT	203-227-7806
Hurd, Jane/4002 Virginia Pl, Bethesda, MD	301-229-7966
Hurwitz, Joyce/7314 Burdette Ct, Bethesda, MD	301-365-0340
Huyssen, Roger/45 Corbin Dr, Darien, CT	203-656-0200

IJ

Inouye, Carol/Gulf Schoolhouse Rd, Cornwallville, NY	518-239-6173
Iosa, Ann/185 Goodhill Rd, Weston, CT	203-226-7674
Irish, Gary/45 Newbury St, Boston, MA	617-247-4168
Irwin, Virginia/67 Spring Park Ave, Jamaica Plain, MA	617-469-3186
Jacobus, Tim/PO Box 142, Glasser, NJ	201-663-4501
Jaeger Design Studio/2025 I St NW #622, Washington, DC	202-785-8434
James, Derek/561 Main St, E Keansburg, NJ	201-787-0231
Jean, Carole/45 Oriole Dr, Roslyn, NY	516-742-3322
Johnson, B E/366 Oxford St, Rochester, NY	716-461-4240
Johnson, David A/299 South Ave, New Canaan, CT	203-966-3269
Jones, Barry/2725 Mary St, Easton, PA	215-253-3709
Jones, Donald/15 Dehart Pl, Madison, NJ	201-765-9750
Jones, George/52 Old Highway, Wilton, CT	203-762-7242
Jones, John R/335 Town St, East Haddam, CT	203-873-9950
Jones, Marilyn/25 Sylvan Rd, Verona, NJ	201-239-6488
Jones, Robert/47 W Stewart, Lansdowne, PA	215-626-1245
Jones, Roger/15 Waldo Ave, Somerville, MA	617-628-1487
Jordan, Laurie/185 Goodhill Rd, Weston, CT	203-226-7674
Jordan, Polly/29 Warren Ave, Somerville, MA	617-776-0329
Juhasz, Victor/576 Westminster Ave, Elizabeth, NJ	201-351-4227

K

Kane, Kid/9 W Bridge St, New Hope, PA	215-862-0392
Karp, Julie/1 Ash Pl #3G, Great Neck, NY	516-466-4093
Kidd, Tom/59 Cross Brook Rd	212-569-1421
Kilroy, John/28 Fairmount Way, Nantasket, MA	617-925-0582
Kingham, Dave/42 Blue Spruce Circle, Weston, CT	203-226-3106
Kingsbery, Guy/305 High St, Milford, CT	203-878-8939
Kinstrey, Jim/1036 Broadway, W Longbranch, NJ	201-229-0312
Kline, Rob/39 Newbury St 2nd Fl, Boston, MA	617-536-2132
Kluglein, Karen/37 Cary Rd, Great Neck, NY	516-487-1323
Knabel, Lonnie/20 Berkeley Ct, Brookline, MA	617-232-1291
Koeppel, Gary/368 Congress, Boston, MA	617-426-8887
Kossin, Sanford/143 Cowneck Rd, Port Washington, NY	516-883-3038
Kovarsky, Anatol/PO Box 8, Westport, CT	203-227-7806
Krosnick Studio/686 Undercliff Ave, Edgewater, NJ	201-224-5495
Kulczak, Frank/412 Diller Rd, Hanover, PA	717-637-2580
Kupper, Ketti/21 Old Stone Rd, Darien, CT	203-656-0010
Kyriacos, Betty/2221 Penfield Ln, Bowie, MD	301-249-3606

L

LaCaourse, Carol/506 Windsor Dr, Framingham, MA	617-451-6528
Langdon, John/106 S Marion Ave, Wenonah, NJ	609-468-7868
Lanza, Barbara/PO Box 118, Pine Island, NY	914-258-4601
Lasasso, Gary/49 Foxhall Ave, Kingston, NY	914-331-3333
Lawton, April/31 Hampshire Dr, Farmingdale, NY	516-454-0868
Layman, Linda J/Hill Rd, South Hamilton, MA	617-468-4297
Lazarevich, Mila/185 Goodhill Rd, Weston, CT	203-226-7674
Lazarus, Robin/814 Edgewood Dr, Westbury, NY	516-334-8609
Leamon, Tom/18 Main St, Amherst, MA	413-256-8423
Lee, Bryce/120 77th St, N Bergen, NJ	201-662-9106
Lee, Robert/444 Bedford Rd, Pleasantville, NY	914-747-2220
Lehew, Ron/17 Chestnut St, Salem, NJ	609-935-1422
Leibow, Paul/369 Lantana Ave, Englewood, NJ	201-567-2561
Levine, Ned/301 Frankel Blvd, Merrick, NY	516-378-8122
Levy, Robert S/1023 Fairway Rd, Franklin Square, NY	516-872-3713

Illustrators

Continued

Please send us your additions and updates.

Lewczak, Scott/95 Kimberly Rd, Colonia, NJ	201-388-5262
Leyburn, Judy/123 Charles St, Boston, MA	617-227-2443
Leyonmark, Roger/229 Berkeley #52, Boston, MA	617-266-3858
Lidbeck, Karin/185 Goodhill Rd, Weston, CT	203-226-7674
Loccisano, Karen/185 Goodhill Rd, Weston, CT	203-226-7674
Lofaro, Jerry/22 Bruce Lane, Farmingdale, NY	516-752-7519
Logan, Ron/PO Box 306, Brentwood, NY	516-273-4693
Longacre, Jimmy/185 Goodhill Rd, Weston, CT	203-226-7674
Lorenz, Al/185 Goodhill Rd, Weston, CT	516-354-5530
Lose, Hal/533 W Hortter St, Philadelphia, PA	215-849-7635
Lowes, Tom/41 Hartsen St, Rochester, NY	716-442-8325
Lubey, Dick/726 Harvard, Rochester, NY	716-442-6075
Luzak, Dennis/88 Main St, New Canaan, CT	203-966-5681
Lyhus, Randy/4853 Cordell Ave #3, Bethesda, MD	301-986-0036
Lynn, Kathy/1741 Bainbridge, Philadelphia, PA	215-545-5039
M MacArthur, Dave/147 E Bradford Ave #B, Cedar Grove, NJ	201-857-1046
MacFarland, Jean/Laurel Lake Rd, Lenox, MA	413-637-3647
MacNeill, Scott/74 York St, Lambertville, NJ	609-397-4631
Maffia, Daniel/44 N Dean St, Englewood, NJ	201-871-0435
Mager, Janet/229 Berkeley #52, Boston, MA	617-266-3858
Mahoney, Katherine/60 Hurd Rd, Belmont, MA	617-489-0406
Mandel, Saul/163 Maytime Dr, Jericho, NY	516-681-3530
Marchesi, Steve/185 Goodhill Rd, Weston, CT	203-226-7674
Mardon, John/185 Goodhill Rd, Weston, CT	203-226-7674
Mariuzza, Pete/146 Hardscrabble Rd, Briarcliff Manor, NY	914-769-3310
Marmo, Brent/4 Davis Ct, Brookline, MA	617-566-7330
Martin, Henry/PO Box 8, Westport, CT	203-227-7806
Martin, Richard/485 Hilda St, East Meadow, NY	516-221-3630
Mascio, Tony/4 Teton Ct, Voorhees, NJ	609-424-5278
Mattelson, Marvin/37 Cary Rd, Great Neck, NY	516-487-1323
Mattingly, David/1112 Bloomfield St, Hoboken, NJ	201-659-7404
Mattiucci, Jim/247 N Goodman St, Rochester, NY	716-271-2280
Mayforth, Hal/19 Irma Ave, Watertown, MA	617-923-4668
Mayo, Frank/265 Briar Brae, Stamford, CT	203-322-3650
Mazzini, John/161 Wadsworth Ave, Plainedge, NY	516-796-6118
McCURDY, MICHAEL/145 LAKE BUEL RD, GREAT BARRINGTON, MA (P 27)	**413-528-2749**
McElfish, Susan/5725 Phillips Ave, Pittsburgh, PA	412-521-6041
McGovern, Mike/PO Box 187, Reading, MA	617-944-2326
McGuire, Arlene Phoebe/495 Old York Rd, Jenkintown, PA	215-576-5123
McIntosh, Jon C/268 Woodward St, Boston, MA	617-277-9530
McManimon, Tom/2700 Route 22, Union, NJ	201-688-2700
McVicker, Charles/4 Willow St, Princeton, NJ	609-924-2660
MDB Communications/932 Hungerford Dr #23, Rockville, MD	301-279-9093
Meeker, Carlene/24 Shore Dr, Winthrop, MA	617-846-5117
Melgar, Fabian/14 Clover Dr, Smithtown, NY	516-543-7561
Melius, John/3028 New Oak Ln, Bowie, MD	301-249-3709
Menk, France/PO Box 350, Pound Ridge, NY	212-628-7546
Metcalf, Roger/132 Hendrie Ave, Riverside, CT	203-637-9524
Michael, Lillian/23 W Mt Pleasant Ave, Philadelphia, PA	215-247-4298
Miles, Elizabeth/185 Goodhill Rd, Weston, CT	203-226-7674
Miller, Warren/PO Box 8, Westport, CT	203-227-7806
Milnazik, Kim/73-2 Drexelbrook Dr, Drexel Hill, PA	215-259-1565
Mistretta, Andrea/5 Bohnert Pl, Waldwick, NJ	201-652-7531
Miyake, Yoshi/185 Goodhill Rd, Weston, CT	203-226-7674
Mladinich, Charles/7 Maspeth Dr, Melville, NY	516-271-8525
Modell, Frank/PO Box 8, Westport, CT	203-227-7806
Montague, Andrea/59 Cross Brook Rd, New Milford, CT	212-569-1421
Mooney, Gerry/2 Main St #3S, Dobbs Ferry, NY	914-693-8076
Moore, Jack/131 Cedar Lake West, Denville, NJ	201-627-6931
Moores, Jeff/72 S Maple Ave, Springfield, NJ	201-379-4657
Morales, Manuel/PO Box 1763, Bloomfield, NJ	201-429-0848
Moran, Mike/25 Anthony Dr, Madison, NJ	201-966-6229
Morecraft, Ron/97 Morris Ave, Denville, NJ	201-627-6728
Morrissey, Belinda/541 Hillcrest St, Teaneck, NJ	201-836-7016
Morrow, Skip/Ware Rd/Box 123, Wilmington, VT	802-464-5523
Moscowitz, Stephen/701 Monroe Ave, Rochester, NY	716-442-8433
MOSS, DONALD/232 PEACEABLE ST, RIDGEFIELD, CT (P 30,31)	**203-438-5633**
Musy, Mark/PO Box 755, Buckingham, PA	215-764-8851

Myers, Lou/58 Lakeview Ave, Peekskill, NY	914-737-2307
N Nachbar, Amy/57 Lorimar Ave, Providence, RI	401-274-4591
Nacht, Merle/374 Main St, Weathersfield, CT	203-563-7993
Neibart, Wally/1715 Walnut St, Philadelphia, PA	215-564-5167
Neider, Alan/151 Penn Common, Milford, CT	203-878-9260
Newman, Robert/420 Springbrook Ln, Hatboro, PA	215-672-8079
Nix, Jonathon J/Carter Rd, Becket, MA	413-684-0441
Noome, Mike/55 Bulkey Ave, N Westport, CT	203-255-5977
Norman, Marty/5 Radcliff Blvd, Glen Head, NY	516-671-4482
Noyes, David/20 Hemenway St #26, Boston, MA	617-262-3611
Noyse, Janet/118 Woodland Rd, Wyncote, PA	215-572-6975
O O'Leary, John/547 N 20th St, Philadelphia, PA	215-561-7377
Oh, Jeffrey/2635 Ebony Rd, Baltimore, MD	301-661-6064
Olsen, Jimmy/50 New York Ave, Clark, NJ	201-388-0967
Olson, Victor/Fanton Meadows, West Redding, CT	203-938-2863
Otnes, Fred/Chalburn Rd, West Redding, CT	203-938-2829
Oughton, Taylor/Jamison, Bucks County, PA	215-598-3246
P Page, Don/112 Chamounix Rd, St Davids, PA	216-293-9673
Palladini, David/PO Box 991, Water Mill, NY	212-983-1362
Palulian, Dickran/18 McKinley St, Rowayton, CT	203-866-3734
Parker, Earl/5 New Brooklyn Rd, Cedar Brook, NJ	609-567-2925
Parker, Ed Assoc/9 Carlisle St, Andover, MA	617-475-2659
Parry, Ivor A/4 Lorraine Dr, Eastchester, NY	212-889-0707
Passalacqua, David/325 Versa Pl, Sayville, NY	516-589-1663
Pate, Rodney/185 Goodhill Rd, Weston, CT	203-226-7674
Patrick, Pamela/398-A Burrows Run, Chadds Ford, PA	215-388-7654
Pavia, Cathy/185 Goodhill Rd, Weston, CT	203-226-7674
Payne, Thomas/11 Colonial Ave, Albany, NY	518-482-1756
Pels, Winslow Pinney/Hack Green Rd, Pound Ridge, NY	914-764-8470
Pennor, Robert/928 Summit Rd, Cheshire, CT	203-758-4008
Pentick, Joseph/RD 4 Box 231, Kingston, NY	914-331-8197
Perina, Jim/33 Regent St, N Plainfield, NJ	201-757-3010
Pidgeon, Jean/38 W 25th St, Baltimore, MD	301-235-1558
Piejko, Alex/5796 Morris Rd, Marcy, NY	315-732-4852
Pinkney, Jerry/41 Furnace Dock Rd, Croton-on-Hudson, NY	914-271-5238
Pirk, Kathy/5112 45th St NW, Washington, DC	202-244-5736
Pisano, Al/21 Skyline Dr, Upper Saddle River, NJ	212-213-3204
Pizzo, Robert/26 Pondfield Rd W #4F, Bronxville, NY	914-961-5020
Perina, Platania, Nancy Anne/44 Cornell, Williston Park, NY	516-747-2417
Plotkin, Barnett/126 Wooleys Ln, Great Neck, NY	516-487-7457
Porzio, Ed/131 Bartlett Rd, Winthrop, MA	617-846-3875
Presnall, Terry/91 Hundred Rd, Wellesly Hills, MA	617-235-8658
Price, George/PO Box 8, Westport, CT	203-227-7806
Printz, Larry/1840 London Rd, Abington, PA	215-572-0331
Prokell, Jim/307 4th Ave #200, Pittsburgh, PA	412-232-3636
Provensen, Alice/Meadowbrook Ln Box 171, Staatsburg, NY	914-266-3245
R Rabl, Lorraine/249 Queen Anne Rd, Bogota, NJ	201-342-4647
Radiomayonnaise/112-A Appleton St, Boston, MA	617-536-5440
Ramage, Alfred/5 Irwin St #7, Winthrop, MA	617-846-5955
Ravel, Ken/2 Myrtle Ave, Stoney Creek, PA	215-779-2105
Recchia, Dennis & Janet/94 Oak St, Tenafly, NJ	201-569-6136
Reeser, Tracy P (Mr)/254 Andover Rd, Glenmoore, PA	215-942-2597
Regnier, Mark/97 Wachusett, Jamaica Plain, MA	617-522-5295
Reiner, John/107 Jackson Ave, Huntington, NY	516-360-3049
Reinert, Kirk/, , RI	401-884-8434
Rera, Lou/340 Linwood Ave, Buffalo, NY	716-885-0015
Richter, Mische/PO Box 8, Westport, CT	203-227-7806
Rickerd, David/22 Canvas Back Rd, Manalapan, NJ	201-446-2119
Riley, Frank/108 Bamford Ave, Hawthorne, NJ	201-423-2659
Roberts & Van Heusen/1153 Narragansett Blvd, Cranston, RI	401-785-4490
Roberts, Cheryl/1153 Narragansett Blvd, Cranston, RI	401-785-4490
Rodericks, Michael/129 Lounsbury Rd, Trumbull, CT	203-268-1551
Roffo, Sergio/42 Shepard St #3, Boston, MA	617-787-5861
Rogers, Glenda/318 Lexington Ave, Syracuse, NY	315-478-4509
Roman, Irena & John/369 Thom Clapp Rd Box 571, Scituate, MA	617-545-6514
Roselius, Elizabeth/7309 Balt Nat'l Pike, Frederick, MD	301-473-4058
Rosenbaum, Harry/444 Bedford Rd, Pleasantville, NY	914-747-2220

ILLUSTRATORS

Rosenbaum, Jonathan/444 Bedford Rd, Pleasantville, NY	914-747-2220
Ross, Larry/53 Fairview Ave, Madison, NJ	201-377-6859
Roth, Gail/185 Goodhill Rd, Weston, CT	203-226-7674
Roth, Shoshanna/720 Washington St, Hoboken, NJ	201-653-8865
Rutherford, Jenny/185 Goodhill Rd, Weston, CT	203-226-7674
Ryan, Carol/14 Adams St, Port Washington, NY	516-944-3953

S

Sahli, Barbara/8212 Flower Ave, Takoma Park, MD	301-585-5122
Salerno, Steve/204 Edwards St, New Haven, CT	203-777-0107
Sanders, Bruce/229 Berkeley #52, Boston, MA	617-266-3858
Sanderson, Ruth/185 Goodhill Rd, Weston, CT	203-226-7674
Santa, Monica/185 Goodhill Rd, Weston, CT	203-226-7674
Santoliquido, Delores/60 W Broad St #6H, Mt Vernon, NY	914-667-3199
Santore, Charles/138 S 20th St, Philadelphia, PA	215-563-0430
Saunders, Rob/368 Congress St 5th Fl, Boston, MA	617-542-6114
Saxon, Charles/PO Box 8, Westport, CT	203-227-7806
Schenker, Bob/31 W Circular Ave, Paoli, PA	215-640-9993
Schleinkofer, David/344 Crown St, Morrisville, PA	215-295-8622
Schlemme, Roy/585 Center St, Oradell, NJ	212-921-9732
Schneider, Rick/260 Montague Rd, Leverett, MA	413-548-9304
Schofield, Glen/214 Washington Pl, Cliffside Pl, NJ	201-941-8853
Schorr, Kathy Staico/PO Box 142, Roxbury, CT	203-266-4084
Schorr, Todd/PO Box 142, Roxbury, CT	203-266-4084
Schreck, John/371 Beacon St #2, Boston, MA	617-236-0350
Schroeder, Michael/1327 Walnut St, Reading, PA	215-375-9055
Schroeppel, Richard/31 Walnut Hill Rd, Amherst, NH	603-673-0997
Schweigert, Carol/791 Tremont St #E406, Boston, MA	617-262-8909
Sekeris, Pim/570 Milton St #10, Montreal H2X 1W4, QU	514-844-0510
Selwyn, Paul/287 Laurel St, Hartford, CT	203-278-6757
Shachat, Andrew/66 Katydid Dr, Somerville, NJ	201-722-1667
Sharpe, Jim/21 Ten O'Clock Ln, Weston, CT	203-226-9984
Shaw, Barclay/49 Elbow Hill Rd, Brookfield, CT	203-775-8477
Sherman, Gene/500 Helendale Rd, Rochester, NY	716-288-8000
Sherman, Oren/30 Ipswich #301, Boston, MA	617-437-7368
Shiff, Andrew Z/153 Clinton St, Hopkinton, MA	617-435-3607
Sikorski, Tony/2304 Clark Bldg, Pittsburgh, PA	412-391-8366
Sims, Blanche/185 Goodhill Rd, Weston, CT	203-226-7674
Sisti, Jerald/34 Wiedmann Ave, Clifton, NJ	201-478-7488
Smallwood, Steve/2417 3rd St Bsmt, Fort Lee, NJ	201-585-7923
Smith, Douglas/405 Washington St #2, Brookline, MA	617-566-3816
Smith, Elwood H/2 Locust Grove Rd, Rhinebeck, NY	914-876-2358
Smith, Gail Hunter/PO Box 217, Barnegat Light, NJ	609-494-9136
Smith, Marcia/112 Linden St, Rochester, NY	716-461-9348
Smith, Raymond/222 Willow Ave, Hoboken, NJ	201-653-6638
Smith, Susan B/290 Newbury #2F, Boston, MA	617-266-4441
Snyder, Emilie/50 N Pine St #107, Marietta, PA	215-426-2906
Soileau, Hodges/350 Flax Hill Rd, Norwalk, CT	203-852-0751
Sokolowski, Ted/RD #2 Box 408, Lake Ariel, PA	717-937-4527
Somerville, Kevin/120 Sylvan Ave, Englewood Cliffs, NJ	201-944-2632
Sorensen, Robert/59 Granville Ave, Milford, CT	203-874-6381
Soyka, Ed/231 Lafayette Ave, Peekskill, NY	914-737-2230
Spanfeller, Jim/Mustato Rd, Katonah, NY	914-232-3546
Sparacio, Mark & Erin/30 Rover Ln, Hicksville, NY	516-579-6679
Sparkman, Gene/15 Bradley Lane, Sandy Hook, CT	203-426-0061
Sparks, Richard & Barbara/2 W Rocks Rd, Norwalk, CT	203-866-2002
Spellman, Susan/91 Hundred Rd, Wellesley Hills, MA	617-235-8658
Spence, Jim/33 Elsie St, Patchogue, NY	516-654-4650
Spiak, Sharon/35 Monroe Ave, Dumont, NJ	201-387-9395
Springer, Sally/317 S Lawrence Ct, Philadelphia, PA	215-925-9697
Sprouls, Kevin/335 Readington Rd, Sommerville, NJ	201-722-5408
Sprovach, Craig/604 Fairfield Ave, Stamford, CT	203-327-2529
Stahl, Benjamin F/134 Washington St, S Norwalk, CT	203-838-5308
Stasolla, Mario/162-A Spice Bush Ln, Tuxedo, NY	203-637-3366
Steig, William/PO Box 8, Westport, CT	203-227-7806
Steinberg, Herb/PO Box 65, Roosevelt, NJ	609-448-4724
Steiner, Joan/Plattekill Rd, Greenville, NY	518-966-8908
Sternberg, Robert/8 Prince St, Rochester, NY	716-244-6327
Stevens, John/18 Manos Pl, Huntington Sta, NY	516-351-9263
Stevenson, James/PO Box 8, Westport, CT	203-227-7806
Stewart, Jonathan/113 South 20th St, Philadelphia, PA	215-546-3649
Stirweis, Shannon/31 Fawn Pl, Wilton, CT	203-762-7058
Stone, David K/6 Farmview Rd, Port Washington, NY	516-627-7040

Sturrock, Walt/57 E Shawnee Trl, Wharton, NJ	201-663-0069
Syverson, Henry/PO Box 8, Westport, CT	203-227-7806
Szabo, Leslie/4 S Main St #204, S Norwalk, CT	203-838-2155

T

Tandem Graphics/5313 Waneta Rd, Bethesda, MD	301-320-5008
Tarlow, Phyllis/42 Stafford Rd, New Rochelle, NY	914-235-9473
Tatore, Paul/10 Wartburg Pl, Valhalla, NY	914-769-1061
Tauss, Herb/S Mountain Pass, Garrison, NY	914-424-3765
Taylor, Dahl/508 Grand St, Troy, NY	518-274-6379
TeleVision Corp/928 Mt Carmel Rd, Parkton, MD	301-343-1111
Tennison, James/117 Ironworks Rd, Clinton, CT	203-669-7883
Thompson, Arthur/39 Prospect Ave, Pompton Plains, NJ	201-835-3534
Thompson, John M/64 Ganung Rd, Ossining, NY	201-653-1675
Tiani, Alex/4 Lafayette Court, Greenwich, CT	203-661-3891
Tinkelman, Murray/75 Lakeview Ave W, Peekskill, NY	914-737-5960
Toelke, Cathleen/16 Tremont St, Boston, MA	617-242-7414
Toelke, Ron/229 Berkeley #52, Boston, MA	617-266-3858
Torrisi, Gary/91 Hundred Rd, Wellesley Hills, MA	617-235-8658
Traub, Patricia/25-30 Aspen St, Philadelphia, PA	215-769-1378
Treatner, Meryl/721 Lombard St, Philadelphia, PA	215-627-2297
Two-H Studio/45 Corbin Dr, Darien, CT	203-656-0200

V

Van Horn, Michael/RD 2/Box 442/Milan Hill Rd, Red Hook, NY	914-758-8407
VanHouten, Norbert/RD 1/Roxbury Rd, Hudson, NY	518-672-4738
Vann, Bob/5306 Knox St, Philadelphia, PA	215-843-4841
Vargo, Kurt/94 New Monmouth Rd, Middletown, NJ	201-671-8679
Vartanoff, Ellen/6825 Wilson Ln, Bethesda, MD	301-229-3846
Vella, Ray/345 Main St #7D, White Plains, NY	914-997-1424
Veno, Joe/20 Cutler Rd, Hamilton, MA	617-468-3165
Vernaglia, Michael/1251 Bloomfield St, Hoboken, NJ	201-659-7750
Viskupic, Gary/7 Westfield Dr, Center Port, NY	516-757-9021
Vissichelli, Joe/100 Mayfield Ln, Valley Stream, NY	516-872-3867

W

Walczak, Larry/803 Park Ave, Hoboken, NJ	201-798-6176
Waldman, Neil/47 Woodlands Ave, White Plains, NY	914-693-2782
Walker, Norman/37 Stonehenge Rd, Weston, CT	203-226-5812
Wallerstein, Alan/61 Tenth St, Ronkonkoma, NY	516-981-3589
Waters, Julian/924 Pennsylvania Ave SE, Washington, DC	202-544-5258
Watson, Karen/100 Churchill Ave, Arlington, MA	617-641-1420
Watts, Mark/616 Iva Ln, Fairless HIlls, PA	215-945-9422
Weber, Robert/PO Box 8, Westport, CT	203-227-7806
Wehrman, Richard/247 N Goodman St, Rochester, NY	716-271-2280
Weissman, Bari/41 Atkins St, Brighton, MA	617-783-0230
Welkis, Alan/53 Heights Rd, Fort Salonga, NY	516-261-4160
Weller, Linda Boehm/185 Goodhill Rd, Weston, CT	203-226-7674
Westlake, Laura/7 Dublin Hill Dr, Greenwich, CT	203-869-8010
Whelan, Michael/23 Old Hayrake Rd, Danbury, CT	203-798-6063
White, Caroline/1 Langdon St #22, Cambridge, MA	617-661-1283
Whiting, Ann/2627 Woodley Place NW, Washington, DC	202-462-1519
Wilcox, David/PO Box 232, Califon, NJ	201-832-7368
Willert, Beth Anne/303 Brook Ave, N Plainfield, NJ	201-755-4327
Williams, Frank/731 North 24th St, Philadelphia, PA	215-232-6666
Williams, Marcia/84 Duncklee St, Newton Highlands, MA	617-332-5823
Williams, Ted/170 Elder Dr, Macedon, NY	315-986-3770
Williges, Mel/2 Hepworth Ct, W Orange, NJ	201-731-4086
Wilson, Gahan/PO Box 8, Westport, CT	203-227-7806
Wilson, Mary Lou/247 N Goodman St, Rochester, NY	716-271-2280
Witschonke, Alan/28 Tower St #2, Somerville, MA	617-628-5601
Wolfe, Jean/27 E Central Ave #B9, Paoli, PA	215-644-2941
Woodman, Bill/PO Box 8, Westport, CT	203-227-7806
Wright, Bob Creative Group Inc/247 North Goodman St, Rochester, NY	716-271-2280
Wu, Leslie/65 Greenfield Ln, Rochester, NY	716-385-3722

YZ

Young, Debby/8 Steephill Rd, Weston, CT	203-227-5672
Young, Robert Assoc/78 North Union St, Rochester, NY	716-546-1973
Young, Wally/7 Birch Hill Rd, Weston, CT	203-227-5672
Ziegler, Bill/PO Box 8, Westport, CT	203-227-7806
Ziegler, Kathy/40201 Delaire Landing, Philadelphia, PA	215-632-8238
Zinn, Ron/117 Village Dr, Jerico, NY	516-933-2767
Zuba, Bob/105 W Saylor Ave, Plains, PA	717-824-9730

Illustrators

Continued

Please send us your additions and updates.

Zuckerman, Craig/724 W Walnut St, Long Beach, NY — 516-432-9483

Southeast

AB

Armstrong, Lynn/2510 Whisper Wind Ct, Roswell, GA — 404-642-5512
The Artsmith/440 College Ave/Box 391, Athens, GA — 404-543-5555
Arunski, Joe & Assoc/8600 SW 86th Ave, Miami, FL — 305-271-8300
Azzinaro, Lewis/11872 St Trinians Ct, Weston, VA — 703-620-5155
Bailey, R.C./255 Westward Dr, Miami Springs, FL — 305-888-6309
Barklew, Pete/110 Alpine Way, Athens, GA — 404-546-5058
Boone, Joe/ PW Inc/PO Box 99337, Louisville, KY — 502-499-9220
Bowles, Aaron/1686 Sierra Woods Ct, Reston, VA — 703-471-4019
Boyter, Charles/1956 Bramblewood Dr NE, Atlanta, GA — 404-727-5665
Burke, Gary/14418 NE Third Ct, N Miami, FL — 305-893-1998
Butler, Meryl/PO Box 991, Virginia Beach, VA — 804-491-2280

C

Carey, Mark/1209 Anne Ave, Chesapeake, VA — 804-482-7646
Carey, Wayne/532 Hardendorp Ave, Atlanta, GA — 404-378-0426
Carter, Kip/225 Beaverdam Dr, Winterville, GA — 404-542-5384
Carter, Zane/1008 N Randolph St #100, Arlington, VA — 703-527-7338
Castellanos, Carlos/20150-08 NE 3rd Ct, Miami, FL — 305-651-9524
Chaffee, Doug/Rt 3 Groveland Dr, Taylors, SC — 803-877-9826
Coastline Studios/6959 Stapoint Ct #J, Winterpark, FL — 305-657-6355
Collins, Samuel/PO Box 73004, Birmingham, AL — 205-991-0557
Correnti, Sandra/Rt 1 Box 256, Leesburg, VA — 703-777-9113
Covington, Neverne/2919 56th St South, Gulfport, FL — 813-347-0746
Crane, Gary/523 W 24th St, Norfolk, VA — 804-627-0717
Crunk, Matt/Rte 5 Box 39, Killen, AL — 205-757-2029

DEF

DeBro, James/2725 Hayden Dr, Eastpoint, GA — 404-344-2971
DeLahoussaye, Jeanne/816 Foucher, New Orleans, LA — 504-581-2167
Dove Design Studio/275 14th St NW, Atlanta, GA — 404-873-2209
Dunlap, Leslie/3745 Keller Ave, Alexandria, VA — 703-379-9692
Eldredge, Ernie/2683 Vesclub Cir, Birmingham, AL — 205-822-3879
Faure, Renee/600 Second St, Neptune Beach, FL — 904-246-2781
Findley, John/213 Elizabeth St, Atlanta, GA — 404-659-7103
Firestone, Bill/1506 N Ivanhoe St, Alexandria, VA — 703-532-2923
Fisher, Mike/3811 General Pershing, New Orleans, LA — 504-827-0382
Fleck, Tom/One Park Pl #120, Atlanta, GA — 404-355-0729
Frank, Cheryll/2216 Eastgate Way, Tallahasse, FL — 904-385-3717

G

Gaadt, David/2103 Tennyson Dr, Greensboro, NC — 919-288-9727
Galey, Chuck/211 Lea Circle, Jackson, MS — 601-372-5103
George, Eugene/2905 Saint Anne St, New Orleans, LA — 504-482-3774
Gordon, Jack/3201 S 5th St, Arlington, VA — 703-979-3236
Gorman, Martha/3057 Pharr Ct Nrth NW #E6, Atlanta, GA — 404-261-5632
Graphics Group/6111 PchtreeDunwdy Rd#G101, Atlanta, GA — 404-391-9929
Graphics Illustrated/5720-E North Blvd, Raleigh, NC — 919-878-7883
Greathead, Ian/2975 Christopher's Court, Marietta, GA — 404-952-5067
Guthrie, Dennis/645 Raven Springs Tr, Stone Mtn, GA — 404-874-6733

HI

Hamilton, Marcus/12225 Ranburne Rd, Charlotte, NC — 704-545-3121
Havaway, Jane/806 Briarcliff Rd, Atlanta, GA — 404-872-7284
Henderling, Lisa/800 West Ave #345, Miami Beach, FL — 305-531-1771
Herring & Klem/PO Box 48453, Atlanta, GA — 404-945-8652
Hickey, John/3821 Abingdon Circle, Norfolk, VA — 804-853-2956
Hicks, Richard Edward/3635 Pierce Dr #76, Chamblee, GA — 404-457-8928
Hilfer, Susan/PO Box 50552, Columbia, SC — 803-799-0689
Hinojosa, Albino/1802 Furman, Ruston, LA — 318-255-2820
Hogenkamp, Johnna/704 W 46th St, Kansas City, MO — 816-753-5312
Hunter, Katherine/1120 Scaly Bark Rd #115-D, Charlotte, NC — 704-332-9118
Hyatt, Mitch/4171 Buckingham Ct, Marietta, GA — 404-924-1241
Hyatt, Steven/4171 Buckingham Ct, Marietta, GA — 404-924-1241
Image Electronic Inc/3525 Piedmont Rd NE #110, Atlanta, GA — 404-262-7610
Irvin, Trevor/330 Southerland Terrace, Atlanta, GA — 404-377-4754

JKL

James, Bill/15840 SW 79th Ct, Miami, FL — 305-238-5709
Jarvis, David/275 Indigo Dr, Daytona Beach, FL — 904-255-1296
Johnson, Pamela R/1415 N Key Blvd, Arlington, VA — 703-525-5012
Jones, Jack/401 W Peachtree St NW #1720, Atlanta, GA — 404-881-6627
Kanelous, George/2864 Lake Valencia Blvd E, Palm

Harbor, FL — 813-784-8528
Kerns, Jeffrey/48 Peachtree Ave, Atlanta, GA — 404-233-5158
Kilgore, Susi/2905 Bay Villa, Tampa, FL — 813-837-9759
Lam, John/5209 N Stanford Dr, Nashville, TN — 615-297-5669
Landis, Jeff/1372 Fiftieth Ave NE, St Petersburg, FL — 813-525-0757
Lee, Kelly/3511 N 22nd St, Arlington, VA — 703-527-4089
Left, Stephen/1351 S Dixie Hwy #E8, Pompano Beach, FL — 305-942-1851
Lester, Mike/1001 Eulalia Rd, Atlanta, GA — 404-233-3093
Lewis, Chris/597 Coolidge Ave, Atlanta, GA — 404-876-0288
Little, Pam/321 Niagara St, Orange City, FL — 904-755-2919
Lovell, Rick/2860 Lakewind Ct, Alpharetta, GA — 404-442-3943
Lunsford, Annie/515 N Hudson St, Arlington, VA — 301-320-3912

MN

Marks, David/750 Clemont Dr, Atlanta, GA — 404-872-1824
Martin, Don/5110 S W 80th St, Miami, FL — 305-665-2376
Matthews, Lu/107 E Cary St, Richmond, VA — 804-782-9895
Mayer, Bill/240 Forkner Dr, Decatur, GA — 404-378-0686
McGary, Richard/180 NE 39th St #125, Miami, FL — 305-757-5720
McKelvey, David/3022 Huntshire Pl, Atlanta, GA — 404-938-1949
McKinney-Levine, Deborah/95-50 Regency Sq Blvd,
  Jacksonville, FL — 904-723-6000
McKissick, Randall/PO Box 21811, Columbia, SC — 803-798-3688
McManus, Eugenia/PO Box 39, Mayhew, MS — 601-328-5534
Mollica, Pat/75 Bennett St NW #D2, Atlanta, GA — 404-355-1200
Montgomery, Michael/PO Box 161031, Atlanta, GA — 404-366-1511
Moore, Connie Illus/4242 Inverness Rd, Duluth, GA — 404-449-9553
Moore, William "Casey"/4242 Inverness Rd, Duluth, GA — 404-449-9553
Myers, Sherwood/9770 Sterling Dr, Miami, FL — 305-238-0488
Nelson, Bill/1402 Wilmington Ave, Richmond, VA — 804-358-9637

OP

Olson, Linda/1 Charter Plaza, Jacksonville, FL — 904-723-6000
Overacre, Gary/RD 2/3802 Vineyard Trace, Marietta, GA — 404-973-8878
Ovies, Joe/1900 Emery St NW #120, Atlanta, GA — 404-355-0729
Pardue, Jack/2307 Sherwood Hall Ln, Alexandria, VA — 703-765-2622
Park, William B/110 Park Ave S, Winter Park, FL — 305-644-1553
Parrish, George/2401 Old Concord Rd, Smyrna, GA — 404-435-4189
Passarelli, Charles/919 Lenox Hill Ct, Atlanta, GA — 404-262-1209
Pate, Martin/401 W Peachtree NW, Atlanta, GA — 404-881-6627
Pawelka, Rick/5720 E North Blvd, Raleigh, NC — 919-878-7883
Penca, Gary/3184 NW 39th Ct, Lauderdale Lakes, FL — 305-733-5847

R

Rabon, Elaine Hearn/PO Box 125, Carlton, GA — 404-783-3134
RAINOCK, NORMAN/10226 PURCELL RD, GLEN ALLEN, VA
(P 35) — **804-264-8123**
Rauchman, Bob/7021 SW 58th St, Miami, FL — 305-445-5628
Rebeiz, Kathryn D/526 Druid Hill Rd, Vienna, VA — 703-938-9779
Robinette, John/3745 Woodland, Memphis, TN — 901-452-9853
Rudnak, Theo/1151 W Peachtree St NW, Atlanta, GA — 404-892-6303

S

Saffold, Joe/719 Martina Dr NE, Atlanta, GA — 404-231-2168
Salmon, Paul/5826 Jackson's Oak Ct, Burke, VA — 703-250-4943
Sams, B B/PO Box A, Social Circle, GA — 404-464-2956
Scheffer, Jules/240 Causeway Blvd, Dunedin, FL — 813-734-1265
Seif, Sue Solomon/10207 Stonemill Rd, Richmond, VA — 804-747-9684
Sheets, Jeff/8350 Rose Terrace N, Largo, FL — 813-536-1941
Shelly, Ron/6396 Manor Lane, S Miami, FL — 305-667-0154
Shepherd, Bob/8371 W Weyburn Rd, Richmond, VA — 804-320-8600
Sloan, Michael/PO Box 1397, Madison, TN — 615-865-7018
Smith, Donald/PO Box 391, Athens, GA — 404-543-5555
Soper, Patrick/214 Stephens, Lafayette, LA — 318-233-1635
Spetseris, Steve/401 W Peachtree NW #1720, Atlanta, GA — 404-881-6627
Stanton, Mark/67 Jonesboro St, McDonough, GA — 404-957-5966
Stanton, Reggie/411 Park Ave N #11, Winter Park, FL — 305-645-1661
Stenstrom, William/1107 Peachtree Rd, Augusta, GA — 404-828-3266

TUV

Taylor, Creed/206 Media Bldg/VA Tech,
  Blacksburg, VA — 703-961-5314
Thompson, Del/108 Sutton Dr, Taylors, SC — 803-268-0883
Tull, Bobbi/317 N Howard St, Alexandria, VA — 703-370-3451
Turner, Pete/938 Pamlico Dr, Cary, NC — 919-467-8466
Ulan, Helen Cerra/4227 San Juan Dr, Fairfax, VA — 703-691-0474
Vaughn, Rob/600 Curtis Pkwy/Box 660706, Miami Springs, FL — 305-885-1292

ILLUSTRATORS

Vintson, Sherry/430 Appian Way NE, St Petersburg, FL	813-822-2512
Vondracek, Woody/420 Lincoln Rd #408, Old Miami Beach, FL	305-531-7558

WXY

Wasiluck Associates/7115 University Blvd, Winter Park, FL	305-678-6964
Webber, Warren/401 W Peachtree NW, Atlanta, GA	404-221-0700
Whitver, Harry K/208 Reidhurst Ave, Nashville, TN	615-320-1795
Wilkinson, Joel/707 E McBee Ave, Greenville, SC	803-235-4483
Williams, Tim/520 Country Glen Rd, Alpharetta, GA	404-475-3146
Xenakis, Thomas/523 W 24th St #25, Norfolk, VA	804-622-2061
Yarnell, David Andrew/PO Box 286, Occoquan, VA	202-690-2987
Young, Bruce/1262 Pasadena Ave NE, Atlanta, GA	404-892-8509

Midwest

A

Ahearn, John D/151 S Elm, St Louis, MO	314-781-3389
AIR Studio/203 E Seventh St, Cincinnati, OH	513-721-1193
Allen, David/18108 Martin Ave #2F, Homewood, IL	312-798-3283
Anastas, Nicolette/535 N Michigan Ave, Chicago, IL	312-943-1668
Andic, Mike/PO Box 500, Woodstock N4S 7Y5, ON	519-439-4661
Appleoff, Sandy/3852 W 75th St, Prairie Village, KS	913-432-2821
Art Force Inc/21700 NW Hwy #570, Southfield, MI	313-569-1074
Artist Studios/666 Euclid Ave, Cleveland, OH	216-241-5355

B

Backes, Nick/405 N Wabash Ave #3203, Chicago, IL	312-329-1370
Baker, Strandell/505 N Lake Shore Dr #5307, Chicago, IL	312-661-1555
Barrows, Scott/341 Kings Cove, Lisle, IL	312-969-8056
Beck, Joan/2521 11th Ave S, Minneapolis, MN	612-870-7159
Behum, Cliff/26384 Aaron Ave, Euclid, OH	216-261-9266
Biggerstaff, Don/PO Box 3926, S Ill Univ/Med Sch, IL	217-782-2326
Blanchette, Dan/185 N Wabash Ave, Chicago, IL	312-332-1339
Boehm, Roger/529 South 7th St #539, Minneapolis, MN	612-332-0787
Boies, Alexandra/438 Portland Ave #8, St Paul, MN	612-224-6767
Boswick, Steven/3342 Capital, Skokie, IL	312-328-2042
Bowman, Bob/163 Cedarwood Ct, Palatine, IL	312-966-2770
Boyer-Pennington, Lyn/3904 Sherwood Forest Dr, Traverse City, MI	616-938-1911
Bradley, Tracy/PO Box 10719, Chicago, IL	312-334-0541
Braught, Mark/629 Cherry St #18, Terre Haute, IN	812-234-6135
Brooks, Dick/11712 N Michigan Rd #100, Zionsville, IN	317-873-1117
Busch, Lonnie/11 Meadow Dr, Fenton, MO	314-343-1330
Butler, Chris/743 N Dearborn, Chicago, IL	312-280-2288
Buttram, Andy/1636 Hickory Glen Dr, Miamisburg, OH	513-859-7428

C

Call, Ken/405 N Wabash #2613, Chicago, IL	312-644-3017
Carloni, Kurt/7392 S Delaine Dr, Oak Creek, WI	414-762-5975
Carr, Ted/43 E Ohio #1001, Chicago, IL	312-467-6865
Carroll, Michael/1228 E 54th St, Chicago, IL	312-752-6262
Centaur Studios/10 Broadway, St Louis, MO	314-421-6485
Cigliano, William/832 W Gunnison St, Chicago, IL	312-878-1659
Clarke, Tate/575 W Madison, Chicago, IL	312-440-1444
Clay, Steve/245 W North Ave, Chicago, IL	312-280-7945
Clifford, Keesler/6642 West H Ave, Kalamazoo, MI	616-375-0688
Clifford, Lawrence/3552 Halliday, St Louis, MO	314-771-6177
Clyne, Dan/535 N Michigan Ave #1416, Chicago, IL	312-943-1668
Cobane, Russell/8291 Allen Rd, Clarkston, MI	313-625-6132
Cochran, Bobbye/730 N Franklin #403, Chicago, IL	312-943-5912
Cole, Grace/4342 N Clark, Chicago, IL	312-935-8605
Collier, John/2309 Willow Creek Ln, Lawrence, KS	913-841-6442
Collins & Lund Studios/1950 Craig Rd, St Louis, MO	314-576-0003
Collins, Britt Taylor/114 Lorraine Rd, Wheaton, IL	312-938-8937
Cosgrove, Dan/405 N Wabash #4307, Chicago, IL	312-527-0375
Coulter, Marty/10129 Conway Rd, St Louis, MO	314-432-2721
Craig, John/RT 2 Box 81 Tower Rd, Soldiers Grove, WI	608-872-2371
Creative Source Inc/360 N Michigan Ave #805, Chicago, IL	312-649-9777
Crnkovich, Tony/5706 S Narragansett, Chicago, IL	312-586-9696
Csicsko, David/19 E Pearson, Chicago, IL	312-787-3256

D

Deal, Jim/2558 W Wilson Ave, Chicago, IL	312-242-3846
Deart, Greg/4041 Beal Rd, Franklin, OH	513-746-5970
Devarj, Silva/116 W Illinois, Chicago, IL	312-266-1358

DiCianni, Ron/340 Thompson Blvd, Buffalo Grove, IL	312-634-1848
Dickens, Holly/65 E South Water, Chicago, IL	312-346-1777
Dinyer, Eric/111 Jefferson Rd, St Louis, MO	314-961-1670
Doney, Todd/5123 Mango, Chicago, IL	312-463-7895
Doyle, Pat/333 N Michigan Ave, Chicago, IL	312-263-2065
Duggan, Lee/52 S Washington, Hinsdale, IL	312-986-9009
Dunlevy, Brad/3660 Jefferson, Kansas City, MO	816-931-8945
Dypold, Pat/26 E Huron St, Chicago, IL	312-337-6919
Dzielak, Dennis/323 S Franklin #600, Chicago, IL	312-786-9364

EF

Eastwood, Peter/3854 N Janssen, Chicago, IL	312-327-4704
Eaton & Iwen/307 N Michigan, Chicago, IL	312-332-3256
Eberbach, Andrea/5301 N Delaware, Indianapolis, IN	317-253-0421
Elins, Michael/155 N Michigan Ave, Chicago, IL	312-565-0030
Ellis, Christie/914 N Winchester, Chicago, IL	312-342-6343
English, Mark/Rt 3 PO Box 325, Kearney, MO	816-635-4433
Fanning, Jim/116 W 3rd St, Kansas City, MO	816-474-3922
Feldkamp-Malloy/185 N Wabash, Chicago, IL	312-263-0633
Flood, Dick/2210 S Lynn, Urbana, IL	217-328-3642
Foty, Tom/126 N 3rd St, Minneapolis, MN	612-332-8648
Frampton, Bill/49 Henderson, Toronto M6J 2B9, ON	416-535-1931
Fruzyna, Frank/435 N Michigan Ave #1832, Chicago, IL	312-644-5558

G

Gehold-Smith, William/1442 W Landt St 2nd Fl, Chicago, IL	312-262-1423
Gieseke, Thomas/7909 W 61st St, Merriam, KS	913-677-4593
Goldammer, Ken/405 N Wabash #3611, Chicago, IL	312-836-0143
Gonnella, Rick/230 N Michigan Ave, Chicago, IL	312-368-8777
Grace, Rob/7516 Lamar Ave #81, Prairie Village, KS	913-341-9135
Graef, Renee/403 W Washington Ave, Madison, WI	608-256-7796
Graham, Bill/116 W Illinois, Chicago, IL	312-467-0330
Graning, Ken/1975 Cragin Dr, Bloomfield Hills, MI	313-851-3665
Groff, David/2265 Avalon Ave, Kettering, OH	513-294-7700
Gsrmon, Van/1601 22nd St #201, W Des Moines, IA	515-225-0001
Gustafson, Glenn/405 N Wabash #4601, Chicago, IL	312-944-5680

H

Hamblin, George/944 Beach St, LaGrange Pk, IL	312-352-1780
Hammond, Franklin/1179-A W King St #310, Toronto M6K 3C5, ON	416-533-4434
Handelan-Pedersen/333 N Michigan #1005, Chicago, IL	312-782-6833
Harris, Scott/1519 W Sunnyside Ave, Chicago, IL	312-271-8476
Havlicek, Karel/405 N Wabash Ave #3203, Chicago, IL	312-329-1370
Hayes, John/224 W Huron #7E, Chicago, IL	312-266-0531
Haynes, Michael/3070 Hawthorn Blvd, St Louis, MO	314-772-3156
Heda, Jackie/3 Playter Blvd #3, Toronto M4K 2V6, ON	416-463-8692
Heyden, Yvette/30 E Huron #4005, Chicago, IL	312-472-6550
Hodde, Julie/20 Lynnray Circle, Dayton, OH	513-433-8383
Hodge, Gerald/1241 Bending Rd, Ann Arbor, MI	313-764-6163
Holladay Prints/1510 E Rusholme, Davenport, IA	319-323-2343
Horn, Robert/405 N Wabash #2815, Chicago, IL	312-644-0058
Hrabe, Curtis/2944 Greenwood Ave, Highland Park, IL	312-432-4632

IJ

Izold, Donald/20475 Bunker Hill Dr, Fairview Park, OH	216-333-9988
J H Illustration/1415 W 6th St, Cedar Falls, IA	319-277-2475
Jacobsen, Bill/405 N Wabash #1801, Chicago, IL	312-321-9558
Jamerson, David/6367 N Guilford Ave, Indianapolis, IN	317-257-8752
James, Freelance/1521 W Sunnyside, Chicago, IL	312-784-2352
Jay/17858 Rose St, Lansing, IL	312-474-9704
Johannes, Greg/233 E Wacker Dr, Chicago, IL	312-822-0560
Johnson, Diane/323 S Franklin #600, Chicago, IL	312-786-0939
Johnson, Rick/323 S Franklin, Chicago, IL	312-987-0935
Johnston, David McCall/81 Humphrey St, Birmingham, MI	313-644-2251
Jones, Jan/2332 N Halstead, Chicago, IL	312-929-1851
Juenger, Richard/1324 S 9th St, St Louis, MO	314-231-4069

K

Kahl, Konrad/26039 German Hill, Franklin, MI	313-851-7064
Kalisch, John W/4201 Levenworth, Omaha, NE	402-734-5064
Kauffman, George/, Topeka, KS'	913-897-4342
Kecman, Milan/2730 Somia Dr, Cleveland, OH	216-741-8755
Kelen, Linda/1922 W Newport, Chicago, IL	312-975-9696
Kelley, Gary/301 1/2 Main St, Cedar Falls, IA	212-683-1362
Kessler Hartsock Assoc/5624 Belmont Ave, Cincinnati, OH	513-542-8775
Kessler, Clifford/6642 West H Ave, Kalamazoo, MI	616-375-0688

Illustrators

Continued

Please send us your additions and updates.

Kirov, Lydia/4008 N Hermitage Ave, Chicago, IL	312-248-8764
Kocar, George F/24213 Lake Rd, Bay Village, OH	216-871-8325
Kock, Carl/311 N Desplaines Ave, Chicago, IL	312-559-0440
Kordic, Vladimir/35351 Grovewood Dr, Eastlake, OH	216-951-4026
Krainik, David/4645 N Manor, Chicago, IL	312-539-4475
Kriegshauser, Shannon/12421 W Grafleman Rd, Hanna City, IL	309-565-7110
Kueker, Don/832 S Ballas, St Louis, MO	314-965-6073

L

Lackner, Paul/29 E Ohio, Chicago, IL	312-565-0030
LaFever, Greg/20 Lynnray Circle, Dayton, OH	513-433-8383
Lambert, John/1911 E Robin Hood Ln, Arlington Heights, IL	312-392-6349
Langeneckert, Donald/4939 Ringer Rd, St Louis, MO	314-487-2042
Langeneckert, Mark/704 Dover Pl, St Louis, MO	314-752-0199
Larson, David/405 N Wabash, Chicago, IL	312-661-0811
Laurent, Richard/1132 W Columbia Ave, Chicago, IL	312-245-9014
Lawson, Robert/1523 Seminole St, Kalamazoo, MI	616-345-7607
Lee, Denis Charles/1120 Heatherway, Ann Arbor, MI	313-973-2795
Lee, Jared D/2942 Old Hamilton Rd, Lebanon, OH	513-932-2154
Leonard, Martha/1515 South Blvd, Evanston, IL	312-864-8638
Lesh, David/6332 Guilford Ave, Indianapolis, IN	317-253-3141
Letostak, John/7801 Fernhill Ave, Parma, OH	216-885-1753
Loos, Jean/5539 Arnsby Pl, Cincinnati, OH	513-561-8472
Loveless, Jim/4137 San Francisco, St Louis, MO	314-533-7914

M

MacNair, Greg/7515 Wayne, University City, MO	314-721-3781
Magdich, Dennis/1914 N Dayton, Chicago, IL	312-248-6492
Maggard, John/102 Marian Lane, Terrace Park, OH	513-831-8801
Mahan, Benton/PO Box 66, Chesterville, OH	419-768-2204
Manchess, Gregory/233 E Wacker Dr, Chicago, IL	312-565-2701
Mayerik, Val/20466 Drake Rd, Strongsville, OH	216-238-9492
Mayes, Kevin/1202 Tulsa St, Wichita, KS	316-522-6742
McDermott, Teri/514 S State St, Elgin, IL	312-888-2206
McGinnis, Renee/907 E Fairchild, Iowa City, IA	319-395-9060
McMahon, Mark/321 S Ridge Rd, Lake Forest, IL	312-295-2604
McMann, Brian/2108 Payne NE #907, Cleveland, OH	216-566-1605
McNicholas, Michael/7804 W College Dr, Palos Hts, IL	312-361-2850
Meade, Roy/240 Tenth St, Toledo, OH	419-244-9074
MedTech Communications/3552 Halliday, St Louis, MO	314-771-6177
Miller, Doug/2648 Glen Mawr Ave, Columbus, OH	614-267-6533
Miller, Jean/350 Esna Park Dr, Markham, ON	416-883-4114
Miller, William (Bill)/1355 N Sandburg Ter #2002, Chicago, IL	312-787-4093
Morgan, Leonard/1163 E Ogden Ave #705, Naperville, IL	312-759-3987
Munger, Nancy/PO Box 125, Richland, MI	616-623-5458

N

Nelson, Diane/2816 Birchwood, Wilmette, IL	312-256-6200
Nelson, Fred/3 E Ontario #25, Chicago, IL	312-935-1707
Nichols, Garry/1449 N Pennsylvania St, Indianapolis, IN	317-637-0250
Nighthawk Studio/1250 Riverbed Rd, Cleveland, OH	216-522-1809
Norcia, Ernest/3451 Houston Rd, Waynesville, OH	513-862-5761
Novack, Bob/6878 Fry Rd, Middlebury Hts, OH	216-234-1808
Noyes, Mary Albury/716 First St N #245, Minneapolis, MN	612-338-1270

O

O'Connell, Mitch/6165 N Winthrop #603, Chicago, IL	312-743-3848
O'Malley, Kathy/10350 Komensky, Oak Lawn, IL	312-499-1069
O'Neill, Brian/17006 Woodbury Ave, Cleveland, OH	216-252-6238
Olson, Robert A/15215 Buchanan Ct, Eden Prairie, MN	612-934-5767
Ortman, John/535 N Michigan Ave, Chicago, IL	312-266-1417
Ostresh, Michael/2034 13th St, Granite City, IL	618-876-8861
Otto, Brian/368 W Huron, Chicago, IL	312-787-6826

PQ

Pappas, Chris/323 S Franklin, Chicago, IL	312-236-6862
Pastucha, Ron/336 McNeans Ave, Winnipeg R2C 2J7, MB	204-222-3178
Petrauskas, Kathy/155 N Michigan Ave, Chicago, IL	312-565-0030
Pitt Studios/1370 Ontario St #1430, Cleveland, OH	216-241-6720
Pitts, Ted/20 Lynnray Circle, Dayton, OH	513-433-8383
Pope, Kevin/328 N Lincoln Ave, Mundelein, IL	312-566-5534
Prepera, Fred/405 N Wabash #3203, Chicago, IL	312-329-1370
Probert, Jean/1022 N Bompart, St Louis, MO	314-968-5076
Quinn, Colleen/535 N Michigan, Chicago, IL	312-943-1668

R

Rainey, Tim/PO Box 1500, Hesston, KS	316-327-2669
Raney, Ken/PO Box 1500, Hesston, KS	316-327-2669
Rasmussen, Bonnie/8828 Pendleton, St Louis, MO	314-962-1842
Rawley, Don/7520 Blaisdell Ave S, Richfield, MN	612-866-1023
Rawson, Jon/750 N Dearborn #2703, Chicago, IL	312-266-4884
Renaud, Phill/2830 W Leland, Chicago, IL	312-583-2681
Roberts, A Hardy/6512 Charlotte, Kansas City, MO	816-444-8210
Robinson, Brenda/718 19th Ave, Coralville, IA	319-353-6622
Rossi, Pam/39 Linden St, Winnetka, IL	312-441-5256
Roth, Hy/1300 Ashland St, Evanston, IL	312-491-1937
Rybka, Stephen/535 N Michigan, Chicago, IL	312-943-1668

S

Sanford, John/5038 W Berteau, Chicago, IL	312-685-0656
Sauck, Mark/155 N Michigan Ave, Chicago, IL	312-565-0030
Schmelzer, J P/1002 S Wesley Ave, Oak Park, IL	312-386-4005
Schrag, Allan/8530 W Ninth, Wichita, KS	316-722-4585
Schrier, Fred/9058 Little Mtn Rd, Kirtland Hills, OH	216-255-7787
Scibilia, Dom/2902 Franklin Blvd, Cleveland, OH	216-861-2561
Selfridge, MC/817 Desplaines St, Plainfield, IL	815-439-7197
Sellars, Joseph/2423 W 22nd St, Minneapolis, MN	612-377-8766
Seltzer, Meyer Design & Illustration/744 W Buckingham Pl, Chicago, IL	312-348-2885
Sereta, Bruce/3010 Parklane Dr, Cleveland, OH	216-241-5355
Shaw, Ned/2770 N Smith Pike, Bloomington, IN	812-333-2181
Shay, RJ/3301 S Jefferson Ave, St Louis, MO	314-773-9989
Sheldon, David/20 Lynnray Circle, Dayton, OH	513-433-8383
Sinenkowski, Laurie/3660 New Castle, Grand Rapids, MI	616-247-0127
Sirrell, Terry/388 E Lambert Dr, Schaumburg, IL	312-980-7047
Sisson-Schlesser, Kathryn/707 W Wrightwood Ave, Chicago, IL	312-472-3877
Skidmore Sahratian Inc/2100 W Big Beaver Rd, Troy, MI	313-643-6000
Slack, Chuck/9 Cambridge Ln, Lincolnshire, IL	312-948-9226
Songero, Jay/17858 Rose St, Lansing, IL	312-849-5676
Soukup, James/Route 1, Seward, NE	402-643-2339
Speer, Terry/181 Forest St, Oberlin, OH	216-774-8319
Staake, Bob/1507 Lanvale Dr, St Louis, MO	314-961-2303
Stearney, Mark/405 N Wabash #2809, Chicago, IL	312-644-6669
Stephens Biondi Decicco/666 N Lake Shore Dr #1020, Chicago, IL	312-944-3340
Storyboard Studio/535 N Michigan Ave, Chicago, IL	312-266-1417
Streff, Michael/2766 Wasson Rd, Cincinnati, OH	513-731-0360
Sumichrast, Jozef/860 N Northwoods, Deerfield, IL	312-945-6353

T

Tate, Clark/1120 N LaSalle, Chicago, IL	312-943-5407
Tate, Don/575 W Madison, Chicago, IL	312-440-1444
Taylor, David/1449 N Pennsylvania St, Indianapolis, IN	317-634-2728
Taylor, Richard/155 N Michigan Ave, Chicago, IL	312-565-0030
Thacker, Kat/40335 Plymouth Rd #203, Plymouth, MI	313-455-2765
Theodore, Jim/15735 Pearl Rd, Strongsville, OH	216-238-6188
Thiewes, Sam/111 N Andover Ln, Geneva, IL	312-232-0980
Thomas, Bob/1002 E Washington St, Indianapolis, IN	317-638-1002
Thomas, Pat/711 Carpenter, Oak Park, IL	312-383-8505
Thornton, Shelley/1600 S 22nd St, Lincoln, NE	212-683-1362
Townley, Jon/61 Sunnyside Lane, Columbus, OH	614-268-9717
Triad Productions/4350 Johnson Dr #228, Shawnee Mission, KS	913-432-2821
Trusilo, Jim/535 N Michigan Ave, Chicago, IL	312-943-1668
Tughan, James/1179-A King St W #310, Toronto M6K3C5, ON	416-535-9149
Turgeon, James/233 E Wacker Dr #1102, Chicago, IL	312-861-1039
Tyrrell, Robert/405 N Wabash Ave #3203, Chicago, IL	312-329-1370

V

Vaccarello, Paul/505 N Lake Shore Dr, Chicago, IL	312-664-2233
Vanderbeek, Don/235 Monteray Ave, Dayton, OH	513-293-5326
Vann, Bill Studio/1706 S 8th St, St Louis, MO	314-231-2322
Vanselow, Holly/1313 W Fletcher, Chicago, IL	312-975-5880
Villani, Ron/405 N Wabash Ave #3203, Chicago, IL	312-329-1370
Vokac, Lucy/24 W Ohio Ave, Naperville, IL	312-357-7671
Vuksanovich, Bill & Fran/3224 N Nordica, Chicago, IL	312-283-2138

W

WALD, CAROL/217 FARNSWORTH AVE, DETROIT, MI (P 38,39)	**313-832-5805**
Walker, John/307 N Michigan Ave #1008, Chicago, IL	312-346-0720
Walker, Ken/116 W 3rd St, Kansas City, MO	816-931-7975

Illustrators
Continued

Please send us your additions and updates.

Walsh, Cathy/323 S Franklin, Chicago, IL	312-944-2985
Walter, Nancy Lee/PO Box 611, Elmhurst, IL	312-833-3898
Westphal, Ken/7616 Fairway, Prairie Village, KS	913-381-8399
Westwood, William/211 23rd Ave SW, Rochester, MN	507-282-7140
Whitney, Bill/116 W Illinois 5th Fl, Chicago, IL	312-527-2455
Wickart Brothers/405 N Wabash #1511, Chicago, IL	312-645-0836
Willey, Chris/3202 Windsor #2E, Kansas City, MO	816-483-1475
Williams, Gordon/1030 Glenmoor Ln, Glendale, MO	314-821-2032
Willson Graphics/100 E Ohio #314, Chicago, IL	312-642-5328
Wimmer, Chuck/5000 Ira Ave, Cleveland, OH	216-526-2820
Wolek, Guy/323 S Franklin, Chicago, IL	312-341-1282
Wolf, Leslie/3 E Ontario #25, Chicago, IL	312-935-1707
Wolf, Paul/510 Tauromee, Kansas City, KS	913-621-4748
Woolery, Lee/7026 Corp Way #211, Dayton, OH	513-433-7912
Wozniak, Elaine & Dorothy/15520 Clifton Blvd, Cleveland, OH	216-226-3565

YZ
Young & Laramore/6367 N Guilford Ave, Indianapolis, IN	317-257-8752
Young, David Jemerson/6367 N Guilford, Indianapolis, IN	317-257-8752
Youssi, John/Rt 1, 220 Powers Rd, Gilberts, IL	312-428-7398
Zadnik, Pat/11900 Edgewater Dr, Cleveland, OH	216-521-6273
Zaresky, Don/41 Leonard Ave, Northfield Center, OH	216-467-5917
Zimnicki Design/774 Parkview Ct, Roselle, IL	312-893-2666
Zumbo, Matthew/2105 N Summit #201, Milwaukee, WI	414-277-9541

Southwest
AB
Alexander, Cynthia/4506 Gilbert Ave, Dallas, TX	214-528-1273
Andrew, Bill/1709 Dryden #709, Houston, TX	713-791-4924
Andrews, Chris/1515 N Beverly Ave, Tucson, AZ	602-325-5126
Archon/2211 S Interregional #308, Austin, TX	512-447-0265
Atha, Jim/1000 W Wilshire #428, Oklahoma City, OK	405-840-3201
Bates, Greg/2811 McKinney #224, Dallas, TX	214-855-0055
Battes, Greg Design & Illus/2954 Satsuma Dr, Dallas, TX	214-620-7685
Bleck, Cathie/1019 N Clinton, Dallas, TX	214-942-4639
Brazeal, Lee Lee/PO Box 430995, Houston, TX	713-877-1823
Brown, Rod Design/2 Dals Com Cmplx Nxus 20, Irving, TX	214-869-9393

C
Carlson, Robert/923 McKelligon, El Paso, TX	915-542-2322
Cheatham, Margaret Kasahara/5914 Oram, Dallas, TX	214-827-3172
Cheney, May/1300 N 12th St #403, Phoenix, AZ	602-239-4230
Cherry, Jim/3600 N Hayden Rd #3308, Scottsdale, AZ	602-941-2883
Chinchar, Alan/1718 Capstan, Houston, TX	713-480-3227
Collier, Steve/5512 Chaucer Dr, Houston, TX	713-522-0205
Connally, Connie/3333 Elm, Dallas, TX	214-742-4302
Cornelius, Ray-Mel/4512 Swiss Ave #3, Dallas, TX	214-826-8988
Criswell, Ron/703 McKinney Ave #201, Dallas, TX	214-954-4497
Curry, Tom/302 Lakehills Dr, Austin, TX	512-263-3407

DE
Dean, Michael/5512 Chaucer, Houston, TX	713-527-0295
Depew, Bob/2755 Rollingdale, Dallas, TX	214-241-9206
Dewy, Jennifer/102 W San Francisco #16, Santa Fe, NM	505-988-2924
Dunnick, Regan/1110 Lovett #202, Houston, TX	713-523-6590
Durbin, Mike/4034 Woodcraft, Houston, TX	713-667-8129
Eckles, Jane/6666 Harwin #540, Houston, TX	713-781-5170
Eubank, Mary Grace/6222 Northwood, Dallas, TX	214-692-7579
Eudy, Mike/3800 Commerce, Dallas, TX	214-826-1361
Evans, Eleanor/965 Slocum, Dallas, TX	214-760-8232

FGH
Falk, Rusty/707 E Alameda Dr, Tempe, AZ	602-966-1626
Forbes, Bart/2706 Fairmount, Dallas, TX	214-748-8436
Garns, G Allen/3314 East El Moro, Mesa, AZ	602-830-7224
Girden, J M/2125 Cerrada Nopal E, Tucson, AZ	602-628-2740
Grimes, Don/3514 Oak Grove, Dallas, TX	214-526-0040
Grimes, Rick/703 McKinney #432, Dallas, TX	214-954-0310
Hall, Bill/1235-B Colorado Ln, Arlington, TX	817-274-0817
High, Richard/4500 Montrose #D, Houston, TX	713-521-2772
Huey, Kenneth/4413 Sycamore St, Dallas, TX	214-821-3042

KL
Kampa, David/2317 Kinney Rd, Austin, TX	512-440-1475
Karas, Brian/4518 N 12th St #108, Phoenix, AZ	602-263-9193
Kirkman, Rick/815 N 1st Ave #3, Phoenix, AZ	602-257-0097

Kohler, Mark/701 W 7th Ave, Austin, TX	512-476-4283
Kramer, Dave/27112 Cooks Cr #4104, Dallas, TX	214-247-7616
Lapsley, Bob/3707 Nottingham, Houston, TX	713-667-4393
Lebo, Narda/4851 Cedar Springs, Dallas, TX	214-528-0375
Lewis, Maurice/3704 Harper St, Houston, TX	713-664-1807
Lindlof, Ed/603 Carolyn Ave, Austin, TX	512-472-0195
Lisieski, Peter/135 Pine St, Nacogdoches, TX	409-564-4244

MN
MacPherson, Kevin/815 N 1st Ave #3, Phoenix, AZ	602-257-0097
Martin, Larry/3040 Sundial, Dallas, TX	214-521-8700
Martin, Lisa/2643 Manana, Dallas, TX	214-352-4387
Martini, John/8742 Welles Dale, San Antonio, TX	512-699-9318
McClain, Lynn/8730 Vinewood, Dallas, TX	214-321-9374
McCullough, Greg/1412 Summerbrook Cir #144, Arlington, TX	817-861-5813
McCullough, Lenndy/708 Canyon Rd #3, Santa Fe, NM	505-982-1964
McElhaney, Gary/5205 Airport Blvd #201, Austin, TX	512-451-3986
McGar, Michael/3330 Irwindell Blvd, Dallas, TX	214-339-0672
Nadon, Jean/7 Lincrest Dr, Galveston, TX	409-763-2162
Nelson, John/345 E Windsor, Phoenix, AZ	602-279-1131

P
Payne, Chris F/6333 Goliad, Dallas, TX	214-421-3993
Pendleton, Nancy/815 N 1st Ave #3, Phoenix, AZ	602-257-0097
Peters, Bob/PO Box 7014, Phoenix, AZ	602-375-2360
Phelps, Timothy/4018 Grennoch Ln, Houston, TX	413-666-7687
Phillips, Barry/, Dallas, TX	214-869-7157
Pietzsch, Steve/3057 Larry Drive, Dallas, TX	214-279-8851
Poli, Kristina/4211 Pebblegate Ct, Houston, TX	713-353-6910

RS
Ricks, Thom/6511 Adair Dr, San Antonio, TX	512-680-6540
Roberts, Mark/Art Direction/2127 Banks St, Houston, TX	713-623-0748
Rogers, Randy/1759 Harold, Houston, TX	713-523-3774
Rose, Lee/4250 TC Jester Blvd, Houston, TX	713-686-4799
Ruland, Mike/8946 Long Point Rd, Houston, TX	713-465-2413
Salem, Kay/13418 Splintered Oak, Houston, TX	713-469-0996
Senkarik, Mickey/PO Box 104, Helotes, TX	512-695-9327
Sims, Thomas/4303 Junius St, Dallas, TX	214-828-0366
Sketch Pad/2605 Westgate Dr, Arlington, TX	817-469-8151
Skistimas, James/7701 N Stemmons Frwy #854, Dallas, TX	214-630-2574
Smith, James Noel/1011 North Clinton, Dallas, TX	214-946-4255
Smith, Malcolm/1309 Main #504-B, Dallas, TX	214-742-5229
Steirnagle, Michael/4141 Pinnacle #132, El Paso, TX	915-533-9295

TVW
Taylor, Michael/9434 Viscount #180, El Paso, TX	915-594-7100
Traylor, Janet/329 W Vernon Ave, Phoenix, AZ	602-254-8232
VAS Communications/4800 N 22nd St, Phoenix, AZ	602-955-1000
Verzaal, Dale/2445 E Pebble Beach, Tempe, AZ	602-839-5536
Waltman, Lynne/PO Box 470889, Ft Worth, TX	817-738-1545
Warner, Michele/1011 North Clinton, Dallas, TX	214-946-4255
Washington, Bill/330 Glenarm, San Antonio, TX	512-734-6216
Watford, Wayne/815 N 1st Ave #3, Phoenix, AZ	602-257-0097
Weakley, Mark/105 N Alamo #618, San Antonio, TX	512-222-9543
Wells, Steve/754 International #T-38, Houston, TX	713-629-6330

Rocky Mountain
AB
Alexander, Hugh/3655 S Verbena St #G201, Denver, CO	303-796-9208
Anderson, Jon/1465 Ellendale Ave, Logan, UT	801-752-8936
Aragon, Art/1376 Eudora St, Denver, CO	303-934-5801
Barber, David/1804 Hollywood Ave, Salt Lake Ctiy, UT	801-485-8366
Bhakti, LeVon/179 S 1200 E #3, Salt Lake City, UT	801-531-6951
Brownd, Elizabeth/470 Woodland Rd, Golden, CO	303-526-0209

CDE
Christensen, James C/656 West 550 South, Orem, UT	801-224-6237
Cuneo, John/2629 18th St, Denver, CO	303-458-7086
Dazzeland Studios/209 Edison, Salt Lake City, UT	801-355-8555
Dolack, Monte/132 W Front St, Missoula, MT	406-549-3248
Eastman, Jody/564 South 2 West, Logan, UT	801-752-3590
English, David/643 East 500 North, Logan, UT	801-752-6144
Enright, Cindy/2629 18th St, Denver, CO	303-458-7086

Illustrators

Continued

Please send us your additions and updates.

F G H J
Farley, Malcolm/3870 Newland, Wheatridge, CO — 303-420-9135
Fujisaki, Pat/5917 S Kenton Way, Englewood, CO — 303-698-0073
Graphics Studio/219 E 7th St, Denver, CO — 303-830-1110
Hardiman, Miles/30 Village Dr, Littleton, CO — 303-798-9143
Harris, Ralph/PO Box 1091, Sun Valley, ID — 208-726-8077
Heiner, Joe & Kathy/850 N Grove Dr, Alpine, UT — 801-756-3332
Hull, Richard/776 W 3500 South, Bountiful, UT — 801-298-1632
Jensen, Patricia/6030 Belmont Way, Parker, CO — 303-841-8899

L M
Lediard, Al/2216 Kensington Ave, Salt Lake City, UT — 801-328-0573
Lyman, Kenvin/209 Edison St, Salt Lake City, UT — 801-355-8555
Masami/3144 W 26th Ave, Denver, CO — 303-756-8983
Maughan, William/PO Box 133, Millville, UT — 801-752-9340
McGowan, Daniel/28325 Little Big Horn Dr, Evergreen, CO — 303-674-0203
Meents, Len/Estes Industries, Penrose, CO — 303-372-3080
Millard, Dennis/240 W 300 N, Salt Lake City, UT — 801-359-8334

N P S
Nelsen, Randy/2343 Dexter St, Denver, CO — 303-860-7070
Nelson, Will/1517 W Hays, Boise, ID — 208-345-3131
Price, Jeannette/1164 E 820 N, Provo, UT — 801-377-3958
Sauter, Ron/3113 E 3rd St #220, Denver, CO — 303-399-3851
Snyder, Teresa & Wayne/10155 Grant Creek Rd, Missoula, MT — 406-549-6772
Strawn, Susan/1216 W Olive St, Ft Collins, CO — 303-493-0679

U V W Z
Uhl, David/2536 Gilpin St, Denver, CO — 303-860-7070
Van Schelt, Perry L/6577 Cyclamen Way, W Jordan, UT — 801-968-3034.
Weller, Don/2240 Monarch Dr, Park City, UT — 801-649-9859
Whitesides, Kim/PO Box 2189, Park City, UT — 801-649-0490
Winborg, Larry/464 South, 275 East, Farmington, UT — 801-451-5310
Zilberts, Ed/1070-A Race St, Denver, CO — 303-399-6539

West Coast

A
Abe, George/1822 NE Ravenna Rd, Seattle, WA — 206-443-0326
Ace, Katherine/16060 Broadway Terrace, Oakland, CA — 415-420-0429
Allaire, Michel J/405 Union St #2, San Francisco, CA — 415-982-5598
Allen, Pat/131 E Portola, Los Altos, CA — 416-941-3570
Allison, Gene/1808 Stanley Ave, Placentia, CA — 714-524-5955
Alvin, John/15942 Londelius, Sepulveda, CA — 213-471-0232
Ambler, Barbara Hoopes/2769 Nipoma St, San Diego, CA — 619-222-7535
Amit, Emanuel/2822 Denby Ave, Los Angeles, CA — 213-666-7414
Anderson, Kevin/1267 Orkney Ln, Cardiff, CA — 619-753-8410
Anderson, Sara/117 W Denny Way #214, Seattle, WA — 206-285-1520
Anderson, Terry/5902 W 85th Pl, Los Angeles, CA — 213-645-8469
Andreoli, Rick/467 Fair Dr #207, Costa Mesa, CA — 714-556-2280
Ansley, Frank/860 Second Ave, San Francisco, CA — 415-644-0585
Arkle, Dave/259 W Orange Grove, Pomona, CA — 714-865-2967
Arshawsky, David/9401 Alcott St, Los Angeles, CA — 213-276-6058
Artists In Print/Fort Mason Bldg D, San Francisco, CA — 415-673-6941
Atkins, Bill/PO Box 1091, Laguna Beach, CA — 714-499-3857
August, Bob/11147 La Maida, N Hollywood, CA — 818-769-3592

B
Backus, Michael/200-A Westminster Ave, Venice, CA — 213-392-4877
Baker, Don/1822 NE Ravenna Blvd, Seattle, WA — 606-443-0326
Banthien, Barbara/902 Marylyn Circle, Petaluma, CA — 707-762-1616
Banyai, Istvan/1241 9th St #3, Santa Monica, CA — 213-394-8035
Barbaria, Steve/1990 Third St #400, Sacramento, CA — 916-442-3200
Barbee, Joel/209 San Pablo, San Clemente, CA — 714-498-0067
Barnard, Bryn/1211 Emerald Bay, Laguna Beach, CA — 714-494-6564
Batcheller, Keith/1438 Calle Cecilia, San Dimas, CA — 818-331-0439
Beach, Lou/5424 W Washington Blvd, Los Angeles, CA — 213-934-7335
Beck, David/6376 W 5th St, Los Angeles, CA — 213-934-3395
Beckerman, Carol/PO Box 8566, Long Beach, CA — 213-420-8407
Beerworth, Roger/618 S Western Ave #201, Los Angeles, CA — 213-392-4877
Beigle, David/5632 Meinhardt Rd, Westminster, CA — 714-893-7749
Bell, Karen/8126 Blackburn Ave, Los Angeles, CA — 213-858-0946
Bennett, Mark/2650 Creston Dr, Los Angeles, CA — 213-462-0109
Bergendorff, Roger/17106 Sims St #A, Huntington Beach, CA — 714-840-7665
Bernstein, Sol/649 Encino Vista Dr, Thousand Oaks, CA — 805-497-7967
Bettoli, Delana/737 Vernon Ave, Venice, CA — 213-396-0296

Bingham, Sid/360 1/2 N Mansfield Ave, Los Angeles, CA — 213-935-4696
Biomedical Illustrations/804 Columbia St, Seattle, WA — 206-682-8197
Birnbaum, Dianne/17301 Elsinore Circle, Huntington Beach, CA — 714-847-7631
Bjorkman, Steve/1711 Langley, Irvine, CA — 714-261-1411
Blackshear, Tom/108 Prof Ctr Pky, San Rafael, CA — 415-897-9486
Blair, Barry/PO Box 156, Dana Point, CA — 714-249-1577
Blank, Jerry/1048 Lincoln Ave, San Jose, CA — 408-289-9095
Blonder, Ellen/PO Box 5513, Mill Valley, CA — 415-388-9158
Bohn, Richard/595 W Wilson St, Costa Mesa, CA — 714-548-6669
Bolourchian, Flora/2800 28th St #105, Santa Monica, CA — 213-450-4881
Borkenhagen, Susan/3558 1/2 Fifth Ave, San Diego, CA — 619-295-6891
Boyle, Neil/5455 Wilshire Blvd #1212, Los Angeles, CA — 213-937-4472
Bradley, Barbara/750 Wildcat Canyon Rd, Berkeley, CA — 415-673-4200
Bringham, Sherry/1440 Bush St, San Francisco, CA — 415-775-6564
Broad, David/100 Golden Hinde Blvd, San Rafael, CA — 415-479-5505
Brown, Bill & Assoc/1054 S Robertson Blvd #203, Los Angeles, CA — 213-652-9380
Brown, Charley/716 Montgomery St, San Francisco, CA — 415-433-1222
Brown, Janis/Rt3 Box 456 #A, Escondido, CA — 619-743-1795
Brown, Rick/1502 N Maple, Burbank, CA — 818-842-0726
Brugger, Bob/1830 S Robertson Blvd, Los Angeles, CA — 213-204-1771
Buechler, Barbara/13929 Marquessa Way #108A, Marina Del Ray, CA — 213-827-5106
Buerge, Bill/734 Basin Dr, Topanga, CA — 213-455-3181
Bull, Michael/2350 Taylor, San Francisco, CA — 415-776-7471
Burnside, John E/4204 Los Feliz Blvd, Los Angeles, CA — 213-665-8913
Busacca, Mark/269 Corte Madera Ave, Mill Valley, CA — 415-381-9048

C
Caldwell, Kirk/1844 Union St, San Francisco, CA — 415-567-3727
Callanta, Al/13010 Miller Ave, Norwalk, CA — 213-921-2369
Carroll, Justin/1118 Chautauqua, Pacific Palisades, CA — 213-459-3104
Catom, Don/638 S Van Ness Ave, Los Angeles, CA — 213-382-6281
Chase, Margo/120 S Sycamore Ave, Los Angeles, CA — 213-937-4421
Chewning, Randy/360 1/2 N Mansfield Ave, Los Angeles, CA — 213-935-4696
Chiodo, Joe/2124 Froude St, San Diego, CA — 619-222-2476
Chorney, Steven/10855 Beckford Ave, Northridge, CA — 818-985-8181
Clark, Tim/8800 Venice Blvd, Los Angeles, CA — 213-202-1044
Clarke, Coralie/PO Box 6057, Bonsall, CA — 619-941-1476
Coconis, Ted/2244 Santa Ana, Palo Alto, CA — 415-856-9055
Coe, Wayne/1707 Michetorena #416, Los Angeles, CA — 213-662-1259
Cole, Dick/25 Hotaling Pl, San Francisco, CA — 415-986-8163
Commander, Bob/8126 Blackburn Ave, Los Angeles, CA — 213-858-0946
The Committee/15468-B Ventura Blvd, Sherman Oaks, CA — 818-986-4420
Consani, Chris/2601 Walnut Ave, Manhattan Bch, CA — 213-316-2929
Cook, Anne/1580 Treat Ave, San Francisco, CA — 415-695-0210
Coppock, Chuck/638 S Van Ness Ave, Los Angeles, CA — 213-382-6281
Cotter, Debbie/248 Alhambra, San Francisco, CA — 415-331-9111
Coviello, Ron/1682 Puterbaugh, San Diego, CA — 619-265-6647
Creative Source/6671 W Sunset Blvd #1519, Los Angeles, CA — 213-462-5731
Criss, Keith/4329 Piedmont Ave, Oakland, CA — 415-547-2528
Critz, Carl/638 S Van Ness Ave, Los Angeles, CA — 213-382-6281
Cummings, B D/3845 E Casselle, Orange, CA — 714-633-3322
Curtis, Todd/2032 14th St #7, Santa Monica, CA — 213-452-0738

D
Daniels/1352 Hornblend St, San Diego, CA — 619-272-8147
Daniels, Shelley/7247 Margerun Ave, San Diego, CA — 619-286-8087
Darrow, David R/9655 Derald Rd, Santee, CA — 619-697-7408
Davidson, Kevin/505 S Grand St, Orange, CA — 714-633-9061
Davis, Jack/3785 Mt Everest Blvd, San Diego, CA — 619-565-0336
Dean, Bruce/360 1/2 N Mansfield Ave, Los Angeles, CA — 213-935-4696
Dean, Donald/3960 Rhoda Ave, Oakland, CA — 415-644-1139
DeAnda, Ruben/550 Oxford St #407, Chula Vista, CA — 619-427-7765
DeLeon, Cam/1725 Berkeley St, Santa Monica, CA — 213-453-4418
Dellorco, Chris/18350 Hatteras #229, Tarzana, CA — 818-342-7890
Dennewill, Jim/5823 Autry Ave, Lakewood, CA — 213-920-3895
Devaud, Jacques/1165 Bruin Tr/Box 260, Fawnskin, CA — 714-866-4563
Dietz, James/2203 13th Ave E, Seattle, WA — 206-325-2857
Diffenderfer, Ed/32 Cabernet Ct, Lafayette, CA — 415-254-8235
Dismukes, John Taylor/2820 Westshire Dr, Hollywood, CA — 213-467-2787
Doe, Bart/3300 Temple St, Los Angeles, CA — 213-383-9707
Dohrmann, Marsha J/144 Woodbine Dr, Mill Valley, CA — 415-383-0188

Illustrators

Continued

Please send us your additions and updates.

ILLUSTRATORS

Doty, Eldon/1106 Santolina Dr, Novato, CA	415-897-7626
Drake, Bob/1556 N Faifax Ave, Los Angeles, CA	213-850-6808
Drayton, Richard/5018 Dumont Pl, Woodland Hills, CA	818-347-2227
Drennon, Tom/916 N Formosa #D, Hollywood, CA	213-874-1276
Duell, Nancy/1046 N Orange Dr, Los Angeles, CA	213-462-5622
Duffus, Bill/1745 Wagner, Pasadena, CA	818-792-7921
Duke, Lawrence W/Star Route Box 93, Woodside, CA	415-861-0941
Duranona, Leo/6340 Lankershim Blvd #105, N Hollywood, CA	818-761-0128
Durfee, Tom/25 Hotaling Pl, San Francisco, CA	415-781-0527

E
Eastside Illustration/1807 SE 7th Ave, Portland, OR	503-235-6878
Eckart, Chuck/166 South Park, San Francisco, CA	415-552-4252
Edelson, Wendy/215 Second Ave S, Seattle, WA	206-728-1300
Eichenberger, Dave/11607 Clover Ave, Los Angeles, CA	213-828-9653
Ellescas, Richard/321 N Martel, Hollywood, CA	213-939-7396
Ellmore, Dennis/3245 Orange Ave, Long Beach, CA	213-424-9379
Elstad, Ron/18253 Solano River Ct, Fountain Valley, CA	714-964-7753
Endicott, James R/3509 N College, Newberg, OR	503-538-5466
Ente, Anke/50 Kings Rd, Brisbane, CA	415-467-8108
Ericksen, Marc/1045 Sansome St #306, San Francisco, CA	415-362-1214
Erickson, Kernie/Box 2175, Mission Viejo, CA	714-831-2818
Erramouspe, David/2337 Kelton Ave, Los Angeles, CA	213-473-7656
Etow, Carole/221 17th St #B, Manhattan Beach, CA	213-545-0795
Evans, Bill/2030 First Ave #201, Seattle, WA	206-623-9459
Evans, Jan/8126 Blackburn Ave, Los Angeles, CA	213-858-0946
Evans, Robert/1045 Sansome, San Francisco, CA	415-397-5322
Evenson, Stan/1830 S Robrtsn Blvd #203, Los Angeles, CA	213-204-1995

F
Feigeles, Neil/1815 N Harvard Blvd, Los Angeles, CA	213-856-9849
Ferrero, Felix/215 Liedesdorff, San Francisco, CA	415-981-1162
Finch, Ken/108 S Jackson St #207, Seattle, WA	206-467-8669
Forrest, William/817 12th St #2, Santa Monica, CA	213-458-9114
Foster, Matt/1555 Fifth Ave 3304, San Francisco, CA	415-759-5642
Fox, Ronald/2274 237th St, Torrance, CA	213-325-4970
Francuch, George/638 S Van Ness Ave, Los Angeles, CA	213-382-6281
Franks, Bill/638 S Van Ness Ave, Los Angeles, CA	213-382-6281
Fraze, Jon/17081 Kenyon Dr #C, Tustin, CA	714-731-8493
Frazee, Marla/5114 1/2 La Roda Ave, Los Angeles, CA	213-258-3846
French, Lisa/489 Norton St, Long Beach, CA	213-423-8741
Fulp, Jim/834 Duboce Ave, San Francisco, CA	415-621-5462

G
Galloway, Nixon/5455 Wilshire Blvd #1212, Los Angeles, CA	213-937-4472
Garcia, Manuel/1352 Hornblend St, San Diego, CA	619-272-8147
Garland, Gil/4928 Hartwick St, Los Angeles, CA	213-933-0610
Garner, Tracy/1830 S Robertson Blvd, Los Angeles, CA	213-204-1771
Garnett, Joe/1100 Glendon #732, Los Angeles, CA	213-279-1539
Garo, Harry/7738 E Allen Grove, Downey, CA	213-978-5104
Geary, Rick/2124 Froude St, San Diego, CA	619-222-2476
Gellos, Nancy/20 Armour St, Seattle, WA	206-285-5838
General Graphics/746 Brannan, San Francisco, CA	415-777-3333
George, Jeff/2204-D Matthews, Redondo Beach, CA	213-371-0280
Gerrie, Dean/222 W Main St #101, Tustin, CA	714-838-0234
Gibson, Mike/1317 California St, Burbank, CA	818-785-8928
Girvin, Tim Design/911 Western Ave #408, Seattle, WA	206-623-7918
Gisko, Max/2629 Wakefield Dr, Belmont, CA	415-469-8030
Glad, Deanna/PO Box 3261, Santa Monica, CA	213-393-7464
Glass, Randy/716 Montgomery St, San Francisco, CA	415-433-1222
Gleason, Bob/11607 Clover Ave, Los Angeles, CA	213-828-9653
Gleeson, Madge/Art Dept/Wstrn Wash Univ, Bellingham, WA	206-676-3000
Gleeson, Tony/2525 Hyperion Ave #4, Los Angeles, CA	213-668-2704
Gleis, Linda/6671 Sunset Blvd #1519, Los Angeles, CA	213-461-6376
Goddard, John/2774 Los Alisos Dr, Fallbrook, CA	619-728-5473
Gohata, Mark/1492 W 153 St, Gardena, CA	213-327-6595
Goldstein, Howard/7031 Aldea Ave, Van Nuys, CA	818-987-2837
Gomez, Ignacio/812 Kenneth Rd, Glendale, CA	818-243-2838
Gordon, Barry/1407 Montana, Los Angeles, CA	213-394-6545
Gordon, Duane/638 S Van Ness Ave, Los Angeles, CA	213-382-6281
Gould, Ron/8119 Shady Glade Ave, N Hollywood, CA	818-504-9513
Graphic Designers Inc/2975 Wilshire Blvd #210, Los Angeles, CA	213-381-3977
Graphicswork/1159 Carrot Wood Glen, Escondido, CA	619-743-8736
Gray, Steve/8126 Blackburn Ave, Los Angeles, CA	213-858-0946
Green, Peter/4433 Forman Ave, Toluca Lake, CA	818-760-1011
Gribbitt Ltd/5419 Sunset Blvd, Los Angeles, CA	213-462-7362
Griffith, Linda/13972 Hilo Ln, Santa Ana, CA	714-832-8536
Grim, Elgas/638 S Van Ness Ave, Los Angeles, CA	213-382-6281
Gross, Daerick/318 W 9th St #204, Los Angeles, CA	213-489-1380
Grossman, Myron/8800 Venice Blvd, Los Angeles, CA	213-559-9349
Grove, David/382 Union St, San Francisco, CA	415-433-2100
Guidice, Rick/9 Park Ave, Los Gatos, CA	408-354-7787
Gurvin, Abe/1129 Tait, Oceanside, CA	619-941-1838

H
Haasis, Michael/941 N Croft Ave, Los Angeles, CA	213-654-5412
Hale, Bruce/2916 5th Ave W, Seattle, WA	206-282-1191
Hall, June/PO Box 203, Three Rivers, CA	209-561-4529
Hall, Patricia/5402 Ruffin Rd #103, San Diego, CA	619-268-0176
Hamagami, John/7822 Croydon Ave, Los Angeles, CA	213-641-1522
Hamilton, Jack/1040 E Van Bibber Ave, Orange, CA	714-250-0560
Hamilton, Pamela/351 1/2 N Sycamore St, Los Angeles, CA	213-933-8660
Hamlin, Barbara/308 Hillcrest Dr, Leucadia, CA	619-944-3751
Hammond, Cris/166 South Park, San Francisco, CA	415-552-4252
Hammond, Roger/5455 Wilshire Blvd #1212, Los Angeles, CA	213-937-4472
Hampton, Gerry Inc/PO Box 2792, Seal Beach, CA	213-431-6979
Hand, Guy/5158 Highland View Ave, Los Angeles, CA	213-255-5115
Hannah, Halsted (Craig)/5320 College Ave #1, Oakland, CA	415-654-6018
Harwin, Fredric/9101 SW 15th Ave, Portland, OR	503-246-8900
Hasenbeck, George/612 Prospect St #401, Seattle, WA	206-283-0980
Hasselle, Bruce/8691 Heil, Westminster, CA	714-848-2924
Hatzer, Fred/5455 Wilshire Blvd #1212, Los Angeles, CA	213-937-4472
Haydock, Robert/49 Shelley Dr, Mill Valley, CA	415-383-6986
Haynes, Bryan/1733 Ellincourt Dr #F, South Pasadena, CA	818-799-7989
Hays, Jim/3809 Sunnyside Blvd, Marysville, WA	206-334-7596
Hegedus, James C/913 Le Doux, Los Angeles, CA	213-657-1972
Heimann, Jim/1548 18th St, Santa Monica, CA	213-828-1041
Heinecke, Stu/9665 Wilshire Blvd #400, Los Angeles, CA	213-837-3212
Heinrich, Pam & Paul/20134 Leadwell St #225, Canoga Park, CA	818-882-2621
Hendricks, Steve/1050 Elsiemae Dr, Boulder Creek, CA	408-338-6639
Herrero, Lowell/433 Bryant St, San Francisco, CA	415-543-6400
Hession, Kathleen/6671 Sunset Blvd #1519, Hollywood, CA	213-462-5731
Hilliard, Fred/5425 Crystal Springs Dr NE, Bainbridge Island, WA	206-842-6003
Hilton-Putnam, Denise/4758 Jean Dr, San Diego, CA	619-565-7568
Hinds, Joe/25200 Crenshaw Blvd #203, Torrance, CA	213-539-3252
Hinton, Hank/6118 W 6th St, Los Angeles, CA	213-938-9893
Hitch, Jeff/3001 Redhill Ave #6-210, Costa Mesa, CA	714-432-1802
Hoburg, Maryanne Regal/1695 8th Ave, San Francisco, CA	415-731-1870
Hodges, Ken/12401 Bellwood, Los Alamitos, CA	213-431-4343
Holmes, Matthew/126 Mering Ct, Sacramento, CA	916-484-6080
Hoover, Anne Nelson/8457 Paseo Del Ocaso, La Jolla, CA	714-454-4294
Hopkins, Christopher/2932 Wilshire #202, Santa Monica, CA	213-828-6455
Hord, Bob/1760 Monrovia #B-9, Costa Mesa, CA	714-631-3890
Hoyos, Andy/6671 W Sunset Blvd #1519, Los Angeles, CA	213-462-5731
Hubbard, Roger/7461 Beverly Blvd #405, Los Angeles, CA	213-938-5177
Hudson, Dave/1807 E Redwood Ave, Anaheim, CA	714-533-0533
Hudson, Ron/725 Auahi St, Honolulu, HI	808-536-2692
Huhn, Tim/4718 Kester Ave #208, Sherman Oaks, CA	818-986-2352
Hulsey, Kevin/5306 Norwich Ave, Van Nuys, CA	818-501-7105
Hume, Kelly/912 S Los Robles, Pasadena, CA	818-793-8344
Hunt, Robert/4376 21st St, San Francisco, CA	415-824-1824
Hwang, Francis/999 Town & Country Rd, Orange, CA	714-538-1727

IJ
Irvine, Rex John/6026 Dovetail Dr, Agoura, CA	818-991-2522
Ito, Joel/505 NW 185th St, Beaverton, OR	503-645-1141
Jacobi, Kathryn/17830 Osborne St, Northridge, CA	213-396-8955
Jacobs, Ellen Going/312 90th St, Daly City, CA	415-994-8800
Jacobsen, Gary/2030 First Ave #201, Seattle, WA	206-441-0606
Jenks, Aleta/780 Bryant St, San Francisco, CA	415-495-4278
Jensen, David/1150 Fremont St, San Jose, CA	408-295-5974
Jones, Reginald/197 Zinfandel Ln, St Helena, CA	707-963-7532
Jones, Steve/1081 Nowita Pl, Venice, CA	213-396-9111
Jost, Larry/3916 E Garfield St, Seattle, WA	206-328-1841
Joy, Pat/247 Alestar #3, Vista, CA	619-726-2781
Judd, Jeff/827 1/2 N McCadden Pl, Los Angeles, CA	213-469-0333

288

Illustrators
Continued

Please send us your additions and updates.

K

Kabaker, Gayle/1440 Bush St, San Francisco, CA	415-775-6564
Kamifuji, Tom/780 Bryant St, San Francisco, CA	415-495-4278
Kari, Morgan/3516 Sawtelle Blvd #226, Los Angeles, CA	213-390-1343
Katayama, Mits/425 Randolph Ave, Seattle, WA	206-324-1199
Keefer, Mel/847 5th St #108, Santa Monica, CA	213-395-1147
Keeling, Gregg Bernard/659 Boulevard Way, Oakland, CA	415-444-8688
Kenyon, Chris/14 Wilmot, San Francisco, CA	415-923-1363
Kimble, David/711 S Flower, Burbank, CA	213-849-1576
King, Heather/1218 Cayetano Dr, Napa, CA	707-226-1232
KITCHELL, JOYCE/2755 EAGLE ST, SAN DIEGO, CA (P 25)	**619-291-1378**
Koester, Michael/272 Gresham, Ashland, OR	503-488-0153
Koulian, Jack/442 W Harvard, Glendale, CA	818-956-5640
Kramer, Moline/854 S Sycamore, Los Angeles, CA	213-934-6280
Kratter, Paul/7461 Beverly Blvd #405, Los Angeles, CA	213-938-5177
Kriegler, Richard/2814 Third St, Santa Monica, CA	213-396-9087
Kriss, Ron/6671 W Sunset #1519, Los Angeles, CA	213-462-5731
Krogle, Bob/11607 Clover Ave, Los Angeles, CA	213-828-9653
Kung, Allan/15219 Normandie #12, Gardena, CA	213-372-6691

L

Labadie, Ed/1971 Glen Ave, Pasadena, CA	818-794-7705
Lagerstrom, Wendy/10462 Vanora Dr, Sunland, CA	818-352-5173
Lake, Larry/360 1/2 N Mansfield Ave, Los Angeles, CA	213-935-4696
Lamb, Dana/PO Box 1091, Yorba Linda, CA	714-996-3449
LaRose, Lou/8126 Blackburn Ave, Los Angeles, CA	213-858-0946
Larson, Ron/940 N Highland Ave, Los Angeles, CA	213-465-8451
Lauderbaugh, Lindah/2002 N Bronson, Los Angeles, CA	213-467-5444
Leary, Catherine/1830 S Robertson Blvd, Los Angeles, CA	213-204-1771
Lee, Warren/88 Meadow Valley Rd, Corte Madera, CA	415-924-0261
Leech, Richard & Associates/725 Filbert St, San Francisco, CA	415-981-4840
Leeds, Beth Whybrow/3916 Sacramento St, San Francisco, CA	415-221-8833
Leedy, Jeff/209 North St, Sausalito, CA	415-331-1354
Levine, Bette/149 N Hamilton Dr #A, Beverly Hills, CA	213-653-9765
Lew, Rictor/3 Damon Ct, Alameda, CA	415-769-7130
Lewis, Dennis/6671 Sunset #1519, Los Angeles, CA	213-462-5731
Lindsay, Martin/4469 41st St, San Diego, CA	619-281-8851
Livermore, Joanie/PO Box 828, Lake Oswego, OR	503-656-1399
Livingston, Francis/1537 Franklin St #105, San Francisco, CA	415-776-1531
Lloyd, Gregory/5534 Red River Dr, San Diego, CA	619-582-3487
Locke, Charles/PO Box 61986, Sunnyvale, CA	408-734-5298
Lohstoeter, Lori/278 Glen Arm, Pasadena, CA	818-244-3299
Losch, Diana/Pier 33 N Embarcadero, San Francisco, CA	415-956-5648
Lozano, Henry Jr/3205 Belle River Dr, Hacienda, CA	818-330-2095
Lulich, Ted/7033 SW Macadamia Ave #107, Portland, OR	503-244-6188
Lund, Gary/360 1/2 N Mansfield Ave, Los Angeles, CA	213-935-4696
Lundgren-Ellis, Alvalyn/1343 Thayer Ave, Los Angeles, CA	213-202-6197
Luth, Tom/2506 Spaulding #8, Long Beach, CA	213-434-5340
Lytle, John/PO Box 5155, Sonora, CA	209-928-4849

M

Machat, Mike/4426 Deseret Dr, Woodland Hills, CA	818-702-9433
MacLeod, Lee/200-A Westminster Ave, Venice, CA	213-392-4877
Mahoney, Patricia/251 Kearny St #511, San Francisco, CA	415-441-4384
Mann, David/186 Silas Ln, Newbury Park, CA	
Manzelman, Judy/9 1/2 Murray Ln, Larkspur, CA	415-461-9685
Maraldo, Vshanna/23316 Burbank Blvd, Woodland Hills, CA	818-703-8348
Marsh, Cynthia/4434 Matilija Ave, Sherman Oaks, CA	818-789-5232
Marshall, Craig/28 Abbey St, San Francisco, CA	415-641-1010
Martin, David/2131 Elsinore St, Los Angeles, CA	213-413-4600
Martin, Greg/731 Fourth St, Encinitas, CA	619-753-4073
Mattos, John/1546 Grant Ave, San Francisco, CA	415-397-2138
Mayeda, Kaz/243 Bickwell #A, Santa Monica, CA	213-452-0054
Mazzetti, Alan/244 Ninth St, San Francisco, CA	415-621-2992
McConnell, Jim/7789 Greenly Dr, Live Oak, CA	415-569-0852
McDonald, Mercedes/25 Montgomery St, Los Gatos, CA	408-395-6540
McDougall, Scott/712 N 62nd St, Seattle, WA	206-783-1403
McElroy, Darlene/2038 Calvert Ave, Costa Mesa, CA	714-556-8133
McKee, Ron/5455 Wilshire Blvd #1212, Los Angeles, CA	213-937-4472
McKiernan, James E/2501 Cherry Ave #310, Signal Hill, CA	213-427-1953
McMahon, Bob/6820 Independence Ave #31, Canoga Park, CA	818-999-4127

Merritt, Norman/5455 Wilshire Blvd #1212, Los Angeles, CA	213-937-4472
Metz Air Art/2817 E Lincoln Ave, Anaheim, CA	714-630-3071
Meyer, Gary/227 W Channel Rd, Santa Monica, CA	213-454-2174
Mikkelson, Linda S/1624 Vista Del Mar, Hollywood, CA	213-463-3116
Millsap, Darrel/1744 6th Ave, San Diego, CA	619-543-0122
Mitchell, Kathy/828 21st St #6, Santa Monica, CA	213-828-6331
Mitoma, Tim/1200 Dale Ave #17, Mountain View, CA	415-965-9734
Moats, George/PO Box 1187, Hanford, CA	209-584-9026
Moch, Paul/1414 Oakland Blvd #4, Walnut Creek, CA	415-932-5815
Monahan, Leo/1624 Vista Del Mar, Los Angeles, CA	213-463-3116
Montana Room Dsgn/2400 E 42nd Ave #403R, Seattle, WA	206-329-5489
Montoya, Ricardo/1025 E Lincoln Ave #D, Anaheim, CA	714-533-0507
Moreau, Alain/1461 1/2 S Beverly Dr, Los Angeles, CA	213-553-8529
Morse, Bill/173 18th Ave, San Francisco, CA	415-221-6711
Mortensen, Chris/140 University Ave #102, Palo Alto, CA	415-321-4787
Mortensen, Gordon/140 University Ave #102, Palo Alto, CA	415-321-4787
Mouri, Gary/25002 Reflejo, Mission Viejo, CA	714-951-8136
Moyna, Nancy/1125 6th St #4, Santa Monica, CA	213-458-1291
Mukai, Dennis/, , CA	213-452-9060
Murov, Debra/504 Strand St, Santa Monica, CA	213-396-6537
Murphy, Michael/333 Kearny St #607, San Francisco, CA	415-391-5153

N

Nasser, Christine/PO Box 3881, Manhattan Beach, CA	213-546-5106
Navarro, Arlene & Larry/1921 Comstock Ave, Los Angeles, CA	213-201-4744
Neila, Anthony/500 Sutter St #4215, San Francisco, CA	415-956-6344
Nelson, Craig/6010 Graciosa Dr, Los Angeles, CA	818-363-4494
Nelson, Mike/1836 Woodsdale Ct, Concord, CA	707-746-0800
Nelson, R Kenton/8800 Venice Blvd, Los Angeles, CA	213-838-1815
Nelson, Susan/2363 N Fitch Mtn Rd, Healdsburg, CA	707-431-7166
Nethery, Susan/1548 18th St, Santa Monica, CA	213-828-1931
Nicholson, Norman/21 Columbus #221, San Francisco, CA	415-421-2555
Nikosey, Tom/7417 Melrose Ave, Los Angeles, CA	213-655-2184
Noble, Larry/18603 Arminta, Reseda, CA	818-609-1605
Nolan, Dennis/579 Beresford Ave, Redwood City, CA	415-364-0366
Nordell, Dale/425 Randolph Ave, Seattle, WA	206-324-1199
Nordell, Marilyn/425 Randolph Ave, Seattle, WA	206-324-1199
Norman, Gary/11607 Clover Ave, Los Angeles, CA	213-828-9653
Nunez, Manuel/1073 W 9th St, San Pedro, CA	213-832-2471
Nye, Linda S/10951 Srrnto Val Rd #1H, San Diego, CA	619-455-5500

O

O'Brien, Kathy/401 Alameda del Prado, Navato, CA	415-883-2964
O'Mary, Tom/8418 Menkar Rd, San Diego, CA	619-578-5361
O'Neil, Sharron/409 Alberto Way #6, Los Gatos, CA	408-354-3816
Obrero, Rudy/1830 S Robertson Blvd, Los Angeles, CA	213-204-1771
Oden, Richard/631 Cliff Dr, Laguna Blvd, CA	714-760-7001
Olson, Mary Ann/19001 S Western Ave, Torrance, CA	213-618-4701
Oppenheim, Jenny/2163 Turstead Ave, St Anselmo, CA	
ORVIDIS, KEN/242 YALE AVE, KENSINGTON, CA (P 34)	**415-525-6626**
Osborne, Jacqueline & Stephen/101 Middlefield Rd, Palo Alto, CA	415-326-2276

P

Pace, Julie/130 N Jackson #101, Glendale, CA	818-246-3721
Page, Frank/11731 Crescenta, Los Angeles, CA	213-471-0232
Palay/Beaubois/724 Pine St, San Francisco, CA	415-362-0331
Pansini, Tom/16222 Howland Ln, Huntington Bch, CA	714-847-9329
Paris Productions/2207 Garnet, San Diego, CA	619-272-4992
Parkinson, Jim/6170 Broadway Terrace, Oakland, CA	415-547-3100
Parmentier, Henri/10462 Vanora Dr, Sunland, CA	818-352-5173
Passey, Kim/1319 Fremont Ave #1, S Pasadena, CA	818-441-4384
Pavesich, Vida/1152 Arch St, Berkeley, CA	415-528-8233
Peck, Everett/1352 Hornblend St, San Diego, CA	619-272-8147
Pederson, Sharleen/7742 Redland St #H3036, Playa Del Rey, CA	213-306-7847
Penido, Anthony/9336 W Washington Blvd Bldg O, Culver City, CA	818-796-4807
Peringer, Stephen/6046 Lakeshore Dr So, Seattle, WA	206-725-7779
Peterson, Barbara/2629 W Northwood, Santa Ana, CA	714-546-2786
Peterson, Eric/270 Termino Avenue, Long Beach, CA	213-438-2785
Pierazzi, Gary/1928 Cooley Ave #49, Palo Alto, CA	415-325-2677
Pina, Richard/600 Moulton #401, Los Angeles, CA	213-227-5213
Platz, Henry III/15922 118th Pl NE, Bothell, WA	206-488-9171

Illustrators

Continued

Please send us your additions and updates.

Pluym, Todd Vander/425 Via Anita, Redondo Beach, CA	213-378-5559
Podevin, J F/223 South Kenmore #4, Los Angeles, CA	213-739-5083
Pound, John/2124 Froude St, San Diego, CA	619-222-2476
Precision Illustration/11731 Crescenta, Los Angeles, CA	213-471-0232
Prochnow, Bill/1717 Union, San Francisco, CA	415-673-0825
Przewodek, Camille/4029 23rd St, San Francisco, CA	415-826-3238
Puchalski, John/8126 Blackburn Ave, Los Angeles, CA	213-858-0946
Putnam, Jamie/10th and Parker, Berkeley, CA	415-549-2500
Pyle, Chuck/146 10th Ave, San Francisco, CA	415-751-8087

R

Raess Design/424 N Larchmont Blvd, Los Angeles, CA	213-659-4928
Ramsay/ In the Black/119 Merchant St, Honolulu, HI	808-732-5700
Rand, Ted/425 Randolph Ave, Seattle, WA	206-324-1199
Ray, Christian/2022 Jones St, San Francisco, CA	415-928-0457
Raymond, T/1010 Urania Ave, Leucadia, CA	619-753-3341
Renz, Michael/1903-B E Denny Way, Seattle, WA	206-323-9257
Rhodes, Barbara/6455 La Jolla Blvd #338, La Jolla, CA	619-459-2045
Richardson, Nelva/2619 American River Dr, Sacramento, CA	916-482-7438
Rieser, William/419 Via Linda Vista, Redondo Beach, CA	213-373-4762
Rinaldi, Linda/5717 Chicopee, Encino, CA	818-881-1578
Robles, Bill/5455 Wilshire Blvd #1212, Los Angeles, CA	213-937-4472
Rodriguez, Robert/1548 18th St, Santa Monica, CA	213-828-2840
Rogers, Mike/7461 Beverly Blvd #405, Los Angeles, CA	213-938-5177
Rogers, Paul/6376 W 5th St, Los Angeles, CA	213-934-3395
Ross, Mary/652 Bair Isl Rd, Redwood City, CA	415-363-2130
Rother, Sue/1537 Franklin St #103, San Francisco, CA	415-387-7578
Rowe, Ken/36325 Panorama Dr, Yucaipa, CA	714-797-7030
Rutherford, John/55 Alvarado Ave, Mill Valley, CA	415-383-1788

S

Saint John, Bob/1036 S 6th Ave, Arcadia, CA	818-447-0375
Sakahara, Dick/28826 Cedarbluff Dr, Rancho Palos Verdes, CA	213-541-8187
Salk, Larry/7461 Beverly Blvd #405, Los Angeles, CA	213-938-5177
Salvati, Jim/983 S Euclid Ave, Pasadena, CA	818-441-2544
Sanford, James/1153 Oleander Rd, Lafayette, CA	415-284-9015
Sano, Kazu/105 Stadium Ave, Mill Valley, CA	415-381-6377
Saputo, Joe/4024 Jasper Rd, Springfield, OR	503-746-1737
Saunders, Alan/540 Seaver Dr, Mill Valley, CA	415-981-6612
Scanlan, David/145 N Orange, Los Angeles, CA	213-933-2500
Scanlon, Dave/1600 18th St, Manhattan Beach, CA	213-545-0773
Schields, Gretchen/4556 19th St, San Francisco, CA	415-558-8851
Schilens, Tim/1372 Winston Ct, Upland, CA	714-623-4999
Schmidt, Eric/1224-A North Brand, GLendale, CA	818-507-0263
Schumacher, Michael/2030 First Ave #201, Seattle, WA	206-623-9459
Schwegler, Janice/365 Carroll Park E, Long Beach, CA	213-439-3838
Scribner, Jo Anne L/3314 N Lee, Spokane, WA	509-484-3208
Seckler, Judy/12 S Fair Oaks Ave, Pasadena, CA	818-508-8778
Shehorn, Gene/1672 Lynwood Dr, Concord, CA	415-687-4516
Shepherd, Roni/1 San Antonio Pl, San Francisco, CA	415-421-9764
Shields, Bill/14 Wilmot, San Francisco, CA	415-346-0376
Sigwart, Forrest/1033 S Orlando Ave, Los Angeles, CA	213-655-7734
Silberstein, Simon/1131 Alta Loma Rd #516, W Hollywood, CA	213-652-5226
Sizemore, Ted/10642 Vanora Dr, Sunland, CA	818-352-5173
Smith, J J/4239 1/2 Lexington Ave, Los Angeles, CA	213-668-2408
Smith, John C/2030 First Ave #201, Seattle, WA	206-623-9459
Smith, Terry/10642 Vanora Dr, Sunland, CA	818-352-5173
Sobel, June/706 Marine St, Santa Monica, CA	213-392-2842
Solvang-Angell, Diane/425 Randolph Ave, Seattle, WA	206-324-1199
South, Randy/1724 20th St, San Francisco, CA	415-695-9606
Spear, Jeffrey A/1228 11th St #201, Santa Monica, CA	213-395-3939
Spear, Randy/4325 W 182nd St #20, Torrance, CA	213-370-6071
Specht/Watson Studio/1246 S La Cienega Blvd, Los Angeles, CA	213-652-2682
Speidel, Sandy/14 Wilmot, San Francisco, CA	415-923-1363
Spencer, Joe/11201 Valley Spring Ln, Studio City, CA	818-760-0216
Sprattler, Rob/360 1/2 N Mansfield Ave, Los Angeles, CA	503-692-6940
Starkweather, Teri/4633 Galendo St, Woodland Hills, CA	818-992-5938
Steele, Robert/14 Wilmot, San Francisco, CA	415-923-0741
Stehrenberger, Mark/11731 Crescenta, Los Angeles, CA	213-471-0232
Stein, Mike/4340 Arizona, San Diego, CA	619-295-2455
Stein, Richard/3037 20th Ave W, Seattle, WA	206-282-4856
Steine, Debra/6561 Green Gables Ave, San Diego, CA	619698-5854

Stepp, Don/275 Marguerita Ln, Pasadena, CA	818-799-0263
Stermer, Dugald/1801 Franklin St #404, San Francisco, CA	415-441-4384
Stewart, Barbara/1640 Tenth Ave #5, San Diego, CA	619-238-0083
Stewart, Walt/PO Box 621, Sausalito, CA	415-868-0481
Steine, Debra/6561 Green Gables Ave, San Diego, CA	619-698-5854
Stoll, Bruce/1534 Queens Ct, Claremont, CA	714-621-9316
Stout, William G/812 S LaBrea, Hollywood, CA	213-936-6342
Strange, Jedd/4684 Saratoga St, San Diego, CA	619-225-9733
Suma, Doug/448 Bryant St, San Francisco, CA	415-777-2120
Suvityasiri, Sarn/1811 Leavenworth St, San Francisco, CA	415-928-1602
Svoboda, John/3211-B S Shannon, Santa Ana, CA	714-979-8992

T

Tanenbaum, Robert/5505 Corbin Ave, Tarzana, CA	818-345-6741
Tarbox, Marla/2611 Morningside St, Pasadena, CA	818-584-1004
Tarleton, Suzanne/1740 Stanford St, Santa Monica, CA	213-478-9412
Taylor, C Winston/17008 Lisette St, Granada Hills, CA	818-363-5761
Thompson, Brian/805-A E Mobeck, West Covina, CA	818-338-9002
Thon, Bud/410 View Park Ct, Mill Valley, CA	415-332-5319
Thornton, Blake/48 Mozden Lane, Pleasant Hill, CA	415-676-7166
Tilley, Debbie/2821 Camino Del Mar #78, Del Mar, CA	619-481-3251
Timmons, Bonnie/1046 N Orange Dr, Los Angeles, CA	213-462-5622
Tomita, Tom/3568 E Melton, Pasadena, CA	818-796-4213
Tompkins, Tish/1660 Redcliff St, Los Angeles, CA	213-662-1660
Tsuchiya, Julie/780 Bryant St, San Francisco, CA	415-495-4278
Tucker, Ezra/4634 Woodman Ave #202, Sherman Oaks, CA	818-905-0758
Twomey, Catherine/4700 4th Ave NE, Seattle, WA	206-632-4717

U V

Unger, Joe/17120 NE 96th St, Redmond, WA	206-883-1419
Unger, Judy/14160 Oro Grande St, Sylmar, CA	818-362-6470
Unruh, Jack/716 Montgomery St, San Francisco, CA	415-433-1222
Vance, Jay/676 Lafayette Park Place, Los Angeles, CA	213-387-1171
Vandervoort, Gene/3201 S Ramona Dr, Santa Ana, CA	714-549-3194
Vanderwielen Designs/19000 MacArthur Blvd #1141, Irvine, CA	714-733-0921
Vanle, Jay/638 S Van Ness Ave, Los Angeles, CA	213-382-6281
Vargas, Kathy/5082 Tasman Dr, Huntington Beach, CA	213-721-5960
Vigon, Jay/708 S Orange Grove Ave, Los Angeles, CA	213-937-0355
Vinson, W T/4118 Vernon, Glen Avon, CA	714-685-7697
Voss, Tom/525 West B St #G, San Diego, CA	619-238-1673

W

Wack, Jeff/3614 Berry Dr, Studio City, CA	818-508-0348
Walden, Craig/425 Randolph Ave, Seattle, WA	206-324-1199
Walstead, Curt/398 Via Colinas, Westlake Village, CA	818-706-2304
Waters Art Studio/1820 E Garry St #207, Santa Ana, CA	714-250-4466
Watson, Richard Jesse/PO Box 1470, Murphys, CA	209-728-2701
Watts, Stan/3896 San Marcus Ct, Newbury Park, CA	805-499-4747
Weston, Will/135 S LaBrea, Los Angeles, CA	213-854-3666
Wexler, Ed/4701 Don Pio Dr, Woodland Hills, CA	818-888-3858
Whidden Studios/11772 Sorrnto Val Rd #260, San Diego, CA	619-455-1776
White, Charles William/1725 Berkeley St, Santa Monica, CA	213-453-4418
Whitten, Leesa/507 South Euclid, Pasadena, CA	818-957-7899
Wicks, Ren/5455 Wilshire Blvd #1212, Los Angeles, CA	213-937-4472
Willardson + Assoc/103 W California, Glendale, CA	818-242-5688
Wilson, Dick/11607 Clover Ave, Los Angeles, CA	213-828-9653
Wilson, Rowland/7501 Solano St, La Costa, CA	619-944-3631
Winston, Jeannie/8800 Venice Blvd, Los Angeles, CA	213-558-0141
Winters, Greg/2139 Pinecrest Dr, Altadena, CA	818-798-7666
Witus, Edward/2932 Wilshire Blvd #202, Santa Monica, CA	213-828-6521
Wolfe, Bruce/206 El Cerrito Ave, Piedmont, CA	415-655-7871
Wolin, Ron/4501 Firmament, Encino, CA	818-783-0523
Woodward, Teresa/544 Paseo Miramar, Pacific Palisades, CA	213-459-2317
Wray, Greg/6376 W 5th St, Los Angeles, CA	213-934-3395
Wright, Jonathan/2110 Holly Dr, Los Angeles, CA	213-461-1091

X Y Z

Xavier, Roger/23200 Los Codona Ave, Torrance, CA	213-375-1663
Yenne, Bill/111 Pine St, San Francisco, CA	415-989-2450
Yeomans, Jeff/820 Deal Ct #C, San Diego, CA	619-488-2502
Zaslavsky, Morris/228 Main St #6, Venice, CA	213-399-3666
Zebot, George/PO Box 4295, Laguna Beach, CA	714-499-5027
Zick, Brian/3251 Primera Ave, Los Angeles, CA	213-855-8855
Zito, Andy/135 S La Brea Ave, Los Angeles, CA	213-931-1181
Zitting, Joel/2404 Ocean Park Blvd #A, Santa Monica, CA	213-452-7009

Photographers

New York City

A

Abatelli, Gary/80 Charles St #3W	212-254-2142
Abel, Jim/112 E 19th St	212-460-5374
Abramowitz, Ellen/166 E 35th St #4H	212-686-2409
Abramowitz, Jerry/680 Broadway	212-420-9500
Abramson, Michael/84 University Pl	212-737-1890
Adamo, Jeff/50 W 93rd St #8P	212-866-4886
Adams, Eddie/29 E 22nd St #68	212-477-5346
Adams, George G./15 W 38th St	212-391-1345
Adelman, Barbara Ellen/267 Mayfair Dr	718-531-8054
Adelman, Bob/151 W 28th St	212-736-0537
Adelman, Menachem Assoc/156 Fifth Ave #323	212-675-1202
Adler, Arnie/70 Park Terrace W	212-304-2443
Aerographics/514 W 24th St	212-362-9546
Agor, Alexander/108-28 Flatlands 7 St	212-777-1775
Aharoni, Oudi/704 Broadway	212-777-0847
Aich, Clara/218 E 25th St	212-686-4220
Akis, Emanuel/6 W 18th St #803	212-620-0299
Albert, Jade/59 W 19th St #3B	212-242-0940
Albert, Peter/59 W 71st St	212-787-1759
Alberts, Andrea/100 Fifth Ave	212-242-5794
Alcorn, Richard/160 W 95th St #7A	212-866-1161
Alexander, Robert/50 W 29th St	212-684-0496
Alexanders, John W/308 E 73rd St	212-734-9166
Allen, Jim/175 Fifth Ave #1112	212-473-8020
Allison, David/42 E 23rd St	212-460-9056
Alper, Barbara/202 W 96th St	212-316-6518
Alpern/Lukoski/250 W 88th St	212-724-5017
Alt, Howard/24 W 31st St	212-594-3300
Amato, Paul/154 W 57th St	212-541-4787
Ambrose, Ken/44 E 23rd St	212-260-4848
Amplo, Nick/271 1/2 W 10th St	212-741-2799
Amrine, Jamie/30 W 22nd St	212-243-2178
Andracke, Gregory/207 W 86th St	212-580-9964
Andrews, Bert/PO Box 20707	212-662-6732
Anik, Adam/111 Fourth Ave #1-I	212-228-4148
Antonio/Stephen Photo/45 E 20th St	212-674-2350
Apple, Richard/80 Varick St #4B	212-966-6782
Arakawa, Nobu/40 E 21st St	212-475-0206
Aranita, Jeffrey/60 Pineapple St	718-625-7672
Arky, David/57 W 19th St #2A	212-242-4760
Arlak, Victoria/40 East End Ave	212-879-0250
Arma, Tom/38 W 26th St	212-243-7904
Arndt, Dianne/400 Central Park West	212-866-1902
ARSLANIAN, OVAK/344 W 14TH ST (P 50,51)	**212-255-1519**
Ashe, Bill/534 W 35th St	212-695-6473
Ashley, Pat/920 Broadway	212-473-6180
Atkin, Jonathan/23 E 17th St	212-242-5218
Aubry, Daniel/365 First Ave	212-598-4191
Augustine, Paula/50 Park Terr E	212-304-0234
Aurora Retouching/19 W 21st St	212-255-0620
Auster, Walter/35 W 38th St	212-354-0456
Avedis/381 Park Ave S	212-685-5888
Avedon, Richard/407 E 75th St	212-879-6325
Axon, Red/17 Park Ave	212-532-6317
Azzato, Hank/348 W 14th St 3rd Fl	212-929-9455
Azzi, Robert/415 Madison Ave	212-750-1020

B

Baasch, Diane/41 W 72nd St #11F	212-724-2123
Babushkin, Mark/110 W 31st St	212-239-6630
Back, John/15 Sheridan Sq	212-243-6347
Bahrt, Irv/310 E 46th St	212-661-5260
Baillie, Allan & Gus Francisco/220 E 23rd St 11th Fl	212-683-0418
Bak, Sunny/876 Broadway 4th Fl	212-677-1712
Baker, Chuck/1630 York Ave	212-517-9060
Baker, Gloria/415 Central Park W	212-222-2866
BAKER, JOE/35 WOOSTER ST (P 52)	**212-925-6555**
Bakerman, Nelson/342 W 56th St #1D	212-489-1647
Baldwin, Joel/29 E 19th St	212-533-7470
Bancroft, Monty/161 W 15th St	212-807-8650

Barash, Howard/349 W 11th St	212-242-6182
Baratta, Nicholas/511 W 33rd St	212-239-0999
Barba, Dan/201 E 16th St	212-420-8611
Barber, James/873 Broadway	212-598-4500
Barboza, Tony/108 E 16th St	212-807-8233
Barcellona, Marianne/36 E 20 St 5th Floor	212-460-8740
Barclay, Bob Studios/5 W 19th St 6th Fl	212-255-3440
Barkentin, George/15 W 18th St	212-243-2174
Barnell, Joe/164 Madison Ave	212-686-8850
Barnett, Peggy/26 E 22nd St	212-673-0500
Barns, Larry/21 W 16th St	212-242-8833
Barr, Neal/222 Central Park South	212-765-5760
Barrett, John/164 E 66th St	212-517-5210
Barrett, John E/40 E 20th St 7th Fl	212-777-7309
Barrick, Rick/12 E 18th St 4th Fl	212-741-2304
Barrow, Scott/214 W 30th St #6	212-736-4567
Barrows, Wendy/205 E 22nd St #4H	212-685-0799
Barton, Paul/101 W 18th St 4th Fl	212-533-1422
Batlin, Lee/37 E 28th St 8th Fl	212-685-9492
Baum, Charles/320 West End Ave	212-724-8013
Baumel, Ken/119 W 23rd St	212-929-7550
Bava, John/51 Station Ave	718-967-9175
Bealmear, Brad/54 Barrow St	212-675-8060
Bean, John/5 W I9th St	212-242-8106
Beaudin, Ted/450 W 31st St	212-563-6065
Bechtold, John/117 E 31st St	212-679-7630
Beck, Arthur/119 W 22nd St	212-691-8331
Becker, Jonathan/450 West 24th St	212-929-3180
Beckhard, Robert/130 E 24th St	212-777-1411
Beebe, Rod/790 Amsterdam #4D	212-678-7832
Beglieter, Steven/2025 Broadway #19K	212-580-7409
Belinsky, Jon/119 E 17th St	212-627-1246
Beller, Janet/568 Broadway	212-334-0281
Benedict, William/5 Tudor City	212-697-4460
Bennett, Philip/1181 Broadway	212-683-3906
Bercow, Larry/209 W 38th St	212-221-1598
Berenholtz, Richard/600 W 111th St #6A	212-222-1302
BERGER, JOSEPH/121 MADISON AVE #3B (P 53)	**212-685-7191**
Bergman, Beth/150 West End Ave	212-724-1867
Bergren, John/27 W 20th St #1003	212-989-4423
Berkun, Phil/199 Amity St #2	718-237-2648
Berkwit, Lane/262 Fifth Ave	212-889-5911
Berman, Brad/295 Ecksford St	718-383-8950
Berman, Howard/5 E 19th St #303	212-473-3366
Berman, Malcolm/256 Fifth Ave	212-431-4446
Bernson, Carol/119 Fifth Ave #806	212-473-3884
Bernstein, Alan/365 First Ave 2nd Fl	212-254-1355
Bernstein, Bill/59 Thompson St #9	212-925-6853
Bester, Roger/55 Van Dam St 11th Fl	212-645-5810
Betz, Charles/50 W 17th St	212-807-0457
Bevan, David/536 W 50th St	212-582-5045
Bevilacqua, Joe/202 E 42nd St	212-490-0355
Bickford, Christopher/55 W 11th St	212-243-6638
Biddle, Geoffrey/5 E 3rd St	212-505-7713
Bies, William/221 W 21st St	212-924-6997
Big City Prodctns/5 E 19th St #303	212-473-3366
Bijur, Hilda/190 E 72nd St	212-737-4458
Bisbee, Terry/290 W 12th St	212-242-4762
Bishop, David/251 W 19th St	212-929-4355
Blachut, Dennis/145 W 28th St 8th Fl	212-947-4270
Blackburn, Joseph M/116 W 29th St #2C	212-947-7674
Blackman, Barry/115 E 23rd St 10th Fl	212-473-3100
Blackman, Jeffrey/2323 E 12th St	718-769-0986
Blackstock, Ann/400 W 43rd St #4E	212-695-2525
Blake, Rebecca/35 W 36th St	212-695-6438
Blechman, Jeff/591 Broadway	212-966-1455
BLECKER, CHARLES/380 BLEECKER ST #3G (P 55)	**212-242-8390**
Blegen, Alana/	718-769-2619
Blinkoff, Richard/147 W 15th St 3rd Fl	212-620-7883
Block, Ira Photography/215 W 20th St	212-242-2728
Bloom, Teri/300 Mercer St #6C	212-475-2274
Blosser, Robert/741 West End Ave #3C	212-662-0107

Photographers
Continued

Please send us your additions and updates.

Bobbe, Leland/51 W 28th St	212-685-5238
Bodi Studios/340 W 39th St	212-947-7883
Bodick, Gay/11 E 80th St	212-772-8584
Bogertman, Ralph Inc/34 W 28th St	212-889-8871
BOLESTA, ALAN/11 RIVERSIDE DR #13SE (P 56,57)	**212-873-1932**
Boljonis, Steven/555 Ft Washington Ave #4A	212-740-0003
Bono, Mary/PO Box 1502	212-475-6266
Bonomo, Louis/118 W 27th St #2F	212-242-4630
Bordnick, Barbara/39 E 19th St	212-533-1180
Borowski, Steve/236 E 74th St	212-772-0811
Bosch, Peter/477 Broome St	212-925-0707
Boszko, Ron/140 W 57th St	212-541-5504
Bottomley, Jim/125 Fifth Ave	212-677-9646
Bracco, Bob/43 E 19th St	212-228-0230
BRADY, STEVE/507 E 30TH ST (P 58,59)	**212-213-6024**
Brandt, Peter/73 Fifth Ave #6B	212-242-4289
Braun, Yenachem/666 West End Ave	212-873-1985
Braune, Peter/134 W 32nd St #602	212-244-4270
Braverman, Alan/PO Box 865	212-674-1925
Brenner, George/15 W 24th St	212-691-7436
Brenner, Jay/18 E 17th St	212-741-2244
Breskin, Michael/324 Lafayette	212-925-2858
Brewster, Don/235 West End Ave	212-874-0548
Bridges, Kiki/147 W 26th St	212-807-6563
Brill Studio/270 City Island Ave	212-885-0802
Brill, James/160 W 16th St	212-645-9414
Britton, Peter/315 E 68th St	212-737-1664
Brizzi, Andrea/175 Washington Park	212-627-2341
Brody, Bob/5 W 19th 2nd Fl	212-741-0013
Bronstein, Steve/5 E 19th St #303	212-473-3366
Brooke, Randy/179 E 3rd St	212-677-2656
Brosan, Roberto/873 Broadway	212-473-1471
Brown, David/Nancy/6 W 20th St 2nd Fl	212-675-8067
Brown, Kirk Q/353 Lexington Ave 15th Fl	212-687-9224
Brown, Owen Studio/134 W 29th St 2nd Fl	212-947-9470
Bruderer, Rolf/443 Park Ave S	212-684-4890
Bruno Burklin/873 Broadway	212-420-0208
Bruno Photo/43 Crosby St 1st Fl	212-925-2929
Brunswick, Cecile/127 W 96th St	212-222-2088
Bryce, Sherman E/269 W 90th St #3B	212-580-9639
Bryson, John/12 E 62nd St	212-755-1321
Buceta, Jaime/56 W 22nd St 6th Fl	212-807-8485
Buck, Bruce/39 W 14th St	212-645-1022
Buckler, Susanne/344 W 38th St	212-279-0043
Buckner, Bill/21 W 17th St	212-242-5129
Burns, Tom/534 W 35th St	212-927-4678
Burquez, Felizardo/22-63 38th St #1	718-274-6139
Burrell, Fred/54 W 21st St #1207	212-691-0808
Butler, Dennis/200 E 37th St 4th Fl	212-686-5084

C

Cadge, Bill & Jeff/15 W 28th St	212-685-2435
Cailor/Resnick/237 W 54th St 4th Fl	212-977-4300
Calicchio, Tom/30 E 21st St	212-473-8990
Callis, Chris/91 Fifth Ave	212-243-0231
Camera Communications/110 Greene St	212-925-2722
Camp, E J/101 W 18th St	212-741-2872
Campbell, Barbara/147 W 22nd St	212-929-5620
Campos, John/132 W 21st St	212-675-0601
Canady, Philip/1411 Second Ave	212-737-3855
Cannon, Gregory/876 Broadway 2nd Fl	212-724-6196
Cantor, Phil/75 Ninth Ave 8th Fl	212-243-1143
Cardacino, Michael/20 Ridge Rd	212-947-9307
Cargasacchi, Gianni/175 Fifth Ave	212-473-8020
Carlton, Chuck/36 E 23rd St 7th Fl	212-777-1099
Carrino, John/160 Fifth Ave #914	212-243-3623
Carron, Les/15 W 24th St 2nd Fl	212-255-8250
Carson, Donald/115 W 23rd St	212-807-8987
Carter, Dwight/11 W 17th St	212-627-1266
Casey/10 Park Ave #3E	212-984-1397
Cashin, Art/5 W 19th St	212-255-3440
Casper, Mike/70 Wooster St	212-219-1257
Castellano, Peter/162 W 21st St	212-206-6320

Castelli, Charles/41 Union Sq W #425	212-620-5536
Castillo, Luis A/60 Pineapple St	718-834-1380
Caulfield, Patricia/115 W 86th St #2E	212-362-1951
Caverly, Kat/414 W 49th St	212-757-8388
Cearley, Guy/25 W 31st St	212-714-0075
Celnick, Edward/36 E 12th St	212-420-9326
Cenicola, Tony Studio/503 W 43rd St	212-239-6634
Cerniglio, Tom/594 Broadway #8W	212-925-9583
Chakmakjian, Paul/35 W 36th St 8th Fl	212-563-3195
Chalk, David/265 37th St PH-A	212-564-0693
Chalkin, Dennis/5 E 16th St	212-929-1036
Chan, T S/174 Duane St	212-219-0574
Chaney, Scott/5 W 30th St	212-736-1720
Chanteau, Pierre/209 W 38th St	212-221-5860
Chao, John/51 W 81st St #6B	212-580-7912
Chapman, Mike/37 E 4th St	212-529-3626
Charlas, Jacques/134 Beaumont	718-648-5345
Charles, Bill/265 W 37th St #PH-D	212-719-9156
Charles, Frederick/254 Park Ave S #7F	212-505-0686
Charles, Lisa/119 W 23rd St	212-807-8600
Chauncy, Kim/123 W 13th St	212-242-2400
Checani, Richard/1133 Broadway	212-645-8634
Chelsea Photo/Graphics/641 Ave of Americas	212-206-1780
Chen, Paul Inc/133 Fifth Ave	212-674-4100
Chernin, Bruce/330 W 86th St	212-496-0266
Chestnut, Richard/236 W 27th St	212-255-1790
Chiba/303 Park Ave S #506	212-674-7575
Chin, Ted/118 W 27th St #3R	212-691-7612
Chokel, Dan/135 W 29th St	212-947-5795
Choucroun, Irit/450 Broome St #3E	212-226-0191
Christensen, Paul H/286 Fifth Ave	212-279-2838
Chrynwski, Walter/154 W 18th St	212-675-1906
Chu, H L & Co Ltd/39 W 29th St	212-889-4818
Church, Diana/31 W 31st St	212-736-4116
Cipolla, Karen/103 Reade St 3rd Fl	212-619-6114
Cirone, Bettina/57 W 58th St	212-888-7649
Clarke, Kevin/900 Broadway 9th Fl	212-460-9360
Clayton, Tom/568 Broadway #601	212-431-3377
Clementi, Joseph Assoc/133 W 19th St 3rd Fl	212-924-7770
Clough, Terry/147 W 25th St	212-255-3040
CLYMER, JONATHAN/146 W 29TH ST (P 61)	**212-714-9041**
Cobb, Jan/381 Park Ave S #922	212-889-2257
Cobin, Martin/145 E 49th St	212-758-5742
Cochran, George/381 Park Ave S	212-689-9054
Coggin, Roy/64 W 21st St	212-929-6262
Cohen, James/580 Eighth Ave	212-719-2790
Cohen, Joel/27 E 13th St #7E	212-691-5129
Cohen, Lawrence/277 E 10th St	212-777-3346
Cohen, Lawrence Photo/247 W 30th St	212-967-4376
Cohen, Marc David/5 W 19th	212-741-0015
Cohen, Robert/175 Fifth Ave #1112	212-473-8020
Cohn, Ric/137 W 25th St #1	212-924-6749
COLABELLA, VINCENT/304 E 41ST ST (P 62)	**212-949-7456**
Colby, Ron/140 E 28th St	212-684-3084
Cole, Bob/131-03 233rd St	718-525-7471
Coleman, Bruce/381 Fifth Ave 2nd Fl	212-683-5227
Coleman, Gene/250 W 27th St	212-691-4752
Colen, Corrine/519 Broadway	212-431-7425
Collins, Arlene/64 N Moore St #3E	212-431-9117
Collins, Chris/381 Park Ave S	212-725-0237
Collins, Joe J/208 Garfield Pl	718-965-4836
Collins, Sheldon/27 W 24th St	212-242-0076
Colliton, Paul/310 Greenwich St	212-619-6102
Colton, Robert/1700 York Ave	212-831-3953
Connelly, Hank/6 W 37th St	212-563-9109
Connors, William/310 E 46th St	212-490-3801
Contact Press Images/135 Central Park West	212-496-5300
Cook, Irvin/534 W 43rd St	212-925-6216
Cook, Rod/29 E 19th St	212-995-0100
Cooke, Colin/380 Lafayette St	212-254-5090
Cooper, Martha/310 Riverside Dr #805	212-222-5146
Cooper, Steve/5 W 31st St	212-279-4543

Photographers
Continued

Please send us your additions and updates.

Cope, Gil/135 W 26th St	212-929-1777
Corbett, Jane/303 Park Ave S #512	212-505-1177
Cornicello, John/245 W 29th St	212-564-0874
Cornish, Dan/594 Broadway #1204	212-226-3183
Corporate Photographers Inc/45 John St	212-964-6515
Cosimo/43 W 13th St	212-206-1818
Couzens, Larry/16 E 17th St	212-620-9790
Cowan, Frank/5 E 16th St	212-675-5960
Craig Jr, Stuart L/381 Fifth Ave 2nd Floor	212-683-5475
Crampton, Nancy/35 W 9th St	212-254-1135
Crocker, Ted/117 E 30th St	212-686-8684
Croner, Ted/15 W 28th St	212-685-3944
Cronin, Casey/115 Wooster St	212-334-9253
Crum, John R Photography/450 W 31st St	212-736-2693
Cserna, George/80 Second Ave #2	212-477-3472
Culberson, Earl/119 W 23rd St	212-473-3366
Cunningham, Peter/214 Sullivan St	212-475-4866
Curatola, Tony/18 E 17th St	212-243-5478
Cutler, Craig/536 W 50th St	212-315-3440
Czaplinski, Czeslaw/90 Dupont St	718-389-9606

D
D'Addio, James/41 Union Sq W #1428	212-645-0267
D'Innocenzo, Paul/368 Broadway #604	212-925-9622
Daley, James D/568 Broadway	212-925-7192
Daly, Jack/247 W 30th St	212-695-2726
Dantuono, Paul/433 Park Ave So	212-683-5778
Dantzic, Jerry/910 President St	718-789-7478
Dauman, Henri/4 E 88th St	212-737-1434
David, Gabrielle/109-35 Ditmars Blvd	718-429-0751
Davidson, Bruce/251 Park Ave S 11th Fl	212-475-7600
Davidson, Darwin K/32 Bank Street	212-242-0095
Davis, Dick/400 E 59th St	212-751-3276
Davis, Don/61 Horatio St	212-989-2820
Davis, Hal/131 Spring St	212-334-8113
Davis, Harold/874 Broadway #407	212-228-0866
Davis, Richard/17 E 16th St 9th Fl	212-675-2428
Day, Bob/29 E 19th St	212-475-7387
Day, Olita/239 Park Ave South	212-673-9354
De Zanger, Arie/80 W 40th St	212-354-7327
DeFrancis, Peter/424 Broome St	212-966-1357
DeGrado, Drew/250 W 40th St 5th Fl	212-302-2760
DeLessio, Len/7 E 17th St	212-206-8725
DeMarchelier, Patrick/162 W 21st St	212-924-3561
DeMelo, Antonio/126 W 22nd St	212-929-0507
DeMenil, Adelaide/222 Central Park South	212-541-8265
DeMilt, Ronald/873 Broadway 2nd Fl	212-228-5321
Denner, Manuel/249 W 29th St 4th Fl	212-947-6220
Dennis, Lisl/135 E 39th St	212-532-8226
Denson, Walt/70 W 83rd St Dplx B	212-496-7305
DePaul, Raymond/252 W 76th St #1A	212-769-2550
DePra, Nancy/15 W 24th St	212-242-0252
Derex, David/247 W 35th St	212-947-9302
Dermer, Ronald/Falmouth St	718-332-2464
DeRosa, Peter/117 W 95th St	212-864-3007
DERR, STEPHEN/420 W 45TH ST (P 63)	**212-246-5920**
DeSanto, Thomas/134 Fifth Ave 2nd Fl	212-989-5622
DeToy, Ted/205 W 19th St	212-675-6744
Deutsch, Jack/165 W 83rd St	212-799-7179
DeVito, Bart/43 E 30th St 14th Fl	212-889-9670
DeVito, Michael Jr/48 W 25th St	212-243-5267
DeVoe, Marcus E/34 E 81st St	212-737-9073
DeWys, Leo/1170 Broadway	212-689-5580
DeZitter, Harry/57 W 19th St	212-242-3124
Diamond, Joe/915 West End Ave	212-316-5295
Dian, Russell/432 E 88th St #201	212-722-4348
Diaz, Jorge/142 W 24th St 12th Fl	212-675-4783
Dibue, Robert/40 W 20th St	212-490-0486
Dicran Studio/35 W 36th St 11th Fl	212-695-6438
DiFranza Williamson Photography/1414 Ave of Americas	212-832-2343
DiMartini, Sally/201 W 16th St	212-989-8369
Dodge, Jeff/133 Eighth Ave	212-620-9652
Doerzbacher, Cliff/12 Cottage Ave	718-984-7522

Doherty, Marie/43 E 22nd St	212-674-8767
Dominis, John/1271 6th Ave Rm 2850	212-841-2340
Dorf, Myron Jay/205 W 19th St 3rd Fl	212-255-2020
Dorot, Didier/48 W 21st St 9th Fl	212-206-1608
Doubilet, David/1040 Park Ave #6J	212-348-5011
Drabkin, Si Studios Inc/236 W 27th St	212-206-7040
Drew Studio/250 W 40th St	212-302-2760
Drew, Rue Faris/177 E 77th St	212-794-8994
Drivas, Joseph/15 Beacon Ave	718-667-0696
Duchaine, Randy/200 W 18th St #4F	212-243-4371
Duke, Dana/620 Broadway	212-260-3334
Dunand, Frank/18 W 27th St	212-686-3478
Duncan, Nena/24 W 30th St 8th Fl	212-696-9652
Dunkley, Richard/175 Fifth Ave #1112	212-473-8020
Dunning, Hank/50 W 22nd St	212-675-6040
Dunning, Robert & Deane/57 W 58th St	212-688-0788
Duomo Photo Inc/133 W 19th St	212-243-1150

E
Eagan, Timothy/319 E 75th St	212-517-7665
Eastep, Wayne/443 Park Ave S #1006	212-686-8404
Eberstadt, Fred/791 Park Ave	212-794-9471
Eckstein, Ed/234 Fifth Ave 5th Fl	212-685-9342
Edahl, Edward/236 W 27th St	212-929-2002
Edgeworth, Anthony/333 Fifth Ave	212-679-6031
Edwards, Gregory/30 East End Ave	212-879-4339
Eguiguren, Carlos/139 E 57th St 3rd Fl	212-888-6732
Ehrenpreis, Dave/156 Fifth Ave	212-242-1976
Eisenberg, Steve/448 W 37th St	212-563-2061
Elbers, Johan/18 E 18th St	212-929-5783
Elgort, Arthur/300 Central Park West	212-219-8775
Elios-Zunini Studio/142 W 4th St	212-228-6827
Elkins, Joel/5 E 16th St	212-989-4500
Ellis, Ray/176 Westminster Rd	718-282-6449
Ellis, Roz/37 W 26th St 5th Fl	212-481-3770
Elmer, Jo/200 E 87th St	212-369-7077
Elmore, Steve/1640 York Ave #3B	212-472-2463
Elness, Jack/236 W 26th St	212-242-5045
Elz, Barry/13 Worth St	212-431-7910
Emberling, David/38 W 26th St	212-242-7455
Emil, Pamela/327 Central Park West	212-749-4716
Endress, John Paul/254 W 31st St	212-736-7800
Englander, Maury/43 Fifth Ave	212-242-9777
Englehardt, Duk/80 Varick St #4E	212-226-6490
Epstein, Mitch/353 E 77th St	212-517-3648
Epstein, S Karin/233 E 70th St	212-472-0771
ESSEL, ROBERT/39 W 71ST ST #A (P 64)	**212-877-5228**
Estrada, Sigrid/902 Broadway	212-673-4300
Everett, Michael/15 W 28th St	212-243-0627

F
Farber, Robert/232 E 58th St	212-486-9090
Faria, Rui/304 Eighth Ave #3	212-243-6343
Farrell, Bill/381 Park Ave S	212-683-1425
Farrell, John/611 Broadway #905	212-460-9001
Favero, Jean P/208 Fifth Ave #3E	212-683-9188
Fay, Stephen Studios/154 W 57th St	212-757-3717
Feibel, Theodor/102-10 66th Rd #15C	718-897-2445
Feinstein, Gary/19 E 17th St	212-242-3373
Feintuch, Harvey/1440 E 14th St	718-339-0301
Feldman, Andy/515 10th St	718-788-6585
Feller, Nora/269 W 25th St	212-620-3155
Fellerman, Stan/152 W 25th St	212-243-0027
Fellman, Sandi/548 Broadway	212-925-5187
Ferguson, Phoebe/289 Cumberland St	718-643-1675
Ferri, Mark/463 Broome St	212-431-1356
Ferris, William/208 W 23rd St	212-691-7108
Fetter, Frank/400 E 78th St	212-249-3138
Fields, Bruce/71 Greene St	212-431-8852
Finkelman, Allan/118 E 28th St #608	212-684-3487
Finlay, Alastair/38 E 21st St 9th Fl	212-260-4297
Finley, Calvin/59 Franklin St	212-219-8759
Firman, John/434 E 75th St	212-794-2794
Fischer, Carl/121 E 83rd St	212-794-0400

Fishbein, Chuck/276 Fifth Ave #1103	212-532-4452
Fisher, Jon/236 W 27th St	212-206-6311
Fishman, Chuck/69 1/2 Morton St	212-242-3987
Fishman, Robert/153 W 27th St #502	212-620-7976
Fiur, Lola Troy/360 E 65th St	212-861-1911
Flash Flood Enterprises/PO Box 1955/Old Chelsea Sta	212-627-7157
Flatow, Carl/20 E 30th St	212-683-8688
Floret, Evelyn/3 E 80th St	212-472-3179
Floyd, Bob/PO Box 216	212-684-0795
Flying Camera/114 Fulton St	212-619-0808
Flynn, Richard/306 W 4th St	212-243-0834
Forastieri, Marili/156 Fifth Ave #1301	212-431-1846
Forelli, Chip/316 Fifth Ave	212-564-1835
Forrest, Bob/273 Fifth Ave 3rd Fl	212-288-4458
Forschmidt, Don S/160 St John's Pl	212-878-7454
Forte, John/162 W 21st St	212-620-0584
Foto Shuttle Japan/47 Greene St	212-966-9641
Foulke, Douglas/28 W 25th St	212-243-0822
Fox, Jeffrey/6 W 20th St	212-620-0147
Foxx, Stephanie/274 W 71st St	212-580-9158
Francais, Isabelle/873 Broadway	212-678-7508
Francekevich, Al/73 Fifth Ave	212-691-7456
FRANCES, SCOTT/175 FIFTH AVE #2401 (P 67)	**212-749-8026**
Francisco, Gus/220 E 23rd St	212-683-0418
Francki, Joe/575 Madison Ave 10th Fl	212-481-7744
Frank, Dick/11 W 25th St	212-242-4648
Fraser, Douglas/9 E 19th St	212-777-8404
Fraser, Gaylene/211 Thompson St	212-677-4589
Fraser, Rob/211 Thompson St #1E	212-677-4589
Freed, Leonard/251 Park Ave S	212-475-7600
French, Larry/273 Fifth Ave 3rd Fl	212-685-2644
Freni, Al/381 Park Ave S #809	212-679-2533
Freson, Robert/881 Seventh Ave	212-246-0679
Fried, Richard/430 W 14th St	212-929-1052
Friedman, Benno/26 W 20th St	212-255-6038
Friedman, Jerry/873 Broadway	212-505-5600
Friedman, Steve/545 W 111th St	212-864-2662
Friedman, Walter/58 W 68th St	212-874-5287
FROOMER, BRETT/39 E 12TH ST (P 68)	**212-533-3113**
Funk, Mitchell/500 E 77th St	212-988-2886
Furones, Claude Emile/40 Waterside Plaza	212-683-0622
Fusco, Paul/251 Park Ave S	212-475-7600
G Gairy, John/11 W 17th St 2nd Fl	212-242-5805
Galante, Dennis/9 W 31st St	212-239-0412
Gallucci, Ed/568 Broadway	212-226-2215
Galton, Beth/130 W 25th St	212-242-2266
Ganges, Halley/35 W 36th St	212-868-1810
Gans, Hank/40 Waterside Plaza	212-683-0622
Garetti, John/140 W 22nd St	212-242-1154
Garik, Alice/ Photo Comm/173 Windsor Pl	718-499-1456
Garn, Andrew/207 Eighth Ave #2R	212-532-7213
Gartel, Larry/152-18 Union Tnpk	718-969-8616
Gatehouse, Don/356 E 89th St	212-410-5961
Gee, Elizabeth/280 Madison #1109	212-683-6924
Geller, Bonnie/57 W 93rd St	212-864-5922
Gelsobello, Paul/245 W 29th St #1200	212-947-0317
Generico, Tony/130 W 25th St 4th Fl	212-685-3031
Gentieu, Penny/87 Barrow St	212-691-1994
Gentil, Gerard/310 E 46th St	212-599-1806
George, Michael/525 Hudson St	212-627-5868
Geradi, Marcia/38 W 21st St	212-243-8400
Germana, Michael/64 Hett Ave	718-667-1275
Gesar, Aram/417 Lafayette St	212-228-1852
Gescheidt, Alfred/175 Lexington Ave	212-889-4023
Gibbons, George/292 City Islnd Ave	212-885-0769
Gidion Inc/140 W 22nd St	212-627-4769
Gigli, Ormond/327 E 58th St	212-758-2860
Gillardin, Andre/6 W 20th St	212-675-2950
Gillette, Bruce/11 W 29th St	212-683-4626
Gioiello, Rick/1105 Stadium Ave	212-409-0023
Giordano, John A/60 E 9th St #538	212-477-3273

Giovanni, Raeanne/156 Fifth Ave #1230	212-206-7757
Giraldi, Frank/54 W 39th St	212-840-8225
GLADSTONE, GARY/237 E 20TH ST #2H (P 70,71)	**212-777-7772**
Glancz, Jeff/38 W 21st St 12th Fl	212-741-2504
Glaser, Harold/143-30 Roosevelt Ave	718-939-1829
Glassman, Carl/80 N Moore St #37G	212-732-2458
Glassman, Keith/237 E 28th St #2A	212-213-5396
Glaviano, Marco/40 W 27th St 9th Fl	212-683-8680
Glinn, Burt/41 Central Park W	212-877-2210
Globus Brothers/44 W 24th St	212-243-1008
Goff, Lee/32 E 64th St	212-223-0716
Gold, Bernie/873 Broadway #301	212-677-0311
Gold, Charles/56 W 22nd St	212-242-2600
Goldberg, Ken/141 Fifth Ave	212-807-5559
Goldman, Richard/36 W 20th St	212-675-3021
Goldring, Barry/568 Broadway #608	212-334-9494
Goldsmith, Gary/201 E 66th St	212-288-4851
Goldstein, Arthur/149 Church St	212-233-6504
Goll, Charles R/404 E 83rd St	212-628-4881
Golob, Stanford/40 Waterside Plaza	212-532-7166
Gonzalez, Gilbert/322 W 53rd St #1	212-245-3762
Gonzalez, Luis/85 Livingston St	718-834-0426
Gonzalez, Manuel/127 W 26th St	212-254-2200
Goodman, Michael/115 Central Park W #32F	212-226-4541
Goodwin, Gary P/134 W 93rd St	212-866-7396
Gordon, Andrew/48 W 22nd St	212-807-9758
Gordon, Brad/259 W 12th St	212-206-7758
Gordon, Joel/112 Fourth Ave	212-254-1688
Gorin, Bart/1160 Broadway	212-683-3743
Gorodnitzki, Diane/160 W 71st St	212-724-6259
Gotfryd, Bernard/46 Wendover Rd	718-261-8039
Gottheil, Philip/236 W 27th St	212-645-5639
Gottlieb, Dennis/5 Union Sq W	212-620-7050
Gould, Peter/ Images/7 E 17th St	212-675-3707
Gove, Geoffrey/117 Waverly Pl	212-260-6051
Gozo Studio/40 W 17th St	212-620-8115
Graff, Randolph/160 Bleecker St	212-254-0412
Graig, Eric/10 E 18th St	212-206-8695
Grand, Paul/1800 Ocean Pkwy	718-375-0138
Grant, Robert/62 Greene St	212-925-1121
Graphic Media/12 W 27th St 12th Fl	212-696-0880
Graves, Tom/136 E 36th St	212-683-0241
Gray, Mitchell/169 E 86th St	212-427-2287
Gray, Robert/160 West End Ave	212-496-0462
Green, Allen/1601 Third Ave	212-534-1718
Green, Anthony/335 W 35th St 11th Fl	212-627-4599
Green, Gary/200 W 95th St	914-757-4443
Green-Armytage, Stephen/171 W 57th St #7A	212-247-6314
Greenberg, David/54 King St	212-316-9196
Greenberg, Joel/265 Water St	212-285-0979
Greene, Jim/20 W 20th St	212-674-1631
Greene, Joshua/448 W 37th St	212-243-2750
Greene, Richard/18 E 17th St	212-242-5282
Greenwald, Seth/195 Adams St	718-802-1531
Gregoire, Peter/329 W 87th St #7	212-496-0584
Gregory, John/105 Fifth Ave #9C	212-691-1797
Gregory, Kevin/237 W 26th St	212-807-9859
Grehan, Farrell/245 W 51st St #306	212-677-3999
Griffiths, Philip Jones/251 Park Ave S	212-475-7600
Grill, Tom/32 E 31st St	212-989-0500
Griner/Cuesta & Assoc/720 Fifth Ave	212-246-7600
Gross, Cy/59 W 19th St	212-243-2556
Gross, David/922 Third Ave #3R	212-688-4729
Gross, Garry/907 Broadway	212-807-7141
Gross, Geoffrey/119 W 23rd St 10th Fl	212-645-5793
Gross, Pat/315 E 86th St #1S East	212-427-9396
Grossman, Eugene/80 N Moore St Ste 14J	212-962-6795
Grossman, Henry/37 Riverside Dr	212-580-7751
Grotell, Al/170 Park Row	212-349-3165
Gruen, John/20 W 22nd St	212-242-8415
Gscheidle, Gerhard E/381 Park Ave S	212-532-1374
Gudnason, Torkil/58 W 15th St	212-929-6680

Photographers

Continued

Please send us your additions and updates.

Guice, Brad Studio/132 W 21st St	212-206-0966
Gurovitz, Judy/207 E 74th St	212-988-8685
Guyaux, Jean-Marie/29 E 19th St	212-529-5395

H
Haar, Thomas/463 West St	212-929-9054
Haas, David/330 W 86th St	212-673-8576
HAAS, KENNETH/15 SHERIDAN SQUARE (P 73)	**212-255-0707**
Haft, Emily/435 E 65th St #100	212-517-5123
Hagen, Boyd/448 W 37th St #6A	212-244-2436
Haggerty, David/17 E 67th St	212-879-4141
Halaska, Jan/PO Box 6611 FDR Sta	718-389-8923
HALING, GEORGE/231 W 29TH ST #302 (P 74,75)	**212-736-6822**
Hall, Clayton/247 W 35th St	212-245-6366
Hamilton, Keith/749 FDR Dr	212-982-3375
Hammond, Maury/9 E 19th St	212-460-9990
Han, Anthony/143 Guernsey St	718-389-8973
Hanlon, Gary Inc/40 W 20th St	212-206-9144
Hansen, Constance/78 Fifth Ave	212-691-5162
HANSON, KENT/147 BLEECKER ST #3R (P 77)	**212-777-2399**
Hardin, Ted/119 W 23rd St #505	212-242-2958
Harrington, Grace/300 W 49th St	212-246-1749
Harris, Leslie/20 W 20th St #703	212-206-1934
Harris, Michael/18 W 21st St	212-255-3377
Harris, Ronald G/119 W 22nd St	212-255-2330
Harrison, Howard/20 W 20th St 8th Fl	212-989-9233
Hartman, Harry/61 W 23rd St 3rd Fl	212-675-5454
Hartmann, Erich/251 Park Ave S	212-475-7600
Harvey, Ned/129 W 22nd St	212-807-7043
Hashi Studio/49 W 23rd St 3rd Fl	212-675-6902
Hathon, Elizabeth/8 Greene St	212-219-0685
Hausherr, Rosemary/145 W 17th St	212-691-3216
Hausman, George/1181 Broadway	212-686-4810
Haviland, Brian/34 E 23rd St 6th Fl	212-598-0070
Hayes, Kerry/35 Taft Ave	718-442-4804
Haynes, Richard/383 Madison Ave 2nd Fl	212-872-1927
Hayward, Bill/596 Broadway 8th Fl	212-966-6490
Hedrich, David/7 E 17th St	212-924-3324
Heery, Gary/577 Broadway 2nd Fl	212-966-6364
Hege, Laszlo/13 E 30th St	718-706-0833
Heiberg, Milton/71 W 23rd St	212-741-6405
Hein, George/13 E 16th St 8th Fl	212-741-3211
Heir, Stuart/17 W 17th St	212-620-0754
Heisler, Gregory/568 Broadway #800	212-777-8100
Hellerstein, Stephen A/120 W 25th St #2E	212-741-2685
Helms, Bill/1175 York Ave	212-759-2079
Henze, Don Studio/126 Fifth Ave 7th Fl	212-989-3576
Heron, Michal (Ms)/28 W 71st St	212-787-1272
Herr, H Buff/56 W 82nd St	212-595-4783
Herrenbruck, David/119 Fifth Ave	212-477-5419
Hess, Brad/1201 Broadway	212-684-3131
Heuberger, William/28 W 25th St	312-242-1532
Heyert, Elizabeth/251 W 30th St	212-594-1008
Hill, Pat/37 W 26th St	212-532-3479
Hiller, Geoffrey/601 W 113th St	212-222-8823
Hine, Skip/34 W 17th St 9th Fl	212-691-5903
Hing/ Norton Photography/24 W 30th St 8th Fl	212-683-4258
Hiro/50 Central Park West	212-580-8000
Hirst, Michael/300 E 33rd St	212-689-7352
Hitz, Brad/377 W 11th St #2B	212-929-1432
Hochman, Allen Studio/9-11 E 19 St	212-777-8404
Hodgson, David/550 Riverside Dr	212-864-6941
Hogan, David/352 E 91st St	212-369-4575
Holbrooke, Andrew/50 W 29th St	212-889-5995
Holland, Robin/430 Greenwich St	212-431-5351
Hollyman, Tom/300 E 40th St #19R	212-867-2383
Holtzman Photography/269 W 11th St	212-242-7985
Hooper, Thomas/126 Fifth Ave	212-691-0122
Hopkins, Douglas/636 Sixth Ave	212-243-1774
Hopkins, Stephen/475 Carlton Ave #6F	718-783-6461
Hopson, Gareth/22 E 21st St	212-535-3800
Horn, Lawrence/599 Sixth Ave	212-242-3280
Horowitz, Ross M/206 W 15th St	212-206-9216

Horowitz, Ryszard/103 Fifth Ave	212-243-6440
HOROWITZ, TED/465 WEST END AVE (P 78,79)	**212-595-0040**
Horst/166 E 63rd St	212-751-4937
Horvath, Jim/95 Charles St	212-741-0300
Howard, Ken/130 W 17th St 9th Fl	212-777-1412
Howard, Rosemary/902 Broadway	212-473-5552
Huang, Ming/3174 44th St	718-204-5912
Hughes, Pinder/536 W 111th St	212-662-5105
Huibregtse, Jim/318 E 39th St	212-679-8125
Hume, Adam/12 E 89th St	212-758-8929
Huntzinger, Bob/514 W 37th St	212-645-9035
Huszar/156 Fifth Ave #836	212-929-2593
Hutchings, Richard/PO Box 45	212-885-0846
Hyatt, Morton/352 Park Ave S 2nd Fl	212-889-2955
Hyman, Barry/319 E 78th St #3C	212-879-3294
Hyman, Paul/236 W 26th St	212-255-1532

I
Ichi/303 Park Ave S #506	212-254-4168
Ihara/568 Broadway #507	212-219-9363
Ikeda, Shig/636 Sixth Ave	212-924-4744
Illography/49 Crosby St	212-219-0244
Image Makers/310 E 23rd St #9F	212-533-4498
Ing, Francis/112 W 31st St 5th Fl	212-279-5022
Intrater, Roberta/1212 Beverly Rd	718-462-4004
Iooss, Walter/344 W 72nd St	212-769-1552
Irgens, O Christian/192-10 69th Ave #B	718-454-3157
Irish, Len/11 W 17th St	212-242-2237
Irwin, William/70 Remsen St #9B	718-237-2598
Isgar, Scott/50 W 22nd St	212-675-1349
Ishimuro, Eisuke/130 W 25th St 10th Fl	212-255-9198
Ivany, Sandra/6 W 90th St #6	212-580-1501

J
Jackson, Martin/181 E 78th St	212-288-3875
Jacobs, Marty/34 E 23rd St 5th Fl	212-475-1160
Jacobs, Robert/116 Lexington Ave	212-683-3629
Jacobsen, Paul/150 Fifth Ave	212-243-4732
Jacobson, Alan/250 W 49th St #800	212-265-0170
Janeart Ltd/161 W 15th St #1C	212-691-9701
Jann, Gail/352 E 85th St	212-861-4335
Janoff, Dean/514 W 24th St	212-362-9546
Jawitz, Louis H/13 E 17th St #PH	212-929-0008
Jeffery, Richard/119 W 22nd St	212-255-2330
Jeffrey, Lance/30 E 21st St #4A	212-674-0595
Jeffry, Alix/71 W 10th St	212-982-1835
Jem, Jason/164-52 84th Ave	718-658-2373
Jenkinson, Mark/142 Bleecker St Box 6	212-529-0488
Jensen, Peter M/22 E 31st St	212-689-5026
Jenssen, Buddy/34 E 29th St	212-686-0865
Joel, Seth Photography/440 Park Ave S	212-685-3179
Joern, James/125 Fifth Ave	212-260-8025
Johansky, Peter/27 W 20th St	212-242-7013
Jones, Chris/240 E 27th St	212-685-0679
Jones, Liz/633 Third Ave 2nd Fl	212-529-6700
Jones, Spencer/400 E 71st St	212-734-2798
Jones, Steve Photo/120 W 25th St #3E	212-929-3641
Joseph, Meryl/158 E 82nd St	212-861-5057
Jurado, Louis/170 Fifth Ave	212-242-7480

K
Kachaturian, Armen/20 West 20th St 8th Fl	212-645-8865
Kahan, Eric/410 W 24th St	212-243-9727
Kahn, R T/156 E 79th St	212-988-1423
Kahn, Steve/60 Thomas St	212-619-7932
Kalan, Mark R/922 President St	718-857-3677
Kalinsky, George/4 Pennsylvania Plaza	212-563-8095
Kamp, Eric/98-120 Queens Blvd	718-896-7780
Kamsler, Leonard/140 Seventh Ave	212-242-4678
Kan Photography/122 W 26th St	212-989-1083
Kana, Titus/876 Broadway	212-473-5550
Kanakis, Michael/144 W 27th St 10th Fl	212-807-8232
Kane, Art/568 Broadway	212-925-7334
Kane, Peter T/236 W 26th St #502	212-924-4968
Kane, Thomas/351 E 12th St #A	212-475-6383

Photographers
Continued

Please send us your additions and updates.

PHOTOGRAPHERS

Kaniklidis, James/1270 E 18th St	718-338-0931
Kaplan, Alan/7 E 20th St	212-982-9500
Kaplan, Barry/323 Park Ave S	212-254-8461
Kaplan, Peter B/126 W 23rd St	212-989-5215
Kaplan, Peter J/924 West End Ave	212-222-1193
Karales, James H/147 W 79th St	212-799-2483
Karia, Bhupendra/9 E 96th St #15B	212-860-5479
Kasoff, Brian/28 W 25th St	212-243-4880
Kassabian Photography/127 E 59th St	212-421-1950
Katvan, Moshe/40 W 17th St	212-242-4895
Katz, Paul/381 Park Ave S	212-684-4395
Katzenstein, David/99 Commercial St	718-383-8528
Kaufman, Micky/144 W 27th St	212-255-1976
Kaufman, Ted/121 Madison Ave #4E	212-685-0349
Kawachi, Yutaka/33 W 17th St 2nd Fl	212-929-4825
Kaye, Nancy/77 Seventh Ave #7U	212-845-6463
Keaveny, Francis/260 Fifth Ave	212-481-9187
Keegan, Marcia/140 E 46th St	212-953-9023
Keller, Tom/440 E 78th St	212-472-3667
Kelley, Charles W Jr/649 Second Ave #6C	212-686-3879
Kelley, David/265 W 37th St	212-869-7896
Kellner, Jeff/16 Waverly Pl	212-475-3719
Kelly, Bill/140 Seventh Ave #1N	212-989-2794
Kennedy, David Michael/10 W 18th St	212-255-9212
Kennedy, Donald J/521 W 23rd St 10th Fl	212-206-7740
Kent, Karen/29 John St	212-962-6793
Kerr, Justin and Barbara/14 W 17th St	212-741-1731
Khornak, Lucille/425 E 58th St	212-593-0933
Kiernan, Jim/34 W 17th St	212-243-3547
Kilkelly, James/30 W 73rd St #2B	212-496-2291
King, Bill/100 Fifth Ave	212-675-7575
Kingsford, Michael Studio/874 Broadway	212-475-0553
Kinmonth, Rob/85 E 10th St #5H	212-475-6370
Kirk, Barbara/447 E 65th St	212-734-3233
Kirk, Charles/333 Park Ave S	212-677-3770
Kirk, Malcolm/12 E 72nd St	212-744-3642
Kirk, Russell/31 W 21st St	212-206-1446
Kirkpatrick, Charla/348 E 92nd St	212-410-3496
Kiss, Bob/29 E 19th St	212-505-6650
Kitchen, Dennis/873 Broadway	212-674-7658
Kittle, Kit/511 E 20th St	212-673-0596
Klauss, Cheryl/463 Broome St	212-431-3569
Klein, Arthur/35-42 80th St	718-278-0457
Klein, Matthew/104 W 17th St	212-255-6400
Klein, Robert/215 W 90th St	212-580-0381
Klein, Rudi/873 Broadway	212-460-8245
Kligge, Robert/578 Broadway	212-226-7113
Klonsky, Arthur/161 W 15th St	212-691-9701
KNOWLES, ROBERT M/2 FORDHAM HILL OVAL #9C (P 81)	**212-367-4430**
Kolansky, Palma/291 Church St	212-431-5858
Komar, Greg/30 Waterside Sq #18A	212-685-0275
Kopelow, Paul/135 Madison Ave	212-689-0685
Koppelman, Jozef/1717 Ave N	718-645-3548
Korsh, Ken/118 E 28th St	212-685-8864
Kosoff, Brian/28 W 25th St 6th Fl	212-243-4880
Koudis, Nick/40 E 23rd St	212-475-2802
Kouirinis, Bill/381 Park Ave S #710	212-696-5674
Kozan, Dan/32 W 22nd St	212-691-2288
Kozlowski, Mark/39 W 28th St	212-684-7487
Kozyra, James/568 Broadway	212-431-1911
Kramer, Bill/33 W 17th St 4th Fl	212-242-7007
Kramer, Daniel/110 W 86th St	212-873-7777
Krein, Jeffrey/119 W 23rd St #800	212-741-5207
Krementz, Jill/228 E 48th St	212-688-0480
Kresch, Jerry/175 W 76th St	212-787-7396
Krieger, Harold/225 E 31st St	212-308-1997
Kristofik, Robert/334 E 90th St #2A	212-534-5541
Kroll, Eric/118 E 28th St #1005	212-684-2465
Kron, Dan/154 W 18th St	212-924-4432
Krongard, Steve/212-A E 26th St	212-689-5634
Krueger, Mike/300 E 95th St #6C	212-722-7638
Kuehn, Karen/49 Warren St	212-406-3005
Kufert, Lowell/160 W 96th St	212-663-2143
Kugler, Dennis/43 Bond St	212-677-3826
Kuhn, Ann Spanos/1155 Broadway	212-685-1774
Kupinski, Steven/50 W 17th St	212-206-0436

L

Labar, Elizabeth/327 W 18th St	212-929-7463
Lambray, Maureen/	212-879-3960
LaMonica, Chuck/121 E 24th St	212-673-4848
Langley, David/536 W 50th St	212-581-3930
Larrain, Gilles/95 Grand St	212-925-8494
Laszlo Studio/28 W 39th St	212-736-6690
Lategan, Barry/502 LaGuardia Pl	212-228-6850
Laurance, Bruce Studio/253 W 28th St	212-947-3451
Laure, Jason/8 W 13th St 11th Fl	212-691-7466
Laurence, Mary/PO Box 1763	212-903-4025
Lavine, Arthur/1361 Madison Ave	212-348-2642
Lawrence, Christopher/12 E 18th St	212-807-8028
Lawrence, Matthew/127 W 24th St	212-620-7301
Lax, Ken/239 Park Ave S	212-228-6191
Layman/Newman/6 W 18th St 6th Fl	212-989-5845
Lazzarini, Bob/25 Park Place	212-513-7163
LeBaube, Guy/310 E 46th St	212-986-6981
Lederman, Ed/166 E 34th St #12H	212-685-8612
Leduc, Lyle/320 E 42nd St #1014	212-697-9216
Lee, Jung/132 W 21st St 3rd Fl	212-807-8107
Lee, Vincent/5 Union Sq West	212-354-7888
Leeds, Karen/43 W 13th St	212-206-1818
LEFKOWITZ, LESTER/370 LEXINGTON AVE #1805 (P 84-87)	**212-627-8088**
Legrand, Michel/152 W 25th St 12th Fl	212-807-9754
Leibovitz, Annie/101 W 18th St	212-807-0220
Leicmon, John/353 W 39th St #204	212-563-5592
Leighton, Thomas/321 E 43rd St	212-370-1835
Leiter, Saul/111 E 10th St	212-475-6034
Lenore, Dan/249 W 29th St #2N	212-967-7115
Leo, Donato/170 Fifth Ave	212-989-4200
Leonian, Phillip/220 E 23rd St	212-989-7670
Lerner, Richard/34 E 23d St	212-598-0070
Lesinski, Martin/49 Willow St #3H	718-624-8475
Let There Be Neon/PO Box 337/Canal St	212-226-4883
Leung, Jook/110 E 23rd St	212-254-8334
Levin, James/1570 First Ave #3D	212-734-0315
Levine, Jonathan/11 W 9th St	212-673-4698
Levine, Nancy/60 E 9th St	212-473-0015
Levinson, Ken/35 East 10th St	212-254-6180
Levy, Peter/119 W 22nd St	212-691-6600
Levy, Richard/5 W 19th St	212-243-4220
Lewin, Gideon/25 W 39th St	212-921-5558
Lewin, Ralph/156 W 74th St	212-580-0482
Lewis, Robert/333 Park Ave S 4th Fl	212-475-6564
Lewis, Ross/460 W 24th St	212-691-6878
Lieberman, Allen/5 Union Sq 4th Fl	212-243-2240
Liebman, Phil/315 Hudson	212-269-7777
Ligeti Inc/415 W 55th St	212-246-8949
Lindner, Steven/18 W 27th St	212-683-1317
Lipton, Trina/60 E 8th St	212-533-3148
Lisi-Hoeltzell Ltd/156 Fifth Ave	212-255-0303
Little, Christopher/4 W 22nd St	212-691-1024
Lloyd, Harvey/310 E 23rd St	212-533-4498
Lobell, Richard/25-12 Union St	718-445-6864
Loete, Mark/33 Gold St #405	212-571-2235
Loew, Anthony/32 E 22nd St	212-226-1499
Logan, Kevin/119 W 23rd St	212-206-0539
Lombardi, Frederick/180 Pinehurst Ave	212-568-0740
Lombroso, Dorit/67 Vestry St #B	212-219-8722
Lomeo, Angelo/336 Central Park W	212-663-2122
Londener, Hank/18 W 38th St	212-354-0293
Lonsdale, William J/35 Orange St	718-788-6652
LOPPACHER, PETER/56 JANE ST (P 88)	**212-929-1322**
Lorenz, Robert/873 Broadway	212-505-8483
Love, Robin/676 Broadway 4th Fl	212-777-3113

Photographers
Continued

Please send us your additions and updates.

Lubianitsky, Leonid/1013 Ave of Americas	212-391-0197
Luce, Marcia Photography/132 W 21st St	212-807-6348
Lucka, Klaus/35 W 31st St	212-594-5910
Luftig, Allan/873 Broadway	212-533-4113
Luria, Dick/5 E 16th St 4th Fl	212-929-7575
Lusk, Frank/25 E 37th St	212-679-1441
Lustica, Tee/156 Fifth Ave #920	212-255-0303
Luttenberg, Gene/20 W 22nd St	212-620-8112
Lypides, Chris/119 W 23rd St	212-741-1911
M Macedonia, Carmine/866 Ave of Americas	212-889-8520
Mack, Donald/69 W 55th St	212-246-6086
Mackiewicz, Jim/208 E 28th St	212-689-0766
MACLAREN, MARK/430 E 20TH ST (P 89)	**212-674-8615**
MacWeeney, Alen Inc/171 First Ave	212-473-2500
Madere, John/306 W 80th St	212-213-2595
Maguire, William/111 W 24th St #7R	212-724-3089
Maisel, Jay/190 Bowery	212-431-5013
Malignon, Jacques/34 W 28th St	212-532-7727
Maloof, Karen/110 W 94th St #4C	212-678-7737
Mangia, Tony/11 E 32nd St #3B	212-889-6340
Mani, Monsor/40 E 23rd St	212-947-9116
Manna, Lou/20 E 30th St	212-683-8689
Manno, John/20 W 22nd St #802	212-243-7353
Mansour, Gozo/40 W 17th St	212-620-8115
Marchese, Jim/200 W 20th St	212-242-1087
Marco, Phil/104 Fifth Ave 4th Fl	212-929-8082
Marcus, Helen/120 E 75th St	212-879-6903
Marcusson, Eric E/85 Barrow St #2R	212-924-5437
Maresca, Frank/236 W 26th St	212-620-0955
Margerin, Bill/41 W 25th St	212-645-1532
Markowitz, Joel/PO Box 6242	212-744-6863
Marks, Michael/6 W 20th St 8th Fl	212-255-0740
Marshall, Alec/308 E 73rd St	212-772-8523
Marshall, Elizabeth/200 Central Pk S #31A	212-333-2012
Marshall, Lee/201 W 89th St	212-799-9717
Martin, Bard/142 W 26th St	212-929-6712
Martin, Butch/244 Madison Ave #2F	212-370-4959
Martin, Dennis/11 W 25th St	212-929-2221
Martinez, Oscar/303 Park Ave S #408	212-673-0932
Marvullo Photomontage/141 W 28th St #502	212-564-6501
Marx, Richard/8 W 19th St	212-929-8880
Masca/109 W 26th St	212-929-4818
Mason, Donald/101 W 18th St 4th Fl	212-675-3809
Mass, Rita/119 W 23rd St 10th Fl	212-645-9120
Masser, Randy/953 President	718-622-8274
Massey, Philip/475 W 186th St	212-928-8210
Masullo, Ralph/33 W 17th St	212-929-4825
Masunaga, Ryuzo/57 W 19th St #2D	212-807-7012
Mathews, Barbara Lynn/16 Jane St	212-691-0823
Matsumoto/PO Box 242 Cooper Station	212-228-7192
Matsuo, Toshi/105 E 29th St	212-532-1320
Matthews, Cynthia/200 E 78th St	212-288-7349
Maucher, Arnold/154 W 18th St	212-206-1535
May Tell, Susan/277 W 10th St	212-741-0189
Maynard, Chris/297 Church St	212-255-8204
Mayor, Randy/139 W 82nd St #7H	212-595-0896
Mazzurco, Phil/150 Fifth Ave #319	212-989-1220
McCabe, David/39 W 67th St #1403	212-874-7480
McCabe, Robert/117 E 24th St	212-677-1910
McCarthy, Margaret/31 E 31st St	212-696-5971
McCartney, Susan/902 Broadway #1608	212-533-0660
McCavera, Tom/450 W 31st St 9th Fl	212-714-9122
McConnell, Chester/31 W 21st St	212-255-8141
McCurdy, John Chang/156 Fifth Ave	212-243-6949
McFarland, Lowell/128 E 28th St	212-686-6346
McFarland, Nancy/128 E 28th St	212-686-6346
McGlynn, David/18-23 Astoria Blvd	718-626-9427
McGrath, Norman/164 W 79th St #16	212-799-6422
McKiernan, Scott/129 Front St	212-825-0073
McLaughlin-Gill, Frances/454 W 46th St #3D-S	212-664-7637
McLoughlin, James Inc/148 W 24th St 5th Fl	212-206-8207
McMullen, Mark/304 Eighth Ave #3	212-243-6343
McNally, Brian T/234 E 81st St #1A	212-744-1263
McNally, Joe/307-09 W Broadway	212-219-1014
McQueen, Hamilton/373 Park Ave S	212-689-7367
McSpirit, Jerry/413 E 82nd St	212-879-2332
Mead, Chris/108 Reade St	212-619-5616
Megna, Richard/210 Forsyth St	212-473-5770
Meiselas, Susan/251 Park Ave S	212-475-7600
Melford, Michael/32 E 22nd St	212-473-3095
Melillo, Nick/118 W 27th St #3R	212-691-7612
Mella, Michael/217 Thompson St	212-777-6012
Mellon/69 Perry St	212-691-4166
Meltzer, Irwin & Assoc/3 W 18th St	212-807-7464
Meltzer, Lee/2271 W 1st St	718-998-2597
Memo Studio/39 W 67th St #1402	212-787-1658
MENASHE, ABRAHAM/306 E 5TH ST #27 (P 91)	**212-254-2754**
Menda, George/568 Broadway #403	212-431-7440
Menken, Howard Studios/119 W 22nd St	212-924-4240
Meola, Eric/535 Greenwich St	212-255-5150
Merle, Michael G/5 Union Square West	212-741-3801
Mervar, Louis/29 W 38th St 16th Fl	212-354-8024
Messin, Larry/64 Carlyle Green	718-948-7209
Meyerowitz, Joel/151 W 19th St	212-242-0740
Michals, Duane/109 E 19th St	212-473-1563
Michelson, Eric T/101 Lexington Ave #4B	212-687-6190
Milbauer, Dennis/15 W 28th St	212-532-3702
Miles, Ian/313 E 61st St	212-688-1360
Miljakovich, Helen/114 Seventh Ave #3C	212-242-0646
Miller, Bert/30 Dongan Pl	212-567-7947
Miller, Bill Photo/36 E 20th St	212-674-8026
MILLER, DONALD L/295 CENTRAL PARK WEST (P 92,93)	**212-496-2830**
Miller, Eileen/28 W 38th St	212-944-1507
Miller, Myron/23 E 17th St	212-242-3780
Miller, Sue Ann/16 W 22nd St #406	212-645-5172
Miller, Wayne F/251 Park Ave S	212-475-7600
Ming Photo/1200 Broadway #2E	212-213-1166
Ming Studio/110 E 23rd St	212-254-8570
Minh Studio/200 Park Ave S #1507	212-477-0649
Mitchell, Andrew/220 Berkeley Pl	718-783-6727
Mitchell, Benn/119 W 23rd St	212-255-8686
Mitchell, Diane/175 W 73rd St	212-877-7624
Mitchell, Jack/356 E 74th St	212-737-8940
Molkenthin, Michael/31 W 31st St #6E	212-594-0144
Moon, Sarah/215 Park Ave S	212-674-8080
Moore, Chris/20 W 22nd St #810	212-242-0553
Moore, Jimmy/38 E 19th St	212-674-7150
Moore, Marvin/234 Fifth Ave 5th Fl	212-696-4001
Moore, Truman/873 Broadway 4th Fl	212-533-3655
Moran, Nancy/568 Broadway	212-505-9620
More, Carla/485 Madison Ave 21st Fl	212-355-2323
Morello, Joe/40 W 28th St	212-684-2340
Moretz, Charles/141 Wooster St	212-714-1357
Morgan, Jeff/27 W 20th St #604	212-924-4000
Morris, Bill/34 E 29th St 6th Fl	212-685-7354
Morris, Leonard/200 Park Ave S	212-473-8485
Morrison, Ted/286 Fifth Ave	212-279-2838
Morsch, Roy J/1200 Broadway #2B	212-679-5537
Morsillo, Les/20 St Marks Pl	212-674-3124
Morton/ Riggs Studio/39 W 29th St	212-889-6643
Moscati, Frank/5 E 16th St	212-255-3434
Moskowitz, Sonia/5 W 86th St #18B	212-877-6883
Mougin, Claude/227 W 17th St	212-691-7895
Mucci, Tina/129 W 22nd St	212-206-9402
Mullane, Fred/415 Madison Ave	212-580-4045
Muller, Rudy/318 E 39th St	212-679-8124
Munro, Gordon/381 Park Ave S	212-889-1610
Munson, Russell/458 Broadway 5th Fl	212-226-8875
Muresan, Jon/56 W 22nd St 5th Fl	212-242-1227
Murphey, Gregory/353 E 77th St	212-517-2648
Murray, Robert/149 Franklin St	212-226-6860
Murrow, Robert/226 W 47th St	212-302-2550
Myers, Robert J/407 E 69th St	212-249-8085

Myriad Communications Inc/208 W 30th St	212-564-4340

N
Naar, Jon/230 E 50th St	212-752-4625
Nadelson, Jay/116 Mercer St	212-226-4266
Nahoum, Ken/260 W Broadway #4G	212-219-0592
Naideau, Harold/233 W 26th St	212-691-2942
Nakamura, Tohru/112 Greene St	212-334-8011
Nakano, George/119 W 22nd St	212-228-9370
Namuth, Hans/20 W 22nd St	212-691-3220
Nardi, Bob/568 Broadway	212-219-8298
Nardiello, Carl/143 W 20th St	212-242-3106
Nathan, Simon/275 W 96th St	212-873-5560
Nault, Corky/25 W 23rd St 3rd Fl	212-807-7310
Needham, Steven/6 W 18th St 10th Fl	212-206-1914
Neil, Joseph/247 W 20th St	212-961-1881
Neleman, Hans/205 E 14th St	212-973-1132
Nelken, Dan/43 W 27th St	212-532-7471
Nelson, Michael/7 E 17th St 5th Fl	212-924-2892
Nemeth Studio/220 E 23rd St #700	212-686-3272
Neumann, Peter/30 E 20th St	212-420-9538
Newler, Michael/119 W 23rd St #409	212-242-2449
Newman, Allan/6 W 18th St 6th Fl	212-989-5845
Newman, Arnold/39 W 67th St	212-877-4510
Newman, Irving/900 Broadway	212-228-2760
Newman, Marvin E/227 Central Park West	212-219-1228
Ney, Nancy/108 E 16th St 6th Fl	212-260-4300
Ng, Norman Kaimen/36 E 20th St	212-982-3230
Niccolini, Dianora/356 E 78th St	212-564-4953
Nicholas, Peter/29 Bleecker St	212-529-5560
Nicholson, Nick/121 W 72nd St #2E	212-362-8418
Nicolaysen, Ron/130 W 57th St	212-947-5167
Niederman, Mark/230 W 72nd St	212-362-3902
Niefield, Terry/12 W 27th St 13th Fl	212-686-8722
Nisnevich, Lev/133 Mulberry St	212-219-0535
Nivelle, Serge/36 Grammercy Pk E #3N	212-473-2802
Niwa-Ogrudek Ltd/30 E 23rd St	212-982-7120
Nobart NY Inc/33 E 18th St	212-475-5522
Nons, Leonard/5 Union Sq West	212-741-3990
Norstein. Marshall/248 6th Ave	718-768-0786

O
O'Connor, Michael/216 E 29th St	212-679-0396
O'CONNOR, THOM/74 FIFTH AVE (P 94)	**212-620-0723**
O'Neill, Michael/134 Tenth Ave	212-807-8777
O'Reilly, Robert/311 E 50th St	212-832-8992
O'Rourke, J Barry/578 Broadway #707	212-226-7113
Obremski, George/1200 Broadway #2A	212-684-2933
Ochi, Toru/636 Sixth Ave	212-807-7711
Oelbaum, Zeva/600 W 115th St #84L	212-864-7926
Ogilvy, Stephen/876 Broadway	212-505-9005
Ohara, Ken/Pier 62/12th Ave @23rd St	212-255-0798
Ohringer, Frederick/514 Broadway	212-737-6487
Ohta Studio/15 E 11th St	212-243-2353
Okada, Tom/45 W 18th St	212-569-0726
Olds, H F/12 W 21st St	212-691-5614
Olivier, Paul/141 W 28th St	212-947-1077
Olivo, John/545 W 45th St	212-765-8812
Olman, Bradley/15 W 24th St	212-243-0649
Oppersdorff, Mathias/1220 Park Ave	212-860-4778
Orenstein, Ronn/55 W 26th St	212-967-6075
Oringer, Hal/568 Broadway #503	212-219-1588
Ort, Samuel/3323 Kings Hwy	718-377-1218
Ortner, Jon/64 W 87th St	212-873-1950
Osonitsch, Robert/112 Fourth Ave	212-533-1920
Otfinowski, Danuta/420 E 10th St	212-254-5799
Otsuki, Toshi/241 W 36th St	212-594-1939
Oudi/704 Broadway 2nd Fl	212-777-0847
Outerbridge, Graeme/PO Box 182	809-298-0888
Owens, Sigrid/221 E 31st St	212-686-5190

PQ
Paccione/73 Fifth Ave	212-691-8674
Page, Lee/310 E 46th St	212-286-9159
Paglailunga, Albert/450 Clarkson Ave Box 18	718-271-2760
Pagliuso, Jean/315 Central Pk West	212-873-6594
Pagnano, Patrick/217 Thompson St	212-475-2566
Palmisano, Georgio/309 Mott St	212-431-7719
Palubniak, Jerry/144 W 27th St	212-645-2838
Palubniak, Nancy/144 W 27th St	212-645-2838
Papadopolous, Peter/78 Fifth Ave	212-675-8830
Pappas, Tony/110 W 31st St 3rd Fl	212-868-2032
Paras, Michael N/28-40 34th St	718-278-6768
Parks, Claudia/210 E 73rd St #1G	212-879-9841
Passmore, Nick/150 W 80th St	212-724-1401
Pastner, Robert L/166 E 63rd St	212-838-8335
Pateman, Michael/155 E 35th St	212-685-6584
Peacock, Christian/118 W 88th St	212-645-9837
Peden, John/155 W 19th St 6th Fl	212-255-2674
Pederson/Erwin/76 Ninth Ave 16th Fl	212-929-9001
Peltz, Stuart/33 W 21st St	212-929-4600
Pemberton, John/37 E 28th St	212-532-9285
Pendleton, Bruce/5 Union Sq West 4th Fl	212-691-5544
Penn, Irving/443 W 50th St	212-695-0290
Penny, Donald Gordon/505 W 23rd St #PH	212-243-6453
Peress, Gilles/251 Park Ave S	212-475-7600
Perkell, Jeff/132 W 22nd St	212-645-1506
Perweiler, Gary/873 Broadway	212-254-7247
Peterson, Grant/876 Broadway	212-475-2767
Peticolas, Kip/210 Forsyth St	212-473-5770
Petoe, Denes/22 W 27th St	212-213-3311
Pettinato, Anthony/156 Fifth Ave #200	212-929-6016
Pfeffer, Barbara/40 W 86th St	212-877-9913
Pfizenmaier, Edward/42 E 23rd	212-475-0910
Phillips, James/82 Greene St	212-219-1799
Phillips, Robert/101 W 57th St	212-757-5190
Photoquest International/521 Madison Ave	212-986-1224
Pich, Tom/2870 Dudley Ave	212-863-1837
Piel, Denis/458 Broadway 9th Fl	212-925-8929
Pierce, Richard/241 W 36th St #8F	212-947-8241
Pilgreen, John/91 Fifth Ave #300	212-243-7516
Pilossof, Judd/142 W 26th St	212-989-8971
Pioppo, Peter/50 W 17th St	212-243-0661
Pipinou, Tom/35 Union Sq West	212-929-0098
Piscioneri, Joe/333 Park Ave S	212-533-7982
Pite, Jonathan/430 W 14th St #502	212-206-7377
Pittman, Dustin/45 W 18th St	212-243-2956
Plotkin, Bruce/3 W 18th St 7th Fl	212-691-6185
Plotkin, Burt/400 Lafayette St	212-260-5900
Pobereskin, Joseph/51 Warren St	212-619-3711
Pobiner, Ted/381 Park Ave S	212-679-5911
Pollack, David/132 W 15th St #4A	212-242-2115
Pollard, Kirsty/5 Union Sq West	212-243-2240
Polsky, Herb/1024 Sixth Ave	212-730-0508
Popper, Andrew J/330 First Ave	212-982-9713
Porta, Art/29 E 32nd St	212-685-1555
Portnoy Studio/135 W 29th St	212-868-0521
Poster, James Studio/210 Fifth Ave #402	212-206-4065
Pottle, Jock/301 W 89th St #15	212-874-0216
Powell, Dean/32 Union Sq East	212-674-6280
Powers, Guy/534 W 43rd St	212-563-3177
Pozarik, Jim/43-19 168th St	718-539-7836
Pressman, Herb/118 E 28th St #908	212-683-5055
Prezant, Steve Studios/1181 Broadway 9th Fl	212-684-0822
Pribula, Barry/59 First Ave	212-777-7612
Price, Clayton J/205 W 19th St	212-929-7721
Price, David/4 E 78th St	212-794-9040
Priggen, Leslie/215 E 73rd St	212-772-2230
Probst, Kenneth/251 W 19 St	212-929-2031
Prochnow, Bob/43-40 161st St	212-627-3244
Proctor, Keith/78 Fifth Ave	212-807-1044
Prozo, Marco/122 Duane St	212-766-4490
Pruitt, David/156 Fifth Ave	212-807-0767
Pruzan, Michael/1181 Broadway	212-686-5505
Puhlmann, Rico/156 Fifth Ave #1218	212-620-4211
Purvis, Charles/84 Thomas St #3	212-619-8028

Photographers

Continued

Please send us your additions and updates.

Quat, Dan/57 Leonard St	212-431-7780

R

R J Photo/711 Amsterdam Ave	212-865-8155
Raab, Michael/831 Broadway	212-533-0030
Rajs, Jake/36 W 20th St 11th Fl	212-675-3666
Rattner, Robert/106-15 Jamaica Ave	718-441-0826
Ratzkin, Lawrence/392 Fifth Ave	212-279-1314
RAY, BILL/350 CENTRAL PARK WEST (P 97)	**212-222-7680**
Raymond, Lelo/212 E 14th St	212-362-9546
Rea, Jimmy/151 W 19th St 10th Fl	212-627-1473
Reed, Robert/25-09 27th St	718-278-2455
Regan, Ken/6 W 20th St	212-989-2004
Regen, David/227 E 11th St #3D	212-533-5183
Reichert, Robert/68-50 Burns St	718-263-7654
Reinhardt, Mike/881 Seventh Ave #405	212-541-4787
Reinmiller, Mary Ann/163 W 17th St	212-243-4302
Rentmeester, Co/4479 Douglas Ave	212-757-4796
Reznicki, Jack/568 Broadway	212-925-0771
Rezny, Aaron/119 W 23rd St	212-691-1894
Rezny, Abe/28 Cadman Plz W/Eagle Wrhse	212-226-7747
Rhodes, A Photography/325 E 64th St	212-249-3974
Ricucci, Vincent/59 W 19th St	212-691-5860
Ries, Henry/204 E 35th St	212-689-3794
Ries, Stan/48 Great Jones St	212-533-1852
Riggs, Robert/502 Laguardia Pl	212-254-7352
Riley, David-Carin/152 W 25th St	212-741-3662
RILEY, JON/12 E 37TH ST (P 98,99)	**212-532-8326**
Rivelli, William/303 Park Ave S #204	212-254-0990
Rivera, Al/139 W 14th St	212-691-3930
Rizzo, Alberto/220 E 23rd St	212-736-1100
Roberts, Grant/11 W 20th St	212-620-7921
Roberts, John/433 W 21st St #5A	212-645-4439
Roberts, Stefan K/155 E 47th St	212-688-9798
Robins, Lawrence/50 W 17th St	212-206-0436
Robinson, CeOtis/4-6 W 101st St #49A	212-663-1231
Robinson, James/1255 Fifth Ave #3G	212-996-5486
Robison, Chuck/21 Stuyvesant Oval	212-777-4894
Rockfield, Bert/31 E 32nd St	212-689-3900
Rodin, Christine/38 Morton St	212-242-3260
Rohr, Robert/325 E 10th St #5W	212-674-1519
Rolo Photo/214 W 17th St	212-691-8355
Romanelli, Marc/244 Riverside Dr	212-865-5214
Romano, Robert/1155 Broadway	212-696-0264
Rose, Uli/234 W 21st St #33	212-505-5234
Rosen, David/238 E 24th St	212-684-5193
Rosenberg, Ken/514 West End Ave	212-362-3149
Rosenfeld, Stanley/175 Riverside Dr #8K	212-787-6653
Rosenthal, Barry/205 W 19th St	212-645-0433
Rosenthal, Marshall M/231 W 18th St	212-807-1247
Ross, Ken/312 E 84th St #5C	212-734-2687
Ross, Mark/345 E 80th St	212-744-7258
Ross, Steve/10 Montgomery Pl	718-783-6451
Rossi, Emanuel/78-29 68th Rd	718-894-6163
Rossum, Cheryl/310 E 75th St	212-628-3173
Roth, Peter/8 W 19th St	212-242-4853
Rothaus, Ede/34 Morton St	212-989-8277
Rotkin, Charles E/1697 Broadway	212-757-9255
Roto Ad Print Studio/252 W 37th St	212-279-6590
Rozsa, Nick/325 E 64th St	212-734-5629
Rubenstein, Raeanne/8 Thomas St	212-964-8426
Rubin, Al/250 Mercer St #1501	212-674-4535
Rubin, Daniel/126 W 22nd St 6th Fl	212-989-2400
Rubin, Darleen/159 Christopher St	212-243-6973
Rubinstein, Eva/145 W 27th St	212-243-4115
Rudnick, James/799 Union St	718-783-4156
Rudolph, Nancy/35 W 11th St	212-989-0392
Rugen-Kory/150 E 18th St	212-777-3889
Ruggeri, Francesco/71 St Marks Pl #9	212-505-8477
Russell, Ted/67-25 Clyde St	718-263-3725
Russell, Tom/636 Ave of Americas	212-989-9755
Ryan, Will/16 E 17th St 2nd Fl	212-242-6270
Rysinski, Edward/636 Ave of Americas	212-807-7301

S

Sabal, David/807 Ave of Americas	212-242-8464
Sacco, Vittorio/126 Fifth Ave #602	212-929-9225
SACHA, BOB/370 CENTRAL PARK W (P 100)	**212-749-4128**
Sailors, David/123 Prince St	212-505-9654
Sakas, Peter/400 Lafayette St	212-254-6096
Salaff, Fred/322 W 57th St	212-246-3699
Salaverry, Philip/20 W 20th St	212-807-0896
Salvati, Jerry/206 E 26th St	212-696-0454
Salzano, Jim/29 W 15th St	212-242-4820
Samardge, Nick/568 Broadway #706	212-226-6770
Sanchez, Alfredo/14-23 30th Dr	718-726-0182
Sanders, Chris/133 Eighth Ave 2nd Fl	212-724-6129
Sandone, A J/132 W 21st St 9th Fl	212-807-6472
Sanford, Tobey/888 Eighth Ave	212-245-2736
Sarapochiello, Jerry/47-A Beach St	212-219-8545
Sartor, Vittorio/32 Union Square E	212-674-2994
Sasson, Bob/352 W 15th St	212-675-0973
Sato Photo/152 W 26th St	212-741-0688
Satterwhite, Al/515 Broadway #2B	212-219-0808
Satterwhite, Steve/13 Avenue A	212-254-8844
Saunders, Michele/141 W 20th St	212-929-5705
Savas, James/37 W 20th St	212-620-0067
Savides, Harris/1425 Third Ave	212-772-8745
Saylor, H Durston/219 W 16th St #4B	212-620-7122
Scarlett, Nora/37 W 20th St	212-741-2620
Scavullo, Francesco/212 E 63rd St	212-838-2450
Schecter, Lee/440 Park Ave S	212-431-0088
Scheer, Stephen/9 Murray St #12NW	212-233-7195
Schein, Barry/118-60 Metropolitan Ave	718-849-7808
Schenk, Fred/112 Fourth Ave	212-677-1250
Schiavone, Carmen/271 Central Park West	212-496-6016
Schiff, Nancy Rica/24 W 30th St 7th Fl	212-679-9444
Schillaci, Michael/320 W 30th St #3A	212-564-2364
Schillaci/Jones Photo/400 E 71st St #14-O	212-734-2798
Schiller, Leif/244 Fifth Ave	212-532-7272
Schinz, Marina/222 Central Park S	212-246-0457
Schlachter, Trudy/160 Fifth Ave	212-741-3128
Schneider, Josef/119 W 57th St	212-265-1223
Schneider, Peter/902 Broadway	212-982-9040
Schneider, Roy/59 W 19th St	212-691-9588
Schreck, Bruno/873 Broadway #304	212-254-3078
Schulze, Fred/38 W 21st St	212-242-0930
Schupf, John/568 Broadway #106	212-226-2250
Schurink, Yonah (Ms)/666 West End Ave	212-362-2860
Schuster, Sharon/320 W 90th St	212-877-1559
Schwartz, Marvin/223 W 10th St	212-929-8916
Schwartz, Sing-Si/15 Gramercy Park S	212-228-4466
Schweitzer, Andrew/333 Park Ave S	212-473-2395
Schwerin, Ron/889 Broadway	212-228-0340
Sclight, Greg/146 W 29th St	212-736-2957
Scocozza, Victor/117 E 30th St	212-686-9440
Secunda, Sheldon/112 Fourth Ave	212-477-0241
Seesselberg, Charles/119 W 23rd St	212-807-8730
Seghers, Carroll/441 Park Ave S	212-679-4582
Seidman, Barry/85 Fifth Ave	212-255-6666
Seitz, Sepp/530 W 25th St	212-255-5959
Selby, Richard/113 Greene St	212-431-1719
Seligman, Paul/163 W 17th St	212-242-5688
Selkirk, Neil/515 W 19th St	212-243-6778
Seltzer, Abe/524 W 23d St	212-807-0660
Seltzer, Kathleen/25 E 4th St	212-475-0314
Sewell, Jim/720 W 181st St	212-923-7686
Shaffer, Stan/2211 Broadway	212-807-7700
Shaman, Harvey/109 81st St	718-793-0434
Shapiro, Pam/11 W 30th St 2nd Fl	212-967-2363
SHARE, JED/TOKYO/63 ADRIAN AVE (P 101)	**212-562-8931**
Sharko, Greg/103-56 103rd St	718-738-9694
Sharratt, Paul/20 W 20th St #703	212-243-3281
Shelley, George/873 Braodway 8th Fl	212-473-0519
Sherman, Guy/108 E 16th St 6th Fl	212-675-4983
Shiki/119 W 23rd St #504	212-929-8847

Photographers

Continued

Please send us your additions and updates.

Shipley, Christopher/18-23 Astoria Blvd	718-626-9427
Shiraishi, Carl/137 E 25th St 11th Fl	212-679-5628
Silano, Bill/138 E 27th St	212-889-0505
Silbert, Layle/505 LaGuardia Pl	212-677-0947
Silver, Larry/236 W 26th St	212-807-9560
Simko, Robert/437 Washington St	212-431-6974
SIMON, PETER ANGELO/568 BROADWAY #701 (P 102)	**212-925-0890**
Simpson, Coreen/599 West End Ave	212-877-6210
Simpson, Jerry/28 W 27th St	212-696-9738
Singer, Michelle/251 W 19th St #5C	212-924-8485
Sirdofsky, Arthur/112 W 31st St	212-279-7557
Skalski, Ken/866 Broadway	212-777-6207
Skelley, Ariel/249 W 29th St #3E	212-868-1179
Skogsbergh, Ulf/5 E 16th St	212-255-7536
Skolnik, Lewis/135 W 29th St	212-239-1455
Skott, Michael/244 Fifth Ave #PH	212-686-4807
Slade, Chuck/12 E 14th St #4B	212-807-1153
Slavin, Fred/42 E 23rd St 7th Fl	212-505-1420
Slavin, Neal/62 Greene St	212-925-8167
Sleppin, Jeff/3 W 30th St	212-947-1433
Sloan-White, Barbara/372 Fifth Ave	212-760-0057
Small, John/156 Fifth Ave #834	212-645-4720
Smilow, Stanford/333 E 30th St/Box 248	212-685-9425
Smith, Jeff/30 E 21st St	212-674-8383
Smith, Kevin/446 W 55th St	212-757-4812
Smith, Michael/140 Claremont #5A	212-724-2800
Smith, Rita/666 West End Ave #10N	212-580-4842
Smith, Robert Photo/421 Seventh Ave	212-563-2535
Smith, William E/498 West End Ave	212-877-8456
Snedeker, Katherine/16 E 30th St	212-684-0788
Snider, Lee/221 W 82nd St #9D	212-873-6141
Snyder, Norman/514 Broadway #3H	212-219-0094
So Studio/34 E 23rd St	212-475-0090
Sobel, Jane/161 W 15th St	212-691-9701
Sochurek, Howard/680 Fifth Ave	212-582-1860
Solomon, Chuck/622 Greenwich St	212-243-4036
Solomon, Paul/440 W 34th St #13E	212-760-1203
Solowinski, Ray/154 W 57th St #826	212-757-7940
Soluri, Michael/95 Horatio St #633	212-645-7999
Somekh, Rick/13 Laight St	212-219-1613
Soot, Olaf/419 Park Ave S	212-686-4565
Sorce, Wayne/20 Henry St #5G	718-237-0497
Sorensen, Chris/PO Box 1760	212-684-0551
Sotres, Craig/40 W 17th St #2B	212-627-4599
Spagnolo, David/144 Reade St	212-226-4392
Spahn, David/381 Park Ave S #915	212-689-6120
Spatz, Eugene/264 Sixth Ave	212-777-6793
Specht, Diane/167 W 71st St #10	212-877-8381
Speier, Leonard/190 Riverside Dr	212-595-5480
Spindel, David M/18 E 17th St	212-989-4984
Spinelli, Frank/12 W 21st St 12th Fl	212-243-7718
Spinelli, Paul/1619 Third Ave #21K	212-410-3320
Spinelli, Phil/12 W 21st St	212-243-7718
Spiro, Edward/82-01 Britten	718-424-7162
Spreitzer, Andy/225 E 24th St	212-685-9669
Springston, Dan/135 Madison Ave	212-689-0685
St John, Lynn/308 E 59th St	212-308-7744
Stahman, Robert/1200 Broadway #2D	212-679-1484
Standard, Venus/115 Pendleton Pl	718-816-8702
Standart, Joe/5 W 19th St	212-924-4545
Stanton, Brian/175 Fifth Ave #3086	212-678-7574
Stanton, William/160 W 95th St #9D	212-662-3571
Stark, Philip/245 W 29th St 15th Fl	212-868-5555
Steadler, Lance/154 W 27th St	212-243-0935
Steedman, Richard C/214 E 26th St	212-684-7878
STEELE, KIM/640 BROADWAY #7W (P 103)	**212-777-7753**
Stegemeyer, Werner/377 Park Ave S	212-686-2247
Steigman, Steve/5 E 19th St #303	212-473-3366
Stein, Larry/568 Broadway #706	212-219-9077
Steinbrenner, Karl Photography/140 W 22nd St	212-807-8936
Steiner, Charles/61 Second Ave	212-777-0813
Steiner, Christian/300 Central Park West	212-724-1990
Stember, John/154 W 57th St	212-757-0067
Stern, Anna/261 Broadway #3C	212-349-1134
Stern, Bert/66 Crosby St	212-925-5909
Stern, Bob/12 W 27th St	212-889-0860
Stern, John/451 W Broadway	212-477-0656
Stern, Laszlo/57 W 19th St	212-691-7696
Sternfeld, Joel/353 E 77th St	212-517-3648
Stetson, David/251 W 30th St #16W	212-279-1515
Stettner, Bill/118 E 25th St	212-460-8180
Stevens, D David/175 Fifth Ave #3216	212-677-2200
Stiles, James/413 W 14th St	212-627-1766
Stock, Dennis/251 Park Ave S	212-475-7600
Stone, Erika/327 E 82nd St	212-737-6435
Stratigakis, John/2258 43rd St	718-274-1697
Stratos, Jim/150 W 36th St	212-695-5674
The Strobe Studio/91 Fifth Ave	212-532-1977
Strode, Mark/2026 E 29th St	718-332-1241
Stroili, Elaine/416 E 85th St #3G	212-879-8587
STRONGIN, JEANNE/61 IRVING PL (P 105)	**212-473-3718**
Stuart, John/80 Varick St #4B	212-966-6783
Stucker, Hal/295 Washington Ave #5D	718-789-1180
Stupakoff, Otto/80 Varick St	212-334-8032
Sugarman, Lynn/40 W 22nd St	212-691-3245
Sun Photo/19 E 21st St	212-505-9585
Sussman, David/115 E 23rd St	212-254-9380
Sutton, Humphrey/18 E 18th St	212-989-9128
Svensson, Steen/52 Grove St	212-242-7272
Swedowsky, Ben/381 Park Ave S	212-684-1454
Swick, Danille/276 First Ave	212-777-0653
Symons, Abner/27 E 21st St 10th Fl	212-777-6660

T
Takeyama, Kimio/154 W 70th St	212-873-0908
Tannenbaum, Ken/16 W 21st St	212-675-2345
Tanous, Dorothy/110 W 30th St #5R	212-563-2017
Taufic, William/166 W 22nd St	212-620-8143
Taylor, Curtise/29 E 22nd St #2S	212-473-6886
Taylor, Jonathan/5 W 20th St	212-741-2805
TCHEREVKOFF, MICHEL/873 BROADWAY (P 106,107)	**212-228-0540**
Tedesco, Frank/Union Sq West	212-777-3376
Terk, Neil/400 E 59th St	212-838-1213
Tervenski, Steve/421 E 54th St	212-753-6990
Tessler, Stefan/115 W 23rd St	212-924-9168
Testa, Michelle/5 W 30th St 5th Fl	212-947-3364
Thomas, Mark/141 W 26th St 4th Fl	212-741-7252
Thompson, Eleanor/147 W 25th St	212-675-6773
Thompson, Kenneth/220 E 95th St	212-348-3530
Tillman, Denny/39 E 20th St	212-674-7160
Today's Photos Inc/17 E 28th St	212-686-0071
Togashi/36 W 20th St	212-929-2290
Tornberg-Coghlan Assoc/6 E 39th St	212-685-7333
Toto, Joe/148 W 24th St	212-620-0755
Truran, Bill/31 W 21st St 6th Fl	212-741-2285
Trzeciak, Erwin/145 E 16th St	212-254-4140
Tullis, Marcus/400 Lafayette St	212-460-9096
Tully, Roger/344 W 38th St	212-947-3961
Tung, Matthew/5 Union Sq West	212-741-0570
Turbeville, Deborah/160 Fifth Ave #907	212-924-6760
Turner, Pete Photography/154 W 57th St	212-765-1733
Turner, Sam/321 E 21st St #3E	212-777-8715
Tweedy-Holmes, Karen/180 Claremont Ave #51	212-866-2289
Tweel, Ron/241 W 36th St	212-563-3452
Tyler, Mark/233 Broadway #822	212-962-3690

U V
Umans, Marty/29 E 19th St	212-995-0100
Unangst, Andrew/381 Park Ave S	212-889-4888
Underhill, Les/10 W 18th St	212-691-9920
Ursillo, Catherine/1040 Park Ave	212-722-9297
Vaeth, Peter/295 Madison Ave	212-685-4700
Valente, Jerry/193 Meserole Ave	718-389-0469
Valentin, Augusto/202 E 29th St 6th Fl	212-888-1371
Vallini Productions/43 E 20th St 2nd Fl	212-674-6581
Vanglintenkamp, Rik/5 E 16th St 12th Fl	212-924-9210

PHOTOGRAPHERS

Varnedoe, Sam/12 W 27th St #603	212-679-1230
Varon, Malcolm/125 Fifth Ave	212-473-5957
Vartoogian, Jack/262 W 107th St #6A	212-663-1341
Vega, Julio/417 Third Ave #3B	212-889-7568
Veldenzer, Alan/160 Bleecker St	212-420-8189
Vendikos, Tasso/59 W 19th St	212-206-6451
Vest, Michael/40 W 27th St 3rd Fl	212-532-8331
Vhandy Productions/225-A E 59th St	212-759-6150
Vicari, Jim/8 E 12th St	212-675-3745
Vickers, Camille/200 W 79th St PH #A	212-580-8649
Victor, Thomas/131 Fifth Ave	212-777-6004
Vidal, Bernard/853 Seventh Ave	212-582-3284
Vidol, John/37 W 26th St	212-889-0065
Viesti, Joe/PO Box 20424	212-734-4890
Vincenzo/327 W 30th St #1D	212-564-4100
Vine, David/873 Broadway 2nd Fl	212-505-8070
Vishniac, Roman/219 W 81st St	212-787-0997
Visual Impact Productions/15 W 18th St 10th Fl	212-243-8441
Vitale, Peter/157 E 71st St	212-249-8412
Vogel, Allen/126 Fifth Ave	212-675-7550
Volpi, Rene/121 Madison Ave #11-I	212-532-7367
Von Hassell, Agostino/277 W 10th St PH-D	212-242-7290
Vos, Gene/440 Park Ave S	212-714-1155

W
Wadler, Lois/341 E 6th St	212-777-5638
Wagner Int'l Photos/216 E 45th St	212-661-6100
WAGNER, DANIEL/50 W 29TH ST (P 110)	**212-532-8255**
Wagner, David/568 Broadway	212-925-5149
Wagoner, Robert/150 Fifth Ave	212-807-6050
Wahlund, Olof/7 E 17th St	212-929-9067
Waine, Michael/873 Broadway	212-533-4200
Waldo, Maje/873 Broadway	212-475-7886
Waldron, William/463 Broome St	212-226-0356
Wallace, Randall/43 W 13th St #3F	212-242-2930
Wallach, Louis/594 Broadway #8W	212-925-9553
Walsh, Bob/401 E 34th St	212-684-3015
Waltzer, Bill/110 Greene St #96	212-925-1242
Waltzer, Carl/873 Broadway #412	212-475-8748
Walz, Barbra/143 W 20th St	212-242-7175
Wang, John Studio Inc/30 E 20th St	212-982-2765
Wang, Tony/108 E 16th St 6th Fl	212-260-0271
Warchol, Paul/133 Mulberry St	212-431-3461
Ward, Bob Studio/151 W 25th St	212-473-7584
Warsaw Photographic Assocs/36 E 31st St	212-725-1888
Watabe, Haruo/37 W 20th St #905	212-505-8800
Watanabe, Nana/130 W 25th St 10th Fl	212-741-3248
Watson, Albert M/80-82 Greene St	212-925-8552
Watson, Michael/133 W 19th St	212-620-3125
Watt, Elizabeth/141 W 26th St	212-929-8504
Watts, Cliff/536 W 50th St	212-581-3930
Weaks, Dan/175 Fifth Ave #3344	212-242-2105
Weatherly, Karl/235 E 11th St	212-736-1100
Webb, Alex/251 Park Ave S	212-475-7600
Weber, Bruce/37 W 26th St	212-685-5025
Weckler, Chad/210 E 63rd St	212-355-1135
Weidlein, Peter/122 W 26th St	212-989-5498
Weinberg, Michael/5 E 16th St	212-691-1000
WEINBERG, STEVE/47 E 19TH ST 3RD FL (P 112,113)	**212-254-9571**
Weinstein, Todd/47 Irving Pl	212-254-7526
Weir, John/38 E 19th St 8th Fl	212-475-3798
Weiss, Michael Photo/10 W 18th St 2nd Fl	212-929-4073
West, Bonnie/156 Fifth Ave #1232	212-929-3338
West, Charles/233 Court St	718-624-5920
Wettenstein, Raphael/165 Madison Ave	212-679-5555
Wexler, Mark/400 W 43rd St	212-564-7733
Wheatman, Truckin/251 W 30th St	212-239-1081
White, Bill/34 W 17th St	212-243-1780
White, Joel/36 W 20th St	212-620-3085
White, John/11 W 20th St 6th Fl	212-691-1133
White, Timothy/430 W 14th St #502	212-206-7377
Whitehurst, William/32 W 20th St	212-206-8825
Whitely Presentations/60 E 42nd St #419	212-490-3111

Whitman, Robert/1181 Broadway 7th Fl	212-213-6611
Wick, Walter/119 W 23rd St #201	212-243-3448
Wien, Jeffrey/160 Fifth Ave #912	212-243-7028
Wier, John Arthur/38 E 19th St 8th Fl	212-477-5107
Wier, Terry/38 E 19th St 8th Fl	212-477-5107
Wiesehahn, Charles/249 W 29th St #2E	212-563-6612
WILCOX, SHORTY/DPI/19 W 21ST ST #901 (P 44,45)	**212-246-6367**
Wilkes, Stephen/48 E 13th St	212-475-4010
Wilks, Harry/234 W 21st St	212-929-4772
Williams, Larry/43 W 29th St	212-684-1317
Williamson, Richie/514 W 24th St	212-362-9546
Wills, Bret/407 E 78th St	212-570-1843
Wilson, Mike/441 Park Ave S	212-683-3557
Wing, Peter/56-08 138th St	718-762-3617
Winkel, Peter/1413 York Ave	212-861-2563
Wolf, Bernard/214 E 87th St	212-427-0220
Wolf, Bruce/123 W 28th St	212-695-8042
Wolf, Henry/58 W 15th St 6th Fl	212-741-2539
Wolff, Brian R/503 Broadway	212-925-7772
Wolfson Photography/156 Fifth Ave #327	212-924-1510
Wolfson, Steve and Jeff/13-17 Laight St 5th Fl	212-226-0077
Wong, Daniel Photography/652 Broadway #3	212-260-7058
Wong, Leslie/303 W 78th St	212-595-0434
Wood, Merrell/319 W 38th St/Twnhse	212-868-0262
Wood, Susan/641 Fifth Ave	212-371-0679
Woodward, Herbert/555 Third Ave	212-685-4385
Wormser, Richard L/800 Riverside Dr	212-928-0056
Wynn, Dan/170 E 73rd St	212-535-1551

YZ
Yalter, Memo/14-15 162nd St	718-767-3330
Yamashiro, Tad/224 E 12th St	212-473-7177
Yee, Tom/141 W 28th St	212-947-5400
YOAV/4523 BROADWAY (P 114)	**212-942-8185**
Yoshitomo Photography/119 Fifth Ave #305	212-505-8800
Young, Donald/166 E 61st St #3C	212-593-0010
Young, James/56 W 22nd St	212-924-5444
Young, Rick/27 W 20th St	212-929-5701
Young, Steve/6 W 18th St	212-691-5860
Zager, Howard/450 W 31st St	212-239-8082
Zakarian, Aram/25 E 20th St	212-679-6203
Zander, George/141 W 28th St	212-971-0874
Zander, Peter/312 E 90th St #4A	212-348-2647
Zanetti, Gerry/36 E 20th St	212-473-4999
Zapp, Carl/873 Broadway	212-505-0510
Zappa, Tony/28 E 29th St	212-532-3476
Zegre, Francois/124 E 27th St	212-684-6517
Zehnder, Bruno/PO Box 5996	212-840-1234
Zenreich, Alan/78 Fifth Ave 3rd Fl	212-807-1551
Zens, Michael/15 W 29th St	212-683-7258
Zimmerman, David/119 W 23rd St #909	212-243-2718
Zimmerman, Marilyn/119 W 23rd St #909	212-243-2718
Zingler, Joseph/18 Desbrosses St	212-226-3867
Zitz, Peter/6126 Firestone Rd	543-547-7896
Zoiner, John/12 W 44th St	212-972-0357
Zwiebel, Michael/42 E 23rd St	212-477-5629

Northeast

A
Aaron, Peter/222 Valley Pl, Mamaroneck, NY	914-698-4060
Abarno, Richard/11 Dean Ave, Newport, RI	401-846-5820
ABDELNOUR, DOUG/RT 22 PO BOX 64, BEDFORD VILLAGE, NY (P 46)	**914-234-3123**
Abell, Ted/51 Russell Rd, Bethany, CT	203-777-1988
Abend, Jay/511 East 5th St, Boston, MA	617-268-3334
Abrams, Larry/7 River St, Milford, CT	203-878-5090
Abramson, Dean/PO Box 610, Raymond, ME	207-655-7386
Adams Studio Inc/1523 22nd St NW Courtyard, Washington, DC	202-785-2188
Adamstein, Jerome/3720 39th St NW #E167, Washington, DC	202-362-9315
Addis, Kory/144 Lincoln St #4, Boston, MA	617-451-5142
Agelopas, Mike/2510 N Charles St, Baltimore, MD	301-235-2823

Photographers
Continued

Please send us your additions and updates.

Ahrens, Gene/544 Mountain Ave, Berkeley Heights, NJ	201-464-4763
Aiello, Frank/35 S Van Brunt St, Englewood, NJ	201-894-5120
ALEXANDER, JULES/9 BELMONT AVE, RYE, NY (P 47)	**914-967-8985**
Allen, C J/89 Orchard St, Boston, MA	617-524-1925
Alonso, Manuel/425 Fairfield Ave, Stamford, CT	203-359-2838
Althus, Mike/5161 River Rd Bldg 2B, Bethesda, MD	301-652-1303
ALTMAN, STEVE/79 GRAND ST, JERSEY CITY, NJ (P 49)	**201-434-0022**
Ames, Thomas Jr/Miller Pond Rd Box 66, Thetford Center, VT	603-643-5523
Ancona, George/Crickettown Rd, Stony Point, NY	914-786-3043
Anderson, Richard Photo/2523 N Calvert St, Baltimore, MD	301-889-0585
Anderson, Robert/Jordon's Valley Mall, Atlantic City, NJ	609-347-1098
ANDERSON, THEODORE/235 N MADISON ST, ALLENTOWN, PA (P 118,119)	**215-437-6468**
Andris-Hendrickson Photo/314 N 13th #404, Philadelphia, PA	215-925-2630
Ankers Photo/316 F St NE, Washington, DC	202-543-2111
Ansin, Mikki/2 Ellery Square, Cambridge, MA	617-661-1640
Anthony, Greg/15 East St, Boston, MA	617-423-4983
Anyon, Benjamin/206 Spring Run Ln, Downington, PA	215-363-0744
Apoian, Jeffrey/202 Lincoln St, Kennett Square, PA	215-353-2210
Appleton, Hal/Kingston, Doug/44 Mechanic St PO Box 421, Newton, MA	617-969-5772
Arbor Studios/56 Arbor St, Hartford, CT	203-232-6543
Arce Studios/219 Henry St, Stanford, CT	203-323-1343
Areman, Scott/5708 Warburton Ave, Yonkers, NY	914-969-5814
Armstrong, Christine/916 N Charles, Baltimore, MD	301-727-8800
Armstrong, James/127 Mill St, Springfield, MA	413-734-7337
Arruda, Robert/144 Lincoln St, Boston, MA	617-482-1425
Auerbach, Scott/32 Country Rd, Mamaroneck, NY	914-698-9073
Augenstein, Ron/509 Jenne Dr, Pittsburgh, PA	412-653-3583
Avanti Studios/46 Waltham St, Boston, MA	617-574-9424
Aviation Photo Service/65 Riverside Ave, Concord, MA	617-371-2079
Avis, Paul/310 Bedford, Manchester, NH	603-627-2659

B
b & h photographics/1210 Race St Box 1319, Philadelphia, PA	215-425-0888
Baehr, Sarah/708 South Ave, New Canaan, CT	203-966-6317
Baer, Rhoda/1648-A Beeckman Pl NW, Washington, DC	202-332-2879
Baese, Gary/2229 N Charles St, Baltimore, MD	301-235-2226
Bain, Christopher/11 Orchard Farm Rd, Port Washington, NY	516-883-2163
Baker, Bill Photo/1045 Pebble Hill Rd RD3, Doylestown, PA	215-348-9743
Baldwin, Steve/8 Eagle St, Rochester, NY	716-325-2907
Barber, Doug/1634 E Baltimore St, Baltimore, MD	301-276-1634
Bardes, Harold/1812 Kennedy Blvd, Union City, NJ	201-867-7808
Bareish Photo/3 Briarfield Dr, Great Neck, NY	516-829-4778
Barlow, Curtis/PO Box 8863, Washington, DC	202-543-5506
Barlow, Len/392 Boylston, Boston, MA	617-266-4030
Barnes, Christopher/122 Winnisimmet St, Chelsea, MA	617-884-2745
Barocas, Melanie Eve/78 Hart Rd, Guilford, CT	203-457-0898
Barone, Christopher/381 Wright Ave, Kingston, PA	717-287-4680
Barrett, Bob/RD 1 Box 219 Creek Rd, High Falls, NY	914-687-0716
Barrow, Pat/3602 Spring St, Chevy Chase, MD	301-588-3131
Bartlett, Linda/3316 Runnymede Pl NW, Washington, DC	202-362-4777
Basch, Richard/2627 Connecticut Ave NW, Washington, DC	202-232-3100
Baskin, Gerry/12 Union Park St, Boston, MA	617-482-3316
Bavendam, Fred/PO Box 276, Kittery, ME	207-439-0600
Bean, Jeremiah/96 North Ave, Garwood, NJ	201-789-2200
Beards, James/409 Pine St, Providence, RI	401-273-9055
Beardsley, John/322 Summer St 5th Fl, Boston, MA	617-482-0130
Beauchesne Photo/4 Bud Way/Vantage Pt III/#2, Nashua, NH	603-880-8686
Beaudin, Ted/56 Arbor St, Hartford, CT	203-232-6198
Bedford Photo-Graphic Studio/PO Box 64 Rt 22, Bedford, NY	914-234-3123
Beigel, Daniel/2024 Chesapeake Road, Annapolis, MD	301-261-2494
Belmonte, William/43 Homestead Ave, Greenfield, MA	413-773-7744
Bender, Frank/2215 South St, Philadelphia, PA	215-985-4664
Benedetto, Angelo/1903 Chestnut St, Philadelphia, PA	215-627-1990
Benn, Nathan/925 1/2 F St NW, Washington, DC	202-638-5705
Bennett, George/1206 Tribbett Ave, Sharon Hill, PA	215-586-7095
Bennett, William/128 W Northfield Rd, Livingston, NJ	201-992-7967
Benson, Gary/50 Hillcrest Rd, Martinsville, NJ	201-356-6705
Benvenuti, Judi/12 N Oak Ct, Madison, NJ	201-377-5075
Berg, Hal/67 Hilary Circle, New Rochelle, NY	914-235-9356
Bergman, LV & Assoc/East Mountain Rd S, Cold Spring, NY	914-265-3656

Berinstein, Martin/215 A St 6th Fl, Cambridge, MA	617-268-4117
Bernsau, W Marc/PO Box 1152, Sanford, ME	207-324-1741
Bernstein, Daniel/7 Fuller St, Waltham, MA	617-894-0473
Berry, Michael/838 S Broad St, Trenton, NJ	609-396-2413
Bethoney, Herb/1222 Washington St, Boston, MA	617-749-1124
Bezushko, Bob/1311 Irving St, Philadelphia, PA	215-735-7771
Bezushko, George/1311 Irving St, Philadelphia, PA	215-735-7771
Bibikow, Walter/76 Batterymarch St, Boston, MA	617-451-3464
Biegun, Richard/56 Cherry Ave, West Sayville, NY	516-567-2645
Bilyk, I George/314 E Mt Airy Ave, Philadelphia, PA	215-242-5431
Bindas Studio/205 A St, Boston, MA	617-268-3050
Bingham, Jack/8 Abbot St, E Rochester, NH	603-742-7718
Binzen, Bill/Indian Mountain Rd, Lakeville, CT	203-435-2485
Birn, Roger/150 Chestnut St, Providence, RI	401-421-4825
Bishop, Jennifer/2732 St Paul St, Baltimore, MD	301-366-6662
Blake, Mike/107 South Street, Boston, MA	617-451-0660
Blakeslee Lane Studios/916 N Charles St, Baltimore, MD	301-727-8800
Blank, Bruce/228 Clearfield Ave, Norristown, PA	215-539-6166
Blevins, Burgess/103 E Read St, Baltimore, MD	301-685-0740
Bliss, Brad/42 Audubon St, Rochester, NY	716-461-9794
Bloomberg, Robert/172 Kohanza St, Danbury, CT	203-794-1764
Blouin, Craig/14 Main St, Rollinsford, NH	603-742-0104
Boehm, J Kenneth/96 Portland Ave, Georgetown, CT	203-544-8524
Bognovitz, Murray/4980 Wyaconda Rd, Rockville, MD	301-984-7771
Bohm, Linda/7 Park St, Montclair, NJ	201-746-3434
Boisvert, Paul/305 South Beach Rd, S Burlington, VT	802-862-7249
Bolster, Mark/1235 Monterey St, Pittsburgh, PA	412-231-3757
Bolton, Bea/15 East St, Boston, MA	617-423-2050
Bookbinder, Sigmund/Box 833, Southbury, CT	203-264-5137
Borkoski, Matthew/1506 Noyes Dr, Silver Spring, MD	301-589-4858
Bossart, Bob/PO Box 734/Cathedral St, Boston, MA	617-423-2323
Bowen, Dave/RD #5 Box 176, Wellsboro, PA	717-326-1212
Bowman, Jo/1102 Manning St, Philadelphia, PA	215-625-0200
Bowman, Ron/PO Box 4071, Lancaster, PA	717-898-7716
Boxer, Jeff Photography/14 Newbury St, Boston, MA	617-266-7755
Boyer, Beverly/17 Llanfair Rd, Ardmore, PA	215-649-0657
Bradley, Dave/840 Summer St, Boston, MA	617-268-6644
Bradley, Roy/760 State St, Schenectady, NY	518-377-9457
Brady, Joseph/Rt 179 RD2 Box 198, Ringoes, NJ	201-788-5550
Braverman, Ed/337 Summer St, Boston, MA	617-423-3373
Bravo, David/1649 Main St, Bridgeport, CT	203-384-8524
Brignolo, Joseph B/Oxford Springs Rd, Chester, NY	914-496-4453
Brown, Jim/48 S Main St, S Norwalk, CT	203-853-0271
Brown, Martin/Cathance Lake, Grove Post Office, ME	207-454-7708
Brown, Stephen R/1882 Columbia Rd NW, Washington, DC	202-667-1965
Brownell, David/PO Box 97, Hamilton, MA	617-468-4284
Brownell, William/1411 Saxon Ave, Bay Shore, NY	516-665-0081
brt Photographic Illustrations/911 State St, Lancaster, PA	717-393-0918
Bruemmer, Fred/5170 Cumberland Ave, Montreal H4V 2N8, QU	514-482-5098
Brundage, Kip/66 Union St, Belfast, ME	207-338-5210
Bubbenmoyer, Kevin/RD #2 Box 110, Orefield, PA	215-395-9167
BUCHANAN, ROBERT/466 LAKEVIEW AVE, VALHALLA, NY (P 60)	**914-592-1204**
Buckman, Sheldon/15 Kiley Dr, Randolph, MA	617-986-4773
Buff, Cindy/55 Marina Bay Dr, Long Beach, NJ	201-870-3222
Bulkin, Susan/Photogphy Works/548 Fairway Terrace, Philadelphia, PA	215-483-8814
Bulvony, Matt/1003 E Carson St, Pittsburgh, PA	412-431-5344
Burak, Jonathan/50 Woodward, Quincy, MA	617-770-3380
Burdick, Gary Photography/9 Parker Hill, Brookfield, CT	203-775-2894
Burger, Oded/670 South St, Waltham, MA	617-527-1024
Burke, John/31 Stanhope St, Boston, MA	617-536-4912
Burke, John & Judy/116 E Van Buren Ave, New Castle, DE	302-322-8760
Burns, George/3909 State St, Schenectady, NY	518-393-3633
Burris, Ken/PO Box 592, Shelburne, VT	802-985-3263
Burwell, John/3519 Bradley Ln, Chevy Chase, MD	301-986-1290
Buschner & Faust/450 W Menlo Park, Rochester, NY	716-475-1170
Butler, Herbert/200 Mamaroneck Ave, White Plains, NY	914-683-1767

C
C L M Photo/272 Nassau Rd, Huntington, NY	516-423-8890
Cali, Guy/Layton Rd, Clarics Summit, PA	717-587-1957

Photographers

Continued

Please send us your additions and updates.

Callahan, Charles/54 Applecross Circle, Chalfont, PA	215-822-8258
Carbone, Fred/1041 Buttonwood St, Philadelphia, PA	215-236-2266
Carrier, John/601 Newbury St, Boston, MA	617-262-4440
Carrino, Nick/710 S Marshall St, Philadelphia, PA	215-925-3190
Carroll, Hanson/11 New Boston Rd, Norwich, VT	802-649-1094
Carruthers, Alan/3605 Jeanne-Mamce, Montreal H2X 2K4, QU	514-288-4333
Carstens, Don/1021 Cathedral St, Baltimore, MD	301-385-3049
Carter, J Pat/3000 Chestnut Ave #116, Baltimore, MD	301-256-2982
Carter, Philip/Seventeen Sunset Dr, Bedford Hills, NY	914-241-4901
Cassaday, Bruce/RD 1 Box 345 Lockwood Rd, Peekskill, NY	914-528-4343
Cataffo, Linda/30 W Harriet Ave, Palisades Park, NJ	201-694-5047
Catiero, Jeff/410 Church Ln, New Brunswick, NJ	201-297-8979
CAVANAUGH, JAMES/PO BOX 158, BUFFALO, NY (P 120)	**716-837-0697**
Cavellero, Cheryl/PO Box 224, Dobbs Ferry, NY	914-693-7919
Certo, Rosemarie/2519 Parrish St, Philadelphia, PA	215-232-2814
Chadman, Bob/595-603 Newbury St, Boston, MA	617-426-4926
Chalifour, Benoit/1030 St Alexandre #812, Montreal H2Z 1P3, QU	514-879-1869
Chandoha, Walter/RD 1 PO Box 287, Annandale, NJ	201-782-3666
Chapman, Peter/28 Randolph St, Boston, MA	617-357-5670
Chaput, Chuck/17 Stilling St, Boston, MA	617-542-8272
Chatwin, Jim/5459 Main St, Williamsville, NY	716-634-3436
Chauhan, Dilip/145 Ipswich St, Boston, MA	617-262-2359
Chawtsky, Ann/85 Andover Rd, Rockville Centre, NY	516-766-2417
Chiusano, Michael/39 Glidden St, Beverly, MA	617-927-7067
Choroszewski, Walter J/10 Mohvale Path, Branchburg, NJ	201-526-2018
Ciaglia, Joseph/2036 Spruce St, Philadelphia, PA	215-985-1092
Clark, Conley/9814 Rosensteel Ave, Silver Spring, MD	301-585-4739
Clarke, Marna G/1571 Boulevard, West Hartford, CT	203-521-5127
Clayton-Hall, Gary/PO Box 38, Shelburne, VT	802-985-8380
Cleff, Bernie Studio/715 Pine St, Philadelphia, PA	215-922-4246
Clemens, Clint/346 Newbury St, Boston, MA	617-437-1309
Clemens, Peter/153 Sidney St, Oyster Bay, NY	516-922-1759
Clifford, Geoffrey C/Craggle Ridge, Reading, VT	802-484-5047
Cohen, Daniel/744 Park Ave, Hoboken, NJ	201-659-0952
Cohen, Marc Assoc/23 Crestview Dr, Brookfield, CT	203-775-1102
Collette, Roger/PO Box 215, Woodsville, NH	603-226-1856
Colucci, Joe/128 Broadway #106, Patterson, NJ	201-881-7618
Conaty, Jim/174 Farm Hill Rd, Sherborn, MA	617-482-0660
Conboy, John/1225 State St, Schenectady, NY	518-346-2346
Confer, Holt/2016 Franklin Pl, Wyomissing, PA	215-678-0131
Congalton, David/206 Washington St, Pembroke, MA	617-826-2788
Conner, Marian/456 Rockaway Rd #15, Dover, NJ	201-328-1823
Connor, Donna/PO Box 272/Fourth Ave, Sweetwater, NJ	609-965-3396
Cooke, Doug/202 Beacon St, Boston, MA	617-267-1754
Coolidge, Jeffrey/322 Summer St, Boston, MA	617-338-6869
Corcoran, John/310 Eighth St, New Cumberland, PA	717-774-0652
Cordingley, Ted/Way Rd, Gloucster, MA	617-283-2591
Cortesi, Wendy/3034 'P' St NW, Washington, DC	202-965-1204
Cough, George/8 Bryant Dr, Huntington, NY	516-673-9376
Coughlin, Suki/Main St, New London, NH	603-526-4645
Crane, Tom/113 Cumberland Pl, Bryn Mawr, PA	215-525-2444
Crawford, Carol/14 Fortune Dr Box 221, Billerica, MA	617-663-8662
Creative Images/122 Elmcroft Rd, Rochester, NY	716-482-8720
Crossley, Dorothy/Mittersill Rd, Franconia, NH	603-823-8177
Cunningham, Chris/9 East St, Boston, MA	617-542-4640
Curtis, Bruce/70 Belmont Dr, Roslyn Heights, NY	516-484-2570
Curtis, Jackie/Alewives Rd, Norwalk, CT	203-866-9198
Curtis, John/50 Melcher St, Boston, MA	617-451-9117
Cushner, Susie/354 Congress St, Boston, MA	617-542-4070
Czamanske, Marty/61 Commercial St, Rochester, NY	716-546-1434

D

D'Angelo, Andy/309 Madison Ave, Reading, PA	215-921-8430
Daigle, James/109 Broad St, Boston, MA	617-233-1284
Dannenberg, Mitchell/261 Averill Ave, Rochester, NY	716-473-6720
Dapkiewicz, Steve/121 Beach St, Boston, MA	617-357-6809
Davidson, Josiah Scenic Photography/PO Box 434, Jenkintown, PA	215-572-5757
Davis, Howard/19 E 21st St, Baltimore, MD	301-625-3838
Davis, Pat Photo/14620 Pinto Ln, Rockville, MD	301-279-8828
Davis, Rick/210 Carter Dr #9/Matlack Ind, West Chester, PA	215-436-6050

De Lucia, Ralph/120 E Hartsdale Ave, Hartsdale, NY	914-472-2253
Dean, Floyd M/2-B S Poplar St, Wilmington, DE	302-655-7193
Debren, Allen/355 Pearl St, Burlington, VT	802-864-5916
Degginger, Phil/PO Box 186, Convent Station, NJ	201-455-1733
Delbert, Christian/19 Linell Circle, Billerica, MA	617-273-3138
Dempsey-Hart/241 A St, Boston, MA	617-338-6661
Denuto, Ellen/3100 Stevens Rd #3133, Wallington, NJ	201-773-5345
Derenzis, Philip/PO Box 19, Wind Gap, PA	215-437-7832
DeVito, Mary/2528 Cedar Ave, Ronkonkoma, NY	516-981-4547
DEWAELE, JOHN/14 ALMY ST, LINCOLN, RI (P 121)	**401-726-0084**
DiBenedetto, Emilo/32 Touro Ave, Medford, MA	617-396-0550
Dickens, James/1255 University Ave, Rochester, NY	716-244-6334
Dickstein, Bob/101 Hillturn Lane, Roslyn Heights, NY	516-621-2413
Diebold, George/416 Bloomfield Ave, Montclair, NJ	201-744-5789
Dietz, Donald/PO Box 177, Dorchester, MA	617-265-3436
DiGiacomo, Melchior/32 Norma Rd, Harrington Park, NJ	201-767-0870
Dillon, George/275 Tremont St, Boston, MA	617-482-6154
DiMarco, Salvatore C Jr/1002 Cobbs St, Drexel Hill, PA	215-789-3239
DiMarzo, Bob/109 Broad St, Boston, MA	617-720-1113
Dittmar, Warren/217 Main St, Ossining, NY	914-762-6311
Dixon, Mel/PO Box 468, Ossining, NY	914-941-9336
Dixon, Rodney/PO Box 113, Cedar Grove, NJ	214-307-7232
Dodson, George/PO Box 525, Bowie, MD	301-262-0702
Dolin, Penny Ann/190 Henry St, Stamford, CT	203-359-9932
Donovan, Bill/165 Grand Blvd, Scarsdale, NY	914-472-0938
Douglas Associates/3 Cove of Cork Ln, Annapolis, MD	301-266-5060
Douglass, James/5161 River Rd Bldg 2B, Bethesda, MD	301-652-1303
Dow, Norman/52 Concord Ave, Cambridge, MA	617-492-1236
Dowling, John/521 Scott Ave, Syracuse, NY	315-446-8189
Dreyer, Peter H/916 Pleasant St, Norwood, MA	617-762-8550
Dunham, Tom/335 Gordon Rd, Robinsville, NJ	609-259-6042
Dunn, Jeffery/32 Pearl St, Cambridge, MA	617-864-2124
Dunn, Paul/239 A Street, Boston, MA	617-542-9554
DUNN, PHOEBE/20 SILVERMINE RD, NEW CANAAN, CT (P 234)	**203-966-9791**
Dunoff, Rich/407 Bowman Ave, Merion Station, PA	215-627-3690
Dunwell, Steve/20 Winchester St, Boston, MA	617-423-4916
Durrance, Dick/Dolphin Ledge, Rockport, ME	207-236-3990
Dwiggins, Gene/204 Westminster Mall, Providence, RI	401-421-6466
Dyekman, James E/14 Cherry Hill Circle, Ossining, NY	914-941-0821

E

Earle, John/PO Box 63, Cambridge, MA	617-628-1454
Eastern Light Photo/113 Arch St, Philadelphia, PA	215-238-0655
Edelman, Harry/1335 Brinton Rd, Pittsburgh, PA	412-371-6865
Edmunds, Skip/25 E Huron, Buffalo, NY	716-842-2272
Edson, Franz Inc/26 Watch Way, Huntington, NY	516-692-4345
Edson, Steven/107 South St, Boston, MA	617-357-8032
Egan, Jim/Visualizations/220 W Exchange St, Providence, RI	401-521-7052
Ehrlich, George/PO Box 186, New Hampton, NY	914-355-1757
Elder, Tommy/Chapelbrook & Ashfield Rds, Williamsburg, MA	413-628-3243
Ellis, Bob/15 Washington Ave, Emerson, NJ	212-874-5300
Elson, Paul/8200 Blvd East, North Bergen, NJ	201-662-2882
Emmott, Bob/700 S 10th St, Philadelphia, PA	215-925-2773
Epstein, Alan Photography/694 Center St, Chicopee, MA	413-736-8532
Ernest Creative Photo/47 Somerset St, N Plainfield, NJ	201-753-6342
Esposito, Anthony Jr/48 Old Amity Rd, Bethany, CT	203-393-2231
ESTO PHOTO/222 VALLEY PL, MAMARONECK, NY (P 65)	**914-698-4060**
Evans, John C/808 Centennial Ave, Sewickley, PA	412-741-5580
Evans, Michael/5520 33rd St NW, Washington, DC	202-362-4901
Everett Studios/22 Barker Ave, White Plains, NY	914-997-2200
Eyle, Nicolas Edward/304 Oak St, Syracuse, NY	315-422-6231

F

F-90 Inc/60 Sindle Ave, Little Falls, NJ	201-785-9090
Falkenstein, Roland/Strawberry St #4, Philadelphia, PA	215-592-7138
Faragan, George/1621 Wood St, Philadelphia, PA	215-564-5711
Farris, Mark/3733 Benton St NW, Washington, DC	202-269-5963
Fatta, C/25 Dry Dock Ave, Boston, MA	617-423-6638
FAULKNER, ROBERT I/52 COMSTOCK ST, NEW BRUNSWICK, NJ (P 66)	**201-828-6984**
Feehan, Stephen/86 Donaldson Ave, Rutherford, NJ	201-438-1514
Feil, Charles W III/7 Fox Court, Portland, ME	207-773-3754
Feiling, David/7804 Ravenswood Ln, Manlius, NY	315-445-2881

Photographers

Continued

Please send us your additions and updates.

Feingersh, Jon/18533 Split Rock Ln, Germantown, MD	301-428-9525
Felker, Richard/20 Melville St, Augusta, ME	207-623-2223
Fennell, Mary/57 Maple Ave, Hastings on Hudson, NY	914-478-3627
Feraulo, Richard/518 First Parish Rd, Scituate, MA	617-545-6654
Fernando Photo/2901 James St, Syracuse, NY	315-432-0065
Ferreira, Al/237 Naubuc Ave, East Hartford, CT	203-569-8812
Ferrino, Paul/PO Box 3641, Milford, CT	203-878-4785
Ficara Studios Ltd/880 Canal St, Stamford, CT	203-327-4535
Filipe, Tony/239 A St, Boston, MA	617-542-8330
Findlay, Christine/Hwy 36 Airport Plaza, Hazlet, NJ	201-264-2211
Fine, Jerome/4594 Brookhill Dr N, Manlius, NY	315-682-7272
Fine, Ron/8600 Longacre Ct, Bethesda, MD	301-469-7960
Finlayson, Jim/PO Box 337, Locust Valley, NY	516-676-5816
Finnegan, Michael/PO Box 901, Plandome, NY	516-365-7942
Fischer, John/9 Shore View Rd, Port Washington, NY	516-883-3225
Fish, Charles/240 Noroton Ave, Darien, CT	203-655-6798
Fish, Dick/40 Center St, Northampton, MA	413-584-6500
Fisher, Al/601 Newbury St, Boston, MA	617-536-7126
Fisher, Patricia/2234 Cathedral Ave NW, Washington, DC	202-232-3781
Fitzgerald, Mark/87 Daly Rd, E Northport, NY	516-462-5628
Fitzhugh, Susan/3809 Beech Ave, Baltimore, MD	301-243-6112
Five Thousand K/281 Summer St, Boston, MA	617-542-5995
Fland, Peter/20 Park St, Moravia, NY	315-497-3528
Flanigan, Jim/1325 N 5th St #F4, Philadelphia, PA	215-236-4448
Flowers, Morocco/520 Harrison Ave, Boston, MA	617-426-3692
Fogliani, Tom/600 Thurnau Dr, River Vale, NJ	201-391-2245
Foley, Paul/791 Tremont, Boston, MA	617-266-9336
Folti, Arthur/8 W Mineola Ave, Valley Steam, NY	516-872-0941
Foote, James/22 Tomac Ave, Old Greenwich, CT	203-637-3228
Forbes, Fred/1 South King St, Gloucester City, NJ	609-456-1919
Forbes, Pat (Ms)/528 'F' St Ter SE, Washington, DC	703-478-0434
Fordham, Mark/2 Roselle Ave, Cranford, NJ	201-276-9515
Foster, Frank/323 Newbury St, Boston, MA	617-536-8267
Foster, Nicholas/143 Claremont Rd, Bernardsville, NJ	201-766-7526
Fournier, Walter/185 Forest St, S Hamilton, MA	617-468-2892
Fox, Peggy/701 Padonia Rd, Cockeysville, MD	301-252-0003
Fox, Seth/8 Roundtree Circle, Hockessin, DE	302-239-3182
Francois, Emmett W/208 Hillcrest Ave, Wycoff, NJ	201-652-5775
Frank, Richard/48 Woodside Ave, Westport, CT	203-227-0496
Frank-Adise, Gale/9012 Fairview Rd, Silver Spring, MD	301-585-7085
Fraser, Renee/1167 Massachusetts Ave, Arlington, MA	617-646-4296
Fredericks, Michael Jr/RD 2 Box 292, Ghent, NY	518-672-7616
Freer, Bonnie/265 S Mountain Rd, New City, NY	212-535-3666
Freeze Frame Studios/255 Leonia Ave, Bogota, NJ	201-343-1233
Freid, Joel Carl/812 Loxford Terr, Silver Spring, MD	301-681-7211
Frerking, Erich Photography Inc/1 Bridge St, Irvington, NY	914-591-6047
Freund, Bud/1425 Bedford St #9C, Stamford, CT	203-359-0147
Fries, Janet/4439 Ellicott St NW, Washington, DC	202-362-4443
Furman, Michael/115 Arch St, Philadelphia, PA	215-925-4233
Furore, Don/49 Sugar Hollow Rd, Danbury, CT	203-792-9395

G G/Q Studios/1217 Spring Garden St, Philadelphia, PA	215-236-7770
Gale, John & Son/712 Chestnut St, Philadelphia, PA	215-629-0506
Galella, Ron/17 Glover Ave, Yonkers, NY	914-237-2988
Gallery, Bill/86 South St, Boston, MA	617-542-0499
Gallo, Peter/1238 Callowhill St, Philadelphia, PA	215-925-5230
Galvin, Kevin/PO Box 30, Hanover, MA	617-826-4795
Gans, Harriet/50 Church Lane, Scarsdale, NY	914-723-7017
Ganson, John/14 Lincoln Rd, Wayland, MA	617-358-2543
Garber, Ira/150 Chestnut St, Providence, RI	401-274-3723
Gardner, Charles/12 N 4th St, Reading, PA	215-376-8086
Garfield, Peter/3401 K St NW, Washington, DC	202-333-1379
Garrett-Stow, Liliane/18 Tuthill Point Rd, East Moriches, NY	516-878-8587
Gates, Ralph/364 Hartshorn Dr Box 233, Short Hills, NJ	201-379-4456
GEER, GARRY/183 ST PAUL ST, ROCHESTER, NY (P 69)	**716-232-2393**
George, Fred/737 Canal St, Stamford, CT	203-348-7454
George, Walter/863 Mountain Ave, Berkeley Heights, NJ	201-464-2180
Geraci, Steve/125 Wilbur Place, Bohemia, NY	516-567-8777
Giandomenico & Fiore/13 Fern Ave, Collingswood, NJ	609-854-2222
Giese, Al/RR 1/Box 302, Poundridge, NY	914-764-5512
Giglio, Harry/925 Penn Ave #305, Pittsburgh, PA	412-261-3338
Gillette, Guy/133 Mountaindale Rd, Yonkers, NY	914-779-4684

Glasofer, David/176 Main St, Metuchen, NJ	201-549-1845
Glass, Mark/310 9th St, Hoboken, NJ	201-798-0219
Glass, Peter/63 Penn Dr, West Hartford, CT	203-233-2898
Gluck, Mike/2 Bronxville Rd, Bronxville, NY	914-961-1677
Goell, Jonathan J/109 Broad St, Boston, MA	617-423-2057
Goembl, Ponder/617 S 10th St, Philadelphia, PA	215-928-1797
Gold, Gary D/One Madison Pl, Albany, NY	518-434-4887
Goldblatt, Steven/32 S Strawberry St, Philadelphia, PA	215-925-3825
Goldenberg, Barry/1 Baltimore Ave Box 412, Cranford, NJ	201-276-1510
Goldklang, Jay/778 New York Ave, Huntington, NY	516-421-3860
Goldman, Mel/329 Newbury St, Boston, MA	617-536-0539
Goldsmith, Alan/PO Box 260, Washington Depot, CT	203-263-3841
Gooch, Tom/1728 Cherry St, Philadelphia, PA	215-567-3608
Good, Richard/5226 Osage Ave, Philadelphia, PA	215-472-7659
Goodman, Howard/PO Box 433, Croton Falls, NY	914-277-3133
Goodman, John/337 Summer St, Boston, MA	617-482-8061
Goodman, John D/One Mill Street, Burlington, VT	802-864-0200
Goodman, Lou/322 Summer St, Boston, MA	617-542-8254
Gorchev & Gorchev/11 Cabot Rd, Woburn, MA	617-933-8090
Gordon, David A/1413 Hertel Ave, Buffalo, NY	716-833-2661
Gordon, Lee/725 Boylston St, Boston, MA	617-423-1985
Gorrill, Robert B/PO Box 206, North Quincy, MA	617-328-4012
Grace, Arthur/1928 35th Pl NW, Washington, DC	202-333-6568
Graham, Jim/720 Chestnut St, Philadelphia, PA	215-592-7272
Grant, Gail/7006 Valley Ave, Phildelphia, PA	215-482-9857
GRANT, JARVIS/1650 HARVARD ST NW #709, WASHINGTON, DC (P 143)	**202-387-8584**
Graphic Accent/446 Main St PO Box 243, Wilmington, MA	617-658-7602
Gray, Sam/886 Gay St, Westwood, MA	617-326-2624
Graybeal, Sharon/PO Box 896, Hockessin, DE	302-998-4037
Grayson, Jay/9 Cockenoe Dr, Westport, CT	203-222-0072
Green, Jeremy/15117 Wheeler Lane, Sparks, MD	301-366-0123
Greenberg, Steven/28 Randolph St, Boston, MA	617-423-7646
Gregoire, Rogier/107 South St 2nd Fl, Boston, MA	617-574-9554
Greniers Commercial Photo/127 Mill St, Springfield, MA	413-532-9406
Griebsch, John/183 St Paul St, Rochester, NY	716-546-1303
Grohe, Stephen F/186 South St, Boston, MA	617-426-2290
Gross, Lance/PO Box 388, Manchester, CT	203-871-2641
Guarinello, Greg/252 Highwood St, Teaneck, NJ	201-836-2333
Gude, Susann/Slip 1-A/Spruce Dr, E Patchogue, NY	516-654-8093

H Hagerman, Ron/385 Westminster St, Providence, RI	401-272-1117
Hahn, Bob/3522 Skyline Dr, Bethlehem, PA	215-868-0339
Halliwell, Harry/PO Box 1690 GMF, Boston, MA	617-623-7225
Halstead, Dirck/3332 P St NW, Washington, DC	202-338-2028
Hambourg, Serge/Box 753, Crugers, NY	212-866-0085
Hamor, Robert/2308 Columbia Cir, Merrimack, NH	603-424-6737
Handerhan, Jerome/ JJH Photo/113 Edgewood Ave, Pittsburgh, PA	412-242-6308
Hansen, Steve/1260 Boylston St, Boston, MA	617-236-2211
Hanstein, George/389 Belmont Ave, Haledon, NJ	201-790-0505
Haritan, Michael/1701 Eben St, Pittsburgh, PA	412-343-2112
Harkey, John/90 Larch Rd, Providence, RI	401-831-1023
Harrington, Phillip A/Wagner Ave/ PO Box 10, Fleischmann's, NY	914-254-5227
Harrington, Blaine/374 Old Hawleyville Rd, Bethel, CT	203-798-2866
Harrington, John/455 Old Sleepy Hollow Rd, Pleasantville, NY	914-939-0702
Harris, Bill/286 Summer St, Boston, MA	617-426-0989
Harris, Brownie/249 McGuire Lane, Croton-on-Hudson, NY	914-271-6426
Harrison, Jim/PO Box 266, Charleston, MA	617-242-4314
Harting, Christopher/327 Summer St, Boston, MA	617-451-6330
Harvey, Scott/273 Speedwell, Morristown, NJ	201-538-9410
Hatos, Kathleen/3418 Keins St, Philadelphia, PA	215-425-3960
Hausner, Clifford/10 Wayne Rd, Fairlawn, NJ	201-791-7409
Hayes, Eric/Rural Route #1, Jrdn Fls B0T1J0, NS	902-875-4260
Heayn, Mark/17 W 24th St, Baltimore, MD	301-235-1608
Hecker, David/285 Aycrigg Ave, Passaic, NJ	201-471-2496
Heilman, Grant/PO Box 317, Lititz, PA	717-626-0296
Heinz, F Michael Photography/17 Rose Hill, Southport, CT	203-259-7456
Heist, Scott/616 Walnut St, Emmaus, PA	215-965-5479
Helmar, Dennis/134 Beach St, Boston, MA	617-451-1496
Herwig/36 Gloucester St, Boston, MA	617-353-1262

Photographers

Continued

Please send us your additions and updates.

Hewitt, Malcolm/179 Massachusetts Ave, Boston, MA	617-262-7227
Hill, Brian/PO Box 1823, Nantucket, MA	617-228-2210
Hill, John T/388 Amity Rd, New Haven, CT	203-393-0035
Hines, Harry/PO Box 10061, Newark, NJ	201-242-0214
Hirshfeld, Max/923 F Street NW, Washington, DC	202-638-3131
Hodges, Sue Anne/34 North St, Wilmington, MA	617-657-6417
Hoffman, Dave/PO Box 1299, Summit, NJ	201-277-6285
Hoffman, Steven/780 Eden Rd, Lancaster, PA	717-569-2631
Holland, James R/208 Commonwealth Ave, Boston, MA	617-321-3638
Hollander, David/11 S Springfield Ave/POB 443, Springfield, NJ	201-467-0870
Holmes, Greg/2007 Hickory Hill Ln, Silver Spring, MD	301-295-3338
Holniker, Barry/400 E 25th St, Baltimore, MD	301-889-1919
Holoquist, Marcy/424 N Craig St, Pittsburgh, PA	412-963-8021
Holt, Chuck/535 Albany St, Boston, MA	617-338-4009
Holt, John/145 South St, Boston, MA	617-426-7262
Holt, Walter/PO Box 936, Media, PA	215-565-1977
Holz, Thomas Jay/PO Box 4, Tribes Hill, NY	518-842-7730
Hone, Stephen/2130 Arch St, Philadelphia, PA	215-568-5434
Hopkins, Tom/15 Orchard Park, Box 7A, Madison, CT	203-245-0824
Hornick/ Rivlin/25 Dry Dock, Boston, MA	617-482-8614
Horowitz, Abby/922 Chestnut, Philadelphia, PA	215-925-3600
Hotshots/35 Congress St, Salem, MA	617-744-1557
Houck, Julie/535 Albany St, Boston, MA	617-338-4009
Houser, Robert/PO Box 299, Litchfield, CT	203-567-4241
Houser-Tartaglia Photoworks/23 Walnut Ave, Clark, NJ	201-388-8531
Howard, Alan B Assoc/27 Cleveland St, Valhalla, NY	914-946-0404
Howard, Jerry/12 Main St, Natick, MA	617-653-7610
Howard, Richard/144 Holworthy St, Cambridge, MA	617-628-5410
Hoyt, Russell/171 Westminister Ave, S Attleboro, MA	617-399-8611
Hoyt, Wolfgang/222 Valley Pl, Mamaroneck, NY	914-698-4060
Hubbell, William/99 East Elm St, Greenwich, CT	203-629-9629
Hulbert, Steve/3642 N 3rd St, Harrisburg, PA	717-236-1906
Hundertmark, Charles/6264 Oakland Mills Rd, Sykesville, MD	301-242-8150
Hungaski, Andrew/Merribrook Lane, Stamford, CT	203-327-6763
Hunsberger, Douglas/115 W Fern Rd, Wildwood Crest, NJ	609-522-6849
Hunter, Allan/56 Main St 3rd Fl, Milburn, NJ	201-467-4920
Hurwitz, Harrison/100 E Hartsdale Ave #6NW, Hartsdale, NY	914-725-4086
Hurwitz, Joel/PO Box 1009, Leominster, MA	617-537-6476
Hutchinson, Gardiner/280 Friend St, Boston, MA	617-523-5180
Huyler, Willard/218 South Ave E, Cranford, NJ	201-272-8874
Hyde, Dana/PO Box 1302, South Hampton, NY	516-283-1001

IJ

Iannazzi, Robert F/450 Smith Rd, Rochester, NY	716-624-1285
Ickow, Marvin/1824 35th St NW, Washington, DC	202-342-0250
Iglarsh, Gary/2229 N Charles St, Baltimore, MD	301-235-3385
Image Source Inc/PO Box 1929, Wilmington, DE	302-658-5897
Impact Multi Image Inc/53 Laurel Dr, Somers Point, NJ	609-484-8100
Iverson, Bruce/, , MA	617-433-8429
Jackson, Reggie/135 Sheldon Terr, New Haven, CT	203-787-5191
Jagger, Warren/150 Chestnut St Box 3330, Providence, RI	401-351-7366
Joachim, Bruno/326 A Street, Boston, MA	617-451-6156
Joel, Yale/ Woodybrook Ln, Croton-On-Hudson, NY	914-271-8172
Johnson, Paul/38 Athens St, Boston, MA	617-269-4043
Jones, Lou/22 Randolph St, Boston, MA	617-426-6335
Jones, Peter/43 Charles St, Boston, MA	617-227-6400
Joseph, Nabil/445 St Pierre St #402, Montreal H2Y 2M8, QU	514-842-2444

K

Kaetzel, Gary/PO Box 3514, Wayne, NJ	201-696-6174
Kalfus, Lonny/226 Hillside Ave, Leonia, NJ	201-944-3909
Kalischer, Clemens/Main St, Stockbridge, MA	413-298-5500
Kalish, Joanne/512 Adams St, Centerport, NY	516-271-6133
Kalisher, Simpson/North St, Roxbury, CT	203-354-8893
Kaminsky, Saul/36 Sherwood Ave, Greenwich, CT	203-531-4953
KAMPER, GEORGE/62 NORTH UNION ST, ROCHESTER, NY (P 80)	**716-454-7006**
Kan, Dennis/4200 Wisconsin Ave #106, Washington, DC	301-428-9417
Kane, Alice/3380 Emeric Ave, Wantagh, NY	516-781-7049
Kane, Martin/555 Chester Pike #2, Sharon Hills, PA	215-237-6897
Kannair, Jon/65 Water St, Worcester, MA	617-757-3417
Kaplan, Carol/20 Beacon St, Boston, MA	617-720-4400
Kasper, Ken/1232 Cobbs St, Drexel Hill, PA	215-446-0108

Katz, Dan/36 Aspen Rd, W Orange, NJ	201-731-8956
Katz, Geoffrey/156 Francestown Rd, New Boston, NH	603-487-3819
Kauffman, Ken/1617 Briar Hill Rd, Gladwyne, PA	215-649-4474
Kaufman, Robert/58 Roundwood Rd, Newton Upper Falls, MA	617-964-4080
KAWALERSKI, TED/7 EVERGREEN WAY, NORTH TARRYTOWN, NY (P 42,43)	**212-242-0198**
Keene Studio/10510 Insley St, Silver Spring, MD	301-949-4722
Keller, Michael/15 S Grand Ave, Baldwin, NY	516-223-9604
Kelley, Edward/20 White St, Red Bank, NJ	201-747-0596
Kelly/Mooney Photography/87 Willow Ave, North Plainfield, NJ	201-757-5924
Kenik, David Photography/21 Countryside Dr, Nashua, NH	603-880-8108
Kernan, Sean/576 Leetes Island Rd, Stony Creek, CT	203-481-4478
Kerper, David/1018 E Willow Grove Ave, Philadelphia, PA	215-836-1135
Kim, Chang H/9425 Bethany Pl, Gaithersburg, MD	301-840-5741
King, Ralph/103 Broad St, Boston, MA	617-426-3565
Kinum, Drew/Glen Avenue, Scotia, NY	518-382-7566
Kirkman, Tom/18 Annetta Ave, Northport, NY	516-261-1559
Kittle, James Kent/49 Brinckerhoff Ln, New Canann, CT	203-966-2442
Klapatch, David/350 Silas Deane Hwy, Wethersfield, CT	203-563-3834
Kligman, Fred/4733 Elm St, Bethesda, MD	301-652-6333
Klinefelter, Eric/10963 Hickory Ridge Rd, Columbia, MD	301-964-0273
Knapp, Stephen/74 Commodore Rd, Worcester, MA	617-757-2507
Kobrin, Harold/PO Box 115, Newton, MA	617-332-8152
Korona, Joseph/178 Superior Ave, Pittsburgh, PA	412-761-4349
Kovner, Mark/14 Cindy Lane, Highland Mills, NY	914-928-6543
Krist, Bob/228 Overlook Ave, Leonia, NJ	201-585-9464
Krubner, Ralph/4 Juniper Court, Jackson, NJ	201-364-3640
Kruper, Alexander Jr/70 Jackson Dr Box 152, Cranford, NJ	201-276-1510
Kugielsky, Joseph/Little Brook Ln, Newtown, CT	203-426-7123

L

L M Associates/20 Arlington, Newton, MA	617-232-0254
Labranche, Rick/3 Crestview Rd, Terryville, CT	203-589-7543
LaBua, Frank/37 N Mountain Ave, Montclair, NJ	201-783-6318
Labuzetta, Steve/180 St Paul St, Rochester, NY	716-546-6825
Lacko, Steve/902 Main St, Belmont, NJ	201-280-1199
LaCourciere, Mario/1 Rue Hamel, Quebec G1R 4J6, QU	418-694-1744
Lamar Photographics/PO Box 470, Framingham, MA	617-881-2512
Lampel, Pat/901 Bonifant Rd, Silver Spring, MD	301-256-6800
Landsman, Gary D/12115 Parklawn Dr, Rockville, MD	301-468-2588
Landwehrle, Don/9 Hother Ln, Bayshore, NY	516-665-8221
LANE, WHITNEY/109 SOMERSTOWN RD, OSSINING, NY (P 83)	**914-762-5335**
Lanman, Jonathan/41 Bristol St, Boston, MA	617-574-9420
Lapides, Susan Jane/451 Huron Ave, Cambridge, MA	617-864-7793
LaRiche, Michael/30 S Bank St, Philadelphia, PA	215-922-0447
Latham, Sid/3635 Johnson Ave, Riverdale, NY	212-543-0335
Laurino, Don Studio/220 Ferris Ave, White Plains, NY	914-693-1199
Lautman, Robert C/4906 41 St NW, Washington, DC	202-966-2800
Lavine, David S/4016 The Alameda, Baltimore, MD	301-467-0523
Lawfer, Larry/107 South St, Boston, MA	617-451-0628
Lawrence, Stephanie/2422 Chetwood Circle, Timonium, MD	301-252-3704
Leach, Peter/118 S Seventh St, Philadelphia, PA	215-574-0230
Leaman, Chris/105 Plant Ave, Wayne, PA	215-647-8455
LeBlond, Jerry/7 Court Sq, Rutland, VT	802-422-3115
Lee, Carol/214 Beacon St, Boston, MA	617-523-5930
Lee, Raymond/PO Box 9743, Baltimore, MD	301-323-5764
Leeming Studios Inc/222 Richmond St, Providence, RI	401-421-1916
Lefcourt, Victoria/3207 Coquelin Terr, Chevy Chase, MD	301-652-1658
Lehman, Amy/115 Old Short Hills Rd, W Orange, NJ	201-376-8734
Leney, Julia/PO Box 434, Wayland, MA	617-358-7229
Lent, Max/24 Wellington Ave, Rochester, NY	716-328-5126
Lent, Michael/PO Box 825, Hoboken, NJ	201-798-4866
Leomporra, Greg/2607 Barton Dr, Cinnaminson, NJ	609-829-3159
LEONARD, BARNEY/518 PUTNAM RD, MERION, PA (P 122,123)	**215-664-2525**
Levart, Herb/566 Secor Rd, Hartsdale, NY	914-946-2060
Leveille, David/27-31 St Bridget's Dr, Rochester, NY	716-423-9474
Levin, Aaron M/3000 Chestnut Ave #102, Baltimore, MD	301-467-8646
Lewitt, Peter/39 Billings Park, Newton, MA	617-244-6552
Ley, Russell/103 Ardale St, Boston, MA	617-325-2500

Photographers

Continued

Please send us your additions and updates.

Lidington, John/2 "C" St, Hull, MA	617-246-0300
Lieberman, Fred/2426 Linden Ln, Silver Spring, MD	301-565-0644
Lightstruck Studio/519 W Pratt St #105, Baltimore, MD	301-727-2220
Lilley, Weaver/125 S 18th St, Philadelphia, PA	215-567-2881
Lillibridge, David/Rt 4 Box 1172, Burlington, CT	203-673-9786
Linck, Tony/2100 Linwood Ave, Fort Lee, NJ	201-944-5454
Lincon, James/30 St John Pl, Westport, CT	203-226-3724
Lineham, Clark/74 Mt Pleasant Ave, Gloucester, MA	617-281-3903
Littlehales, Breton/9520 Seminole St, Silver Spring, MD	202-737-6222
Littlewood, John/PO Box 141, Woodville, MA	617-435-4262
Lockwood, Lee/27 Howland Rd, West Newton, MA	617-965-6343
Loescher, Mark/29 Webb Rd, Westport, CT	203-227-5855
Lokmer, John/PO Box 2782, Pittsburgh, PA	412-765-3565
Long Shots/4421 East West Hwy, Bethesda, MD	301-654-0279
Longley, Steven/2224 North Charles St, Baltimore, MD	301-467-4185
Lowe, T J II/1420 E Front St, Plainfield, NJ	201-769-8485
Lukowicz, Jerome/122 Arch St, Philadelphia, PA	215-922-7122
Lunan, David/535 Albany St, Boston, MA	617-542-7875
M Machalaba, Robert/4 Brentwood Dr, Livingston, NJ	201-992-4674
MacKay, Kenneth/127 Hillary Lane, Penfield, NY	716-385-1116
MacKenzie, Maxwell/2641 Garfield St NW, Washington, DC	202-232-6686
MacLeod, Richard/551 Boylston St, Boston, MA	617-267-6364
Maggio, Chris/180 St Paul St, Rochester, NY	716-454-3929
Maggio, Donald/Brook Hill Ln #5E, Rochester, NY	716-381-8053
Maglott, Larry/249 A St, Boston, MA	617-482-9347
Magnet, Jeff/628B 1620 Worchester Rd, Framingham, MA	617-547-8226
Magno, Thomas/19 Peters St, Cambridge, MA	617-492-5197
Makris, Dave/10 Newbold Dr, Hyde Park, NY	914-229-5012
MALITSKY, ED/337 SUMMER ST, BOSTON, MA (P 124)	**617-451-0655**
Malka, Daniel/1030 St Alexandre #203, Montreal H2Z 1P3, QU	514-397-9704
Maltz, Alan/182 Beach #136, Belle Harbour, NY	718-318-0110
Malyszko, Michael/90 South St, Boston, MA	617-426-9111
Mandelkorn, Richard/309 Waltham St, W Newton, MA	617-332-3246
Manheim, Michael Philip/PO Box 35, Marblehead, MA	617-631-3560
Mann, Richard J/PO Box 2712, Dix Hills, NY	516-266-3658
Marchese, Frank/56 Arbor St, Hartford, CT	203-232-4417
Marcus, Joan/2311 Calvert St NW, Washington, DC	202-332-2828
Mares, Manuel/185 Chestnut Hill Ave, Brighton, MA	617-782-4208
Margolis, David/682 Howard Ave, New Haven, CT	203-777-7288
Margolis, Paul/77 S Broadway, Nyack, NY	914-358-6749
Marinelli, Jack/673 Willow St, Waterbury, CT	203-756-3273
Marinelli, Mary Leigh/48 Essex St, Salem, MA	617-745-7035
Mark Color Studios/7106 Ridge Rd, Baltimore, MD	301-687-1222
Markel, Brad/639 'E' St NE, Washington, DC	703-920-2791
Marshall, John/344 Boylston St, Boston, MA	617-536-2988
Martin Paul Ltd/247 Newbury St, Boston, MA	617-536-1644
Martin, Bruce/266-A Pearl St, Cambridge, MA	617-492-8009
Martin, Jeff/6 Industrial Way W, Eatontown, NJ	201-389-0888
Martin, Marilyn/130 Appleton St #2l, Boston, MA	617-262-5507
Massar, Ivan/296 Bedford St, Concord, MA	617-369-4090
Mastalia, Francesco/2 Midland Ave, Hawthorne, NJ	212-772-8449
Matt, Philip/PO Box 10406, Rochester, NY	716-461-5977
Mattei, George Photography/179 Main St, Hackensack, NJ	201-342-0740
Mauss, Peter/222 Valley Pl, Mamaroneck, NY	914-698-4060
Mavodones, Bill/46 Waltham St #105, Boston, MA	617-423-7382
Mayernik, George/41 Wolfpit Ave #2N, Norwalk, CT	203-846-1406
Mazzone, James/1201 82nd St, N Bergen, NJ	201-861-8992
McCarron, Marc/1018 E Willow Grove Ave, Philadelphia, PA	215-836-1135
McConnell, Jack/182 Broad St, Old Wethersfield, CT	203-563-6154
McConnell, Russ/8 Adler Dr, E Syracuse, NY	315-433-1005
McCormick & Nelson, Inc/34 Piave St, Stamford, CT	203-348-5062
McCoy, Dan/Main St, Housatonic, MA	413-274-6211
McDermott, Brian/14 Sherwood Ave, Ossining, NY	914-941-6012
McDonald, Kevin R/319 Newtown Turnpike, Redding, CT	203-938-9276
McDonough Studio/3224 Kennedy Blvd, Jersey City, NJ	201-420-1056
McGrail, John/6576 Senator Ln, Bensalem, PA	215-750-6070
McKean, Thomas R/742 Cherry Circle, Wynnewood, PA	215-642-1412
McLaren, Lynn/42 W Cedar, Boston, MA	617-227-7448
McLean, Alex/65 E India Row #10D, Boston, MA	617-523-6446
McMullin, Forest/183 St Paul St, Rochester, NY	716-262-3944

McNeill, Brian/840 W Main St, Lansdale, PA	215-368-3326
McQueen, Ann/791 Tremont St #401, Boston, MA	617-267-6258
McWilliams, Jack/15 Progress Ave, Chelmsford, MA	617-256-9615
Meacham, Joseph/229 Brown St, Philadelphia, PA	215-925-8122
Mecca, Jack/1508 72nd St, North Bergen, NJ	201-869-7956
Mednick, Seymour/316 S Camac, Philadelphia, PA	215-735-6100
Medvec, Emily/151 Kentucky Ave SE, Washington, DC	202-546-1220
Meech, Christopher/20 Forest St, Stamford, CT	203-348-1158
Meek, Richard/8 Skyline Dr, Huntington, NY	516-271-0072
Mehne, Ralph/1501 Rose Terrace, Union, NJ	201-686-0668
Meiller, Henry Studios/1026 Wood St, Philadelphia, PA	215-922-1525
Melino, Gary/235 Simmonsville Ave, Johnston, RI	401-781-6320
Mellor, D W/1020 Mt Pleasant Rd, Bryn Mawr, PA	215-527-9040
Melton, Janice Munnings/692 Walkhill St, Boston, MA	617-298-1443
Mendelsohn, David/Sky Farm Rd, Northwood, NH	603-942-7622
MERCER, RALPH/239 'A' ST, BOSTON, MA (P 125)	**617-482-2942**
Merchant, Martin/22 Barker Ave, White Plains, NY	914-997-2200
Merz, Laurence/215 Georgetown Rd, Weston, CT	203-222-1936
Michael's/481 Central Ave, Cedarhurst, NY	516-374-3456
Michael, Shawn/240 Prospect Ave, Hackensack, NJ	201-487-2865
Millard, Howard/220 Sixth Ave, Pelham, NY	914-738-3689
Miller, Bruce Photography/9 Tall Oaks Dr, East Brunswick, NJ	201-257-0211
Miller, Don/60 Sindle Ave, Little Falls, NJ	201-785-9090
Miller, Gary/PO Box 136, Bedford Hills, NY	914-666-4174
Miller, J T/12 Forest Edge Dr, Titusville, NJ	609-737-3116
Miller, Melabee/29 Beechwood Pl, Hillside, NJ	201-527-9121
Miller, Roger/1411 Hollins St Union Sq, Baltimore, MD	301-566-1222
Millman, Lester Jay/23 Court St #23, White Plains, NY	914-946-2093
Mincey, Dale/113 Brunswick St, Jersey City, NJ	201-420-9387
Mindell, Doug/811 Boylston St, Boston, MA	617-262-3968
Mink, Mike/180 St Paul St 5th Fl, Rochester, NY	716-325-4865
Miraglia, Elizabeth/29 Drummer Ln, W Redding, CT	203-938-2261
Mirando, Gary/27 Cleveland St, Valhalla, NY	914-997-6588
Mitchell, Mike/930 'F' St #800, Washington, DC	202-347-3223
Moerder, Dan/2115 Wallace St, Philadelphia, PA	215-978-7414
Mogerley, Jean/1262 Pines Lake Dr W, Wayne, NJ	201-839-2355
Molinaro, Neil R/15 Walnut Ave, Clark, NJ	201-396-8980
Monroe, Robert/Kennel Rd, Cuddebackville, NY	914-754-8329
Mopsik, Eugene/419 S Perth St, Philadelphia, PA	215-922-3489
Moran, Richard/201 S Main St, Wilkes-Barre, PA	717-826-6184
Morgan, Bruce/55 S Grand Ave, Baldwin, NY	516-546-3554
Morley, Bob/129 South St, Boston, MA	617-482-7279
Morrow, Christopher W/163 Pleasant St, Arlington, MA	617-648-6770
Morse, Timothy/1133 Curve St, Carlisle, MA	617-369-8036
MOZO PHOTO DESIGN/282 SHELTON RD (RT 110), MONROE, CT (P 127)	**203-261-7400**
Mullen, Stephen/825 N 2nd St, Philadelphia, PA	215-574-9770
Mulligan, Bob/109 Broad St, Boston, MA	617-542-7308
Mulligan, Joseph/239 Chestnut St, Philadelphia, PA	215-592-1359
Munster, Joseph/Old Rt 28, Phoenicia, NY	914-688-5347
Murray, Ric/150 Chestnut St, Providence, RI	401-751-8806
Musto, Tom/225 S Main St, Wilkes-Barre, PA	717-822-5798
Mydans, Carl/212 Hommocks Rd, Larchmont, NY	212-841-2345
Myers Studios Inc/21 Princeton Place, Orchard Park, NY	716-662-6002
Myers, Steve/Drawer 2, Almond, NY	607-276-6400
Myron/127 Dorrance St, Providence, RI	401-421-1946
N Nadel, Lee/443 Albany St, Boston, MA	617-451-6646
Nagler, Lanny/56 Arbor St, Hartford, CT	203-233-4040
Nelder, Oscar/Box 661 Main St, Presque Isle, ME	207-769-5911
Nelson, Janet/Finney Farm, Croton-On-Hudson, NY	914-271-5453
Nerney, Dan/137 Rowayton Ave, Rowayton, CT	203-853-2782
Nettis, Joseph/1717 Walnut St, Philadelphia, PA	215-563-5444
Neudorfer, Brien/46 Waltham St, Boston, MA	617-451-9211
Neumann, William/96 Carmita Ave, Rutherford, NJ	201-939-0370
Neumayer, Joseph/Chateau Rive #102, Peekskill, NY	914-739-3005
Nible, R C/408 Vine St 4th Fl, Philadelphia, PA	215-625-0638
Nichols, Don/1241 University Ave, Rochester, NY	716-461-9666
Nighswander, Tim/315 Peck St, New Haven, CT	203-789-8529
Noble Inc/611 Cathedral St, Baltimore, MD	301-244-0292
Nochton, Jack/1238 W Broad St, Bethlehem, PA	215-691-2223
Noel, Peter/18 Bartlett St, Malden, MA	617-321-1264

Photographers
Continued

Please send us your additions and updates.

Norris, Robert/RFD 1 Box 4480, Pittsfield, ME	207-487-5981
Northlight Visual Comm Group Inc/21-23 Quine St, Cranford, NJ	201-272-1155
Nurnberg, Paul/193 Florence St #3R, Roslindale, MA	617-327-3920

O
O'Connell, Bill/791 Tremont St, Boston, MA	617-437-7556
O'Donnell, John/179 Westmoreland St, White Plains, NY	914-948-1786
O'Donoghue, Ken/8 Union Park St, Boston, MA	617-542-4898
O'Neill, James/1543 Kater St, Philadelphia, PA	215-545-3223
O'Neill, Martin/1914 Mt Royal Terr 1st Fl, Baltimore, MD	301-225-0522
O'Neill, Michael Photo/162 Lakefield Rd, E Northport, NY	516-754-0459
O'Shaughnessy, Bob/50 Melcher, Boston, MA	617-542-7122
Obermeyer, Eva/PO Box 1722, Union, NJ	201-375-3322
Ogiba, Joseph/PO Box M, Somerville, NJ	201-725-4595
Olbrys, Anthony/41 Pepper Ridge Rd, Stamford, CT	203-322-9422
Oliver, Lou/8 Adler Dr, E Syracuse, NY	315-433-1005
Olivera, Bob/42 Weybossett St, Providence, RI	401-272-1170
Olmstead Studio/118 South St, Boston, MA	617-542-2024
Opfer, Robert M/20-35 Richmond St, Philadelphia, PA	215-563-0888
Orel, Mano/PO Box E, Dove Court, Croton-On-Hudson, NY	914-271-5542
Orkin, Pete/80 Washington St, S Norwalk, CT	203-866-9978
Orlando, Fran/329 Spruce St, Philadelphia, PA	215-629-9968
Orling, Alan S/Hawley Rd, North Salem, NY	914-669-5405
Orrico, Charles/72 Barry Ln, Syosset, NY	516-364-2257
Ouzer, Louis/120 East Ave, Rochester, NY	716-454-7582
Owens, John/93 Massachusetts Ave, Boston, MA	617-423-2452

PQ
Painter, Joseph/205 Fairmont Ave, Philadelphia, PA	215-592-1612
PALMER, GABE/FIRE HILL FARM, WEST REDDING, CT (P 95)	**203-938-2514**
Panioto, Mark/95 Mohawk Ln, Weathersfield, CT	203-241-3202
Pantages, Tom/7 Linden Ave, Gloucester, MA	617-525-3678
Paradigm Productions/6437 Ridge Ave, Philadelphia, PA	215-482-8404
Paredes, Cesar/322 Clarksville Rd, Princeton Junction, NJ	609-799-4097
Parker, Bruce/Box 341 Eastwood Sta, Syracuse, NY	315-487-2828
Paskevich, John/1500 Locust St #3017, Philadelphia, PA	215-735-9868
Patrey, Dan/3 Cornell Pl, Great Neck, NY	516-466-4396
Patten, Michael/24-D Bartle Ct, Highland Park, NJ	201-846-8662
Paxenos, Dennis F/2125 Maryland Ave #103, Baltimore, MD	301-837-1029
PEASE, GREG/23 E 22ND ST, BALTIMORE, MD (P 144,145)	**301-332-0583**
Peckham, Lynda/65 S Broadway, Tarrytown, NY	914-631-5050
Pehlman, Barry/806 King Rd, Malvern, PA	215-296-7966
Pellegrini, Lee/381 Newtonville Ave, Newtonville, MA	617-964-7925
Pelletier, Herve/329 A Street, Boston, MA	617-423-6724
Peluso, Frank/2 Columbine Rd, Whitehouse Station, NJ	201-534-9637
Penneys, Robert/147 N 12th St, Philadelphia, PA	215-925-6699
The Peregrine Group/375 Sylvan Ave, Englewood Cliffs, NJ	201-567-8585
Perez, Paul R/143 W Hoffman Ave, Lindenhurst, NY	516-226-0846
Perlmutter, Steven/246 Nicoll St, New Haven, CT	203-789-8493
Peterson, Brent/15 Davenport Ave #2G, New Rochelle, NY	212-573-7195
Petronio, Frank/74 Westchester Ave, Rochester, NY	716-288-4642
Pevarnik, Gervose/180 St Paul St, Rochester, NY	716-262-3579
Philiba, Allan A/3408 Bertha Dr, Baldwin, NY	516-623-7841
Photo Synthesis/524 Parkway View Dr, Pittsburgh, PA	412-787-7287
Photo-Coloitura/PO Box 1749, Boston, MA	617-522-5132
Photographic Illustration Ltd/7th & Ranstead, Philadelphia, PA	215-925-7073
Photown Studio/190 Vandervoort St, North Tonawanda, NY	716-693-2912
Pickerell, Jim H/110-E Frederick Ave, Rockville, MD	301-251-0720
Picture That Inc/880 Briarwood, Newtown Square, PA	215-353-8833
Picturehouse Assoc Inc/22 Elizabeth St, Norwalk, CT	203-852-1776
PIETERSEN, ALEX/29 RAYNOR RD, MORRISTOWN, NJ (P 96)	**201-267-7003**
Piperno, Lauren/215 E Dean St, Freeport, NY	718-935-1550
Plank, David/981 River Rd, Reading, PA	215-376-3461
Platteter, George/82 Colonnade Dr, Rochester, NY	716-334-4488
Poggenpohl, Eric/1816 S Street NW, Washington, DC	202-387-0826
Pohuski, Michael/36 S Paca St #215, Baltimore, MD	301-962-5404
Polansky, Allen/1431 Park Ave, Baltimore, MD	301-383-9021
Polumbaum, Ted/326 Harvard St, Cambridge, MA	617-491-4947
Pope-Lance, Elton/125 Stockfarm Rd, Sudbury, MD	609-695-1040
Porcella, Phil/109 Broad St, Boston, MA	617-426-3222

Portsmouth Photography/259 Miller Ave, Portsmouth, NH	603-431-3351
Potter, Anthony/509 W Fayette St, Syracuse, NY	315-428-8900
Powell, Bolling/1 Worcester Sq, Boston, MA	617-536-1199
Pownall, Ron/7 Ellsworth Ave, Cambridge, MA	617-354-0846
Praus, Edgar G/176 Anderson Ave, Rochester, NY	716-442-4820
Profit, Everett R/533 Massachusetts Ave, Boston, MA	617-267-5840
Prue, Sara/, Washington, DC	202-232-2330
Quin, Clark/241 A Street, Boston, MA	617-451-2686
Quindry, Richard/200 Loney St, Philadelphia, PA	215-742-6300

R
Raab, Timothy/163 Delaware Ave, Delmar, NY	518-439-2298
Ranck, Rosemary/323 W Mermaid Ln, Philadelphia, PA	215-242-3718
Rapp, Frank/327 A St, Boston, MA	617-542-4462
Rauch, Bonnie/Crane Rd, Somers, NY	914-277-3986
Rawle, Johnathan/7 Railroad Ave, Bedford, MA	617-275-3030
Ray, Dean/13 W 25th St, Baltimore, MD	301-243-3441
Raycroft/McCormick/326 A Street #C, Boston, MA	617-542-7229
Redding, Jim/105 Beach St, Boston, MA	617-482-2833
Reis, Jon Photography/141 The Commons, Ithaca, NY	607-272-1966
Renard, Jean/142 Berkeley St, Boston, MA	617-266-8673
Renckly, Joe/1200 Linden Pl, Pittsburgh, PA	412-323-2122
RESNICK, SETH/15 SLEEPER ST #507, BOSTON, MA (P 128,129)	**617-423-7475**
Retallack, John/207 Erie Station Rd, West Henrietta, NY	716-334-1530
Richard, George/PO Box 392, Walker Valley, NY	914-733-4300
Richards, Toby/244 Alexander St, Princeton, NJ	609-921-6830
Richmond, Jack/12 Farnsworth St, Boston, MA	617-482-7158
Riemer, Ken/183 St Paul St, Rochester, NY	716-232-5450
Riley, George/Sisquisic Trail PO Box 840, Yarmouth, ME	207-846-5787
Riley, Laura/Hidden Spng Fm PO Box 186, Pittstown, NJ	201-735-7707
Rimi, Jim/PO Box 2134, West New York, NJ	201-866-7463
Ritter, Frank/2414 Evergreen St, Yorktown Hts, NY	914-962-5385
Rizzi, Leonard F/5161 River Rd Bldg 2B, Bethesda, MD	301-652-1303
Rizzo, John/36 St Paul St, Rochester, NY	716-232-5140
Robb, Steve/535 Albany St, Boston, MA	617-542-6565
Roberts, Mathieu/200 Henry St, Stamford, CT	203-324-3582
Robins, Susan/124 N Third St, Philadelphia, PA	215-238-9988
Robinson, George A/4-A Stonehedge Dr, S Burlington, VT	802-862-6902
Robinson, Mike/2413 Sarah St, Pittsburgh, PA	412-431-4102
Rocheleau, Paul/Canaan Rd, Richmond, MA	413-698-2676
Rockhill, Morgan/204 Westminster Mall, Providence, RI	401-274-3472
Rode, Robert/2670 Arleigh Rd, East Meadow, NY	516-485-6687
Roseman, Shelly/1238 Callowhill St, Philadelphia, PA	215-922-1430
Rosier, Gerald/PO Box 470, Framingham, MA	617-881-2512
Rosner, Eric/1133 Arch St 9th Fl, Philadelphia, PA	215-629-1240
Rosner, Stu/One Thompson Sq, Charlestown, MA	617-242-2112
Ross, Alex F/1622 Chestnut St, Philadelphia, PA	215-843-1274
Rossow, Lee/641 Van Doren Ct, Valley Cottage, NY	914-358-6931
Roth, Eric/337 Summer St, Boston, MA	617-338-5358
Roth, Seth/264 9th St, Jersey City, NJ	201-792-9234
Rothstein, Jennifer/192-C Columbus Dr #1, Jersey City, NJ	201-435-5701
ROTMAN, JEFFREY L/14 COTTAGE AVE, SOMERVILLE, MA (P 130)	**617-666-0874**
Rowan, Norm R/106 E 6th St, Clifton, NJ	201-772-5126
Roytos, Richard/PO Box 4000, Princeton, NJ	609-921-4983
Ruggeri, Lawrence/10 Old Post Office Rd, Silver Spring, MD	301-588-3131
Ruggieri, Ignazio/49 Prospect St, Little Falls, NJ	201-890-0660
Rummel, Hal/36 S Paca St #515, Baltimore, MD	301-244-8517
Runyon, Paul/113 Arch St, Philadelphia, PA	215-238-0655
Russ, Clive/82 Barlett St, Charlestown, MA	617-242-5234
Russel, Rae/75 Byram Lake Rd, Mount Kisco, NY	914-241-0057
Russell Studios/14 Hawk St, Scotia, NY	518-370-3600
Russo, Rich/11 Clinton St, Morristown, NJ	201-538-6954
Ryder Photo/141 First St, Liverpool, NY	315-622-3499

S
Sa'Adah, Jonathan/PO Box 247, Hartford, VT	802-295-5327
Sagala, Steve/53-A Parsippany Rd, Whippany, NJ	201-377-1418
Sakmanoff, George/179 Massachusetts Ave, Boston, MA	617-262-7227
Salamone, Anthony/1277 Commonwealth Ave, Boston, MA	617-254-5427
Salant, Robin/216 Wadsworth Ave, South Plainfield, NJ	201-272-7195
Salomone, Frank/296 Brick Blvd, Bricktown, NJ	201-920-1525
Salsbery, Lee/14 Seventh St NE, Washington, DC	202-543-1222

Photographers

Continued

Please send us your additions and updates.

Salstrand, Duane/503 Boylston #4, Brookline, MA	617-232-1795
Samara, Thomas/713 Erie Blvd West, Syracuse, NY	315-476-4984
Samuels Studio/8 Waltham St, PO Box 201, Maynard, MA	617-897-7901
Sanford, Eric/219 Turnpike Rd, Manchester, NH	603-624-0122
Sansone, Nadine/7 River St, Milford, CT	203-878-5090
Sapienza, Louis A/96 West St, Colonia, NJ	201-382-5933
Saraceno, Paul/46 Waltham St, Boston, MA	617-542-2779
Sasso, Ken/116 Mattabaffa, Meriden, CT	203-235-1421
Sauter, Ron Photo/183 St Paul St, Rochester, NY	716-232-1361
Savage, Sally/99 Orchard Terrace, Piermont, NY	914-359-5735
Saydah, Gerard/, , NJ	201-768-2582
Sayers, Jim/325 Valley Rd, West Orange, NJ	201-325-7826
Schadt, Bob/23 Ransom Rd, Brighton, MA	617-782-3734
Schaefer, Dave/48 Grove St, Belmont, MA	617-371-2850
SCHAEFFER, BRUCE/631 N POTTSTOWN PIKE, EXTON, PA	
(P 131)	**215-363-5230**
Schembri, Joseph/PO Box 4393, Metuchen, NJ	201-287-8561
Schenk, Andy/28 Mulberry Ln, Colts Neck, NJ	201-946-9459
Scherer, James/35 Kingston St, Boston, MA	617-338-5678
Scherzi, James/116 Town Line Rd, Syracuse, NY	315-455-7961
Schlanger, Irv/946 Cherokee Rd, Huntington Valley, PA	215-663-0663
Schlegel, Robert/2 Division St #10-11, Somerville, NJ	201-231-1212
SCHLEIPMAN, RUSS/298-A COLUMBUS AVE, BOSTON, MA	
(P 132)	**617-267-1677**
Schlowsky Studios/145 South St, Boston, MA	617-338-4664
Schmitt, Steve/337 Summer St, Boston, MA	617-482-5482
Schoen, Robert/241 Crescent St, Waltham, MA	617-647-5546
Schoon, Tim/PO Box 7446, Lancaster, PA	717-291-9483
Schroeder, H Robert/PO Box 7361, W Trenton, NJ	609-883-8643
Schulmeyer, LT/2124 Maryland Ave, Baltimore, MD	301-332-0767
Schultz, Jurgen/Rt 100 N/Box 19, Londonderry, VT	802-824-3475
Schweikardt, Eric/PO Box 56, Southport, CT	203-375-8181
Sculnick, Herb/7 2nd St, Athens, NY	518-945-1598
Sedik, Joe/342 Perkiomen Ave, Lansdale, PA	215-368-6832
Segal Panorama Photo/, , IL	815-256-2240
Seng, Walt/810 Penn Ave #400, Pittsburgh, PA	412-391-6780
Serbin, Vincent/304 Church Rd, Bricktown, NJ	201-477-5620
Serio, Steve/535 Albany St, Boston, MA	617-542-2644
Severi, Robert/813 Richmond Ave, Silver Spring, MD	301-585-1010
Shafer, Bob/3554 Quebec St N W, Washington, DC	202-362-0630
Sharp, Steve/153 N 3rd St, Philadelphia, PA	215-925-2890
Shelton, Sybil/416 Valley View Rd, Englewood, NJ	201-568-8684
Shepherd, Francis/PO Box 204, Chadds Ford, PA	215-347-6799
Sherer, Larry/5233 Eliots Oak Rd, Columbia, MD	301-730-3178
Sherman, Steve/49 Melcher St, Boston, MA	617-542-1496
Sherriff, Bob/963 Humphrey St, Swampscott, MA	617-599-6955
Shotwell, John/17 Stillings St, Boston, MA	617-357-7456
Shoucais, Bill/460 Harrison Ave 3rd Fl, Boston, MA	617-423-1774
Siciliano, Richard/707 Union St, Schenectady, NY	518-370-0312
Sickles Photo Reporting/PO Box 98, Maplewood, NJ	201-763-6355
Siegel, Hyam Photography/PO Box 356, Brattleboro, VT	802-257-0691
Siegler, William A/38 Orange Ave, Walden, NY	914-778-7300
Silk, Georgiana B/190 Godfrey Rd E, Weston, CT	203-226-0408
Silver, David/35 N Third St, Philadelphia, PA	215-925-7277
Silverman, Paul/49 Ronald Dr, Clifton, NJ	201-472-4339
Silverstein, Abby/3315 Woodvalley Dr, Baltimore, MD	301-486-5211
Simian, George/9 Hawthorne Pl, Boston, MA	617-267-3558
Simmons, Erik Leigh/241 A St, Boston, MA	617-482-5325
Simon, David/263 110th St, Jersey City, NJ	201-795-9326
Simpson/Flint/2133 Maryland Ave, Baltimore, MD	301-837-9923
Singer, Arthur/Sedgewood RD 12, Carmel, NY	914-225-6801
Singer, Jay/20 Russell Park Rd, Syosset, NY	516-935-8991
Sint, Steven/6 Second Rd, Great Neck, NY	516-487-4918
SITEMAN, FRANK/136 POND ST, WINCHESTER, MA (P 133)	**617-729-3747**
Sitkin, Marc B/23 Lincoln St, Hartford, CT	203-727-0605
Siuccoli, Stephen/152-A Prospect Ave, Shelton, CT	203-736-6100
Skalkowski, Bob/310 Eighth St, New Cumberland, PA	717-774-0652
Sklute, Kenneth/210 E Nassau St, Islip Terrace, NY	516-581-7276
Skoogford, Leif/415 Church Rd #B2, Elkins Park, PA	215-635-5186
Slide Graphics/262 Summer St, Boston, MA	617-542-0700
Sloan Photo/443 Albany St, Boston, MA	617-542-3215
Smith & Warren Photography/PO Box 205, Pittsburgh, PA	412-687-7500
Smith, Chris/19 E 22nd St, Baltimore, MD	301-659-0986
Smith, Gary & Russell/65 Washington St, S Norwalk, CT	203-866-8871
Smith, Gordon E/65 Washington St, S Norwalk, CT	203-866-8871
Smith, Hugh R/2515 Burr St, Fairfield, CT	203-255-1942
Smith, Philip W/1589 Reed Rd #2A, W Trenton, NJ	609-737-3370
Smith, Stuart/68 Raymond Lane, Wilton, CT	203-762-3158
Snyder, Clarence/717 Porter St, Easton, PA	215-252-2109
Solomon Assoc/PO Box 237, Glyndon, MD	301-833-5678
Soorenko, Barry/5161 River Rd Bldg 2B, Bethesda, MD	301-652-1303
Speedy, Richard/244 Alexander St, Princeton, NJ	609-921-6830
Spelman, Steve/15 A St Mary's Ct, Brookline, MA	617-566-6578
Spencer, Michael/735 Mt Hope Ave, Rochester, NY	716-475-6817
Sperduto, Stephen/18 Willett Ave, Port Chester, NY	914-939-0296
Spiegel, Ted/RD 2 Box 353 A, South Salem, NY	914-763-3668
Spiro, Don/137 Summit Rd, Sparta, NJ	212-484-9753
St Niell Studio/209 Parker Ave, Clifton, NJ	201-340-1212
Staccioli, Marc/1480 Rt 46 #321B, Parsippany, NJ	201-334-7620
Stafford, Rick/26 Wadsworth, Allston, MA	617-495-2389
Stapleton, John/6854 Radbourne Rd, Upper Darby, PA	215-626-0920
Stearns, Stan/1814 Glade Ct, Annapolis, MD	301-268-5777
Stein, Geoffrey R/348 Newbury St, Boston, MA	617-536-8227
Stein, Howard/18 Willett Ave, Port Chester, NY	914-939-0242
Steiner, Chuck/111 Newark Ave, Union Beach, NJ	201-739-0629
Steiner, Lisl/'El Retscho' Trinity Pass, Pound Ridge, NY	914-764-5538
Steiner, Peter/183 St Paul St 3rd Fl, Rochester, NY	716-454-1012
Stevens, Lee/2 Phillips Dr, Newburyport, MA	617-462-9385
Stier, Kurt/93 Massachusetts Ave #402, Boston, MA	617-247-3822
Stierer, Dennis/34 Plympton St, Boston, MA	617-357-9488
Still, John/17 Edinboro St, Boston, MA	617-451-8178
STILLINGS, JAMEY/87 N CLINTON AVE 5TH FL,	
ROCHESTER, NY (P 134,135)	**716-232-5296**
Stills/1 Winthrop Sq, Boston, MA	617-482-0660
Stock, Jack/Newberg, Art/155 Myrtle St, Shelton, CT	203-735-3388
Stoller, Bob/30 Old Mill Rd, Great Neck, NY	516-829-8906
Storch, Otto/Box 712, 22 Pondview Ln, East Hampton, NY	516-324-5031
Stromberg, Bruce/PO Box 2052, Philadelphia, PA	215-735-3520
Stuart, Stephen Photography/10 Midland Ave, Port Chester,	
NY	914-939-0302
Studio 185/185 Forest St, S Hamilton, MA	617-468-2892
Studio Assoc/30-6 Plymouth St, Fairfield, NJ	201-575-2640
The Studio Inc/818 Liberty Ave, Pittsburgh, PA	412-261-2022
Studio Tech/25 Congress St, Salem, MA	617-745-5070
Sullivan, Sharon/325 1/2 4th St, Jersey City, NJ	201-795-1930
Sunshine Photography/192 Newtown Rd, Plainview, NY	516-293-3376
Susoeff, Bill/3025 Wahangton Rd, McMurray, PA	412-941-8606
Sutphen, Chazz/22 Crescent Beach Dr, Burlington, VT	802-862-5912
Swann/ Niemann/1258 Wisconsin Ave NW 4th Fl, Washington,	
DC	201-342-6300
Sweeney, Dan/337 Summer St, Boston, MA	617-482-5482
Sweet, Ozzie/Mill Village Hill, Francestown, NH	603-547-6611
Swertfager, Amy/343 Manville Rd, Pleasantville, NY	914-747-1900
Swift, Dick/31 Harrison Ave, New Canaan, CT	203-966-8190
Swisher, Mark/5107 Herring Run Dr, Baltimore, MD	301-426-6665
Swoger, Arthur/18 Medway St #3, Providence, RI	401-331-0440
Szabo, Art/156-A Depot Rd, Huntington, NY	516-549-1699

T Tadder, Morton/1010 Morton St, Baltimore, MD — 301-837-7427

Tango, Rick/11 Pocconock Terrace, Ridgefield, CT	203-431-0514
Tardi, Joseph/125 Wolf Rd #108, Albany, NY	518-438-1211
Taylor, Alan/RD 1 Box 649, Saratoga Springs, NY	518-584-7937
Tchakirides, Bill/ Photography Assoc/140-50 Huyshope Ave,	
Hartford, CT	203-525-5117
TECH PHOTO/37 HUYLER CT, SETAUKET, NY (P 84-87)	**516-751-5193**
Tenin, Barry/PO Box 2660 Saugatuck Sta, Westport, CT	203-226-9396
Tepper, Peter/195 Tunxis Hill Rd, Fairfield, CT	203-367-6172
Tesa, Rudi/194 Knickerbocker Rd, Demarest, NJ	201-767-4012
Tesi, Mike/12 Kulick Rd, Fairfield, NJ	201-575-7780
Thauer, Bill/542 Higgens Crowell Rd, W Yarmouth, MA	617-362-8222
Thayer, Mark/25 Dry Dock, Boston, MA	617-542-9532
Thellmann, Mark D/19 W Park Ave, Merchantville, NJ	609-488-9093
Thomas, Edward/140-50 Huyshope Ave, Hartford, CT	203-246-3293
Tkatch, James/2307 18th St NW, Washington, DC	202-462-2211

Photographers

Continued

Please send us your additions and updates.

Tollen, Cynthia/50 Fairmont St, Arlington, MA — 617-641-4052
Tong, Darren/28 Renee Terrace, Newton, MA — 617-527-3304
Tornallyay, Martin/77 Taft Ave, Stamford, CT — 203-357-1777
Total Concept Photo/95-D Knickerbocker Ave, Bohemia, NY — 516-567-6010
Touchton, Ken/PO Box 9435, Washington, DC — 703-476-3628
Traub, Willard/PO Box 2429, Framingham, MA — 617-872-2010
Traver, Joseph/187 Hodge Ave, Buffalo, NY — 716-884-8844
Trefethen, Jim/14 Soley St Box 165, Charlestown, MA — 617-242-0064
TREIBER, PETER/917 HIGHLAND AVE, BETHLEHEM, PA
  (P 117) — **215-867-3303**
Tretick, Stanley/4365 Embassy Park Dr NW, Washington, DC — 202-537-1445
Tribulas, Michael/1879 Old Cuthbert Rd #14, Cherry Hill, NJ — 609-354-1903
Tritsch, Joseph/507 Longstone Dr, Cherry Hill, NJ — 609-424-0433
Troha, John/12258 St James Rd, Potomac, MD — 301-340-7220
Trola, Bob/1216 Arch St 2nd Fl, Philadelphia, PA — 215-977-7078
Truslow, Bill/855 Islington St, Ponsborough, PA — 603-436-4600
Trzoniec, Stanley/58 W Main St, Northboro, MA — 617-393-3800
Tur, Stefan/, , NY — 914-557-8857

UV
Uniphoto/1071 Wisconsin Ave, Washington, DC — 202-333-0500
Urban, John/1424 Canton Ave, Milton, MA — 617-333-0343
Urbina, Walt/7208 Thomas Blvd, Pittsburgh, PA — 412-242-5070
Uzzle, Burk/537 Hilaire Rd, St Davids, PA — 215-688-0507
VADNAI, PETER/180 VALLEY RD, KATONAH, NY (P 108) — **914-232-5328**
Valerio, Gary/278 Jay St, Rochester, NY — 716-352-0163
Van Petten, Rob/109 Broad St, Boston, MA — 617-426-8641
Van Schalkwyk, John/50 Melcher St, Boston, MA — 617-542-4825
Van Valkenburgh, Larry/26 E High St, Ballston Spa, NY — 518-885-8406
Van Zandbergen Photo/187 Riverside Dr, Binghamton, NY — 607-625-3408
Vandermark, Peter/523 Medford St, Charlestown, MA — 617-242-2277
Vanderwarker, Peter/56 Boyd St, Newton, MA — 617-964-2728
Vandevanter, Jan/909 'C' St SE, Washington, DC — 202-546-3520
Vaughan, Ted/423 Doe Run Rd, Manheim, PA — 717-665-6942
VECCHIO, DAN/129 E WATER ST, SYRACUSE, NY (P 136) — **315-471-1064**
Vega, Eloise/1 Cobblestone Rd, Monsey, NY — 212-512-1818
VERICKER, JOE/111 CEDAR ST 4TH FL, NEW ROCHELLE,
  NY (P 109) — **914-632-2072**
Verno, Jay/344 Third Ave, Pittsburgh, PA — 412-562-9880
Vickery, Eric/4 Genetti Circle, Bedford, MA — 617-275-0314
Vidor, Peter/70 Chestnut St, Morristown, NJ — 201-267-1104
Visual Productions/2121 Wisconsin Ave NW #470,
  Washington, DC — 202-337-7332
Vogt, Laurie/1210 Park Ave #3, Hoboken, NJ — 201-792-0485
Von Hoffmann, Bernard/2 Green Village Rd, Madison, NJ — 201-377-0317
Voscar The Maine Photographer/PO Box 661, Presque Isle,
  ME — 207-769-5911

W
Waggaman, John/2746 N 46 St, Philadelphia, PA — 215-473-2827
Wagner, William/208 North Ave, Cranford, NJ — 201-276-2002
Walch, Robert/310 W Main St, Kutztown, PA — 215-683-5701
Waldemar/386 Brook Ave, Passaic Park, NJ — 201-471-3033
Waldman, Ed/109 Rochelle Ave, Philadelphia, PA — 215-560-2088
Wallen, Jonathan/41 Lewis Pkwy, Yonkers, NY — 914-476-8674
Walp's Photo Service/182 S 2nd St, Lehighton, PA — 215-377-4370
Walsh, Dan/409 W Broadway, Boston, MA — 617-268-7615
Walters, Day/PO Box 5655, Washington, DC — 202-362-0022
Walther, Michael/2185 Brookside Ave, Wantagh, NY — 516-783-7636
Wanamaker, Roger/PO Box 2800, Darien, CT — 203-655-8383
Ward, Jack/221 Vine St, Philadelphia, PA — 215-627-5311
WARD, TONY/704 SOUTH 6TH ST, PHILADELPHIA, PA
  (P 111) — **215-238-1208**
Warner, Lee/2300 Walnut St #421, Philadelphia, PA — 215-567-0187
Warren, Marion E/1935 Old Annapolis Blvd, Annapolis, MD — 301-974-0444
Watson, Ed/972 E Broadway, Stratford, CT — 203-375-3384
Watson, H Ross/859 Lancaster Ave, Bryn Mawr, PA — 215-527-2028
Watson, Linda M/38 Church St/Box 14, Hopkinton, MA — 617-498-9638
Watson, Tom/2172 West Lake Rd, Skaneateles, NY — 315-685-6033
Wee, John/2100 Mary St, Pittsburh, PA — 412-381-5555
Weems, Bill/2030 Pierce Mill Rd NW, Washington, DC — 202-667-2444
Weems, Samuel/One Arcadia Pl, Boston, MA — 617-288-8888
Weese, Carl/140-50 Huyshope Ave, Hartford, CT — 203-246-6016
Weidman, H Mark/2112 Goodwin Lane, North Wales, PA — 215-646-1745

Weigand, Tom/717 North 5th St, Reading, PA — 215-374-4431
Weinberg, Abe/1230 Summer St, Philadelphia, PA — 215-567-5454
Weinrebe, Steve/354 Congress St, Boston, MA — 617-423-9130
Weisenfeld, Stanley/135 Davis St, Painted Post, NY — 607-962-7314
Weisgrau, Richard/1107 Walnut St 2nd Fl, Philadelphia, PA — 215-923-0348
Weiss, Michael/212 Race St, Philadelphia, PA — 215-629-1685
Weitz, Allan/147 Harbinson Pl, E Windsor, NJ — 609-443-5549
Wells, David/222 W Rittenhouse Sq #14A, Philadelphia, PA — 215-732-1028
Wendler, Hans/RD 1 Box 191, Epsom, NH — 603-736-9383
Werner, Perry/21 Sheridan Ave, Mt Vernon, NY — 914-699-3637
Westwood Photo Productions/PO Box 85, Mansfield, MA — 617-339-4141
Wexler, Ira/4893 MacArthur Blvd NW, Washington, DC — 202-337-4886
Wheeler, Edward F/1050 King of Prussia Rd, Radnor, PA — 215-964-9294
Wheeler, Nick/Turner Rd, Townsend Harbor, MA — 617-597-2919
White, Frank/18 Milton Pl, Rowayton, CT — 203-866-9500
White, Sharon/107 South St, Boston, MA — 617-423-0577
Whitman, Edward/519 W Pratt St, Baltimore, MD — 301-727-2220
Wickenheis, A/143 W Hoffman Ave, Lindenhurst, NY — 516-226-0846
Wilcoxson, Steve/1820 Bolton St, Baltimore, MD — 301-669-7447
Wiley, John Jay/147 Webster St, Boston, MA — 617-567-0506
Williams, Lawrence S/9101 W Chester Pike, Upper Darby, PA — 215-789-3030
Willinger, Dave/74 Pacific Blvd, Long Beach, NY — 516-889-0678
Wilson, John/2416 Wynnefield Dr, Havertown, PA — 215-446-4798
Wilson, Paul S/6384 Overbrook Ave, Philadelphia, PA — 215-473-4455
WILSON, ROBERT L/PO BOX 1742, CLARKSBURG, WV
  (P 137) — **304-623-5368**
Windman, Russell/348 Congress St, Boston, MA — 617-357-5140
Wolff, Randolph/5811 Edson Lane #301, Rockville, MD — 301-468-0833
Wood, Jeffrey C/808 Monroe Ave, Ardsley, PA — 215-572-6848
Wood, Richard/169 Monsgnr O'Brien Hwy, Cambridge, MA — 617-661-6856
Woodard, Steve/2003 Arbor Hill Ln, Bowie, MD — 301-249-7705
Worth, Courtia Jay/Box 911 Springtown Rd, Tillson, NY — 914-658-9517
Wrenn, Bill/14 Rockland Pl, Old Greenwich, CT — 203-637-1145
Wright, Jeri/PO box 7, Wilmington, NY — 518-946-2658
Wu, Ron/179 St Paul St, Rochester, NY — 716-454-5600
Wurster, George/22 Hallo St, Edison, NJ — 201-352-2134
Wyatt, Ronald/846 Harned St, Perth Amboy, NJ — 201-442-7527
Wyman, Ira/14 Crane Ave, West Peabody, MA — 617-535-2880

YZ
Yablon, Ron/PO Box 128, Exton, PA — 215-363-2596
Yamashita, Michael/Roxticus Rd, Mendham, NJ — 201-543-4473
Yoch, Philip/314 Cralside Dr, Tonowanda, NY — 716-691-3037
Young, Don/PO Box 249, Exton, PA — 215-363-2596
Yourman, Steve & Lisa/317 Plaza Rd N, Fairlawn, NJ — 201-796-8091
Yuichi, Idaka/RR 2 Box 229D Wood Ave, Rindge, NH — 603-899-6165
Zane, Steven/227 Grand St, Hoboken, NJ — 201-420-8868
Zappala, John/Candlewood Echoes, Sherman, CT — 203-354-6420
Zimbel, George/1538 Sherbrooke W #813, Montreal H3G1L5,
  QU — 514-931-6387
Zimmerman, Larry/50 Grove St, Salem, MA — 617-745-7117
Zmiejko, Tom/246 Center St #110, Freeland, PA — 717-636-2304
Zuckerman, Robert/100 Washington St, South Norwalk, CT — 203-853-2670
Zungoli, Nick/Box 5, Sugar Loaf, NY — 914-469-9382
Zurich, Robert/105 Church St, Aberdeen, NJ — 201-566-7076
Zutell, Kirk/911 State St, Lancaster, PA — 717-393-0918

Southeast

A
Abel, Wilton/2609 Commonwealth Ave, Charlotte, NC — 704-372-6354
Adcock, James/3108 1/2 W Leigh St #8, Richmond, VA — 804-358-4399
Alexander, Ric & Assoc Inc/212 S Graham St, Charlotte, NC — 704-332-1254
Allard, William Albert/Marsh Run Farm Box 549, Somerset, VA

— 804-823-5951

Allen, Bob/710 W Lane St, Raleigh, NC — 919-833-5991
Alston, Cotten/Box 7927-Station C, Atlanta, GA — 404-876-7859
Alterman, Jack/285 Meeting St, Charleston, SC — 803-577-0647
Alvarez, Jorge/3105 W Granada, Tampa, FL — 813-831-6765
Anderson, Susanne/PO Box 6, Waterford, VA — 703-882-3244
Andrea, Michael/225 South Mint St, Charlotte, NC — 704-334-3992
Ashcraft, Jeff/3611 Tanglewood Dr NW, Atlanta, GA — 404-438-1287
Atlantic Photo/319 N Main St, High Point, NC — 919-884-1474

Photographers

Continued

Please send us your additions and updates.

B Bachmann, Bill/PO Box 833, Lake Mary, FL 305-322-4444
Baker, I Wilson/PO Box 647, Mount Pleasant, SC 803-881-0811
Balbuza, Joseph/25 NE 210 St, Miami, FL 305-652-1728
Ball, Roger/225 West 4th St #A, Charlotte, NC 704-335-0479
Ballenberg, Bill/200 Cortland Ln, Virginia Beach, VA 804-463-3505
Baptie, Frank/1426 9th St N, St Petersburg, FL 813-823-7319
Barley, Bill/PO Box 2388, Columbia, SC 803-755-1554
Barnes, Billy E/313 Severin St, Chapel Hill, NC 919-942-6350
Barnett, Bob/819 Leigh Mill Rd, Great Falls, VA 703-759-4582
Barr, Ian/2640 SW 19th St, Fort Lauderdale, FL 305-584-6247
Barrera, Louis/157-79 75 Ave North, Palm Beach Gardens, FL 305-744-6916
Barreras, Anthony/731-D Highland Ave, Atlanta, GA 404-681-2370
Barrs, Michael/6303 SW 69th St, Miami, FL 305-665-2047
Bartlett & Assoc/3007 Edgewater Dr, Orlando, FL 305-425-7308
Bassett, Donald/9185 Green Meadows Way, Palm Beach
  Gardens, FL 305-694-1109
Beck, Charles/2721 Cherokee Rd, Birmingham, AL 205-871-6632
Beck, G & Assoc/176 Ottley Dr NE, Atlanta, GA 404-872-0728
Becker, Joel/5121 Virginia Beach Blvd, Norfolk, VA 804-461-7886
Bedgood, Bill/1292 Logan Cir, Atlanta, GA 404-351-4852
Behrens, Bruce/2920 N Orange Ave, Orlando, FL 305-898-2346
Belenson, Mark/8056 NW 41st Ct, Sunrise, FL 305-749-0675
Bennett, Ken/1001 Lockwood Ave, Columbus, GA 404-324-1182
**BENNETT, ROBERT/819 LEIGH MILL RD, GREAT FALLS, VA
  (P 140)** **703-759-4582**
Bentley, Gary/240 Great Circle Rd #330, Nashville, TN 615-242-4038
Berger, Erica/One Herald Plaza, Miami, FL 305-376-3750
Beswick, Paul/4479 Westfield Dr, Mableton, GA 404-944-8579
Bewley, Glen/428 Armour Circle, Atlanta, GA 404-872-7277
Bilby, Glade/1715 Burgundy, New Orleans, LA 504-949-6700
Blanton, Jeff/2086 Gatlin Ave, Orlando, FL 305-851-7279
Blow, Jerry/PO Box 1615, Wilmington, NC 919-763-3835
Boatman, Mike/PO Box 11131, Memphis, TN 901-382-1656
Bollman, Brooks/1183 Virginia Ave NE, Atlanta, GA 404-876-2422
Bondarenko, Marc/212 S 41st St, Birmingham, AL 205-933-2790
Borchelt, Mark/4398-D Eisenhower Ave, Alexandria, VA 703-243-7850
Borum, Michael/625 Fogg St, Nashville, TN 615-259-9750
Bose, Patti/1245 W Fairbanks #300, Winter Park, FL 305-629-5650
Bostick, Rick/6959-J Stapoint Ct, Winterpark, FL 305-677-5717
Boyd, Richard/PO Box 5097, Roanoke, VA 703-366-3140
Boyle, Jeffrey/7752 NW 54th St, Miami, FL 305-592-7032
Brack, Dennis/3609 Woodhill Pl, Fairfax, VA 703-280-2285
Brasher/Rucker Photography/3373 Park Ave, Memphis, TN 901-324-7447
Brill, David/Route 4, Box 121-C, Fairbourn, GA 404-461-5488
Brinson, Rob/486 14th St, Atlanta, GA 404-874-2497
Brooks, Charles/800 Luttrell St, Knoxville, TN 615-525-4501
Broomell, Peter/901 N Columbus St, Alexandria, VA 703-548-5767
Brown, Billy/2700 Seventh Ave S, Birmingham, AL 205-251-8327
Brown, Richard Photo/PO Box 1249, Asheville, NC 704-253-1634
Browne, Turner/1634 Washington Ave, New Orleans, LA 504-899-8883
Bruce, Thomas/79-25 4th St N, St Petersburg, FL 813-577-5626
Bryant, Donne/PO Box 80155, Baton Rouge, LA 504-769-1419
Bumpus, Ken/1770 W Chapel Dr, Deltona, FL 305-695-0668
Burgess, Ralph/PO Box 36, Chrstnsted/St Croix, VI 809-773-6541
Burns, Jerry/331-B Elizabeth St, Atlanta, GA 404-522-9377
Burris, Ned/2603 Treehouse Pkwy, Norcross, GA 404-938-8405
Byrd, Syndey/7932 S Clairborne #6, New Orleans, LA 504-865-7218

C Calamia, Ron & Assoc/8140 Forshey St, New Orleans, LA 504-482-8062
Camera Graphics/1230 Gateway Rd, Lake Park, FL 305-844-3399
Carnes, John/3307 Orleans Dr, Nashville, TN 615-383-1693
**CARPENTER, MICHAEL/5127 HARTFORD LN, BURKE, VA
  (P 141)** **703-978-2196**
Carriker, Ronald/565 Alpine Rd, Winston Salem, NC 919-765-3852
Case, Sam/PO Box 1139, Purcellville, VA 703-338-2725
Caswell, Sylvia/807 9th Court S, Birmingham, AL 205-252-2252
Caudle, Rod Studio/1708 Defoor Pl, Atlanta, GA 404-351-6385
Cavedo, Brent/9 W Main St, Richmond, VA 804-344-5374
Centner, Ed Productions/12950 SW 122nd Ave, Miami, FL 305-238-3338
Cerri, Robert Noel/612-A NE Fourteenth Ave, Ft Lauderdale,
  FL 305-764-7259

Chalfant, Flip/283 Hope St, Marietta, GA 404-422-1796
Chambers, Terrell/6843 Tilton Lane, Doraville, GA 404-396-4648
Chamowitz, Mel/3931 N Glebe Rd, Arlington, VA 703-536-8356
Chapple, Ron/501 N College, Charlotte, NC 704-377-4217
Chernush, Kay/3855 N 30th St, Arlington, VA 703-528-1195
Chesler, Donna & Ken/6941 NW 12th St, Plantation, FL 305-581-6489
Choiniere, Gerin/900 Greenleaf Ave, Charlotte, NC 704-372-0220
Clark, Marty/1105 Peachtree St NE, Atlanta, GA 404-873-4618
Clayton, Al/141 The Prado NE, Atlanta, GA 404-577-4141
Cochrane, Craig/PO Box 2316, Virginia Beach, VA 804-468-1065
Cody, Dennie/5820 SW 51st Terrace, Miami, FL 305-666-0247
Colbroth, Ron/4421 Airlie Way, Annandale, VA 703-354-2729
Collins, Michael/250 23rd St SW, Winterhaven, FL 813-294-2572
Compton, Grant/7004 Sand Nettles Dr, Savannah, GA 912-897-3771
Contorakes, George/PO Box 430901, South Miami, FL 305-661-0731
Cook, Jamie/653 Ethel St, Atlanta, GA 404-892-1393
Cooke, Bill/7761 SW 88th St, Miami, FL 305-596-2454
Copeland, Jim/2135-F Defoor Hills Rd, Atlanta, GA 404-352-2025
Corn, Jack/27 Dahlia Dr, Brentwood, TN 615-373-3301
Cornelia, William/PO Box 5304, Hilton Head Island, SC 803-671-2576
Cosby-Bower Inc/209 N Foushee St, Richmond, VA 804-643-1100
Cox, Whitney/2042 W Grace St #3, Richmond, VA 804-358-3061
Cromer, Peggo/1206 Andora Ave, Coral Gables, FL 305-667-3722
Crum, Lee/PO Box 15229, New Orleans, LA 504-529-2156

D Dale, John/576 Armour Circle NE, Atlanta, GA 404-872-3203
Daniel, Ralph/915 Argonne Ave #2, Atlanta, GA 404-872-3946
David, Alan/1186-D N Highland Ave, Atlanta, GA 404-872-2142
Davidson, Cameron/1720 Dogwood Dr, Alexandria, VA 202-328-3344
Dawson, Bill/1853 Madison Ave, Memphis, TN 901-726-6043
Degast, Robert/Rt 1 Box 323, Onancock, VA 804-787-8060
DeKalb, Jed/PO Box 22884, Nashville, TN 615-331-8527
Demolina, Raul/3903 Ponce De Leon, Coral Gables, FL 305-448-8727
Design & Visual Effects/1228 Zonolite Rd, Atlanta, GA 404-872-3283
DeVault, Jim/2400 Sunset Pl, Nashville, TN 615-269-4538
Diaz, Rick/7395 SW 42nd St, Miami, FL 305-264-9761
Dickerson, John/1895 Annwicks Dr, Marietta, GA 404-977-4138
Dickinson, Dick/1854 University Pkwy, Sarasota, FL 813-351-2036
DiModica, James/139 Sevilla Ave, Coral Gables, FL 305-666-7710
Dix, Paul/106 W Bonito Dr, Ocean Springs, MS 601-875-7691
Dixon, Tom/3404-D W Windover Ave, Greensboro, NC 919-294-6076
Dobbs, David/1536 Monroe Dr NE #110, Atlanta, GA 404-885-1460
Donica, John/4204 Wallace Ln, Nashville, TN 615-269-5024
Dorin, Jay/, Miami, FL 305-534-1534
Doty, Gary/PO Box 23697, Ft Lauderdale, FL 305-928-0644
Douglas, Keith/405 NE 8th Ave, Ft Lauderdale, FL 305-763-5883
Draper, Fred/259 S Willow Ave, Cookeville, TN 615-526-1315
Dressler, Brian/3529 Yale Ave, Columbia, SC 803-254-7171
Drymon, Terry/6308 Benjamin Rd, Tampa, FL 813-888-7779
Dugas, Henri/PO Box 250, Amelia, LA 501-631-0687
Duvall, Thurman III/1021 Northside Dr NW, Atlanta, GA 404-875-0161

E Eastmond, Peter/PO Box 856 E, Barbados,W Indies, 809-429-7757
Edwards, Jack/209 N Rocheblave St, New Orleans, LA 504-822-2111
Edwards, Jim/416 Armour Circle NE, Atlanta, GA 404-875-1005
Eighme, Bob/PO Box 7083, Ft Lauderdale, FL 305-527-8445
Elliot, Tom/19756 Bel Aire Dr, Miami, FL 305-251-4315
Ellis, Bill/406 Edwards Dr, Greensboro, NC 919-299-5074
Ellis, Gin/1203 Techwood Dr, Atlanta, GA 404-892-3204
Elmore, James/4807 5th St W, Bradenton, FL 813-755-0546
Engelman, Suzanne/1621 Woodbridge Lk Cir, W Palm Beach,
  FL 305-969-6666
English, Melissa Hayes/1195 Woods Circle NE, Atlanta, GA 404-261-7650
Erickson, Jim/302 Jefferson St #300, Raleigh, NC 919-833-9955

F Felipe, Giovanni/3465 SW 73rd Ave, Miami, FL 305-266-5308
Fernandes, Jose/1011 Valencia, Coral Gables, FL 305-443-6501
Findel, Stefan/1133 Spring St NW, Atlanta, GA 404-872-8103
Fineman, Michael/7521 SW 57th Terrace, Miami, FL 305-666-1250
Fisher, Ray/10700 SW 72nd Ct, Miami, FL 305-665-7659
Fitzgerald, Barry/808 Charlotte St, Fredericksburg, VA 703-371-3253
Foley, Roger/519 N Monroe St, Arlington, VA 703-524-6274

Forer, Dan/1970 NE 149th St, North Miami, FL — 305-949-3131
Fowley, Douglas/103 N Hite Ave, Louisville, KY — 502-897-7222
Frazier, Steve/1425 US 19 S Bldg 26 #102, Clearwater, FL — 813-531-3631
Freeman, Tina/2113 Decatur Sr, New Orleans, LA — 504-949-1863
Frink, Stephen/PO Box 19-A, Key Largo, FL — 305-451-3737

G
Gandy, Skip/302 East Davis Blvd, Tampa, FL — 813-253-0340
Gardella Photography & Design/781 Miami Cr NE, Atlanta, GA — 404-231-1316
Garrett, Kenneth/PO Box 208, Broad Run, VA — 703-347-5848
Garrison, Gary/4608 Tchoupitoulas, New Orleans, LA — 504-899-8445
Gefter, Judith/1725 Clemson Rd, Jacksonville, FL — 904-733-5498
Gelberg, Bob/7035-E SW 47th St, Miami, FL — 305-665-3200
Gemignani, Joe/13833 NW 19th Ave, Miami, FL — 305-685-7636
Genser, Howard/1859 Seventh Ave, Jacksonville, FL — 904-734-9688
Gentile, Arthur Sr/7335 Connan Lane, Charlotte, NC — 704-541-0227
Gerlich, Fred/1220 Spring St NW, Atlanta, GA — 404-872-3487
Gibbs, Ernest/300 Regency Rd #C4, Spartanburg, SC — 803-582-0471
Glaser, Ken & Assoc/5270 Annunciation St, New Orleans, LA — 504-895-7170
Gleasner, Bill/132 Holly Ct, Denver, NC — 704-483-9301
Godfrey, Mark/3526 N Third St, Arlington, VA — 703-527-8293
Gornto, Bill/590 Ponce De Leon Ave, Atlanta, GA — 404-876-1331
Graham, Curtis/648 First Ave S, St Petersburg, FL — 813-821-0444
Granberry/Anderson Studios/1211 Spring St NW, Atlanta, GA — 404-874-2426
Greer, Greg/2032 Adams, New Orleans, LA — 504-861-7100
Grigg, Roger Allen/PO Box 52851, Atlanta, GA — 404-876-4748
Groendyke, Bill/6344 NW 201st Ln, Miami, FL — 305-625-8293
Guider, John/517 Fairground Ct, Nashville, TN — 615-255-4495
Gupton, Charles/Route 2 Box 206, Wake Forest, NC — 919-556-6511
Guravich, Dan/PO Box 891, Greenville, MS — 601-335-2444

H
Haggerty, Richard/656 Ward St, High Point, NC — 919-889-7744
Hall, Don/2922 Hyde Park st, Sarasota, FL — 813-365-6161
Hall, Ed/7100 Citrus Point, Winter Park, FL — 305-657-8182
Hamilton, Tom/1095 Greenleaf Rd, Atlanta, GA — 404-622-0100
Hannau, Michael/3800 NW 32nd Ave, Miami, FL — 305-633-1100
Hansen, Eric/3005 7th Ave S/Box 55492, Birmingham, AL — 205-251-5587
Harbison, Steve/1516 Crestwood Dr, Greeneville, TN — 615-638-2535
Hardy, Frank/1003 N 12th Ave, Pensacola, FL — 904-438-2712
Harkins, Lynn S/1900 Byrd Ave #101, Richmond, VA — 804-285-2900
Harrelson, Keith/4505 131st Ave N, Clearwater, FL — 813-577-9812
Harris, Christopher/PO Box 2926, Covington, LA — 504-893-4898
Haviland, Patrick/3642 Tryclan Dr, Charlotte, NC — 704-527-8795
HENDERSON/MUIR PHOTO/5700 NEW CHAPEL HILL RD, RALEIGH, NC (P 148) — **919-851-0458**
Hendley, Arington/454 Irwin St, Atlanta, GA — 404-577-2300
Henley & Savage/113 S Jefferson St, Richmond, VA — 804-780-1120
Higgins, Neal/1540 Monroe Dr, Atlanta, GA — 404-876-3186
Hill, Dan/9132 O'Shea Ln, W Springfield, VA — 703-451-4705
HILL, JACKSON/2032 ADAMS ST, NEW ORLEANS, LA (P 149) — **504-861-3000**
Hill, Tom/207 E Parkwood Rd, Decatur, GA — 404-377-3833
Hillyer, Jonathan/450-A Bishop St, Atlanta, GA — 404-351-0477
Hirsch, Alan/1259 Ponce de Leon #6C, San Juan, PR — 809-723-2224
Hoflich, Richard/544 N Angier Ave NE, Atlanta, GA — 404-584-9159
Hogben, Steve/468 Armour Dr, Atlanta, GA — 404-266-2894
Holland, Ralph/3706 Alliance Dr, Greensboro, NC — 919-855-6422
Holland, Robert/PO Box 162099, Miami, FL — 305-255-6758
Holt Group/403 Westcliff Rd/Box 35488, Greensboro, NC — 919-668-2770
Hood, Robin/1101 W Main St, Franklin, TN — 615-794-2041
Hopkins, Allen W/627 King St, Alexandria, VA — 703-671-7734
Horan, Eric/PO Box 6373, Hilton Head Island, SC — 803-842-3233
Hosack, Loren/2301-F Sabal Ridge Ct, Palm Beach Gardens, FL — 305-627-8313
Hunter, Bud/1917 1/2 Oxmoor Rd, Birmingham, AL — 205-879-3153
Huntley, Robert/1210 Spring St NW, Atlanta, GA — 404-892-6450

IJ
International Defense Images/2419 Mt Vernon Ave, Alexandria, VA — 703-548-7217
Isaacs, Lee/807 9th Court South, Birmingham, AL — 205-252-2698
Jamison, Chipp/2131 Liddell Dr NE, Atlanta, GA — 404-873-3636
Jeffcoat, Russell/620 Saluda Ave, Columbia, SC — 803-799-8578

Jeffcoat, Wilber L/1864 Palomino Cir, Sumter, SC — 803-773-3690
Jenkins, Dave Prdctns/1084 Duncan Ave, Chattanooga, TN — 615-629-5380
Jimison, Tom/5929 Annunciation, New Orleans, LA — 504-891-8587
Johns, Douglas/2535 25th Ave N, St Petersburg, FL — 813-321-7235
Johnson, George L/16603 Round Oak Dr, Tampa, FL — 813-963-3222
Johnson, Silvia/6110 Brook Dr, Falls Church, VA — 703-532-8653
Jones, Wesley/, , FL — 305-483-8376
Jordan/Rudolph Studios/1446 Mayson St NE #5L, Atlanta, GA — 404-874-1829
Jureit, Robert A/916 Aguero Ave, Coral Gables, FL — 305-667-1346

K
Kaplan Studio/PO Box 7206, McLean, VA — 703-893-1660
Kaplan, Al/PO Box 611373, North Miami, FL — 305-891-7595
Kappiris, Stan/PO Box 14331, Tampa, FL — 813-254-4866
Katz, Arni/PO Box 724507, Atlanta, GA — 404-953-1168
Kaufman, Len/5119 Arthur St, Hollywood, FL — 305-920-7822
Kearney, Mitchell/301 E 7th St, Charlotte, NC — 704-377-7662
Kennedy, M Lewis/2700 7th Ave S, Birmingham, AL — 205-252-2700
Kern Photography/1243 N 17th Ave, Lake Worth, FL — 305-582-2487
Kersh, Viron/PO Box 51201, New Orleans, LA — 504-524-4515
King, J Brian/1267 Coral Way, Miami, FL — 305-856-6534
King, Tom/2806 Edgewater Dr, Orlando, FL — 305-841-4421
Kinney, Greg/912 Burford Pl, Nashville, TN — 615-297-8084
Kinsella, Barry/1010 Andrews Rd, West Palm Beach, FL — 305-832-8736
Klass, Rubin & Erika/5200 N Federal Hwy #2, Fort Lauderdale, FL — 305-565-1612
Klemens, Susan/7423 Foxleigh Way, Alexandria, VA — 703-971-1226
Kling, David Photography/502 Armour Circle, Atlanta, GA — 404-881-1215
KNIBBS, TOM/5907 NE 27TH AVE, FT LAUDERDALE, FL (P 150) — **305-491-6263**
Knight, Steve/1212 E 10th St, Charlotte, NC — 704-334-5115
Kohanim, Parish/1130 W Peachtree NW, Atlanta, GA — 404-892-0099
Kollar, Robert E/1431 Cherokee Trail #52, Knoxville, TN — 615-573-8191
Koplitz, William/729 N Lime St, Sarasota, FL — 813-366-5905
Kralik, Scott/210 N Fillmore, Arlington, VA — 703-522-8261
Kufner, Gary/305 NW 10th Terr, Hallendale, FL — 305-944-7740
Kunz, Grace/1104 W Newtown St, Dothan, AL — 205-793-5723

L
Lackey, Larry/2400 Poplar Ave #514, Memphis, TN — 901-323-0811
Lair, John/1122 Roger St, Louisville, KY — 502-589-7779
Langone, Peter/516 NE 13th St, Ft Lauderdale, FL — 305-467-0654
Lanpher, Keith/865 Monticello Ave, Norfolk, VA — 804-627-3051
Latham, Charles/559 Dutch Valley Rd NE, Atlanta, GA — 404-873-5858
Lathem, Charles & Assoc/559 Dutch Valley Rd NE, Atlanta, GA — 404-873-5858
Lavenstein, Lance/4605 Pembroke Lake Cir, Virginia Beach, VA — 804-499-9959
Lawrence, David/PO Box 835, Largo, FL — 813-586-2112
Lawrence, John R/Box 330570, Coconut Grove, FL — 305-447-8621
Lawson, Slick/3801 Whitland Ave, Nashville, TN — 615-383-0147
Lazzo, Dino/655 SW 20th Rd, Miami, FL — 305-856-1148
Lee, Chung P/7820 Antiopi St, Annandale, VA — 703-560-3394
Lee, George/PO Box 3923, Greenville, SC — 803-232-4119
Lee, Joe/846 N President St, Jackson, MS — 601-948-5255
Leggett, Albert/1415 Story Ave, Louisville, KY — 502-584-0255
Leo, Victor/7100 Greenlawn Rd, Louisville, KY — 502-423-8374
Little, Chris/PO Box 467221, Atlanta, GA — 404-641-9688
Llewellyn, Robert/PO Drawer L, Charlottesville, VA — 804-973-8000
Long, Lewis/3130 SW 26th St, Miami, FL — 305-448-7667
Loumakis, Constantinos/826 SW 13th St, Ft Lauderdale, FL — 305-525-7367
Lubin, Jeff/8472 Rainbow Bridge Ln, Springfield, VA — 703-569-5086
Lucas, Steve/7925 SW 104th St #E-202, Miami, FL — 305-271-0778
Luttrell, David/1500 Highland Dr, Knoxville, TN — 615-523-7121
Lynch, Warren/306 Production Ct, Louisville, KY — 502-491-8233

M
Magee, Ken/3519 Live Oak, New Orleans, LA — 504-484-6779
Magruder, Mary and Richard/2156 Snap Finger Rd, Decatur, GA — 404-289-8985
Mahen, Rich/4301 SW 10th St, Ft Lauderdale, FL — 305-792-5429
Malles, Ed/355 Needle Blvd, Merritt Island, FL — 305-452-0880
Mann, James/1007-B Norwalk, Greensboro, NC — 919-292-1190
Mann, Rod/5082 Woodleigh Rd, Knotts Island, NC — 919-429-3009

Photographers

Continued

Please send us your additions and updates.

Maratea, Ronn/4338 Virginia Beach Blvd, Virginia Beach, VA	804-340-6464
Marden, Bruce F Productions/1379 Chattahoochee Ave, Atlanta, GA	404-351-8152
Markatos, Jerry/Rt 2 Box 419/Rock Rest Rd, Pittsboro, NC	919-542-2139
Marquez, Toby/1709 Wainwright Dr, Reston, VA	703-471-4666
Mason, Chuck/14115 NW 5th Court, North Miami, FL	305-769-0911
May, Clyde/1037 Monroe Dr NE, Atlanta, GA	404-873-4329
Mazey, Jon/2724 NW 30th Ave, Ft Lauderdale, FL	305-731-3300
McCannon, Tricia/1536 Monroe Dr, Atlanta, GA	404-873-3070
McCarthy, Tom/8960 SW 114th St, Miami, FL	305-233-1703
McClure, Dan/320 N Milledge, Athens, GA	404-354-1234
McCord, Fred/2720 Piedmont Rd NE, Atlanta, GA	404-262-1538
McCoy, Frank T/131 Donmond Dr, Hendersonville, TN	615-822-4437
McGee, E Alan/1816-E Briarwd Ind Ct, Atlanta, GA	404-633-1286
McIntyre, William/3746 Yadkinville Rd, Winston-Salem, NC	919-922-3142
McKee, Lee/1004 Ruth Jordano Ct, Ocoee, FL	305-656-9289
McKenzie & Dickerson/133 W Vermont Ave/Box 152, Southern Pines, NC	919-692-6131
McLaughlin, Ken/623 7th Ave S, Nashville, TN	615-256-8162
McNabb, Tommy/4015 Brownsboro Rd, Winston-Salem, NC	919-723-4640
McNeely, Burton/PO Box 338, Land O'Lakes, FL	813-996-3025
McVicker, Sam/PO Box 880, Dunedin, FL	813-734-9660
Melyana Assoc/2740 Alton Rd, Miami Beach, FL	305-673-0094
Meredith, David/2900 NE 30th Ave #4E, Ft Lauderdale, FL	305-564-4579
Michot, Walter/1520 E Sunrise Blvd, Ft Lauderdale, FL	305-527-8445
Mikeo, Rich/5399 N E 14th Ave, Ft Lauderdale, FL	305-491-5399
Miller, Brad/3645 Stewart, Coconut Grove, FL	305-666-1617
Miller, Bruce/9401 61st Court SW, Miami, FL	305-666-4333
Miller, Frank Lotz/1115 Washington Ave, New Orleans, LA	504-899-5688
Miller, Randy/6666 SW 96th St, Miami, FL	305-667-5765
Mills, Henry/5514 Starkwood Dr, Charlotte, NC	704-535-1861
Mims, Allen/107 Madison Ave, Memphis, TN	901-527-4040
Minardi, Mike/PO Box 14247, Tampa, FL	813-684-7138
Moede, Ronald/Daniel Bldg, Greenville, SC	803-298-2053
Molony, Bernard/PO Box 15081, Atlanta, GA	404-457-6934
Moore, George Photography/1301 Admiral St, Richmond, VA	804-355-1862
Morgan, Frank/2414 Arctic Ave #5, Virginia Beach, VA	804-422-9328
Morgan, Red/970 Hickory Trail, W Palm Beach, FL	305-793-6085
Morrah, Linda/201 E Coffee St, Greenville, SC	803-242-9108
Morris, Paul/5420 NW 169th St, Miami, FL	305-758-8150
Murphy Jr, Lionel/2311 Waldemere, Sarasota, FL	813-365-0595
Murray, Kevin/1424 W 4th St, Winston-Salem, NC	919-722-5107
Murray, Steve/1330 Mordecai Dr, Raleigh, NC	919-828-0653
Myers, Fred/114 Regent Ln, Florence, AL	205-386-2207
Myhre, Gordon/PO Box 1226, Ind Rocks Beach, FL	813-584-3717
Mykietyn, Walt/10110 SW 133 St, Miami, FL	305-235-2342

NO
Nelson, Jon/PO Box 8772, Richmond, VA	804-359-0642
Nemeth, Judy/PO Box 37108, Charlotte, NC	704-375-9292
Neubauer, John/1525 S Arlington Ridge Rd, Arlington, VA	703-920-5994
Nicholson, Nick/1503 Brooks Ave, Raleigh, NC	919-787-6076
Norling Studios Inc/221 Swathmore Ave/Box 7167, High Point, NC	919-434-3151
North Light Studio/1803 Hendricks Ave, Jacksonville, FL	904-398-2501
Norton, Mike/4917 W Nassau, Tampa, FL	813-876-3390
NOVAK, JACK/PO BOX 971, ALEXANDRIA, VA (P 236)	**703-836-4439**
Novicki, Norb/6800 North West 2nd St, Margate, FL	305-971-8954
O'Boyle, Erin/7001 N Atlantic Ave #122, Cape Canaveral, FL	305-783-1923
O'Brian, Brian/102 W Clinton Ave #404, Huntsville, AL	205-539-0407
O'Kain, Dennis/219 Gilmer St, Lexington, GA	404-743-3140
O'Sullivan, Brian/1401 SE 8th St, Deerfield Beach, FL	305-429-0712
Olive, Tim/754 Piedmont Ave NE, Atlanta, GA	404-872-0500
Olson, Carl/3325 Laura Way, Winston, GA	404-949-1532
Osborne, Mitchel L/920 Frenchman St, New Orleans, LA	504-949-1366

P
Parker, Phillip M/192 Williford, Memphis, TN	901-529-9200
Patterson, M N/1615 Brown Ave #2, Cookeville, TN	615-528-8025
Patterson, Pat/1635 Old Louisburg Rd, Raleigh, NC	919-834-2223
Payne, Steve/1524 Virginia St E, Charleston, WV	304-343-7254
Pelosi & Chambers/684 Greenwood Ave NE, Atlanta, GA	404-872-8117
Peters, J Dirk/PO Box 15492, Tampa, FL	813-884-6272
Petrey, John/670 Clay St/Box 2401, Winter Park, FL	305-645-1718

Photo-Synthesis/1239 Kensington Rd, McLean, VA	703-734-8770
Photographic Group/7407 Chancery Ln, Orlando, FL	305-855-4306
Photographic Ideas/PO Box 285, Charleston, SC	803-577-7020
Photography Unlimited/3662 S West Shore Blvd, Tampa, FL	813-839-7710
Pierce, Nancy J/1715 Merry Oaks Rd, Charlotte, NC	704-535-7409
Pocklington, Mike/9 W Main St, Richmond, VA	804-783-2731
Posey, Mike/3524 Canal St, New Orleans, LA	504-488-8000
Prism Studios/1027 Elm Hill Pike, Nashville, TN	615-255-1919
Purin, Thomas/14190 Harbor Lane, Lake Park, FL	305-622-4131

R
Ramirez, George/303 Canals St, Santurce, PR	809-724-5727
Ramos, Victor/8390 SW 132 St, Miami, FL	305-255-3111
Randolph, Bruce/132 Alan Dr, Newport News, VA	804-877-0992
Rank, Don/1980 Will Ross Ct, Atlanta, GA	404-452-1658
Rathe, Robert A/8451-A Hilltop Rd, Fairfax, VA	703-560-7222
RAYMOND, TOM/RT 6 BOX 424-C, JONESBOROUGH, TN (P 151)	**615-753-9061**
Reus-Breuer, Sandra/Cal Josefa Cabrera Final #3, Rio Piedras, PR	809-767-1568
Rickles, Tom/2655 Pinetree Dr, Miami Beach, FL	305-866-5762
Riggall, Michael/403 8th St NE, Atlanta, GA	404-872-8242
Riley, Richard/34 N Ft Harrison, Clearwater, FL	813-446-2626
Rippey, Ray/PO Box 50093, Nashville, TN	615-646-1291
Rodgers, Ted/544 Plasters Ave, Atlanta, GA	404-892-0967
Rogers, Brian/689 Antone St NW, Atlanta, GA	404-355-8069
Rogers, Chuck/508 Armour Cir NE, Atlanta, GA	404-872-0062
Rosen, Olive/3415 Arnold Ln, Falls Church, VA	703-560-5557
Rosenblum, Bruce/1380 SW 82nd Terr #732, Plantation, FL	305-475-8351
Rossmeissl, Kirk/1921 Woodford Rd, Vienna, VA	301-989-4866
Rubio, Manny/1203 Techwood Dr, Atlanta, GA	404-892-0783
Runion, Britt/6414 Orange Bay Ave, Orlando, FL	305-351-3203
Russell, John/PO Box 2141, High Point, NC	919-887-1163
Rutherford, Michael W/623 Sixth Ave S, Nashville, TN	615-242-5953
Rutledge, Don/13000 Edgetree Ct, Midlothian, VA	804-353-0151

S
Saenz, C M/PO Box 117, Alachua, FL	904-462-5670
Sahuc, Louis/530 Royal St, New Orleans, LA	504-523-2809
Salmon, George/10325 Del Mar Circle, Tampa, FL	813-961-8687
Sander, Neil/PO Box 819, Maggie Valley, NC	704-456-9912
Saylor, Ted/2312 Farwell Dr, Tampa, FL	813-879-5636
Schaedler, Tim/PO Box 1081, Safety Harbor, FL	813-796-0366
Schatz, Bob/112 Second Ave N, Nashville, TN	615-254-7197
Schenck, Gordon H/PO Box 35203, Charlotte, NC	704-332-4078
Schenker, Richard/6304 Benjamin Rd #504, Tampa, FL	813-885-5413
Schermerhorn, Tim/325 Model Farm Rd, High Point, NC	919-889-6121
Schiavone, George/355 NE 59th Terr, Miami, FL	305-662-6057
Schiff, Ken/4406 SW 74th Ave, Miami, FL	305-262-2022
Schlinkert, Richard/5816 Sixth Ave, Birmingham, AL	205-595-7134
Schneider, John/3702-B Alliance Dr, Greensboro, NC	919-855-0261
Schulke, Flip/PO Box 570669, Miami, FL	305-251-7717
Schumacher, Karl/6254 Park Rd, McLean, VA	703-241-7424
Schwartz, Alan/8400 SW 133rd Ave Rd #409, Miami, FL	305-596-6720
Seifried, Charles/Rt 3 Box 162, Decatur, AL	205-355-5558
Seitelman, M D/PO Box 2477, Alexandria, VA	703-548-7217
Seitz, Arthur/615 NE 12th Ave #109, Ft Lauderdale, FL	305-764-5635
Sharpe, David/816 N St Asaph St, Alexandria, VA	703-683-3773
Shea, David/114 S Elgin Pkwy, Ft Walton Beach, FL	904-244-3602
Sheffield, Scott/2707 W Broad St, Richmond, VA	804-358-3266
Sheldon, Mike/Rt 2 Box 61A, Canton, NC	704-235-8345
Sherbow, Robert/1607 Colonial Terr, Arlington, VA	202-522-3644
Sherman, Pam/103 Bonnie Brae Way, Hollywood, FL	305-652-0566
SHERMAN, RON/PO BOX 28656, ATLANTA, GA (P 152)	**404-993-7197**
Shooters Photographic/PO Box 36464, Charlotte, NC	704-334-7267
Shrout, Bill/Route 1 Box 317, Theodore, AL	205-973-1379
Silla, Jon/229 S Brevard St, Charlotte, NC	704-377-8694
Sink, Richard/1225 Cedar Dr, Winston Salem, NC	919-784-8759
Sisson, Barry/6813 Bland St, Springfield, VA	703-569-6051
Smeltzer, Robert/10-B Sevier St, Greenville, SC	803-235-2186
Smith, Clark/314 E Tyler, Dalken, GA	404-226-2508
Smith, Richard & Assoc/1007 Norwalk St #B, Greensboro, NC	919-292-1190
Smith, Richard Photo/5907 NE 27th Ave, Ft Lauderdale, FL	305-491-6263
Smith/Garner Studios/1114 W Peachtree St, Atlanta, GA	404-875-0086

Snow, Chuck/2700 7th Ave S, Birmingham, AL — 205-251-7482
Sparkman, Clif/161 Mangum St SW #301, Atlanta, GA — 404-588-9687
Sparks, Don/670 11th St NW, Atlanta, GA — 404-876-7354
Speidell, Bill/PO Box 426, Madison Heights, VA — 804-846-2133
St John, Chuck/2724 NW 30th Ave, Ft Lauderdale, FL — 305-731-3300
St John, Michael/PO Box 1202, Oldsmar, FL — 813-725-4817
**STANSFIELD, ROSS/4938-D EISENHOWER AVE,
   ALEXANDRIA, VA (P 146)** — **703-370-5142**
Stanwycks, Vicki/PO Box 70592, New Orleans, LA — 504-943-7957
Staples, Neil/1231 NE 9th Ave, Ft Lauderdale, FL — 305-527-4
Stein Photo/20240 SW 92nd Ave, Miami, FL — 305-251-2868
Stein, Art/1845 MacArthur Dr, McLean, VA — 703-684-0675
Stein, Marc/402 Rustic Trail, Birmingham, AL — 205-987-1359
Stewart, Harvey & Co Inc/836 Dorse Rd, Lewisville, NC — 919-945-2101
Stoppee Photographics Group/13 W Main St, Richmond, VA — 804-644-0266
Strode, William A/1008 Kent Rd, Prospect, KY — 502-228-4446
Sustendal, Michael/147 Carondelet St #1076, New Orleans, LA — 504-891-8373
Swann, David/776 Juniper St, Atlanta, GA — 404-873-3003
Sweetman, Gary Photography/2904 Manatee Ave W,
   Bradenton, FL — 813-748-4004
Symmes Jr, Edwin C/PO Box 8101, Atlanta, GA — 404-876-7620

T
Tapp, Eddie/955 Smoketree Dr, Tucker, GA — 404-446-2131
Tast, Jerry/7932 Southside Blvd #2303, Jacksonville, FL — 904-642-8300
Taylor, Randy/600 NE 36th St #218, Miami, FL — 305-573-5200
Telesca, Chris/PO Box 51449, Raliegh, NC — 919-846-0101
Tesh, John/904-A Norwalk St, Greenboro, NC — 919-299-1400
Thomas, J Clark/2305 Elliston Place, Nashville, TN — 615-327-1757
Thomas, Larry/1212 Spring St, Atlanta, GA — 404-881-8850
Thompson & Thompson/5180 NE 12th Ave, Ft Lauderdale, FL — 305-772-4411
Thompson, Darrell/124 Rhodes Dr, Marietta, GA — 404-641-2020
Thompson, Ed C/2381 Drew Valley Rd, Atlanta, GA — 404-636-7258
Thompson, Michael Photography/1579-F #240 Monroe Dr,
   Atlanta, GA — 404-874-4054
Thompson, Rose/1802 NW 29th St, Oakland Park, FL — 305-485-0148
Thompson, Thomas L/3210 Peachtree Rd NW #14, Atlanta,
   GA — 404-524-6929
Tilley, Arthur/1925 College Ave NE, Atlanta, GA — 404-371-8086
Tilson, Mark/419 Sinclair Ave NE, Atlanta, GA — 404-524-8569
Tobias, Jerry/2117 Opa-Locka Blvd, Miami, FL — 305-685-3003
Traves, Stephen/360 Elden Dr, Atlanta, GA — 404-255-5711
Trufant, David/1902 Highland Rd, Baton Rouge, LA — 504-344-9690
Truman, Gary/PO Box 7144, Charleston, WV — 304-755-3078
Tucker, Mark Studio/117 Second Ave N, Nashville, TN — 615-254-5555
Turnau, Jeffrey/7210 Red Rd #216, Miami, FL — 305-666-5454
Turner, Sam Photo/720 Parkridge Cir, Marietta, GA — 404-365-2128
Tutino, Aldo/407 N Washington St, Alexandria, VA — 703-549-8014

U V
Ustinick, Richard/12 North 18th St, Richmond, VA — 804-649-1477
Uzzell, Steve/2505 N Custis Rd, Arlington, VA — 703-522-2320
Valada, M C/8451 Hilltop Rd #A, Fairfax, VA — 703-573-3006
Van Calsem, Bill/824 Royal St, New Orleans, LA — 504-522-7346
Van Camp, Louis/713 San Juan Rd, New Bern, NC — 919-633-6081
Vance, David/150 NW 164th St, Miami, FL — 305-685-2433
Vaughn, Marc/600 Curtis Pkwy/Box 660706, Miami Springs,
   FL — 305-888-4926
Victor, Ira/2026 Prairie Ave, Miami Beach, FL — 305-532-4444
Visual Zone/3804 Veterans Blvd, Metairie, LA — 504-454-2409
Von Matthiessen, Maria/251 Royal Palm Way Ste 201, Palm
   Beach, FL — 305-655-6889
Vullo, Phillip Photography/565 Dutch Valley Rd NE, Atlanta,
   GA — 404-874-0822

W
Wagoner, Mark/12-H Wendy Ct Box 18974, Greensboro, NC — 919-854-0406
Walker Jr, Reuel F/PO Box 5421, Greenville, SC — 803-834-9836
Walters, Tom/804 Atando Ave, Charlotte, NC — 704-333-6294
Webb, Jon/2023 Kenilworth Ave, Louisville, KY — 502-459-7081
Webster & Co/2401 Euclid Ave, Charlotte, NC — 704-522-0647
Weinlaub, Ralph/81 SW 6th St, Pompano Beach, FL — 305-941-1368
Weithorn, Mark/13740 NW 19th Ave #6, Miami, FL — 305-688-7070
Westerman, Charlie/Central Amer Bldg/Bowman Fld,
   Louisville, KY — 502-458-1532

Wheless, Rob/2239 Faulkner Rd NE, Atlanta, GA — 404-321-3557
White, Drake/PO Box 40090, Augusta, GA — 404-733-4142
White, Ellis/2286 Central Ave, Memphis, TN — 901-725-4740
Whitman, Alan/PO Box 8446, Mobile, AL — 205-478-5520
Whitman, John/604 N Jackson St, Arlington, VA — 703-524-5569
Wiener, Ray/4300 NE 5th Terrace, Oakland Park, FL — 305-565-4415
Wiley Jr, Robert/1145 Washington Ave, Winter Park, FL — 305-629-5823
Williams, Jimmy/3801 Beryl Rd, Raleigh, NC — 919-832-5971
Williams, Ron/105 Space Park Dr #A, Nashville, TN — 615-331-2500
Williamson, Thomas A/9511 Colonial Dr, Miami, FL — 305-255-6400
Willis, Joe/105 Lake Emerald Dr #314, Ft Lauderdale, FL — 305-485-7185
Wilson, Andrew/1720 Cumberland Point Dr #20, Marietta, GA — 404-980-1289
Wilson, Vickie/, , FL — 305-348-4906
Wilt, Greg/PO Box 212, Clearwater, FL — 813-442-4360
Winner, Alan/20151 NE 15th Court, Miami, FL — 305-653-6778
Wolf, David/1770 Quail Ridge Rd, Raleigh, NC — 919-876-1387
Wray, Michael/3501 Royal Palm Ave, Ft Lauderdale, FL — 305-564-3433
Wright, Chris (Ms)/4131 Walnut Grove, Memphis, TN — 901-761-5215
Wright, Christopher/2001-A Dekle Ave, Tampa, FL — 813-251-5206
Wrisley, Bard/55 Bennett St NW, Atlanta, GA — 404-524-6929

Y Z
Yankus, Dennis/223 S Howard Ave, Tampa, FL — 813-254-4156
Yarbrough, Hal/12119 Muriel Ave #511, Baton Rouge, LA — 504-275-6753
Young, Chuck/1199-R Howell Mill Rd, Atlanta, GA — 404-351-1199
Zeck, Gerry/1939 S Orange Ave, Sarasota, FL — 813-953-4888
Zimmerman, Mike/7821 Shalimar, Mira Mar, FL — 305-987-8482
Zinn, Arthur/2661 S Course Dr, Pompano Beach, FL — 305-973-3851
Zonner, Anthony/850 Montrose St, Shreveport, LA — 318-865-0307

Midwest

A
Abel Photographics/7035 Ashland Dr, Cleveland, OH — 216-526-5732
Abramson, Michael Photo/3312 W Belle Plaine, Chicago, IL — 312-267-9189
Accola, Harlan J/210 W 29th St, Marshfield, WI — 715-387-8682
Adamo, Sam/490 Parkview Dr, Seven Hills, OH — 216-447-9249
Adams, Steve Studio/3101 S Hanley, Brentwood, MO — 314-781-6676
AGS & R Studios/425 N Michigan Ave, Chicago, IL — 312-836-4500
Alan, Andrew/20727 Scio Church Rd, Chelsea, MI — 313-475-2310
Albiez, Scott/4144 N Clarendon, Chicago, IL — 312-327-8999
Albright, Dave/200 S Main, Northville, MI — 313-348-2248
Alexander, Gordon/1848 Porter St SW, Wyoming, MI — 616-531-1204
Allan-Knox Studios/1014 N Van Buren St, Milwaukee, WI — 414-272-4999
Altman, Ben/820 N Franklin, Chicago, IL — 312-944-1434
Amenta/555 W Madison #3802, Chicago, IL — 312-248-2488
Anderson Studios Inc/546 S Meridian #300, Indianapolis, IN — 317-632-9405
Anderson, Craig/105 7th St, W Des Moines, IA — 515-279-7766
Anderson, Curt/Box 3213, Minneapolis, MN — 612-332-2008
Anderson, John/401 W Superior, Chicago, IL — 312-944-3311
Anderson, Rob/900 W Jackson, Chicago, IL — 312-666-0417
Anderson, Whit/219 W Chicago, Chicago, IL — 312-973-5683
Andre, Bruce/436 N Clark, Chicago, IL — 312-661-1060
Apolinski Photography/735 N Oriole Ave, Park Ridge, IL — 312-696-3156
Ardisson Photography/436 N Clark, Chicago, IL — 312-951-8393
**ARMOUR, TONY/1726 N CLYBOURN AVE, CHICAGO, IL
   (P 157)** — **312-664-2256**
Arndt, David M/4620 N Winchester, Chicago, IL — 312-334-2841
Arndt, Jim/400 First Ave N #510, Minneapolis, MN — 612-332-5050
Arsenault, Bill/570 W Fulton, Chicago, IL — 312-454-0544
Askenas, Ulf/409 W Huron, Chicago, IL — 312-944-4630
ATEVICH, ALEX/325 N HOYNE AVE, CHICAGO, IL (P 158) — **312-942-1453**
Atkinson, David/3923 W Pine Blvd, St Louis, MO — 314-535-6484
Audio Visual Impact Group/233 E Erie, Chicago, IL — 312-664-6247
Ayala/431 E Illinois, Chicago, IL — 312-329-0787
Azuma, Don/1335 N Wells, Chicago, IL — 312-337-2101

B
Baer, Gordon/PO Box 2467, Cincinnati, OH — 513-281-2339
Bagnoli, Susan/74-24 Washington Ave, Eden Prairie, MN — 612-944-5750
Bahm, Dave/711 Commercial, Belton, MO — 816-331-0257
Baker, Jim/1905 Main, Kansas City, MO — 816-471-5565
Balterman, Lee/910 N Lake Shore Dr, Chicago, IL — 312-642-9040
Banks, Mikes/1915 Parmenter #10, Royal Oak, MI — 313-435-4031

Photographers

Continued

Please send us your additions and updates.

Banner & Burns Inc/153 W Ohio, Chicago, IL	312-644-4770
Bannister, Will/2312 N Lincoln, Chicago, IL	312-327-2143
Barge, Mike/7618 W Myrtle, Chicago, IL	312-762-1749
Barkan Keeling Photo/905 Vine St, Cincinnati, OH	513-721-0700
Barlow Photography Inc/1125 S Brentwood Blvd, Richmond Hts, MO	314-721-2385
Barnett, Jim/1502 S Keystone Ave, Indianapolis, IN	317-783-6797
Barrett, Robert/3733 Pennsylvania, Kansas City, MO	816-753-3208
Bartholomew, Gary/263 Columbia Ave, Des Plaines, IL	312-824-8473
Bartone, Tom/436 N Clark St, Chicago, IL	312-836-0464
Bartz, Carl Studio Inc/321 N 22nd St, St Louis, MO	314-231-8690
Basdeka, Pete/1254 N Wells, Chicago, IL	312-944-3333
Bass, Alan/126 W Kinzie, Chicago, IL	312-280-9140
Battrell, Mark/1611 N Sheffield, Chicago, IL	312-642-6650
Baver, Perry L/2923 W Touhy, Chicago, IL	312-674-1695
Bayles, Dal/4431 N 64th St, Milwaukee, WI	414-464-8917
Beasley, Michael/1210 W Webster, Chicago, IL	312-248-5769
Beaulieu, Allen/127 N 7th St #208, Minneapolis, MN	612-338-2327
Beck, Peter/3409 W 44th St, Minneapolis, MN	612-920-4741
Beckett Photography/510 N Water St, Milwaukee, WI	414-271-2061
Beckett Studios/340 W Huron St, Chicago, IL	312-943-2648
Bellville, Cheryl Walsh/2823 8th St S, Minneapolis, MN	612-333-5788
Belter, Mark/640 N LaSalle St #555, Chicago, IL	312-337-7676
Benda, James/13282 Glendale Rd, Savage, MN	612-890-5914
Benda, Tom/20555 LaGrange, Frankfurt, IL	815-469-3600
Bender/Bender/281 Klingel Rd, Waldo, OH	614-726-2470
Benkert, Christine/27 N 4th St #501, Minneapolis, MN	612-340-9503
Benoit, Bill/1708 1/2 Washington, Wilmette, IL	312-251-7634
Bentley, David/208 West Kinzie, Chicago, IL	312-836-0242
Berglund, Peter/126 N 3rd St #402, Minneapolis, MN	612-371-9318
Bergos, Jim Studio/122 W Kinzie St, Chicago, IL	312-527-1769
Berkman, Elie/125 Hawthorn Ave, Glencoe, IL	312-835-4158
Berlin Chic Photo/1120 W Barry St, Chicago, IL	312-327-2266
Berliner, Sheri/2815 N Pine Grove #1A, Chicago, IL	312-477-6692
Berlow, Marc Photography/325 W Huron St #406, Chicago, IL	312-787-6528
Bernard, Jerry/2023 Beard St, Detroit, MI	313-841-9284
Berr, Keith/1220 W 6th St #608, Cleveland, OH	216-566-7950
BERTHIAUME, TOM/1008 NICOLLET MALL, MINNEAPOLIS, MN (P 159)	**612-338-1999**
Bidak, Lorne/570 W Fulton, Chicago, IL	312-263-0010
Bieber, Tim/3312 W Belle Plaine, Chicago, IL	312-463-3590
Biel Photographic Studios/2289-91 N Moraine Blvd, Dayton, OH	513-298-6621
Bilsley, Bill/218 South Patton, Arlington Heights, IL	312-259-7633
Bishop, Robert/5622 Delmar #103, St Louis, MO	314-367-8787
Bjornson, Howard/671 N Sangamon, Chicago, IL	312-829-8516
Blasdel, John/3030 Roanoke, Kansas City, MO	816-561-8989
Block, Ernie/1138 Cambridge Cir Dr, Kansas City, KS	913-321-3080
Block, Stuart/1242 W Washington Blvd, Chicago, IL	312-733-3600
Bochsler, Tom/3514 Mainway, Burlington L7M 1A8, ON	416-529-9011
Bock, Edward/400 N First Ave #207, Minneapolis, MN	612-332-8504
Bodenhansen, Gary/306 W 8th St, Kansas City, MO	816-221-2456
Bolber Studio/6706 Northwest Hwy, Chicago, IL	312-763-5860
Bornefeld, William/586 Hollywood Pl, St Louis, MO	314-962-5596
Boschke, Les/4200 N Hermitage, Chicago, IL	312-929-1119
Bosek, George/118 W Kinzie, Chicago, IL	312-828-0988
Bosy, Peter/564 W Randolph, Chicago, IL	312-559-0042
Boucher, Joe/5765 S Melinda St, Milwaukee, WI	414-281-7653
Bowen, Paul/Box 3375, Wichita, KS	316-263-5537
Boyer, Dick/100 W Chicago, Chicago, IL	312-337-7211
Brackenbury, Vern/1516 N 12th St, Blue Springs, MO	816-229-6703
Braddy, Jim/PO Box 11420, Chicago, IL	312-337-5664
Brandenburg, Jim/708 N 1st St, Minneapolis, MN	612-341-0166
Brandt & Assoc/Route 5 Box 148, Barrington Hills, IL	312-428-6363
Braun Photography/3966 W Bath Rd, Akron, OH	216-666-4540
Brettell, Jim/2122 Morrison Ave, Lakewood, OH	216-228-0890
Brewer, William/6252 S MLK Dr, Chicago, IL	312-493-1147
Brimacombe, Gerald/7212 Mark Terrace, Minneapolis, MN	612-941-5860
Broderson, Fred/215 W Huron, Chicago, IL	312-787-1241
Brody, David & Assoc/6001 N Clark, Chicago, IL	312-761-2735
Brody, Jerry/70 W Hubbard, Chicago, IL	312-329-0660
Brookins, Carl/PO Box 80096, St Paul, MN	612-636-1733
Brooks, John/5663 Carrollton Ave, Indianapolis, IN	317-253-5663
Brosilow, Michael/208 W Kinzie 4th Fl, Chicago, IL	312-645-0628
Brown, Alan J/145 W 4th St, Cincinnati, OH	513-421-5588
Brown, David/900 Jorie Blvd #70, Oak Brook, IL	312-355-4661
Brown, James F/1349 E McMillan St, Cincinnati, OH	513-221-1144
Brown, Ron/1324 N Street, Lincoln, NE	402-476-1760
Brown, Steve/107 W Hubbard, Chicago, IL	312-467-4666
Bruno, Sam/1630 N 23rd, Melrose Park, IL	312-345-0411
Bruton, Jon/3838 W Pine Blvd, St Louis, MO	314-533-6665
Brystrom, Roy/6127 N Ravenswood, Chicago, IL	312-973-2922
Bukva, Walt/118 Anchor Rd, Michigan City, IN	219-872-9469
Bundt, Nancy/4001 Forest Rd, Minneapolis, MN	612-927-7493
Burjoski, David/18 S Kings Hwy, St Louis, MO	314-367-4060
Burns Copeland Photography/6651 N Artesian, Chicago, IL	312-465-3240
Burress, Cliff/343 S Dearborn #608, Chicago, IL	312-427-3335
Burris, Zack/230 E Ohio, Chicago, IL	312-951-0131
Bush, Tim/1138 W 9th St, Cleveland, OH	216-621-2500

C

C-H Studios/600 W Jackson, Chicago, IL	312-726-7830
Cabanban, Orlando/410 S Michigan Ave, Chicago, IL	312-922-1836
CABLE, WAYNE/2212 N RACINE, CHICAGO, IL (P 160)	**312-525-2240**
Cain, C C/420 N Clark, Chicago, IL	312-644-2371
Cairns, Robert/2035 W Charleston #4-SE, Chicago, IL	312-384-3114
Camacho, Mike/124 W Main St, West Dundee, IL	312-428-3135
Camera Works Inc/1260 Carnegie Ave, Cleveland, OH	216-687-1788
Camerawork, Ltd/1032 N LaSalle, Chicago, IL	312-666-8802
Camlen Studio/3695-H N 126th St, Brookfield, WI	414-781-9477
Campbell, Bob/722 Prestige, Joliet, IL	815-725-1862
Candee & Assoc/1212 W Jackson, Chicago, IL	312-829-1212
Caporale, Michael/6710 Madison Rd, Cincinnati, OH	513-561-4011
Carell, Lynn/3 E Ontario #25, Chicago, IL	312-935-1707
Carney, Joann/368 W Huron, Chicago, IL	312-266-7620
Carosella, Tony/4138-A Wyoming, St Louis, MO	314-664-3462
Carr, Steve/311 N Desplaines #608, Chicago, IL	312-454-0984
Carter, Garry/179 Waverly, Ottawa K2P 0V5, ON	613-233-3306
Carter, Mary Ann/5954 Crestview, Indianapolis, IN	317-255-1351
Casalini, Tom/10 1/2 N Main St, Zionsville, IN	317-873-5229
Cascarano, John/657 W Ohio, Chicago, IL	312-733-1212
Caswell, George/700 Washington Ave N #308, Minneapolis, MN	612-332-2729
Cates, Gwendolen/1942 N Dayton, Chicago, IL	312-880-5571
Caulfield, James/430 W Erie, Chicago, IL	312-951-7260
Ceolla, George/5700 Ingersoll Ave, Des Moines, IA	515-279-3508
Cermak Photo/96 Pine Ave, Riverside, IL	312-447-6446
Chadwick Taber Inc/617 W Fulton, Chicago, IL	312-454-0855
Chambers, Tom/153 W Ohio, Chicago, IL	312-828-9488
Chapman, Cam/126 W Kinzie, Chicago, IL	312-222-9242
Chapman, John/125 W Hubbard, Chicago, IL	312-337-7347
Chare, Dave/1045 N Northwest Hwy, Park Ridge, IL	312-696-3188
Charlie Company/2000 Superior Ave #2, Cleveland, OH	216-566-7464
Chauncey, Paul C/1029 N Wichita #13, Wichita, KS	316-262-6733
Cherup, Thomas/PO Box 84, Dearborn Hts, MI	313-561-9376
Chicago Photographers/60 W Superior, Chicago, IL	312-944-4828
Chin, Ruth/108 E Jackson, Muncie, IN	317-284-4582
Chobot, Dennis/2857 E Grand Blvd, Detroit, MI	313-875-6617
Christian Studios Inc/5408 N Main St, Dayton, OH	513-275-3775
Christman, Gerald/985 Ridgewood Dr, Highland Park, IL	312-433-2279
Clark, Harold/9 Lloyd Manor, Islington M9B 5H5, ON	416-236-2958
Clark, Junebug/30419 W Twelve Mile Rd, Farmington Hills, MI	313-478-3666
Clarke, Jim/689 Craig Rd, St Louis, MO	314-872-7506
Clawson, David/6800 Normal Blvd, Lincoln, NE	402-489-1302
CLAWSON, KENT/2530 W WILSON AVE, CHICAGO, IL (P 161)	**312-583-0001**
Clemens, Jim/1147 W Ohio, Chicago, IL	312-280-2289
Click* Chicago/213 W Institute Pl #503, Chicago, IL	312-787-7880
Cloudshooters/Aerial Photo/4620 N Winchester, Chicago, IL	312-334-2841
Clough, Jean/1059 W Columbia, Chicago, IL	312-583-8681
Coats & Greenfield Inc/2928 Fifth Ave S, Minneapolis, MN	612-827-4676
Cocase, Ellen/18 W Hubbard St, Chicago, IL	312-384-0718
Cochrane, Jim/25 1/2 York St #1, Ottawa K1N 5S7, ON	613-234-3099
Cocose, Ellen/18 W Hubbard, Chicago, IL	312-384-0718
Coha, Dan/9 W Hubbard, Chicago, IL	312-664-2270
Coil, Ron Studio/15 W Hubbard St, Chicago, IL	312-321-0155

Photographers

Continued

Please send us your additions and updates.

Compton, Ted/112 N Washington, Hinsdale, IL	312-654-8781
Condie, Thomas M/527 N 27th St, Milwaukee, WI	414-342-6363
Copeland, Burns/6651 N Artesian, Chicago, IL	312-465-3240
Corey, Carl/222 S Morgan, Chicago, IL	312-421-3232
Coster-Mullen, John E/PO Box 1637, Appleton, WI	414-733-9001
Cowan, Ralph/452 N Halsted St, Chicago, IL	312-243-6696
Cox, D E/5856 Hartwell, Dearborn, MI	313-581-0116
CR Studio/1859 W 25th St, Cleveland, OH	216-861-5360
Cralle, Gary/83 Elm Ave #205, Toronto M4W 1P1, ON	416-923-2920
Crane, Arnold/666 N Lake Shore Dr, Chicago, IL	312-337-5544
Crane, Michael/1717 Wyandotte St, Kansas City, MO	816-221-9382
Creightney, Dorrell/116 W Illinois, Chicago, IL	312-528-0816
Crofoot, Ron/6140 Wayzata Blvd, Minneapolis, MN	612-546-0643
Crofton, Bill/205 Ridge Rd #102, Wilmette, IL	312-256-7862
Crosby, Paul/1701 E 79th St #17B, Minneapolis, MN	612-854-3060
Crosson, Milton/700 Walnut St, Cincinnati, OH	513-721-7444
Crowther Photography/2210 Superior Viaduct W, Cleveland, OH	216-566-8066
Culbert-Aguilar, Kathleen/1338 W Carmen, Chicago, IL	312-561-1266
Culver, Steve/115 N Washington Ave #200, Minneapolis, MN	612-332-2425
Cunningham, Elizabeth/1122 W Lunt Ave, Chicago, IL	312-998-1505
Curtis, Lucky/1540 N Park Ave, Chicago, IL	312-787-4422

D

D'Orio, Tony/1147 W Ohio, Chicago, IL	312-421-5532
Dacuisto, Todd/4455 W Bradley Rd #204, Milwaukee, WI	414-352-7527
Dale, LB/7015 Wing Lake Rd, Birmingham, MI	313-851-3296
Dali, Michael/1737 McGee, Kansas City, MO	816-931-0570
Dapkus, Jim/Westfield Photo/Rte 1 Box 247, Westfield, WI	608-296-2623
Davito, Dennis/638 Huntley Heights, Manchester, MO	314-394-0660
Day, Michael/264 Seaton St, Toronto M5A 2T4, ON	416-920-9135
Daytons/701 Industrial Blvd, Minneapolis, MN	612-623-7086
Deahl, David/70 W Hubbard, Chicago, IL	312-644-3187
Debacker, Michael/231 Ohio, Wichita, KS	316-265-2776
Debold, Bill/1801 N Halsted, Chicago, IL	312-337-1177
DeLaittre, Bill/1307 5th St South, Minneapolis, MN	612-936-9840
Delich, Mark/304 W 10th St #200, Kansas City, MO	816-474-6699
DeMarco Photographers/7145 W Addison, Chicago, IL	312-282-1422
DeNatale, Joe/215 W Ohio, Chicago, IL	312-329-0234
Denning, Warren/27 Laurel, Wichita, KS	316-262-4163
Deutsch, Owen/1759 N Sedgewick, Chicago, IL	312-943-7155
DIERINGER, RICK/19 WEST COURT ST, CINCINNATI, OH (P 162)	**513-621-2544**
Dinerstein, Matt/606 W 18th St, Chicago, IL	312-243-4766
Ditlove, Michel/18 W Hubbard, Chicago, IL	312-644-5233
Ditz, Michael/8138 W 9 Mile Rd, Oak Park, MI	313-546-1759
Dollahan, Sam/1043 W Grand, Chicago, IL	312-226-5620
Donner, Michael/5534 S Dorchester, Chicago, IL	312-241-7896
Donofrio, Randy/6459 S Albany, Chicago, IL	312-737-0990
Dovey, Dean/531 S Plymouth Ct #303, Chicago, IL	312-427-0189
Doyle, Tim/1550 E 9 Mile Rd, Ferndale, MI	313-543-9440
Drew, Terry-David/219 W Chicago, Chicago, IL	312-943-0301
Drickey, Pat/406 S 12th St, Omaha, NE	402-344-3786
Drier, David/804 Washington St #3, Evanston, IL	312-475-1992
Dublin, Rick/1019 Currie Ave N, Minneapolis, MN	612-332-8924
DuBroff, Don/2031 W Cortez, Chicago, IL	312-252-7390

E

Eagle, Joe/415 W Superior, Chicago, IL	312-280-1919
Eagle, Lin/415 W Superior, Chicago, IL	312-664-7650
Ebel, Bob Photography/1376 W Carroll, Chicago, IL	312-222-1123
Ebenoh, Tom/8439 Lake Dr, Cedar Hill, MO	314-285-2467
Ebert Photography/227 S Marion, Chicago, IL	312-386-6222
Eckhard, Kurt/1306 S 18th St, St Louis, MO	314-241-1116
Eggebenn, Mark/1217 Center Ave, Dostburg, WI	414-564-2344
Eiler, Lynthia & Terry/330-B Barker Rd Rt 2, Athens, OH	614-592-1280
Einhorn, Mitchell/175 E Delaware Pl, Chicago, IL	312-944-7028
Eisner, Scott Photography/314 W Superior, Chicago, IL	312-670-2217
Elledge, Paul/1808 W Grand Ave, Chicago, IL	312-733-8021
Ellingsen/1411 Peterson, Park Ridge, IL	312-823-0192
Elliott, Peter/405 N Wabash Ave, Chicago, IL	312-329-1370
Elmore, Bob and Assoc/315 S Green St, Chicago, IL	312-641-2731
Englehard, J Versar/522 W Eugene St, Chicago, IL	312-787-2024
Ernst, Elizabeth/1020 Elm St, Winnetka, IL	312-441-8993

ETM Studios/130 S Morgan, Chicago, IL	312-666-0660
Evans, Patricia/1153 E 56th St, Chicago, IL	312-288-2291
Ewert, Steve/17 N Elizabeth, Chicago, IL	312-733-5762

F

Faitage, Nick Photography/1910 W North Ave, Chicago, IL	312-276-9321
Farber, Gerald/10910 Whittier, Detroit, MI	313-371-4161
Farmer, Jerry/620 E Adams, Springfield, IL	217-785-6102
Faverty, Richard/340 W Huron, Chicago, IL	312-943-2648
Feferman, Steve/462 Fern Dr, Wheeling, IL	312-644-5767
Fegley, Richard/6083 N Kirkwood, Chicago, IL	312-527-1114
Feher, Paul/3138 Flame Dr, Oregon, OH	419-698-4254
Feldman, Stephen L/2705 W Agatite, Chicago, IL	312-539-0300
Ferguson, Ken/920 N Franklin St, Chicago, IL	312-642-6255
Ferguson, Scott/7110 Oakland Ave, St Louis, MO	314-647-7466
Ficht, Bill/1207 Ford St, Geneva, IL	312-232-2874
Fichter, Russ/159 W Goethe, Chicago, IL	312-787-9768
Fine Art Photography/1619 Winchester, Schaumberg, IL	312-351-1702
Finlay & Finlay Photo/141 E Main St, Ashland, OH	419-289-3163
Firak Photography/11 E Hubbard, Chicago, IL	312-467-0208
First Light Assoc/78 Rusholme Rd, Toronto M6J 3H6, ON	416-532-6108
Fish Studios/125 W Hubbard, Chicago, IL	312-944-1570
Fitzsimmons, J Kevin/2380 Wimbledon Rd, Columbus, OH	614-457-2010
Fleming, Larry/1029 N Wichita #3, Wichita, KS	316-267-0780
Fletcher, Mike/7467 Kingsbury, St Louis, MO	314-721-2279
Flood, Kevin/1329 Macklind St, St Louis, MO	314-647-2485
Floyd, Bill/215 W Ohio, Chicago, IL	312-321-1770
Fong, John/13 N Huron St, Toledo, OH	419-243-7378
Fontayne Studios Ltd/4528 W Oakton, Skokie, IL	312-676-9872
Ford, Madison/2616 Industrial Row, Troy, MI	313-280-0640
Forrest, Michael/2150 Plainfield Ave NE, Grand Rapids, MI	616-361-2556
Forsyte, Alex/1180 Oak Ridge Dr, Glencoe, IL	312-835-0307
Forth, Ron/316 W 4th St, Cincinnati, OH	513-621-0841
Foss Studio/1711 N Honore, Chicago, IL	312-771-9347
Foss, Kurt/4147 Pleasant Ave S, Minneapolis, MN	612-822-4694
Foster, Richard/157 W Ontario St, Chicago, IL	312-943-9005
Foto-Graphics/2402 N Shadeland Ave, Indianapolis, IN	317-353-6259
Foto/Ed Sacks/Box 7237, Chicago, IL	312-871-4700
Fox Commercial Photo/119 W Hubbard, Chicago, IL	312-664-0162
Fox, Fred & Sons/2746 W Fullerton, Chicago, IL	312-342-3233
Frantz, Ken/706 N Dearborn, Chicago, IL	312-951-1077
Franz, Bill/820 E Wisconsin, Delavan, WI	414-728-3733
Freeman, George/1061 W Balmoral, Chicago, IL	312-275-1122
Frerck, Robert/4158 N Greenview 2nd Fl, Chicago, IL	312-883-1965
Frick, Ken/2255 Barry Dr, Colombus, OH	614-471-3090
Friedman, Susan J/215 W Ohio, Chicago, IL	312-527-1880
Fritz, Tom/2320 N 11th St, Milwaukee, WI	414-263-6700
Futran, Eric/6347 N Lakewood, Chicago, IL	312-338-3735

G

Gabriel Photo/160 E Illinois, Chicago, IL	312-787-2915
Gale, Bill/3041 Aldrich Ave S, Minneapolis, MN	612-827-5858
Gallagher, Colleen/300 W Grand St #440, Chicago, IL	312-467-0021
Galloway, Scott/177 Benson Rd, Akron, OH	216-666-4477
Gardner, Al/7120 Eugene, St Louis, MO	314-752-5278
Gates, Bruce/356 1/2 S Main St, Akron, OH	216-375-5282
Gaymont, Gregory/1812 N Hubbard St, Chicago, IL	312-421-3146
Gerding, Gary/8025 W Dodge Rd, Omaha, NE	402-390-2677
Gerlach, Monte/422 N Taylor, Oak Park, IL	312-848-1193
Getsug, Don/610 N Fairbanks Ct, Chicago, IL	312-440-1311
Giannetti, Joseph/127 N 7th St #402, Minneapolis, MN	612-339-3172
Gibbs, Stu/3244 N Cicero, Chicago, IL	312-725-8457
Gillette, Bill/2917 Eisenhower, Ames, IA	515-294-4340
Gilo, Dave/121 N Broadway, Milwaukee, WI	414-273-1022
GILROY, JOHN/2407 WEST MAIN ST, KALAMAZOO, MI (P 163)	**616-349-6805**
Girard, Connie/316 Telford Ave, Dayton, OH	513-294-2095
Glenn, Eileen/123 W Chestnut, Chicago, IL	312-944-1756
Gluth, Bill/621 W Randolph, Chicago, IL	312-207-0055
Goddard, Will/1496 N Albert St, St Paul, MN	612-483-9068
Goez, Bill/9657 S Winchester, Chicago, IL	312-881-1964
Goff, D R/66 W Wittier St, Columbus, OH	614-443-6530
Goldberg, Lenore/210 Park Ave, Glencoe, IL	312-835-4226
Goldstein, Steven/14982 Country Ridge, St Louis, MO	314-532-0660

Photographers

Continued

Please send us your additions and updates.

Goodman, Anne Margaret/411 N LaSalle, Chicago, IL	312-670-3660
Gorecki Studio/5011 W Fullerton, Chicago, IL	312-622-8146
Goss, James M/1737 McGee St, Kansas City, MO	816-471-8069
Goss, Michael/1548 W Devon, Chicago, IL	312-262-6719
Gould, Christopher/224 W Huron, Chicago, IL	312-944-5545
Gould, Rick Studios/217 N 10th St, St Louis, MO	314-241-4862
Graenicher, Kurt/112 Seventh Ave, Monroe, WI	608-328-8400
Graham-Henry, Diane/2943 N Seminary, Chicago, IL	312-327-4493
Grajczyk, Chris/126 North 3rd St #405, Minneapolis, MN	612-333-6265
Graphic Arts Photo/100 E Ohio, Chicago, IL	312-944-1577
Gray, Walter/1035 W Lake, Chicago, IL	312-733-3800
Grayson, Dan/831 W Cornelia, Chicago, IL	312-477-8659
Greenblatt, William/20 Nantucket Ln, St Louis, MO	314-726-6151
Gregg, Rene/4965 McPherson, St Louis, MO	314-361-1963
Gregg, Robb T/4715 N Ronald St, Harwood Heights, IL	312-867-5445
Gremmler, Paul/221 W Walton, Chicago, IL	312-664-0464
Griffith, Sam/345 N Canal, Chicago, IL	312-648-1900
Griffith, Walter/719 S 75th St, Omaha, NE	402-391-8474
Grignon Studios/1300 W Altgeld Dr, Chicago, IL	312-975-7200
Grippentrag, Dennis/70 E Long Lake Rd, Bloomfield Hills, MI	313-645-2222
Groen, John/676 N LaSalle, Chicago, IL	312-266-2331
Grondin, Timothy/145 W 4th St, Cincinnati, OH	513-421-5588
Gross, Frank/125 W Hubbard, Chicago, IL	312-822-9374
Gross, Werner/465 S College, Valparaiso, IN	219-462-3453
Grubman, Steve/219 W Chicago, Chicago, IL	312-787-2272
Grunewald, Jeff/161 W Harrison St, Chicago, IL	312-663-5799
GSP/156 N Jefferson, Chicago, IL	312-944-3000
Gubin, Mark/2893 S Delaware Ave, Milwaukee, WI	414-482-0640
Guenther, Stephen/1939 Sherman Ave, Evanston, IL	312-864-5381
Guerry, Tim/411 S Sangamon #3B, Chicago, IL	312-666-0303
H Haberman, Mike/529 S 7th St #427, Minneapolis, MN	612-338-4696
Haefner, Jim/1407 B Allen, Troy, MI	313-583-4747
Haines, W C (Bill)/3101 Mercier Ste 484, Kansas City, MO	816-531-0561
Halbe, Harrison/744 Office Pkwy #175, St Louis, MO	314-993-1145
Hall, Brian/1015 N LaSalle St, Chicago, IL	312-642-6764
Haller, Pam/215 W Huron, Chicago, IL	312-649-0920
Hamill, Larry/77 Deshler, Columbus, OH	614-444-2798
Hammarlund, Vern/135 Park St, Troy, MI	313-588-5533
Hampton, Chris/120 W Kinzie St, Chicago, IL	312-467-0135
Handley, Robert E/1920 E Croxton, Bloomington, IL	309-828-4661
Harbron, Patrick/366 Adelaide St E #331, Toronto, ON	416-863-9412
Harding Studio/727 Hudson, Chicago, IL	312-943-4010
Harlan, Bruce/52922 Camellia Dr, South Bend, IN	219-239-7350
Harquail, John/67 Mowat Ave #40, Toronto M6K 3E3,	416-535-1620
Harrig, Rick/3316 South 66th Ave, Omaha, NE	402-397-5529
Harris, Bart/70 W Hubbard St, Chicago, IL	312-751-2977
Hart, Bob/116 W Illinois, Chicago, IL	312-644-3636
Harvey, Jeff/PO Box 262, Palos Hts, IL	312-535-4900
Hatcher, Lois/32 W 58th St, Kansas City, MO	816-361-6230
Hauser, Marc/1810 W Cortland, Chicago, IL	312-486-4381
Hawker, Chris/119 N Peoria, Chicago, IL	312-829-4766
Hedrich-Blessing/11 W Illinois St, Chicago, IL	312-321-1151
Heil, Peter/213 W Institute Pl #707, Chicago, IL	312-544-9130
Heilbron, Kenneth/1357 N Wells, Chicago, IL	312-787-1238
Helmick, William/129 Geneva, Elmhurst, IL	312-834-4798
Henebry, Jeanine/1154 Locust Rd, Wilmette, IL	312-251-8747
Henning, Paul/PO Box 92218, Milwaukee, WI	414-765-9441
Hermann, Dell/676 N LaSalle, Chicago, IL	312-664-1461
Hertzberg, Richard/436 N Clark, Chicago, IL	312-836-0464
Hetisimer, Larry/1630 5th Ave, Moline, IL	309-797-1010
Hill, Roger/4040 W River Dr, Comstock Park, MI	616-784-9620
Hillery, John/PO Box 2916, Detroit, MI	313-345-9511
Hirneisen, Richard/306 S Washington St #218, Royal Oak, MI	313-399-2410
Hirschfeld, Corson/316 W Fourth St, Cincinnati, OH	513-241-0550
Hodes, Charles S/233 E Erie, Chicago, IL	312-951-1186
Hodges, Charles/539 W North Ave, Chicago, IL	312-664-8179
Hoffman-Wilber Inc/618 W Jackson, Chicago, IL	312-454-0303
Holcepl, Robert/2479 W 11th St, Cleveland, OH	216-621-3838
Holographics Design System/1134 W Washington, Chicago, IL	312-226-1007
Holzemer, Buck/3448 Chicago Ave, Minneapolis, MN	612-824-3874

Honor, David/415 W Superior, Chicago, IL	312-751-1644
Hooke Photography/1147 W Ohio, Chicago, IL	312-829-4568
Hoppe, Ed Photography/401 W Superior, Chicago, IL	312-787-2136
HOSKINS, SARAH/1206 ISABELLA, WILMETTE, IL (P 165)	**312-256-5724**
Houghton, Michael/Studiohio/55 E Spring St, Columbus, OH	614-224-4885
Howrani, Armeen/2820 E Grand Blvd, Detroit, MI	313-875-3123
Hrdlicka, Mitch/4201 Levinworth, Omaha, NE	402-551-0887
Hsi, Kai/160 E Illinois, Chicago, IL	312-642-9853
Hurling, Robert/225 W Huron, Chicago, IL	312-944-2022
Hutson, David/8120 Juniper, Prairie Village, KS	913-383-1123
Hyman, Randy/7709 Carnell Ave, St Louis, MO	314-721-7489
I Iann-Hutchins/2044 Euclid Ave, Cleveland, OH	216-579-1570
Image Productions/115 W Church, Libertyville, IL	312-680-7100
Image Studio/1100 S Lynndale, Appleton, WI	414-739-7824
Imagematrix/2 Garfield Pl, Cincinnati, OH	513-381-1380
Imagination Unlimited/PO Box 268709, Chicago, IL	312-764-1880
Imbrogno/411 N LaSalle St, Chicago, IL	312-644-7333
Inflight Photo/3114 St Mary's, Omaha, NE	402-345-2164
INGRAM, RUSSELL/1000-02 W MONROE ST, CHICAGO, IL (P 166,167)	**312-829-4652**
Ingve, Jan & Assoc/128 Wedgewood Dr, Barrington, IL	312-381-3456
International Photo Corp/1035 Wesley, Evanston, IL	312-475-6400
Irving, Gary/PO Box 38, Wheaton, IL	312-653-0641
Isenberg, Bill/27059 Arden Park Circle, Farmington Hills, MI	313-478-9709
Isenberger, Brent/1710-J Gutherie Ave, Des Moines, IA	515-262-5466
Issacs, Michael/517 W 3rd St #306, Cincinnati, OH	513-721-6596
Itahara, Tets/676 N LaSalle, Chicago, IL	312-649-0606
Iwata, John/336 W 15th Ave, Oshkosh, WI	414-424-0317
Izokaitis, Kastytis/441 N Clark, Chicago, IL	312-321-1388
Izquierdo, Abe/325 W Huron, Chicago, IL	312-787-9784
Izui, Richard/315 W Walton, Chicago, IL	312-266-8029
J Jackson, David/1021 Hall St, Grand Rapids, MI	616-243-3325
Jackson, Jack/207 E Buffalo #514, Milwaukee, WI	414-289-0890
Jacob, David/6412 N Glenwood, Chicago, IL	312-274-9191
Jacobs, Todd/3336 N Sheffield, Chicago, IL	312-472-4401
Jacobson, Scott/3435 N County Rd 18, Plymouth, MN	612-546-9191
Jacquin Enterprise/1219 Holly Hills, St Louis, MO	314-832-4221
James Studio/730 Lee St, Des Plaines, IL	312-824-0007
James, E Michael/10757 S Peoria, Chicago, IL	312-928-5908
JAMES, PHILLIP MACMILLAN/2300 HAZELWOOD AVE, ST PAUL, MN (P 168)	**612-777-2303**
Jedd, Joseph/5931 N Keating, Chicago, IL	312-685-0641
Jenkins, David/1416 S Michigan Ave, Chicago, IL	312-922-2299
Jennings, Bill/1322 S Wabash, Chicago, IL	312-987-0124
Jensen, Michael/1101 Stinson Blvd NE, Minneapolis, MN	612-379-1944
Jilling, Helmut/1759 State Rd, Cuyahoga Falls, OH	216-928-1330
Jo, Isac/4344 N Wolcott, Chicago, IL	312-472-1607
Jochim, Gary/1324 1/2 N Milwaukee, Chicago, IL	312-252-5250
JOEL, DAVID/1342 W HOOD AVE, CHICAGO, IL (P 169)	**312-262-0794**
Johnson, Dave/679 E Mandoline, Madison Hts, MI	313-589-0066
Johnson, Donald/2807 Brindle, Northbrook, IL	312-480-9336
Johnson, Jim/802 W Evergreen, Chicago, IL	312-943-8864
Johnson, Wayne/6727 12th Ave S, Minneapolis, MN	612-899-0100
Jones, Arvell/8232 W McNichols, Detroit, MI	313-342-2000
Jones, Brent/9121 S Merrill Ave, Chicago, IL	312-933-1174
Jones, Dawson/46 E Franklin St, Dayton, OH	513-435-1121
Jones, Dick/325 W Huron St, Chicago, IL	312-642-0242
Jones, Duane/5605 Chicago Ave S, Minneapolis, MN	612-823-8173
Jones, Harrison/727 N Hudson #405, Chicago, IL	312-337-4997
Jons Studio/35 E Wacker, Chicago, IL	312-236-0243
Jordan, Jack/840 John St, Evansville, IN	812-423-7676
Jordano, Dave/1335 N Wells, Chicago, IL	312-280-8212
Joseph, Mark/1007 N La Salle, Chicago, IL	312-951-5333
Justice Patterson Studio/7613 Production Dr, Cincinnati, OH	513-761-4023
K Kahn, Dick/21750 Doral Rd, Waukesha, WI	414-784-1994
Kalyniuk, Jerry/4243 N Winchester, Chicago, IL	312-975-8973
Kapal Photo Studio/233 Ridge Rd, Munster, IN	219-836-2176
Kaplan, Dick/1694 First St, Highland Park, IL	312-432-0632
Karant & Assoc/215 W Ohio St, Chicago, IL	312-527-1880

Kaspar, Tom/650 S Clark, Chicago, IL	312-987-0956
Kauck, Jeff/205 W Fourth, Cincinnati, OH	513-241-5435
KAUFFMAN, KIM/444 LENTZ COURT, LANSING, MI (P 170)	**517-371-3036**
Kavula, Ken/19 E Pearson, Chicago, IL	312-280-9060
Kazu Studio/1211 W Webster, Chicago, IL	312-348-5393
KEAN, CHRISTOPHER/624 WEST ADAMS ST, CHICAGO, IL	
(P 154,155)	**312-559-0880**
Keeling, Robert/26 E Huron St, Chicago, IL	312-944-5680
Keisman & Keisman/920 N Franklin St, Chicago, IL	312-268-7955
Kelly, Tony/828 Colfax, Evanston, IL	312-864-0488
Kem, Patrick/1832 E 38th St, Minneapolis, MN	612-729-8989
Ketchum, Art/1 E Oak, Chicago, IL	312-544-1222
Kezar, Mitch/2207 Oakview Ln N, Minneapolis, MN	612-559-1733
Kinast, Susan/1035 Lake St, Chicago, IL	312-738-0068
King, Budde/1914 Gardner Rd, Westchester, IL	312-865-8316
King, Jay Studios/1024 W Armitage, Chicago, IL	312-327-0011
Kingsbury, Andrew/700 N Washington #306, Minneapolis, MN	612-340-1919
Kitahara, Joe/304 W 10th St, Kansas City, MO	816-474-6699
Klein Photography/952 W Lake, Chicago, IL	312-226-1878
Klein, Daniel/306 W 8th, Kansas City, MO	816-474-6491
Klutho, Dave/4617 Brookroyal Ct, St Louis, MO	314-487-3626
Knize, Karl/1024 W Armitage, Chicago, IL	312-243-5503
Kodama, Kiyoshi/424 N Benton, St Charles, MO	314-946-9247
KOGAN, DAVID/1313 W RANDOLPH ST #314, CHICAGO, IL	
(P 171)	**312-243-1929**
Kolesar, Jerry Photographics/679 E Mandoline, Madison Hts, MI	313-589-0066
Kolze, Larry/22 W Erie, Chicago, IL	312-266-8352
Kompa, Jeff/25303 Lorain Rd, N Olmstead, OH	216-777-1611
Kondas, Thom Assoc/PO Box 1162, Indianapolis, IN	317-637-1414
Kondor, Linda/430 N Clark St, Chicago, IL	312-642-7365
Korab, Balthazar/PO Box 895, Troy, MI	313-641-8881
Krantz, John/1791 W 31st Pl, Cleveland, OH	216-241-3411
Krantzen Studios/100 S Ashland, Chicago, IL	312-942-1900
Kraus, Gregor/213 W Institute Pl, Chicago, IL	312-266-6068
Krejci, Donald/1825 E 18th St, Cleveland, OH	216-831-4730
Krinsky, Jon A/85 Tahlequah Trail, Springboro, OH	513-746-5230
Krueger, Dick/660 W Grand Ave, Chicago, IL	312-243-2730
Kufrin, George/500 N Dearborn, Chicago, IL	312-787-2854
Kulp, Curtis/222 W Ontario, Chicago, IL	312-266-0477
Kusel, Bob/1651 W Touhy, Chicago, IL	312-787-8220
L Lacey, Ted/4733 S Woodlawn, Chicago, IL	312-624-2419
Lacroix, Pat/25 Brant St, Toronto, ON	416-864-1858
Laden, Murray/110 W Kinzie, Chicago, IL	312-222-0555
Landau, Allan/1147 West Ohio, Chicago, IL	312-942-1382
Landis, Mike/447 N Rochester Rd #14, Clawson, MI	313-589-1788
Lane, Jack Studio/5 W Grand Ave, Chicago, IL	312-337-2326
Lanza, Scott/, Milwaukee, WI	414-482-4114
LaRoche, Andre/32588 Deguinder, Warren, MI	313-978-7373
Larsen, Kim/ Soren Studio/325 N Hoyne, Chicago, IL	312-666-5885
LaTona, Tony/1317 E 5th, Kansas City, MO	816-474-3119
Lauth, Lyal/833 N Orleans, Chicago, IL	312-787-5615
Leavenworth Photo Inc/929 West St, Lansing, MI	517-482-4658
Leavitt, Debbie/2756 N Pine Grove Ave #212, Chicago, IL	312-348-2833
Leavitt, Fred/916 Carmen, Chicago, IL	312-784-2344
Lecat, Paul/820 N Franklin, Chicago, IL	312-664-7122
Lee, Robert Photo/1512 Northlin Dr, St Louis, MO	314-965-5832
Lee, Terry/4420 N Paulina, Chicago, IL	312-561-1153
LeGrand, Peter/413 Sandburg, Park Forest, IL	312-747-4923
Lehn, John/2601 E Franklin Ave, Minneapolis, MN	612-338-0257
Leick, Jim/1709 Washington Ave, St Louis, MO	314-241-2354
Leinwohl, Stef/439 W Oakdale #3, Chicago, IL	312-348-5862
Leonard, Steve/825 W Gunnison, Chicago, IL	312-275-8833
Leslie, William F/53 Tealwood Dr, Creve Coeur, MO	314-993-8349
Levey, Don/15 W Delaware Pl, Chicago, IL	312-329-9040
Levin, Jonathan/1035 W Lake St, Chicago, IL	312-226-3898
Levin, Marty/215 W Ohio, Chicago, IL	312-787-2586
Lewandowski, Leon/325 W Huron, Chicago, IL	312-467-9577
Lieberman, Archie/1135 Asbury, Evanston, IL	312-475-8508
Lightfoot, Robert/311 Good Ave, Des Plaines, IL	312-297-5447
Linc Studio/1163 Tower, Schaumberg, IL	312-882-1311
Lindblade, George R/PO Box 1342, Sioux City, IA	712-255-4346
Lindwall, Martin/1269 Briarwood Ln, Libertyville, IL	312-680-1578
Lipschis, Helmut Photography/903 W Armitage, Chicago, IL	312-871-2003
Liss, Leroy/6243 N Ridgeway Ave, Chicago, IL	312-539-4540
Little, Scott/1515 Linden, Des Moines, IA	515-243-4428
Lohbeck, Stephen/1226 Ambassador Blvd, St Louis, MO	314-991-4657
Lords Studio Ltd/162 N Clinton, Chicago, IL	312-332-0208
Lowenthal, Jeff/20 E Randolph #7948, Chicago, IL	312-938-0130
Lowry, Miles/222 S Morgan #3B, Chicago, IL	312-666-0882
Loynd, Mel/208 Queen St S, Streetsville L5M1L5, ON	416-821-0477
Lucas, John V/4100 W 40th St, Chicago, IL	312-927-4500
Lucas, Joseph/20 N Wacker Dr #1425, Chicago, IL	312-782-6905
Ludwigs, David/3600 Troost St, Kansas City, MO	816-531-1363
Lvles, David/401 W Superior 5th Fl, Chicago, IL	312-642-1223
M **MAAS, CURT/5860 MERLE HAY RD/BOX 127, JOHNSTON, IA (P 176)**	**515-270-3732**
MacDonald, Al/32 Martin Lane, Elk Grove, IL	312-437-8850
MACK, RICHARD/2119 LINCOLN, EVANSTON, IL (P 172)	**312-869-7794**
MacTavish Arndt, David/4620 N Winchester, Chicago, IL	312-334-2841
Maguire, Jim/144 Lownsdale, Akron, OH	216-630-9050
Maki & Smith Photo/6156 Olson Mem Hwy, Golden Valley, MN	612-541-4722
Malinowski, Stan/1150 N State #312, Chicago, IL	312-951-6715
Mally Assoc/20 W Hubbard #3E, Chicago, IL	312-644-4367
Maloney, Michael/517 W Third St, Cincinnati, OH	513-721-2384
Manarchy, Dennis/229 W Illinois, Chicago, IL	312-828-9117
Mandel, Avis/40 E Cedar, Chicago, IL	312-642-4776
Mankus, Gary/1520 N LaSalle, Chicago, IL	312-787-5438
Mann, Milton & Joan/PO Box 413, Evanston, IL	312-777-5656
Manning, Russell/905 Park Ave, Minneapolis, MN	612-338-7761
Mar, Jan/111 Westgate, Oak Park, IL	312-524-1898
Marcus, Joel/23309 Commerce Park Rd, Cleveland, OH	216-831-0688
Marienthal, Michael/1832 S Halsted, Chicago, IL	312-226-5505
Marovitz, Bob/3450 N Lake Shore Dr, Chicago, IL	312-975-1265
Marsalle/PO Box 300063, Minneapolis, MN	612-872-8717
Marshall, Don Photography/361 W Superior, Chicago, IL	312-944-0720
Marshall, Paul/117 N Jefferson St #304, Chicago, IL	312-559-1270
Marshall, Simeon/1043 W Randolph, Chicago, IL	312-243-9500
Martin, Barbara E/46 Washington Terrace, St Louis, MO	314-361-0838
Marvy, Jim/41 Twelfth Ave N, Minneapolis, MN	612-935-0307
Masheris, R Assoc Inc/1338 Hazel Ave, Deerfield, IL	312-945-2055
Mathews, Bruce/16520 Ellison Way, Independence, MO	816-373-2920
Matlow, Linda/300 N State St #3926, Chicago, IL	312-321-9071
Matusik, Jim/3714 N Racine, Chicago, IL	312-327-5615
Mauney, Michael/1405 Judson Ave, Evanston, IL	312-869-7720
May, Ron/PO Box 8359, Ft Wayne, IN	219-483-7872
May, Sandy/18 N 4th St #506, Minneapolis, MN	612-332-0272
McCabe, Mark/1301 E 12th St, Kansas City, MO	816-474-6491
McCall Photo/900 N Franklin, Chicago, IL	312-951-5525
McCann, Larry/666 W Hubbard, Chicago, IL	312-942-1924
McCann, Michael/27 N 4th St, Minneapolis, MN	612-333-2115
McCay, Larry Inc/PO Box 927, Mishawaka, IN	219-259-1414
McClelan, Thompson/206 S First St, Champaign, IL	217-356-2767
McConnell & McConnell/1313 W Randolph #317, Chicago, IL	312-738-1444
McDonald, Neal/1515 W Cornelia, Chicago, IL	312-525-5401
McDunn, James/PO Box 8053, Rolling Meadows, IL	312-934-4288
McGleam, Patrick/5422 N Paulina, Chicago, IL	312-989-0248
McHale Studios Inc/2349 Victory Pkwy, Cincinnati, OH	513-961-1454
McInturff, Steve/1795 E Kings Creek, Urbana, OH	513-789-3590
McKay, Doug/7830 Cornell, St Louis, MO	314-863-7167
McKinley, William/847 W Jackson, Chicago, IL	312-666-5400
McLuckie Graphic Photo/121 S Wheeling, Wheeling, IL	312-639-8900
McMahon, Franklin/1319 Chestnut, Wilmette, IL	312-256-5528
McNichol, Greg/1638 W Greenleaf Ave, Chicago, IL	312-973-1032
Mead, Robert/711 Hillgrove Ave, La Grange, IL	312-354-8300
Meier, Lori/9100 Guthrie, St Louis, MO	314-428-0120
Meineke, David/703 E Golf Rd, Schaumburg, IL	312-884-6006
Melkus, Larry/679-E Mandoline, Madison Hts, MI	313-589-0066
Meoli, Rick/710 N Tucker #306, St Louis, MO	314-231-6038
Merrithew, Jim/PO Box 1510, Almonte K0A 1A0, ON	613-729-3862
Meyer, Fred/415 N Dearborn, Chicago, IL	312-527-4873

Photographers

Continued

Please send us your additions and updates.

Meyer, Gordon/216 W Ohio, Chicago, IL	312-642-9303
Meyer, Jim/7727 Frontier Trail, Chanhassen, MN	612-934-2908
Meyer, Robert/208 W Kinzie St, Chicago, IL	312-467-1430
Michael, William/225 W Hubbard, Chicago, IL	312-644-6137
Michl, Joe/252 First Ave N, Minneapolis, MN	612-375-0180
Micus Photo/2777 S Finley, Downers Grove, IL	312-627-8181
Mignard Associates/1950-R South Glenstone, Springfield, MO	417-881-7422
Mihalevich, Mike/9235 Somerset Dr, Overland Park, KS	913-642-6466
Miller Photo/7237 W Devon, Chicago, IL	312-631-1255
Miller, Buck/PO Box 33, Milwaukee, WI	414-273-0985
Miller, Daniel D/1551 North Orleans, Chicago, IL	312-944-7192
Miller, Frank/6016 Blue Circle Dr, Minnetonka, MN	612-935-8888
Miller, Pat/1101 Stinson Blvd NE, Minneapolis, MN	612-378-9043
Miller, Spider/833 North Orleans, Chicago, IL	312-944-2880
Miller, William F/618 W Jackson, Chicago, IL	312-648-1818
Milne, Brian/78 Rusholme Rd, Toronto M6J 3H6, ON	416-532-6108
Mitchell, John Sr/2617 Greenleaf, Elk Grove, IL	312-956-8230
Mitchell, Rick/652 W Grand, Chicago, IL	312-829-1700
Mitzit, Bruce/331 S Peoria/Box 6638, Chicago, IL	312-508-1937
Mohlenkamp, Steve/632 West Pleasant, Freeport, IL	815-235-1918
Moore, Bob c/o Mofoto Graphics/1615 S 9th St, St Louis, MO	314-231-1430
Moore, Dan/1029 N Wichita #9, Wichita, KS	316-264-4168
Morrill, Dan/1811 N Sedgewick, Chicago, IL	312-787-5095
Morris, Merle Photography/614 Fifth Ave S, Minneapolis, MN	612-338-7829
Morton White & Cunningham/6665-H Huntley Rd, Columbus, OH	614-885-8687
Moshman Photo/401 W Superior, Chicago, IL	312-869-6770
Moss, Jean/222 W Ontario, Chicago, IL	312-787-0260
Mottel, Ray/760 Burr Oak Rd, Westmont, IL	312-323-3616
Moustakas, Daniel/1255 Rankin, Troy, MI	313-589-0100
Moy, Clinton Photography/4728 N Spaulding, Chicago, IL	312-539-4297
Moy, Willie/364 W Erie, Chicago, IL	312-943-1863
Mueller, Linda/1900 Delmar, St Louis, MO	314-621-2400
Musich, Jack/325 W Huron, Chicago, IL	312-644-5000
Mutrux, John L/5217 England, Shawnee Missn, KS	913-722-4343

NO

Nagler, Monte/38881 Lancaster Dr, Farmington Hills, MI	313-661-0826
Nano, Ed/3413 Rocky River Rd, Cleveland, OH	216-941-3373
Nathanson, Neal/7531 Cromwell, St Louis, MO	314-727-7244
Nawrocki, William S/PO Box 43-007, Chicago, IL	312-445-8920
Neal, Les/319 N Albany, Chicago, IL	312-722-0116
Nelson, Tom/400 First Ave N, Minneapolis, MN	612-339-3579
Neumann, Robert/101 S Mason St, Saginaw, MI	517-790-9000
Nexus Productions/10-A Ashdale Ave, Toronto M4L 2Y7, ON	416-463-5078
Niedorf, Steve/700 N Washington, Minneapolis, MN	612-332-7124
Norris, James/2301 N Lowell, Chicago, IL	312-342-1050
Northlight Studio/1539 E 22nd St, Cleveland, OH	216-621-3111
Novak, Ken/2483 N Bartlett Ave, Milwaukee, WI	414-962-6953
Novak, Sam/230 W Huron, Chicago, IL	312-664-6733
Nozicka, Steve/314 W Institute Pl, Chicago, IL	312-787-8925
Nugent Wenckus Inc/110 Northwest Hwy, Des Plaines, IL	312-694-4151
O'BARSKI, DON/17239 PARKSIDE, S HOLLAND, IL (P 173)	**312-596-0606**
O'Rourke, John/PO Box 52, Wilmington, OH	513-382-3782
Oakes, Kenneth Ltd/902 Yale Ln, Highland Park, IL	312-432-4809
Oberle, Frank/309 N Riverside Dr, St Charles, MO	314-946-0554
Officer, Hollis/819 Broadway 6th Fl, Kansas City, MO	816-474-5501
Okita, Clyde/865 N Sangamon 5th Fl, Chicago, IL	312-829-8283
OLAUSEN, JUDY/213 1/2 N WASHINGTON AVE, MINNEAPOLIS, MN (P 156)	**612-332-5009**
Olsson, Russ/215 W Illinois, Chicago, IL	312-329-9358
Ontiveros, Don/5516 N Kenmore Ave, Chicago, IL	312-878-9009
Oscar & Assoc/63 E Adams, Chicago, IL	312-922-0056
Oxendorf, Eric/1442 N Franklin Pl Box 92337, Milwaukee, WI	414-273-0654

P

Pacific Studio/632 Krenz Ave, Cary, IL	312-639-5654
Palmisano, Vito/1147 W Ohio St, Chicago, IL	312-565-0524
Panama, David/1100 N Dearborn, Chicago, IL	312-642-7095
Panich, Wil/20 W Hubbard, Chicago, IL	312-828-0742
Parker, Norman/710 N 2nd St #300N, St Louis, MO	314-621-8100
Parks, Jim/210 W Chicago, Chicago, IL	312-321-1193
Passman, Roger/719 W Willow, Chicago, IL	312-664-4085

Paszkowski, Rick/1637 W Estes, Chicago, IL	312-761-3018
Paternite, David/1245 S Clevelnd-Massilon Rd #3, Akron, OH	216-666-7720
Paulson, Bill/5358 Golla Rd, Stevens Point, WI	715-341-6100
Payne, John/430 W Erie, Chicago, IL	312-280-8414
Payne, Scott/611 Lunt Unit B, Schaumburg, IL	312-980-3337
Pazovski, Kazik/2340 Laredo Ave, Cincinnati, OH	513-281-0030
Perkins, Ray/222 S Morgan St, Chicago, IL	312-421-3438
Perman, Craig/1645 Hennepin #311, Minneapolis, MN	612-338-7727
Perno, Jack/1147 W Ohio, Chicago, IL	312-829-5292
Perraud, Gene/535 N Michigan #2601, Chicago, IL	312-564-5278
Perspective Inc/2322 Pennsylvania St, Fort Wayne, IN	219-424-8136
Peterson, Garrick/216 W Ohio St, Chicago, IL	312-266-8986
Peterson, Richard Photo/529 S 7th St #315, Minneapolis, MN	612-341-0480
Petroff, Tom/19 W Hubbard, Chicago, IL	312-836-0411
Phelps Photo/1057 W Dakin, Chicago, IL	312-248-2536
Phillips, David R/1230 W Washington Blvd, Chicago, IL	312-733-3277
Photo Concepts Inc/23042 Commerce Dr #2001, Farmington Hills, MI	313-477-4301
Photo Design/815 Main St, Cincinnati, OH	513-421-5588
Photo Group/1945 Techny Rd, Northbrook, IL	312-564-9220
Photo Ideas Inc/804 W Washington Blvd, Chicago, IL	312-666-3100
PHOTO IMAGES/430 W ERIE ST, CHICAGO, IL (P 175)	**312-664-5953**
The Photo Place/4739 Butterfield, Hillside, IL	312-544-1222
Photographic Arts/624 W Adams, Chicago, IL	312-876-0818
Photographic Illustrators/405 1/2 E Main, Muncie, IN	317-288-1454
The Picture Place/689 Craig Rd, St Louis, MO	314-872-7506
Pierce, Rod/236 Portland Ave, Minneapolis, MN	612-332-2670
Pintozzi, Peter/42 E Chicago, Chicago, IL	312-266-7775
PIONEER HI-BRED INTERNATIONAL/5860 MERLE HAY RD/ BOX 127, JOHNSTON, IA (P 176,177)	**515-270-3732**
Pitt, Tom/1201 W Webster, Chicago, IL	312-281-5662
Pohlman Studios Inc/527 N 27th St, Milwaukee, WI	414-342-6363
Pokempner, Marc/1453 W Addison, Chicago, IL	312-525-4567
Polaski, James/9 W Hubbard, Chicago, IL	312-644-3686
Poli, Frank/158 W Huron, Chicago, IL	312-944-3924
Polin, Jack Photography/7306 Crawford, Lincolnwood, IL	312-676-4312
Pomerantz, Ron/325 W Huron #406, Chicago, IL	312-787-6407
Poon On Wong, Peter/516 First Ave #305, Minneapolis, MN	612-340-0798
Poplis, Paul/3599 Refugee Rd Bldg B, Columbus, OH	614-231-2942
Portnoy, Lewis/5 Carole Lane, St Louis, MO	314-567-5700
Powell, Jim/326 W Kalamazoo, Kalamazoo, MI	616-381-2302
Price, Paul/8138 W Nine Mile Rd, Oak Park, MI	313-546-1759
Pritzner, Al/8192 Nieman Rd, Lenexa, KS	913-492-0396
Proctor & Proctor Photo/18126 Center Ave, Homewood, IL	312-798-6849
Progressive Visuals/2550 Northridge Ave, Arlington Hgts, IL	312-949-0886
PRZEKOP, HARRY J/332 S CUYLER, OAK PARK, IL (P 178)	**312-524-9743**
Puffer, David/213 W Institute, Chicago, IL	312-266-7540
Puza, Greg/PO Box 1986, Milwaukee, WI	414-444-9882
Pyrzynski, Larry/691 N Sangamon, Chicago, IL	312-472-6550

QR

Quinn, James/518 S Euclid, Oak Park, IL	312-383-0654
Quist, Bruce/1370 N Milwaukee, Chicago, IL	312-252-3921
Rack, Ron/215 E Ninth St, Cincinnati, OH	513-421-6267
Raczynski, Walter/117 North Jefferson, Chicago, IL	312-454-0680
Radencich, Michael/1007 McGee, Kansas City, MO	816-421-5076
Radlund & Associates/4704 Pflaum Rd, Madison, WI	608-222-8177
Randall, Bob/325 W Huron, Chicago, IL	312-235-4613
Reames-Hanusin Studio/3306 Commercial Ave, Northbrook, IL	312-564-2706
Reed, Dick/1330 Coolidge, Troy, MI	313-280-0090
Reeve, Catherine/822 Madison St, Evanston, IL	312-864-8298
Reffner, Wayne/4178 Dayton-Xenia Rd, Dayton, OH	513-429-2760
Reid, Ken/800 W Huron #3S, Chicago, IL	312-733-2121
Reiss, Ray/2144 N Leavitt, Chicago, IL	312-384-3245
Remington, George/1455 W 29th St, Cleveland, OH	216-241-1440
Renerts, Peter Studio/633 Huron Rd, Cleveland, OH	216-781-2440
Renken, Roger/PO Box 11010, St Louis, MO	314-394-5055
Reuben, Martin/1231 Superior Ave, Cleveland, OH	216-781-8644
Ricco, Ron/207 E Buffalo #619, Milwaukee, WI	414-271-4360
Rice, Ted/2599 N 4th St, Columbus, OH	614-263-8656
Rich, Larry/29731 Everett, Southfield, MI	313-557-7676
Ritter, Gene/2440 W 14th St, Cleveland, OH	216-781-9461

Robert, Francois/740 N Wells, Chicago, IL	312-787-0777
Robinson, David/1147 W Ohio, Chicago, IL	312-942-1650
Roessler, Ryan/401 W Superior, Chicago, IL	312-951-8702
Rogers, Bill Arthur/846 Wesley, Oak Park, IL	312-848-3900
Rogowski, Tom/214 E 8th St, Cincinnati, OH	513-621-3826
Rohman, Jim/2254 Marengo, Toledo, OH	419-865-0234
Rosmis, Bruce/118 W Ohio, Chicago, IL	312-787-9046
Ross, Allan/3221 S Morgan, Chicago, IL	312-376-1011
Rostron, Philip/489 Wellington St W, Toronto, ON	416-596-6587
Rothrock, Douglas/215 W Ohio, Chicago, IL	312-951-9045
Rottinger, Ed/5409 N Avers, Chicago, IL	312-583-2917
Rowley, Joe/368 W Huron, Chicago, IL	312-266-7620
Rubin, Laurie/719 W Willow St, Chicago, IL	312-266-1131
Rush, Michael/415 Delaware, Kansas City, MO	816-471-1200
Russetti, Andy/1260 Carnegie St, Cleveland, OH	216-687-1788
Rustin, Barry/934 Glenwood Rd, Glenview, IL	312-724-7600
Rutt, Don/324 Munson St, Traverse City, MI	616-946-2727
Rutten, Bonnie/414 Sherburne Ave, St Paul, MN	612-224-5777
Ryan, Gary/23245 Woodward, Ferndale, MI	313-861-8199

S

S T Studio/325 W Huron St #711, Chicago, IL	312-943-2565
Sacco Photography Ltd/833 North Orleans St, Chicago, IL	312-943-5757
SACKS, ANDREW/20727 SCIO CHURCH RD, CHELSEA, MI (P 179)	**313-475-2310**
Sacks, Ed/Box 7237, Chicago, IL	312-871-4700
Sadin-Schnair Photo/820 N Franklin, Chicago, IL	312-944-1434
Sala, Don/950 W Willow, Chicago, IL	312-751-2858
Salter, Tom/685 Pallister, Detroit, MI	313-874-1155
Saltzman, Ben/700 N Washington, Minneapolis, MN	612-332-5112
Sanders, Kathy/368 W Huron, Chicago, IL	312-943-2627
Sanderson, Glenn/2936 Gross St, Green Bay, WI	414-336-6500
Sandoz Studios/415 Huron #3, Chicago, IL	312-440-0004
Sapecki, Roman/2479 W 11th St, Cleveland, OH	216-621-3838
Sarnacki, Michael/18101 Oakwood Blvd, Dearborn, MI	313-548-1149
Sauer, Neil W/1554 S 7th St, St Louis, MO	314-241-9300
Schaefer, Ginzy/4336 Genesse, Kansas City, MO	816-753-4068
Schanuel, Anthony/10901 Oasis Dr, St Louis, MO	314-849-3495
Schaugnessy, Abe/32 Martin Ln, Elk Grove Village, IL	312-437-8850
Schewe, Jeff/624 West Willow, Chicago, IL	312-951-6334
Schnaible, Gerry/1888 Jamestown Cir, Hoffman Estates, IL	312-289-6090
Scholtes, Marc/726 Central Ave NE, Minneapolis, MN	612-378-1888
Schrempp, Erich/932 W Washington Blvd, Chicago, IL	312-454-3237
Schridde, Charles/600 Ajax Dr, Madison Hts, MI	313-589-0111
Schroeder, Loranelle/400 N First Ave 6th Fl, Minneapolis, MN	612-339-3191
Schube-Soucek/1735 Carmen Dr, Elk Grove Village, IL	312-439-0640
Schuemann, Bill/1591 S Belvoir Blvd, South Euclid, OH	216-382-4409
Schuessler, Dave/40 E Delaware, Chicago, IL	312-787-6868
Schuette, Bob/1221 Sixth Ave, Grafton, WI	414-377-2298
Schulman, Bruce/1102 W Columbia, Chicago, IL	312-338-0619
Schulman, Lee/669 College Ave Box 09506, Columbus, OH	614-235-5307
Schultz, Tim/2000 N Clifton, Chicago, IL	312-943-3318
Schwartz, Linda/72 E Oak #3E, Chicago, IL	312-266-7868
Scott, Denis/216 W Ohio St, Chicago, IL	312-467-5663
Secreto, Jim/2626 Industrial Row, Troy, MI	313-280-0640
Seed, Brian/213 W Institute Pl #503, Chicago, IL	312-787-7880
Seed, Suzanne/175 E Delaware, Chicago, IL	312-266-0621
Segal, Mark/230 N Michigan Ave, Chicago, IL	312-236-8545
Segielski, Tony/1886 Thunderbird, Troy, MI	313-362-3111
Semeniuk, Robert/78 Rusholme Rd, Toronto M6J 3H6, ON	416-532-6108
Sereta, Greg/2108 Payne Ave #400, Cleveland, OH	216-861-7227
Severson, Kent/529 S 7th St #637, Minneapolis, MN	612-375-1870
Seymour, Ronald/314 W Superior, Chicago, IL	312-642-4030
Shafer, Ronald/4428 N Malden, Chicago, IL	312-878-1346
Shaffer, Mac/526 E Dunedin Rd, Columbus, OH	614-268-2249
Shambroom, Paul/529 S 7th St #537, Minneapolis, MN	612-340-9179
Shanoor Photo/116 W Illinois, Chicago, IL	312-266-1358
SHAPIRO, TERRY/1147 W OHIO ST, CHICAGO, IL (P 180)	**312-226-3384**
Sharp, Joe/Owens Corning Fiberglass Tower, Toledo, OH	419-248-8041
Shaughnessy & MacDonald/32 Martin Ln, Elk Grove Village, IL	312-437-8850
SHAY, ARTHUR/618 INDIAN HILL RD, DEERFIELD, IL (P 181)	**312-945-4636**
Shelli, Bob/PO Box 2062, St Louis, MO	314-772-8540

Sheppard, Richard/421 N Main St, Mt Prospect, IL	312-259-4375
Shigeta-Wright Assoc/1546 N Orleans St, Chicago, IL	312-642-8715
Shirmer, Bob/11 W Illinois St, Chicago, IL	312-321-1151
Shoots, Jim Weiner/230 E Ohio #402, Chicago, IL	312-337-0220
Shotwell, Chuck/2111 N Clifton, Chicago, IL	312-929-0168
Shoulders, Terry/676 N LaSalle, Chicago, IL	312-642-6622
Siede/Preis Photo/1526 N Halsted, Chicago, IL	312-787-2725
Sieracki, John/676 N LaSalle, Chicago, IL	312-664-7824
Sigman, Gary/2941 N Racine, Chicago, IL	312-871-8756
Silber, Gary Craig/300 Main St, Racine, WI	414-637-5097
Silker, Glenn/5249 W 73rd St #A, Edina, MN	612-835-1811
Sills, Anne Margaret/411 N LaSalle St, Chicago, IL	312-670-3660
Sills, Casey/411 N Lasalle, Chicago, IL	312-670-3660
Silver, Jared N/660 La Salle Pl, Chicago, IL	312-433-3866
Simmons Photography Inc/326 Chicago Ave, Chicago, IL	312-944-0326
Sindelar, Dan/2517 Grove Springs Ct, St Louis, MO	314-846-4775
Singer, Beth/25741 River Dr, Franklin, MI	313-626-4860
Sinkler, Paul/510 N First Ave #307, Minneapolis, MN	612-343-0325
SINKLIER, SCOTT/5860 MERLE HAY RD/BOX 127, JOHNSTON, IA (P 177)	**515-270-3732**
Skalak, Carl/47-46 Grayton Rd, Cleveland, OH	216-676-6508
Skrebneski, Victor/1350 N LaSalle St, Chicago, IL	312-944-1339
Skutas, Joe/17 N Elizabeth, Chicago, IL	312-733-1266
Sladcik, William/215 W Illinois, Chicago, IL	312-644-7108
Slaughter, Michael/2051 Osage Ln, Hanover Park, IL	312-250-8508
Smetzer, Donald/2534 N Burling St, Chicago, IL	312-327-1716
Smith, Bill/600 N McClurgh Ct #802, Chicago, IL	312-787-4686
Smith, Doug Photo/2911 Sutton, St Louis, MO	314-645-1359
Smith, Mike/521 Cottonwood Circle, Bolingbrook, IL	312-759-0262
Smith, R Hamilton/1021 W Montana Ave, St Paul, MN	612-488-9068
Smith, Richard/PO Box 455, Round Lake, IL	312-546-0977
Smith, Robert/496 W Wrightwood Ave, Elmhurst, IL	312-941-7755
Snook, Allen/1433 W Fullerton, Addison, IL	312-495-3939
Snook, J J/118 W Ohio, Chicago, IL	312-495-3939
Snow, Andy/346 Shadywood Dr, Dayton, OH	513-836-8566
Snyder, John/368 W Huron, Chicago, IL	312-440-1053
Solis Studio/4161 S Archer, Chicago, IL	312-890-0555
Soluri, Tony/1147 W Ohio, Chicago, IL	312-243-6580
Sorokowski, Rick/1051 N Halsted, Chicago, IL	312-280-1256
SPAHR, DICK/1133 E 61ST ST, INDIANAPOLIS, IN (P 182)	**317-255-2400**
Spectra Studios/213 W Institute #512, Chicago, IL	312-787-0667
Spencer, Gary/3546 Dakota Ave S, Minneapolis, MN	612-929-7803
Spingola, Laurel/6225 N Forest Glen, Chicago, IL	312-883-0020
Spitz, Robert/317 Howard, Evanston, IL	312-869-4992
Sroka, Michael/5722 W Fillmore Dr, West Allis, WI	414-543-0512
Stansfield, Stan/215 W Ohio, Chicago, IL	312-337-3245
Starkey, John/2250 Rome Dr, Indianapolis, IN	317-299-5758
Starmark Photo/706 N Dearborn, Chicago, IL	312-922-3388
Stealey, Jonathan/PO Box 611, Findlay, OH	419-423-1149
Steele, Charles/531 S Plymouth Ct #22, Chicago, IL	312-922-0201
Stegbauer, Jim/421 Transit, Roseville, MN	612-333-1982
Stein, Frederic/409 W Huron St, Chicago, IL	312-642-7171
Steinbacher, Ed/5745 Overture Way, Clinton, OH	216-825-9138
STEINBERG, MIKE/633 HURON RD, CLEVELAND, OH (P 183)	**216-589-9953**
Steinhart Photography/325 W Huron, Chicago, IL	312-944-0226
Stemo Photo/1880 Holste Rd, Northbrook, IL	312-498-4844
Stenberg, Pete Photography/225 W Hubbard, Chicago, IL	312-644-6137
Sterling, Joseph/2216 N Cleveland, Chicago, IL	312-348-4333
Stewart, Ron/314 E Downer Pl, Aurora, IL	312-897-4317
Stornello, Joe/4319 Campbell St, Kansas City, MO	816-756-0419
Straus, Jerry/247 E Ontario, Chicago, IL	312-787-2628
Strouss, Sarah/134 Upland Ave, Youngstown, OH	216-744-2774
Struse, Perry L Jr/232 Sixth St, West Des Moines, IA	515-279-9761
The Studio, Inc/730 N Franklin, Chicago, IL	312-337-1490
Stump Studio/3260 W Irving Park Rd, Chicago, IL	312-649-0084
Summers Studio/153 W Ohio, Chicago, IL	312-527-0908
Sundlof, John/401 W Superior, Chicago, IL	312-951-8701
Swan, Tom/2417 N Burling, Chicago, IL	312-871-8370
Swanson, Michael/215 W Ohio, Chicago, IL	312-337-3245

T

Taback, Sidney/415 Eastern Ave, Toronto M4M1B7, ON	416-463-5718

Taber, Gary/305 S Green St, Chicago, IL 312-726-0374
Taxel, Barney/4614 Prospect Ave, Cleveland, OH 216-431-2400
Taylor, Dale E/8505 Midcounty Ind Ctr, St Louis, MO 314-426-2655
Technigraph Studio/1212 Jarvis, Elk Grove Village, IL 312-437-3334
Teeter, Brian/5607 Green Circle Dr #217, Minnetonka, MN 612-935-5666
Teschl, Josef/31 Brock Ave #203, Toronto, ON 416-743-5146
Teufen, Al/600 E Smith Rd, Medina, OH 216-723-3237
Thien, Alex/2754 N Prospect Ave, Milwaukee, WI 414-964-4349
Thill, Nancy/70 W Huron St, Chicago, IL 312-944-7164
Thoen, Greg/14940 Minnetonka Rd, Minnetonka, MN 612-938-2433
Thoman, Fred/6710 Madison Rd, Cincinnati, OH 513-561-4011
Thomas, Bill/Rt 4 Box 387, Nashville, IN 812-988-7865
Thomas, Tony/676 N Lasalle St 6th Fl, Chicago, IL 312-337-2274
Thompson, Dale/224 S Michigan Ave 14th Fl, Chicago, IL 312-347-2081
Thompson, Ken/225 W Huron, Chicago, IL 312-951-6356
Tillis, Harvey/501 N Wells, Chicago, IL 312-828-0731
Tolchin, Robert/2522 Fontana Dr, Glenview, IL 312-729-2522
Torno, Laurent/1709 Washington #9000, St Louis, MO 314-231-4883
Toro, Mark/778 S Wall St, Columbus, OH 614-460-4635
Tower Photo/4327 N Elston, Chicago, IL 312-478-8494
Townsend, Wesley/, Lombard, IL 312-620-7118
TPS Studio/4016 S California, Chicago, IL 312-847-1221
Tracy, Janis/213 W Institute Pl, Chicago, IL 312-787-7166
Trantafil, Gary/3926 N Spaulding Ave, Chicago, IL 312-539-0150
Trotter, Jim/12342 Conway Rd, St Louis, MO 314-878-0777
Trujillo, Edward/345 N Canal St #1604, Chicago, IL 312-454-9798
Tucker, Bill/114 W Illinois, Chicago, IL 312-321-1570
Tunison, Richard/5511 E Lake Dr, Lisle, IL 312-944-1188
Tushas, Leo/111 N Fifth Ave #309, Minneapolis, MN 612-333-5774

U V Uhlmann, Gina/1611 N Sheffield, Chicago, IL 312-642-6650
Umland, Steve/600 Washington Ave N, Minneapolis, MN 612-332-1590
Upitis, Alvis/620 Morgan Ave S, Minneapolis, MN 612-374-9375
Urba, Alexis/148 W Illinois, Chicago, IL 312-644-4466
Van Allen, John/U of Iowa Fndtn/Alumni Ctr, Iowa City, IA 319-354-9512
Van Marter, Robert/1209 Alstott Dr S, Howell, MI 517-546-1923
Vander Lende, Craig/214 East Fulton, Grand Rapids, MI 616-458-4415
Vander Veen, David/5151 N 35th St, Milwaukee, WI 414-527-0450
VanKirk Photography/1230 W Washington Blvd, Chicago, IL 312-226-4060
Vanmarter, Robert/1209 Alstott Dr S, Howell, MI 517-546-1923
Variakojis, Danguole/5743 S Campbell, Chicago, IL 312-776-4668
Vaughan, Jim/321 S Jefferson, Chicago, IL 312-663-0369
Vedros, Nick/215 W 19th St, Kansas City, MO 816-471-5488
Ventola, Giorgio/230 W Huron, Chicago, IL 312-951-0880
Vergos Studio/122 W Kinzie 3rd Fl, Chicago, IL 312-527-1769
Viernum, Bill/1629 Mandel Ave, Westchester, IL 312-562-4143
Villa, Armando/1872 N Clybourne, Chicago, IL 312-472-7003
Visual Data Systems Inc/5617 63rd Pl, Chicago, IL 312-585-3060
Vizanko Advertising Photo/11511 K-Tel Drive, Minnetonka, MN 612-933-1314
Vollan, Michael/175 S Morgan, Chicago, IL 312-644-1792
Von Baich, Paul/78 Rusholme Rd, Toronto M6J 3H6, ON 416-532-6108
Von Photography/685 W Ohio, Chicago, IL 312-243-8578
Voyles, Dick & Assoc/2822 Breckenridge Ind Ctr, St Louis, MO 314-968-3851
Vuksanovich/401 W Superior St, Chicago, IL 312-664-7523

W Wagenaar, David/1035 W Lake St, Chicago, IL 312-942-0943
Waite, Tim/717 S Sixth St, Milwaukee, WI 414-643-1500
Walker, Jessie Assoc/241 Fairview, Glencoe, IL 312-835-0522
Wans, Glen/325 W 40th, Kansas City, MO 816-931-8905
Ward, Les/17371 Beechwood, Birmingham, MI 313-548-4400
Warkenthien, Dan/117 South Morgan, Chicago, IL 312-666-6056
Warren, Lennie/401 W Superior, Chicago, IL 312-664-5392
Watt, John/2479 W 11th St, Cleveland, OH 216-621-3838
Watts, Dan/245 Plymouth, Grand Rapids, MI 616-451-4693
Watts, Ron/78 Rusholme Rd, Toronto M6J 3H6, ON 416-532-6108
Wedlake, James/750 Jossman Rd, Ortonville, MI 313-627-2711
Weidemann, Skot/1123 Sherman Ave, Madison, WI 608-251-7932
Weiner, Jim/540 N Lakeshore Dr, Chicago, IL 312-644-0040
Weinstein, John/3119 N Seminary Ave, Chicago, IL 312-327-8184
Weinstein, Michael/123 N Jefferson, Chicago, IL 312-207-5430
Weinstein, Phillip/343 S Dearborn, Chicago, IL 312-922-1945

Weispfenning, Donna/815 W 53rd St, Minneapolis, MN 612-823-8405
Welzenbach, John/368 W Huron St, Chicago, IL 312-337-3611
Wengroff, Sam/2052 N Dayton, Chicago, IL 312-248-6623
West, Stu/430 First Ave #210, Minneapolis, MN 612-375-0404
Westerman, Charlie/59 E Cedar St, Chicago, IL 312-440-9422
White, Christopher/169 MacKay St #3, Ottawa K1M 2B5, ON 613-741-3246
Whitford, T R/1709 Washington 7th Fl, St Louis, MO 314-231-3522
Whitmer, Jim/125 Wakeman, Wheaton, IL 312-653-1344
Wicks, L Photography/1235 W Winnemac Ave, Chicago, IL 312-878-4925
Wigodsky, Steve/10326 Wright St, Omaha, NE 402-397-2697
Wilder, J David/2300 Payne Ave, Cleveland, OH 216-771-7687
Willett, Mike/221 W Walton, Chicago, IL 312-642-4282
Willette, Brady T/2720 W 43rd St, Minneapolis, MN 612-926-4261
Williams, Alfred G/5230 S Blackstone Ave #306, Chicago, IL 312-947-0991
Williams, Barry/2361 N High St, Columbus, OH 614-291-9774
Williams, Basil/4068 Tanglefoot Terrace, Bettendorf, IA 319-355-7142
Williamson, John/224 Palmerston Ave, Toronto M6J 2J4, ON 416-530-4511
Wilson, Dave & Assoc/1533 Seventh Ave, Moline, IL 309-762-1922
Wilson, Jack/2133 Bellvue, St Louis, MO 314-645-2211
Wilson, Tim/2330 N Sacramento, Chicago, IL 312-227-6914
Wimer, Scott K/555 W Adams #6E, Chicago, IL 312-372-7828
Wirthlin, Walter/6406 Morganford, St Louis, MO 314-351-7369
Witkin, L/11 E Hubbard, Chicago, IL 312-661-1099
Witte, Scott J/3025 W Highland Blvd, Milwaukee, WI 414-933-3223
Woburn/4715 N Ronald St, Harwood Heights, IL 312-867-5445
Woehrle, Mark/1709 Washington Ave, St Louis, MO 314-231-9949
Wojcik, Richard R/151 Victor Ave, Highland Park, MI 313-868-2200
Wolf, Bobbe/1011 W Armitage, Chicago, IL 312-472-9503
Wolf, Don/301 W 17th St, Kansas City, MO 816-421-0004
Wolff, Ed/11357 S Second St, Schoolcraft, MI 616-679-4702
Wooden, John/219 N 2nd St J#306, Minneapolis, MN 612-339-3032
Woodward, Greg/401 W Superior, Chicago, IL 312-337-5838
Worzala, Lyle/2954 W 57th St, Chicago, IL 312-434-7156
Wright, James/5740 S Kenwood #1, Chicago, IL 312-856-1838

Y Z Yamashiro, Paul Studio/125 W Hubbard St, Chicago, IL 312-321-1009
Yapp, Charles/932 W Washington, Chicago, IL 312-558-9338
Yates, Peter/515 Spring St, Ann Arbor, MI 313-995-0839
Yaworski, Don/10108 W 69th Terrace, Merriam, KS 913-384-2225
Zamiar, Thomas/210 W Chicago, Chicago, IL 312-787-4976
Zann, Arnold/502 N Grove Ave, Oak Park, IL 312-386-2864
Zarlengo, Joseph/419 Melrose Ave, Boardman, OH 216-782-7797
Zena Photography/633 Huron Rd SE 5th Fl, Cleveland, OH 216-621-6366
Zimion/Marshall Studio/1043 W Randolph, Chicago, IL 312-243-9500
Zoom Photo/427 Queen St West, Toronto M5V 2A5, ON 416-593-0690
Zukas, R/311 N Desplaines #500, Chicago, IL 312-648-0100

Southwest

A Abraham, Joe/11944 Hempstead Rd #C, Houston, TX 713-460-4948
AKER/BURNETTE STUDIO/4710 LILLIAN, HOUSTON, TX (P 186,187) **713-862-6343**
Alford, Jess/1800 Lear St #3, Dallas, TX 214-421-3107
Allen, Jim Photo/4410 Lovers Lane, Dallas, TX 214-368-0563
Anderson, Derek Studio/3959 Speedway Blvd E, Tucson, AZ 602-881-1205
Anderson, Randy/1606 Lewis Trail, Grand Prairie, TX 214-660-1071
Angle, Lee/1900 Montgomery, Fort Worth, TX 817-737-6469
Annerino, John/PO Box 1545, Prescott, AZ 602-445-4094
Ashe, Gil/Box 686, Bellaire, TX 713-668-8766
Ashley, Constance/2024 Farrington St, Dallas, TX 214-747-2501
Assid, Al/6311 N O'Connor #166, Irving, TX 214-869-7766
Associated Photo/2344 Irving Blvd, Dallas, TX 214-630-8730
Austin, David/2412 Fifth Ave, Fort Worth, TX 817-335-1881

B Badger, Bobby/1355 Chemical, Dallas, TX 214-634-0222
Bagshaw, Cradoc/603 High St NE, Albuquerque, NM 505-243-1096
Baird, Darryl/830 Exposition #215, Dallas, TX 214-826-3348
Baker, Bobbe C/1119 Ashburn, College Station, TX 409-696-7185
Baker, Jeff/2401 S Ervay #302, Dallas, TX 214-720-0178
Baker, Lane/7145 N 59th Ave, Glendale, AZ 602-937-4477
Baldwin/Watriss Assoc/1405 Branard St, Houston, TX 713-524-9199

Photographers
Continued

Please send us your additions and updates.

Ballingham, Rodney/PO Box 35171, Dallas, TX	214-528-5434
Baraban, Joe/2426 Bartlett #2, Houston, TX	713-526-0317
Barker, Kent/2039 Farrington, Dallas, TX	214-760-7470
Bayanduryan, Rubik/PO Box 1791, Austin, TX	512-451-8960
Beebower Brothers/9995 Monroe #209, Dallas, TX	214-358-1219
Bender, Robert/1345 Chemical, Dallas, TX	214-631-4538
Bennett, Sue/PO Box 1574, Flagstaff, AZ	602-774-2544
Bennett, Tony R/122 Parkhouse, Dallas, TX	214-747-0107
Benoist, John/PO Box 20825, Dallas, TX	214-692-8813
Berman, Bruce/140 N Stevens #301, El Paso, TX	915-544-0352
Bernhard, John/3700 Watonga #2210, Houston, TX	713-893-3555
Berrett, Patrick L/2425-C NE Monroe, Albuquerque, NM	505-881-0935
Berry, George S Photography/Rt 2 Box 325B, San Marcos, TX	512-396-4805
Bishop, Gary/PO Box 12394, Dallas, TX	214-368-0889
Blackwell, J Michael/2032 Farrington, Dallas, TX	214-760-8742
Bland, Ron/2424 S Carver Pkwy #107, Grand Prairie, TX	214-660-6600
Blue, Janice/1708 Rosewood, Houston, TX	713-522-6899
Bondy, Roger/PO Box 3, Oklahoma City, OK	405-424-5224
Booth, Greg/1322 Round Table, Dallas, TX	214-688-1855
Bouche, Len/PO Box 5188, Sante Fe, NM	505-471-2044
Boulanger, Gary/2330 E Monterosa, Phoenix, AZ	602-264-1151
Bowman, Matt/3613 Parry, Dallas, TX	214-824-2142
Bradley, Matt/15 Butterfield Ln, Little Rock, AR	501-224-0692
Bradshaw, Reagan/PO Box 12457, Austin, TX	512-458-6101
BRADY, STEVE/5250 GULFTON #2G, HOUSTON, TX (P 188,189)	**713-660-6663**
Branner, Phillip/2700 Commerce St, Dallas, TX	214-939-0550
BROUSSEAU, J/2408 FARRINGTON, DALLAS, TX (P 190)	**214-638-1248**
Bryant, Ray/8235 Douglass #615, Dallas, TX	214-691-9335
Buffington, David/2401 S Ervay #105, Dallas, TX	214-428-8221
Bumpass, R O/2404 Farrington, Dallas, TX	214-630-0180
Bunch, Fred C/1809 Binz, Houston, TX	713-529-6211
Burger, Steven/544 E Dunlap Ave, Phoenix, AZ	602-997-4625
Burkes, Marsha/905 Iwo St, Alvin, TX	713-792-4266
Burkey, J W/2739 Irving Blvd, Dallas, TX	214-630-1369

C

Cabluck, Jerry/Box 9601, Fort Worth, TX	817-336-1431
CALDWELL, JIM/2422 QUENBY, HOUSTON, TX (P 191)	**713-527-9121**
Campbell, Doug/5617 Matalee, Dallas, TX	214-823-9151
Cannedy, Carl/2408 Farrington, Dallas, TX	214-638-1247
Captured Image Photography/5131 E Lancaster, Fort Worth, TX	817-457-2302
Carr, Fred/8303 Westglen Dr, Houston, TX	713-266-2872
Case, Bob/126 E Texas St, Grapevine, TX	817-481-4854
Cathey Graphics Group/8585 Stemmons Frwy, Dallas, TX	214-638-0731
Chavanell, Joe/PO Box 32383, San Antonio, TX	512-377-1552
Chenn, Steve/6301 Ashcroft, Houston, TX	713-271-0631
Chisholm, Rich & Assoc/3233 Marquart, Houston, TX	713-623-8790
Clair, Andre/11415 Chatten Way, Houston, TX	713-465-5507
Clark, H Dean/18405 FM 149, Houston, TX	713-469-7021
Claussen, Peter/6901-C Mullins, Houston, TX	713-661-7498
Clintsman, Dick/3001 Quebec #102, Dallas, TX	214-630-1531
Cobb, Lynn/3505 Turtle Creek #109, Dallas, TX	214-528-6694
Cole, Alan Michael/Route A Box 197, Flippin, AR	501-425-9107
Colombo, Michel/2707 Stemmons Frwy #160, Dallas, TX	214-630-5317
Connolly, Danny F/PO Box 1290, Houston, TX	713-862-8146
Cook, Robert Ames/2608 Irving Blvd, Dallas, TX	214-634-7196
Cotter, Austin/1350 Manufacturing #211, Dallas, TX	214-742-3633
Countryman, Mike/1609 Grantland Circle, Fort Worth, TX	817-496-6348
Cowlin, James/PO Box 34205, Phoenix, AZ	602-264-9689
Craig, George/314 E 13th St, Houston, TX	713-862-6008
Crane, Christopher/5455 Dashwood #300, Bellaire, TX	713-661-1098
Creighton, Jim/5933 Bellaire #117, Houston, TX	713-669-1119
Crittendon, James/5914 Lake Crest, Garland, TX	214-226-2196
Cruff, Kevin/2318 E Roosevelt, Phoenix, AZ	602-267-8845
Crump, Bill/1357 Chemical, Dallas, TX	214-630-7745

D

David, Jerry/3314 Silver Maple Court, Garland, TX	214-495-9600
Davis, David/749 E Lola Dr, Phoenix, AZ	602-992-9770
Davis, Mark/8718 Boundbrook Ave, Dallas, TX	214-348-7679
Dawson, Greg/2211 Beall St, Houston, TX	713-862-8301

Dean, Don/5925 Maple #106/Box 36365, Dallas, TX	214-939-0005
Debenport, Robb/2412 Converse, Dallas, TX	214-631-7606
Denman, Merv/514 E Pipeline, Hurst, TX	817-268-2400
Doering, Douglas/2823 W Davis St, Dallas, TX	214-330-0304
Douglas, King Studio/1319 Conant St, Dallas, TX	214-630-4700
Drews, Buzzy/1555 W Mockingbird #202, Dallas, TX	214-351-9968
DuBose, Bill/5538 Dyer, Dallas, TX	214-630-0086
Duran, Mark/66 East Vernon, Phoenix, AZ	602-279-1141
Dyer, John/211 Richmond, San Antonio, TX	512-223-1891
Dykinga, Jack/3808 Calle Barcelona, Tucson, AZ	602-326-6094

E

Echo Image/1350 Manufacturing #206, Dallas, TX	214-742-1014
ECLIPSE/2727 E 21ST ST #600, TULSA, OK (P 192)	**918-747-1991**
Edens, Swain/104 Heiman, San Antonio, TX	512-226-2210
Edwards, Bill/3820 Brown, Dallas, TX	214-521-8630
Eglin, Tom/3950 W Mais St, Tucson, AZ	602-748-1299
Eilers, Rick/4030 Swiss, Dallas, TX	214-823-2103
Enriquez, Arturo & Vallarie/1109 Arizona Ave, El Paso, TX	915-533-9688
Evenson, Martin/5512 Dyer St, Dallas, TX	214-369-0798

F

Fantich, Barry/PO Box 70103, Houston, TX	713-520-5434
Faustino/PO Box 771234, Houston, TX	713-864-8454
Findysz, Mary/5740 E 22nd St, Tucson, AZ	602-745-8069
Fittipaldi, Mary Ann/3775 W Fourth St, Fort Worth, TX	817-735-9010
Fontenot, Dallas/6002 Burning Tree Dr, Houston, TX	713-988-2183
Ford, Bill/202 S Center Valley, Irving, TX	214-986-7887
Forsyth, Mimi/PO Box 992, Santa Fe, NM	505-982-8891
Foxall, Steve/3417 Main St, Dallas, TX	214-939-9120
Frady, Connie/2808 Fifth Ave, Fort Worth, TX	817-927-7589
Freeman, Charlie/3333-A Elm St, Dallas, TX	214-742-1446
Fry, Kristen Pearce/5416 Wateka, Dallas, TX	214-350-9565
Fuller, Timothy Woodbridge/135 1/2 S Sixth Ave, Tucson, AZ	602-622-3900

G

Gaber, Brad/4946 Glen Meadow, Houston, TX	713-723-0030
Galloway, Jim/2201 N Lamar, Dallas, TX	214-954-0355
Gary & Clark Photographic Studio/2702 Main, Dallas, TX	214-939-9070
Gatz, Larry/5250 Gulfton #3B, Houston, TX	713-666-5203
Gayle, Rick/2318 E Roosevelt, Phoenix, AZ	602-267-8845
Geffs, Dale/15715 Amapola, Houston, TX	713-933-3876
GENDREAU, RAYMOND/2039 FARRINGTON, DALLAS, TX (P 193)	**214-760-1999**
Gerczynski, Tom/2211 N 7th Ave, Phoenix, AZ	602-252-9229
Germany, Robert/11163 Shady trail #103, Dallas, TX	214-241-1950
Gilbert, Bruce/12335 Braesridge, Houston, TX	713-723-1486
Giles-Cardellino Inc/315 9th St #2, San Antonio, TX	512-224-9606
Gilmore, Dwight/2437 Hillview, Fort Worth, TX	817-536-4825
Gilstrap, L C/132 Booth Calloway, Hurst, TX	817-284-7701
Glentzer, Don Photography/3814 S Shepherd Dr, Houston, TX	713-529-9686
Gomel, Bob/10831 Valley Hills, Houston, TX	713-977-6390
Gonzalez, Peter/PO Box 2775, Austin, TX	512-444-9737
Goodman, Robert/2025 Levee, Dallas, TX	214-653-1120
Graham, Boyce/2707 Stemmons Frwy #160, Dallas, TX	214-631-4019
Grass, Jon/1345 Chemical St, Dallas, TX	214-634-1455
GREEN, MARK/2406 TAFT ST, HOUSTON, TX (P 194,195)	**713-523-6146**
Grider, James/732 Schilder, Fort Worth, TX	817-732-7472
Guerrero, Charles/2207 Comal St, Austin, TX	512-477-6642

H

Hagler, Skeeter/PO Box 628, Red Oak, TX	214-576-5620
Hale, Butch Photography/1319 Conant, Dallas, TX	214-637-3987
Halpern, David/7420 E 70th St, Tulsa, OK	918-252-4973
Hamburger, Jay/1817 State St, Houston, TX	713-869-0869
Hamilton, Jeffrey/6719 Quartzite Canyon Pl, Tucson, AZ	602-299-3624
Handel, Doug/3016 Selma, Dallas, TX	214-241-1549
Hart, Michael/7320 Ashcroft #105, Houston, TX	713-271-8250
Hartman, Gary/911 South St Marys St, San Antonio, TX	512-225-2404
Hatcok, Tom/113 W 12th St, Deer Park, TX	713-479-2603
Hawks, Bob/1345 E 15th St, Tulsa, OK	918-584-3351
Hawn, Gray Photography/1608 W 35th St, Austin, TX	512-451-7561
Haynes, Mike/2700 Commerce St, Dallas, TX	214-939-0550
Heiner, Gary/2039 Farrington, Dallas, TX	214-760-7471
Heinsohn, Bill/5455 Dashwood #200, Bellaire, TX	713-666-6515
Heit, Don/8502 Eustis Ave, Dallas, TX	214-324-0305

PHOTOGRAPHERS

321

Photographers

Continued

Please send us your additions and updates.

Henry, Steve/7403 Pierrepont Dr, Houston, TX	713-937-4514
Hicks, Tracy/4228 Main, Dallas, TX	214-939-9085
Hight, George C/1404 Linda Dr Box 327, Gallup, NM	505-863-3222
Hix, Steve/209 E Ben White Blvd #109, Austin, TX	512-441-2600
Hollenbeck, Phil/9010 Windy Crest, Dallas, TX	214-340-1117
Hollingsworth, Jack/3141 Irving Blvd #209, Dallas, TX	214-634-2632
Hood, Bob/2312 Grand, Dallas, TX	214-428-6080
Hubbard, Tim/Box 44971/Los Olivos Sta, Phoenix, AZ	602-274-6985
Huber, Phil/13562 Braemar Dr, Dallas, TX	214-243-4011
Hulsey, Jim Photography/8117 NW 80th St, Oklahoma City, OK	405-720-2767

IJ
IVES, MICHAEL/1000 CORNELL PKWY #200, OKLAHOMA CITY, OK (P 196)	**405-947-0606**
Ives, Tom/2250 El Moraga, Tucson, AZ	602-743-0750
Jacka, Jerry/PO Box 9043, Phoenix, AZ	602-944-2793
Jacoby, Doris/1317 Conant, Dallas, TX	214-631-5533
JENNINGS, STEVE/PO BOX 33203, TULSA, OK (P 197)	**918-745-0836**
Jew, Kim/4013 Central NE, Albuquerque, NM	505-255-6424
Johnson, Michael/830 Exposition #215, Dallas, TX	214-828-9550
Jones, C Bryan/PO Box 7687, Houston, TX	713-861-5299
Jones, Jerry/6207 Edloe, Houston, TX	713-668-4328

K
Kaluzny, Zigy/4700 Strass Dr, Austin, TX	512-452-4463
Kasie Photos/2123 Avignon, Carrollton, TX	214-492-7837
Katz, John/5222 Red Field, Dallas, TX	214-637-0844
Kenny, Gill/3515 N Camino De Vista, Tucson, AZ	602-743-0963
Kern, Geof/1337 Crampton, Dallas, TX	214-630-0856
Kirkley, Kent/1345 Conant St, Dallas, TX	214-630-0051
Klumpp, Don/804 Colquitt, Houston, TX	713-521-2090
Knowles, Jim/6102 E Mockingbird Ln #499, Dallas, TX	214-699-5335
Knudson, Kent/PO Box 10397, Phoenix, AZ	602-277-7701
Koelsch, David/PO Box 178, Jones, OK	405-399-5212
Kopacka, Greg/PO Box 680824, San Antonio, TX	512-688-9202
Koppes, Neil/1611 N 36th St, Phoenix, AZ	602-231-0918
Korab, Jeanette/2264 Vantage, Dallas, TX	214-337-0114
Kretchmar, Phil Photography/3333 Elm, Dallas, TX	214-744-2039
Kroninger, Rick/105 N Alamo #615, San Antonio, TX	512-222-8141
Kuper, Holly/5522 Anita St, Dallas, TX	214-827-4494

L
Lallo, Edward L/1350 Manufacturing #211, Dallas, TX	214-741-9226
Langhammer, Gary/1350 Manufacturing #215, Dallas, TX	214-744-2255
Larson, Dennis/5353 Maple #102, Dallas, TX	214-630-3418
Latorre, Robert/2336 Farrington St, Dallas, TX	214-630-8977
Lawrence, David/2720 Stemmons #1206, Dallas, TX	214-637-4686
Lawrie, Bill/313 Sundial Dr, Dallas, TX	214-243-4188
Lettner, Hans/830 North 4th Ave, Phoenix, AZ	602-258-3506
LJM Studios/216 W Main, Azle, TX	817-444-2712
Loven, Paul/2301 N 16th St, Phoenix, AZ	602-253-0335
Luker, Tom/PO Box 6112, Coweta, OK	918-486-5264

M
Mader, Bob/2570 Promenade Center N, Richardson, TX	214-690-5511
Magee, Mike/1325 Conant St, Dallas, TX	214-638-6868
Mageors & Rice Photo Service Inc/240 Turnpike Ave, Dallas, TX	214-941-3777
Maloney, John W/170 Leslie, Dallas, TX	214-741-6320
Manley, Dan/1350 Manufacturing Suite 215, Dallas, TX	214-748-8377
Manske, Thaine/7313 Ashcroft #216, Houston, TX	713-771-2220
Manstein, Ralph/5353 Institute Ln, Houston, TX	713-523-2500
Maples, Carl/1811 Cohn, Houston, TX	713-868-1289
Markham, Jim/2739 S E Loop 410, San Antonio, TX	512-648-0403
Markow, Paul/2222 E McDowell Rd, Phoenix, AZ	602-273-7985
Marshall, Jim/7451 Long Rifle Rd/Box 2421, Carefree, AZ	602-488-3373
Matthews, Michael/2727 Cancun, Dallas, TX	214-492-5580
Maxham, Robert/319 E Huisache, San Antonio, TX	512-735-3537
Mayer, George H/933 Stonetrail, Plano (Dallas), TX	214-424-4409
McCormick, Mike/5950 Westward Ave, Houston, TX	713-988-0775
McCoy, Gary/2700 Commerce St, Dallas, TX	214-939-0550
McIntosh, W S/12201 Merit Dr #222, Dallas, TX	214-783-1711
McKee, Crane/9113 Sovereign Rd, Dallas, TX	214-638-1498
McMichael, Garry D/RT 1 Box 312, Paris, AR	501-963-6429
McNee, Jim/PO Box 741008, Houston, TX	713-796-2633

Messina, John/4440 Lawnview, Dallas, TX	214-388-8525
Meyerson, Arthur/4215 Bellaire Blvd, Houston, TX	713-660-0405
Meyler, Dennis/7315 Ashcroft #110, Houston, TX	713-778-1700
Mills, Jack R/PO Box 32583, Oklahoma City, OK	405-787-7271
Moberley, Connie/215 Asbury, Houston, TX	713-864-3638
Molen, Roy/3302 N 47 Pl, Phoenix, AZ	602-840-5439
Montoya, Andy/1800 Lear #5, Dallas, TX	214-421-3993
Moore, Terrence/PO Box 41536, Tucson, AZ	602-623-9381
Moot, Kelly/6606 Demoss #508, Houston, TX	713-683-6400
Morgan, Roger/828 Birdsong, Bedford, TX	817-282-2170
Morris, Garry/9281 E 27th St, Tucson, AZ	602-795-2334
Morris, Mike/4003 Gilbert #6, Dallas, TX	214-528-3600
Morrison, Chet Photography/3102 Commerce St, Dallas, TX	214-939-0903
Muir, Robert/Box 42809 Dept 404, Houston, TX	713-784-7420
Murdoch, Lane/2707 Stemmons Frwy, Dallas, TX	214-634-2240
Murphy, Dennis/101 Howell St, Dallas, TX	214-651-7516
Myers, Jim/165 Cole, Dallas, TX	214-698-0500

NO
Neely, David/11163 Shady Trail #103, Dallas, TX	214-241-1950
Netzer, Don/8585 Stemmons #M29, Dallas, TX	214-869-0826
Newby, Steve/4501 Swiss, Dallas, TX	214-821-0231
Newman, David/3319 Knight #1, Dallas, TX	214-522-8612
Noland, Lloyd (Weaver)/PO Box 9456, Santa Fe, NM	505-982-2488
Norrell, J B/7320 Ashcroft #106, Houston, TX	713-981-6409
Olvera, Jim/235 Yorktown St, Dallas, TX	214-760-0025

P
Palmetto, Chuck/2707 Stemmons #160, Dallas, TX	214-638-1885
Pantin, Tomas/PO Box 1146, Austin, TX	512-474-9968
Parsons, Bill/518 W 9th St, Little Rock, AR	501-372-5892
Patrick, Richard/215 W 4th St #B, Austin, TX	512-472-9092
Payne, A F/830 North 4th Ave, Phoenix, AZ	602-258-3506
Payne, C Ray/2643 Manana, Dallas, TX	214-350-1055
Payne, Richard/2029 Haddon St, Houston, TX	713-524-7525
Payne, Tom/2425 Bartlett, Houston, TX	713-527-8670
Perlstein, Mark/1844 Place One Ln, Garland, TX	214-690-0168
Peterson, Bruce/1222 E Edgemont, Phoenix, AZ	602-265-6505
Pettit, Steve/206 Weeks, Arlington, TX	817-265-8776
Pfuhl, Chris/PO Box 542, Phoenix, AZ	602-253-0525
Phelps, Greg/2360 Central Blvd, Brownsville, TX	512-541-4909
Photo Media, Inc/2805 Crockett, Fort Worth, TX	817-332-4172
Poulides, Peter/PO Box 202505, Dallas, TX	214-350-5395
Prosen, Philip M/69-47 Coronado, Dallas, TX	214-321-2938

QR
The Quest Group/3007 Paseo, Oklahoma City, OK	405-525-6591
Quilia, Jim/3125 Ross, Dallas, TX	214-826-8327
Raphaele Inc/616 Hawthorne, Houston, TX	713-524-2211
Raymond, Ray/1244 E Utopia, Phoenix, AZ	602-581-8160
Records, Bill/505 W 38, Austin, TX	512-458-1017
Redd, True/2328 Farrington, Dallas, TX	214-638-0602
REENS, LOUIS/4814 SYCAMORE, DALLAS, TX (P 198)	**214-827-3388**
REESE, DONOVAN/4801 LEMMON AVE, DALLAS, TX (P 199)	**214-526-5851**
Reisch, Jim/Studio 2025 Levee St, Dallas, TX	214-748-0456
Rich, Wilburn/3233 Marquart, Houston, TX	713-623-8790
Robbins Jr, Joe D/7320 Ashcroft Ste 213, Houston, TX	713-271-1111
Robbins, Mark/2520 Oakland Blvd, Ft Worth, TX	817-536-5061
Roe, Cliff/47 Woodelves Pl, The Woodlands, TX	713-363-5661
Rogers, John/PO Box 35753, Dallas, TX	214-351-1751
Rubin, Janice/705 E 16th St, Houston, TX	713-868-6060
Running, John/PO Box 1237, Flagstaff, AZ	602-774-2923
Rusing, Rick/22 E 15th St, Tempe, AZ	602-967-1864
Russell, Gail/PO Box 241, Taos, NM	505-776-8474
Russell, Nicholas/849-F Harvard, Houston, TX	713-864-7664
Ryan, Tom/1821 Levee, Dallas, TX	214-651-7085

S
Sall, Narinder/2024 Karbach #3, Houston, TX	713-680-3717
Savant, Joseph/4756 Algiers St, Dallas, TX	214-951-0111
Sawada, Spencer/2810 S 24th St #109, Phoenix, AZ	602-275-5078
Saxon, John/1337 Crampton, Dallas, TX	214-630-5160
Scheer, Tim/1521 Centerville Rd, Dallas, TX	214-328-1016
Scheyer, Mark/3317 Montrose #A1003, Houston, TX	713-861-0847
Schlesinger, Terrence/PO Box 32877, Phoenix, AZ	602-957-7474

Photographers

Continued

Please send us your additions and updates.

Schneps, Michael/21 Pinedale #6, Houston, TX	713-520-8224
Schultz, David/4220 Main St, Dallas, TX	214-827-1453
Schuster, Ellen/3719 Gilbert, Dallas, TX	214-526-6712
SCOTT, RON/EFX/1000 JACKSON BLVD, HOUSTON, TX	
(P 200,201)	**713-529-5868**
Scruggs, Jim/2410 Taft, Houston, TX	713-523-6146
Segrest, Jerry Photography/1707 S Arvay, Dallas, TX	214-426-6360
Segroves, Jim/170 Leslie, Dallas, TX	214-827-5482
Sellers, Dan/2258 Vantage, Dallas, TX	214-631-4705
Shackelford, Robert/1515 Lomita Ave, Richardson, TX	214-234-4736
Shands, Nathan/1107 Bryan, Mesquite, TX	214-285-5382
Shaw, Robert/1723 Kelly SE, Dallas, TX	214-428-1757
Shultz, Dave/PO Box 59737, Dallas, TX	214-438-1549
Siegel, David Martin/224 N 5th Ave, Phoenix, AZ	602-257-9509
Sieve, Jerry/PO Box 1777, Cave Creek, AZ	602-488-9561
Simon, Frank/1012 N Seventh Ave, Phoenix, AZ	602-254-4018
SIMPSON, MICHEAL/415 N BISHOP AVE, DALLAS, TX	
(P 202)	**214-943-9347**
Smith, Louis/9101 Jameel #190, Houston, TX	713-451-8094
Smith, Seth/1228 North 8th St, Abilene, TX	915-673-7505
Smith/Garza Photography/PO Box 10046, Dallas, TX	214-941-4611
Smothers, Brian/834 W 43rd St, Houston, TX	713-695-0873
Smusz, Ben/7313 Ashcroft #216, Houston, TX	713-772-5026
Southan, Ron/2905 Sun Valley, Irving, TX	214-255-3741
Sperry, Bill/3300 E Stanford, Paradise Valley, AZ	602-955-5626
St Angelo, Ron/350 Turtle Creek #109, Dallas, TX	214-254-7703
St Gil & Associates/2230 Ashford Hollow Ln, Houston, TX	713-870-9458
Staarjes, Hans/20 Lana Lane, Houston, TX	713-621-8503
Starnes, Mac/2703 Fondren #136, Dallas, TX	214-692-1720
Stibbens, Steve/104 Cole St, Dallas, TX	214-651-8224
Stiller, Rick/1311 E 35th St, Tulsa, OK	918-749-0297
Stites, Bill/1600 Park St, Houston, TX	713-523-6439
Stroud, Dan/1350 Manufacturing #211, Dallas, TX	214-745-1933
Studio Nine/283 N University, Provo, UT	801-374-6463
Suddarth, Robert/3402 73rd St, Lubbock, TX	806-795-4553
Sumner, Bill/122 Parkhouse, Dallas, TX	214-748-3766
Svacina, Joe/2209 Summer, Dallas, TX	214-748-3260
Swindler, Mark/206 Santa Rita, Odessa, TX	915-332-3515

T

Tenney, Bob/PO Box 17236, Dallas, TX	214-288-9291
Terry, Phillip/1222 Manufacturing St, Dallas, TX	214-749-0515
Thatcher, Charles/4220 Main St, Dallas, TX	214-823-4356
Thompson, Dennis/4153 S 87th Ave, Tulsa, OK	918-582-8850
Thompson, Wesley/800 W Airport Frwy #301, Irving, TX	214-438-7762
Timmerman, Bill/2301 N 16th St, Phoenix, AZ	602-252-6501
Tomlinson, Doug/5651 East Side Ave, Dallas, TX	214-821-1192
Trent, Rusty/7205 Cecil, Houston, TX	713-797-1405
Turner, Rick/1117 Welch, Houston, TX	713-524-2576
Turtle Creek Studio/1405-B Turtle Creek Blvd, Dallas, TX	214-742-1045

UV

Untersee, Chuck/2747 Seelcco, Dallas, TX	214-358-2306
Van Warner, Steven/1637 W Wilshire, Phoenix, AZ	602-254-2618
Vener, Ellis/3601 Allen Pkwy #123, Houston, TX	713-523-0456
Viewpoint Photographers/217 McKinley, Phoenix, AZ	602-245-0013
Vine, Terry/5455 Dashwood, Houston, TX	713-664-2920
Vinson, Phil/6216 Devonshire Terrace, Fort Worth, TX	817-451-4907
Von Helms, Michael/4212 San Felipe, Houston, TX	713-666-1212
Vracin, Andrew/4501 Swiss Ave, Dallas, TX	214-821-0231

WY

Walker, Balfour/1838 E 6th St, Tucson, AZ	602-624-1121
Wells, Craig/537 W Granada, Phoenix, AZ	602-252-8166
Welsch, Diana/PO Box 1791, Austin, TX	512-451-8960
WERRE, BOB/2437 BARTLETT ST, HOUSTON, TX (P 203)	**713-529-4841**
Wheeler, Don/220 N Main, Tulsa, OK	918-592-5099
White, Frank Photo/2702 Sackett, Houston, TX	713-524-9250
Wilke, Darrell/2608 Irving Blvd, Dallas, TX	214-631-6459
Willecke, Brian/PO Box 16603, Ft Worth, TX	817-346-6121
Williams, Oscar/8535 Fairhaven, San Antonio, TX	512-690-8807
Wilson, Sandy/PO Box 49391, Austin, TX	512-452-1299
Wolenski, Stan/2201 N Lamar, Dallas, TX	214-720-0044
Wolfhagen, Vilhelm/4916 Kelvin, Houston, TX	713-522-2787
WOLLAM, LES/5215 GOODWIN AVE, DALLAS, TX (P 204)	**214-760-7721**

Wood, Keith/1308 Conant St, Dallas, TX	214-634-7344
Wristen, Don/2025 Levee St, Dallas, TX	214-748-5317
Yeung, Ka Chuen/4901 W Lovers Lane, Dallas, TX	214-350-8716

Rocky Mountain

A

Aiuppy, Larry/PO Box 26, Livingston, MT	406-222-7308
Alaxandar/820 Humboldt St #6, Denver, CO	303-863-8844
Allen, Lincoln/1705 Woodbridge Dr, Salt Lake City, UT	801-277-1848
Alston, Bruce/PO Box 2480, Steamboat Springs, CO	303-879-1675
Anderson, Borge/234 South 200 East, Salt Lake City, UT	801-359-7703
Appleton, Roger/1224 E Platte, Colorado Springs, CO	303-635-0393
Appleton/ Kidder/1420 N Weber, Colorado Springs, CO	303-635-0393
Auben, Steven/590 Dover, Lakewood, CO	303-232-0243

B

Bako, Andrew/3047 4th St SW, Calgary T2S 1X9, AB	403-243-9789
Barry, Dave/6669 S Kit CArson St, Littleton, CO	303-798-9995
Bartay Studio/721 Santa Fe Dr, Denver, CO	303-628-0700
Bartek, Patrick/PO Box 26994, Las Vegas, NV	702-368-2901
Batchlor, Paul/655 Wolff St #42, Denver, CO	303-623-4465
Bator, Joe/2011 Washington Ave, Golden, CO	303-279-4163
Bauer, Erwin A/Box 543, Teton Village, WY	307-733-4023
Beery, Gale/150 W Byers, Denver, CO	303-777-0458
Benschneider, Ben/1711 Alamo, Colorado Springs, CO	303-473-4294
Berchert, Jim/PO Box 903, Denver, CO	303-466-7414
Berge, Melinda/1280 Ute Ave, Aspen, CO	303-925-2317
Birnbach, Allen/3600 Tejon St, Denver, CO	303-455-7800
Blake, John/4132 20th St, Greeley, CO	303-330-0980
Bluebaugh, David Studio/1594 S Acoma St, Denver, CO	303-778-7214
Bonmarito, Jim/PO Box 599, Durango, CO	303-247-1166
Bosworth/Graves Photo Inc/1055 S 700 W, Salt Lake City, UT	801-972-6128
Brantley, Robert/1414 S 7th West, Salt Lake City, UT	801-972-8293
Burggraf, Chuck/2941 W 23rd Ave, Denver, CO	303-480-9053
Busath, Drake/701 East South Temple St, Salt Lake City, UT	801-364-6645

C

CAMBON, JIM/216 RACQUETTE DR, FORT COLLINS, CO (P 206)	**303-221-4545**
Carduino, Tony/1706 Palm Dr #3, Ft Collins, CO	303-493-4648
Chatman, Donna/13474 W 65th Dr, Arvada, CO	303-422-8743
Chesley, Paul/Box 94, Aspen, CO	303-925-1148
Christensen, Barry/4505 South 2300 West, Roy, UT	801-731-3521
Clasen, Norm/PO Box 4230, Aspen, CO	303-925-4418
Coca, Joe/213 1/2 Jefferson St, Ft Collins, CO	303-482-0858
Collector, Stephen/1836 Mapleton Ave, Boulder, CO	303-442-1386
Colman, Mark/1505 E 13th Ave #9, Denver, CO	303-832-1243
Conrad, Bruce/PO Box 2606, Durango, CO	303-385-4265
Cook, James/PO Box 11608, Denver, CO	303-433-4874
Coppock, Ron/1443 Wazee St, Denver, CO	303-893-2299
Cravens, Karen/PO Box 26307, Lakewood, CO	303-423-1230
Cronin, Bill/2543 Xavier, Denver, CO	303-458-0883
Crowe, Steven/1150 S Cherry #1-202, Denver, CO	303-782-0346
Cruickshank/505 C Street, Lewiston, ID	208-743-9411
Cupp, David/2520 Albion St, Denver, CO	303-321-3581

D

Dahlquist, Ron/PO Box 1606, Steamboat Springs, CO	303-879-7075
Daly, Michael Kevin/PO Box 1987, Zephyr Cove, NV	916-577-7095
Dean, Bill/621 West 1000 North, West Bountiful, UT	801-295-9746
DeHoff, RD/632 N Sheridan, Colorado Springs, CO	303-635-0263
DELESPINASSE, HANK/2300 E PATRICK LN #21, LAS VEGAS, NV (P 218)	**702-798-6693**
Delmancznk, Phillip/1625 Wilber Pl, Reno, NV	702-329-0339
Dennis, Steven/350 N Santa Fe Dr, Denver, CO	303-534-8400
DeSciose, Nick/2700 Arapahoe St #2, Denver, CO	303-296-6386
DeVore, Nicholas III/1280 Ute, Aspen, CO	303-925-2317
Dickey, Marc/2500 Curtis #115, Denver, CO	303-298-7691
Dimond, Craig/615 Simpson Ave, Salt Lake City, UT	801-484-7003
Dolan, J Ross/6094 S Ironton Ct, Englewood, CO	303-770-8454
Donovan, David/437 Engel Ave, Henderson, NV	702-564-3598
Douglass, Dirk/2755 S 300 W #D, Salt Lake City, UT	801-485-5691
Downs, Jerry/1315 Oak Ct, Boulder, CO	303-444-8910

Photographers

Continued

Please send us your additions and updates.

PHOTOGRAPHERS

E F

Elder, Jim/PO Box 1600, Jackson Hole, WY	307-733-3555
Fader, Bob/14 Pearl St, Denver, CO	303-744-0711
Farace, Joe Photo/14 Inverness #B100, Englewood, CO	303-799-6606
Feld, Stephen/1572 E 9350 S, Sandy, UT	801-571-1752
Firth, Peter/5100 S 300 W #B, Murray, UT	801-262-3177
Ford, David/954 S Emerson, Denver, CO	303-778-7044
FRAZIER, VAN/2770 S MARYLAND PKWY, LAS VEGAS, NV	
(P 220)	**702-735-1165**
Freeman, Hunter/852 Santa Fe Dr, Denver, CO	303-893-5730

G H

Gallian, Dirk/PO Box 4573, Aspen, CO	303-925-8268
Gamba, Mark/705 19th St, Glenwood Springs, CO	303-945-5903
Goetze, David/3215 Zuni, Denver, CO	303-458-5026
Gorfkle, Gregory D/6901 E Baker Pl, Denver, CO	303-759-2737
Graf, Gary/1870 S Ogden St, Denver, CO	303-722-0547
H B R Studios/3310 South Knox Court, Denver, CO	303-789-4307
Harris, Richard/935 South High, Denver, CO	303-778-6433
Haun, Lora/8428 Fenton St, Arvada, CO	303-428-8834
Havey, James/1836 Blake St #203, Denver, CO	303-296-7448
Held, Patti/PO Box 44441, Denver, CO	303-341-7248
Henderson, Gordon/182 Gariepy Crescent, Edmonton	403-483-8049
Herridge, Brent/736 South 3rd West, Salt Lake City, UT	801-363-0337
Hiser, David C/1280 Ute Ave, Aspen, CO	303-925-2317
Holdman, Floyd/1908 Main St, Orem, UT	801-224-9966
Hooper, Robert Scott/4330 W Desert Inn Rd, Las Vegas, NV	702-873-5823
Hunt, Steven/1139 W Shepard Ln, Farmington, UT	801-451-6552
Huntress, Diane/3337 W 23rd Ave, Denver, CO	303-480-0219

J K

J T Photographics/10490-C West Fair Ave, Littleton, CO	303-972-8847
Jensen, Curt/915 Walnut #A 305, Rock Spring, WY	307-382-7794
Johns, Rob/1075 Piedmont, Boulder, CO	303-449-9192
JOHNSON, JIM PHOTO/16231 E PRINCETON CIRCLE,	
DENVER, CO (P 207)	**303-680-0522**
Johnson, Ron/2460 Eliot St, Denver, CO	303-458-0288
Kay, James W/4463 Wander Ln, Salt Lake City, UT	801-277-4489
Kehrwald, Richard J/32 S Main, Sheridan, WY	307-674-4679
Kidder, Jeanne/1420 N Weber, Colorado Springs, CO	303-635-0393
Kitzman, J R/1285 Acropolis Dr, Lafayette, CO	303-440-7623
Koropp, Robert/901 E 17th Ave, Denver, CO	303-830-6000
Kramer, Andrew/PO Box 6023, Boulder, CO	303-449-2280
Krause, Ann/2450 8th St, Boulder, CO	303-447-9711

L

Lammers, Kathi/PO Box 8480, Breckenridge, CO	303-453-1860
Laszlo, Larry/1100 Acoma St, Denver, CO	303-893-1199
LeCoq, John Land/640 S University, Denver, CO	303-295-3907
Lee, Jess/6799 N Derek Ln, Idaho Falls, ID	208-529-4535
LeGoy, James M/PO Box 21004, Reno, NV	702-322-0116
LEVY, PATRICIA BARRY/4467 UTICA, DENVER, CO (P 208)	**303-458-6692**
Lichter, Michael/3300 14th St, Boulder, CO	303-443-9198
Lissy, David/14472 Applewood Ridge Rd, Golden, CO	303-277-0232
Lokey, David/PO Box 7, Vail, CO	303-949-5750
Lonczyna, Longin/257-R S Rio Grande St, Salt Lake City, UT	801-355-7513
Lotz, Fred/4220 W 82nd Ave, Westminster, CO	303-427-2875

M

MacDonald, Dan/PO Box 5133, Greeley, CO	303-352-5812
Mangelson, Tom/PO Box 205, Moose, WY	307-733-6179
Marlow, David/PO Box 4934, Aspen, CO	303-925-8882
Masamori, Ron/1261 Glenarm Pl, Denver, CO	303-892-6666
Mathews, T R/9206 W 100th St, Broomfield, CO	303-469-1436
McDonald, Kirk/350 Bannock, Denver, CO	303-733-2958
McDowell, Pat/PO Box 283, Park City, UT	801-649-3403
McManemin, Jack/662 S State St, Salt Lake City, UT	801-533-0435
Meleski, Mike/1134 S Broadway, Denver, CO	303-297-0632
Melick, Jordan/1250 W Cedar St, Denver, CO	303-744-1414
Messineo, John/PO Box 1636, Fort Collins, CO	303-482-9349
MILES, KENT/25 SOUTH 300 EAST, SALT LAKE CITY, UT	
(P 209)	**801-364-5755**
Miller, Kenneth L/PO Box 57, Silver City, NV	702-847-9076
Milmoe, James O/14900 Cactus Cr, Golden, CO	303-279-4364
Milne, Lee/3615 W 49th Ave, Denver, CO	303-458-1520
Mitchell, Paul/1517 S Grant, Denver, CO	303-722-8852

Mock, Wanda/PO Box 85, Roberts, MT	406-445-2356
Moore, Janet/3250 S Elati St, Englewood, CO	303-781-0035
Mosbisch, Dick/5480 E Gill Pl, Denver, CO	303-333-9651
Munro, Harry/2355 W 27th Ave, Denver, CO	303-355-5612

O P

O'Hara, Timothy/PO Box 1802, Ft Collins, CO	303-224-2186
Oswald, Jan/921 Santa Fe, Denver, CO	303-893-8038
Patryas, David/26 Birch Ct #4, Long Mont, CO	303-678-0959
Paul, Howard/2460 Eliot St, Denver, CO	303-458-0288
Paul, Ken/1523 E Montana Dr, Golden, CO	303-526-1162
Payne, Brian/2685 Forest, Denver, CO	303-355-5373
Peregrine Studio/1541 Platte St, Denver, CO	303-455-6944
Perkin, Jan/3194 Kaibob Way, Salt Lake City, UT	801-485-8100
Phillips, Ron/6500-K Stapleton S Dr, Denver, CO	303-321-6777

Q R

Quinney Group/423 E Broadway, Salt Lake City, UT	801-363-0434
Rafkind, Andrew/1702 Fairview Ave, Boise, ID	208-344-9918
Ramsey, Steve/4800 N Washington St, Denver, CO	303-295-2135
Ranson Photographers Ltd/26 Airport Rd, Edmonton T5G	
0W7, AB	403-454-9674
Rawls, Ray/4344 E 127th Pl, Denver, CO	303-452-5587
Redding, Ken/PO Box 717, Vail, CO	303-949-6123
Reed, Joe/9859 Orangewood Dr, Denver, CO	303-452-2894
Reynolds, Roger/3310 S Knox Ct, Englewood, CO	303-789-4307
Rosen, Barry/1 Middle Rd, Englewood, CO	303-758-0648
Rosenberg, David/1545 Julian SE, Denver, CO	303-893-0893
Rosenberger, Edward/2248 Emerson Ave, Salt Lake City, UT	801-355-9007
Russell, John/PO Box 4739, Aspen, CO	303-920-1431

S

Saehlenou, Kevin/3478 W 32nd Ave, Denver, CO	303-455-1611
Sahula, Peter/, , CO	303-927-3475
Sammons, Steve/776 Santa Fe Dr, Denver, CO	303-623-1171
Saviers, Trent/2606 Rayma Ct, Reno, NV	702-747-2591
Scherer, William D/PO Box 274, Greeley, CO	303-353-6674
Schlack, Greg/1510 Lehigh St, Boulder, CO	303-499-3860
Schmiett, Skip/740 W 1700 S #10, Salt Lake City, UT	801-973-0642
Schneider, Beth/1666 Race St, Denver, CO	303-388-4909
Schoenfeld, Michael/925 SW Temple, Salt Lake City, UT	801-532-2006
Shupe, John R/4090 Edgehill Dr, Ogden, UT	801-392-2523
Simons, Randy/3320 S Knox Ct, Englewood, CO	303-761-1458
SMITH, DAVID SCOTT/1437 AVE E, BILLINGS, MT (P 210)	**406-259-5656**
Smith, Derek/925 SW Temple, Salt Lake City, UT	801-863-6346
Smith, Dorn/1201-A Santa Fe, Denver, CO	303-571-4331
Snyder, John P/PO Box 7429 University Sta, Provo, UT	801-373-5748
Sokol, Howard/3006 Zuni St, Denver, CO	303-433-3353
St John, Charles/PO Box 6580, Denver, CO	303-292-6019
Staver, Barry/5122 S Iris Way, Littleton, CO	303-973-4414
STEARNS, DOUG/1738 WYNKOOP ST #102, DENVER, CO	
(P 211)	**303-296-1133**
Stewert, Sandy/17618 W 14th Ave #1, Golden, CO	303-278-8039
Stott, Barry/2427 Chamonix Rd, Vail, CO	303-476-5774
Stouder, Carol/5421 W Geddes Pl, Littleton, CO	303-979-5402
Studio Nine/283 N University, Provo, UT	801-374-6463
Swartz, Bill/5992 S Eudora Ct, Littleton, CO	303-773-2776
Sweitzer, David/4800 Washington, Denver, CO	303-295-0703

T

Tanner, Scott/2755 South 300 West #D, Salt Lake City, UT	801-466-6884
TEJADA, DAVID X/1553 PLATTE ST #205, DENVER, CO	
(P 212)	**303-458-1220**
Tharp, Brenda/901 E Seventeenth Ave, Denver, CO	303-830-0845
Till, Tom/796 Westwood, Moab, UT	801-259-5327
Tobias, Philip/3614 Morrison Rd, Denver, CO	303-936-1267
Tradelius, Bob/738 Santa Fe Dr, Denver, CO	303-825-4847
Travis, Tom/1219 S Pearl St, Denver, CO	303-377-7422
Tregeagle, Steve/2994 S Richards St #C, Salt Lake City, UT	801-484-1673
Trice, Gordon/2046 Arapahoe St, Denver, CO	303-298-1986
Twede, Brian L/430 S State St, Salt Lake City, UT	801-534-1459

V W

Van Hemert, Martin/5481 Cyclamen Ct, Salt Lake City, UT	801-969-3569
Vandenberg, Greg/1901 E 47th Ave, Denver, CO	303-295-2525
Viggio Studio/2400 Central Ave, Boulder, CO	303-444-3342
Walker, Rod/PO Box 2418, Vail, CO	303-926-3210

Photographers
Continued

Please send us your additions and updates.

Wankelman, Peter/633 S College Ave, Ft Collins, CO	303-482-9424
Wapinski, David/10 Valdez Circle, Dugway, UT	801-522-4214
Warren, Cameron A/PO Box 10588, Reno, NV	702-825-5565
Wayda, Steve/5725 Immigration Canyon, Salt Lake City, UT	801-582-1787
Weeks, Michael/PO Box 6965, Colorado Springs, CO	303-632-2996
Wellisch, Bill/2325 Clay St, Denver, CO	303-455-8766
Welsh, Steve/518 Americana Blvd, Boise, ID	208-336-5541
Wheeler, Geoffrey/721 Pearl St, Boulder, CO	303-449-2137
White, Stuart/4229 Clark Ave, Great Falls, MT	406-761-6666
Wiseman, Jay/6429 South 300 East, Murray, UT	801-261-2933
Wordal, Eric/3640 Keir Lane, Helena, MT	406-475-3304
Worden, Kirk/16 W 13th Ave, Denver, CO	303-629-5574

West Coast

A

Abecassis, Andree L/756 Neilson St, Berkeley, CA	415-526-5099
Abraham, Russell/17 Brosnan St, San Francisco, CA	415-558-9100
Abramowitz, Alan/PO Box 45121, Seattle, WA	206-527-8111
Ackroyd, Hugh S/Box 10101, Portland, OR	503-227-5694
Addor, Jean-Michel/1311 63rd St, Emeryville, CA	415-653-1745
Adler, Allan S/PO Box 2251, Van Nuys, CA	818-901-6555
Adler, Gale/3740 Veteran Ave #1, Los Angeles, CA	213-837-9224
Agee, Bill & Assoc/715 Larkspur Box 612, Corona Del Mar, CA	714-760-6700
Ahrend, Jay/1046 N Orange Dr, Hollywood, CA	213-462-5256
Albert, Betty/4900 Burrett Ave, Richmond, CA	415-235-2856
Alexander, David/1545 N Wilcox #202, Hollywood, CA	213-464-8361
Alexanian, Nubar/1821 Fifth Ave W, Seattle, WA	206-285-3787
All Sport Photo/23335 Lake Manor Dr, Chatsworth, CA	818-704-5118
Allan, Larry/3503 Argonne St, San Diego, CA	619-270-1850
Allen, Charles/537 S Raymond Ave, Pasadena, CA	818-795-1053
Allen, Judson Photo/654 Gilman St, Palo Alto, CA	415-324-8177
Allensworth, Jim/PO Box 2224, Newport Beach, CA	714-970-1395
Allison, Glen/PO Box 1833, Santa Monica, CA	213-392-1388
Alt, Tim/3699 Wilshire Blvd #870, Los Angeles, CA	213-387-8384
Ambrose, Paul Studios/1931-J Old Middlefield Wy, Mountain View, CA	415-965-3555
Amer, Tommy/1858 Westerly Terrace, Los Angeles, CA	213-664-7624
Andersen, Kurt/250 Newhall, San Francisco, CA	415-641-4276
ANDERSON, KAREN/1170 N WESTERN AVE, LOS ANGELES, CA (P 214)	**213-461-9100**
Anderson, Rick/8871-B Balboa Ave, San Diego, CA	619-268-1957
Angelo, Michael/PO Box 2039, Mill Valley, CA	415-381-4224
Ansa, Brian/2605 N Lake Ave, Altadena, CA	818-797-2233
Aperture PhotoBank/1530 Westlake Ave N, Seattle, WA	206-282-8116
Apton, Bill/577 Howard St, San Francisco, CA	415-543-6313
Arend, Christopher/5401 Cordova St Ste 204, Anchorage, AK	907-562-3173
Armas, Richard/6913 Melrose Ave, Los Angeles, CA	213-931-7889
Arnesen, Erik/605 25th St, Manhattan Beach, CA	213-546-2363
Arnold, Robert Photo/1379 Natoma, San Francisco, CA	415-621-6161
Arnone, Ken/3886 Ampudia St, San Diego, CA	619-298-3141
Aron, Jeffrey/17801 Sky Park Cir #H, Irvine, CA	714-250-1555
Aronovsky, James/3356-C Hancock St, San Diego, CA	619-296-4858
Ashley, Chuck/329 San Francisco Blvd, San Anselmo, CA	415-453-2967
Askew, Don/8148 Ronson Rd #L, San Diego, CA	619-569-6274
The Association/151 Kalmuf #H 10, Costa Mesa, CA	714-631-4634
Atkinson Photo/505 S Flower B Level, Los Angeles, CA	213-624-5970
Atlas Photo-Video/11416 Harrisburg Rd, Los Alamitos, CA	213-430-8379
Aurness, Craig/1526 Pontius Ave #A, Los Angeles, CA	213-477-0421
Avery, Franklin/800 Duboce #101, San Francisco, CA	415 986-3701
Avery, Ron/820 N La Brea, Los Angeles, CA	213-465-7193
Avery, Sid/820 N La Brea, Los Angeles, CA	213-465-7193
Ayres, Robert Bruce/5635 Melrose Ave, Los Angeles, CA	213-461-3816

B

Bacon, Garth/18576 Bucknall Rd, Saratoga, CA	408-866-5858
Baer, Morley/PO Box 222537, Carmel, CA	408-624-3530
Bagley, John/730 Clemintina, San Francisco, CA	415-861-1062
Bailey, Brent P/759 W 19th St, Costa Mesa, CA	714-548-9683
Baker, Bill/265 29th St, Oakland, CA	415-832-7685
BAKER, FRANK/15031-B PARKWAY LOOP, TUSTIN, CA (P 215)	**714-259-1462**
Balderas, Michael/5837-B Mission Gorge Rd, San Diego, CA	619-563-7077
Baldwin, Doug/10518-2 Sunland Blvd, Sunland, CA	818-353-7270
Banko, Phil/1249 First Ave S, Seattle, WA	206-621-7008
Banks, Ken/135 N Harper Ave, Los Angeles, CA	213-930-2831
Bardin, James/111 Villa View Dr, Pacific Palisades, CA	213-459-4775
Bare, John/3001 Red Hill Ave #4-102, Costa Mesa, CA	714-979-8712
Barkentin, Pamela/1218 N LaCienega, Los Angeles, CA	213-854-1941
Barnes, David/PO Box 31498, Seattle, WA	206-282-8116
Barnes, John/637 Natoma St, San Francisco, CA	415-431-5264
Barnhurst, Noel/1417 15th St, San Francisco, CA	415-431-0401
Barros, Robert/E1813 Sprague, Spokane, WA	509-535-6455
Bartholick, Robin/89 Yesler Way 4th Fl, Seattle, WA	206-467-1001
Barton, Hugh G/230 Polk St, Eugene, OR	503-342-7072
Bartone, Laurence/335 Fifth St, San Francisco, CA	415-974-6010
Bartruff, Dave/PO Box 800, San Anselmo, CA	415-457-1482
Bates, Frank/5158 Highland View Ave, Los Angeles, CA	213-258-5272
Batista-Moon Studio/444 Pearl #B-1, Monterey, CA	408-373-1947
Bauer, Karel M/141 10th St, San Francisco, CA	415-863-5155
Bayer, Dennis/1261 Howard St, San Francisco, CA	415-552-6575
Bear, Brent/8566 W Pico Blvd, Los Angeles, CA	213-652-1156
Beatie, Chris/25952 Via Del Rey, San Juan Capistrano, CA	714-240-3311
Becker Bishop Studios/1830 17th St, San Francisco, CA	415-552-4254
Bedilion, Michael/7272 Carlton Ave, Westminster, CA	714-894-3900
Beebe, Morton/150 Lombard St #207, San Francisco, CA	415-362-3530
Beer, Rafael/207 S Catalina Ste 4, Los Angeles, CA	213-384-9532
Behrman, C H/8036 Kentwood, Los Angeles, CA	213-216-6611
Belcher, Richard/2565 Third St #206, San Francisco, CA	415-641-8912
Benchmark Photo/1442 N Hundley, Anaheim, CA	714-630-7965
Bencze, Louis/2442 NW Market St #86, Seattle, WA	206-783-8033
Benet, Ben/333 Fifth St #A, San Francisco, CA	415-974-5433
Bennett, James Photo/280 Cajon St, Laguna Beach, CA	714-497-4309
Bennion, Chris/5234 36th Ave NE, Seattle, WA	206-526-9981
Benson, Hank/653 Bryant St, San Francisco, CA	415-543-8153
Benson, John/1261 Howard St 2nd Fl, San Francisco, CA	415-621-5247
Benton, Richard/4773 Brighton Ave, San Diego, CA	619-224-0278
Bergman, Alan/8241 W 4th St, Los Angeles, CA	213-852-1408
Berman, Ellen/5425 Senford Ave, Los Angeles, CA	213-641-2783
Berman, Steve/7955 W 3rd, Los Angeles, CA	213-933-9185
Bernstein, Andrew/1415 N Chester, Pasadena, CA	818-797-3430
Bernstein, Gary/8735 Washington Blvd, Culver City, CA	213-550-6891
Bertholomey, John/17962 Sky Park Cir #J, Irvine, CA	714-261-0575
Betz, Ted R/527 Howard 2nd Fl, San Francisco, CA	415-777-1260
Bez, Frank/1880 Santa Barbara Ave, San Luis Obispo, CA	805-541-2878
Bielenberg, Paul/2447 Lanterman Terr, Los Angeles, CA	213-669-1085
Biggs, Ken/1147 N Hudson Ave, Los Angeles, CA	213-462-7739
Bilecky, John/5047 W Pico Blvd, Los Angeles, CA	213-931-1610
Bilyell, Martin/600 NE Couch St, Portland, OR	503-238-0349
Bishop, David/Photopia/PO Box 2309, San Francisco, CA	415-441-5611
Bjoin, Henry/146 N La Brea Ave, Los Angeles, CA	213-937-4097
Blakeley, Jim/1061 Folsom St, San Francisco, CA	415-558-9300
Blakeman, Bob/710 S Santa Fe, Los Angeles, CA	213-624-6662
Blattel, David/740 S Mariposa St, Burbank, CA	213-937-0366
Blaustein, John/911 Euclid Ave, Berkeley, CA	415-525-8133
Bleyer, Pete/807 N Sierra Bonita Ave, Los Angeles, CA	213-653-6567
Blumensaadt, Mike/306 Edna, San Francisco, CA	415-333-6178
Bodnar, Joe/2817 Selby, Los Angeles, CA	213-838-6587
Boonisar, Peter/PO Box 2274, Atascadero, CA	805-466-5577
Bortvent, Jim/9100 SW Washington, Portland, OR	503-297-2976
Boudreau, Bernard/1015 N Cahuenga, Hollywood, CA	213-467-2602
Boulevard Photographic/5701 Buckingham Pky #F, Culver City, CA	213-649-0202
Boulger & Kanuit/503 S Catalina, Redondo Beach, CA	213-540-6300
Bourret, Tom/930 Alabama, San Francisco, CA	415-282-2525
Bowen, John E/PO Box 1115, Hilo, HI	808-959-9460
Boyd, Bill/614 Santa Barbara St, Santa Barbara, CA	805-962-9193
Boyd, Jack/2038 Calvert Ave, Costa Mesa, CA	714-556-8133
Boyer, Dale/PO Box 391535, Mountainview, CA	415-968-9656
Boyer, Neil/1416 Aviation Blvd, Redondo Beach, CA	213-374-0443
Brabant, Patricia/245 S Van Ness 3rd Fl, San Francisco, CA	415-864-0591
Bracke, Vic/560 S Main St #4N, Los Angeles, CA	213-623-6522
Bradley, Leverett/Box 1793, Santa Monica, CA	213-394-0908
Bragstad, Jeremiah O/1041 Folsom St, San Francisco, CA	415-776-2740

Photographers

Continued

Please send us your additions and updates.

Brandon, Randy/PO Box 1010, Girdwood, AK	907-783-2773
Braun, Ernest/PO Box 627, San Anselmo, CA	415-454-2791
Brenneis, Jon/2576 Shattuck, Berkeley, CA	415-845-3377
Brewer, Art/27324 Camino Capistrano #161, Laguna Nigel, CA	714-582-9085
Brian, Rick/555 S Alexandria Ave, Los Angeles, CA	213-387-3017
Britt, Jim/140 N LaBrea, Los Angeles, CA	213-936-3131
Broberg, Ed/PO Box 1892, Walla Walla, WA	509-529-5189
Brod, Garry/6502 Santa Monica Blvd, Hollywood, CA	213-463-7887
Brown, George/1417 15th St, San Francisco, CA	415-621-3543
Brown, Matt/420 Commercial Ave, Anacortes, WA	206-293-3540
Brown, Michael/PO Box 45969, Los Angeles, CA	213-379-7254
Browne, Rick/145 Shake Tree Ln, Scotts Valley, CA	408-438-3919
Brum, Kim/5555-L Santa Fe St, San Diego, CA	619-483-2124
Bubar, Julie/12559 Palero Rd, San Diego, CA	619-234-4020
Buchanan, Bruce/PO Box 48892, Los Angeles, CA	213-462-7086
Buchanan, Craig/1026 Folsom St #207, San Francisco, CA	415-861-5566
Budnik, Victor/125 King St, San Francisco, CA	415-541-9050
BURKE, KEVIN/1015 N CAHUENGA BLVD, LOS ANGELES, CA (P 216)	**213-467-0266**
Burke, Leslie/947 La Cienega, Los Angeles, CA	213-652-7011
Burke/Triolo Photo/940 E 2nd St #2, Los Angeles, CA	213-687-4730
Burkhart, Howard Photography/8513 1/2 Horner St, Los Angeles, CA	213-671-2283
BURMAN & STEINHEIMER/2648 FIFTH AVE, SACRAMENTO, CA (P 217)	**916-457-1908**
Burr, Bruce/2867 1/2 W 7th St, Los Angeles, CA	213-388-3361
Burr, Lawrence/76 Manzanita Rd, Fairfax, CA	415-456-9158
Burroughs, Robert/6713 Bardonia St, San Diego, CA	619-469-6922
Burry, D L/PO Box 1611, Los Gatos, CA	408-354-1922
Burt, Pat/1412 SE Stark, Portland, OR	503-284-9989
Bush, Chan/PO Box 819, Montrose, CA	818-957-6558
Bush, Charles/940-N Highland, Los Angeles, CA	213-937-8246
Bush, Dave/2 St George St, San Francisco, CA	415-981-2874
Busher, Dick/7042 20th Place NE, Seattle, WA	206-523-1426
Bussey, Bill/7915 Via Stefano, Burbank, CA	818-767-5078
Butchofsky, Jan/7219 Hampton Ave, Los Angeles, CA	213-874-5313
Butler, Erik/161 King St, San Francisco, CA	415-777-1656

C	
C & I Photography/3523 Ryder St, Santa Clara, CA	408-733-5855
Cable, Ron/17835 Skypark Cir #N, Irvine, CA	714-261-8910
Caccavo, James/10002 Crescent Hts Blvd, Los Angeles, CA	213-939-9594
Cacitti, Stanley R/589 Howard, San Francisco, CA	415-974-5668
Caddow, Thomas/1944 University #10, Palo Alto, CA	415-329-0334
Cahoon, John/613 S LaBrea Ave, Los Angeles, CA	213-930-1144
Camera Hawaii/875 Waimanu St #110, Honolulu, HI	808-536-2302
Cameron, Robert/543 Howard, San Francisco, CA	415-777-5582
Camp, James Lee/1248 Jedburgh St, Glendora, CA	818-966-9240
Campbell Comm Photo/8586 Miramar Pl, San Diego, CA	619-587-0336
Campbell, David/244 Ninth St, San Francisco, CA	415-864-2556
Campbell, Kathleen Taylor/4751 Wilshire Blvd, Los Angeles, CA	213-931-6202
Campos, Michael/705 13th St, San Diego, CA	619-233-9914
Cannon, Bill/516 Yale Ave North, Seattle, WA	206-682-7031
Caplan, Stan/7014 Santa Monica Blvd, Los Angeles, CA	213-462-1271
Capps, Alan/137 S La Peer Dr, Los Angeles, CA	213-276-3724
Caputo, Tony/6636 Santa Monica Blvd, Hollywood, CA	213-464-6636
Carey, Ed/60 Federal St, San Francisco, CA	415-543-4883
Carlson, Craig/266 J Street, Chula Vista, CA	619-422-4937
Carofano, Ray/1011 1/4 W 190th St, Gardena, CA	213-515-0310
Carpenter, Mert/2020 Granada Wy, Los Gatos, CA	408-370-1663
Carr, Melanie/2120 J Durante Blvd #U, Del Mar, CA	619-755-1200
Carroll, Bruce/517 Dexter Ave N, Seattle, WA	206-623-2119
Carroll, Tom/26712 Calle Los Alamos, Capistrano Beach, CA	714-493-2665
Carroon, Chip/PO Box 590451, San Francisco, CA	415-864-1082
Carruth, Kerry/7153 Helmsdale Circle, Canoga Park, CA	818-704-6570
Carry, Mark/3375 Forest Ave, Santa Clara, CA	408-248-7872
Casemore, Rick/111 N Tamarind Ave, Los Angeles, CA	213-461-9384
Casilli, Mario/2366 N Lake Ave, Altadena, CA	213-681-4476
Casler, Christopher/1600 Viewmont Dr, Los Angeles, CA	213-854-7733
Cato, Eric/3456 1/2 Floyd Terr, Los Angeles, CA	213-851-5606
Caulfield, Andy/PO Box 41131, Los Angeles, CA	213-258-3070

Chamberlain, Paul/319 1/2 S Robertson Blvd, Beverly Hills, CA	213-659-4647
Chaney, Brad/370 4th St, San Francisco, CA	415-543-2525
Charles, Cindy/1040 Noe St, San Francisco, CA	415-821-4457
Chen, James/1917 Anacapa St, Santa Barbara, CA	805-569-1849
Cherin, Alan/220 S Rose St, Los Angeles, CA	213-680-9893
Chernus, Ken/9531 Washington Blvd, Culver City, CA	213-838-3116
Chesser, Mike/6632 Santa Monica Blvd, Los Angeles, CA	213-463-5678
Chester, Mark/PO Box 99501, San Francisco, CA	415-922-7512
Chiarot, Roy/846 S Robertson Blvd, Los Angeles, CA	213-659-9173
Chin, K P/PO Box 421737, San Francisco, CA	415-282-3041
Chmielewski, David/230-C Polaris, Mountain View, CA	415-969-6639
Chun, Mike/35 Russia St #H, San Francisco, CA	415-469-7220
Chung, Ken-Lei/5200 Venice Blvd, Los Angeles, CA	213-938-9117
Church, Jim & Cathy/PO Box 80, Gilroy, CA	408-842-9682
Ciskowski, Jim/2444 Wilshire Blvd #B100, Santa Monica, CA	213-829-7375
Clark, Richard/334 S LaBrea, Los Angeles, CA	213-933-7407
Claxton, William/1368 Angelo Dr, Beverly Hills, CA	213-854-2222
Clayton, John/160 South Park, San Francisco, CA	415-495-4562
Cobb, Bruce/1537-A 4th St #102, San Rafael, CA	415-454-0619
Coccia, Jim/PO Box 81313, Fairbanks, AK	907-479-4707
Cogen, Melinda/1112 N Beachwood Dr, Hollywood, CA	213-467-9414
Cohn, Steven/2036 Eunice St, Berkeley, CA	415-525-0982
Coit, Jim/5555-L Santa Fe St, San Diego, CA	619-272-2255
Coleberd, Frances/1273 Mills St Apt 3, Menlo Park, CA	415-325-4731
Coleman, Arthur Photography/303 N Indian Ave, Palm Springs, CA	619-325-7015
Colladay, Charles/711 12th Ave, San Diego, CA	619-231-2920
Collison, James/6950 Havenurst, Van Nuys, CA	818-902-0770
Coluzzi, Tony Photography/897 Independence Ave #2B, Mountain View, CA	415-969-2955
Cook, Kathleen Norris/PO Box 2159, Laguna Hills, CA	714-770-4619
Corell, Volker/6614 Aldama St, Los Angeles, CA	213-255-3336
Cormier, Glenn/ PO Box 351, Santa Barbara, CA	805-963-4853
Cornfield, Jim/454 S La Brea Ave, Los Angeles, CA	213-938-3553
Correll, Volker/6614 Aldama St, Los Angeles, CA	213-255-3336
Corwin, Jeff/CPC Assoc/1910 Weepah Way, Los Angeles, CA	213-656-7449
Courbet, Yves/6516 W 6th St, Los Angeles, CA	213-655-2181
Courtney, William/4524 Rutgers Way, Sacramento, CA	916-487-8501
Cowin, Morgin/325 Bocana St, San Francisco, CA	415-648-2600
Crane, Wally/PO Box 81, Los Altos, CA	415-960-1990
Crawford, Dick/PO Box 747, Sanger, CA	209-875-3800
Crowley, Eliot/706 W Pico Blvd, Los Angeles, CA	213-742-0367
Cummings, Ian/2400 Kettner Blvd, San Diego, CA	619-231-1270
Cummins, Jim/1527 13th Ave, Seattle, WA	206-322-4944

D	
Dahlstrom Photography Inc/2312 NW Savier St, Portland, OR	503-222-4910
Dancs, Andras/518 Beatty St #603, Vancouver V6B 2L3, BC	604-684-6760
Dang, Tai/426 Jefferson St, Oakland, CA	415-832-8642
Daniel, Hank/PO Box 15779, Sacramento, CA	916-321-1278
Daniel, Jay/517 Jacoby St #11, San Raphael, CA	415-459-1495
Davey, Robert/PO Box 69291, Los Angeles, CA	213-659-3542
David/Gayle Photo/911 Western Ave #510, Seattle, WA	206-624-5207
Davidson, Dave/25003 S Beeson Rd, Beavercreek, OR	503-632-7650
Davidson, Jerry/3923 W Jefferson Blvd, Los Angeles, CA	213-735-1552
Davis, Tim/PO Box 1278, Palo Alto, CA	415-327-4192
Dayton, Ted/1112 N Beachwood, Los Angeles, CA	213-462-0712
DeCastro, Mike/2415 De La Cruz, Santa Clara, CA	408-988-8696
DeCruyenaere, Howard/1825 E Albion Ave, Santa Ana, CA	714-997-4446
DeGennaro, George Assoc/902 South Norton Ave, Los Angeles, CA	213-935-5179
Degler, Curtis/1050 Carolan Ave #311, Burlingame, CA	415-342-7381
Del Re, Sal/211-E East Columbine Ave, Santa Ana, CA	714-432-1333
Delancie, Steve/1129 Folsom St, San Francisco, CA	415-864-2640
Demerdjian, Jacob/3331 W Beverly Blvd, Montebello, CA	213-724-9630
DeMont, Debbi/3736 E 7th St, Long Beach, CA	213-433-1087
Denman, Frank B/1201 First Ave S, Seattle, WA	206-325-9260
Denny, Michael/2631 Ariane Dr, San Diego, CA	619-272-9104
DePaola, Mark/1560 Benedict Cnyn Dr, Beverly Hills, CA	213-550-5910
Der, Rick Photography/50 Mandell St #10, San Francisco, CA	415-824-8580
Derhacopian, Ronald/3109 Beverly Blvd, Los Angeles, CA	213-388-6724

Photographers

Continued

Please send us your additions and updates.

Devine, W L Studios/PO Box 67, Maple Falls, WA	206-599-2927
DeWilde, Roc/139 Noriega, San Francisco, CA	415-681-4612
DeYoung, Skip/1112 N Beachwood, Los Angeles, CA	213-462-0712
Diaz, Armando/19 S Park, San Francisco, CA	415-495-3552
Digital Art/3699 Wilshire Blvd #870, Los Angeles, CA	213-387-8384
Dinn, Peter/2776 Humboldt Ave, Oakland, CA	415-532-7792
Dogra, Narinder/15890 La Miranda Ct, Morgan Hill, CA	408-779-8811
Dolgins, Alan/1640 S La Cienega Blvd, Los Angeles, CA	213-273-5794
Dominick/833 N LaBrea Ave, Los Angeles, CA	213-934-3033
Donaldson, Peter/118 King St, San Francisco, CA	415-957-1102
Dow, Larry/1537 W 8th St, Los Angeles, CA	213-483-7970
Dowbanko, Uri/PO Box 1201, Aguroa Hills, CA	818-706-8838
Drake, Brian/407 Southwest 11th Ave, Portland, OR	503-241-4532
Dreiwitz, Herb/145 N Edgemont St, Los Angeles, CA	213-383-1746
Dressler, Rick/1322 Bell Ave #M, Tustin, CA	714-730-9113
Driver, Wallace/2510 Clairemont Dr #113, San Diego, CA	619-275-3159
Drumbor, David C/1147 Longfellow Ave, Campbell, CA	408-559-7876
Dudley, Hardin & Yang/3839 Stone Way North, Seattle, WA	206-632-3001
Dudley, Hardin & Yang/ Bellvue/13000 Bel-Red Rd, Bellevue, WA	206-455-4041
Duff, Rodney/4901 Morena Blvd #323, San Diego, CA	619-270-4082
Duffey, Robert/9691 Campus Dr, Anaheim, CA	714-956-4731
Duka, Lonnie/919 Oriole Dr, Laguna Beach, CA	714-494-7057
Dull, Ed/1745 NW Marshall, Portland, OR	503-224-3754
Dumentz, Barbara/39 E Walnut St, Pasadena, CA	213-467-6397
Dunbar, Clark/1260-B Pear Ave, Mountain View, CA	415-964-4225
Dunmire, Larry/PO Box 338, Balboa Island, CA	714-673-4058

E

Eadon, Jack/15031-B Parkway Loop, Tustin, CA	714-770-4300
Ealy, Dwayne/2 McLaren #B, Irvine, Ca	714-951-5089
Eastabrook, William R/3281 Oakshire Dr, Los Angeles, CA	213-851-3281
Eclipse Anonymous/PO Box 689, Haines, AK	907-766-2670
Edmunds, Dana/188 N King St, Honolulu, HI	808-521-7711
Edwards, Grant P/6837 Nancy Ridge Dr #G, San Diego, CA	619-458-1999
Elias, Robert Studio/959 N Cole, Los Angeles, CA	213-460-2988
Elk, John III/583 Weldon, Oakland, CA	415-834-3024
Emanuel, Manny/2257 Hollyridge Dr, Hollywood, CA	213-465-0259
Emberly, Gordon/1479 Folsom, San Francisco, CA	415-621-9714
Enkelis, Liane/764 Sutter Ave, Palo Alto, CA	415-326-3253
Esgro, Dan/PO Box 38536, Los Angeles, CA	213-932-1919
Estel, Suzanne/2325 3rd St, San Francisco, CA	415-864-3661
Evans, Marty/11112 Ventura Blvd, Studio City, CA	818-762-5400

F

Falk, Randolph/123 16th Ave, San Francisco, CA	415-751-8800
Fallon, Bernard/524 N Juanita Ave #3, Redondo Beach, CA	213-318-6006
Faries, Tom/16431 Sandalwood, Fountain Valley, CA	714-775-5767
Farruggio, Matthew J/3239 Kempton, Oakland, CA	415-444-0665
Faubel, Warren/627 S Highland Ave, Los Angeles, CA	213-939-8822
Feldman, Marc/6442 Santa Monica Blvd, Hollywood, CA	213-463-4829
Felt, Jim/1316 SE 12th Ave, Portland, OR	503-238-1748
Felzman, Joe/421 NW Fourth Ave, Portland, OR	503-224-7983
Finn, Dennis/1520 Tower Grove Dr, Beverly Hills, CA	213-274-4014
Finnegan, Kristin/3045 NW Thurman St, Portland, OR	503-241-2701
Firebaugh, Steve/6750 55th Ave S, Seattle, WA	206-721-5151
Fischer, Curt/51 Stillman, San Francisco, CA	415-974-5568
Fischer, David/340 Harriet, San Francisco, CA	415-495-4585
Fisher, Arthur Vining/271 Missouri St, San Francisco, CA	415-626-5483
Fitch, Wanelle/17845-D Sky Pk Cir, Irvine, CA	714-261-1566
Flavin, Frank/PO Box 141172, Anchorage, AK	907-561-1606
Flinn, Jim/8617 Sandpoint Way NE, Seattle, WA	206-524-1409
Flood, Alan/206 14th Ave, San Mateo, CA	415-572-0439
Fogg, Don/259 Clara St, San Francisco, CA	415-974-5244
Foothorap, Robert/426 Bryant St, San Francisco, CA	415-957-1447
Ford Photography/906 1/2 S Robertson Blvd, Los Angeles, CA	213-655-7655
Forsman, John/8696 Crescent Dr, Los Angeles, CA	213-933-9339
Forster, Bruce/431 NW Flanders, Portland, OR	503-222-5222
Forsyth, Dan/2311 Fifteenth Ave, San Francisco, CA	415-753-8451
Fort, Daniel/PO Box 11324, Costa Mesa, CA	714-546-5709
Fortson, Ed/Shoshana/400 S June St, Los Angeles, CA	213-934-6368
Fowler, Bradford/1946 N Serrano Ave, Los Angeles, CA	213-464-5708
Fox, Arthur/2194 Cable St, San Diego, CA	619-223-4784

Frankel, Tracy/7250 Hillside Ave #308, Los Angeles, CA	213-851-9668
Franklin, Charly/3352 20th St, San Francisco, CA	415-543-5400
Franzen, David/746 Ilaniwai St #200, Honolulu, HI	808-537-9921
FRAZIER, KIM ANDREW/PO BOX 6132, HAYWARD, CA (P 219)	**415-889-7050**
Freed, Jack/749 N La Brea, Los Angeles, CA	213-931-1015
Freis, Jay/416 Richardson St, Sausalito, CA	415-332-6709
French, Gerald/550 15th St #31/Showpl Sq, San Francisco, CA	415-397-3040
French, Peter/PO Box 100, Kamuela, HI	808-889-6488
Friedlander, Ernie/82 Ringold Alley, San Francisco, CA	415-626-6111
Friedman, Todd/PO Box 3737, Beverly Hills, CA	213-550-0831
Friend, David/3886 Ampudia St, San Diego, CA	619-260-1603
Frigge, Eric/	714-854-2985
Frisch, Stephen/ICB - Gate 5 Rd, Sausalito, CA	415-332-4545
Frisella, Josef/340 S Clark Dr, Beverly Hills, CA	213-462-2593
Fritz, Steve/1023 S Santa Fe Ave, Los Angeles, CA	213-629-8052
Fritze, Jack/2106 S Grand, Santa Ana, CA	714-545-6466
Fronk, Peter/203 Indian Way, Novato, CA	415-883-5253
Fruchtman, Jerry/8735 Washington Blvd, Culver City, CA	213-839-7891
Fry, George B III/PO Box 2465, Menlo Park, CA	415-323-7663
Fujioka, Robert/715 Stierlin Rd, Mt View, CA	415-960-3010
Fukuda, Curtis/2239-F Old Middlefield Way, Mountain View, CA	415-962-9131
Fukuda, Steve/454 Natoma, San Francisco, CA	415-543-9339
Fukuhara, Richard Yutaka/1032-2 Taft Ave, Orange, CA	714-998-8790
Furuta, Carl/7360 Melrose Ave, Los Angeles, CA	213-655-1911
Fusco, Paul/7 Melody Ln, Mill Valley, CA	415-388-8940

G

Gage, Rob/789 Pearl St, Laguna Beach, CA	714-494-7265
Gallagher, John/PO Box 4070, Seattle, WA	206-937-2422
Galvan, Gary/4626 1/2 Hollywood Blvd, Los Angeles, CA	213-667-1457
Gardner, Robert/800 S Citrus Ave, Los Angeles, CA	213-931-1108
Garrabrandts, Doug/431 Winchester Ave, Glendale, CA	818-502-0271
Garretson, Jim/333 Fifth St, San Francisco, CA	415-974-6464
Gascon, Enrique Jr/143 S Edgemont St, Los Angeles, CA	213-383-9157
Gatley, David/14341 Aedan Ct, Poway, CA	619-748-0405
Geissler, Rick/1729 Vista Del Valle, El Cajon, CA	619-440-5594
Gelineau, Val/1041 N McCadden Pl, Los Angeles, CA	213-465-6149
Gerba, Peter/50 Ringold St, San Francisco, CA	415-864-5474
Gerretsen, Charles/1714 N Wilton Pl, Los Angeles, CA	213-462-6342
Gersten, Paul/1021 1/2 N La Brea, Los Angeles, CA	213-850-6045
Gervase, Mark/732 N Highland Ave, Los Angeles, CA	213-464-2775
Giannetti Photography/730 Clementina St, San Francisco, CA	415-864-0270
Gibbs, Christopher/4640 Business Pk Blvd, Anchorage, AK	907-563-6112
Gibson, Mark/PO Box 14542, San Francisco, CA	415-524-8118
Giefer, Sebastian/3132 Hollyridge Dr, Hollywood, CA	213-461-1122
Gilbert, Elliot/311 N Curson Ave, Los Angeles, CA	213-939-1846
Gillman, Mitchell/610 22nd St #307, San Francisco, CA	415-621-5334
Gilmore, Ed/9000 Broadway Terrace, Oakland, CA	415-547-2194
Giraud, Steve/2960 Airway Ave #B-103, Costa Mesa, CA	714-751-8191
Gleis, Nick/4040 Del Rey #7, Marina Del Rey, CA	213-823-4229
Glenn, Joel/439 Bryant St, San Francisco, CA	415-957-1273
Gnass, Jeff/PO Box 2196, Oroville, CA	916-533-6788
Goavec, Pierre/1464 La Plaza #303, San Francisco, CA	415-564-2252
Goble, James/620 Moulton Ave #205, Los Angeles, CA	213-222-7661
Godwin, Bob/1427 E 41st St #1, Los Angeles, CA	213-269-8001
Going, Michael/1117 N Wilcox Pl, Los Angeles, CA	213-465-6853
Goldman, Larry/5310 Circle Dr #206, Van Nuys, CA	818-995-4121
Goldner, David/833 Traction Ave, Los Angeles, CA	213-617-0761
Goldstein, Larry/214-1265 W 13th Ave, Vancouver V6H 1N5, BC	604-687-6660
Goodman, Jamison/1001 E 1st St, Los Angeles, CA	213-617-1900
Goodman, Todd/1417 26th #E, Santa Monica, CA	213-453-3621
Gordon, Charles M/19226 35th Pl NE, Seattle, WA	206-365-2132
Gordon, Jon/2052 Los Feliz Dr, Thousand Oaks, CA	805-496-1485
Gordon, Larry Dale/2047 Castilian Dr, Los Angeles, CA	213-874-6318
Gorman, Greg/1351 Miller Dr, Los Angeles, CA	213-650-5540
Gottlieb, Mark/1915 University Ave, Palo Alto, CA	415-321-8761
Gowans, Edward/10316 NW Thompson Rd, Portland, OR	503-297-5110
Grady, Noel/277 Rodney Ave, Encinitas, CA	619-753-8630

PHOTOGRAPHERS

Graham, Don/1545 Marlay Dr, Los Angeles, CA	213-656-7117
Graham, Ellen/614 N Hillcrest Rd, Beverly Hills, CA	213-275-6195
Gray, Dennis/250 Newhall St, San Francisco, CA	415-641-4009
Gray, Keehn/625 Locust Rd, Sausalito, CA	415-332-8831
Gray, Marion/42 Orben Pl, San Francisco, CA	415-931-5689
Gray, Todd/1962 N Wilcox, Los Angeles, CA	213-466-6088
Greenleigh, John/756 Natoma, San Francisco, CA	415-864-4147
Grigg, Robert/1050 N Wilcox Ave, Hollywood, CA	213-469-6316
Grimm, Tom & Michelle/PO Box 83, Laguna Beach, CA	714-494-1336
Groenekamp, Greg/2922 Oakhurst Ave, Los Angeles, CA	213-838-2466
Gross, Richard/1810 Harrison St, San Francisco, CA	415-558-8075
Groutage, Monty/2214 S Fairview Rd, Santa Ana, CA	714-751-8734
Gullette, William/3410 Villa Terr, San Diego, CA	619-692-3801
Gurente, Paul/1005 W Olive Ave, Burbank, CA	818-841-4050

H

Hagopian, Jim/915 N Mansfield Ave, Hollywood, CA	213-856-0018
Hagyard, Dave/1205 E Pike, Seattle, WA	206-322-8419
Haislip, Kevin/PO Box 1862, Portland, OR	503-254-8859
Hale, Don/460 NE 70th St, Seattle, WA	206-524-5220
Hall, Alice/1033 N Myra Ave, Los Angeles, CA	213-666-0535
Hall, George/82 Macondray Ln, San Francisco, CA	415-775-7373
Hall, Steven/645 N Eckhoff St #P, Orange, CA	714-634-1132
Hall, William/19881 Bushard St, Huntington Bch, CA	714-968-2473
Halle, Kevin/11125-D Flintkote Ave, San Diego, CA	619-452-7759
Hamilton, David W/511 The Alameda, San Anselmo, CA	415-461-5901
Hammid, Tino/PO Box 69-A109, Los Angeles, CA	213-652-6626
Hampton, Ralph/PO Box 480057, Los Angeles, CA	213-934-5781
Hanauer, Mark/1717 N Vine St #12, Los Angeles, CA	213-462-2421
Handleman, Doris/10108 Lovelane, Los Angeles, CA	213-838-0088
Hands, Bruce/PO Box 16186, Seattle, WA	206-938-8620
Hansen, Jim/2800 S Main St #1, Santa Ana, CA	714-545-1343
Hara/245 Prado Rd #4, San Luis Obispo, CA	805-543-6907
Harding, C B/660 N Thompson St, Portland, OR	503-281-9907
Harmel, Mark/714 N Westbourne, West Hollywood, CA	213-659-1633
Harrington, Lewis/746 Ilaniwai #200, Honolulu, HI	808-533-3696
Harrington, Marshall/2775 Kurtz St #2, San Diego, CA	619-291-2775
Harris, Paul/4601 Larkwood Ave, Woodland Hills, CA	818-347-8294
Hart, G K/780 Bryant St, San Francisco, CA	415-495-4278
Hartman, Raiko/6916 Melrose, Los Angeles, CA	213-278-4700
Harvey, Stephen/7801 W Beverly Blvd, Los Angeles, CA	213-934-5817
Hathaway, Steve/173 Bluxome 4th Fl, San Francisco, CA	415-495-3473
Hawkes, William/5757 Venice Blvd, Los Angeles, CA	213-931-7777
Hawley, Larry/6502 Santa Monica Blvd, Hollywood, CA	213-466-5864
Healy, Brian/333-A 7th St, San Francisco, CA	415-861-1008
Heffernan, Terry/352 6th St, San Francisco, CA	415-626-1999
Henderson, Tom/11722 Sorrento Vly Rd #A, San Diego, CA	619-481-7743
Henneg, Robert/3435 Army St #336, San Francisco, CA	415-282-7302
Herrmann, Karl/3165 S Barrington Ave #F, Los Angeles, CA	213-397-5917
Herron, Matt/PO Box 1860, Sausalito, CA	415-479-6994
Hewett, Richard/5725 Buena Vista Terr, Los Angeles, CA	213-254-4577
Hicks, Alan/333 N W Park, Portland, OR	503-226-6741
Hicks, Jeff & Assoc/41 E Main, Los Gatos, CA	408-395-2277
Higgins, Donald/201 San Vincente Blvd #14, Santa Monica, CA	213-393-8858
Higgins, Errol/2 McLaren #B, Irvine, CA	714-951-5089
Hildreth, James/40 Lundys Lane, San Francisco, CA	415-821-7398
Hill, Dennis/20 N Raymond Ave #14, Pasadena, CA	818-795-2589
Hines, Richard/734 E 3rd St, Los Angeles, CA	213-625-2333
Hirshew, Lloyd/750 Natoma, San Francisco, CA	415-861-3902
Hishi, James/612 S Victory Blvd, Burbank, CA	213-849-4871
Hixson, Richard/1468 Huston Rd, Lafayette, CA	415-621-0246
Hodge, Nettie/9687 Adams Ave, Huntington Beach, CA	714-964-3166
Hodges, Rose/2325 3rd St #401, San Francisco, CA	415-550-7612
Hodges, Walter/1605 Twelfth Ave #25, Seattle, WA	206-325-9550
Hoffman, Davy/1923 Colorado Ave, Santa Monica, CA	213-453-4661
Hoffman, Paul/4500 19th St, San Francisco, CA	415-863-3575
Hofmann, Mark/827 N Fairfax Ave, Los Angeles, CA	213-658-7376
Hogg, Peter/1221 S La Brea, Los Angeles, CA	213-937-0642
Holcomb, Mark/15 1/2 Holcomb Court, Walnut Creek, CA	415-932-8126
Hollenbeck, Cliff/Box 4247 Pioneer Sq, Seattle, WA	206-682-6300
Hollingsworth, Mike/164 N La Brea Ave, Los Angeles, CA	213-936-0310
Holmes, Mark/347 S Wilton Pl, Los Angeles, CA	213-933-5242

Holmes, Robert/PO Box 556, Mill Valley, CA	415-383-6783
Holt, David/1624 Cotner Ave #B, Los Angeles, CA	213-478-1188
Holz, William/7630 W Norton Ave, Los Angeles, CA	213-656-4061
Honolulu Creative Group/424 Nahua St, Honolulu, HI	808-926-6188
Honowitz, Ed/512 N Hobart Blvd, Los Angeles, CA	213-669-1785
Hooper, H Lee/30708 Monte Lado Dr, Malibu, CA	213-457-2897
Hopkins, Stew/345 5th Ave, Venice, CA	213-396-8649
Horikawa, Michael/508 Kamakee St, Honolulu, HI	808-538-7378
Housel, James F/84 University Pl #409, Seattle, WA	206-682-6181
Houser, Dave/249 S Hwy 101 #336, Solana Beach, CA	619-755-2828
Hudetz, Larry/11135 SE Yamhill, Portland, OR	503-245-6001
Hunt, Phillip/3435 Army St #206, San Francisco, CA	415-821-9879
HUNTER, JEFF/4626 1/2 HOLLYWOOD BLVD, LOS ANGELES, CA (P 221)	**213-669-0468**
Hussey, Ron/1499 Bluebird Canyon, Laguna Beach, CA	714-494-6988
Hylen, Bo/1640 S LaCienega, Los Angeles, CA	213-271-6543
Hyun, Douglass/6546 Hollywood Blvd #220, Hollywood, CA	213-467-4455

I

Illusion Factory/4657 Abargo St, Woodland Hills, CA	818-883-4501
Illustration West/4020 N Palm #207, Fullerton, CA	714-773-9131
Imstepf, Charles/620 Moulton Ave #216, Los Angeles, CA	213-222-8773
In Vision/2004 Martin Ave, Santa Clara, CA	408-496-6030
Inahara, Sharon/178 N Mansfield, Los Angeles, CA	213-463-8318
Iri, Carl/5745 Scrivener, Long Beach, CA	213-658-5822
Isaacs, Robert/1646 Mary Ave, Sunnyvale, CA	408-245-1690
Iverson, Michele/1527 Princeton #2, Santa Monica, CA	213-829-5717

J

Jacobs, Lou/296 Avenida Andorra, Cathedral City, CA	619-324-5505
Jacobs, Michael/646 N Cahuenga Blvd, Los Angeles, CA	213-461-0240
James, Patrick/1412 Santa Cruz, San Pedro, CA	213-519-1357
Jarrett, Michael/16812 Red Hill, Irvine, CA	714-250-3377
Jasmine Photography/1746 N Ivar, Hollywood, CA	213-851-2775
Jay, Michael/1 Zeno Pl #345 Folsom Cmplx, San Francisco, CA	415-543-7101
Jenkin, Bruce/11577-A Slater Ave, Fountain Valley, CA	714-546-2949
Jensen, John/449 Bryant St, San Francisco, CA	415-957-9449
Johnson, Dave Photo/2081 Bering Dr #F, San Jose, CA	408-436-8778
Johnson, Diane Photo/3018 Columbia St, San Diego, CA	619-295-2369
Johnson, Payne B/4650 Harvey Rd, San Diego, CA	619-299-4567
Jones, Aaron/608 Folsom St, San Francisco, CA	415-495-6333
Jones, DeWitt/Box 116, Bolinas, CA	415-868-0674
Jones, Douglas/918 Lombard St, Costa Mesa, CA	714-631-3891
Jones, William B/2171 India St #B, San Diego, CA	619-235-8892

K

Kaestner, Reed/2120 J Durante Blvd #4, Del Mar, CA	619-755-1200
Kaldor, Kurt/1011 Grandview Dr, S San Francisco, CA	415-583-8704
Karageorge, Jim/610 22nd St #309, San Francisco, CA	415-648-3444
Karjalas' Photo Vision/231 E Imperial Hwy #260, Fullerton, CA	714-992-1210
Kasmier, Richard/441 E Columbine #I, Santa Ana, CA	714-545-4022
Kasparowitz, Josef/PO Box 14408, San Luis Obispo, CA	805-544-8209
Katano, Nicole/2969 Jackson #104, San Francisco, CA	415-563-2646
Katzenberger, George/211-D E Columbine St, Santa Ana, CA	714-545-3055
Kauffman, Helen/9017 Rangeley Ave, Los Angeles, CA	213-275-3569
Kaufman, Robert/259 Ridge Rd, San Carlos, CA	415-369-5908
Kauschke, Hans-Gerhard/16 Una Way #D, Mill Valley, CA	415-383-4230
Keenan, Elaine Faris/90 Natoma St, San Francisco, CA	415-546-9246
KEENAN, LARRY/421 BRYANT ST, SAN FRANCISCO, CA (P 223)	**415-495-6474**
Kehl, Robert/769 22nd St, Oakland, CA	415-452-0501
Keller, Greg/769 22nd St, Oakland, CA	415-452-0501
Kelley, Tom/8525 Santa Monica Blvd, Los Angeles, CA	213-657-1780
Kent, Betty McAlinden/2317 Cliff Dr, Newport Beach, CA	714-631-1141
Kermani, Shahn/109 Minna St #210, San Francisco, CA	415-567-6073
Kessler/McKinnon Photo/2101 Las Palmas, Carlsbad, CA	619-931-9299
Kiesow, Paul/7247 Camellia Ave, N Hollywood, CA	213-655-1897
Kilberg, James/3371 Cahuenga Blvd W, Los Angeles, CA	213-874-9514
Killian, Glen/1270 Rio Vista, Los Angeles, CA	213-263-6567
Kimball, Ron/2582 Sun-Mor Ave, Mt View, CA	415-948-2939
Kimball-Nanessence/3421 Tripp Ct #4, San Diego, CA	619-453-1922
King, Nicholas/3356 Hancock St #B, San Diego, CA	619-296-8200
Kinon, Ed/PO Box 590805, San Francisco, CA	415-752-0807

Photographers

Continued

Please send us your additions and updates.

Kious, Gary/9800 Sepulvada Blvd #304, Los Angeles, CA	213-536-4880
Kirkendall/ Spring/18819 Olympic View Dr, Edmonds, WA	206-776-4685
Kirkland, Douglas/9060 Wonderland Park Ave, Los Angeles, CA	213-656-8511
Kirkpatrick, Mike/1115 Forest Way, Brookdale, CA	408-395-1447
Kleinman, Kathryn/542 Natoma St, San Francisco, CA	415-864-2406
Klimek & Weislein/, Los Angeles, CA	213-253-1049
Koch, Jim/1360 Logan Ave #106, Costa Mesa, CA	714-957-5719
Kodama & Moriarty Photo/4081 Glencoe Ave, Marina Del Rey, CA	213-306-7574
Koehler, Rick/1622 Moulton Pkwy #A, Tustin, CA	714-259-8787
Koga, Dean/20219 SW Birch St, Santa Ana Hts, CA	714-756-9185
Kohler, Heinz/163 W Colorado Blvd, Pasadena, CA	213-681-9195
Kopp, Pierre/PO Box 8337, Long Beach, CA	213-430-8534
Kosta, Jeffrey/2565 Third St #306, San Francisco, CA	415-285-7001
Kramer, David/5121 Santa Fe St #A, San Diego, CA	619-270-5501
Krasner, Carin/5923 W Pico Blvd, Los Angeles, CA	213-937-4686
Kredenser, Peter/2551 Angelo Dr, Los Angeles, CA	213-278-6356
Krisel, Ron/1925 Pontius Ave, Los Angeles, CA	213-477-5519
Krosnick, Alan/2800 20th St, San Francisco, CA	415-285-1819
Krueger, Gary/PO Box 543, Montrose, CA	818-249-1051
Krupp, Carl/PO Box 910, Merlin, OR	503-479-6699
Kubly, Jon/604 Moulton, Los Angeles, CA	213-747-7259
Kuhn, Chuck/206 Third Ave S, Seattle, WA	206-624-4706
Kuhn, Robert/3022 Valevista Tr, Los Angeles, CA	213-461-3656
Kupersmith, Dan/823 N LaBrea, Los Angeles, CA	213-935-6232
Kurihara, Ted/601 22nd St, San Francisco, CA	415-285-3200
Kurisu/819 1/2 N Fairfax, Los Angeles, CA	213-655-7287
Kuslich, Lawrence J/3386 SE 20th Ave, Portland, OR	503-236-3454

L
Lachata, Carol/77 S Michigan Ave, Pasadena, CA	818-794-6860
Lamb & Hall/7318 Melrose, Los Angeles, CA	213-931-1775
Lammers, Bud/211-A East Columbine, Santa Ana, CA	714-546-4441
Lamont, Dan/117 W Denny Way #213, Seattle, WA	206-285-8252
Lamotte, Michael/828 Mission St, San Francisco, CA	415-777-1443
Landau, Robert/7275 Sunset Blvd #4, Los Angeles, CA	213-851-2995
Landecker, Tom/1028 Folsom St, San Francisco, CA	415-864-8888
Lane, Bobbi/7213 Santa Monica Blvd, Los Angeles, CA	213-874-0557
Langdon, Harry/8275 Beverly Blvd, Los Angeles, CA	213-651-3212
LaRocca, Jerry/3734 SE 21st Ave, Portland, OR	503-232-5005
Larson, Dean/7668 Hollywood Blvd, Los Angeles, CA	213-876-1033
LaTona, Kevin/159 Western Ave W #454, Seattle, WA	206-285-5779
Lawder, John/2672 S Grand, Santa Ana, CA	714-557-3657
Lawlor, John/6101 Melrose, Hollywood, CA	213-468-9050
Lea, Thomas/181 Alpine, San Francisco, CA	415-864-5941
Leach, David/7408 Beverly Blvd, Los Angeles, CA	213-932-1234
Leatart, Brian/520 N Western, Los Angeles, CA	213-856-0121
LeBon, David/732 N Highland Ave, Los Angeles, CA	213-464-2775
Lee, Larry/PO Box 4688, North Hollywood, CA	818-766-2677
Lee, Roger Allyn/1628 Folsom St, San Francisco, CA	415-861-1147
Lee, Sherwood/909 Micheltorena St, Los Angeles, CA	213-660-4230
Legname, Rudi/389 Clementina St, San Francisco, CA	415-777-9569
Lehman, Danny/6643 W 6th St, Los Angeles, CA	213-652-1930
Leighton, Ron/1360 Logan #105, Costa Mesa, CA	714-641-5122
Leng, Brian/1021 1/2 N La Brea, Los Angeles, CA	213-469-8624
Lennon Photographer/1015 N Cahuenga Blvd, Hollywood, CA	213-469-2212
Levasheff, Michael/1112 N Beachwood, Los Angeles, CA	213-946-2511
Levy, Paul/2830 S Robertson Blvd, Los Angeles, CA	213-838-2252
Lewin, Elyse/820 N Fairfax, Los Angeles, CA	213-655-4214
Lewine, Rob/8929 Holly Pl, Los Angeles, CA	213-654-0830
Lewis, Cindy/3960 Laurel Canyon Blvd #310, Studio City, CA	818-761-2911
Lewis, Don/2350 Stanley Hills Dr, Los Angeles, CA	213-656-2138
Li, Jeff/234 N Juanita Ave, Los Angeles, CA	213-383-3077
Lidz, Jane/33 Nordhoff St, San Francisco, CA	415-587-3377
LIGHTRA/1545 N WILCOX AVE #102, HOLLYWOOD, CA (P 229)	**213-461-3529**
Liles, Harry/1060 N Lillian Way, Hollywood, CA	213-466-1612
Lind, Lenny/832 Folsom St #810, San Francisco, CA	415-563-2020
Lindsey, Gordon/2311 Kettner Blvd, San Diego, CA	619-234-4432
Lindstrom, Eric/414 Olive Way #B29, Seattle, WA	206-583-0601
Lindstrom, Mel/2510-H Old Middlefld Way, Mountain View, CA	415-962-1313
Linn, Alan/5121 Santa Fe St #B, San Diego, CA	619-483-2122

Livzey, John/1510 N Las Palmas, Hollywood, CA	213-469-2992
Lockwood, Scott/1317 Willow St, Los Angeles, CA	213-617-2222
Loeser, Peter/1431 Ocean Ave #819, Santa Monica, CA	213-393-5576
London, Matthew/10391 Camino Ruiz #95, San Diego, CA	619-457-3251
Long, John/815 High St, Palo Alto, CA	415-328-5664
Lopez, Bret/533 Moreno Ave, Los Angeles, CA	213-393-8841
Lorenzo/4654 El Cajon Blvd, San Diego, CA	619-280-6010
Lovell, Craig/Rt 1 Box 53A, Carmel, CA	408-624-5241
Luhn, Jeff/ Visioneering/2565 3rd St #339, San Francisco, CA	415-282-6630
Lund, John M/860 Second St, San Francisco, CA	415-957-1775
Lund, John William/741 Natoma St, San Francisco, CA	415-552-7764
Lyon, Fred/237 Clara St, San Francisco, CA	415-974-5645
Lyons, Marv/2865 W 7th St, Los Angeles, CA	213-384-0732

M
Madden, Daniel J/PO Box 965, Los Alamitos, CA	213-429-3621
Madison, David/2330 Old Middlefield Rd, Mountain View, CA	415-961-6297
Maharat, Chester/74 Clearbrook, Irvine, CA	714-832-6203
Maher, John/10413 NW Laidlaw Rd, Portland, OR	503-297-7451
Mahieu, Ted/PO Box 42578, San Francisco, CA	415-641-4747
Maloney, Jeff/2646 Taffy Dr, San Jose, CA	408-274-6027
Malphettes, Benoit/816 S Grand St, Los Angeles, CA	213-629-9054
Mangold, Steve/Po Box 1001, Palo Alto, CA	415-969-9897
Manning, Lawrence/15507 Doty Ave, Lawndale, CA	213-679-4774
Mar, Tim/PO Box 3488, Seattle, WA	206-583-0093
Marcus, Ken/6916 Melrose Ave, Los Angeles, CA	213-937-7214
Mareschal, Tom/5816 182nd Pl SW, Lynnwood, WA	206-771-6932
Margolies, Paul/480 Potrero, San Francisco, CA	415-621-3306
Marley, Stephen/1160 Industrial Way, San Carlos, CA	415-966-8301
Marriott, John/1830 McAllister, San Francisco, CA	415-922-2920
Marsden, Dominic/3783 W Cahuenga Blvd, Studio City, CA	818-508-5222
Marshall, Jim/3622 16th St, San Francisco, CA	415-864-3622
Marshutz, Roger/1649 S La Cienega Blvd, Los Angeles, CA	213-273-1610
Martin Photography/1053 Blossom Dr, Santa Clara, CA	408-985-9378
Martin, John F/118 King St, San Francisco, CA	415-957-1355
Martinelli, Bill/608 S Railroad Ave, San Mateo, CA	415-347-3589
Martinez, David/2325 Third St #433, San Francisco, CA	415-558-8088
Mason, Pablo/3026 North Park Way, San Diego, CA	619-298-2200
Masterson, Ed/11211-S Sorrento Val Rd, San Diego, CA	619-457-3251
Matoso, Gary/161 King St, San Francisco, CA	415-777-1656
Mauskopf, Norman/615 W California Blvd, Pasadena, CA	818-578-1878
McAfee, Lynn//12745 Moor Park St #10, Studio City, CA	818-761-1317
McAfee, Tom/930 Alabama, San Francisco, CA	415-282-2525
McCall, Stuart/518 Beatty St #603, Vancouver V6B 2L3, BC	604-684-6760
McClain, Stan/39 E Walnut St, Pasadena, CA	818-795-8828
McCracken, Sabra K/200 W 34th St #190, Anchorage, AK	907-345-5941
MCCRARY, JIM/211 S LABREA AVE, LOS ANGELES, CA (P 224,225)	**213-936-5115**
McCumsey, Robert/2600 E Coast Hwy, Corona Del Mar, CA	714-720-1624
McDermott, John/31 Genoa Place, San Francisco, CA	415-982-2010
McGraw, Chelsea/1722 Mackinnon, Cardiff by the Sea, CA	619-436-0602
McIntyre, Don/515 S Harbor Blvd, Anaheim, CA	714-635-9491
McIntyre, Gerry/3385 Lanatt Way #B, Sacramento, CA	916-736-2108
McIntyre, Mark/380 Del Mar Blvd, Pasadena, CA	818-796-1841
McKinney, Andrew/1628 Folsom St, San Francisco, CA	415-621-8415
McMahon, Steve/1164 S LaBrea, Los Angeles, CA	213-937-3345
McVay, Matt/PO Box 1103, Mercer Island, WA	206-236-1343
Meisels, Penina/917 20th St, Sacramento, CA	916-443-3330
Melgar Photographers Inc/2971 Corvin Dr, Santa Clara, CA	408-733-4500
Mendenhall, Jim/PO Box 10547, Santa Ana, CA	714-834-9240
Menzel, Peter J/136 N Deer Run Lane, Napa, CA	707-255-3528
Menzie, W Gordon/2311 Kettner Blvd, San Diego, CA	619-234-4431
Merfeld, Ken/3951 Higuera St, Culver City, CA	213-837-5300
Merkel, Dan/PO Box 1025, Haleiwa, HI	808-373-2710
Merken, Stefan/900 N Citrus Ave, Los Angeles, CA	213-466-4533
Meyers, Deborah/405 1/2 S Fairfax Ave, Los Angeles, CA	213-655-4444
MIAD Photography/3220 S Susan St, Santa Ana, CA	714-549-4101
Micoine, Christian/, Los Angeles, CA	213-856-0008
Mihulka, Chris/PO Box 1515, Springfield, OR	503-741-2289
Miles, Reid/1136 N Las Palmas, Hollywood, CA	213-462-6106
Milholland, Richard/8271 W Norton, Los Angeles, CA	213-650-5458
Milkie Studio Inc/127 Boylston Ave E, Seattle, WA	206-324-3000
Miller, Bill/7611 Melrose Ave, Los Angeles, CA	213-651-5630

Photographers

Continued

Please send us your additions and updates.

PHOTOGRAPHERS

Miller, Donald/415 Molino, Los Angeles, CA	213-680-1896
Miller, Earl/3212 Bonnie Hill Dr, Los Angeles, CA	213-851-4947
Miller, Ed/705 32nd Ave, San Francisco, CA	415-221-5687
Miller, Jim/1122 N Citrus Ave, Los Angeles, CA	213-466-9515
Miller, Jordan/506 S San Vicente Blvd, Los Angeles, CA	213-655-0408
Miller, Peter Read/3413 Pine Ave, Manhattan Beach, CA	213-545-7511
Miller, Ray/PO Box 450, Balboa, CA	714-646-5748
Miller, Wynn/4083 Glencoe Ave, Marina Del Rey, CA	213-821-4948
Milliken, Brad/583 Vista Ave, Palo Alto, CA	415-424-8211
Milne, Robbie/2717 Western, Seattle, WA	206-682-6828
Milroy/ McAleer/3857 Birch St #170, Newport Beach, CA	714-957-0219
Mineau, Joe/8921 National Blvd, Los Angeles, CA	213-558-3878
Mishler, Clark/1238 G St, Anchorage, AK	907-179-0892
Mitchell, David Paul/564 Deodar Ln, Bradbury, CA	818-358-3328
Mitchell, Josh/706 W Pico Blvd 4th Fl, Los Angeles, CA	213-742-0368
Mitchell, Margaretta K/280 Hillcrest Rd, Berkeley, CA	415-655-4920
Mizono, Robert/14 Otis St 3rd Fl, San Francisco, CA	415-558-8663
Montague, Chuck/18005 Skypark Cir #E, Irvine, CA	714-250-0254
Monteaux, Michele/8741 Washington Blvd, Culver City, CA	213-839-6439
Montes de Oca, Arthur/4302 Melrose Ave, Los Angeles, CA	213-665-5141
Moore, Charles/PO Box 1876, Columbia, CA	415-451-1088
Moore, Gary/1125 E Orange Ave, Monrovia, CA	818-359-9414
Moran, Edward/5264 Mount Alifan Dr, San Diego, CA	619-693-1041
Moratti, Brian/27411 Lindvog Rd NE, Kingston, WA	206-297-3158
Morduchowicz, Daniel/2020 N Main St #223, Los Angeles, CA	213-223-1867
Morfit, Mason/897 Independence Ave #D, Mountain View, CA	415-969-2209
Morgan, Scott/2210 Wilshire #433, Santa Monica, CA	213-829-5318
Morrell, Paul/300 Brannan St #207, San Francisco, CA	415-543-5887
Mosgrove, Will/250 Newhall, San Francisco, CA	415-282-7080
Motil, Guy/253 W Canada, San Clemente, CA	714-492-1350
Moulin, Tom/465 Green St, San Francisco, CA	415-986-4224
Muckley, Mike Photography/8057 Raytheon Rd #3, San Diego, CA	619-565-6033
Mudford, Grant/5619 W 4th St #2, Los Angeles, CA	213-936-9145
MUENCH, DAVID/PO BOX 30500, SANTA BARBARA, CA (P 235)	**805-967-4488**
Mullenski, Steven/7718 1/2 Herschel Ave, La Jolla, CA	619-454-4331
Muna, R J/63 Encina Ave, Palo Alto, CA	415-328-1131
Murphy, Suzanne/2442 Third St, Santa Monica, CA	213-399-6652
Murphy, William/7771 Melrose Ave, Los Angeles, CA	213-651-4800
Murray, Derik/1128 Homer St, Vancouver V6B 2X6, BC	604-669-7468
Murray, Michael/15431 Redhill Ave #E, Tustin, CA	714-259-9222
Murray, Tom/592 N Rossmore Ave, Los Angeles, CA	213-937-3821
Murray, William III/1507 Belmont Ave, Seattle, WA	206-322-3377
Musilek, Stan/610 22nd St #307, San Francisco, CA	415-621-5336
Myers, Jeffry W Photography/Joseph Vance Bldg #414, Seattle, WA	206-621-7609

N
Nadler, Jeff/520 N Western Ave, Los Angeles, CA	213-467-2135
Nahoum, Ken/6609 Orange St, Los Angeles, CA	213-559-3244
Nakamura, Michael/5429 Russell NW, Seattle, WA	206-784-4323
Nance, Ancil/9217 N Hudson, Portland, OR	503-286-0941
Nation, Bill/1514 S Stanley, Los Angeles, CA	213-937-4888
Nease, Robert/441 E Columbine #E, Santa Ana, CA	714-545-6557
Nebeux, Michael/1633 W 144th St, Gardena, CA	213-532-0949
Nels/811 Traction Ave, Los Angeles, CA	213-680-2414
Newman, Greg/1356 Brampton Rd, Pasadena, CA	213-257-6247
Niedopytalski, Dave/1415 E Union, Seattle, WA	206-329-7612
Noble, Richard/7618 Melrose Ave, Los Angeles, CA	213-655-4711
Nolan, Terry/431 Termino Ave, Long Beach, CA	213-439-1158
Nolton, Gary/107 NW Fifth Ave, Portland, OR	503-228-0844
Normark, Don/1622 Taylor Ave N, Seattle, WA	206-284-9393
Norwood, David/4040 Del Rey Ave #7, Marina Del Rey, CA	213-827-2020
Noyle, Ric/733 Auahi St, Honolulu, HI	808-524-8269
NTA Photo/600 Moulton Ave #101-A, Los Angeles, CA	213-226-0506
Nuding, Peter/3181 Melendy Dr, San Carlos, CA	415-967-4854
Nyerges, Suzanne/413 S Fairfax, Los Angeles, CA	213-938-0151

O
O'Brien, George/1515 Merced St, Fresno, CA	209-226-4000
O'Brien, Tom/450 S La Brea, Los Angeles, CA	213-938-2008
O'Hara, Yoshi/6341 Yucca St, Hollywood, CA	213-466-8031

O'Rear, Chuck/PO Box 361, St Helena, CA	707-963-2663
Odgers, Jayme/703 S Union, Los Angeles, CA	213-461-8173
Ogilvie, Peter/90 Natoma, San Francisco, CA	415-391-1646
Oldenkamp, John/3331 Adams Ave, San Diego, CA	619-283-0711
Olson, George/451 Vermont, San Francisco, CA	415-864-8686
Olson, Jon/4045 32nd Ave SW, Seattle, WA	206-932-7074
Omni Color/4320 Viewridge Ave #C, San Diego, CA	619-565-0672
Orazem, Scott/1150 1/2 Elm Dr, Los Angeles, CA	213-277-7447
Osbourne, Jan/460 NE 70th St, Seattle, WA	206-524-5220
Oshiro, Jeff/2534 W 7th St, Los Angeles, CA	213-383-2774
OTTO, GLENN/10625 MAGNOLIA BLVD, NORTH HOLLYWOOD, CA (P 226)	**818-762-5724**
Ounjian, Michael/612 N Myers St, Burbank, CA	818-842-0880
Outland, Joe/Box 6202 Pt Loma Station, San Diego, CA	619-222-4558
Ovregaard, Keith/765 Clementina St, San Francisco, CA	415-621-0687
Owen & Owen Photo/4114 Kilauea Ave, Honolulu, HI	808-737-9123
Owyang, William/211 Bradford St, San Francisco, CA	415-923-6067

P
Pacheco, Robert/11152 3/4 Morrison, N Hollywood, CA	818-761-1320
Pacura, Tim/756 Natoma St, San Francisco, CA	415-552-3512
Padys, Diane/PO Box 77307, San Francisco, CA	415-285-6443
Pagos, Terry/3622 Albion Pl N, Seattle, WA	206-633-4616
Pan, Richard/722 N Hoover St, Los Angeles, CA	213-661-6638
Parks, Ayako/PO Box 6552, Laguna Nigel, CA	714-240-8347
Parks, Jeff/12936 133rd Pl NE, Kirkland, WA	206-821-5450
Parrish, Al/3501 Buena Vista Ave, Glendale, CA	818-957-3726
Parry, Karl/8800 Venice Blvd, Los Angeles, CA	213-558-4446
Pasquali, Art/1061 Sunset Blvd, Los Angeles, CA	213-250-0134
Patterson, Marion/1745 Croner Ave, Menlo Park, CA	209-379-2838
Patterson, Robert/915 N Mansfield Ave, Hollywood, CA	213-462-4401
Paulus, Bill/612 Lighthouse Ave, Pacific Grove, CA	408-375-0446
Pavloff, Nick/PO Box 2339, San Francisco, CA	415-452-2468
Peais, Larry/95 Minna, San Francisco, CA	415-957-1366
Pearson, Charles R/PO Box 350, Leavenworth, WA	509-763-3333
Pearson, John/1343 Sacramento, Berkeley, CA	415-525-7553
Pearson, Victoria/560 S Main St #4-N, Los Angeles, CA	213-627-9256
Pedrick, Frank/2690 Union st, Oakland, CA	415-465-5080
Peebles, Douglas Photography/1100 Alekea St #221, Honolulu, HI	808-533-6686
Pelton & Assoc/36 14th St, Hermosa Beach, CA	213-376-8061
Percey, Roland/626 N Hoover, Los Angeles, CA	213-660-7305
Perry, David/Box 4165 Pioneer Sq Sta, Seattle, WA	206-932-6614
Peterman, Joan & Herbert/3185 Rossini Pl, Topanga, CA	818-883-1229
Peterson, Bryan/PO Box 892, Hillsboro, OR	503-985-3276
Peterson, Darrell/1004 Turner Way E, Seattle, WA	206-324-0307
Peterson, Richard/733 Auahi St, Honolulu, HI	808-536-8222
Peterson, Richard Studio/711 8th Ave #A, San Diego, CA	619-236-0284
Pett, Laurence J/5907 Cahill Ave, Tarzana, CA	818-344-9453
Pfleger, Mickey/PO Box 280727, San Francisco, CA	415-355-1772
Phillips, Bernard/1810 Harrison St, San Francisco, CA	415-621-7982
Photo Graphics West/15811 Debesor St, Valinda, CA	818-918-5491
Photography Northwest/1415 Elliot Ave W, Seattle, WA	206-285-5249
Pildas, Ave/1568 Murray Circle, Los Angeles, CA	213-664-1313
Pinckney, Jim/PO Box 1149, Carmel Valley, CA	408-375-3534
Piper, Jim/922 SE Ankeny, Portland, OR	503-231-9622
Piscitello, Chuck/6502 Santa Monica Blvd, Los Angeles, CA	213-460-6397
Place, Chuck/2940 Lomita Rd, Santa Barbara, CA	805-682-6089
Pleasant, Ralph B/8755 W Washington Blvd, Culver City, CA	213-202-8997
Poppleton, Eric/1341 Ocean Ave #259, Santa Monica, CA	213-209-3765
Porter, James/3955 Birch St #F, Newport Beach, CA	714-852-8756
Poulsen, Chriss/104-A Industrial Center, Sausalito, CA	415-331-3495
POWERS, DAVID/17 BROSNAN ST, SAN FRANCISCO, CA (P 227)	**415-864-7974**
Powers, Lisa/2073 Outpost Dr, Los Angeles, CA	213-874-5877
Prater, Yvonne/Box 940 Rt 1, Ellensburg, WA	509-925-1774
Preuss, Karen/369 Eleventh Ave, San Francisco, CA	415-752-7545
Pribble, Paul/120 S Vignes St, Los Angeles, CA	213-617-7182
Price, Mark/2337 El Camino Real, San Mateo, CA	415-345-8377
Price, Tony/PO Box 5216, Portland, OR	503-239-4228
Prince, Norman/3245 25th St, San Francisco, CA	415-821-6595
Pritchett, Bill/1771 Yale St, Chula Vista, CA	619-421-6005
Proehl, Steve/916 Rodney Dr, San Leandro, CA	415-483-3683

Photographers

Continued

Please send us your additions and updates.

Professional Photo Services/1011 Buenos Ave #A-B, San Diego, CA — 619-299-4410
Pruitt, Brett/2343-B Rose St, Honolulu, HI — 808-845-3811

R Raabe, Dan/256 S Robertson Blvd #4504, Beverly Hills, CA — 213-461-7060
Rahn, Stephen/259 Clara St, San Francisco, CA — 415-495-3556
Ramey, Michael/612 Broadway, Seattle, WA — 206-329-6936
Rampy, Tom/PO Box 3980, Laguna Hills, CA — 714-850-4048
Ramsey, Gary/1412 Ritchey #A, Santa Ana, CA — 714-547-0782
Rand, Marvin/13432 Beach, Marina Del Rey, CA — 213-306-9779
Randklev, James/1471 S Bradford St, Los Angeles, CA — 213-825-5893
Randlett, Mary/Box 10536, Bainbridge Island, WA — 206-842-3935
Ransier, Richard/3923 W Jefferson Blvd, Los Angeles, CA — 213-450-6265
Ranson, James/PO Box 501, Laguna Beach, CA — 714-634-6688
Rapoport, Aaron/3119 Beverly Blvd, Los Angeles, CA — 213-738-7277
Rausin, Chuck/1020 Woodcrest Ave, La Habra, CA — 213-697-0408
Rawcliffe, David/7609 Beverly Blvd, Los Angeles, CA — 213-938-6287
Ream-Stuart Visual Productions/3405 Industrial Dr, Santa Rosa, CA — 707-523-0125
Reed, Bob/1816 N Vermont Ave, Los Angeles, CA — 213-662-9703
Reiff, Robert/1920 Main St #2, Santa Monica, CA — 213-938-3064
Ressmeyer, Roger/1230 Grant Ave #574, San Francisco, CA — 415-921-1675
Rhoney, Ann/2264 Green St, San Francisco, CA — 415-922-4775
Rich, Bill/109 Minna #459, San Francisco, CA — 415-775-8214
Ricketts, Mark/2809 NE 55th St, Seattle, WA — 206-526-1911
Riggs, Robin/3785 Cahuenga W, N Hollywood, CA — 818-506-7753
Ripley, Michael & Assoc/13985 E 6th St, Corona, CA — 714-737-5118
Ritts, Herb/7927 Hillside Ave, Los Angeles, CA — 213-876-6366
Robbins, Bill/7016 Santa Monica Blvd, Los Angeles, CA — 213-930-1382
Roberge, Earl/764 Bryant, Walla Walla, WA — 509-525-7385
Rodal, Arney A/395 Winslow Way E, Bainbridge Island, WA — 206-842-4989
Rogers, Kenneth/PO Box 3187, Beverly Hills, CA — 213-553-5532
Rojas, Art/1588 N Batavia Unit 2, Orange, CA — 714-921-1710
Rokeach, Barrie/32 Windsor, Kensington, CA — 415-527-5376
Rolston, Matthew/8259 Melrose Ave, Los Angeles, CA — 213-658-1151
Rorke, Lorraine/146 Shrader St, San Francisco, CA — 415-386-2121
Ros-Lynn Photo/405 E Olive, Fresno, CA — 209-266-0305
Rose, Peter/651 N Russell, Portland, OR — 503-249-5864
Rosenberg, Allan/963 North Point St, San Francisco, CA — 415-673-4550
Ross, Alan C/202 Culper Ct, Hermosa Beach, CA — 213-379-2015
Ross, Bill/1526 Pontius Ave #A, Los Angeles, CA — 818-703-7605
Ross, Dave/130 McCormick #106, Costa Mesa, CA — 714-432-1355
Ross, James Studio/2565 3rd St #220, San Francisco, CA — 415-821-5710
Rothman, Michael/1816 N Vermont Ave, Los Angeles, CA — 213-662-9703
Rouse, Victoria/4411 Geary Blvd #244, San Francisco, CA — 415-621-5660
ROWAN, BOB/209 LOS BANOS AVE, WALNUT CREEK, CA (P 228) — **415-930-8687**
Rowell, Galen/1483-A Solano Ave, Albany, CA — 415-524-9343
Rubins, Richard/3757 Wilshire Blvd #204A, Los Angeles, CA — 213-387-9989
Ruppert, Michael/5086 W Pico, Los Angeles, CA — 213-938-3779
Ruscha, Paul/940 N Highland Ave, Los Angeles, CA — 213-465-3516
Ruthsatz, Richard/8735 Washington Blvd, Culver City, CA — 213-838-6312

S Sabransky, Cynthia/3331 Adams Ave, San Diego, CA — 619-283-0711
Sacks, Ron/PO Box 5532, Portland, OR — 503-641-4051
Sadlon, Jim/2 Clinton Park, San Francisco, CA — 415-626-1900
Safron, Marshal/506 S San Vincente Blvd, Los Angeles, CA — 213-653-1234
Sagara, Peter/736 N LaBrea, Los Angeles, CA — 213-933-7531
Saitta, Joseph/2000 Old Page Mill Rd, Palo Alto, CA — 415-494-1684
Salas, Michael/398 Flower St, Costa Mesa, CA — 213-930-2935
Salazar, Tim/4057 Brant St #6, San Diego, CA — 619-574-1176
Saloutos, Pete/11225 Huntley Pl, Culver City, CA — 213-397-5509
Samerjan, Peter/743 N Fairfax, Los Angeles, CA — 213-653-2940
Sanders, Paul/7378 Beverly Blvd, Los Angeles, CA — 213-933-5791
Sandford, Eric/Mazama Meadows, Mazama, WA — 509-996-2250
SANDISON, TERI/1545 N WILCOX #102, HOLLYWOOD, CA (P 229) — **213-461-3529**
Santullo, Nancy/7213 Santa Monica Blvd, Los Angeles, CA — 213-874-1940
Sarpa, Jeff/555 Rose Ave #G, Venice, CA — 213-392-7400
Sassy, Gene/PO Box 3114, Pomona, CA — 714-623-7424
Sato, Garry/645 N Martel Ave, Los Angeles, CA — 213-658-8645
Scharf, David/2100 Loma Vista Pl, Los Angeles, CA — 213-666-8657

Schelling, Susan/1440 Bush St, San Francisco, CA — 415-441-3662
Schenker, Larry/10950 Pickford Way, Culver City, CA — 213-837-2020
Scherl, Ron/1301 Guerrero, San Francisco, CA — 415-285-8865
Schermeister, Phil/472 22nd Ave, San Francisco, CA — 415-386-0218
Schiff, Darryll/8153 W Blackburn Ave, Los Angeles, CA — 213-658-6179
Schmidt, Brad/1417 26th St, Santa Monica, CA — 213-828-0754
Schubert, John/5959 W Third, Los Angeles, CA — 213-935-6044
Schuetz, Frank/, Los Angeles, CA — 213-474-2340
Schwartz, George J/PO Box 413, Bend, OR — 503-389-4062
Schwartz, Stuart/301 8th St #204, San Francisco, CA — 415-863-8393
Schwob, Bill/1033 Heinz St, Berkeley, CA — 415-848-3579
Scoffone, Craig/1169 Husted Ave, San Jose, CA — 408-723-7011
Scott, Mark/7207 Melrose Ave, Hollywood, CA — 213-931-9319
Sebastian Studios/5161-A Santa Fe St, San Diego, CA — 619-581-9111
Sedam, Mike/16907 80th Ave NE, Bothell, WA — 206-488-9375
Segal, Susan/11738 Moor Pk #B, Studio City, CA — 818-763-7612
Seidemann, Bob/703 S Union Ave, Los Angeles, CA — 213-483-6046
Seiffe, Rolf/2022 Jones St, San Francisco, CA — 415-928-0457
Selig, Jonathan/29206 Heathercliff Rd, Malibu, CA — 213-457-5856
Selland Photography/461 Bryant St, San Francisco, CA — 415-495-3633
Serbin, Glen/905 Chelham Way, Montecito, CA — 805-969-9186
Sessions, David/2210 Wilshire Blvd #205, Santa Monica, CA — 213-394-8379
Sexton, Richard/128 Laidley St, San Francisco, CA — 415-550-8345
Shaffer, Bob/1250 Folsom, San Francisco, CA — 415-552-4884
Shahood, Chuck/10725 Ellis Ave #A, Fountain Valley, CA — 714-963-2142
Shaneff, Carl/1100 Alakea St #224, Honolulu, HI — 808-533-3010
Sharpe, Dick/2475 Park Oak Dr, Los Angeles, CA — 213-462-4597
Sheret, Rene/2532 W 7th St, Los Angeles, CA — 213-385-8587
Shipps, Raymond/1325 Morena Blvd #A, San Diego, CA — 619-276-1690
Shirley, Ron/706 W Pico Blvd, Los Angeles, CA — 213-747-6608
Sholik, Stan/15455 Red Hill Ave #E, Tustin, CA — 714-259-7826
Short, Glenn/14641 La Maida, Sherman Oaks, CA — 818-990-5599
Shorten, Chris/60 Federal St, San Francisco, CA — 415-543-4883
Shrum, Steve/PO Box 6360, Ketchikan, AK — 907-225-5453
Shuman, Ronald/1 Menlo Pl, Berkeley, CA — 415-527-7241
Shvartzman, Eddie/224 Barbara Dr, Los Gatos, CA — 408-559-6490
Sibley, Scott/764 Bay, San Francisco, CA — 415-673-7468
Sievert, John/2421 Cabrillo St, San Francisco, CA — 415-751-2369
Silk, Gary Photography/6546 Hollywood Blvd #215, Hollywood, CA — 213-466-1785
Silva, Keith/771 Clementina Alley, San Francisco, CA — 415-863-5655
Silverek, Don/914 Ripley St, Santa Rosa, CA — 707-525-1155
Silverman, Jay Inc/920 N Citrus Ave, Hollywood, CA — 213-466-6030
Sim, Veronica/4961 W Sunset Blvd, Los Angeles, CA — 213-661-7356
Simon, Marc/1031 Sanchez, San Francisco, CA — 415-647-9547
Simon, Wolfgang/PO Box 807, La Canada, CA — 818-790-1605
SIMPSON, STEPHEN/701 KETTNER BLVD #124, SAN DIEGO, CA (P 230) — **619-239-6638**
Sinick, Gary/3246 Ettie St, Oakland, CA — 415-655-4538
Sirota, Peggy/451 N Harper Ave, Los Angeles, CA — 213-653-1903
Sjef's Fotographie/2311 NW Johnson St, Portland, OR — 503-223-1089
Skarsten & Dunn Studios/1062 N Rengstorff #E, Mountain View, CA — 415-969-5759
Slabeck, Bernard/2565 Third St #316, San Francisco, CA — 415-282-8202
Slatery, Chad/11627 Ayres Ave, Los Angeles, CA — 213-477-0734
Slaughter, Paul D/771 El Medio Ave, Pacific Palisades, CA — 213-454-3694
Slenzak, Ron/7106 Waring Ave, Los Angeles, CA — 213-934-9088
Slobin, Marvin/1065 15th St, San Diego, CA — 619-239-2828
Slobodian, Scott/6519 Fountain Ave, Los Angeles, CA — 213-464-2341
Smith, Charles J/7163 Construction Crt, San Diego, CA — 619-271-6625
Smith, Diane/428 Kurdson Way, Spring Valley, CA — 619-470-0861
Smith, Don/1527 Belmont #1, Seattle, WA — 206-324-5748
Smith, Elliott Varner/PO Box 5268, Berkeley, CA — 415-654-9235
Smith, Gil/2865 W 7th St, Los Angeles, CA — 213-384-1016
Smith, Steve/228 Main St #E, Venice, CA — 213-392-4982
Smith, Todd/2643 S Fairfax, Culver City, CA — 213-559-0059
Snyder, Mark/2415 Third St #265, San Francisco, CA — 415-861-7514
Sokol, Mark/6518 Wilkinson Ave, North Hollywood, CA — 818-506-4910
Sollecito, Tony/1120-B W Evelyn Ave, Sunnyvale, CA — 408-773-8118
Solomon, Marc/PO Box 480574, Los Angeles, CA — 213-935-1771
Speier, Brooks/6022 Haviland Ave, Whittier, CA — 213-695-3552
Spitz, Harry Photography/6153 Carpenter Ave, North

Hollywood, CA	818-761-9828
Sporkin, Lee/135 S Detroit, Los Angeles, CA	213-934-6737
Spradling, David/2515 Patricia Ave, Los Angeles, CA	213-477-0467
Spring, Bob & Ira/18819 Olympic View Dr, Edmonds, WA	206-776-4685
Springmann, Christopher/PO Box 745, Point Reyes, CA	415-663-8428
St Jivago Desanges/PO Box 24AA2, Los Angeles, CA	213-931-1984
Staley, Bill/1401 Crown St, Vancouver V7J 1G4, BC	604-986-1174
Starkman, Rick/544 N Rios Ave, Solana Beach, CA	619-481-8259
Steele, Melissa/PO Box 280727, San Francisco, CA	415-355-1772
Stees, M S/PO Box 2775, Costa Mesa, CA	714-545-7993
Stein, Robert/319 1/2 S Robertson Blvd, Beverly Hills, CA	213-652-2030
Steinberg, Bruce/2128 18th St, San Francisco, CA	415-864-0739
Steinberg, Mike Photo/715 S Coast Hwy, Laguna Beach, CA	714-240-2997
Steiner, Glenn Rakowsky/3356 Hancock St #D, San Diego, CA	619-299-0197
Stevens, Bob/9048 Santa Monica Blvd, Los Angeles, CA	213-271-8123
Stewart, Stephen/939 N Alfred #7, West Hollywood, CA	213-656-2270
Stewart, Tom/Studio 3/PO Box 5063, Portland, OR	503-238-1748
Stinson, John/376 W 14th St, San Pedro, CA	213-831-8495
Stoaks, Charles/PO Box 6417, Portland, OR	503-243-2635
Stock, Richard Photography/1767 N Orchid Ave #312, Los Angeles, CA	213-876-7436
Stockton, Michael/567 Prescott St, Pasadena, CA	818-794-6087
Stone, Pete/1410 NW Johnson, Portland, OR	503-224-7125
Stoy, Werner/287 Chestnut St, San Carlos, CA	415-591-4155
Strauss, Andrew/6442 Santa Monica Blvd, Los Angeles, CA	213-464-5394
Streano, Vince/PO Box 662, Laguna Beach, CA	714-497-1908
Street-Porter, Tim/6938 Camrose Dr, Los Angeles, CA	213-874-4278
Streshinsky, Ted/PO Box 674, Berkeley, CA	415-526-1976
Strickland, Steve/Box 3486, San Bernardino, CA	714-883-4792
Stryker, Ray/12029 76th Ave S, Seattle, WA	206-772-5680
Stuart, James Peter/PO Box 84744, Seattle, WA	206-587-0588
Studio AV/1227 First Ave S, Seattle, WA	206-223-1007
Studio B/5121-B Santa Fe St, San Diego, CA	619-483-2122
Su, Andrew/5733 Benner St, Los Angeles, CA	213-256-0598
Sugar, James/45 Midway Ave, Mill Valley, CA	415-388-3344
Sugiyama, Ron/PO Box 665, San Francisco, CA	415-563-8052
Sullivan, Jeremiah S/PO Box 7870, San Diego, CA	619-224-0070
Sund, Harald/PO Box 16466, Seattle, WA	206-938-1080
Surber, Bruce/13600 NE 20th St #E, Bellevue, WA	206-641-6003
Sutton, David/11502 Dona Teresa Dr, Studio City, CA	213-654-7979
Sutton, John/333 Fifth St, San Francisco, CA	415-974-5452
Swanson, Van/41195 Academy Dr, Hemet, CA	714-658-8125
Swarthout, Walter & Assoc/370 Fourth St, San Francisco, CA	415-543-2525
Swartz, Fred/135 S LaBrea, Los Angeles, CA	213-939-2789
Swenson, John/4353 W 5th St #D, Los Angeles, CA	213-384-1782
Tachibana, Kenji/1067 26th Ave East, Seattle, WA	206-325-2121
Taggart, Fritz/1117 N Wilcox Pl, Los Angeles, CA	213-469-8227
Tapp, Carlan/114 Alaskan Way S, Seattle, WA	206-621-8344
Taub, Doug/8712 Duncamp Pl, Los Angeles, CA	213-650-1221
Tauber, Richard/4221 24th St, San Francisco, CA	415-824-6837
Teeter, Jeff/2205 Dixon St, Chico, CA	916-895-3255
Teke/4338 Shady Glade Ave, Studio City, CA	818-985-9066
Theis, Rocky/2955 4th Ave, San Diego, CA	619-295-1923
Thimmes, Timothy/2805 S La Cienega Ave, Los Angeles, CA	213-204-6851
Thomas, Neil/4686 Woodside Dr, Los Angeles, CA	213-202-0051
Thompson, Michael/7811 Alabama Ave #14, Canoga Park, CA	818-883-7870
Thompson, William/PO Box 4460, Seattle, WA	206-621-9069
Thomson, Sydney (Ms)/PO Box 1032, Keaau, HI	808-966-8587
Thornton, Tyler/4706 Oakwood Ave, Los Angeles, CA	213-465-0425
Tichenor, K C/2395 El Camino Ave, Sacramento, CA	916-971-1771
Tilger, Stewart/71 Columbia #206, Seattle, WA	206-682-7818
Tise, David/975 Folsom St, San Francisco, CA	415-777-0669
Tokar, John/1360 Logan Ave #105, Costa Mesa, CA	714-733-8572
Tracy, Tom/37 Crystal Springs, San Mateo, CA	415-340-9811
Trafficanda, Gerald/1111 N Beachwood Dr, Los Angeles, CA	213-466-1111
Trailer, Martin/11125-D Flintkote Ave, San Diego, CA	619-452-7759
Trank, Steven/706 W Pico Blvd, Los Angeles, CA	213-749-1220
Trexler, Pete/5888 Smiley Dr Std B, Culver City, CA	213-558-8226
Trindl, Gene/3950 Vantage Ave, Studio City, CA	213-877-4848
Tucker, Kim/2428 Canyon Dr, Los Angeles, CA	213-465-9233
Turner & DeVries/1200 College Walk #212, Honolulu, HI	808-537-3115
Turner, John Terence/173 37th Ave E, Seattle, WA	206-325-9073
Turner, Richard P/Box 64205 Rancho Pk Sta, Los Angeles, CA	213-279-2127
Tuschman, Mark/300 Santa Monica, Menlo Park, CA	415-322-4157

U V

Ueda, Richard/1816 South Flower St, Los Angeles, CA	213-747-7259
Underwood, Ron/918 Hilldroft Rd, Glendale, CA	818-246-3628
Undheim, Timothy/8535 Arjohns Dr #L, San Diego, CA	619-549-3322
Uniack/8933 National Blvd, Los Angeles, CA	213-938-0287
Upfront Communication/227 5th St #A, Encinitas, CA	619-273-8544
Upton, Tom/1879 Woodland Ave, Palo Alto, CA	415-325-8120
Urie, Walter Photography/1810 E Carnegie, Santa Ana, CA	714-261-6302
Vanderpoel, Fred/1118 Harrison, San Francisco, CA	415-621-4405
Varie, Bill/2210 Wilshire Blvd, Santa Monica, CA	213-395-9337
Vega, Raul/3511 W 6th Tower Suite, Los Angeles, CA	213-387-2058
Veitch, Julie/5757 Venice Blvd, Los Angeles, CA	213-936-4231
Venezia, Jay/1373 Edgecliffe Dr, Los Angeles, CA	213-665-7382
Vereen, Jackson/570 Bryant St, San Francisco, CA	415-777-5272
Viarnes, Alex/Studio 33/Clementina, San Francisco, CA	415-543-1195
Vignes, Michelle/654 28th St, San Francisco, CA	415-550-8039
Villaflor, F/PO Box 883274, San Francisco, CA	415-921-4238
Visually Speaking/3609 E Olympic Blvd, Los Angeles, CA	213-269-9141
Vogt, Jurgen/936 E 28th Ave, Vancouver V5V 2P2, BC	604-876-5817
Vollenweider, Thom/3430 El Cajon Blvd, San Diego, CA	619-280-3070
Vollick, Tom/415 28th St, Hermosa Beach, CA	213-316-3196

W

Wade, Bill/5608 E 2nd St, Long Beach, CA	213-439-6826
Wahlstrom, Richard/650 Alabama St 3rd Fl, San Francsico, CA	415-550-1400
Wallace, Marlene/1624 S Cotner, Los Angeles, CA	213-826-1027
Wallick, Philip/PO Box 3096, Chico, CA	916-893-8464
Warden, John/9201 Shorecrest Dr, Anchorage, AK	907-243-1667
Warren Aerial Photography/1585 E Locust, Pasadena, CA	213-681-1006
Warren, Adrienne/3001 Crown Valley Pkwy, Laguna Niguel, CA	714-643-0333
Warren, William James/509 S Gramercy Pl, Los Angeles, CA	213-383-0500
Watanabe, David/14355 132nd Ave NE, Kirkland, WA	206-823-0692
Waterfall, William/826 15th Ave, Honolulu, HI	808-737-5116
Watson, Alan/710 13th St #300, San Diego, CA	619-239-5555
Watson, Stuart/620 Moulton Ave, Los Angeles, CA	213-221-3886
Waz, Tony/1115 S Trotwood Ave, San Pedro, CA	213-548-3758
Webber, Phil/2466 Westlake Ave N, Seattle, WA	206-282-2423
Weissman, Jeff/3025 Jordan Rd, Oakland, CA	415-482-3891
Werner, Jeffery R/14002 Palawan Way, Marina Del Rey, CA	213-821-2384
Werner, Joel/930 W 16th St #E1, Costa Mesa, CA	714-650-0999
Werts Studio Inc/732 N Highland, Los Angeles, CA	213-464-2775
Werts, Bill/732 N Highland, Los Angeles, CA	213-464-2775
West, Andrew/342 Sycamore Rd, Santa Monica, CA	213-459-7774
Wexler, Glen/736 N Highland, Los Angeles, CA	213-465-0268
Wheeler, Nik/7444 Woodrow Wilson Dr, Los Angeles, CA	213-850-0234
Wheeler, Richard/PO Box 3739, San Rafael, CA	415-457-6914
Whetstone, Wayne/149 W Seventh Ave, Vancouver V5Y1L8, BC	604-873-8471
Whitmore, Ken/PO Box 49373, Los Angeles, CA	213-472-4337
Whittaker, Steve/111 Glen Way #8, Belmont, CA	415-595-4242
Wiener, Leigh/2600 Carman Crest Dr, Los Angeles, CA	213-876-0990
Wietstock, Wilfried/877 Valencia St, San Francisco, CA	415-285-4221
Wilcox, Jed/PO Box 4091, Palm Springs, CA	714-659-3945
Wilhelm, Dave/2565 Third St #303, San Francisco, CA	415-826-9399
Wilkings, Steve/Box 22810, Honolulu, HI	808-732-6288
Willett, Larry/450 S LaBrea, Los Angeles, CA	213-935-6047
Williams, David Jordan/6122 W Colgate, Los Angeles, CA	213-936-3170
Williams, Harold/705 Bayswater Ave, Burlingame, CA	415-648-6644
Williams, Sandra/PO Box 16130, San Diego, CA	619-234-0447
Williams, Steven Burr/5315 Clinton, Los Angeles, CA	213-469-5749
Williams, Wayne/7623 Beverly Blvd, Los Angeles, CA	213-937-2882
Williamson, Scott/1901 E Carnegie #1G, Santa Ana, CA	714-261-2550
Wilson, Don/10754 2nd Ave NW, Seattle, WA	206-367-4075
WILSON, DOUGLAS M/10133 NE 113TH PL, KIRKLAND, WA (P 231)	**206-822-8604**

Photographers

Continued

Please send us your additions and updates.

Wimpey, Christopher/627 Eighth Ave, San Diego, CA	619-232-3222
Wincott, Gary Photography/1087 Robbia Dr, Sunnyvale, CA	408-245-9559
Windus, Scott/916 N Formosa, Beverly Hills, CA	213-276-0968
Winholt, Bryan/PO Box 331, Sacramento, CA	916-725-0592
Winter-Green Photo/7936 Miramar Rd, San Diego, CA	619-565-1652
Wittner, Dale/507 Third Ave #209, Seattle, WA	206-623-4545
Wolfe, Dan E/45 E Walnut, Pasadena, CA	213-681-3130
Wolman, Baron/PO Box 1000, Mill Valley, CA	415-388-0181
Wong, Ken/3522 W Temple St, Los Angeles, CA	213-389-3081
Wood, Darrell/517 Aloha St, Seattle, WA	206-283-7900
Wood, James/1746 N Ivar, Los Angeles, CA	213-461-3861
Woolslair, James/17229 Newhope St #H, Fountain Valley, CA	714-957-0349
Wortham, Robert/521 State St, Glendale, CA	818-243-6400
Wright, Armand/4026 Blairmore Ct, San Jose, CA	408-629-0559
Wyatt, Tom Photography/215 Second St, San Francisco, CA	415-543-2813

YZ

Young, Bill/PO Box 27344, Honolulu, HI	808-595-7324
Young, Edward/860 2nd St, San Francisco, CA	415-543-6633
Youngblood, Lee/501 Forest Ave #608, Palo Alto, CA	415-329-1085
Yudelson, Jim/33 Clementina, San Francisco, CA	415-543-3325
Zajack, Greg/1517 W Alton Ave, Santa Ana, CA	714-432-8400
Zak, Ed/80 Tehama St, San Francisco, CA	415-781-1611
Zanzinger, David/2411 Main St, Santa Monica, CA	213-399-8802
Zaruba, Jeff/833 N Fairfax Ave, Los Angeles, CA	213-653-3341
Zenuk, Alan/POB 3531, Vancouver BC, Canada V6B 3Y6,	604-733-8271
Zimberoff, Tom/PO Box 5212, Beverly Hills, CA	213-271-5900
Zimmerman, Dick/8743 W Washington Blvd, Los Angeles, CA	213-204-2911
Zimmerman, John/9135 Hazen Dr, Beverly Hills, CA	213-273-2642
Zippel, Arthur/2110 E McFadden #D, Santa Ana, CA	714-835-8400
Zlozower, Neil/6341 Yucca, Los Angeles, CA	213-935-0606
Zurek, Nikolay/276 Shipley St, San Francisco, CA	415-777-9210
Zwart, Jeffrey R/1900-E East Warner, Santa Ana, CA	714-261-5844
Zyber, Tom/11577-A Slater Ave, Fountain Valley, CA	714-546-2949

Notes:

Stock

New York City

American Heritage Picture Library/10 Rockefeller Plaza	212-399-8930
American Library Color Slide Co/222 W 23rd St	212-255-5356
Archive Pictures/111 Wooster St	212-431-1610
Argent and Aurum/470 W 24th St	212-807-1186
Arnold, Peter/1181 Broadway 4th Fl	212-481-1190
Art Resource Inc/65 Bleecker St 9th Fl	212-505-8700
Beck's Studio/37-44 82nd St	718-424-8751
The Bethel Agency/513 W 54th St #1	212-664-0455
Bettmann Archive/136 E 57th St	212-758-0362
Camera Five Inc/6 W 20th St	212-989-2004
Camp, Woodfin Assoc/415 Madison Ave	212-750-1020
Coleman, Bruce Inc/381 Fifth Ave 2nd Fl	212-683-5227
COMSTOCK/32 E 31ST ST (P INSIDE FRONT COVER)	**212-889-9700**
Consolidated Poster Service/341 W 44th St	212-581-3105
Contact Stock Images/415 Madison Ave	212-750-1020
Cooke, Jerry/161 E 82nd St	212-288-2045
Culver Pictures Inc/150 W 22nd St 3rd Fl	212-684-5054
Design Conceptions/Elaine Abrams/112 Fourth Ave	212-254-1688
DeWys, Leo Inc/1170 Broadway	212-986-3190
DMI Inc/341 First Ave	212-777-8135
Dot Picture Agency/50 W 29th St	212-684-3441
DPI Inc/19 W 21st St #901	212-752-3930
Ewing Galloway/1466 Broadway	212-719-4720
Flex Inc/342 Madison Ave	212-722-5816
Flying Camera Inc/114 Fulton St	212-619-0808
Focus on Sports/222 E 46th St	212-661-6860
Four by Five Inc/485 Madison Ave	212-355-2323
FPG International/251 Park Ave S	212-777-4214
Fundamental Photographs/210 Forsythe St	212-473-5770
Gabriel Graphic News Service/38 Madison Sq Sta	212-254-8863
Gamma-Liaison Photo Agency/150 E 58th St	212-888-7272
Globe Photos Inc/275 Seventh Ave 21st Fl	212-689-1340
Gottscho-Schleisner Inc/150-35 86th Ave	718-526-2795
The Granger Collection/1841 Broadway	212-586-0971
Gross, Lee Assoc/366 Madison Ave	212-682-5240
Heyman, Ken/3 E 76th St	212-226-3725
THE IMAGE BANK/111 FIFTH AVE (P BACK COVER)	**212-529-6700**
Image Resources/134 W 29th St	212-736-2523
Index Stock International Inc/126 Fifth Ave	212-929-4644
International Stock Photos/113 E 31st St #1A	212-696-4666
Keystone Press Agency Inc/202 E 42nd St	212-924-8123
Kramer, Joan & Assoc Inc/720 Fifth Ave	212-567-5545
Lewis, Frederick Inc/134 W 29th St #1003	212-594-8816
Life Picture Service/Rm 28-58 Time-Life Bldg	212-841-4800
Magnum Photos Inc/251 Park Ave S	212-475-7600
Maisel, Jay/190 Bowery	212-431-5013
Manhattan Views/41 Union Sq W #1027	212-255-1477
MediChrome/271 Madison Ave	212-679-8480
Memory Shop Inc/109 E 12th St	212-473-2404
Monkmeyer Press Photo Agency/118 E 28th St #615	212-689-2242
Omni Photo Communication/521 Madison Ave	212-751-6530
Photo Assoc News Service/PO Box 306 Station A	718-961-0909
Photo Files/1235 E 40th St	718-338-2245
Photo Library Inc/325 W 45th St	212-246-1349
Photo Researchers Inc/60 E 56th St	212-758-3420
Photo Unique/1328 Broadway PH	212-244-5511
Photo World/251 Park Ave S	212-777-4214
Photofile International Ltd/32 E 31st St	212-989-0500
Photography for Industry/230 W 54th St	212-757-9255
PhotoNet/250 W 57th St	212-757-0320
Photoreporters/875 Ave of Americas #1003	212-736-7602
Phototake/4523 Broadway #76	212-942-8185
Phototeque/156 Fifth Ave #415	212-242-6406
Pictorial Parade/130 W 42nd St	212-840-2026
RDR Productions/351 W 54th St	212-586-4432
Reese, Kay/175 Fifth Ave #1304	212-598-4848
Reference Pictures/119 Fifth Ave	212-254-0008
Retna Ltd/36 W 56th St	212-489-1230
Roberts, H Armstrong/1181 Broadway	212-685-3870
Science Photo Library Int'l/118 E 28th St	212-683-4025

Shashinka Photo/501 Fifth Ave #2102	212-490-2180
Shostal Assoc/164 Madison Ave	212-686-8850
SO Studio Inc/34 E 23rd St	212-475-0090
Sochurek, Howard Inc/680 Fifth Ave	212-582-1860
Sovfoto-Eastphoto Agency/25 W 43rd St	212-921-1922
Spano/Roccanova/16 W 46th St	212-840-7450
Sports Illustrated Pictures/Time-Life Bldg 19th Fl	212-841-3663
Steinhauser, Art Ent/305 E 40th St	212-953-1722
The Stock Market/1181 Broadway 10th Fl	212-684-7878
The Stock Shop/271 Madison Ave	212-679-8480
Stockphotos Inc/373 Park Ave S 6th Fl	212-686-1196
The Strobe Studio Inc/91 Fifth Ave	212-691-5270
Sygma Photo News/225 W 57th St 7th Fl	212-765-1820
Tamin Stock Photos/440 West End Ave #4E	212-807-6691
Taurus Photos/118 E 28th St	212-683-4025
UPI Photo Library/48 E 21st St	212-777-6200
Wheeler Pictures/50 W 29th St #11W	212-696-9832
Wide World Photos Inc/50 Rockefeller Plaza	212-621-1930
Winiker, Barry M/173 W 78th St	212-572-7364

Northeast

Authenticated News Int'l/29 Katonah Ave, Katonah, NY	914-232-7726
Bergman, LV & Assoc/East Mountain Rd S, Cold Spring, NY	914-265-3656
Blizzard, William C/PO Box 1696, Beckley, WV	304-755-0094
Camerique Stock Photography/1701 Skippack Pike, Blue Bell, PA	215-272-7649
Camerique Stock Photography NE/45 Newbury St, Boston, MA	617-267-6450
Cape Scapes/542 Higgins Crowell Rd, West Yarmouth, MA	617-362-8222
Chandoha, Walter/RD 1 PO Box 287, Annandale, NJ	201-782-3666
Chimera Productions/PO Box 1742, Clarksburg, WV	304-623-5368
Consolidated News Pictures/209 Pennsylvania Ave SE, Washington, DC	202-543-3203
Cyr Color Photo/PO Box 2148, Norwalk, CT	203-838-8230
DCS Enterprises/12806 Gaffney Rd, Silver Spring, MD	301-622-2323
Devaney Stock Photos/7 High St #308, Huntington, NY	516-673-4477
Dunn, Phoebe/20 Silvermine Rd, New Canaan, CT 234	203-966-9791
Earth Scenes/Animals Animals/17 Railroad Ave, Chatham, NY	518-392-5500
Educational Dimension Stock/PO Box 126, Stamford, CT	203-327-4612
F/Stop Pictures Inc/PO Box 359, Springfield, VT	802-885-5261
First Foto Bank/2637 Connecticut Ave NW, Washington, DC	301-670-0299
Folio/2651 Conn Ave NW 3rd Fl, Washington, DC	202-965-2410
Heilman, Grant/506 W Lincoln Ave, Lititz, PA	717-626-0296
Illustrators Stock Photos/PO Box 1470, Rockville, MD	301-279-0045
Image Photos/Main St, Stockbridge, MA	413-298-5500
The Image Works Inc/PO Box 443, Woodstock, NY	914-679-7172
Jones, G P - Stock/45 Newbury St, Boston, MA	617-267-6450
Lambert, Harold M Studio/2801 W Cheltenham Ave, Philadelphia, PA	215-224-1400
Light, Paul/1430 Massachusetts Ave, Cambridge, MA	617-628-1052
Lumiere/512 Adams St, Centerport, NY	516-271-6133
Mercier, Louis/15 Long Lots Rd, Westport, CT	203-227-1620
Newsphoto Worldwide/902 National Press Bldg, Washington, DC	202-737-0450
Photo Media Ltd/3 Forest Glen Rd, New Paltz, NY	914-255-8661
Photo Stock Unlimited/7208 Thomas Blvd, Pittsburgh, PA	412-242-5070
Picture Group/5 Steeple St, Providence, RI	401-273-5473
The Picture Cube/89 State St, Boston, MA	617-367-1532
Picture Research/6107 Roseland Dr, Rockville, MD	301-230-0043
Positive Images/12 Main St, Natick, MA	617-653-7610
Rainbow/PO Box 573, Housatonic, MA	413-274-6211
Roberts, H Armstrong/4203 Locust St, Philadelphia, PA	215-386-6300
Sandak Inc/180 Harvard Ave, Stamford, CT	203-348-4721
Sequis Stock Photo/PO Box 215, Stevenson, MD	301-583-9177
Sportschrome/270 Sylvan Ave, Englewood Cliffs, NJ	201-568-1412
Starwood/PO Box 40503, Washington, DC	202-362-7404
Stock Boston Inc/36 Gloucester St, Boston, MA	617-266-2300
Undersea Systems/PO Box 29M, Bay Shore, NY	516-666-3127
Unicorn/Photographic Images Div/1148 Parsippany Blvd, Parsippany, NJ	201-334-0353
Uniphoto Picture Agency/1071 Wisconsin Ave NW,	

Stock

Continued

Please send us your additions and updates.

Washington, DC	202-333-0500
View Finder Stock Photo/818 Liberty Ave, Pittsburg, PA	412-391-8720
Weidman, H Mark/2112 Goodwin Lane, North Wales, PA	215-646-1745

Southeast

Cactus Clyde/3623 Perkins Rd Box 14876, Baton Rouge, LA	504-887-3704
Camera MD Studios/8290 NW 26 Pl, Ft Lauderdale, FL	305-741-5560
Florida Image File/222 2nd St N, St Petersburg, FL	813-894-8433
THE IMAGE BANK/2490 PIEDMONT RD NE #1106, ATLANTA, GA (P BACK COVER)	**404-233-9920**
McCarthy's National Stock/8960 SW 114th St, Miami, FL	305-233-1703
Phelps Agency/3210 Peachtree St NW, Atlanta, GA	404-264-0264
Photo Options/1432 Linda Vista Dr, Birmingham, AL	205-979-8412
PHOTRI(PHOTO RESEARCH INT'L)/505 W WINDSOR/PO BOX 971, ALEXANDRIA, VA (P 236)	**703-836-4439**
Sharp Shooters/7210 Red Rd #216, Miami, FL	305-666-1266
Sherman, Ron/PO Box 28656, Atlanta, GA	404-993-7197
Southern Stock Photo/3601 W Commercial Blvd #33, Ft Lauderdale, FL	305-486-7117
Stills Inc/3210 Peachtree Rd NE, Atlanta, GA	404-233-0022
The Waterhouse/PO Box 2487, Key Largo, FL	305-451-3737

Midwest

A-Stock Photo Finder & Photographers/1030 N State St, Chicago, IL	312-645-0611
Artstreet/111 E Chestnut St, Chicago, IL	312-664-3049
Bundt, Nancy/4001 Forest Rd, Minneapolis, MN	612-927-7493
Cameramann International/PO Box 413, Evanston, IL	312-777-5657
Camerique Stock Photography/233 E Wacker Dr #4305, Chicago, IL	312-938-4466
Camerique Stock Photography/45 E Charles St, Toronto M4Y 1S6,	416-925-4323
Campbell Stock Photo/28000 Middlebelt Rd #260, Farmington Hills, MI	313-626-5233
Charlton Photos/11518 N Pt Washington Rd, Mequon, WI	414-241-8634
Click! Chicago Inc/213 W Institute Pl #503, Chicago, IL	312-787-7880
Collectors Series/161 W Harrison, Chicago, IL	312-427-5311
Gartman, Marilyn/5549 N Clark St, Chicago, IL	312-561-5504
Hedrich-Blessing/11 W Illinois St, Chicago, IL	312-321-1151
Historical Picture Service/601 W Randolph St, Chicago, IL	312-346-0599
Ibid Inc/727 N Hudson, Chicago, IL	312-944-0020
THE IMAGE BANK/822 MARQUETTE AVE, MINNEAPOLIS, MN (P BACK COVER)	**612-332-8935**
THE IMAGE BANK/510 N DEARBORN #930, CHICAGO, IL (P BACK COVER)	**312-329-1817**
Journalism Services Stock/118 E 2nd St, Lockport, IL	312-951-0269
Krinsky, Jon A/85 Tahlequah Trail, Springboro, OH	513-746-5230
Miller Services/45 East Charles St, Toronto M4Y 1S6, ON	416-925-4323
Photo Reserve/842 W Lill St, Chicago, IL	312-871-7371
The Photoletter/Pine Lake Farm, Osceola, WI	715-248-3800
Pix International/300 N State #3926, Chicago, IL	312-321-9071
Thill, Nancy/70 W Huron St, Chicago, IL	312-944-7164
Third Coast Stock/PO Box 92397, Milwaukee, WI	414-765-9442
Weathers, Ginny/708 Gage, Topeka, KS	913-272-1190
Zehrt, Jack/PO Box 122A Rt5, Pacific, MO	314-458-3600

Southwest

Cochise Photographics/1500 Martingale Rd, Sierra Vista, AZ	602-458-2400
Far West Photo/1104 Hermosa Dr SE, Albuquerque, NM	505-255-0646
THE IMAGE BANK/1336 CONANT ST, DALLAS, TX (P BACK COVER)	**214-631-3808**
Image Venders/2404 Farrington, Dallas, TX	214-630-0183
Images Unlimited/13510 Floyd #100, Dallas, TX	214-644-6595
McLaughlin, Herb & Dorothy/2344 W Holly, Phoenix, AZ	602-258-6551
Photobank/PO Box 1086, Scottsdale, AZ	602-948-8805
Photoworks/Uniphoto International/215 Asbury, Houston, TX	713-864-3638
Raphaele/Digital Transparencies Inc/616 Hawthorne, Houston, TX	713-524-2211
Running Productions/PO Box 1237, Flagstaff, AZ	602-774-2923

Southern Images/Rt 1 Box 312, Paris, AR	501-963-6429
The Stock House Inc/1622 W Alabama, Houston, TX	713-526-3007
Visual Images West/600 E Baseline Rd #B-6, Tempe, AZ	602-820-5403
Westlake, Jude/PO Box 791, Tempe, AZ	602-968-9078

Rocky Mountain

Amwest Picture Agency/1595 S University, Denver, CO	303-777-2770
Aspen Stock Photo/PO Box 4063, Aspen, CO	303-925-8280
Dannen, Kent & Donna/Moraine Route, Estes Park, CO	303-586-5794
International Photo File/PO Box 343, Magna, UT	801-250-3447
The Photo Bank/271 Second Ave N Box 3069, Ketchum, ID	208-726-5731
Stack, Tom & Assoc/1322 N Academy Blvd #209, Colorado Springs, CO	303-570-1000
The Stock Broker/450 Lincoln St #110, Denver, CO	303-698-1734
Stock Imagery/711 Kalamath St, Denver, CO	303-592-1091
The Stock Solution/6640 South, 2200 West, Salt Lake City, UT	801-569-1155
Visual Media Inc/2661 Vassar St, Reno, NV	702-322-8868

West Coast

After Image Inc/3807 Wilshire Blvd #250, Los Angeles, CA	213-480-1105
Alaska Pictorial Service/Drawer 6144, Anchorage, AK	907-344-1370
AlaskaPhoto/1530 Westlake Ave N, Seattle, WA	206-282-8116
American Stock Photos/6842 Sunset Blvd, Los Angeles, CA	213-469-3908
Aperture PhotoBank/1530 Westlake Ave N, Seattle, WA	206-282-8116
Beebe, Morton & Assoc/150 Lombard St #207, San Francisco, CA	415-362-3530
Burr, Lawrence/76 Manzanita Rd, Fairfax, CA	415-456-9158
Camera Hawaii/875 Waimanu, Honolulu, HI	808-536-2302
Cornwell, David/1311 Kalakaua Ave, Honolulu, HI	808-949-7000
Dae Flights/PO Box 1086, Newport Beach, CA	714-675-3902
Dandelet Interlinks/126 Redwood Rd, San Anselmo, CA	415-456-1260
Eclipse & Suns/PO Box 689, Haines, AK	907-766-2670
Elich, George/PO Box 255016, Sacramento, CA	916-481-5021
Ergenbright, Ric/PO Box 1067, Bend, OR	503-389-7662
Focus West/4112 Adams Ave, San Diego, CA	619-280-3595
French, Peter/PO Box 100, Kamuela, HI	808-889-6488
Gemini Smith/5858 Desert View Dr, La Jolla, CA	619-454-4321
Great American Stock/3955 Pacific Hwy, San Diego, CA	619-297-2205
Grimm, Tom & Michelle/PO Box 83, Laguna Beach, CA	714-494-1336
Grubb, T D/11102 Blix St, N Hollywood, CA	818-760-1236
THE IMAGE BANK/8228 SUNSET BLVD #310, LOS ANGELES, CA (P BACK COVER)	**213-656-9003**
Jeton/483 Index Pl NE, Kenton, WA	206-226-1408
Long Photo Inc/1265 S Cochran, Los Angeles, CA	213-933-7219
Lundberg, Bret/PO Box 7542, Newport Beach, CA	714-631-4177
Peebles, Douglas Photography/1100 Alakea St #221, Honolulu, HI	808-533-6686
Photo File/550 15th St #31/1 Shwplce Sq, San Francisco, CA	415-397-3040
Photo Network/1541 Parkway Loop #J, Tustin, CA	714-259-1244
Photo Vault/1045 17th St, San Francisco, CA	415-552-9682
Photographsanstuff/730 Clementina, San Francisco, CA	415-861-1062
Photophile/2311 Kettner Blvd, San Diego, CA	619-234-4431
Simpson, Ed/PO Box 397, S Pasadena, CA	213-682-3131
Spectrum/115 Sansome St #812, San Francisco, CA	415-340-9811
Stock Orange/2511 W Sunflower #D9, Santa Ana, CA	714-546-0485
Take Stock/2831 7th Street, Berkeley, CA	415-644-2988
Terraphotographics/BPS/PO Box 490, Moss Beach, CA	415-726-6244
TRW/9841 Airport Blvd #1414, Los Angeles, CA	213-536-4880
Visual Impact/733 Auahi St, Honolulu, HI	808-524-8269
West Light/1526 Pontius Ave #A, Los Angeles, CA	213-477-0421
West Stock/157 Yesler Way #600, Seattle, WA	206-621-1611
Zephyr Pictures/2120 Jimmy Durante Blvd, Del Mar, CA	619-755-1200

STOCK

Graphic Designers

New York City

A
Abramson, Michael R Studio	212-683-1271
Adams, Gaylord Design	212-684-4625
Adlemann, Morton	212-564-8258
Adzema, Diane	212-982-5657
AKM Associates	212-687-7636
Album Graphics Inc	212-489-0793
Alexander, Martha	212-772-7382
Aliman, Elie	212-925-9621
Allied Graphic Arts	212-730-1414
American Express Publishing Co	212-382-5600
Amorello, Frank Assoc	212-972-1775
Anagraphics Inc	212-279-2370
Ancona Design Atelier	212-947-8287
And Co	212-213-8888
Anspach Grossman Portugal	212-692-9000
Antler & Baldwin Graphics	212-751-2031
Antupit and Others Inc	212-686-2552
Appelbaum Company	212-593-0003
Art Department	212-391-1826
Athey, Diane	212-787-7415

B
Balasas, Cora	718-633-7753
Bantam Books Inc	212-765-6500
Barmache, Leon Design Assoc Inc	212-752-6780
Barnett Design Group	212-677-8830
Barry, Jim	212-873-6787
Basilion, Nick	212-645-6568
Becker Hockfield Design Assoc	212-505-7050
Beckerman, Ann Design	212-684-0496
Bell, James Graphic Design Inc	212-929-8855
Bellows, Amelia	212-777-7012
Benvenutti, Chris	212-696-0880
Bernhardt/Fudyma	212-889-9337
Besalel, Ely	212-759-7820
Bessen & Tully, Inc	212-838-6406
Binns, Betty Graphic Design	212-679-9200
Biondo, Charles Design Assoc	212-645-5300
Birch, Colin Assoc Inc	212-223-0499
Bloch, Graulich & Whelan, Inc	212-473-7033
BN Associates	914-964-8102
Boker Group	212-686-1132
Bonnell Design Associates Inc	212-921-5390
Bordnick, Jack & Assoc	212-563-1544
Botero, Samuel Assoc	212-935-5155
Bradford, Peter	212-982-2090
Brainchild Designs	212-420-1222
Branin, Max	212-254-9608
Braswell, Lynn	212-222-8761
Bree/Taub Design	212-254-8383
Breth, Jill Marie	212-781-8370
Brochure People	212-696-9185
Brodsky Graphics	212-684-2600
Brown, Alastair Assoc	212-221-3166
Brown, Kim	212-567-5671
Buckley Designs Inc	212-861-0626
Burns, Tom Assoc Inc	212-594-9883
By Design	212-684-0388
The Byrne Group	212-889-0502

C
Cain, David	212-691-5783
Cannan, Bill & Co Inc	212-563-1004
Caravello Studios	212-620-0620
Carnase, Inc	212-679-9880
Carson, Carol	212-580-0514
Cetta, Al	212-989-9696
Chajet Design Group Inc	212-684-3669
Chang, Ivan	212-777-6102
Chapman, Sandra S	718-855-7396
Charles, Irene Assoc	212-765-8000

Chermayeff & Geismar	212-532-4499
Chu, H L & Co Ltd	212-889-4818
Church, Wallace Assoc	212-755-2903
Cliffer, Jill	212-691-7013
Cohen, Norman Design	212-679-3906
Comart Assoc	212-714-2550
Condon, J & M	212-242-7811
Corchia Woliner Assoc	212-977-9778
Corey & Co	212-924-4311
Corpographics, Inc.	212-483-9065
Corporate Annual Reports Inc.	212-889-2450
Corporate Graphics Inc	212-599-1820
Cosgrove Assoc Inc	212-889-7202
Cotler, Sheldon Inc	212-719-9590
Cousins, Morison S & Assoc	212-751-3390
Crane, Susan Inc	212-260-0580
Cranner, Brian Inc	212-582-2030
Creamer Dickson Basford	212-887-8670
Csoka/Benato/Fleurant Inc	212-242-6777
Cuevas, Robert	212-661-7149
Curtis Design Inc.	212-685-0670

D
Daniels Design	212-889-0071
Danne & Blackburn Inc.	212-371-3250
Davis, Jed	212-481-8481
Davis-Delaney-Arrow Inc	212-686-2500
DeHarak, Rudolph	212-929-5445
Deibler, Gordon	212-565-8022
Delgado, Lisa	212-645-0097
Delphan Company	212-371-6700
DeMartin-Marona-Cranstoun-Downes	212-682-9044
DeMartino/Schultz	212-513-0300
DESIGNED TO PRINT (P 242,243)	**212-924-2090**
Designers Three	212-221-5900
Designframe	212-924-2426
Deutsch Design	212-684-4478
Diamond Art Studio	212-685-6622
Dickens, Holly	212-682-1490
DiComo, Charles & Assoc	212-689-8670
DiFranza Williamson Inc	212-832-2343
Displaycraft	718-784-8186
Donovan & Green Inc	212-725-2233
Doret, Michael	212-929-1688
Douglas, Barry Design	212-734-4137
DOWNEY WEEKS + TOOMEY (P 244-247)	**212-564-8260**
Drate, Spencer	212-620-4672
Dreyfuss, Henry Assoc	212-957-8600
Dubins, Milt Designer Inc	212-691-0232
Dubourcq, Hilaire	212-924-1564
Dubrow, Oscar Assoc	212-688-0698
Duffy, William R	212-682-6755
Dwyer, Tom	212-986-7108

E
Edgar, Lauren	212-673-6060
Edge, Dennis Design	212-679-0927
Eichinger, Inc	212-421-0544
Eisenman and Enock	212-431-1000
Emerson, Matt	212-807-8144
Environetics Inc	212-481-9700
Environment Planning Inc	212-661-3744
Erikson Assoc.	212-688-0048
ETC Communications Grp	212-645-6800
Etheridge, Palombo, Sedewitz	212-944-2530
Eucalyptus Tree Studio	212-226-0331

F
Failing, Kendrick G Design	212-677-5764
Falkins, Richard Design	212-840-3045
Farmlett Barsanti Inc	212-691-9398
FDC Planning & Design Corp	212-355-7200
Feucht, Fred Design Group Inc	212-682-0040
Fineberg Associates	212-734-1220
Florville, Patrick Design Research	718-475-2278

Graphic Designers

Continued

Please send us your additions and updates.

Flying Eye Graphics	212-725-0658
Forman, Yale Designs Inc	212-799-1665
Foster, Stephen Design	212-532-0771
Freeman, Irving	212-674-6705
Freyss, Christina	212-571-1130
Friday Saturday Sunday Inc	212-260-8479
Friedlander, Ira	212-580-9800
Fulgoni, Louis	212-243-2959
Fulton & Partners	212-695-1625

G Gale, Cynthia

Gale, Cynthia	212-860-5429
Gale, Robert A Inc	212-535-4791
Gamarello, Paul	212-485-4774
Gardner, Beau Assoc Inc	212-832-2426
Gaster, Joanne	212-686-0860
Gentile Studio	212-986-7743
George, Hershell	212-929-4321
Gerstman & Meyers Inc.	212-586-2535
Gianninoto Assoc, Inc.	212-759-5757
Giber, Lauren	212-473-2062
Giovanni Design Assoc.	212-725-8536
Gips & Balkind & Assoc	212-421-5940
Gladstein, Renee	212-877-2966
Gladych, Marianne	212-925-9712
Glaser, Milton	212-889-3161
GLAZER & KALAYJIAN (P 248,249)	**212-687-3099**
Glusker Group	212-757-4438
Goetz Graphics	212-679-4250
Goldman, Neal Assoc	212-687-5058
Gorbaty, Norman Design	212-684-1665
Gorman, Chris Assoc	212-696-9377
Grant, Bill	718-996-3555
Graphic Art Resource Assoc	212-929-0017
Graphic Chart & Map Co	212-982-2428
The Graphic Expression Inc.	212-759-7788
Graphics 60 Inc.	212-687-1292
Graphics by Nostradamus	212-581-1362
Graphics for Industry	212-889-6202
Graphics Institute	212-887-8670
Graphics to Go	212-889-9337
Gray, George	212-873-3607
Green, Douglas	212-752-6284
Griffler Designs	212-794-2625
Grossberg, Manuel	212-620-0444
Grunfeld Graphics Ltd	212-431-8700
Gucciardo & Shapokas	212-683-9378

H Halle, Doris

Halle, Doris	212-321-2671
Halversen, Everett	718-438-4200
Handler Group Inc	212-391-0951
Haydee Design Studio	212-242-3110
HBO Studio Productions Inc	212-477-8600
Hecker, Mark Studio	212-620-9050
Heimall, Bob Inc	212-245-4525
Herbick, David	718-852-6450
Holden, Cynthia	212-222-4214
Holland, DK	718-789-3112
Holzsager, Mel Assoc Inc	212-741-7373
Hooper, Ray Design	212-924-5480
Hopkins, Will	212-580-9800
Horvath & Assoc Studios Ltd	212-741-0300
Hub Graphics	212-675-8500
Human Factors/Industrial Design Inc	212-730-8010
Huttner & Hillman	212-532-6062

IJ Image Communications Inc

Image Communications Inc	212-807-9677
Infield & D'Astolfo	212-924-9206
Inkwell Inc	212-279-2066
Inner Thoughts	212-674-1277
Intersight Design Inc	212-696-0700
Jaffe Communications, Inc	212-697-4310
Johnson, Dwight	718-834-8529

Johnston, Shaun & Susan	212-663-4686
Jonson Pedersen Hinrichs & Shakery	212-889-9611

K Kacik Design

Kacik Design	212-753-0031
Kaeser & Wilson Design	212-563-2455
Kahn, Al Group	212-580-3517
Kahn, Donald	212-889-8898
Kallir Phillips Ross Inc.	212-878-3700
Kass Communications	212-868-3133
Kass, Milton Assoc Inc	212-874-0418
Kaye Graphics	212-924-7800
Keithley & Assoc	212-807-8388
Kleb Associates	212-246-2847
KLN Publishing Services Inc	212-686-8200
Kneapler, John	212-696-1150
Ko Noda and Assoc International	212-759-4044
Kollberg-Johnson Assoc Inc	212-686-3648
Koons, Irv Assoc	212-752-4130
Koppel & Scher Inc	212-683-0870

L Lacy, N Lee

Lacy, N Lee	212-532-6200
Lake, John	212-644-3850
Lamlee, Stuart	212-844-8991
The Lamplight Group	212-682-6270
LCL Design Assoc Inc	212-758-2604
Leach, Richard	212-869-0972
Lebbad, James A	212-645-5260
Lee & Young Communications	212-689-4000
Lesley-Hille Inc	212-677-7570
Lester & Butler	212-889-0578
Levine, Gerald	212-986-1068
Levine, William V & Assoc	212-683-7177
Levirne, Joel	212-869-8370
Lichtenberg, Al Graphic Art	212-865-4312
Lieberman, Ron	212-947-0653
Liebert Studios Inc	212-686-4520
Lika Association	212-490-3660
Lind Brothers Inc	212-924-9280
Lippincott & Margulies Inc	212-832-3000
Little Apple Art	718-499-7045
Loiacono Adv	212-683-5811
Lubliner/Saltz	212-679-9810
Luckett Slover & Partners	212-620-9770
Lukasiewicz Design Inc	212-581-3344
Lundgren, Ray Graphics	212-370-1686
Luth & Katz Inc	212-644-5777

M M & Co Design Group

M & Co Design Group	212-243-0082
Maddalone, John	212-807-6087
Maggio, Ben Assoc Inc	212-697-8600
Maggio, J P Design Assoc Inc	212-725-9660
Maleter, Mari	718-726-7124
Marchese, Frank	212-988-6267
Marckrey Design Group Inc	212-620-7077
Marcus, Eric	718-789-1799
Mauro, C L & Assoc Inc	212-868-3940
Mauro, Frank Assoc Inc	212-719-5570
Mayo-Infurna Design	212-888-7883
McDonald, B & Assoc	212-869-9717
McGovern & Pivoda	212-840-2912
McNicholas, Florence	718-965-0203
Meier Adv	212-355-6460
Mendola Design	212-986-5680
Mentkin, Robert	212-534-5101
Merrill, Abby Studio Inc	212-753-7565
Millenium Design	212-683-3400
Miller, Irving D Inc	212-755-4040
Mirenburg, Barry	718-885-0835
Mitchell, E M Inc	212-986-5595
Mizerek Design	212-986-5702
Modular Marketing Inc	212-581-4690
Mont, Howard Assoc Inc	212-683-4360

Graphic Designers

Continued

Please send us your additions and updates.

Morris, Dean	212-420-0673
Moshier, Harry & Assoc	212-873-6130
Moskof & Assoc	212-333-2015
Mossberg, Stuart Design Assoc	212-873-6130
Muir, Cornelius, Moore	212-687-4055
Murtha Desola Finsilver Fiore	212-832-4770

N

N B Assoc Inc	212-684-8074
Nelson, George & Assoc Inc	212-777-4300
Nemser, Robert	212-832-9595
New American Graphics	212-532-3551
Newman, Harvey Assoc	212-391-8060
Nicholson Design	212-206-1530
Nightingale, Gordon	212-685-9263
Nitzburg, Andrew	212-686-3514
Nobart NY Inc	212-475-5522
Noneman & Noneman Design	212-473-4090
North, Charles W Studio	212-242-6300
Notovitz & Perrault Design Inc	212-677-9700
Novus Visual Communications Inc	212-689-2424

O

Oak Tree Graphics Inc	212-398-9355
Offenhartz, Harvey Inc	212-751-3241
Ohlsson, Eskil Assoc Inc	212-758-4412
Ong & Assoc	212-355-4343
Orlov, Christian	212-873-2381
Ortiz, Jose Luis	212-831-6138
Oz Communications Inc	212-686-8200

P

Page Arbitrio Resen Ltd	212-421-8190
Pahmer, Hal	212-889-6202
Palladino, Tony	212-751-0068
Paragraphics	718-965-2231
Parsons School of Design	212-741-8900
Patel, Harish Design Assoc	212-686-7425
Peckolick & Prtnrs	212-532-6166
Pellegrini & Assoc	212-686-4481
Pencils Portfolio Inc	212-355-2468
Penpoint Studio Inc	212-243-5435
Penraat Jaap Assoc	212-873-4541
Performing Dogs	212-260-1880
Perlman, Richard Design	212-935-2552
Perlow, Paul	212-758-4358
Peters, Stan Assoc Inc	212-684-0315
Peterson Blythe & Cato	212-557-5566
Pettis, Valerie	212-683-7382
Plumb Design Group Inc	212-673-3490
Podob, Al	212-697-6643
Pop Shots Corporate Design	212-489-1717
Pouget, Evelyn	212-228-7935
Prendergast, J W & Assoc Inc	212-687-8805
Primary Design Group	212-219-1000
Projection Systems International	212-682-0995
Puiying	212-689-5148
Pushpin Group	212-674-8080

Q R

Quon, Mike Design Office	212-226-6024
Rafkin Rubin Inc	212-869-2540
Ratzkin, Lawrence	212-279-1314
RC Graphics	212-755-1383
RD Graphics	212-889-5612
Regn-Califano Inc	212-239-0380
Robinson, Mark	718-638-9067
Rogers, Ana	212-741-4687
Rogers, Richard Inc	212-685-3666
Romero, Javier	212-206-9175
Rosenthal, Herb & Assoc Inc	212-685-1814
ROSS CULBERT HOLLAND & LAVERY (P 252,253)	**212-206-0044**
Ross/Pento Inc	212-757-5604
Rouya, E S	718-937-7197
Russell, Anthony Inc	212-255-0650

S

Sabanosh, Michael	212-947-8161
Saiki & Assoc	212-255-0466
Sakin, Sy	212-688-3141
Saks, Arnold	212-861-4300
Saksa Art & Design	212-255-5539
Salisbury & Salisbury Inc	212-575-0770
Salpeter, Paganucci, Inc	212-683-3310
Saltzman, Mike Group	212-929-4655
Sandgren Associates Inc	212-679-4650
Sawyer, Arnie Studio	212-685-4927
Saxton Communications Group	212-953-1300
Say It In Neon	212-691-7977
Schaefer-Cassety Inc	212-840-0175
Schaeffer/Boehm Ltd	212-947-4345
Schechter Group Inc	212-752-4400
Schecterson, Jack Assoc Inc	212-889-3950
Schumach, Michael P	718-539-5328
Scott, Louis Assoc	212-674-0215
SCR Design Organization	212-752-8496
Shapiro, Ellen Graphic Design	212-221-2625
Shareholder Graphics	212-661-1070
Shareholders Reports	212-686-9099
Sherin & Matejka Inc	212-686-8410
Sherowitz, Phyllis	212-532-8933
Shreeve, Draper Design	212-675-7534
Siegel & Gale Inc	212-730-0101
Silberlicht, Ira	212-595-6252
Silverman, Bob Design	212-371-6472
Singer, Paul Design	718-449-8172
Sloan, William	212-226-8110
Smith, Edward Design	212-255-1717
Smith, Laura	212-206-9162
Sochynsky, Ilona	212-686-1275
Solay/Hunt	212-840-3313
Sorvino, Skip	212-580-9638
St Vincent Milone & McConnells	212-921-1414
Stillman, Linda	212-410-3225
Stuart, Gunn & Furuta	212-689-0077
Studio 42	212-354-7298
The Sukon Group, Inc	212-986-2290
Swatek and Romanoff Design Inc	212-807-0236
Systems Collaborative Inc	212-608-0584

T

Tapa Graphics	212-243-0176
Taurins Design Assoc	212-679-5955
Tauss, Jack George	212-279-1658
Taylor & Ives	212-244-0750
Taylor, Stan Inc	212-685-4741
Teague, Walter Dorwin Assoc	212-557-0920
Tercovich, Douglas Assoc Inc	212-838-4800
Thompson Communications	212-685-4400
Three	212-988-6267
Tobias, William	212-741-1712
Todd, Ann	212-799-1016
Tower Graphics Arts Corp	212-421-0850
Tribich/Glasman Design	212-679-6016
Tscherny, George Design	212-734-3277
Tunstull Studio	718-875-9356

U V

Ultra Arts Inc	212-679-7493
Un, David	212-924-2090
Vecchio, Carmine	212-683-2679
Viewpoint Graphics	212-685-0560
Visible Studio Inc	212-683-8530
Visual Accents Corp	212-777-7766

W

Wajdowicz, Jurek	212-807-8144
Waldman, Veronica	212-260-3552
Waters, John Assoc Inc	212-807-0717
Waters, Pamela Studio Inc	212-620-8100
Webster, Robert Inc	212-677-2966

Graphic Designers
Continued

Please send us your additions and updates.

Weed, Eunice Assoc Inc	212-725-4933
Whelan Design Office	212-691-4404
The Whole Works	212-575-0765
Wijtvliet, Ine	212-319-4444
Wilke, Jerry	212-689-2424
Wilson, Rex Co	212-594-3646
Withers, Bruce Graphic Design	212-599-2388
Wizard Graphics Inc	212-686-8200
Wolf, Henry Production Inc	212-472-2500
Wolff, Rudi Inc	212-873-5800
Wood, Alan	212-889-5195
Word-Wise	212-246-0430
Works	212-696-1666

YZ Yoshimura-Fisher Graphic Design

Yoshimura-Fisher Graphic Design	212-431-4776
Young Goldman Young Inc	212-697-7820
Zahor & Bender	212-686-1121
Zazula, Hy Inc	212-581-2747
Zeitsoff, Elaine	212-580-1282
Zimmerman & Foyster	212-674-0259

Northeast

A

Action Incentive/2 Townlake Cir, Rochester, NY	716-427-2410
Adam Filippo & Moran/1206 Fifth Ave, Pittsburgh, PA	412-261-3720
Adler-Schwartz Graphics/6 N Park Dr #107 Park Ctr, Hunt Valley, MD	301-628-0600
Advertising Design Assoc Inc/1220 Ridgley St, Baltimore, MD	301-752-2181
Another Color Inc/1439 Rhode Island Ave NW, Washington, DC	202-328-1414
Aries Graphics/Massabesic, Manchester, NH	603-668-0811
The Artery/12 W Biddle St, Baltimore, MD	301-752-2979
Arts and Words/1025 Conn Ave NW #300, Washington, DC	202-463-4880
Artwork Unlimited Inc/1411 K St NW, Washington, DC	202-638-6996
Autograph/616 Third St, Annapolis, MD	301-268-3300
The Avit Corp/799 Abbott Blvd, Fort Lee, NJ	201-886-1100

B

Bachman Design Assoc/979 Summer St, Stamford, CT	203-325-9104
Bain, S Milo/3 Shaw Lane, Hartsdale, NY	914-946-0144
Baker, Arthur/PO Box 29, Germantown, NY	518-537-4438
Baldwin, Jim/47 Warren St, Salem, MA	617-745-6462
Bally Design Inc/219 Park Rd, Carnegie, PA	412-621-9009
Banks & Co/607 Boylston St, Boston, MA	617-262-0020
Barancik, Bob/1919 Panama Ave, Philadelphia, PA	215-893-9149
Barton-Gillet/10 S Gay St, Baltimore, MD	301-685-6800
Bedford Photo-Graphic Studio/PO Box 64 Rt 22, Bedford, NY	914-234-3123
Belser, Burkey/1818 N St NW #110, Washington, DC	202-775-0333
Bennardo, Churik Design Inc/1311 Old Freeport Rd, Pittsburgh, PA	412-963-0133
Berns & Kay Ltd/1611 Connecticut Ave, Washington, DC	202-387-7032
Blum, William Assoc/210 Lincoln St, Boston, MA	617-232-1166
Bodzioch, Leon/59 Smith St, Chelmsford, MA	617-250-0265
Bogus, Sidney A & Assoc/22 Corey St, Melrose, MA	617-662-6660
Bomzer Design Inc/66 Canal St, Boston, MA	617-227-5151
Bookmakers/305 N Main St, Westport, CT	203-226-4293
Booth, Margot/2807 N Glade St NW, Washington, DC	202-244-0412
Bowers, John/PO Box 101, Radnor, PA	215-688-5541
Bradbury, Robert & Assoc/26 Halsey Ln, Closter, NJ	201-768-6395
Brady, John Design Consultants/130 7th St, Century Bldg, Pittsburgh, PA	412-288-9300
Breckenridge Designs/2025 I St NW #300, Washington, DC	202-833-5700
Bressler, Peter Design Assoc/301 Cherry St, Philadelphia, PA	215-925-7100
Bridy, Dan/119 First Ave, Pittsburgh, PA	412-288-9362
BRIER, DAVID/51 PROSPECT TERRACE, E RUTHERFORD, NJ (P 238,239)	**201-896-8476**
Brown and Craig Inc/407 N Charles St, Baltimore, MD	301-837-2727
Buckett, Bill Assoc/137 Gibbs St, Rochester, NY	716-546-6580
Byrne, Ford/100 N 20th St, Philadelphia, PA	215-564-0500

C

Cable, Jerry Design/29 Station Rd, Madison, NJ	201-966-0124
Calingo, Diane/3711 Lawrence Ave, Kensington, MD	301-949-3557

Cameron Inc/9 Appleton St, Boston, MA	617-338-4408
Campbell Harrington & Brear/352 W Market St, York, PA	717-846-2947
Carlson, Tim/4 Davis Ct, Brookline, MA	617-566-7330
Carmel, Abraham/7 Peter Beet Dr, Peekskill, NY	914-737-1439
Case/11 Dupont Circle NW #400, Washington, DC	202-328-5900
Casey Mease Inc/917 N Washington St, Wilmington, DE	302-655-2100
Chaparos Productions Limited/1112 6th St NW, Washington, DC	202-289-4838
Charysyn & Charysyn/Route 42, Westkill, NY	518-989-6720
Chase, David O Design Inc/E Genesee St, Skaneateles, NY	315-685-5715
Chronicle Type & Design/1333 New Hampshire Ave NW, Washington, DC	202-828-3519
Clark, Dave/112 Main St #303, Annapolis, MD	301-269-1856
Cleary Design/118-A N Division St, Salisbury, MD	301-546-1040
Cliggett, Jack/703 Redwood Ave, Yeadon, PA	215-623-1606
Colangelo, Ted Assoc/340 Pemberwick Rd (The Mill), Greenwich, CT	203-531-3600
Colopy Dale Inc/850 Ridge Ave, Pittsburgh, PA	412-332-6706
Communications Graphics Group/3717 Columbia Pike #211, Arlington, VA	703-979-8500
Concept Packaging Inc/5 Horizon Rd, Ft Lee, NJ	201-224-5762
Consolidated Visual Center Inc/2529 Kenilworth Ave, Tuxedo, MD	301-772-7300
Cook & Shanosky Assoc/103 Carnegie Ctr #203, Princeton, NJ	609-452-1666
Corcetto, Tony/RD 1 Box 300, Reinholds, PA	215-678-0866
Creative Presentations Inc/1221 Massachusetts Ave NW, Washington, DC	202-737-7152
The Creative Dept/130 S 17th, Philadelphia, PA	215-988-0390
Crozier, Bob & Assoc/1201 Pennsylvania Ave NW, Washington, DC	202-638-7134
Curran & Connors Inc/333 Jericho Tpke, Jericho, NY	516-433-6600

D

D'Art Studio Inc/176 Federal #518, Boston, MA	617-482-4442
Dakota Design/Rte 363, Leighton Bldg, King of Prussia, PA	215-265-1255
Dale, Terry/2824 Hurst Terrace NW, Washington, DC	202-244-3866
Dawson Designers Associates/21 Dean St, Assonet, MA	617-644-2940
Dean, Jane/13 N Duke St, Lancaster, PA	717-295-4638
DeCesare, John/1091 Post Rd, Darien, CT	203-655-6057
DeMartin-Marona-Cranstoun-Downes/911 Washington St, Wilmington, DE	302-654-5277
Design Associates/1601 Kent St #1010, Arlington, VA	703-243-7717
Design Center Inc/210 Lincoln St #408, Boston, MA	617-542-1254
Design Communication Collaboration/1346 Connecticut Ave NW, Washington, DC	202-833-9087
Design for Medicine Inc/301 Cherry St, Philadelphia, PA	215-925-7100
Design Group of Boston/437 Boylston St, Boston, MA	617-437-1084
Design Technology Corp/5 Suburban Park Dr, Billerica, MA	617-272-8890
Design Trends/4 Broadway PO Box 119, Valhalla, NY	914-948-0902
Designworks Inc/5 Bridge St, Watertown, MA	617-926-6286
DiFiore Associates/625 Stanwix St #2507, Pittsburgh, PA	412-471-0608
Dimmick, Gary/47 Riverview Ave, Pittsburgh, PA	412-321-7225
Dohanos, Steven/271 Sturges Highway, Westport, CT	203-227-3541
Downing, Allan/50 Francis St, Needham, MA	617-449-4784
Duffy, Bill & Assoc/3286 M Street NW, Washington, DC	202-965-2216

E

Edigraph Inc/45 Cantitoe St, RFD 1, Katonah, NY	914-232-3725
Educational Media/Graphics Division/GU Med Ctr 3900 Reservoir Rd, Washington, DC	202-625-2211
Egress Concepts/20 Woods Bridge Rd, Katonah, NY	914-232-8433
Erickson, Peter/147 Main St, Maynard, MA	617-369-8060
Eucalyptus Tree Studio/2220 N Charles St, Baltimore, MD	301-243-0211
Evans Garber & Paige/2631 Genesee St, Utica, NY	315-733-2313

F

Fader Jones & Zarkades/797 Boylston St, Boston, MA	617-267-7779
Falcone & Assoc/13 Watchung Ave Box 637, Chatham, NJ	201-635-2900
Fannell Studio/8 Newbury St, Boston, MA	617-267-0895
Fink Graphics/11 W 25th St, Baltimore, MD	301-366-1540
Finnin, Teresa/655 Washington Blvd #602, Stamford, CT	203-348-4104
Forum Inc/1226 Post Rd, Fairfield, CT	203-259-5686
Fossella, Gregory Assoc/479 Commonwealth Ave, Boston, MA	617-267-4940

Graphic Designers

Continued

Please send us your additions and updates.

Fraser, Robert & Assoc Inc/1101 N Calvert St, Baltimore, MD	301-685-3700
Fresh Produce/1307 Warwick Dr, Lutherville, MD	301-821-1815
Froelich Advertising Service/8 Wanamaker Ave, Mahwah, NJ	201-529-1737

G
Gasser, Gene/300 Main St, Chatham, NJ	201-635-6020
Gateway Studios/225 Ross St, Pittsburgh, PA	412-471-7224
Gatter Inc/68 Purchase St, Rye, NY	914-967-5600
Genesis Design/360 Pleasant St, Ashland, MA	617-881-2471
GK+D Communications/2311 Calvert St NW #300, Washington, DC	202-328-0414
Glass, Al/3312 M St NW, Washington, DC	202-333-3993
Glickman, Frank Inc/180 Mosshill Rd, Boston, MA	617-524-2200
Goldner, Linda/709 Rittenhouse Savoy, Philadelphia, PA	215-735-8370
Good, Peter Graphic Design/Pequot Press Bldg, Chester, CT	203-526-9597
Gorelick, Alan & Assoc/999 Raritan Rd, Clark, NJ	201-382-4141
Graham Associates Inc/1899 L St NW, Washington, DC	202-833-9657
Grant Marketing Assoc./1100 E Hector St, Conshohocken, PA	215-834-0550
The Graphic Suite/235 Shady Ave, Pittsburgh, PA	412-661-6699
Graphic Workshop/466 Old Hook Rd, Emerson, NJ	201-967-8500
Graphicenter/1101 2nd St NE, Washington, DC	202-544-0333
Graphics By Gallo/1800-B Swann St NW, Washington, DC	202-234-7700
Graphics Plus Corp/198 Ferry St, St Malden, MA	617-321-7500
Graphicus Corp/2025 Maryland Ave, Baltimore, MD	301-727-5553
Graves Fowler & Assoc/14532 Carona Dr, Silver Spring, MD	301-236-9808
Grear, Malcolm Designers Inc/391 Eddy St, Providence, RI	401-331-5656
Green, Mel/31 Thorpe Rd, Needham Hts, MA	617-449-6777
Greenebaum Design/86 Walnut St, Natick, MA	617-655-8146
Greenfield, Peggy/2 Lewis Rd, Foxboro, MA	617-543-6644
Gregory & Clyburne/59 Grove St, New Canaan, CT	203-966-8343
Groff, Jay Michael/515 Silver Spring Ave, Silver Spring, MD	301-565-0431
GROUP FOUR DESIGN/PO BOX 717, AVON, CT (P 250,251)	**203-678-1570**
Gunn Associates/275 Newbury St, Boston, MA	617-267-0618

H
Hain, Robert Assoc/346 Park Ave, Scotch Plains, NJ	201-322-1717
Hammond Design Assoc/35 Amherst St, Milford, NH	603-673-5253
Harrington-Jackson/10 Newbury St, Boston, MA	617-536-6164
Harvey, Ed/PO Box 23755, Washington, DC	703-671-0880
Hegemann Associates/One S Franklin St, Nyack, NY	914-358-7348
Herbick & Held/1117 Wolfendale St, Pittsburgh, PA	412-321-7400
Herbst Lazar Rogers & Bell Inc/10 N Market St #406, Lancaster, PA	717-291-9042
Herman & Lees/930 Massachusetts Ave, Cambridge, MA	617-876-6463
Hill, Michael/828 Park Ave, Baltimore, MD	301-728-8767
Hillmuth, James/3613 Norton Pl, Washington, DC	202-244-0465
Holl, RJ/ Art Directions/McBride Rd, Wales, MA	413-267-5024
Holloway, Martin/56 Mt Horeb Rd, Plainfield, NJ	201-563-0169
Hough, Jack Inc/25 Seirhill Rd, Norwalk, CT	203-846-2666
Hrivnak, James/10822 Childs Ct, Silver Spring, MD	301-681-9090
Huerta, Gerard/45 Corbin Dr, Darien, CT	203-656-0505
Huyysen, Roger/45 Corbin Dr, Darien, CT	203-656-0200

IJ
Image Consultants/3 Overlook Dr, Amherst, NH	603-673-5512
Innovations & Development Inc/115 River Rd, Edgewater, NJ	201-941-5500
Irish, Gary Graphics/45 Newbury St, Boston, MA	617-247-4168
Itin, Marcel/Visual Concepts/100 Cutler Rd, Greenwich, CT	203-869-1928
Jaeger Design Studio/2025 I St NW, Washington, DC	202-785-8434
Jarrin Design Inc/PO Box 421, Pound Ridge, NY	914-764-4625
Jensen, R S/819 N Charles St, Baltimore, MD	301-727-3411
Jezierny, John Michael/20 Kenter Pl, Westville, CT	203-689-8170
Johnson & Simpson Graphic Design/49 Bleeker St, Newark, NJ	201-624-7788
Johnson Design Assoc/403 Massachusetts Ave, Acton, MA	617-263-5345
Jones, Tom & Jane Kearns/2803 18th ST NW, Washington, DC	202-232-1921

K
Kahana Associates/419 Benjamin #A Fox Pavilion, Jenkintown, PA	215-887-0422
Karp, Rudi/28 Dudley Ave, Landsowne, PA	215-284-5949
Katz-Wheeler Design/37 S 20th St, Philadelphia, PA	215-567-5668
Kaufman, Henry J & Assoc Inc/2233 Wisconsin Ave NW, Washington, DC	202-333-0700
KBH Graphics/1023 St Paul Street, Baltimore, MD	301-539-7916

Kell & Co/110 Fidler Ln #1400, Silver Spring, MD	202-585-4000
Ketchum International/4 Gateway Ctr, Pittsburgh, PA	412-456-3693
King-Casey Inc/199 Elm St, New Canaan, CT	203-966-3581
Klim, Matt & Assoc/PO Box Y, Avon Park N, Avon, CT	203-678-1222
Klotz, Don/296 Millstone Rd, Wilton, CT	203-762-9111
Knox, Harry & Assoc/1312 18th St NW, Washington, DC	202-833-2305
Kostanecki, Andrew Inc/47 Elm St, New Canaan, CT	203-966-1681
Kovanen, Erik/102 Twin Oak Lane, Wilton, CT	203-762-8961
Kramer/Miller/Lomden/Glossman/1528 Waverly, Philadelphia, PA	215-545-7077
Krohne, David/2727 29th St NW, Washington, DC	202-265-2371
Krone Graphic Design/426 S 3rd St, Lemoyne, PA	717-774-7431
Krueger Wright Design/106 Bromfield Rd, Somerville, MA	617-666-4880

L
LAM Design Inc/661 N Broadway, White Plains, NY	914-948-4777
Landersman, Myra/PO Box 346, Malaga, NJ	609-694-1011
Langdon, John/106 S Marion Ave, Wenonah, NJ	609-468-7868
Lapham/Miller Assoc/34 Essex St, Andora, MA	617-367-0110
Latham Brefka Associates/833 Boylston St, Boston, MA	617-536-8787
Lausch, David Graphics/2613 Maryland Ave, Baltimore, MD	301-235-7453
Lebowitz, Mo/2599 Phyllis Dr, N Bellemore, NY	516-826-3397
Leeds, Judith K Studio/14 Rosemont Ct, N Caldwell, NJ	201-226-3552
Lenney, Ann/2737 Devonshire Pl NW, Washington, DC	202-667-1786
Leotta Designers Inc/303 Harry St, Conshohocken, PA	215-828-8820
Lester Associates Inc/100 Snake Hill Rd Box D, West Nyack, NY	914-358-6100
Levinson Zaprauskis Assoc/15 W Highland Ave, Philadelphia, PA	215-248-5242
Lewis, Hal Design/104 S 20th St, Philadelphia, PA	215-563-4461
Lion Hill Studio/1233 W Mt Royal Ave, Baltimore, MD	301-837-6218
Livingston Studio/29 Robbins Ave, Elmsford, NY	914-592-4220
Lizak, Matt/Blackplain Rd RD #1, N Smithfield, RI	401-766-8885
Lose, Hal/533 W Hortter St, Philadelphia, PA	215-849-7635
Loukin, Serge Inc/PO Box 425, Solomons, MD	202-645-2788
Luebbers Inc/2300 Walnut St #732, Philadelphia, PA	215-567-2360
Luma/702 N Eutaw St, Baltimore, MD	301-523-5903
Lussier, Mark/21 First St, E Norwalk, CT	203-852-0363

M
MacIntosh, Rob Communication/93 Massachusetts, Boston, MA	617-267-4912
Maglio, Mark/PO Box 872, Plainville, CT	203-793-0771
Mahoney, Ron/204 Fifth Ave, Pittsburgh, PA	412-261-3824
Major Assoc/1101 N Calvert #1703, Baltimore, MD	301-752-6174
Mandala/520 S Third St, Philadelphia, PA	215-923-6020
Mandle, James/300 Forest Ave, Paramus, NJ	201-967-7900
Mansfield, Malcom/20 Aberdeen St, Boston, MA	617-437-1922
Marcus, Sarna/4720 Montgomery Ln #903, Bethesda, MD	301-951-7044
Mariuzza, Pete/146 Hardscrabble Rd, Briarcliff Manor, NY	914-769-3310
Martucci Studio/116 Newbury St, Boston, MA	617-266-6960
Mason, Kim/1301 Delaware Ave SW, Washington, DC	202-646-0118
MDB Communications Inc/932 Hungerford Dr #23, Rockville, MD	301-279-9093
Media Concepts/14 Newbury St, Boston, MA	617-437-1382
Melanson, Donya Assoc/437 Main St, Charlestown, MA	617-241-7300
Melone, Michael/RD 3 Box 123, Canonsburg, PA	412-746-5165
Micolucci, Nicholas Assoc/515 Schumaker Rd, King of Prussia, PA	215-265-3320
Miho, J Inc/46 Chalburn Rd, Redding, CT	203-938-3214
Mitchell & Company/1029 33rd St NW, Washington, DC	202-342-6025
Monti, Ron/106 W University, Baltimore, MD	301-366-8952
Morlock Graphics/7400 York Rd, Towson, MD	301-825-5080
Moss, John C/4805 Bayard Blvd, Chevy Chase, MD	301-320-3912
Mossman Art Studio/2514 N Charles St, Baltimore, MD	301-243-1963
Mueller & Wister/1211 Chestnut St #607, Philadelphia, PA	215-568-7260
Muller-Munk, Peter Assoc/2100 Smallman St, Pittsburgh, PA	412-261-5161
Murphy, Martha/8 August Ave, Baltimore, MD	301-747-4555
Myers, Gene Assoc/5575 Hampton, Pittsburgh, PA	412-661-6314

NO
Nason Design Assoc/329 Newbury, Boston, MA	617-266-7286
Navratil Art Studio/905 Century Bldg, Pittsburgh, PA	412-471-4322
Nimeck, Fran/RD #4, 358 Riva Ave #A, South Brunswick, NJ	201-821-8741
Nolan & Assoc/4100 Cathedral Ave NW, Washington, DC	202-363-6553

Graphic Designers
Continued

Please send us your additions and updates.

North Charles St Design/222 W Saratoga St, Baltimore, MD — 301-539-4040
Odyssey Design Group/918 F St NW #200, Washington, DC — 202-783-6240
Ollio Studio/Fulton Bldg, Pittsburgh, PA — 412-281-4483
Omnigraphics/19 Mt Auburn St, Cambridge, MA — 617-354-7444
On Target/1185 E Putnam Ave, Riverside, CT — 203-637-8300

P
Paganucci, Bob/17 Terry Ct, Montvale, NJ — 201-391-1752
Paine/ Bluett/ Paine Inc/4617 Edgefield Rd, Bethesda, MD — 301-493-8445
Papazian Design/224 Clarendon St, Boston, MA — 617-262-7848
Parks, Franz & Cox, Inc/2425 18th St NW, Washington, DC — 202-797-7568
Parry, Ivor A/4 Lorraine Dr, Eastchester, NY — 914-961-7338
Parshall, C A Inc/200 Henry St, Stamford, CT — 203-947-5971
Pasinski, Irene Assoc/4951 Centre Ave, Pittsburgh, PA — 412-683-0585
Patazian Design Inc/224 Clarendon St, Boston, MA — 617-262-7848
Peck, Gail M/1637 Harvard St NW, Washington, DC — 202-667-7448
Pentick, Joseph/RD 4 Box 231, Kingston, NY — 914-331-8197
Perspectives In Communications/1637 Harvard St NW, Washington, DC — 202-667-7448
Pesanelli, David Assoc/4301 Connecticut Ave NW, Washington, DC — 202-363-4760
Petty, Daphne/1460 Belmont St NW, Washington, DC — 202-667-8222
Phase One Graphics/315 Market St, Sudbury, PA — 717-286-1111
Phillips Design Assoc/25 Dry Dock Ave, Boston, MA — 617-423-7676
Picture That Inc/880 Briarwood Rd, Newtown Square, PA — 215-353-8833
Pinkston, Steve/24 N New St 2nd Fl, West Chester, PA — 215-692-2939
Planert, Paul Design Assoc/4650 Baum Blvd, Pittsburgh, PA — 412-621-1275
Plataz, George/516 Martin Bldg, Pittsburgh, PA — 412-322-3177
Porter, Al/Graphics Inc/5431 Connecticut Ave NW, Washington, DC — 202-244-0403
Porter, Eric/37 S 20th St, Philadelphia, PA — 215-563-1904
Porter, John/7056 Carroll Ave, Takoma Park, MD — 301-270-8990
Presentation Associates/1346 Connecticut Ave NW, Washington, DC — 202-333-0080
Production Studio/382 Channel Dr, Port Washington, NY — 516-944-6688
Profile Press Inc/40 Greenwood Ave, E Islip, NY — 516-277-6319
Prokell, Jim/307 4th Ave #200, Pittsburgh, PA — 412-232-3636
Publication Services Inc/990 Hope St, PO Box 4625, Stamford, CT — 203-348-7351

R
Ralcon Inc/431 W Market St, West Chester, PA — 215-692-2840
Rand, Paul Inc/87 Goodhill Rd, Weston, CT — 203-227-5375
Redtree Associates/1740 N St NW, Washington, DC — 202-628-2900
Renaissance Communications/7835 Eastern Ave, Silver Spring, MD — 301-587-1505
Research Planning Assoc/1831 Chestnut St, Philadelphia, PA — 215-561-9700
Richardson/Smith/139 Lewis Wharf, Boston, MA — 617-367-1491
Richman, Mel/15 N Presidential Blvd, Bala Cynwyd, PA — 215-667-8900
Rieb, Robert/10 Reichert Circle, Westport, CT — 203-227-0061
Ringel, Leonard Design/18 Wheeler Rd, Kendall Park, NJ — 201-297-9084
Ritter, Richard Design Inc/31 Waterloo Ave, Berwyn, PA — 215-296-0400
Ritzau van Dijk Design/7 Hart Ave, Hopewell, NJ — 609-466-2797
RKM Inc/5307 29th St NW, Washington, DC — 202-364-0148
Rogalski Assoc/186 Lincoln St, Boston, MA — 617-451-2111
Romax Studio/32 Club Circle, Stamford, CT — 203-324-4260
Rosborg Inc/15 Commerce Rd, Newton, CT — 203-426-3171
Roth, J H Inc/13 Inwood Ln E, Peekskill, NY — 914-737-6784
Roth, Judee/103 Cornelia St, Boonton, NJ — 201-316-5411
RSV/437 Boylston St, Boston, MA — 617-262-9450
Rubin, Marc Design Assoc/PO Box 440, Breesport, NY — 607-739-0871
RZA Inc/122 Mill Pond Rd, Park Ridge, NJ — 201-391-8500

S
Sanchez/138 S 20th St, Philadelphia, PA — 215-564-2223
Schneider Design/2633 N Charles St, Baltimore, MD — 301-467-2611
Schoenfeld, Cal/6 Colony Ct #B, Parsippany, NJ — 201-263-1635
Schrecongost, Paul/284 Liberty St, Salem, WV — 304-782-3499
Selame Design Associates/2330 Washington St, Newton Lower Falls, MA — 617-969-6690
Shapiro, Deborah/150 Bentley Ave, Jersey City, NJ — 201-432-5198
Silvia, Ken/15 Story St, Cambridge, MA — 617-451-1995
Simpson Booth Designers/14 Arrow St, Cambridge, MA — 617-661-2630
Smarilli Graphics Inc/602 N Front St, Warmleysburg, PA — 717-737-8141
Smith, Agnew Moyer/850 Ridge Ave, Pittsburgh, PA — 412-322-6333

Smith, Doug/17 Althea Lane, Larchmont, NY — 914-834-3997
Smith, Gail Hunter/PO Box 217, Barnegat Light, NJ — 609-494-9136
Smith, Tyler Art Direction/127 Dorrance St, Providence, RI — 401-751-1220
Smizer Design/59 Wareham St, Boston, MA — 617-423-3350
Snowden Associates Inc/5217 Wisconsin Ave NW, Washington, DC — 202-362-8944
Sparkman & Bartholomew/1144 18th St NW, Washington, DC — 202-785-2414
Spectrum Boston/79-A Chestnut St, Boston, MA — 617-367-1008
Stansbury Ronsaville Wood Inc/17 Pinewood St, Annapolis, MD — 301-261-8662
Star Design Inc/PO Box 30, Moorestown, NJ — 609-235-8150
Steel Art Co Inc/75 Brainerd Rd, Allston, MA — 617-566-4079
Stettler, Wayne Design/2311 Fairmount Ave, Philadelphia, PA — 215-235-1230
Stockman & Andrews Inc/684 Warren Ave, E Providence, RI — 401-438-0694
Stolt, Jill Design/1239 University Ave, Rochester, NY — 716-461-2594
Stuart, Neil/RD 1 Box 64, Mahopac, NY — 914-618-1662
The Studio Group/1713 Lanier Pl NW, Washington, DC — 202-332-3003
Studio Six Design/6 Lynn Dr, Springfield, NJ — 201-379-5820
Studio Three/1617 J F Kennedy Blvd, Philadelphia, PA — 215-665-0141

T
Takajian, Asdur/17 Merlin Ave, N Tarrytown, NY — 914-631-5553
Taylor, Pat/3540 'S' St NW, Washington, DC — 202-338-0962
Telesis/107 E 25th, Baltimore, MD — 301-235-2000
Tetrad Inc/309 Third St, Annapolis, MD — 301-268-8680
Theoharides Inc/303 South Broadway, Tarrytown, NY — 914-631-5363
Thompson, Bradbury/Jones Park, Riverside, CT — 203-637-3614
Thompson, George L/603 Main St, Reading, MA — 617-944-6256
Toelke, Cathleen/16 Tremont St, Boston, MA — 617-242-7414
Torode, Barbara/2311 Lombard St, Philadelphia, PA — 215-732-6792
Total Collateral Grp/992 Old Eagles School Rd, Wayne, PA — 215-687-8016
Town Studios Inc/212 9th St Victory Bldg, Pittsburgh, PA — 412-471-5353
Troller, Fred Assoc Inc/12 Harbor Ln, Rye, NY — 914-698-1405

V
Van Der Sluys Graphics Inc/3303 18th St NW, Washington, DC — 202-265-3443
Vance Wright Adams & Assoc/930 N Lincoln Ave, Pittsburgh, PA — 412-322-1800
VanDine, Horton, McNamara, Manges Inc/100 Ross St, Pittsburgh, PA — 412-261-4280
Vann, Bob/5306 Knox St, Philadelphia, PA — 215-843-4841
Vinick, Bernard Assoc Inc/211 Wethersfield Ave, Hartford, CT — 203-525-4293
Viscom Inc/PO Box 10498, Baltimore, MD — 301-764-0005
Visual Research & Design Corp/360 Commonwealth Ave, Boston, MA — 617-536-2111
The Visualizers/1100 E Carson St, Pittsburgh, PA — 412-488-0944

WYZ
Warkulwiz Design/1704 Locust St, Philadelphia, PA — 215-546-0880
Wasserman's, Myron Graphic Design Group/113 Arch St, Philadelphia, PA — 215-922-4545
Weadock, Rutka/1627 E Baltimore St, Baltimore, MD — 301-563-2100
Webb & Co/839 Beacon St, Boston, MA — 617-262-6980
Weymouth Design/234 Congress St, Boston, MA — 617-542-2647
White, E James Co/5750 B General Washington Dr, Alexandria, VA — 703-750-3680
Wickham & Assoc Inc/1133 15 St, NW, Washington, DC — 202-296-4860
Willard, Janet Design Assoc/4284 Route 8, Allison Park, PA — 412-486-8100
Williams Associates/200 Broadway #206, Lynnfield, MA — 617-599-1818
Wilsonwork Graphic Design/1811 18th St NW, Washington, DC — 202-332-9016
Wood, William/68 Windsor Pl, Glen Ridge, NJ — 201-743-5543
Wright, Kent M Assoc Inc/22 Union Ave, Sudbury, MA — 617-443-9909
Yeo, Robert/746 Park Ave, Hoboken, NJ — 201-659-3277
Yurdin, Carl Industrial Design Inc/2 Harborview Rd, Port Washington, NY — 516-944-7811
Zeb Graphics/1312 18th St NW, Washington, DC — 202-293-1687
Zmiejko & Assoc Design Agcy/PO Box 126, Freeland, PA — 717-636-2304

Southeast

A
Ace Art/171 Walnut St, New Orleans, LA — 504-861-2222
Alphabet Group/1441 Peachtree NE, Atlanta, GA — 404-892-6500
Alphacom Inc/14955 NE Sixth Ave, N Miami, FL — 305-949-5588
Art Services/1135 Spring St, Atlanta, GA — 404-892-2105

Graphic Designers

Continued

Please send us your additions and updates

Arts & Graphics/4010 Justine Dr, Annandale, VA — 703-941-2560
Arunski, Joe & Assoc/8600 SW 86th Ave, Miami, FL — 305-271-8300
The Associates Inc/5319 Lee Hwy, Arlington, VA — 703-534-3940
Aurelio & Friends Inc/11110 SW 128th Ave, Miami, FL — 305-385-0723

B
Baskin & Assoc/1021 Prince St, Alexandria, VA — 703-836-3316
Bender, Diane/2729 S Cleveland St, Arlington, VA — 703-521-1006
Beveridge and Associates, Inc/2020 N 14th St #444, Arlington, VA — 202-243-2888
Blair Incorporated/5819 Seminary Rd, Bailey's Crossroads, VA — 703-820-9011
Bodenhamer, William S Inc/7380 SW 121st St, Miami, FL — 305-253-9284
Bonner Advertising Art/1315 Washington Ave, New Orleans, LA — 504-895-7938
Bono Mitchell Graphics/2118 N Oakland St, Arlington, VA — 703-276-0612
Bowles, Aaron/1686 Sierra Woods Ct, Reston, VA — 703-471-4019
Brimm, Edward & Assoc/140 S Ocean Blvd, Palm Beach, FL — 305-655-1059
Brothers Bogusky/11950 W Dixie Hwy, Miami, FL — 305-891-3642
Bugdal Group/7227 NW 7th St, Miami, FL — 305-264-1860
Burch, Dan Associates/2338 Frankfort, Louisville, KY — 502-895-4881

C
Carlson Design/1218 NW 6th St, Gainesville, FL — 904-373-3153
Chartmasters Inc/3525 Piedmont,7 Pdmt Ctr, Atlanta, GA — 404-262-7610
Clavena, Barbara/6000 Stone Lake, Birmingham, AL — 205-991-8909
Cooper-Copeland Inc/1151 W Peachtree St NW, Atlanta, GA — 404-892-3472
Corporate Design/Plaza Level-Colony Sq, Atlanta, GA — 404-876-6062
Creative Design Assoc/9330 Silver Thorn Rd, Lake Park, FL — 305-627-2467
Creative Services Inc/2317 Esplanade St, New Orleans, LA — 504-943-0842
Creative Services Unlimited/3080 N Tamiami Tr #3, Naples, FL — 813-262-0201
Creative Technologies Inc/7630 Little River Tnpk, Annandale, VA — 703-256-7444
Critt Graham & Assoc/1190 W Orvid Hills Dr #T45, Atlanta, GA — 404-320-1737

D E F
Design Consultants Inc/301 Park Ave, Falls Church, VA — 703-241-2323
Design Inc/9304 St Marks Pl, Fairfax, VA — 703-273-5053
Design Workshop Inc/9791 NW 91st Ct, Miami, FL — 305-884-6300
Designcomp/202 Dominion Rd NE, Vienna, VA — 703-938-1822
Dodane, Eric/8525 Richland Colony Rd, Knoxville, TN — 615-693-6857
Emig, Paul E/3900 N 5th St, Arlington, VA — 703-522-5926
First Impressions/4411 W Tampa Bay Blvd, Tampa, FL — 813-875-0555
Foster, Kim A/1801 SW 11th St, Miami, FL — 305-642-1801
From Us Advertising & Design/273 Connecticut Ave NE, Atlanta, GA — 404-373-0373

G
Gerbino Advertising Inc/2000 W Commercial Blvd, Ft Lauderdale, FL — 305-776-5050
Gestalt Associates, Inc/1509 King St, Alexandria, VA — 703-683-1126
Get Graphic Inc/160 Maple Ave E #201, Vienna, VA — 202-938-1822
Graphic Arts Inc/1433 Powhatan St, Alexandria, VA — 703-683-4303
Graphic Consultants Inc/5133 Lee Hwy, Arlington, VA — 703-536-8377
Graphics Group/6111 PchtreeDunwdy Rd#G101, Atlanta, GA — 404-391-9929
Graphicstudio/12305 NE 12th Ct, N Miami, FL — 305-893-1015
Great Incorporated/601 Madison St, Alexandria, VA — 703-836-6020
Gregg, Bill Advertising Design/2465 SW 18th Ave A-3309, Miami, FL — 305-854-7657
Group 2 Atlanta/3500 Piedmont Rd, Atlanta, GA — 404-262-3239

H I
Haikalis, Stephanie/3310 Coryell Ln, Alexandria, VA — 703-998-8695
Hall Graphics/2600 Douglas Rd #608, Coral Gables, FL — 305-443-8346
Hall, Stephen Design Office/535 Louisville Galleria, Louisville, KY — 502-458-2200
Hannau, Michael Ent. Inc/950 SE 8th St, Hialeah, FL — 305-887-1536
Hauser, Sydney/9 Fillmore Dr, Sarasota, FL — 813-388-3021
Helms, John Graphic Design/4191 Cottonwood, Memphis, TN — 901-363-6589
Identitia Incorporated/1000 N Ashley Dr #515, Tampa, Fl — 813-221-3326

J K L
Jensen, Rupert & Assoc Inc/1800 Peachtree Rd #525, Atlanta, GA — 404-352-1010
Johnson Design Group Inc/3426 N Washington Blvd #102, Arlington, VA — 703-525-0808
Johnson, Charlotte/1614 N Cleveland St, Arlington, VA — 202-544-7936
Jordan Barrett & Assoc/6701 Sunset Dr, Miami, FL — 305-667-7051
Kelly & Co Graphic Design Inc/4639 Lown St N, St

Petersburg, FL — 813-526-1009
Ketchum, Barbara/3948 Browning Pl #200, Raleigh, NC — 919-782-4599
Kjeldsen, Howard Assoc Inc/PO Box 420508, Atlanta, GA — 404-266-1897
Klickovich Graphics/1638 Eastern Parkway, Louisville, KY — 502-459-0295
Lowell, Shelley Design/1449 Bates Ct NE, Atlanta, GA — 404-636-9149

M
Marks, David/750 Clemont Dr, Atlanta, GA — 404-872-1824
Maxine, J & Martin Advertising/1497 Chain Bridge Rd #204, McLean, VA — 703-356-5222
McGurren Weber Ink/705 King St 3rd Fl, Alexandria, VA — 703-548-0003
MediaFour Inc/7638 Trail Run Rd, Falls Church, VA — 703-573-6117
Michael, Richard S/4722 Old Kingston Pike, Knoxville, TN — 615-584-3319
Miller, Hugh K/2473 John Young Pkwy, Orlando, FL — 305-293-8220
Moore, William "Casey"/4242 Inverness Rd, Duluth, GA — 404-449-9553
Morgan-Burchette Assoc/1020 N Fairfax St, Alexandria, VA — 703-549-2393
Morris, Robert Assoc Inc/6015 B NW 31 Ave, Ft Lauderdale, FL — 305-973-4380
Muhlhausen, John Design Inc/1146 Green St, Roswell, GA — 404-642-1146

P Q
Parallel Group Inc/3091 Maple Dr, Atlanta, GA — 404-261-0988
Pertuit, Jim & Assoc Inc/302 Magazine St #400, New Orleans, LA — 504-568-0808
PL&P Advertising Studio/1500 NW 62nd St #202, Ft Lauderdale, FL — 305-776-6505
Platt, Don Advertising Art/1399 SE 9th Ave, Hialeah, FL — 305-888-3296
Point 6/770 40th Court NE, Ft Lauderdale, FL — 305-563-6939
Polizos, Arthur Assoc/220 W Freemason St, Norfolk, VA — 804-622-7033
Positively Main St Graphics/290 Coconut Ave, Sarasota, FL — 813-366-4959
PRB Design Studio/1900 Howell Brnch Rd #3, Winter Park, FL — 305-671-7992
Pre-Press Studio Design/1105N Royal St, Alexandria, VA — 703-548-9194
Prep Inc/2615-B Shirlington Rd, Arlington, VA — 703-979-6575
Price Weber Market Comm Inc/2101 Production Dr, Louisville, KY — 502-499-9220
Promotion Graphics Inc/12787 W Dixie Hwy, N Miami, FL — 305-891-3941
Quantum Communications/1730 N Lynn St #400, Arlington, VA — 703-841-1400

R S T
Rasor & Rasor/1145-D Executive Cir, Cary, NC — 919-467-3353
Rebeiz, Kathryn Dereki/526 Druid Hill Rd, Vienna, VA — 703-938-9779
Reinsch, Michael/32 Palmetto Bay Rd, Hilton Head Island, SC — 803-842-3298
Revelations Studios/3100 Clay Ave #287, Orlando, Fl — 305-896-4240
Richardson, Hank/2675 Paces Ferry Rd #225, Atlanta, GA — 404-433-0973
Rodriguez, Emilio Jr/8270 SW 116 Terrace, Miami, FL — 305-235-4700
Sager Assoc Inc/739 S Orange Ave, Sarasota, FL — 813-366-4192
Salmon, Paul/5826 Jackson's Oak Ct, Burke, VA — 703-250-4943
Santa & Assoc/3960 N Andrews Ave, Ft Lauderdale, FL — 305-561-0551
Schulwolf, Frank/524 Hardee Rd, Coral Gables, FL — 305-665-2129
Showcraft Designworks/603 Pinellas, Clearwater, FL — 813-586-0061
Sirrine, J E/PO Box 5456, Greenville, SC — 803-298-6000
Tash, Ken/6320 Castle Pl, Falls Church, VA — 703-237-1712
Thayer Dana Industrial Design/Route 1, Monroe, VA — 804-929-6359
Thomas, Steve Design/141 Brevard Ct, Charlotte, NC — 704-332-4624
Turpin Design Assoc/1762 Century Blvd #B, Atlanta, GA — 404-320-6963

V W
Unique Communications/1034 Saber Ln, Herndon, VA — 703-471-1406
Varisco, Tom Graphic Design Inc/1925 Esplanade, New Orleans, LA — 504-949-2888
Visualgraphics Design/1211 NW Shore Blvd, Tampa, FL — 813-877-3804
Walton & Hoke/7247 Lee Hwy, Falls Church, VA — 703-538-5727
Whitford, Kim/242 Mead Rd, Decatur, GA — 404-371-0860
Whitver, Harry K Graphic Design/208 Reidhurst Ave, Nashville, TN — 615-320-1795
Winner, Stewart Inc/550 W Kentucky St, Louisville, KY — 502-583-5502
Wood, Tom/3925 Peachtree Rd NE, Atlanta, GA — 404-262-7424

Midwest

A
Aarons, Allan Design/666 Dundee Rd #1701, Northbrook, IL — 312-291-9800
Ades, Leonards Graphic Design/666 Dundee Rd #1103, Northbrook, IL — 312-564-8863

Album Graphics/1950 N Ruby St, Melrose Park, IL	312-344-9100
Allied Design Group/1701 W Chase, Chicago, IL	312-743-3330
Ampersand Assoc/2454 W 38th St, Chicago, IL	312-523-2282
Anderson Studios/209 W Jackson Blvd, Chicago, IL	312-922-3039
Anderson, I K Studios/215 W Huron, Chicago, IL	312-664-4536
Art Forms Inc/5150 Prospect Ave, Cleveland, OH	216-361-3855
Arvind Khatkate Design/200 E Ontario St, Chicago, IL	312-337-1478

B

Babcock & Schmid Assoc/3689 Ira Rd, Bath, OH	216-666-8826
Bagby Design/225 N Michigan, Chicago, IL	312-861-1288
Bal Graphics Inc/314 W Superior, Chicago, IL	312-337-0325
Banka Mango Design Inc/274 Merchandise Mart, Chicago, IL	312-467-0059
Barnes, Jeff/666 N Lake Shore Dr #1408, Chicago, IL	312-951-0996
Bartels & Cartsens/3284 Ivanhoe, St Louis, MO	314-781-4350
Bay Graphics/341 W Superior, Chicago, IL	312-337-0325
Beda Ross Design/310 W Chicago Ave, Chicago, IL	312-944-2332
Benjamin, Burton E Assoc/3391 Summit, Highland Park, IL	312-432-8089
Berg, Don/207 E Michigan, Milwaukee, WI	414-276-7828
Bieger, Walter Assoc/1689 W County Rd F, Arden Hills, MN	612-636-8500
Blake, Hayward & Co/834 Custer Ave, Evanston, IL	312-864-9800
Blau-Bishop & Assoc/401 N Michigan Ave, Chicago, IL	312-321-1420
Boelter Industries Inc/5198 W 76th St, Minneapolis, MN	612-831-5338
Boller-Coates-Spadero/742 N Wells, Chicago, IL	312-787-2798
Bowlby, Joseph A/53 W Jackson #711, Chicago, IL	312-922-0890
Bradford-Cout Graphic Design/9933 Lawler, Skokie, IL	312-539-5557
Brooks Stevens Assoc Inc/1415 W Donges Bay Rd, Mequon, WI	414-241-3800
Busch, Lonnie/11 Meadow Dr, Fenton, MO	314-343-1330

C

Campbell Art Studio/2145 Luray Ave, Cincinnati, OH	513-221-3600
Campbell Creative Group Inc/8705 N Port Washington, Milwaukee, WI	414-351-4150
Carter, Don W/ Industrial Design/8809 E 59th St, Kansas City, MO	816-356-1874
Centaur Studios Inc/10 S Broadway, St Louis, MO	314-421-6485
Chartmasters Inc/150 E Huron St, Chicago, IL	312-787-9040
Chestnut House/200 E Ohio, Chicago, IL	312-822-9090
Claudia Janah Designs Inc/222 N Dearborn, Chicago, IL	312-726-4560
Clifford, Keesler/6642 West H Ave, Kalamazoo, MI	616-375-0688
CMO Graphics/160 E Illinois, Chicago, IL	312-527-0900
Combined Services Inc/1414 Laurel Ave, Minneapolis, MN	612-339-7770
Container Corp of America/1 First National Plaza, Chicago, IL	312-580-5500
Contours Consulting Design Group/864 Stearns Rd, Bartlett, IL	312-837-4100
Coons/Beirise Design Assoc/2344 Ashland Ave, Cincinnati, OH	513-751-7459
Crosby, Bart/676 St Clair St, Chicago, IL	312-951-2800

D

Day, David Design & Assoc/700 Walnut St, Cincinnati, OH	513-621-4060
DeBrey Design/6014 Blue Circle #D, Minneapolis, MN	612-935-2292
DeGoede & Others/435 N Michigan Ave, Chicago, IL	312-951-6066
Dektas Eger Inc/1077 Celestial St, Cincinnati, OH	513-621-7070
Design Alliance Inc/114 E 8th St, Cincinnati, OH	513-621-9373
Design Consultants/505 N Lakeshore Dr #4907, Chicago, IL	312-642-4670
Design Factory/7543 Floyd, Overland Park, KS	913-383-3085
The Design Group/2976 Triverton Pike, Madison, WI	608-274-5393
Design Group Three/1114 W Armitage Ave, Chicago, IL	312-337-1775
Design Innovations Inc/75 Berkeley St, Toronto M5A 2W5, ON	416-362-8470
Design Mark Inc/5455 W 86th St, Indianapolis, IN	317-872-3000
Design Marks Corp/1462 W Irving Park, Chicago, IL	312-327-3669
Design North Inc/8007 Douglas Ave, Racine, WI	414-639-2080
Design One/437 Marshman St, Highland Park, IL	312-433-4140
The Design Partnership/124 N 1st St, Minneapolis, MN	612-338-8889
Design Planning Group/223 W Erie, Chicago, IL	312-943-8400
Design Train/434 Hidden Valley Ln, Cincinnati, OH	513-761-7099
Design Two Ltd/600 N McClurg Ct #330, Chicago, IL	312-642-9888
Dezign House III/1701 E 12th #8FW, Cleveland, OH	216-621-7777
Di Cristo & Slagle Design/741 N Milwaukee, Milwaukee, WI	414-273-0980
Dickens Design Group/13 W Grand, Chicago, IL	312-222-1850
Dimensional Designs Inc/1101 Southeastern Ave, Indianapolis, IN	317-637-1353

Distinction Design/8337 Capton Ln, Darien, IL	
Doty, David Design/661 W Roscoe, Chicago, IL	312-348-1200
Douglas Design/2165 Lakeside Ave, Cleveland, OH	216-621-2558
Dresser, John Design/180 Crescent Knoll E, Libertyville, IL	312-362-4222
Dynamic Graphics Inc/6000 N Forrest Park Dr, Peoria, IL	309-688-9800

E

Eaton and Associates/2116 2nd Ave S, Minneapolis, MN	612-871-1028
Egger/Assoc Inc/812 Busse Hwy, Park Ridge, IL	312-296-9100
Ellies, Dave Indstrl Design/2015 W 5th Ave, Columbus, OH	614-488-7995
Elyria Graphics/147 Winckles St, Elyria, OH	216-365-9384
Emphasis 7 Communications/43 E Ohio #1000, Chicago, IL	312-951-8887
Engelhardt Design/1738 Irving Ave S, Minneapolis, MN	612-377-3389
Environmental Graphics Inc/1101 Southeastern Ave, Indianapolis, IN	317-634-1458
Epstein & Assoc/11427 Bellflower, Cleveland, OH	216-421-1600
Eurographics/727 N Hudson, Chicago, IL	312-951-5110

F

Falk, Robert Design Group/4425 W Pine, St Louis, MO	314-531-1410
Feldkamp-Malloy/185 N Wabash, Chicago, IL	312-263-0633
Ficho & Corley Inc/875 N Michigan Ave, Chicago, IL	312-787-1011
Fleishman-Hillard, Inc/1 Memorial Dr, St Louis, MO	314-982-1700
Fleming Design Office/7101 York Ave S, Minneapolis, MN	612-830-0099
Flexo Design/57 W Grand, Chicago, IL	312-321-1368
Ford & Earl Assoc Inc/28820 Mound Rd, Warren, MI	313-536-1999
Forsythe-French Inc/4115 Broadway, Kansas City, MO	816-561-6678
Frederiksen Design/609 S Riverside Dr, Villa Park, IL	312-343-5882
Frink, Chin, Casey Inc/505 E Grant, Minneapolis, MN	612-333-6539

G

Garmon, Van/1601 22nd St #201, W Des Moines, IA	515-225-0001
Gellman, Stan Graphic Design Studio/4509 Laclede, St Louis, MO	314-361-7676
Gerhardt and Clements/162 W Hubbard St, Chicago, IL	312-337-3443
Glenbard Graphics Inc/333 Kimberly Dr, Carol Stream, IL	312-653-4550
Goldsholl Assoc/420 Frontage Rd, Northfield, IL	312-446-8300
Goldsmith Yamasaki Specht Inc/840 N Michigan Ave, Chicago, IL	312-266-8404
Golon, Mary/1112 Hull Terr, Evanston, IL	312-328-3935
Goodwin, Arnold/730 N Franklin, Chicago, IL	312-787-0466
Goose Graphics/716 First St N, Minneapolis, MN	612-333-3502
Gournoe, M Inc/60 E Elm, Chicago, IL	312-787-5157
Graphic Corp/727 E 2nd St PO Box 4806, Des Moines, IA	515-247-8500
Graphic House Inc/672 Woodbridge, Detroit, MI	313-259-7790
Graphic Productions/162 N Clinton, Chicago, IL	312-236-2833
Graphic Specialties Inc/2426 East 26th St, Minneapolis, MN	612-722-6601
Graphica Corp/3184 Alpine, Troy, MI	313-649-5050
Graphics Group/8 S Michigan Ave, Chicago, IL	312-782-7421
Graphics-Cor Associates/549 W Randolph St, Chicago, IL	312-332-3379
Greenberg, Jon Assoc Inc/2338 Coolidge, Berkley, MI	313-548-8080
Greenlee-Hess Ind Design/750 Beta Dr, Mayfield Village, OH	216-461-2112
Greiner, John & Assoc/8 W Hubbard, Chicago, IL	312-644-2973
Grusin, Gerald Design/232 E Ohio St, Chicago, IL	312-944-4945

H

Handelan-Pedersen/333 N Michigan #1005, Chicago, IL	312-782-6833
Hans Design/663 Greenwood Rd, Northbrook, IL	312-272-7980
Harley, Don E Associates/1740 Livingston Ave, West St Paul, MN	612-455-1631
Harris, Judy/550 Willow Creek Ct, Clarendon Hill, IL	312-789-3821
Herbst Lazar Rogers & Bell Inc/345 N Canal, Chicago, IL	312-454-1116
Higgins Hegner Genovese Inc/510 N Dearborn St, Chicago, IL	312-644-1882
Hirsch, David Design Group Inc/205 W Wacker Dr, Chicago, IL	312-329-1500
Hirsh Co/8051 N Central Park Ave, Skokie, IL	312-267-6777
Hoekstra, Grant Graphics/333 N Michigan Ave, Chicago, IL	312-641-6940
Hoffar, Barron & Co/53 W Jackson #711, Chicago, IL	312-922-0890
Hoffman York & Compton/2300 N Mayfair Rd, Milwaukee, WI	414-259-2000
Horvath, Steve Design/301 N Water St, Milwaukee, WI	414-271-3992

IJ

Identity Center/955 N Plumgrove Rd, Schaumburg, IL	312-843-2378
IGS Design Div of Smith Hinchman & Grylls/455 W Fort St, Detroit. MI	313-964-3000
Indiana Design Consortium/102 N 3rd St 300 Rvr Cty Bldg, Lafayette, IN	317-423-5469
Industrial Technological Assoc/30675 Solon Rd, Cleveland,	

Graphic Designers

Continued

Please send us your additions and updates

OH	216-349-2900
Ing, Victor Design/5810 Lincoln, Morton Grove, IL	312-965-3459
Intelplex/12215 Dorsett Rd, Maryland Hts, MO	314-739-9996
J M H Corp/1200 Waterway Blvd, Indianapolis, IN	317-639-2535
James, Frank Direct Marketing/120 S Central #500 Chrmal Plz, Clayton, MO	314-726-4600
Jansen, Ute/410 S Michigan Ave #919, Chicago, IL	312-922-5048
Johnson, Stan Design Inc/21185 W Gumina Rd, Brookfield, WI	414-783-6510
Johnson, Stewart Design Studio/218 W Walnut, Milwaukee, WI	414-265-3377
Jones, Richmond Designer/1921 N Hudson St, Chicago, IL	312-935-6500
Joss Design Group/232 E Ohio, Chicago, IL	312-828-0055

K

Kaulfuss Design/200 E Ontario St, Chicago, IL	312-943-2161
KDA Industrial Design Consultants Inc/1785-B Cortland Ct, Addison, IL	312-495-9466
Kearns, Marilyn/442 North Wells, Chicago, IL	312-645-1888
Keller Lane & Waln/8 S Michigan #814, Chicago, IL	312-782-7421
Kerr, Joe/405 N Wabash #2013, Chicago, IL	312-661-0097
Kornick & Lindsay/161 E Erie #107, Chicago, IL	312-280-8664
Kovach, Ronald Design/719 S Dearborn, Chicago, IL	312-461-9888

L

Laney, Ron/15 Fern St/Box 423, St Jacob, IL	618-644-5883
Lange, Jim Design/213 W Institute, Chicago, IL	312-943-2589
Larsen Design/7101 York Ave S, Minneapolis, MN	612-835-2271
Larson Design/7101 York Ave South, Minneapolis, MN	612-835-2271
Lehrfeld, Gerald/43 E Ohio, Chicago, IL	312-944-0651
Lenard, Catherine/509 W Wrightwood Ave, Chicago, IL	312-248-6937
Lerdon, Wes Assoc/3070 Riverside Dr, Columbus, OH	614-486-8188
Lesniewicz/Navarre/222 N Erie St, Toledo, OH	419-243-7131
Lipson Associates Inc/2349 Victory Pkwy, Cincinnati, OH	513-961-6225
Lipson Associates Inc/666 Dundee Rd #103, Northbrook, IL	312-291-0500
Liska & Assoc/213 W Institute Pl #605, Chicago, IL	312-943-5910
Loew, Dick & Assoc/1308 N Astor St, Chicago, IL	312-787-9032
Lubell, Robert/2946 E Lincolnshire, Toledo, OH	419-531-2267
LVK Associates Inc/4235 Cinell, St Louis, MO	314-534-2104

M

Maddox, Eva Assoc Inc/440 North Wells, Chicago, IL	312-670-0092
Madsan/Kuester/1 Main @ River Pl #500, Minneapolis, MN	612-378-1895
Manning Studios Inc/613 Main St, Cincinnati, OH	513-621-6959
Market Design/1010 Euclid Ave, Cleveland, OH	216-771-0300
Marsh, Richard Assoc Inc/203 N Wabash #1400, Chicago, IL	312-236-1331
McCoy, Steven/5414 1/2 NW Radio Hwy, Omaha, NE	402-554-1416
McDermott, Bill Graphic Design/1410 Hanley Industrial Ct, St Louis, MO	314-962-6286
McGuire, Robert L Design/7943 Campbell, Kansas City, MO	816-523-9164
McMurray Design Inc/405 N Wabash Ave, Chicago, IL	312-527-1555
Media Corporation/3070 Riverside Dr, Columbus, OH	614-488-7767
Media Loft/7200 France Ave, Minneapolis, MN	612-831-0226
Minnick, James Design/535 N Michigan Ave, Chicago, IL	312-527-1864
Moonink Inc/233 N Michigan Ave, Chicago, IL	312-565-0040
Murrie White Drummond Leinhart/58 W Huron, Chicago, IL	312-943-5995

NO

Naughton, Carol & Assoc/345 N Canal #901, Chicago, IL	312-454-1888
Nemetz, Jeff/900 N Franklin #600, Chicago, IL	312-664-8112
Nobart Inc/1133 S Wabash Ave, Chicago, IL	312-427-9800
Nottingham-Spirk Design Inc/11310 Juniper Rd, Cleveland, OH	216-231-7830
Oak Brook Graphics, Inc/287 W Butterfield Rd, Elmhurst, IL	312-832-3200
Obata Design/1610 Menard, St Louis, MO	314-241-1710
Oberg, Richard/327 15th Ave, Moline, IL	319-359-3831
Osborne-Tuttle/233 E Wacker Dr #2409, Chicago, IL	312-565-1910
Oskar Designs/616 Sheridan Rd, Evanston, IL	312-328-1734
Our Gang Studios/3120 St Marys Ave, Omaha, NE	402-341-4965
Overlock Howe Consulting Group/4484 W Pine, St Louis, MO	314-533-4484

PQ

Pace Studios/3730 W Morse Ave, Lincolnwood, IL	312-676-9770
Painter/Cesaroni Design, Inc/1865 Grove St, Glenview, IL	312-724-8840
Palmer Design Assoc/3330 Old Glenview Rd, Wilmette, IL	312-256-7448
Paragraphs Design/10 E Huron St 4th Fl, Chicago, IL	312-943-4866
Paramount Technical Service Inc/31811 Vine St, Cleveland, OH	216-585-2550
Perlstein, Warren/560 Zenith Dr, Glenview, IL	312-827-7884

Perman, Norman/233 E Erie #2304, Chicago, IL	312-642-1348
Peterson, Ted/23 N Lincoln St, Hinsdale, IL	312-920-1091
Phares Associates Inc/Hills Tech Dr, Farmington Hills, MI	313-553-2232
Pinzke, Herbert/1935 N Kenmore, Chicago, IL	312-528-2277
Pitlock Design/300 N Michigan #200, South Bend, IN	219-233-8606
Pitt Studios/1370 Ontario St #1430, Cleveland, OH	216-241-6720
Polivka-Logan Design/5100 Thimsen Ave, Minnetonka, MN	612-474-1124
Porter-Matjasich/154 W Hubbard #404, Chicago, IL	312-670-4355
Powell/Kleinschmidt Inc/115 S LaSalle St, Chicago, IL	312-726-2208
Pride and Perfomance/970 Raymond Ave, St Paul, MN	612-646-4800
Prodesign Inc/2500 Niagara Ln, Plymouth, MI	612-476-1200
Purviance, George Marketing Comm/7404 Bland Dr, Clayton, MO	314-721-2765
Pycha and Associates/16 E Pearson, Chicago, IL	312-944-3679

R

Qually & Co Inc/30 E Huron #2502, Chicago, IL	312-944-0237
Ramba Graphics/1776 Columbus Rd, Cleveland, OH	216-621-1776
Red Wing Enterprises/666 N Lake Shore Dr #211, Chicago, IL	312-951-0441
Redmond, Patrick Design/1450 Energy Pk Dr #113H/Box 16, St Paul, MN	612-926-3951
Reed, Stan/1900 University Ave, Madison, WI	608-238-1900
RHI Inc/213 W Institute Pl, Chicago, IL	312-943-2585
Richardson/Smith Inc/10350 Olentangy River Rd, Worthington, OH	614-885-3453
Roberts Webb & Co/111 E Wacker Dr, Chicago, IL	312-861-0060
Robinson, Thompson & Wise/8717 W 110th St, Overland Park, KS	913-451-9473
Ross & Harvey/500 N Dearborn, Chicago, IL	312-467-1290
Roth, Randall/535 N Michigan #2312, Chicago, IL	312-467-0140
Rotheiser, Jordan I/1725 McGovern St, Highland Park, IL	312-433-4288

S

Samata Assoc/213 W Main Street, West Dundee, IL	312-428-8600
Sargent, Ann Design/432 Ridgewood Ave, Minneapolis, MN	612-870-9995
Savlin/ Williams Assoc/1335 Dodge, Evanston, IL	312-328-3366
Schlatter Group Inc/40 E Michigan Mall, Battle Creek, MI	616-964-0898
Schmidt, Wm M Assoc/20296 Harper Ave, Harper Woods, MI	313-881-8075
Schultz, Ron Design/838 W Webster, Chicago, IL	312-528-1853
Scott, Jack/600 S Dearborn #1308, Chicago, IL	312-922-1467
Selfridge, Mary/817 Desplaines St, Plainfield, IL	815-436-7197
Seltzer, Meyer Design & Illustration/744 W Buckingham Pl, Chicago, IL	312-348-2885
Sherman, Roger Assoc Inc/13530 Michigan Ave, Dearborn, MI	313-582-8844
Shilt, Jennifer/1010 Jorie Blvd, Oak Brook, IL	312-325-8657
Sigalos, Alex/520 N Michigan Ave #606, Chicago, IL	312-321-0349
Simanis, Vito/4 N 013 Randall Rd, St Charles, IL	312-584-1683
Simons, I W Industrial Design/975 Amberly Pl, Columbus, OH	614-451-3796
Skolnick, Jerome/200 E Ontario, Chicago, IL	312-944-4568
Slavin Assoc Inc/229 W Illinois, Chicago, IL	312-822-0559
Smith, Glen Co/337 Oak Grove, Carriage House, Minneapolis, MN	612-871-1616
Sosin, Bill/415 W Superior St, Chicago, IL	312-751-0974
Source Inc/180 N Michigan Ave, Chicago, IL	312-236-7620
Space Design International Inc/309 Vine St, Cincinnati, OH	513-241-3000
Spatial Graphics Inc/7131 W Lakefield Dr, Milwaukee, WI	414-545-4444
Speare, Ray/730 N Franklin #501, Chicago, IL	312-943-5808
Stepan Design/317 S Prairie, Mt Prospect, IL	312-364-4121
Strandell Design Inc/233 E Wacker Dr #3609, Chicago, IL	312-861-1654
Strizek, Jan/213 W Institute Pl, Chicago, IL	312-664-4772
Stromberg, Gordon H Visual Design/5423 Artesian, Chicago, IL	312-275-9449
Studio One Graphics/16329 Middlebelt, Livonia, MI	313-522-7505
Studio One Inc/4640 W 77th St, Minneapolis, MN	612-831-6313
Swoger Grafik/12 E Scott St, Chicago, IL	312-943-2491
Synthesis Concepts/612 N Michigan Ave #501, Chicago, IL	312-787-1201

T

T & Company/3553 W Peterson Ave, Chicago, IL	312-463-1336
Tassian, George Org/702 Gwynne Bldg, Cincinnati, OH	513-721-5566
Taylor & Assoc/8601 Urbandale Rd, Des Moines, IA	515-276-0992
Tepe Hensler & Westerkamp/632 Vine St #1100, Cincinnati, OH	513-241-0100
Teubner, Peter & Assoc/2341 N Cambridge St, Chicago, IL	312-248-6797

Graphic Designers
Continued

Please send us your additions and updates.

Thorbeck & Lambert Inc/1409 Willow, Minneapolis, MN	612-871-7979
Toth, Joe/20000 Eldra Rd, Rocky River, OH	216-356-0745
Turgeon, James/233 E Wacker Dr #1102, Chicago, IL	312-861-1039

UV
Underwood, Muriel/173 W Madison Ave, #1011, Chicago, IL	312-236-8472
Unicom/4100 W River Ln, Milwaukee, WI	414-354-5440
UVG & N/4415 W Harrison St, Hillside, IL	312-449-1500
Vallarta, Frederick Assoc Inc/875 N Michigan #1545, Chicago, IL	312-944-7300
Vanides-Mlodock/323 S Franklin St, Chicago, IL	312-663-0595
Vann, Bill Studio/1706 S 8th St, St Louis, MO	314-231-2322
Vista Three Design/4820 Excelsior Blvd, Minneapolis, MN	612-920-5311
Visual Image Studio/1599 Selby Ave #22, St Paul, MN	612-644-7314

WXZ
Wallner Harbauer Bruce & Assoc/500 N Michigan Ave, Chicago, IL	312-787-6787
Weber Conn & Riley/444 N Michigan #2440, Chicago, IL	312-527-4260
Weiss, Jack Assoc/820 Davis St, Evanston, IL	312-866-7480
Widmer, Stanley Assoc Inc/Staples Airport Ind Park, RR2, Staples, MN	218-894-3466
Willson, William/100 E Ohio St #314, Chicago, IL	312-642-5328
Winbush Design/444 N Lake Shore Dr 4th Fl, Chicago, IL	312-527-4478
Wooster + Assoc/314 Walnut, Winnetka, IL	312-726-7944
Worrel, W Robert Design/716 N First St, Minneapolis, MN	612-623-3391
Xeno/PO Box 10030, Chicago, IL	312-327-1989
Zender and Associates/3914 Miami Rd, Cincinnati, OH	513-561-8496
Ziegler, Nancy/874 Greenbay Rd, Wilmet, IL	312-446-3707

Southwest

A
A&M Associates Inc/2727 N Central Ave, Box 21503, Phoenix, AZ	602-263-6504
Ackerman & McQueen/5708 Mosteller Dr, Oklahoma City, OK	405-843-9451
The Ad Department/1412 Texas St, Ft Worth, TX	817-335-4012
Ad-Art Studios/813 6th Ave, Ft Worth, TX	817-335-9603
Advertising Inc/2202 E 49th St, Tulsa, OK	918-747-8871
Anderson Pearlstone & Assoc/PO Box 6528, San Antonio, TX	512-826-1897
Apple Graphics/5440 Harvest Hill Rd #235, Dallas, TX	214-522-6261
Ark, Chuck/3825 Bowser Ave, Dallas, TX	214-522-5356
Arnold Harwell McClain & Assoc/4131 N Central Expwy #510, Dallas, TX	214-521-6400
Art Associates/1300 Walnut Hill Ln #103, Irving, TX	214-258-6001
The Art Works/4409 Maple St, Dallas, TX	214-521-2121

B
Baugh, Larry/1417 N Irving Hts, Irving, TX	214-438-5696
Beals Advertising Agency/5005 N Pennsylvania, Oklahoma City, OK	405-848-8513
The Belcher Group Inc/8300 Bissonnet #240, Houston, TX	713-271-2727
Bleu Design Assoc/345 E Windsor, Phoenix, AZ	602-279-1131
Boughton, Cindy/1617 Fannin #2801, Houston, TX	713-951-9113
Brooks & Pollard Co/1650 Union Nat'l Plaza, Little Rock, AR	501-375-5561

C
Central Advertising Agency/1 Tandy Circle #300, Fort Worth, TX	817-390-3011
Chandler, Jeff/PO Box 224427, Dallas, TX	214-946-1348
Chesterfield Interiors Inc/2213 Cedar Springs, Dallas, TX	214-747-2211
Coffee Design Inc/5810 Star Ln, Houston, TX	713-780-0571
Connaster & Co/3111 Cole #1, Dallas, TX	214-744-3555
Cranford/ Johnson & Assoc/1st Commercial Bldg #2200, Little Rock, AR	501-376-6251
Creative Directions/3302 Shore Crest, Dallas, TX	214-358-3433

DE
Design Bank/PO Box 33459, Austin, TX	512-445-7584
Design Enterprises, Inc/9434 Viscount Blvd #180, El Paso, TX	915-594-7100
Designmark/1800 W Loop South #1390, Houston, TX	713-626-0953
Drebelbis, Marsha/2607 Routh St, Dallas, TX	214-951-0266
Eisenberg Inc/4924 Cole, Dallas, TX	214-528-5990
Executive Image/16479 Dallas Pkwy #20, Dallas, TX	214-733-0496

FG
Fischer, Don/3636 Lemmon #204, Dallas, TX	214-522-2995
Ford, Deborah/202 Senter Valley, Irving, TX	214-579-9472

Friesenhahn, Michelle/717 W Ashby, San Antonio, TX	512-342-1997
Funk, Barbara/3174 Catamore Ln, Dallas, TX	214-350-8534
Galen, D/5335 Bent Tree Forest #192, Dallas, TX	214-385-7855
GKD/PO Box 12860, Oklahoma City, OK	405-943-2333
Gluth & Weaver/3911 Stony Brook, Houston, TX	713-784-4141
The Goodwin Co/7598 N Mesa #200, El Paso, TX	915-584-1176
Graphics Hardware Co/3532 W Northern #2, Phoenix, AZ	602-242-4687
Gregory Dsgn Group/3636 Lemmon #302, Dallas, TX	214-522-9360
Grimes, Don/3514 Oak Grove, Dallas, TX	214-526-0040

HI
Hanagriff King Design/4151 SW Freeway, Houston, TX	714-622-4260
Harman, Gary/1025 S Jennings #403, Ft Worth, TX	817-332-7687
Harrison Allen Design/6633 Hillcroft #252B, Houston, TX	713-729-3938
Herman, Ben/701 Pennsylvania, Fort Worth, TX	817-731-9941
Hermsen Design Assoc/5626 Preston Oaks #34-D, Dallas, TX	214-233-5090
Herring, Jerry/1216 Hawthorne, Houston, TX	713-526-1250
High, Richard/4500 Montrose #D, Houston, TX	713-521-2772
Hill, Chris/3512 Lake, Houston, TX	713-523-7363
Hixo/2204 Rio Grande St, Austin, TX	512-477-0050
Hood Hope & Assoc/8023 E 63rd Box 35408, Tulsa, OK	918-250-9511
Hubler-Rosenburg Assoc/1405-A Turtle Creek, Dallas, TX	214-742-2491
Image Excellence/3312 Shore Crest, Dallas, TX	214-352-9958
Image Group Studio/2808 Cole St, Dallas, TX	214-745-1411

JKL
Jacob, Jim/3333 Elm #102, Dallas, TX	214-939-0033
Jettun, Carol/4212 Cumberland Rd, Ft Worth, TX	817-737-4708
Johnson, Carla/9010 Windy Crest, Dallas, TX	214-522-1449
Jones, Don/10529 Sinclair, Dallas, TX	214-327-0819
Kilmer/Geer/5650 Kirby Dr #205, Houston, TX	713-668-1708
Konig Design Group/4001 Broadway, San Antonio, TX	512-824-7387
Ledbetter, James/10818 Ridge Spring, Dallas, TX	214-341-4858
Lindgren Design/5350 Interfirst Two, Dallas, TX	214-742-3573
Loucks Atelier/2900 Weslyan #530, Houston, TX	713-877-8551
Lowe Runkle Co/6801 Broadway Extension, Oklahoma City, OK	405-848-6800
Lyons, Dan/5510 Abrams #109A, Dallas, TX	214-368-4890

M
Mantz & Associates/3707 Rawlins, Dallas, TX	214-521-7432
Martin, Hardy/7701 Stemmons #860, Dallas, TX	214-630-2977
Martin, Randy/701 E Plano Pkwy, Dallas, TX	214-881-1647
McCulley, Mike/412 Knollwood Ct, Euless, TX	214-528-4889
McEuen, Roby/600 Eighth Ave, Ft Worth, TX	817-335-5153
McFarlin, Steven/208 W Keaney #103, Mesquite, TX	214-289-1893
McGrath, Michael Design/1201 Richardson Dr, Richardson, TX	214-644-4358
Moore Co/5427 Redfield, Dallas, TX	214-631-9443
Morales, Frank Design/12770 Coit Rd #905, Dallas, TX	214-233-0667
Morris, Carroll/14970 Trafalgar Ct, Dallas, TX	214-233-6616
Morrison & Assoc/3900 Lemmon #2, Dallas, TX	214-528-7410

NOPQ
Neumann, Steve & Friends/3000 Richmond #103, Houston, TX	713-629-7501
Overton, Janet/2927 Bay Oaks Dr, Dallas, TX	214-357-1272
Owens & Assoc Advertising Inc/2600 N Central Ave #1700, Phoenix, AZ	602-264-5691
Pencil Point/14330 Midway #210, Dallas, TX	214-233-0776
Pirtle Design/4528 McKinney Ave #104, Dallas, TX	214-522-7520
Quad Type & Graphics/14004 Goldmark #260, Dallas, TX	214-238-0733

RS
Richards Brock Miller Mitchell & Assoc/12700 Hillcrest #242, Dallas, TX	214-386-9077
Sawyer, Sandra/1319 Ballinger, Ft Worth, TX	817-332-1611
Serigraphics Etc/4907 W Lovers Ln, Dallas, TX	214-352-6440
Slaton, Richard/3514 Oak Grove #9, Dallas, TX	214-231-3000
Squires, James/2913 N Canton, Dallas, TX	214-939-9194
Stoler, Scott/5015-A N Central Expwy, Dallas, TX	214-521-4024
Strickland, Michael & Co/3000 Post Oak Blvd #140, Houston, TX	713-961-1323
Struthers, Yvonne/2110 Mossy Oak, Arlington, TX	214-469-1377
Studio Renaissance/3200 Main St, Dallas, TX	214-939-0401
Studiographix/411 Northgate Plaza, Dallas, TX	214-258-8446

Graphic Designers

Continued

Please send us your additions and updates.

Sullivan, Jack Design Group/1320 N 7th Ave, Phoenix, AZ	602-271-0117
Suntar Designs/PO Box 1901, Prescott, AZ	602-778-2714
Sweeney, Jim/250 Decker, Irving, TX	214-258-1705

T
Tarasoff, Neal/3019 Caribbean, Mesquite, TX	214-681-0480
Tellagraphics/401-D N Interurban, Richardson, TX	214-238-9297
Texas Art & Media/500 W 13th St #220, Ft Worth, TX	817-334-0443
Total Designers/3511 Pinemont #3, Houston, TX	713-688-7766
3D/International/1900 W Loop South #200, Houston, TX	713-871-7000
Turnipseed, Allan/2719-C Laclede, Dallas, TX	214-871-2828

UVW
Unigraphics/2700 Oak Lawn, Dallas, TX	214-526-0930
Vanmar Assoc/1440 Empire Central #458, Dallas, TX	214-630-7603
Walker Fuld & Assoc/8800 N Central Expwy #458, Dallas, TX	214-692-7775
Warden, Bill/1349 Empire Central #802, Dallas, TX	214-634-8434
A Worthwhile Place Comm/2505 Wedglea #279, Dallas, TX	214-946-1348
WW3 Papagalos/313 E Thomas #208, Phoenix, AZ	602-279-2933

Rocky Mountain
ABC
Allison & Schiedt/219 E 7th Ave, Denver, CO	303-830-1110
Ampersand Studios/315 St Paul, Denver, CO	303-388-1211
Arnold Design Inc/1635 Ogden, Denver, CO	303-832-7156
Barnstorm Studios/2502 1/2 Colorado Ave, Colorado Springs, CO	303-630-7200
BROGREN/KELLY & ASSOC/3113 E THIRD AVE #220, DENVER, CO (P 240,241)	**303-399-3851**
Chen, Shih-chien/2839 35th St, Edmonton T6L5K2, AB	403-462-8617
CommuniCreations/2130 S Bellaire, Denver, CO	303-759-1155
Consortium West/Concept Design/2290 E 4500 St #120, Salt Lake City, UT	801-278-4441
Cuerden Advertising Design/1730 Gaylord St, Denver, CO	303-321-4163

DEFG
Danford, Chuck/1556 Williams St, Denver, CO	303-320-1116
Design Center/734 W 800 S, Salt Lake City, UT	801-532-6122
Duo Graphics/3907 Manhattan Ave, Ft Collins, CO	303-463-2788
Entercom/425 S Cherry St #200, Denver, CO	303-393-0405
Fleming, Ron/724 6th St NW, Great Falls, MT	406-761-7887
Gelotte, Mark/3485 S Arrow #82, Denver, CO	303-750-5941
Gibby, John Design/1140 E 1250 N, Layton, UT	801-544-0736
Graphic Concepts Inc/145 Pierpont Ave, Salt Lake City, UT	801-359-2191
Graphien Design/6950 E Belleview #250, Englewood, CO	303-779-5858
Gritz Visual Graphics/5595 Arapahoe Rd, Boulder, CO	303-449-3840

MOR
Markowitz & Long/900 28th St #203, Boulder, CO	303-449-7394
Martin, Janet/1112 Pearl, Boulder, CO	303-442-8202
Matrix International Inc/3773 Cherry Creek Dr N #690, Denver, CO	303-388-9353
Monigle, Glenn/150 Adams, Denver, CO	303-388-9358
Multimedia/450 Lincoln #100, Denver, CO	303-777-5480
Okland Design Assoc/1970 SW Temple, Salt Lake City, UT	801-484-7861
Radetsky Design Associates/2342 Broadway, Denver, CO	303-629-7375

TVW
Tandem Design Group Inc/217 E 7th Ave, Denver, CO	303-831-9251
Taylor, Robert W Design Inc/2260 Baseline Rd #205, Boulder, CO	303-443-1975
Three B Studio & Assoc/1475 S Pearl St, Denver, CO	303-777-6359
Visual Communications/4475 E Hinsdale Pl, Littleton, CO	303-773-0128
Visual Images Inc/1626 Franklin, Denver, CO	303-388-5366
Walker Design Associates/1873 S Bellaire St #715, Denver, CO	303-773-0426
Weller Institute for Design/2240 Monarch Dr, Park City, UT	801-649-9859
Woodard Racing Graphics Ltd/3116 Longhorn Rd, Boulder, CO	303-443-1986
Worthington, Carl A Partnership/1309 Spruce St, Boulder, CO	303-449-8900

West Coast
A
A & H Graphic Design/11844 Rncho Brndo #120-72, Rancho Bernardo, CA	619-486-0777
Ace Design/310 Industrial Ctr Bldg, Sausalito, CA	415-332-9390
Adfiliation Design/323 W 13th Ave, Eugene, OR	503-687-8262
ADI/1100 W Colorado Blvd, Los Angeles, CA	213-254-7131
Advertising Design & Production Service/1929 Emerald St #3, San Diego, CA	619-483-1393
Advertising/Design Assoc/1906 Second Ave, Walnut Creek, CA	415-421-7000
AGI/424 N Larchmont Blvd, Los Angeles, CA	213-462-0821
Alatorre, Sean/1341 Ocean Ave #259, Santa Monica, CA	213-209-3765
Alvarez Group/1516 N Vista Street, Los Angeles, CA	213-876-3491
Andrysiak, Michele/13534 Cordary Ave #14, Hawthorne, CA	213-973-8480
Antisdel Image Group/3252 De La Cruz, Santa Clara, CA	408-988-1010
Art Zone/404 Piikoi St PH, Honolulu, HI	808-537-6647
Artists In Print/Bldg 314, Fort Mason Center, San Francisco, CA	415-673-6941
Artmaster Studios/547 Library St, San Fernando, CA	818-365-7188
Artworks/115 N Sycamore St, Los Angeles, CA	213-933-5763
Asbury & Assoc/3450 E Spring St, Long Beach, CA	213-595-6481

B
Bailey, Robert Design Group/0121 SW Bancroft St, Portland, OR	503-228-1381
Ballard, Laurie/2400-D Main St, Santa Monica, CA	213-392-9749
Banuelos Design/111 S Orange St, Orange, CA	714-771-4335
Baptiste, Bob/20360 Orchard Rd, Saratoga, CA	408-867-6569
Barile, Michael & Assoc/7062 Saroni Dr, Oakland, CA	415-339-8360
Barnes, Herb Graphics/1844 Monterey Rd, S Pasadena, CA	213-682-2420
Basic Designs Inc/Box 479 Star Rt, Sausalito, CA	415-388-5141
Bass, Yager and Assoc/7039 Sunset Blvd, Hollywood, CA	213-466-9701
Beggs Langley Design/156 University Ave #201, Palo Alto, CA	415-323-6160
Bennett, Douglas Design/1966 Harvard Ave E, Seattle, WA	206-324-9966
Bennett, Ralph Assoc/6700 Densmore Ave, Van Nuys, CA	818-782-3224
Beuret, Janis/404 Piikoi St PH, Honolulu, HI	808-537-6647
Bhang, Samuel Design Assoc/824 S Burnside, Los Angeles, CA	213-382-1126
The Blank Co/1048 Lincoln Ave, San Jose, CA	408-289-9095
Blazej, Rosalie Graphics/127 Mateo St, San Francisco, CA	415-586-3325
Blik, Ty/715 'J' St #102, San Diego, CA	619-232-5707
Bloch & Associates/2800 28th St #105, Santa Monica, CA	213-450-8863
Boelter, Herbert A/246 North Frederic, Burbank, CA	818-845-5055
Bohn, Richard/595 W Wilson St, Costa Mesa, CA	714-548-6669
Boyd, Douglas Design/8271 Melrose Ave, Los Angeles, CA	213-655-9642
Bright & Associates, Inc/8322 Beverly Blvd, Los Angeles, CA	213-658-8844
Briteday Inc/970 Terra Bella #7, Mountain View, CA	415-968-5668
Brookins, Ed/4333 Farmdale Ave, Studio City, CA	213-766-7336
Brosio Design/3539 Jennings St, San Diego, CA	619-226-4322
Brown, Bill/1054 S Robertson Blvd #203, Los Angeles, CA	213-652-9380
Burns & Associates Inc/2700 Sutter St, San Francisco, CA	415-567-4404
Burridge, Robert/4681 Tajo, Santa Barbara, CA	805-964-2087
Business Graphics/1717 N Highland, Los Angeles, CA	213-467-0292

C
Camozzi, Teresa/770 California St, San Francisco, CA	415-392-1202
Campbell, Tom + Assoc/4751 Wilshire Blvd #219, Los Angeles, CA	213-931-9990
Carlson, Keith Advertising Art/251 Kearny St, San Francisco, CA	415-397-5130
Carre Design/1424 4th St #500 Ctr Tower, Santa Monica, CA	213-395-1033
Catalog Design & Production Inc/1485 Bay Shore Blvd, San Francisco, CA	415-468-5500
Chan Design/1334 Lincoln Blvd #150, Santa Monica, CA	213-393-3735
Chartmasters Inc/639 Howard St, San Francisco, CA	415-421-6591
Chase, Margo/120 S Sycamore Ave, Los Angeles, CA	213-937-4421
Chris Von-Veh/143 Finch Pl, Winslow, WA	206-842-1140
Churchill, Steven/4757 Cardin St, San Diego, CA	619-560-1225
Clark, Tim/8800 Venice Blvd, Los Angeles, CA	213-202-1044
Coak, Steve/2870 N Haven Lane, Altadena, CA	818-797-5477
The Coakley Heagerty Co/122 Saratoga Ave # 28, Santa Clara, CA	408-249-6242
Coates Advertising/115 SW Ash St #323, Portland, OR	503-241-1124
Cognata Associates Inc/2247 Webster, San Francisco, CA	415-931-3800
Cojean, Lonnie/1454 W 8th St, Upland, CA	714-985-9335

Graphic Designers

Continued

Please send us your additions and updates.

Conber Creations/3326 NE 60th, Portland, OR	503-288-2938
Corporate Comms Group/310 Washington St, Marina Del Rey, CA	213-821-9086
Corporate Graphics/2800 Van Ness, San Francisco, CA	415-474-2888
Cowart, Jerry/1144-C S Robertson Blvd, Los Angeles, CA	213-278-5605
Crawshaw, Todd Design/345-D Folsom, San Francisco, CA	145-777-3939
Creative Source/6671 W Sunset Blvd #1519, Los Angeles, CA	213-462-5731
Cronan, Michael Patrick/1 Zoe St, San Francisco, CA	415-543-6745
Cross Assoc/113 Stewart St, San Francisco, CA	415-777-2731
Cross, James/10513 W Pico Blvd, Los Angeles, CA	213-474-1484
Crouch + Fuller Inc/853 Camino Del Mar, Del Mar, CA	619-450-9200
Curtis, Todd/2032 14th St #7, Santa Monica, CA	213-452-0738

D

Dahm & Assoc Inc/26735 Shorewood Rd, Rncho Palos Verdes, CA	213-373-4408
Danziger, Louis/7001 Melrose Ave, Los Angeles, CA	213-935-1251
Davis, Pat/818 19th St, Sacramento, CA	916-442-9025
Dawson, Chris/7250 Beverly Blvd #101, Los Angeles, CA	213-937-5867
Dayne, Jeff The Studio/731 NE Everett, Portland, OR	503-232-8777
Daystar Design/4641 Date Ave #1, La Mesa, CA	619-463-5014
Dellaporta Adv & Graphic/2020 14th St, Santa Monica, CA	213-452-3832
DeMaio Graphics & Advertising/7101 Baird St #3, Reseda, CA	818-342-1800
Design & Direction/2275 Torrance Blvd #201, Torrance, CA	213-320-0822
Design Corps/501 N Alfred St, Los Angeles, CA	213-651-1422
Design Direction Group/595 S Pasadena Ave, Pasadena, CA	818-792-4765
Design Element/8624 Wonderland Ave, Los Angeles, CA	213-656-3293
Design Graphics/2647 S Magnolia, Los Angeles, CA	213-749-7347
Design Graphics/30 NE 23rd Pl, Portland, OR	503-223-0678
Design Group West/853 Camino Del Mar, Del Mar, CA	619-450-9200
Design Office/55 Stevenson, San Francisco, CA	415-543-4760
Design Projects Inc/16200 Ventura Blvd #418, Encino, CA	818-995-0303
Design Vectors/408 Columbus Ave #2, San Francisco, CA	415-391-0399
The Design Works/2205 Stoner Ave, Los Angeles, CA	213-477-3577
The Designory Inc/351 E 6th St, Long Beach, CA	213-432-5707
Detanna & Assoc/8200 Wilshire Blvd #400, Beverly Hills, CA	213-852-0808
Diniz, Carlos/676 S Lafayette Park Pl, Los Angeles, CA	213-387-1171
Doane, Dave Studio/215 Riverside Dr, Orange, CA	714-548-7285
Doerfler Design/8742 Villa La Jolla Dr #29, La Jolla, CA	619-455-0506
Dowlen, James/3436 Mendocino Ave, Santa Rosa, CA	707-576-7286
Dupre Design/415 2nd St, Coronado, CA	619-435-8369
Dyer-Cahn/5550 Wilshire Blvd #301, Los Angeles, CA	213-937-4100
Dyna Pac/7926 Convoy St, San Diego, CA	619-560-0280

EF

Earnett McFall & Assoc/2409 NE 133 St, Seattle, WA	206-364-4956
Ehrig & Assoc/4th & Vine Bldg 8th Fl, Seattle, WA	206-623-6666
Engle, Ray & Assoc/626 S Kenmore, Los Angeles, CA	213-381-5001
Exhibit Design Inc/101 S Claremont, San Mateo, CA	415-342-3060
Farber, Melvyn Design Group/406 Bonhill Rd, Los Angeles, CA	213-829-2668
Finger, Julie Design Inc/8467 Melrose Pl, Los Angeles, CA	213-653-0541
Five Penguins Design/269 W Alameda, Burbank, CA	818-841-5576
Floyd Design & Assoc/3451 Golden Gate Way, Lafayette, CA	415-283-1735
Flying Colors/2806 Laguna, San Francisco, CA	415-563-0500
Follis, Dean/2124 Venice Blvd, Los Angeles, CA	213-735-1283
Fox, BD & Friends Advertising Inc/6671 Sunset Blvd, Los Angeles, CA	213-464-0131
Frazier, Craig/173 7th St, San Francisco, CA	415-863-9613
Furniss, Stephanie Design/1327 Via Sessi, San Rafael, CA	415-459-4730
Fusfield, Robert/8306 Wilshire Blvd #2550, Beverly Hills, CA	213-933-2818

G

Garner, Glenn Graphic Design/2366 Eastlake Ave E, Seattle, WA	206-323-7788
Garnett, Joe Design/Illus/1100 Glendon #732, Los Angeles, CA	213-279-1539
Georgopoulos/Imada Design/5410 Wilshire Blvd #405, Los Angeles, CA	213-933-6425
Gerber Advertising Agency/1305 SW 12th Ave, Portland, OR	503-221-0100
Gillian/Craig Assoc/165 Eighth St #301, San Francisco, CA	415-558-8988
Girvin, Tim Design/911 Western Ave #408, Seattle, WA	206-623-7918
Glickman, Abe Design/14547 Titus, #201, Van Nuys, CA	818-989-3223
Global West Studio/201 N Occidental Blvd, Los Angeles, CA	213-384-3331

The Gnu Group/2200 Bridgeway Blvd, Sausalito, CA	415-332-8010
Gohata, Mark/1492 W 153 St #309, Gardena, CA	213-327-6595
Gold, Judi/8738 Rosewood Ave, West Hollywoood, CA	213-659-4690
Gordon, Roger/10799 N Gate St, Culver City, CA	213-559-8287
Gotschalk's Graphics/3157 Third Ave #3, San Diego, CA	619-298-0085
Gould & Assoc/10549 Jefferson, Culver City, CA	213-879-1900
Graformation/5233 Bakman Ave, N Hollywood, CA	818-985-1224
Graphic Data/804 Tourmaline POB 99991, San Diego, CA	619-274-4511
Graphic Designers Inc/2975 Wilshire Blvd #210, Los Angeles, CA	213-381-3977
Graphic Ideas/3108 Fifth Ave, San Diego, CA	619-299-3433
Graphic Studio/811 N Highland Ave, Los Angeles, CA	213-466-2666

H

Hale, Dan Ad Design Co/21241 Ventura Blvd #279, Woodland Hills, CA	818-347-4021
Harper and Assoc/2285 116th Ave NE, Bellevue, WA	206-462-0405
Harrington and Associates/11480 Burbank Blvd, N Hollywood, CA	818-508-7322
Harte-Yamashita & Forest/5735 Melrose Ave, Los Angeles, CA	213-462-6486
Hauser, S G Assoc Inc/24009 Ventura Blvd #200, Calabasas, CA	818-884-1727
Helgesson, Ulf Ind Dsgn/4285 Canoga Ave, Woodland Hills, CA	818-883-3772
Hernandez, Daniel/13443 Mulberry Dr #31, Whittier, CA	213-696-0607
Hornall Anderson Design Works/411 First Ave S, Seattle, WA	206-467-5800
Hosick, Frank Design/PO Box H, Vashon Island, WA	206-463-5454
Hubert, Laurent/850 Arbor Rd, Menlo Park, CA	415-321-5182
Humangraphic/4015 Ibis St, San Diego, CA	619-299-0431
Hyde, Bill/751 Matsonia, Foster City, CA	415-345-6955

IJ

Ikkanda, Richard/2800 28th St #105, Santa Monica, CA	213-450-4881
Imag'Inez/41 Grant Ave, San Francisco, CA	415-254-2444
Image Stream/5450 W Washington Blvd, Los Angeles, CA	213-933-9196
Imagination Creative Services/2415 De La Cruz, Santa Clara, CA	408-988-8696
Imagination Graphics/2760 S Harbor Blvd #A, Santa Ana, CA	714-662-3114
J J & A/405 S Flower, Burbank, CA	213-849-1444
Jaciow Design Inc/201 Castro St, Mountain View, CA	415-962-8860
Jerde Partnership/2798 Sunset Blvd, Los Angeles, CA	213-413-0130
Johnson Rodger Design/704 Silver Spur Rd, Rolling Hills, CA	213-377-8860
Johnson, Paige Graphic Design/535 Ramona St, Palo Alto, CA	415-327-0488
Joly Major Product Design Group/2180 Bryant St, San Francisco, CA	415-641-1933
Jones, Steve/1081 Nowita Pl, Venice, CA	213-396-9111
Jonson Pedersen Hinrichs & Shakery/620 Davis St, San Francisco, CA	415-981-6612
Juett, Dennis & Assoc/672 S Lafayette Pk Pl #48, Los Angeles, CA	213-385-4373

K

K S Wilshire Inc/10494 Santa Monica Blvd, Los Angeles, CA	213-879-9595
Kageyama, David Designer/2119 Smith Tower, Seattle, WA	206-622-7281
Kamins, Deborah/16255 Ventura Blvd #304, Encino, CA	818-905-8536
Keating, Kate Assoc/249 Front St, San Francisco, CA	415-398-6611
Kessler, David & Assoc/1300 N Wilton Pl, Hollywood, CA	213-462-6043
Klein/1111 S Robertson Blvd, Los Angeles, CA	213-278-5600
Kleiner, John A Graphic Design/2627 10th Ct #4, Santa Monica, CA	216-472-7442
Kuey, Patty/20341 Ivy Hill Ln, Yorba Linda, CA	714-970-5286

L

Lacy, N Lee Assoc Ltd/8446 Melrose Pl, Los Angeles, CA	213-852-1414
Lancaster Design/1810 14th St, Santa Monica, CA	213-450-2999
Landes & Assoc/20313 Mason Court, Torrance, CA	213-540-0907
Landor Associates/Ferryboat Klamath Pier 5, San Francisco, CA	415-955-1200
Larson, Ron/940 N Highland Ave, Los Angeles, CA	213-465-8451
Laurence-Deutsch Design/751 N Highland, Los Angeles, CA	213-937-3521
Leong, Russell Design/535 Ramona #33, Palo Alto, CA	415-321-2443
Leonhardt Group/411 First Ave S #400, Seattle, WA	206-624-0551
Lesser, Joan/Etcetera/3565 Greenwood Ave, Los Angeles, CA	213-397-4575
Levine, Steve & Co/228 Main St, #5, Venice, CA	213-399-9336

Logan Carey & Rehag/353 Folsom St, San Francisco, CA — 415-543-7080
Loveless, J R Design/3617 MacArthur Blvd #511, Santa Ana, CA — 714-754-0886
Lumel-Whiteman Assoc/4721 Laurel Canyon #203, North Hollywood, CA — 818-769-5332

M
Mabry, Michael/212 Sutter St, San Francisco, CA — 415-982-7336
Maddu, Patrick & Co/1842 Third Ave, San Diego, CA — 619-238-1340
Manwaring, Michael Office/1005 Sansome St, San Francisco, CA — 415-421-3595
Marketing Comm Grp/124 S Arrowhead Ave, San Bernadino, CA — 714-885-4976
Marketing Tools/384 Trailview Rd, Encinitas, CA — 619-942-6042
Markofski, Don/525 S Myrtle #212, Monrovia, CA — 818-446-1222
Marra & Assoc/2800 NW Thurman, Portland, OR — 503-227-5207
Matrix Design Consultants/2525 W 7th St, Los Angeles, CA — 213-487-6300
Matthews, Robert/1101 Boise Dr, Campbell, CA — 408-378-0878
McCargar Design/652 Bair Island Rd #306, Redwood City, CA — 415-363-2130
McKee, Dennis/350 Townsend St, San Francisco, CA — 415-543-7107
Media Services Corp/10 Aladdin Ter, San Francisco, CA — 415-928-3033
Meek, Kenneth/90 N Berkeley, Pasadena, CA — 818-449-9722
Mikkelson, Linda S/1624 Vista Del Mar, Hollywood, CA — 213-463-3116
Miller, Marcia/425 E Hyde Park, Ingelwood, CA — 213-677-4171
Miura Design/1326 Crenshaw #A, Torrance, CA — 213-320-1957
Mize, Charles Advertising Art/300 Broadway #29, San Francisco, CA — 415-421-1548
Mizrahi, Robert/6256 San Harco Circle, Buena Park, CA — 714-527-6182
Mobius Design Assoc/7250 Beverly Blvd #101, Los Angeles, CA — 213-937-0331
Molly Designs Inc/15 Chrysler, Irvine, CA — 714-768-7155
Murphy, Harry & Friends/225 Miller Ave, Mill Valley, CA — 415-383-8586
Murray/Bradley Inc/1904 Third Ave #432, Seattle, WA — 206-622-7082

N
N Graphic/480 2nd St #101, San Francisco, CA — 415-896-5806
Naganuma, Tony K Design/1100 Montgomery St, San Francisco, CA — 415-433-4484
Nagel, William Design Group/167 Hamilton Ave, Palo Alto, CA — 415-328-0251
Neill, Richard/9724 Olive St, Bloomington, CA — 714-877-5824
New Concepts Industrial Design Corp/1902 N 34th, Seattle, WA — 206-633-3111
Nicholson Design/662 Ninth Ave, San Diego, CA — 619-235-9000
Nicolini Associates/4046 Maybelle Ave, Oakland, CA — 415-531-5569
Niehaus, Don/2380 Malcolm Ave, Los Angeles, CA — 213-279-1559
Nine West/9 West State St, Pasadena, CA — 818-799-2727
Nordenhook Design/901 Dove St #115, Newport Beach, CA — 714-752-8631

O P
Olson Design Inc/853 Camino Del Mar, Del Mar, CA — 619-450-9200
Orr, R & Associates Inc/22282 Pewter Ln, El Toro, CA — 714-770-1277
Osborn, Michael Design/105 South Park, San Francisco, CA — 415-495-4292
Oshima, Carol/1659 E Sachs Place, Covina, CA — 818-966-0796
Pacific Rim Design/720 E 27th Ave, Vancouver V5V2K9, BC — 604-879-6689
Package Deal/18211 Beneta Way, Tustin, CA — 714-541-2440
Pease, Robert & Co/11 Orchard St, Alamo, CA — 415-820-0404
Peddicord & Assoc/2290 Walsh, Santa Clara, CA — 408-727-7800
Pentagram/620 Davis St, San Francisco, CA — 415-981-6612
Persechini & Co/357 S Robertson Blvd, Beverly Hills, CA — 213-657-6175
Petzold & Assoc/11830 SW Kerr Pkwy #350, Lake Oswego, OR — 503-246-8320
Pihas Schmidt Westerdahl Co/517 SW Fourth Ave, Portland, OR — 503-228-4000
Pittard, Billy/6335 Homewood Ave, Hollywood, CA — 213-462-2300
Popovich, Mike/15428 E Valley Blvd, City of Industry, CA — 818-336-6958
Powers Design International/822 Production Pl, Newport Beach, CA — 714-645-2265
Primo Angeli Graphics/508 4th St, San Francisco, CA — 415-974-6100

Q R
The Quorum/305 NE Mapleleaf Pl, Seattle, WA — 206-522-6872
Rand, Vicki/4087 Glencoe Ave, Marina Del Rey, CA — 213-306-9779
Reid, Scott/432 State St, Santa Barbara, CA — 805-963-8926
Reineck & Reineck/1425 Cole St, San Francisco, CA — 415-566-3614
Reineman, Richard Industrial Design/601 Clubhouse Ave, Newport Beach, CA — 714-673-2485
Reis, Gerald & Co/560 Sutter St #301, San Francisco, CA — 415-421-1232
Rickabaugh Design/213 SW Ash #209, Portland, OR — 503-223-2191
Ritola, Roy Inc/714 Sansome St, San Francisco, CA — 415-788-7010
RJL Design Graphics/44110 Old Warm Springs Blvd, Fremont, CA — 415-657-2038
Roberts, Eileen/PO Box 1261, Carlsbad, CA — 619-439-7800
Robinson, David/3607 Fifth Ave #6, San Diego, CA — 619-298-2021
Rogow & Bernstein Dsgn/5971 W 3rd St, Los Angeles, CA — 213-936-9916
Rohde, Gretchen/411 First Ave S #550, Seattle, WA — 206-623-9459
Rolandesign/21833 De La Luz Ave, Woodland Hills, CA — 818-346-9752
Runyan, Richard Design/12016 Wilshire Blvd, West Los Angeles, CA — 213-477-8878
Runyan, Robert Miles & Assoc/200 E Culver Blvd, Playa Del Rey, CA — 213-823-0975
Rupert, Paul Designer/728 Montgomery St, San Francisco, CA — 415-391-2966

S
Sackheim, Morton Enterprises/170 N Robertson Blvd, Beverly Hills, CA — 213-652-0220
San Diego Art Prdctns/2752 Imperial Ave, San Diego, CA — 619-239-6666
Sanchez/Kamps Assoc/60 W Green St, Pasadena, CA — 213-793-4017
Sant'Andrea, Jim West Inc/855 W Victoria St #1A, Compton, CA — 213-979-5449
Schaefer, Robert Television Art/738 N Cahuenga, Hollywood, CA — 213-462-7877
Schorer, R Thomas/27580 Silver Spur Rd #201, Palos Verdes, CA — 213-377-0207
Schwab, Michael Design/118 King St, San Francisco, CA — 415-546-7559
Schwartz, Bonnie/Clem/2941 4th Ave, San Diego, CA — 619-291-8878
Seiniger & Assoc/8201 W 3rd, Los Angeles, CA — 213-653-8665
Shaw, Michael Design/819 17th St, Manhattan Beach, CA — 213-545-0516
Shenon, Mike/576 Cambridge Ave, Palo Alto, CA — 415-493-6878
Shimokochi/Reeves Design/6043 Hollywood Blvd #203, Los Angeles, CA — 213-460-4916
Shoji Graphics/4121 Wilshire Blvd #315, Los Angeles, CA — 213-384-3091
Sidjakov, Nicholas/3727 Buchanan, San Francisco, CA — 415-931-7500
Signworks/7710 Aurora Ave N, Seattle, WA — 206-525-2718
Smidt, Sam/666 High St, Palo Alto, CA — 415-327-0707
The Smith Group/520 NW Davis St #325, Portland, OR — 503-224-1905
Sorensen, Hugh Industrial Design/841 Westridge Way, Brea, CA — 714-529-8493
Soyster & Ohrenschall Inc/575 Sutter St, San Francisco, CA — 415-956-7575
Spear, Jeffrey A/1228 11th St #201, Santa Monica, CA — 213-395-3939
Specht/Watson Studio/1246 S La Cienega BLvd, Los Angeles, CA — 213-652-2682
Sperling, Lauren/128 S Bowling Green Way, Los Angeles, CA — 213-472-9957
Spivey, William Design Inc/21911 Winnebago, Lake Forrest, CA — 714-770-7931
The Stansbury Company/9304 Santa Monica Blvd, Beverly Hills, CA — 213-273-1138
Starr Seigle McCombs Inc/1001 Bishop Sq #19 Pcfc Twr, Honolulu, HI — 808-524-5080
Stein, Richard/3037 20th Ave W, Seattle, WA — 206-282-4856
Stephenz, The Group/145 Dillon Ave Bldg D, Campbell, CA — 408-379-4883
Strong, David Design Group/2030 First Ave #201, Seattle, WA — 206-447-9160
The Studio/45 Houston, San Francisco, CA — 415-928-4400
Studio A/5801-A S Eastern Ave, Los Angeles, CA — 213-721-1802
Sugi, Richard Design & Assoc/844 Colorado Blvd #202, Los Angeles, CA — 213-385-4169
Superior Graphic Systems/1700 W Anaheim St, Long Beach, CA — 213-433-7421
Sussman & Prejza/1651 18th St, Santa Monica, CA — 213-829-3337

T
Tackett/Barbaria/1990 3rd St #400, Sacramento, CA — 916-442-3200
Thomas & Assoc/532 Colorado Ave, Santa Monica, CA — 213-451-8502
Thomas, Greg/2238 1/2 Purdue Ave, Los Angeles, CA — 213-479-8477
Thomas, Keith M Inc/3211 Shannon, Santa Ana, CA — 714-261-1161
Torme, Dave/55 Francisco St, San Francisco, CA — 415-391-2694
Trade Marx/1100 Pike St, Seattle, WA — 206-623-7676
Tribotti Design/15234 Morrison St, Sherman Oaks, CA — 818-784-6101

Trygg Stefanic Advertising/127 Second St #1, Los Altos, CA	415-948-3493
Tycer Fultz Bellack/1731 Embarcadero Rd, Palo Alto, CA	415-856-1600

V Vanderbyl Design/One Zoe St, San Francisco, CA — 415-543-8447

VanNoy & Co Inc/19750 S Vermont, Torrance, CA	213-329-0800
Vantage Advertising & Marketing Assoc/433 Callan Ave POB 3095, San Leandro, CA	415-352-3640
Vigon, Larry/101 S Sycamore Ave #1, Los Angeles, CA	213-394-6502
Visual Resources Inc/1556 N Fairfax, Los Angeles, CA	213-851-6688
Voltec Associates/560 N Larchmont, Los Angeles, CA	213-467-2106

W Walton, Brenda/PO Box 161976, Sacramento, CA — 916-456-5833

Webster, Ken/67 Brookwood Rd #6, Orinda, CA	415-954-2516
Weideman and Associates/4747 Vineland Ave, North Hollywood, CA	818-769-8488
Wertman, Chuck/559 Pacific Ave, San Francisco, CA	415-433-4452
West End Studios/40 Gold St, San Francisco, CA	415-434-0380
West, Suzanne Design/535 Ramona St, Palo Alto, CA	415-324-8068
White + Assoc/137 N Virgil Ave #204, Los Angeles, CA	213-380-6319
Whitely, Mitchell Assoc/716 Montgomery St, San Francisco, CA	415-398-2920
Wilkins & Peterson Graphic Design/206 Third Ave S #300, Seattle, WA	206-624-1695
Willardson + Assoc/103 W California, Glendale, CA	818-242-5688
Williams & Ziller Design/330 Fell St, San Francisco, CA	415-621-0330
Williamson & Assoc Inc/8800 Venice Blvd, Los Angeles, CA	213-836-0143
Winters, Clyde Design/2200 Mason St, San Francisco, CA	415-391-5643
Woo, Calvin Assoc/4015 Ibis St, San Diego, CA	619-299-0431
Workshop West/9720 Wilshire Blvd #700, Beverly Hills, CA	213-278-1370

YZ Yamaguma & Assoc/12 S First St #500, San Jose, CA — 408-279-0500

Yanez, Maurice & Assoc/770 S Arroyo Pky, Pasadena, CA	818-792-0778
Yee, Ray/424 Larchmont Blvd, Los Angeles, CA	213-465-2514
Young & Roehr Adv/6415 SW Canyon Ct, Portland, OR	503-297-4501
Yuguchi Krogstad/3378 W 1st St, Los Angeles, CA	213-383-6915
Zamparelli & Assoc/1450 Lomita Dr, Pasadena, CA	818-799-4370

Production/Support Services

Labs and Retouchers

New York City

Accu-Color Group Inc/103 Fifth Ave	212-989-8235
ACS Studios/2 West 46th St	212-575-9250
Adams Photoprint Co Inc/60 E 42nd St	212-697-4980
Alchemy Color Ltd/125 W 45th St	212-997-1944
American Blue Print Co Inc/7 E 47th St	212-751-2240
American Photo Print Co/285 Madison Ave	212-532-2424
American Photo Print Co/350 Fifth Ave	212-736-2885
Andy's Place/17 E 48th St	212-371-1362
Apco-Apeda Photo Co/250 W 54th St	212-586-5755
Appel, Albert/119 W 23rd St	212-989-6585
Arkin-Medo/30 E 33rd St	212-685-1969
ASAP Photolab/40 E 49th St	212-832-1223
AT & S Retouching/230 E 44th St	212-986-0977
Atlantic Blue Print Co/575 Madison Ave	212-755-3388
Authenticolor Labs Inc/227 E 45th St	212-867-7905
Avekta Productions Inc/164 Madison Ave	212-686-4550
AZO Color Labs/149 Madison Ave	212-982-6610
Bebell Color Labs/416 W 45th St	212-245-8900
Bell-Tait, Carolyn/10 W 33rd St	212-947-9449
Bellis, Dave/15 E 55th St	212-753-3740
Bellis, Dave Studios/155 E 55th St	212-753-3740
Benjamin, Bernard/1763 Second Ave	212-722-7773
Berger, Jack/41 W 53rd St	212-245-5705
Berkey K & L/222 E 44th St	212-661-5600
Bishop Retouching/236 E 36th St	212-889-3525
Blae, Ken Studios/1501 Broadway	212-869-3488
Bluestone Photoprint Co Inc/19 W 34th St	212-564-1516
Bonaventura Studio/307 E 44th St #1612	212-687-9208
Broderson, Charles Backdrops/873 Broadway #612	212-925-9392
Brunel, Jean Inc/11 Jay St	212-226-3009
C & C Productions/445 E 80th St	212-472-3700
Cacchione & Sheehan/1 West 37th St	212-869-2233
Carlson & Forino Studios/230 E 44th St	212-697-7044
Cavalluzzo, Dan/49 W 45th St	212-921-5954
Certified Color Service/2812 41st Ave	212-392-6065
Chapman, Edwin W/20 E 46th St	212-697-0872
Chroma Copy/423 West 55th St	212-399-2420
Chrome Print/104 E 25th St	212-228-0840
CitiChrome Lab/158 W 29th St	212-695-0935
Clayman, Andrew/334 Bowery #6F	212-674-4906
Colmer, Brian-The Final touch/310 E 46th St	212-682-3012
Coln, Stewart/563 Eleventh Ave	212-868-1440
Color Design Studio/19 W 21st St	212-255-8103
Color Masters Inc/143 E 27th St	212-889-7464
Color Perfect Inc/200 Park Ave S	212-777-1210
Color Pro Labs/40 W 37th St	212-563-5599
Color Unlimited Inc/443 Park Ave S	212-889-2440
Color Vision Photo Finishers/642 9th Avenue	212-757-2787
Color Wheel Inc/227 E 45th St	212-697-2434
Colorama Labs/40 W 37th St	212-279-1950
Colorite Film Processing/115 E 31st St	212-532-2116
Colotone Litho Seperator/555 Fifth Ave	212-557-5564
Columbia Blue & Photoprint Co/14 E 39th St	212-532-9424
Commerce Photo Print Co/415 Lexington Ave	212-986-2068
Compo Photocolor/18 E 48th St	212-758-1690
Copy-Line Corp/40 W 37th St	212-563-3535
Copycolor/8 W 30th St	212-725-8252
Copytone Inc/8 W 45th St	212-575-0235
Corona Color Studios Inc/10 W 33rd St	212-239-4990
Cortese, Phyllis/306 E 52nd St	212-421-4664
Crandall, Robert Assoc/306 E 45th St	212-661-4710
Creative Color Inc/25 W 45th St	212-582-3841
The Creative Color Print Lab Inc/25 W 45th St	212-582-6237
Crowell, Joyce/333 E 30th St	212-683-3055
Crown Photo/370 W 35th St	212-279-1950
Dai Nippon Printing/1633 Broadway	212-397-1880
The Darkroom Inc/222 E 46th St	212-687-8920
Davis-Ganes/15 E 40th St	212-687-6537
Diamond Art Studio/11 E 36th St	212-685-6622
Diamond, Richard/50 E 42nd St	212-697-4720
Diana Studio/301 W 53rd St	212-757-0445
Dimension Color Labs Inc/1040 Ave of Amer	212-354-5918
DiPierro-Turiel/210 E 47th St	212-752-2260
Drop Everything/20 W 20th St	212-242-2735
Duggal Color Projects Inc/9 W 20th St	212-924-6363
Dzurella, Paul Studio/15 W 38th St	212-840-8623
Ecay, Thom/49 W 45th St	212-840-6277
Edstan Productions/240 Madison Ave	212-686-3666
Egelston Retouching Services/333 Fifth Ave 3rd Fl	212-213-9095
Evans-Avedisian DiStefano Inc/29 W 38th St	212-697-4240
Filmstat/520 Fifth Ave	212-840-1676
Fine-Art Color Lab Inc/221 Park Ave S	212-674-7640
Finley Photographics Inc/488 Madison Ave	212-688-3025
Flax, Sam Inc/111 Eighth Ave	212-620-3000
Fodale Studio/247 E 50th St	212-755-0150
Forway Studios Inc/441 Lexington Ave	212-661-0260
Four Colors Photo Lab Inc/10 E 39th St	212-889-3399
Foursome Color Litho/30 Irving Pl	212-475-9219
Frenchys Color Lab/10 E 38th St	212-889-7787
Frey, Louis Co Inc/90 West St	212-791-0500
Friedman, Estelle Retouchers/160 E 38th St	212-532-0084
Fromia, John A/799 Broadway	212-473-7930
Gads Color/135 W 41st St	212-221-0923
Gayde, Richard Assoc Inc/515 Madison Ave	212-421-4088
Gilbert Studio/210 E 36th St	212-683-3472
Giraldi, Bob Prodctns/581 Sixth Ave	212-691-9200
Goodman, Irwin Inc/1156 Avenue of the Americas	212-944-6337
Graphic Images Ltd/151 W 46th St	212-869-8370
Gray, George Studios/230 E 44th St	212-661-0276
Greller, Fred/325 E 64th St	212-535-6240
Grubb, Louis D/155 Riverside Dr	212-873-2561
GW Color Lab/36 E 23rd St	212-677-3800
H-Y Photo Service/16 E 52nd St	212-371-3018
Hadar, Eric Studio/10 E 39th St	212-889-2092
Hudson Reproductions Inc/76 Ninth Ave	212-989-3400
J & R Color Lab/29 W 38th St	212-869-9870
J M W Studio Inc/230 E 44th St	212-986-9155
Jaeger, Elliot/49 W 45th St	212-840-6278
Jellybean Photographics Inc/99 Madison Ave 14th Fl	212-679-4888
JFC Color Labs Inc/443 Park Ave S	212-889-0727
Katz, David Studio/6 E 39th St	212-889-5038
Kaye Graphics Inc/151 Lexington Ave	212-889-8240
KG Studios Inc/56 W 45th St	212-840-7930
Kurahara, Joan/611 Broadway	212-505-8589
LaFerla, Sandro/108 W 25th St	212-620-0693
Langen & Wind Color Lab/265 Madison Ave	212-686-1818
Larson Color Lab/123 Fifth Ave	212-674-0610
Lieberman, Ken Laboratories/13 W 36th St	212-564-3800
Loy-Taubman Inc/34 E 30th St	212-685-6871
Lucas, Bob/10 E 38th St	212-725-2090
Lukon Art Service Ltd/56 W 45th St 3rd Fl	212-575-0474
Mann & Greene Color Inc/320 E 39th St	212-481-6868
Manna Color Labs Inc/42 W 15th St	212-691-8360
Marshall, Henry/6 E 39th St	212-686-1060
Martin, Tulio G Studio/140 W 57th St	212-245-6489
Martin/Arnold Color Systems/150 Fifth Ave #429	212-675-7270
Mayer, Kurt Color Labs Inc/1170 Broadway	212-532-3738
McCurdy & Cardinale Color Lab/65 W 36th St	212-695-5140
McWilliams, Clyde/151 West 46th St	212-221-3644
Media Universal Inc/116 W 32nd St	212-695-7454
Medina Studios Inc/141 E 44th St	212-867-3113
Miller, Norm & Steve/17 E 48th St	212-752-4830
Modernage Photo Services/312 E 46th St	212-661-9190
Moser, Klaus T Ltd/127 E 15th St	212-475-0038
Motal Custom Darkrooms/25 W 45th St 3rd Fl	212-757-7874
Murray Hill Photo Print Inc/32 W 39th St	212-921-4175
My Lab Inc/117 E 30th St	212-686-8684

Continued

Please send us your additions and updates.

My Own Color Lab/45 W 45th St	212-391-8638
National Reprographics Co/110 W 32nd St	212-736-5674
New York Camera/131 W 35th St	212-564-4398
New York Film Works Inc/928 Broadway	212-475-5700
New York Flash Rental/156 Fifth Ave	212-741-1165
Olden Camera/1265 Broadway	212-725-1234
Ornaal Color Photos/24 W 25th St	212-675-3850
Paccione, E S Inc/150 E 56th St	212-755-0965
Palevitz, Bob/333 E 30th St	212-684-6026
Pastore dePamphilis Rampone/145 E 32nd St	212-889-2221
Pergament Color/305 E 47th St	212-751-5367
Photo Retouch Inc/160 E 38th St	212-532-0084
Photographics Unlimited/43 W 22nd St	212-255-9678
Photographic Color Specialists Inc./10-36 47th Rd	718-786-4770
Photorama/239 W 39th St	212-354-5280
PIC Color Corp/25 W 45th St	212-575-5600
Portogallo Photo Services/72 W 45th St	212-840-2636
Positive Color Inc/405 Lexington	212-687-9600
Precision Chromes Inc/310 Madison Ave	212-687-5990
Preferred Photographic Co/165 W 46th St	212-757-0237
Procil Adstat Co Inc/7 W 45th St	212-819-0155
Prussack, Phil/155 E 55th St	212-755-2470
Quality Color Lab/305 E 46th St	212-753-2200
R & V Studio/32 W 39th St	212-944-9590
Rahum Supply Co/1165 Broadway	212-685-4784
Rainbow Graphics & Chrome Services/49 W 45th St	212-869-3232
Ram Retouching/380 Madison Ave	212-599-0985
Ramer, Joe Assoc/509 Madison Ave	212-751-0894
Rasulo Graphics Service/36 E 31st St	212-686-2861
Regal Velox/25 W 43rd St	212-840-0330
Reiter Dulberg/157 W 54th St	212-582-6871
Renaissance Retouching/136 W 46th St	212-575-5618
Reproduction Color Specialists/9 E 38th St	212-683-0833
Retouchers Gallery/211 E 53rd St	212-751-9203
Retouching Inc/9 E 38th St	212-683-4188
Retouching Plus/125 W 45th St	212-764-5959
Rio Enterprises/240 E 58th St	212-758-9300
Rivera and Schiff Assoc Inc/21 W 38th St	212-354-2977
Robotti, Thomas/5 W 46th St	212-840-0215
Rogers Color Lab Corp/165 Madison Ave	212-683-6400
Russo Photo Service/432 W 45th St	212-247-3817
Sa-Kura Retouching/123 W 44th St	212-764-5944
San Photo-Art Service/165 W 29th St	212-594-0850
Sang Color Inc/19 W 34th St	212-594-4205
Scala Fine Arts Publishers Inc/65 Bleecker St	212-673-4988
Schiavone, Joe/301 W 53rd St #4E	212-757-0660
Scope Assoc/11 E 22nd St	212-674-4190
Scott Screen Prints/228 E 45th St	212-697-8923
Scott, Diane Assoc/339 E 58th St	212-355-4616
Sharkey, Dick The Studio/301 W 53rd St	212-265-1036
Sharron Photographic Labs/260 W 36th St	212-239-4980
Simmons-Beal Inc/3 E 40th St	212-532-6261
Skeehan Black & White/61 W 23rd St	212-675-5454
Slide by Slide/445 E 80th St	212-879-5091
Slide Shop Inc/220 E 23rd St	212-725-5200
Spano/Roccanova Retouching Inc/16 W 46th St	212-840-7450
Spector, Hy Studios/56 W 45th St	212-221-3656
Spectrum Creative Retouchers Inc/230 E 44th St	212-687-3359
Stanley, Joseph/211 W 58th St	212-246-1258
Steinhauser, Art Retouching/305 E 40th St	212-953-1722
Stewart Color Labs Inc/563 Eleventh Ave	212-868-1440
Studio 55/39 W 38th St	212-840-0920
Studio Chrome Lab Inc/36 W 25th St	212-989-6767
Studio Macbeth Inc/130 W 42nd St	212-921-8922
Studio X/20 W 20th St	212-989-9233
Sunlight Graphics/401 5th Ave	212-683-4452
Super Photo Color Services/165 Madison Ave	212-686-9510
Sutton Studio/112 E 17th St	212-777-0301
T R P Slavin Colour Services/920 Broadway	212-674-5700
Tanksley, John Studios Inc/210 E 47th St	212-752-1150
Tartaro Color Lab/29 W 38th St	212-840-1640
Todd Photoprint Inc/1600 Broadway	212-245-2440

Trio Studio/18 E 48th St	212-752-4875
Truglio, Frank & Assoc/835 Third Ave	212-371-7635
Twenty/Twenty Photographers Place/20 W 20th St	212-675-2020
Ultimate Image/443 Park Ave S 7th Fl	212-683-4838
Van Chromes Corp/311 W 43rd St	212-582-0505
Venezia, Don Retouching/488 Madison Ave	212-688-7649
Verilen Reproductions/3 E 40th St	212-686-7774
Vidachrome Inc/25 W 39th St 6th Fl	212-391-8124
Vogue Wright Studios/423 West 55th St	212-977-3400
Wagner Photoprint Co/121 W 50th St	212-245-4796
Ward, Jack Color Service/220 E 23rd St	212-725-5200
Way Color Inc/420 Lexington Ave	212-687-5610
Weber, Martin J Studio/171 Madison Ave	212-532-2695
Weiman & Lester Inc/21 E 40th St	212-679-1180
Welbeck Studios Inc/39 W 38th St	212-869-1660
Wind, Gerry & Assoc/265 Madison Ave	212-686-1818
Winter, Jerry Studio/333 E 45th St	212-490-0876
Wolf, Bill/212 E 47th St	212-697-6215
Wolsk, Bernard/509 Madison Ave	212-751-7727
Zazula, Hy Assoc/2 W 46th St	212-819-0444

Northeast

Able Art Service/8 Winter St, Boston, MA	617-482-4558
Adams & Abbott Inc/46 Summer St, Boston, MA	617-542-1621
Alfie Custom Color/155 N Dean St, Englewood, NJ	201-569-2028
Alves Photo Service/14 Storrs Ave, Braintree, MA	617-843-5555
Artography Labs/2419 St Paul St, Baltimore, MD	301-467-5575
Asman Custom Photo Service Inc/926 Pennsylvania Ave SE, Washington, DC	202-547-7713
Assoc Photo Labs/1820 Gilford, Montreal, QU	514-523-1139
Blakeslee Lane Studio/916 N Charles St, Baltimore, MD	301-727-8800
Blow-Up/2441 Maryland Ave, Baltimore, MD	301-467-3636
Bonaventure Color Labs/425 Guy St, Montreal, QU	514-989-1919
Boris Color Lab/35 Landsdowne St, Boston, MA	617-437-1152
Boston Photo Service/112 State St, Boston, MA	617-523-0508
Calverts Inc/938 Highland Ave, Needham Hts, MA	617-444-8000
Campbell Photo & Printing/1328 'I' St NW, Washington, DC	202-347-9800
Central Color/1 Prospect Ave, White Plains, NY	914-681-0218
Color Film Corp/440 Summer St, Boston, MA	617-426-5655
Colorama/420 Valley Brook Ave, Lyndhurst, NJ	201-933-5660
Colorlab/5708 Arundel Ave, Rockville, MD	301-770-2128
Colortek/111 Beach St, Boston, MA	617-451-0894
Colotone Litho Seperator/260 Branford Rd/Box 97, North Branford, CT	203-481-6190
Complete Photo Service/703 Mt Auburn St, Cambridge, MA	617-864-5954
The Darkroom Inc/232 First Ave, Pittsburgh, PA	412-261-6056
The Darkroom/443 Broadway, Saratoga Springs, NY	518-587-6465
Delbert, Christian/19 Linell Circle, Billerica, MA	617-273-3138
Dimension Systems/680 Rhd Islnd Ave NE/Upper Lvl, Washington, DC	202-832-5401
Dunigan, John V/62 Minnehaha Blvd, PO Box 70, Oakland, NJ	201-337-6656
Dunlop Custom Photolab Service/2321 4th St NE, Washington, DC	202-526-5000
Durkin, Joseph/25 Huntington, Boston, MA	617-267-0437
Eastman Kodak/343 State St, Rochester, NY	716-724-4688
EPD Photo Service/67 Fulton Ave, Hempstead, NY	516-486-5300
Five-Thousand K/281 Summer St, Boston, MA	617-542-5995
Foto Fidelity Inc/35 Leon St, Boston, MA	617-267-6487
G F I Printing & Photo Co/2 Highland St, Port Chester, NY	914-937-2823
Gould, David/76 Coronado St, Atlantic Beach, NY	516-371-2413
Gourdon, Claude Photo Lab/60 Sir Louis VI, St Lambert, QU	514-671-4604
Graphic Accent/446 Main St PO Box 243, Wilmington, MA	617-658-7602
Iderstine, Van/148 State Hwy 10, E Hanover, NJ	201-887-7879
Image Inc/1919 Pennsylvania Ave, Washington, DC	202-833-1550
Industrial Color Lab/P O Box 563, Framingham, MA	617-872-3280
JTM Photo Labs Inc/125 Rt 110, Huntington Station, NY	516-549-0010
K E W Color Labs/112 Main St, Norwalk, CT	203-853-7888
Leonardo Printing Corp/529 E 3rd St, Mount Vernon, NY	914-664-7890
Light-Works Inc/77 College St, Burlington, VT	802-658-6815
Meyers, Tony/W 70 Century Rd, Paramus, NJ	201-265-6000
Modern Mass Media/Box 950, Chatham, NJ	201-635-6000

Moore's Photo Laboratory/1107 Main St, Charleston, WV	304-357-4541
Muggeo, Sam/63 Hedgebrook Lane, Stamford, CT	212-972-0398
Musy, Mark/PO Box 755, Buckingham, PA	215-794-8851
National Color Labs Inc/306 W 1st Ave, Roselle, NJ	201-241-1010
National Photo Service/1475 Bergen Blvd, Fort Lee, NJ	212-860-2324
Northeast Color Research/40 Cameron Ave, Somerville, MA	617-666-1161
Ogunquit Photo School/PO Box 568, Ogunquit, ME	207-646-7055
Photo Dynamics/PO Box 731, 70 Jackson Dr, Cranford, NJ	201-272-8880
Photo Publishers/1899 'L' St NW, Washington, DC	202-833-1234
Photo-Coloritura/PO Box 1749, Boston, MA	617-522-5132
Regester Photo Service/50 Kane St, Baltimore, MD	301-633-7600
Retouching Graphics Inc/205 Roosevelt Ave, Massapequa Park, NY	516-541-2960
Riter, Warren/2291 Penfield, Pittsford, NY	716-381-4368
Rothman, Henry/6927 N 19th St, Philadelphia, PA	215-424-6927
Select Photo Service/881 Montee de Liesse, Montreal, QU	514-735-2509
Snyder, Jeffrey/915 E Street NW, Washington, DC	202-347-5777
Spaulding Co Inc/301 Columbus, Boston, MA	617-262-1935
Sterling Photo Processing/345 Main Ave, Norwalk, CT	203-847-9145
STI Group/606 W Houstatonic St, Pittsfield, MA	413-443-7900
Stone Reprographics/44 Brattle St, Cambridge, MA	617-495-0200
Subtractive Technology/338-B Newbury St, Boston, MA	617-437-1887
Superior Photo Retouching Service/1955 Mass Ave, Cambridge, MA	617-661-9094
Technical Photography Inc/1275 Bloomfield Ave, Fairfield, NJ	201-227-4646
Trama, Gene/571 South Ave, Rochester, NY	716-232-6122
Universal Color Lab/810 Salaberry, Chomeday, QU	514-384-2251
Van Vort, Donald D/71 Capital Hts Rd, Oyster Bay, NY	516-922-5234
Visual Horizons/180 Metropark, Rochester, NY	716-424-5300
Von Eiff, Damon/7649 Old Georgeton Std 9, Bethesda, MD	301-951-8887
Weinstock, Bernie/162 Boylston, Boston, MA	617-423-4481
Wilson, Paul/25 Huntington Ave, Boston, MA	617-437-1236
Zoom Photo Lab/45 St Jacques, Montreal, QU	514-288-5444

Southeast

AAA Blue Print Co/3649 Piedmont Rd, Atlanta, GA	404-261-1580
Advance Color Processing Inc/1807 Ponce de Leon Blvd, Miami, FL	305-443-7323
Allen Photo/3808 Wilson Blvd, Arlington, VA	703-524-7121
Associated Photographers/19 SW 6th St, Miami, FL	305-373-4774
Atlanta Blue Print/1052 W Peachtree St N E, Atlanta, GA	404-873-5911
B & W Processing/6808 Hanging Moss, Orlando, FL	305-677-8078
Barral, Yolanda/100 Florida Blvd, Miami, FL	305-261-4767
Berkey Film Processing/1200 N Dixie Hwy, Hollywood, FL	305-927-8411
Bristow Photo Service/2018 Wilson St, Hollywood, FL	305-920-1377
Chromatics/625 Fogg St, Nashville, TN	615-254-0063
Clark Studio/6700 Sharon Rd, Charlotte, NC	704-552-1021
Color Copy Center/5745 Columbia Cir, W Palm Beach, FL	305-842-9500
Color Copy Inc/925 Gervais St, Columbia, SC	803-256-0225
Color Image-Atlanta/478 Armour Circle, Atlanta, GA	404-876-0209
The Color Lab/111 NE 21st St, Miami, FL	305-576-3207
Colorcraft of Columbia/331 Sunset Shopping Center, Columbia, SC	803-252-0600
Customlab/508 Armour Cr, Atlanta, GA	404-875-0289
Dixie Color Lab/520 Highland S, Memphis, TN	901-458-1818
E-Six Lab/53 14th St NE, Atlanta, GA	404-885-1293
Eagle Photographics/3612 Swann Ave, Tampa, FL	813-870-2495
Florida Color Lab/PO Box 10907, Tampa, FL	813-877-8658
Florida Photo Inc/781 NE 125th St, N Miami, FL	305-891-6616
Fordyce, R B Photography/4873 NW 36th St, Miami, FL	305-885-3406
Gables Blueprint Co/4075 Ponce De Leone Blvd, Coral Gables, FL	305-443-7146
General Color Corporation/604 Brevard Ave, Cocoa Beach, FL	305-631-1602
Infinite Color/2 East Glebe Rd, Alexandria, VA	703-549-2242
Inter-American Photo/8157 NW 60th St, Miami, FL	305-592-3833
Janousek & Kuehl/3300 NE Expressway #1-I, Atlanta, GA	404-458-8989
Klickovich, Robert Retouching/1638 Eastern Pkwy, Louisville, KY	502-459-0295
Laser Color Labs/Fairfield Dr, W Palm Beach, FL	305-848-2000
Litho Color Plate/7887 N W 55th St, Miami, FL	305-592-1605
Mid-South Color Laboratories/496 Emmet, Jackson, TN	901-422-6691

Northside Blueprint Co/5141 New Peachtree Rd, Atlanta, GA	404-458-8411
Par Excellence/2900 Youree Dr, Shreveport, LA	318-869-2533
Photo-Pros/635 A Pressley Rd, Charlotte, NC	704-525-0551
Plunkett Graphics/1052 W Peachtree St, Atlanta, GA	404-873-5976
A Printers Film Service/904-D Norwalk, Greensboro, NC	919-852-1275
Remington Models & Talent/2480 E Commercial Blvd PH, Ft Lauderdale, FL	305-566-5420
Reynolds, Charles/1715 Kirby Pkwy, Memphis, TN	901-754-2411
Rich, Bob Photo/12495 NE 6th Ave, Miami, FL	305-893-6137
Rothor Color Labs/1251 King St, Jacksonville, FL	904-388-7717
S & S Pro Color Inc/2801 S MacDill Ave, Tampa, FL	813-831-1811
Sheffield & Board/18 E Main St, Richmond, VA	804-649-8870
Smith's Studio/2420 Wake Forest Rd, Raleigh, NC	919-834-6491
Spectrum Custom Color Lab/302 E Davis Blvd, Tampa, FL	813-251-0338
Studio Masters Inc/1398 NE 125th St, N Miami, FL	305-893-3500
Supreme Color Inc/71 NW 29th St, Miami, FL	305-573-2934
Taffae, Syd/3550 N Bayhomes Dr, Miami, FL	305-667-5252
Thomson Photo Lab Inc/4210 Ponce De Leon Blvd, Coral Gables, FL	305-443-0669
Viva-Color Labs/121 Linden Ave NE, Atlanta, GA	404-881-1313
Williamson Photography Inc/9511 Colonial Dr, Miami, FL	305-255-6400
World Color Inc/1281 US #1 North, Ormond Beach, FL	904-677-1332

Midwest

A-1 Photo Service/105 W Madison St #907, Chicago, IL	312-346-2248
Absolute Color Slides/197 Dundas E, Toronto 15A 124, ON	416-868-0413
AC Color Lab Inc/2160 Payne Ave, Cleveland, OH	216-621-4575
Ad Photo/2056 E 4th St, Cleveland, OH	216-621-9360
Advantage Printers/1307 S Wabash, Chicago, IL	312-663-0933
Airbrush Arts/1235 Glenview Rd, Glenview, IL	312-998-8345
Amato Photo Color/818 S 75th St, Omaha, NE	402-393-8380
Anderson Graphics/521 N 8th St, Milwaukee, WI	414-276-4445
Anro Color/1819 9th St, Rockford, IL	815-962-0884
Arrow Photo Copy/523 S Plymouth St, Chicago, IL	312-427-9515
Artstreet/111 E Chestnut St, Chicago, IL	312-664-3049
Astra Photo Service/6 E Lake, Chicago, IL	312-372-4366
Astro Color Labs/61 W Erie St, Chicago, IL	312-280-5500
Benjamin Film Labs/287 Richmond St, Toronto, ON	416-863-1166
BGM Color Labs/497 King St E, Toronto, ON	416-947-1325
Boulevard Photo/333 N Michigan Ave, Chicago, IL	312-263-3508
Brookfield Photo Service/9146 Broadway, Brookfield, IL	312-485-1718
Buffalo Photo Co/60 W Superior, Chicago, IL	312-787-6476
Carriage Barn Studio/2360 Riverside Dr, Beloit, WI	608-365-2405
Chroma Studios/2300 Maryland Ln, Columbus, OH	614-471-1191
Chromatics Ltd/4507 N Kedzie Ave, Chicago, IL	312-478-3850
Cockrell, Ray/1737 McGee, Kansas City, MO	816-471-5959
Color Central/612 N Michigan Ave, Chicago, IL	312-321-1696
Color Corp of Canada/1198 Eglinton W, Toronto, ON	416-783-0320
Color Darkroom Corp/3320 W Vliet St, Milwaukee, WI	414-344-3377
Color Detroit Inc/310 Livernois, Ferndale, MI	313-546-1800
Color Graphics Inc/5809 W Divison St, Chicago, IL	312-261-4143
Color International Labs/593 N York St, Elmhurst, IL	312-279-6632
The Color Market/3177 MacArthur Blvd, Northbrook, IL	312-564-3770
Color Perfect Inc/24 Custer St, Detroit, MI	313-872-5115
Color Service Inc/325 W Huron St, Chicago, IL	312-664-5225
Color Studio Labs/1553 Dupont, Toronto, ON	416-531-1177
Color Systems/5719 N Milwaukee Ave, Chicago, IL	312-763-6664
Color Technique Inc/57 W Grand Ave, Chicago, IL	312-337-5051
Color West Ltd/1901 W Cermak Rd, Broadview, IL	312-345-1110
Coloron Corp/360 E Grand Ave, Chicago, IL	312-265-6766
Colorprints Inc/410 N Michigan Ave, Chicago, IL	312-467-6930
Commercial Colorlab Service/41 So Stolp, Aurora, IL	312-892-9330
Copy-Matics, Div Lith-O-Lux/6324 W Fond du Lac Ave, Milwaukee, WI	414-462-2250
Corley D & S Ltd/3610 Nashua Dr #7, Mississaugua, ON	416-675-3511
Custom Color Processing Lab/1300 Rand Rd, Des Plaines, IL	312-297-6333
Cutler-Graves/535 N Michigan Ave, Chicago, IL	312-828-9310
D-Max Colorgraphics/1662 Headlands Dr, Fenton, MO	314-343-3570
Diamond Graphics/6324 W Fond du Lac Ave, Milwaukee, WI	414-462-2250
Drake, Brady Copy Center/413 N 10th St, St Louis, MO	314-421-1311
Draper St Photolab/1300 W Draper St, Chicago, IL	312-975-7200

Production/Support Services

Continued

Please send us your additions and updates

Duncan, Virgil Studios/4725 E State Blvd, Ft Wayne, IN	219-483-6011
Dzuroff Studios/1020 Huron Rd E, Cleveland, OH	216-696-0120
Eastman Kodak Co/1712 S Prairie Ave, Chicago, IL	312-922-9691
Emulsion Stripping Ltd/4 N Eighth Ave, Maywood, IL	312-344-8100
Fotis Photo/25 E Hubbard St, Chicago, IL	312-337-7300
The Foto Lab Inc/160 E Illinois St, Chicago, IL	312-321-0900
Foto-Comm Corporation/215 W Superior, Chicago, IL	312-943-0450
Fromex/188 W Washington, Chicago, IL	312-853-0067
Gallery Color Lab/620 W Richmond St, Toronto, ON	416-367-9770
Gamma Photo Lab Inc/314 W Superior St, Chicago, IL	312-337-0022
Graphic Lab Inc/124 E Third St, Dayton, OH	513-461-3774
Graphic Spectrum/523 S Plymouth Ct, Chicago, IL	312-427-9515
Greenhow, Ralph/333 N Michigan Ave, Chicago, IL	312-782-6833
Grignon Studios/1300 W Altgeld, Chicago, IL	312-975-7200
Grossman Knowling Co/7350 John C Lodge, Detroit, MI	313-832-2360
Harlem Photo Service/6706 Northwest Hwy, Chicago, IL	312-763-5860
Hill, Vince Studio/119 W Hubbard, Chicago, IL	312-644-6690
Imperial Color Inc/618 W Jackson Blvd, Chicago, IL	312-454-1570
J D H Inc/1729 Superior Ave, Cleveland, OH	216-771-0346
Jahn & Ollier Engraving/817 W Washington Blvd, Chicago, IL	312-666-7080
Janusz, Robert E Studios/1020 Huron Rd, Cleveland, OH	216-621-9845
John, Harvey Studio/823 N 2nd St, Milwaukee, WI	414-271-7170
Jones & Morris Ltd/24 Carlaw Ave, Toronto, ON	416-465-5466
K & S Photographics/180 N Wabash Ave, Chicago, IL	312-207-1212
K & S Photographics/1155 Handley Industrial Ct, St Louis, MO	314-962-7050
Kai-Hsi Studio/160 E Illinois St, Chicago, IL	312-642-9853
Kier Photo Service/1627 E 40th St, Cleveland, OH	216-431-4670
Kitzerow Studios/203 N Wabash, Chicago, IL	312-332-1224
Kluegel, Art/630 Fieldston Ter, St Louis, MO	314-961-2023
Kolorstat Studios/415 N Dearborn St, Chicago, IL	312-644-3729
Kremer Photo Print/228 S Wabash, Chicago, IL	312-922-3297
LaDriere Studios/1565 W Woodward Ave, Bloomfield Hills, MI	313-644-3932
Lagasca, Dick & Others/203 N Wabash Ave, Chicago, IL	312-263-1389
Langen & Wind Color Service Inc/2871 E Grand Blvd, Detroit, MI	313-871-5722
Lim, Luis Retouching/405 N Wabash, Chicago, IL	312-645-0746
Lubeck, Larry & Assoc/405 N Wabash Ave, Chicago, IL	312-726-5580
Merrill-David Inc/3420 Prospect Ave, Cleveland, OH	216-391-0988
Meteor Photo Company/1099 Chicago Rd, Troy, MI	313-583-3090
Midwest Litho Arts/5300 B McDermott Dr, Berkeley, IL	312-449-2442
Multiprint Co Inc/153 W Ohio St, Chicago, IL	312-644-7910
Munder Color/2771 Galilee Ave, Zion, IL	312-764-4435
National Photo Service/114 W Illinois St, Chicago, IL	312-644-5211
NCL Graphics/575 Bennett Rd, Elk Grove Village, IL	312-593-2610
Noral Color Corp/5560 N Northwest Hwy, Chicago, IL	312-775-0991
Norman Sigele Studios/270 Merchandise Mart, Chicago, IL	312-642-1757
O'Brien, Tom & Assoc/924 Terminal Rd, Lansing, MI	517-321-0188
O'Connor-Roe Inc/111 E Wacker, Chicago, IL	312-856-1668
O'Donnell Studio Inc/333 W Lake St, Chicago, IL	312-346-2470
P-A Photocenter Inc/310 W Washington St, Chicago, IL	312-641-6343
Pallas Photo Labs/319 W Erie St, Chicago, IL	312-787-4600
Pallas Photo Labs/207 E Buffalo, Milwaukee, WI	414-272-2525
Parkway Photo Lab/57 W Grand Ave, Chicago, IL	312-467-1711
Photocopy Inc/104 E Mason St, Milwaukee, WI	414-272-1255
Photographic Specialties Inc/225 Border Ave N, Minneapolis, MN	612-332-6303
Photomatic Corp/59 E Illinois St, Chicago, IL	312-527-2929
Precision Photo Lab/5787 N Webster St, Dayton, OH	513-898-7450
Procolor/909 Hennepin Ave, Minneapolis, MN	612-332-7721
Proctor, Jack/2050 Dain Tower, Minneapolis, MN	612-338-7777
Professional Photo Colour Service/126 W Kinzie, Chicago, IL	312-644-0888
Quantity Photo Co/119 W Hubbard St, Chicago, IL	312-644-8288
Race Frog Stats/207 E Michigan Ave, Milwaukee, WI	414-276-7828
Rahe, Bob/220 Findlay St, Cincinnati, OH	513-241-9060
Rees, John/640 N LaSalle, Chicago, IL	312-337-5785
Reichart, Jim Studio/2301 W Mill Rd, Milwaukee, WI	414-228-9089
Reliable Photo Service/415 N Dearborn, Chicago, IL	312-644-3723
Repro Inc/912 W Washington Blvd, Chicago, IL	312-666-3800
The Retouching Co/360 N Michigan Ave, Chicago, IL	312-263-7445
Rhoden Photo & Press Service/7833 S Cottage Grove, Chicago, IL	312-488-4815
Robb Ltd/362 W Erie, Chicago, IL	312-943-2664
Robin Color Lab/2106 Central Parkway, Cincinnati, OH	513-381-5116
Ross-Ehlert/225 W Illinois, Chicago, IL	312-644-0244
Schellhorn Photo Techniques/3916 N Elston Ave, Chicago, IL	312-267-5141
Scott Studio & Labs/26 N Hillside Ave, Hillsdale, IL	312-449-3800
SE Graphics Ltd/795 E Kings St, Hamilton, ON	416-545-8484
Sladek, Dean/8748 Hollyspring Trail, Chagrin Falls, OH	216-543-5420
Speedy Stat Service/566 W Adams, Chicago, IL	312-939-3397
Standard Studios Inc/3270 Merchandise Mart, Chicago, IL	312-944-5300
The Stat Center/666 Euclid Ave #817, Clevland, OH	216-861-5467
Superior Bulk Film/442 N Wells St, Chicago, IL	312-644-4448
Thorstad, Gordy Retouching Inc/119 No 4th St #311, Minneapolis, MN	612-338-2597
Transparency Duplicating Service/847 W Jackson Blvd, Chicago, IL	312-733-4464
Transparency Processing Service/324 W Richmond St, Toronto, ON	416-593-0434
UC Color Lab/3936 N Pulaski Rd, Chicago, IL	312-545-9641
Uhlir, Louis J/2509 Kingston Rd, Cleveland Hts, OH	216-932-4837
Wichita Color Lab/231 Ohio, Wichita, KS	316-265-2598
Williams, Warren E & Assoc/233 E Wacker Dr, Chicago, IL	312-565-2689
Winnipeg Photo Ltd/1468 Victoria Park Ave, Toronto, ON	416-755-7779
Witkowski Art Studio/52098 N Central Ave, South Bend, IN	219-272-9771
Wood, Bruce/185 N Wabash, Chicago, IL	312-782-4287
Yancy, Helen/421 Valentine St, Dearborn Heights, MI	312-278-9345

Southwest

A-1 Blue Print Co Inc/2220 W Alabama, Houston, TX	713-526-3111
Alamo Photolabs/3814 Broadway, San Antonio, TX	512-828-9079
Alied & WBS/6305 N O'Connor #111, Irving, TX	214-869-0100
Baster, Ray Enterprises/246 E Watkins, Phoenix, AZ	602-258-6850
The Black & White Lab/4930 Maple Ave, Dallas, TX	214-528-4200
Casey Color Inc/2115 S Harvard Ave, Tulsa, OK	918-744-5004
Century Copi-Technics Inc/710 N St Paul St, Dallas, TX	214-741-3191
Collins Color Lab/2714 McKinney Ave, Dallas, TX	214-824-5333
Color Mark Laboratories/2202 E McDowell Rd, Phoenix, AZ	602-273-1253
The Color Place/1330 Conant St, Dallas, TX	214-631-7174
The Color Place/4201 San Felipe, Houston, TX	713-629-7080
The Color Place/2927 Morton St, Fort Worth, TX	817-335-3515
Commercial Color Corporation/1621 Oaklawn St, Dallas, TX	214-744-2610
Custom Photographic Labs/601 W ML King Blvd, Austin, TX	512-474-1177
Dallas Printing Co/3103 Greenwood St, Dallas, TX	214-826-3331
Five-P Photographic Processing/2122 E Governor's Circle, Houston, TX	713-688-4488
Floyd & Lloyd Burns Industrial Artist/3223 Alabama Courts, Houston, TX	713-622-8255
H & H Blueprint & Supply Co/5042 N 8th St, Phoenix, AZ	602-279-5701
Hall Photo/6 Greenway Plaza, Houston, TX	713-961-3454
Hot Flash Photographics/5933 Bellaire Blvd #114, Houston, TX	713-666-9510
Hunter, Marilyn Art Svc/8415 Gladwood, Dallas, TX	214-341-4664
Kolor Print Inc/PO Box 747, Little Rock, AR	501-375-5581
Magna Professional Color Lab/2601 N 32nd St, Phoenix, AZ	602-955-0700
Master Printing Co Inc/220 Creath St, Jonesboro, AR	501-932-4491
Meisel Photochrome Corp/9645 Wedge Chapel, Dallas, TX	214-350-6666
NPL/1926 W Gray, Houston, TX	713-527-9300
Optifab Inc/1550 W Van Buren St, Phoenix, AZ	602-254-7171
The Photo Company/124 W McDowell Rd, Phoenix, AZ	602-254-5138
PhotoGraphics/1700 S Congress, Austin, TX	512-447-0963
Pounds/909 Congress, Austin, TX	512-472-6926
Pounds Photo Lab Inc/2507 Manor Way, Dallas, TX	214-350-5671
Pro Photo Lab Inc/2700 N Portland, Oklahoma City, OK	405-942-3743
PSI Film Lab Inc/3011 Diamond Park Dr, Dallas, TX	214-631-5670
Raphaele/Digital Transparencies Inc/616 Hawthorne, Houston, TX	713-524-2211
River City Silver/906 Basse Rd, San Antonio, TX	512-734-2020
Spectro Photo Labs Inc/4519 Maple, Dallas, TX	214-522-1981
Steffan Studio/1905 Skillman, Dallas, TX	214-827-6128
Texas World Entrtnmnt/8133 Chadbourne Rd, Dallas, TX	214-351-6103
Total Color Inc/1324 Inwood Rd, Dallas, TX	214-634-1484
True Color Photo Inc/710 W Sheridan Ave, Oklahoma City, OK	405-232-6441

Production/Support Services

Continued

Please send us your additions and updates.

Rocky Mountain

Cies/Sexton Photo Lab/275 S Hazel Ct, Denver, CO   303-935-3535
Pallas Photo Labs/700 Kalamath, Denver, CO   303-893-0101
Rezac, R Retouching/7832 Sundance Trail, Parker, CO   303-841-0222

West Coast

A & I Color Lab/933 N Highland, Los Angeles, CA   213-464-8361
ABC Color Corp/3020 Glendale Blvd, Los Angeles, CA   213-662-2125
Action Photo Service/251 Keany, San Francisco, CA   415-543-1777
Alan's Custom Lab/1545 Wilcox, Hollywood, CA   213-461-1975
Aristo Art Studio/636 N La Brea, Los Angeles, CA   213-939-0101
Art Craft Custom Lab/1900 Westwood Blvd, Los Angeles, CA   213-475-2986
Atkinson-Stedco Color Film Svc/7610 Melrose Ave, Los Angeles, CA   213-655-1255
Bakes, Bill Inc/265 29th St, Oakland, CA   415-832-7685
Black & White Color Reproductions/38 Mason, San Francisco, CA   415-989-3070
Bogle Graphic Photo/1117 S Olive, Los Angeles, CA   213-749-7461
Boston Media Productions/330 Townsend St #112, San Francisco, CA   415-495-6662
Chrome Graphics/449 N Huntley Dr, Los Angeles, CA   213-657-5055
Chromeworks Color Processing/425 Bryant St, San Francisco, CA   415-957-9481
Coletti, John/333 Kearny #703, San Francisco, CA   415-421-3848
Color Lab Inc/742 Cahuenga Blvd, Los Angeles, CA   213-466-3551
Colorscope/250 Glendale Blvd, Los Angeles, CA   213-250-5555
Colortek/10425 Venice Blvd, Los angeles, CA   213-870-5579
Complete Negative Service/6007 Waring Ave, Hollywood, CA   213-463-7753
CPS Lab/1759 Las Palmas, Los Angeles, CA   213-464-0215
Cre-Art Photo Labs Inc/6920 Melrose Ave, Hollywood, CA   213-937-3390
Croxton, Stewart Inc/8736 Melrose, Los Angeles, CA   213-652-9720
Custom Graphics/15162 Goldenwest Circle, Westminster, CA   714-893-7517
Custom Photo Lab/123 Powell St, San Francisco, CA   415-956-2374
The Darkroom Custom B&W Lab/897-2B Independence Ave, Mountain View, CA   415-969-2955
Faulkner Color Lab/1200 Folsom St, San Francisco, CA   415-861-2800
Focus Foto Finishers/138 S La Brea Ave, Los Angeles, CA   213-934-0013
Frosh, R L & Sons Scenic Studio/4114 Sunset Blvd, Los Angeles, CA   213-662-1134
G P Color Lab/215 S Oxford Ave, Los Angeles, CA   213-386-7901
Gamma Photographic Labs/555 Howard St, San Francisco, CA   415-495-8833
Gibbons Color Lab/606 N Almont Dr, Los Angeles, CA   213-275-6806
Giese, Axel Assoc/544 Starlight Crest Dr, La Canada, CA   213-790-8768
Glusha, Laura/1053 Colorado Blvd #F, Los Angeles, CA   213-255-1997
Good Stats Inc/1616 N Cahuenga Blvd, Hollywood, CA   213-469-3501
Gornick Film Production/4200 Camino Real, Los Angeles, CA   213-223-8914
Graphic Center/7386 Beverly, Los Angeles, CA   213-938-3773
Graphic Process Co/979 N LaBrea, Los Angeles, CA   213-850-6222
Graphicolor/8134 W Third, Los Angeles, CA   213-653-1768
Hollywood Photo Reproduction/6413 Willoughby Ave, Hollywood, CA   213-469-5421
Imperial Color Lab/365 Howard St, San Francisco, CA   415-777-4020
Ivey-Seright/424 8th Ave North, Seattle, WA   206-623-8113
Jacobs, Ed/937 S Spaulding, Los Angeles, CA   213-935-1064
Jacobs, Robert Retouching/6010 Wilshire Blvd #505, Los Angeles, CA   213-931-3751
Johnston, Chuck/1111 Wilshire, Los Angeles, CA   213-482-3362
Kawahara, George/250 Columbus, San Francisco, CA   415-543-1637
Kimbo Color Laboratory Inc/179 Stewart, San Francisco, CA   415-288-4100
Kinney, Paul Productions/818 19th St, Sacramento, CA   916-447-8868
Landry, Carol/8148-L Ronson Rd, San Diego, CA   619-560-1778
Laursen Color Lab/1641 Reynolds, Irvine, CA   714-261-1500
Lee Film Processing/8584 Venice Blvd, Los Angeles, CA   213-559-0296
M P S Photo Services/17406 Mt Cliffwood Cir, Fountain Valley, CA   714-540-9515
M S Color Labs/740 Cahuenga Blvd, Los Angeles, CA   213-461-4591
Maddocks, J H/4766 Melrose Ave, Los Angeles, CA   213-660-1321
Marin Color Lab/41 Belvedere St, San Rafael, CA   415-456-8093
Mark III Colorprints/7401 Melrose Ave, Los Angeles, CA   213-653-0433

MC Photographics/PO Box 1515, Springfield, OR   503-741-2289
Metz Air Art/2817 E Lincoln Ave, Anaheim, CA   714-630-3071
Modern Photo Studio/5625 N Figueroa, Los Angeles, CA   213-255-1527
Modernage/470 E Third St, Los Angeles, CA   213-628-8194
Newell Color Lab/630 Third St, San Francisco, CA   415-974-6870
Olson, Bob Photo Blow-Up Lab/7775 Beverly Blvd, Los Angeles, CA   213-931-6643
Ostoin, Larry/22943 B Nadine Cr, Torrance, CA   213-530-1121
Pacific Production & Location/424 Nahua St, Honolulu, HI   808-924-2513
Paragon Photo/7301 Melrose Ave, Los Angeles, CA   213-933-5865
Personal Color Lab/1552 Gower, Los Angeles, CA   213-467-0721
Petron Corp/5443 Fountain Ave, Los Angeles, CA   213-461-4626
Pevehouse, Jerry Studio/3409 Tweedy Blvd, South Gate, CA   213-564-1336
Photoking Lab/6612 W Sunset Blvd, Los Angeles, CA   213-466-2977
Prisma Color Inc/5619 Washington Blvd, Los Angeles, CA   213-728-7151
Professional Color Labs/96 Jessie, San Francisco, CA   415-397-5057
Quantity Photos Inc/5432 Hollywood Blvd, Los Angeles, CA   213-467-6178
Rapid Color Inc/1236 S Central Ave, Glendale, CA   213-245-9211
Remos, Nona/4053 Eighth Ave, San Diego, CA   619-692-4044
Repro Color Inc/3100 Riverside Dr, Los Angeles, CA   213-664-1951
Retouching Chemicals/5478 Wilshire Blvd, Los Angeles, CA   213-935-9452
Revilo Color/4650 W Washington Blvd, Los Angeles, CA   213-936-8681
Reynolds, Carol Retouching/1428 N Fuller Ave, Hollywood, CA   213-874-7083
RGB Lab Inc/816 N Highland, Los Angeles, CA   213-469-1959
Ro-Ed Color Lab/707 N Stanley Ave, Los Angeles, CA   213-651-5050
Roller, S J/6881 Alta Loma Terrace, Los Angeles, CA   213-876-5654
Ross, Deborah Design/10806 Ventura Blvd #3, Studio City, CA   818-985-5205
Rudy Jo Color Lab Inc/130 N La Brea, Los Angeles, CA   213-937-3804
Schaeffer Photo Rapid Lab/6677 Sunset Blvd, Hollywood, CA   213-466-3343
Schroeder, Mark/70 Broadway, San Francisco, CA   415-421-3691
Snyder, Len/238 Hall Dr, Orinda, CA   415-254-8687
Staidle, Ted & Assocs/544 N Larchmont Blvd, Los Angeles, CA   213-462-7433
Stat House/8126 Beverly Blvd, Los Angeles, CA   213-653-8200
Still Photo Lab/1216 N LaBrea, Los Angeles, CA   213-465-6106
Studio Photo Service/733 N LaBrea Ave, Hollywood, CA   213-935-1223
Technicolor Inc/1738 No Neville, Orange, CA   714-998-3424
Thomas Reproductions/1147 Mission St, San Francisco, CA   415-431-8900
Timars/918 N Formosa, Los Angeles, CA   213-876-0175
Tom's Chroma Lab/514 No LaBrea, Los Angeles, CA   213-933-5637
Trans Tesseract/715 N San Antonio Rd, Los Altos, CA   415-949-2185
Tri Color Camera/1761 N Vermont Ave, Los Angeles, CA   213-664-2952
Universal Color Labs/1076 S La Cienega Blvd, Los Angeles, CA   213-652-2863
Vloeberghs, Jerome/333 Kearny St, San Francisco, CA   415-982-1287
Waters Art Studio/1820 E Garry St #207, Santa Ana, CA
Wild Studio/1311 N Wilcox Ave, Hollywood, CA   213-463-8369
Williams, Alan & Assoc Inc/8032 W Third St, Los Angeles, CA   213-653-2243
Wolf Color Lab/6416 Selma, Los Angeles, CA   213-463-0766
Zammit, Paul/5478 Wilshire Blvd #300, Los Angeles, CA   213-933-8563
Ziba Photographics/591 Howard St, San Francisco, CA   415-543-6221

Lighting

New York City

Altman Stage Lighting Co Inc/57 Alexander   212-569-7777
Artistic Neon by Gasper/75-49 61st St   718-821-1550
Balcar Lighting Systems/15 E 30th St   212-889-5080
Barbizon Electric Co Inc/426 W 55th St   212-586-1620
Bernhard Link Theatrical Inc/104 W 17th St   212-929-6786
Big Apple Cine Service/49-01 25th Ave   718-626-5210
Big Apple Lights Corp/533 Canal St   212-226-0925
Camera Mart/456 W 55th St   212-757-6977
Electra Displays/122 W 27th St   212-924-1022
F&B/Ceco Lighting & Grip Rental/315 W 43rd St   212-974-4640
Feature Systems Inc/512 W 36th St   212-736-0447
Ferco/707 11th Ave   212-245-4800
Filmtrucks, Inc/450 W 37th St   212-868-7065

Fiorentino, Imero Assoc Inc/44 West 63rd St	212-246-0600
Four Star Stage Lighting Inc/585 Gerard Ave	212-993-0471
Kliegl Bros Universal/32-32 48th Ave	718-786-7474
Lee Lighting America Ltd/534 W 25th St	212-924-5476
Litelab Theatrical & Disco Equip/76 Ninth Ave	212-675-4357
Lowel Light Mfg Inc/475 10th St	212-949-0950
Luminere/160 W 86th St	212-724-0583
Metro-Lites Inc/750 Tenth Ave	212-757-1220
Movie Light Ltd/460 W 24th St	212-989-2318
New York Flash/156 Fifth Ave	212-741-1165
Paris Film Productions Ltd/213-23 99th Ave	718-740-2020
Photo-Tekniques/119 Fifth Ave	212-254-2545
Production Arts Lighting/636 Eleventh Ave	212-489-0312
Ross, Charles Inc/333 W 52nd St	212-246-5470
Stage Lighting Discount Corp/346 W 44th St	212-489-1370
Stroblite Co Inc/10 E 23rd St	212-677-9220
Tekno Inc/15 E 30th St	212-887-5080
Times Square Stage Lighting Co/318 W 47th St	212-541-5045
Vadar Ltd/150 Fifth Ave	212-989-9120

Northeast

Barbizon Light of New England/3 Draper St, Woburn, MA	617-935-3920
Blake, Ben Films/104 W Concord St, Boston, MA	617-266-8181
Bogen/PO Box 448, Engelwood, NJ	201-568-7771
Capron Lighting & Sound/278 West St, Needham, MA	617-444-8850
Cestare, Thomas Inc/188 Herricks Rd, Mineola, NY	516-742-5550
Cody, Stuart Inc/300 Putnam Ave, Cambridge, MA	617-661-4540
Dyna-Lite Inc/140 Market St, Kenilworth, NJ	201-245-7222
Film Associates/419 Boylston St #209, Boston, MA	617-266-0892
Filmarts/38 Newbury St, Boston, MA	617-266-7468
Heller, Brian/200 Olney St, Providence, RI	401-751-1381
Lighting Products, GTE Sylvania/Lighting Center, Danvers, MA	617-777-1900
Limelight Productions/Yale Hill, Stockbridge, MA	413-298-3771
Lycian Stage Lighting/P O Box 68, Sugar Loaf, NY	914-469-2285
Martorano, Salvatore Inc/9 West First St, Freeport, NY	516-379-8097
McManus Enterprises/111 Union Ave, Bala Cynwyd, PA	215-664-8600
Norton Assoc/53 Henry St, Cambridge, MA	617-876-3771
Packaged Lighting Systems/29-41 Grant, PO Box 285, Walden, NY	914-778-3515
Penrose Productions/4 Sandalwood Dr, Livingston, NJ	201-992-4264
R & R Lighting Co/813 Silver Spring Ave, Silver Spring, MD	301-589-4997
Reinhard, Charles Lighting Consultant/39 Ocean Ave, Massapequa, NY	516-799-1615

Southeast

Kupersmith, Tony/320 N Highland Ave NE, Atlanta, GA	404-577-5319

Midwest

Duncan, Victor Inc/32380 Howard St, Madison Heights, MI	313-589-1900
Film Corps/3101 Hennepin Ave, Minneapolis, MN	612-338-2522
Frost, Jack/234 Piquette, Detroit, MI	313-873-8030
Grand Stage Lighting Co/630 W Lake, Chicago, IL	312-332-5611
Midwest Cine Service/304 W 79th Terr, Kansas City, MO	816-333-0022
Midwest Stage Lighting/2104 Central, Evanston, IL	312-328-3966
Studio Lighting/1345 W Argyle St, Chicago, IL	312-989-8808

Southwest

ABC Theatrical Rental & Sales/825 N 7th St, Phoenix, AZ	602-258-5265
Astro Audio-Visual/1336 W Clay, Houston, TX	713-528-7119
Chase Lights/1942 Beech St, Amarillo, TX	806-381-0575
Dallas Stage Lighting & Equipment Co/2813 Florence, Dallas, TX	214-827-9380
Duncan, Victor Inc/2659 Fondren Dr, Dallas, TX	214-369-1165
FPS Inc/11250 Pagemill Rd, Dallas, TX	214-340-8545
Gable, Pee Wee Inc/PO Box 11264, Phoenix, AZ	602-242-7660
MFC-The Texas Outfit/5915 Star Ln, Houston, TX	713-781-7703
Southwest Film & TV Lighting/904 Koerner Ln, Austin, TX	512-385-3483

Rocky Mountain

Rocky Mountain Cine Support/1332 S Cherokee, Denver, CO	303-795-9713

West Coast

Aguilar Lighting Works/3230 Laurel Canyon Blvd, Studio City, CA	213-766-6564
American Mobile Power Co/3218 W Burbank Blvd, Burbank, CA	213-845-5474
Astro Generator Rentals/2835 Bedford St, Los Angeles, CA	213-838-3958
B S Rental Co/18857 Addison St, North Hollywood, CA	213-761-1733
B S Rental Co/1082 La Cresta Dr, Thousand Oaks, CA	805-495-8606
Backstage Studio Equipment/5554 Fairview Pl, Agoura, CA	213-889-9816
Casper's Camera Cars/8415 Lankershim Blvd, Sun Valley, CA	213-767-5207
Castex Rentals/591 N Bronson Ave, Los Angeles, CA	213-462-1468
Ceco, F&B of CA Inc/7051 Santa Monica Blvd, Hollywood, CA	213-466-9361
Cine Turkey/2624 Reppert Ct, Los Angeles, CA	213-654-6495
Cine-Dyne Inc/9401 Wilshire Blvd #830, Beverly Hills, CA	213-622-7016
Cine-Pro/1037 N Sycamore Ave, Hollywood, CA	213-461-4794
Cinemobile Systems Inc/11166 Gault St, North Hollywood, CA	213-764-9900
Cineworks-Cinerents/5724 Santa Monica Blvd, Hollywood, CA	213-464-0296
Cool Light Co Inc/5723 Auckland Ave, North Hollywood, CA	213-761-6116
Denker, Foster Co/1605 Las Flores Ave, San Marino, CA	213-799-8656
Fiorentino, Imero Assoc Inc/6430 Sunset Blvd, Hollywood, CA	213-467-4020
Great American Market/PO Box 178, Woodlands Hill, CA	213-883-8182
Grosso & Grosso/7502 Wheatland Ave, Sun Valley, CA	213-875-1160
Hollywood Mobile Systems/7021 Hayvenhurst St, Van Nuys, CA	213-782-6558
Independent Studio Services/11907 Wicks St, Sun Valley, CA	213-764-0840
Kalani Studio Lighting/129-49 Killion St, Van Nuys, CA	213-762-5991
Key Lite/333 S Front St, Burbank, CA	213-848-5483
Leoinetti Cine Rentals/5609 Sunset Blvd, Hollywood, CA	213-469-2987
Mobile Power House/3820 Rhodes Ave, Studio City, CA	213-766-2163
Mole Richardson/937 N Sycamore Ave, Hollywood, CA	213-851-0111
Pattim Service/10625 Chandler, Hollywood, CA	213-766-5266
Picture Package Inc/22236 Cass Ave, Woodland Hills, CA	213-703-7168
Producer's Studio/650 N Bronson St, Los Angeles, CA	213-466-3111
Production Systems Inc/5759 Santa Monica Blvd, Hollywood, CA	213-469-2704
RNI Equipment Co/7272 Bellaire Ave, North Hollywood, CA	213-875-2656
Skirpan Lighting Control Co/1100 W Chestnut St, Burbank, CA	213-840-7000
Tech Camera/6370 Santa Monica Blvd, Hollywood, CA	213-466-3238
Wallace Lighting/6970 Varna Ave, Van Nuys, CA	213-764-1047
Young Generations/8517 Geyser Ave, Northridge, CA	213-873-5135

Studio Rentals

New York City

3G Stages Inc/236 W 61st St	212-247-3130
The 95th St Studio/206 E 95th St	212-831-1946
American Museum of the Moving Image/31-12 36th St	718-784-4520
Antonio/Stephen Ad Photo/45 E 20th St	212-674-2350
Boken Inc/513 W 54th St	212-581-5507
C & C Visual/12 W 27th St 7th Fl	212-684-3830
Camera Mart Inc/456 W 55th St	212-757-6977
Cine Studio/241 W 54th St	212-581-1916
Codalight Rental Studios/151 W 19th St	212-206-9333
Contact Studios/165 W 47th St	212-354-6400
Control Film Service/321 W 44th St	212-245-1574
DeFilippo/207 E 37th St	212-986-5444
Duggal Color Projects/9 W 20th St	212-242-7000
Farkas Films Inc/385 Third Ave	212-679-8212
Gruszczynski Studio/821 Broadway	212-673-1243
Horvath & Assoc Studios/95 Chambers	212-741-0300
Matrix Studios Inc/727 Eleventh Ave	212-265-8500
Mothers Sound Stages/210 E 5th St	212-260-2050
National Video Industries/15 W 17th St	212-691-1300
New York Flash Rental/156 Fifth Ave	212-741-1165

Production/Support Services

Continued

Please send us your additions and updates.

Ninth Floor Studio/1200 Broadway	212-679-5537
North American Video/423 E 90th St	212-369-2552
North Light Studios/122 W 26th St	212-989-5498
Osonitsch, Robert/112 Fourth Ave	212-533-1920
PDN Studio/167 Third Ave	212-677-8418
Phoenix State Ltd/537 W 59th St	212-581-7721
Photo-Tekniques/119 Fifth Ave	212-254-2545
Production Center/221 W 26th St	212-675-2211
Professional Photo Supply/141 W 20th St	212-924-1200
Reeves Teletape Corp/304 E 44th St	212-573-8888
Rotem Studio/259 W 30th St	212-947-9455
Schnoodle Studios/54 Bleecker St	212-431-7788
Silva-Cone Studios/260 W 36th St	212-279-0900
Stage 54 West/429 W 54th St	212-757-6977
Stages 1&2 West/460 W 54th St	212-757-6977
Studio 35/35 W 31st St	212-947-0898
Studio 39/144 E 39th St	212-685-1771
Studio Twenty/6 W 20th St	212-675-8067
Vagnoni, A Devlin Productions/150 W 55th St	212-582-5572
Yellowbox/47 E 34th St	212-532-4010

Northeast

Allscope Inc/PO Box 4060, Princeton, NJ	609-799-4200
Bay State Film Productions Inc/35 Springfield St, Agawam, MA	413-786-4454
Century III/651 Beacon St, Boston, MA	617-267-6400
Color Leasing Studio/330 Rt 46 East, Fairfield, NJ	201-575-1118
D4 Film Studios Inc/109 Highland Ave, Needham, MA	617-444-0226
Penrose Productions/4 Sandalwood Dr, Livingston, NJ	201-992-4264
Pike Productions Inc/47 Galen St, Watertown, MA	617-924-5000
September Productions Inc/171 Newbury St, Boston, MA	617-262-6090
Television Productions & Services/55 Chapel St, Newton, MA	617-965-1626
Ultra Photo Works/468 Commercial Ave, Palisades Pk, NJ	201-592-7730
Videocom Inc/502 Sprague St, Dedham, MA	617-329-4080
WGGB-TV/PO Box 3633, Springfield, MA	413-785-1911
WLNE-TV/430 County St, New Bedford, MA	617-993-2651

Southeast

Enter Space/20 14th St NW, Atlanta, GA	404-885-1139
The Great Southern Stage/15221 NE 21st Ave, North Miami Beach, FL	305-947-0430
Williamson Photography Inc/9511 Colonial Dr, Miami, FL	305-255-6400

Midwest

Emerich Style & Design/PO Box 14523, Chicago, IL	312-871-4659
Gard, Ron/2600 N Racine, Chicago, IL	312-975-6523
Hanes, Jim/1930 N Orchard, Chicago, IL	312-944-6554
Lewis, Tom/2511 Brumley Dr, Flossmoor, IL	312-799-1156
The Production Center/151 Victor Ave, Highland Park, MI	313-868-6600
Rainey, Pat/4031 N Hamlin Ave, Chicago, IL	312-463-0281
Sosin, Bill/415 W Superior St, Chicago, IL	312-751-0974
Stratford Studios Inc/2857 E Grand Blvd, Detroit, MI	313-875-6617
Zawaki, Andy & Jake/1830 W Cermak, Chicago, IL	312-422-1546

Southwest

AIE Studios/3905 Braxton, Houston, TX	713-781-2110
Arizona Cine Equipment/2125 E 20th St, Tucson, AZ	602-623-8268
Hayes Productions Inc/710 S Bowie, San Antonio, TX	512-224-9565
MFC Film Productions Inc/5915 Star Ln, Houston, TX	713-781-7703
Pearlman Productions Inc/2506 South Blvd, Houston, TX	713-523-3601
Stokes, Bill Assoc/5642 Dyer, Dallas, TX	214-363-0161
Tecfilms Inc/2856 Fort Worth Ave, Dallas, TX	214-339-2217

West Coast

Blakeman, Bob Studios/710 S Santa Fe, Los Angeles, CA	213-624-6662
Carthay Studio/5907 W Pico Blvd, Los Angeles, CA	213-938-2101
Chris-Craft Video Tape/915 N LaBrea, Los Angeles, CA	213-850-2236
Cine-Rent West Inc/991 Tennessee St, San Francisco, CA	415-864-4644
Cine-Video/948 N Cahuenga Blvd, Los Angeles, CA	213-464-6200
Columbia Pictures/Columbia Plaza, Burbank, CA	818-954-6000
Design Arts Studios/1128 N Las Palmas, Hollywood, CA	213-464-9118
Disney, Walt Productions/500 S Buena Vista St, Burbank, CA	818-840-1000
Dominick/833 N LaBrea Ave, Los Angeles, CA	213-934-3033
Eliot, Josh Studio/706 W Pico Blvd, Los Angeles, CA	213-742-0367
Goldwyn, Samuel Studios/1041 N Formosa Ave, Los Angeles, CA	213-650-2500
Great American Cinema Co/10711 Wellworth Ave, Los Angeles, CA	213-475-0937
Hill, Dennis Studio/20 N Raymond Ave #14, Pasadena, CA	818-795-2589
Hollywood National Studios/6605 Eleanor Ave, Hollywood, CA	213-467-6272
Hollywood Stage/6650 Santa Monica Blvd, Los Angeles, CA	213-466-4393
Kelley, Tom Studios/8525 Santa Monica Blvd, Los Angeles, CA	213-657-1780
Kings Point Corporation/9336 W Washington, Culver City, CA	213-836-5537
Lewin, Elyse/820 N Fairfax Ave, Los Angeles, CA	213-655-4214
Liles, Harry Productions Inc/1060 N Lillian Way, Los Angeles, CA	213-466-1612
MGM Studios/10202 W Washington, Culver City, CA	213-836-3000
MPI Studios/1714 N Wilton Pl, Los Angeles, CA	213-462-6342
Norwood, David/4040 Del Rey Ave #7, Marina Del Rey, CA	213-827-2020
Paramount/5555 Melrose, Los Angeles, CA	213-468-5000
Raleigh Studio/650 N Bronson Ave, Los Angeles, CA	213-466-7778
Solaris T V Studios/2525 Ocean Park Blvd, Santa Monica, CA	213-450-6227
Studio AV/1227 First Ave S, Seattle, WA	206-223-1007
Studio Center CBS/4024 Radford Ave, Studio City, CA	818-760-5000
Studio Resources/1915 University Ave, Palo Alto, CA	415-321-8763
Sunset/Gower Studio/1438 N Gower, Los Angeles, CA	213-467-1001
Superstage/5724 Santa Monica Blvd, Los Angeles, CA	213-464-0296
Team Production Co Inc/4133 Lankershim Blvd, North Hollywood, CA	818-506-5700
Television Center Studios/846 N Cahuenga Blvd, Los Angeles, CA	213-462-5111
Trans-American Video/1541 Vine St, Los Angeles, CA	213-466-2141
Twentieth Century Fox/10201 W Pico Blvd, Los Angeles, CA	213-277-2211
Universal City Studios/Universal Studios, Universal City, CA	213-985-4321
UPA Pictures/4440 Lakeside Dr, Burbank, CA	213-842-7171
The Videography Studios/8471 Universal Plaza, Universal City, CA	213-204-2000
Vine Street Video Center/1224 Vine St, Pasadena, CA	213-462-1099
Warner Brothers/4000 Warner Blvd, Burbank, CA	213-843-6000
Wolin/Semple Studio/520 N Western Ave, Los Angeles, CA	213-463-2109

Animators

New York City

Abacus Productions Inc/475 Fifth Ave	212-532-6677
ALZ Productions/11 Waverly Pl	212-473-7620
Ani-Live Film Service Inc/45 W 45th St	212-819-0700
Animated Productions Inc/1600 Broadway	212-265-2942
Animation Camera Workshop/49 W 24th St	212-807-6450
Animation Center Inc/15 W 46th St	212-869-0123
Animation Services Inc/221 W 57th St 11th Fl	212-333-5656
Animation Service Center/293 W 4th St	212-924-3937
Animex Inc/1540 Broadway	212-575-9494
Animus Films/15 W 44th St	212-391-8716
A P A/230 W 10th St	212-929-9436
Avekta Productions Inc/164 Madison Ave	212-686-4550
Backle, RJ Prod/321 W 44th St	212-582-8270
Bakst, Edward/160 W 96th St	212-666-2579
Beckerman, Howard/45 W 45th St #300	212-869-0595
Blechman, R O/2 W 47th St	212-869-1630
Broadcast Arts Inc/632 Broadway	212-254-5910
Cel-Art Productions Inc/20 E 49th St	212-751-7515
Charisma Communications/32 E 57th St	212-832-3020

Please send us your additions and updates.

Charlex Inc/2 W 45th St	212-719-4600
Cinema Concepts/321 W 44th St	212-541-9220
Clark, Ian/229 E 96th St	212-289-0998
Computer Graphics Lab/405 Lexington Ave	212-557-5130
D & R Productions Inc/6 E 39th St	212-532-5303
Dale Cameragraphics Inc/12 W 27th St	212-696-9440
Darino Films/222 Park Ave S	212-228-4024
DaSilva, Raul/137 E 38th St	212-696-1657
Devlin Productions Inc/150 W 55th St	212-582-5572
Diamond & Diaferia/12 E 44th St	212-986-8500
Digital Effects Inc/321 W 44 St	212-581-7760
Dolphin Computer Animation/140 E 80th St	212-628-5930
Doros Animation Inc/475 Fifth Ave	212-684-5043
Elinor Bunin Productions Inc/30 E 60th St	212-688-0759
Fandango Productions Inc/15 W 38th St	212-382-1813
The Fantastic Animation Machine/12 E 46th St	212-697-2525
Feigenbaum Productions Inc/25 W 43rd St # 220	212-840-3744
Film Opticals/144 E 44th St	212-697-4744
Film Planning Assoc/38 E 20th	212-260-7140
Friedman, Harold Consortium/420 Lexington Ave	212-697-0858
Gati, John/881 Seventh Ave #832	212-582-9060
Granato Animation Photography/15 W 46th St	212-869-3231
Graphic Motion Group Ltd/16 W 46th St	212-354-4343
Greenberg, R Assoc/240 Madison Ave	212-689-7886
Grossman, Robert/19 Crosby St	212-925-1965
High-Res Solutions Inc/10 Park Ave #3E	212-684-1397
Howard Graphics/36 W 25th St	212-929-2121
I F Studios/15 W 38th St	212-697-6805
ICON Communications/717 Lexington Ave	212-688-5155
Image Factory Inc/18 E 53rd St	212-759-9363
International Production Center/514 W 57th St	212-582-6530
J C Productions/16 W 46th St	212-575-9611
Kim & Gifford Productions Inc/548 E 87th St	212-986-2826
Kimmelman, Phil & Assoc Inc/50 W 40th St	212-944-7766
Kurtz & Friends/130 E 18th St	212-777-3258
Leo Animation Camera Service/25 W 43rd St	212-997-1840
Lieberman, Jerry/76 Laight St	212-431-3452
Locomo Productions/875 West End Ave	212-222-4833
Marz Productions Inc/118 E 25th St	212-477-3900
Metropolis Graphics/28 E 4th St	212-677-0630
Motion Picker Studio/416 Ocean Ave	718-856-2763
Murphy, Neil/208 W 23rd St	212-691-5730
Musicvision, Inc/185 E 85th St	212-860-4420
New York Siggraph/451 W 54th St	212-582-9223
Omnibus Computer Gaphics/508 W 57th St	212-975-9050
Ovation Films/49 W 24th St	212-675-4700
Paganelli, Albert/21 W 46th St	212-719-4105
Perpetual Animation/17 W 45th St	212-840-2888
Polestar Films & Assoc Arts/870 Seventh Ave	212-586-6333
Rankin/Bass Productions/1 E 53rd St	212-759-7721
Rembrandt Films/59 E 54th St	212-758-1024
Robinson, Keith Prod Inc/200 E 21st St	212-533-9078
Seeger, Hal/45 W 45th St	212-575-8900
Shadow Light Prod, Inc/12 W 27th St 7th Fl	212-689-7511
Singer, Rebecca Studio Inc/111 W 57th St	212-944-0466
Stanart Studios/1650 Broadway	212-586-0445
Stark, Philip/245 W 29th St 15th Fl	212-868-5555
Sunflower Films/15 W 46th St	212-869-0123
Telemated Motion Pictures/PO Box 176	212-475-8050
Today Video, Inc/45 W 45th St	212-391-1020
Triology Design/25 W 45th St	212-382-3592
Videart Inc/39 W 38th St	212-840-2163
Video Works/24 W 40th St	212-869-2500
Weiss, Frank Studio/66 E 7th St	212-477-1032
World Effects Inc/20 E 46th St	212-687-7070
Zanders Animation Parlour/18 E 41st St	212-725-1331

Northeast

The Animators/247 Ft Pitt Blvd, Pittsburgh, PA	412-391-2550
Aviation Simulations International Inc/Box 358, Huntington, NY	516-271-6476

Comm Corps Inc/711 4th St NW, Washington, DC	202-638-6550
Consolidated Visual Center/2529 Kenilworth Ave, Tuxedo, MD	301-772-7300
Felix, Luisa/180 12th St, Jersey City, NJ	201-653-1500
Hughes, Gary Inc/PO Box, Cabin John, MD	301-229-1100
Penpoint Prod Svc/331 Newbury St, Boston, MA	617-266-1331
Pilgrim Film Service/2504 50th Ave, Hyattsville, MD	301-773-7072
Symmetry T/A/13813 Willoughby Road, Upper Marlboro, MD	301-627-5050
Synthavision-Magi/3 Westchester Plaza, Elmsford, NY	212-733-1300
West End Film Inc/2121 Newport Pl NW, Washington, DC	202-331-8078

Southeast

Bajus-Jones Film Corp/401 W Peachtree St #1720, Atlanta, GA	404-221-0700
Cinetron Computer Systems Inc/6700 IH 85 North, Norcross, GA	404-448-9463

Midwest

AGS & R Studios/425 N Michigan Ave, Chicago, IL	312-836-4500
Associated Audio-Visual Corp/2821 Central St, Evanston, IL	312-866-6780
Bajus-Jones Film Corp/203 N Wabash, Chicago, IL	312-332-6041
The Beach Productions Ltd/1960 N Seminary, Chicago, IL	312-281-4500
Boyer Studio/1324 Greenleaf, Evanston, IL	312-491-6363
Coast Prod/505 N Lake Shore Dr, Chicago, IL	312-222-1857
Filmack Studios Inc/1327 S Wabash, Chicago, IL	312-427-3395
Freese & Friends Inc/1429 N Wells, Chicago, IL	312-642-4475
Goldsholl Assoc/420 Frontage Rd, Northfield, IL	312-446-8300
Goodrich Animation/405 N Wabash, Chicago, IL	312-329-1344
Kayem Animation Services/100 E Ohio, Chicago, IL	312-664-7733
Kinetics/444 N Wabash, Chicago, IL	312-644-2767
Optimation Inc/9055 N 51st St, Brown Deer, WI	414-355-4500
Pilot Prod/1819 Ridge Ave, Evanston, IL	312-328-3700
Quicksilver Assoc Inc/16 W Ontario, Chicago, IL	312-943-7622
Ritter Waxberg & Assoc/200 E Ontario, Chicago, IL	312-664-3934
Simott & Associates/676 N La Salle, Chicago, IL	312-440-1875

Southwest

Graphic Art Studio/5550 S Lewis Ave, Tulsa, OK	918-743-3915
Media Visions Inc/2716 Bissonnet #408, Houston, TX	713-521-0626

Rocky Mountain

Phillips, Stan & Assoc/865 Delaware, Denver, CO	303-595-9911

West Coast

Abel, Bob & Assoc/953 N Highland Ave, Los Angeles, CA	213-462-8100
Animation Filmakers Corp/7000 Romaine St, Hollywood, CA	213-851-5526
Animedia Productions Inc/10200 Riverside Dr, North Hollywood, CA	213-851-4777
Bass, Saul/Herb Yeager/7039 Sunset Blvd, Hollywood, CA	213-466-9701
Bosustow Entertainment/1649 11th St, Santa Monica, CA	213-394-0218
Cinema Research Corp/6860 Lexington Ave, Hollywood, CA	213-461-3235
Clampett, Bob Prod/729 Seward St, Hollywood, CA	213-466-0264
Cornerstone Productions/5915 Cantelope Ave, Van Nuys, CA	213-994-0007
Court Productions/1030 N Cole, Hollywood, CA	213-467-5900
Craig, Fred Productions/932 S Pine, San Gabriel, CA	213-287-6479
Creative Film Arts/7026 Santa Monica Blvd, Hollywood, CA	213-466-5111
DePatie-Freleng Enterprises/16400 Ventura Blvd #312, Encino, CA	818-906-3375
Duck Soup Productions Inc/1026 Montana Ave, Santa Monica, CA	213-451-0771
Energy Productions/846 N Cahuenga Blvd, Los Angeles, CA	213-462-3310
Excelsior Animated Moving Pictures/749 N LaBrea, Hollywood, CA	213-938-2335
Filmcore/849 N Seward, Hollywood, CA	213-464-7303
Filmfair/10900 Ventura Blvd, Studio City, CA	213-877-3191
Gallerie International Films Ltd/11320 W Magnolia Blvd, Hollywood, CA	213-760-2040

Production/Support Services

Continued

Please send us your additions and updates

Hanna-Barbera/3400 W Cahuenga, Hollywood, CA	213-466-1371
Jacques, Jean-Guy & Assoc/633 N LaBrea Ave, Hollywood, CA	213-936-7177
Kurtz & Friends/2312 W Olive Ave, Burbank, CA	213-461-8188
Littlejohn, William Prod Inc/23425 Malibu Colony Dr, Malibu, CA	213-456-8620
Lumeni Productions/1727 N Ivar, Hollywood, CA	213-462-2110
Marks Communication/5550 Wilshire Blvd, Los Angeles, CA	213-464-6302
Melendez, Bill Prod Inc/439 N Larchmont Blvd, Los Angeles, CA	213-463-4101
Murakami Wolf Swenson Films Inc/1463 Tamarind Ave, Hollywood, CA	213-462-6474
New Hollywood Inc/1302 N Cahuenga Blvd, Hollywood, CA	213-466-3686
Pantomime Pictures Inc/12144 Riverside Dr, North Hollywood, CA	818-980-5555
Pegboard Productions/1310 N Cahuenga Blvd, Hollywood, CA	818-353-4991
Quartet Films Inc/5631 Hollywood Blvd, Hollywood, CA	213-464-9225
R & B EFX/1802 Victory Blvd, Glendale, CA	818-956-8406
Raintree Productions Ltd/666 N Robertson Blvd, Hollywood, CA	213-652-8330
S & A Graphics/3350 Barham Blvd, Los Angeles, CA	213-874-2301
Spungbuggy Works Inc/8506 Sunset Blvd, Hollywood, CA	213-657-8070
Sullivan & Associates/3377 Barham Blvd, Los Angeles, CA	213-874-2301
Sunwest Productions Inc/1021 N McCadden Pl, Hollywood, CA	213-461-2957
Title House/738 Cahuenga Blvd, Los Angeles, CA	213-469-8171
Triplane Film & Graphics Inc/328 1/2 N Sycamore Ave, Los Angeles, CA	213-937-1320
U P A Pictures Inc/875 Century Park East, Los Angeles, CA	213-556-3800
Williams, Richard Animation/5631 Hollywood Blvd, Los Angeles, CA	213-461-4344

Models & Talent

New York City

Abrams Artists/420 Madison Ave	212-935-8980
Act 48 Mgt Inc/1501 Broadway #1713	212-354-4250
Adams, Bret/448 W 44th St	212-246-0428
Agency for Performing Arts/888 Seventh Ave	212-582-1500
Agents for the Arts/1650 Broadway	212-247-3220
Alexander, Willard/660 Madison Ave	212-751-7070
Amato, Michael Theatrical Entrps/1650 Broadway	212-247-4456
Ambrose Co/1466 Broadway	212-921-0230
American Intl Talent/166 W 125th St	212-663-4626
American Talent Inc/888 Seventh Ave	212-977-2300
Anderson, Beverly/1472 Broadway	212-944-7773
Associated Booking/1995 Broadway	212-874-2400
Associated Talent Agency/41 E 11th St	212-674-4242
Astor, Richard/1697 Broadway	212-581-1970
Avantege Model Management/205 E 42nd St #1303	212-687-9890
Baldwin Scully Inc/501 Fifth Ave	212-922-1330
Barbizon Agency/3 E 54th St	212-371-3617
Barbizon Agency of Rego Park/95-20 63rd	718-275-2100
Barry Agency/165 W 46th St	212-869-9310
Bauman & Hiller/250 W 57th St	212-757-0098
Beilin, Peter/230 Park Ave	212-949-9119
Big Beauties Unlimited/159 Madison Ave	212-685-1270
Bloom, J Michael/400 Madison Ave	212-832-6900
Brifit Models/236 E 46th St 4th Fl	212-949-6262
Buchwald, Don & Assoc Inc/10 E 44th St	212-867-1070
Cataldi, Richard Agency/180 Seventh Ave	212-741-7450
Celebrity Lookalikes/235 E 31st St	212-532-7676
Click Model Management/881 Seventh Ave #1013	212-245-4306
Coleman-Rosenberg/667 Madison Ave	212-838-0734
Columbia Artists/165 W 57th St	212-397-6900
Cunningham, W D/919 Third Ave	212-832-2700
Deacy, Jane Inc/300 E 75th St	212-752-4865
DeVore, Ophelia/1697 Broadway	212-586-2144

Diamond Artists/119 W 57th St	212-247-3025
DMI Talent Assoc/250 W 57th St	212-246-4650
Dolan, Gloria Management Ltd/850 Seventh Ave	212-696-1850
Draper, Stephen Agency/37 W 57th St	212-421-5780
Eisen, Dulcina Assoc/154 E 61st St	212-355-6617
Elite Model Management Corp/150 E 58th St	212-935-4500
Faces Model Management/567 Third Ave	212-661-1515
Fields, Marje/165 W 46th St	212-764-5740
Ford Models Inc/344 E 59th St	212-753-6500
Foster Fell Agency/26 W 38th St	212-944-8520
Funny Face/440 E 62nd St	212-752-6090
Gage Group Inc/1650 Broadway	212-541-5250
Greco, Maria & Assoc/888 Eighth Ave	212-757-0681
Hadley, Peggy Ent/250 W 57th St	212-246-2166
Harth, Ellen Inc/149 Madison Ave	212-686-5600
Hartig, Michael Agency Ltd/114 E 28th St	212-684-0010
Henderson-Hogan/200 W 57th St	212-765-5190
Henry, June/175 Fifth Ave	212-475-5130
Hesseltine Baker Assocs/165 W 46th St	212-921-4460
Hunt, Diana Management/44 W 44th St	212-391-4971
Hutto Management Inc/405 W 23rd St	212-807-1234
HV Models/305 Madison Ave	212-751-3005
International Model Agency/232 Madison Ave	212-686-9053
International Creative Management/40 W 57th St	212-556-5600
International Legends/40 E 34th St	212-684-4600
Jacobsen-Wilder Inc/419 Park Ave So	212-686-6100
Jan J Agency/224 E 46th St	212-490-1875
Jordan, Joe Talent Agency/200 W 57th St	212-582-9003
Kahn, Jerry Inc/853 Seventh Ave	212-245-7317
Kay Models/328 E 61st St	212-308-9560
Kennedy Artists/237 W 11th St	212-675-3944
Kid, Bonnie Agency/25 W 36th St	212-563-2141
King, Archer/1440 Broadway	212-764-3905
Kirk, Roseanne/161 W 54th St	212-888-6711
KMA Associates/303 W 42nd St #606	212-581-4610
Kolmar-Luth Entertainment Inc/1501 Broadway #201	212-730-9500
Kroll, Lucy/390 West End Ave	212-877-0556
L B H Assoc/1 Lincoln Plaza	212-787-2609
L'Image Model Management Inc/114 E 32nd St	212-725-2424
The Lantz Office/888 Seventh Ave	212-586-0200
Larner, Lionel Ltd/850 Seventh Ave	212-246-3105
Leach, Dennis/160 Fifth Ave	212-691-3450
Leaverton, Gary Inc/1650 Broadway	212-541-9640
Leigh, Sanford Entrprs Ltd/440 E 62nd St	212-752-4450
Leighton, Jan/205 W 57th St	212-757-5242
Lenny, Jack Assoc/140 W 58th St #1B	212-582-0270
Lewis, Lester Assoc/110 W 40th St	212-921-8370
M E W Company/370 Lexington Ave	212-889-7272
Mannequin Fashion Models Inc/40 E 34th St	212-684-5432
Martinelli Attractions/888 Eighth Ave	212-586-0963
Matama Talent & Models/30 W 90th St	212-580-2236
McDearmon, Harold/45 W 139th St	212-283-1005
McDermott, Marge/216 E 39th St	212-889-1583
McDonald/ Richards/235 Park Ave S	212-475-5401
MMG Ent/Marcia's Kids/250 W 57th St	212-246-4360
Models Models Inc/37 E 28th St #506	212-889-8233
Models Service Agency/1457 Broadway	212-944-8896
Models Talent Int'l/1140 Broadway	212-684-3343
Morris, William Agency/1350 Sixth Ave	212-586-5100
New York Production Studio/250 W 57th St	212-765-3433
Nolan, Philip/184 Fifth Ave	212-243-8900
Oppenheim-Christie/565 Fifth Ave	212-661-4330
Oscard, Fifi/19 W 44th St #1500	212-764-1100
Ostertag, Barna Agency/501 Fifth Ave	212-697-6339
Our Agency/19 W 34th St #700	212-736-9582
Packwood, Harry Talent Ltd/250 W 57th St	212-586-8900
Palmer, Dorothy/250 W 57th St	212-765-4280
Perkins Models/1697 Broadway	212-582-9511
Petite Model Management/123 E 54th St #9A	212-759-9304
Pfeffer & Roelfs Inc/850 Seventh Ave	212-315-2230
Plus Models/49 W 37th St	212-997-1785
PlusModel Model Management Ltd/49 W 37th St	212-997-1785

Production/Support Services

Continued

Please send us your additions and updates.

Powers, James Inc/12 E 41st St	212-686-9066
Prelly People & Co/296 Fifth Ave	212-714-2060
Premier Talent Assoc/3 E 54th St	212-758-4900
Prestige Models/80 W 40th St	212-382-1700
Rogers, Wallace Inc/160 E 56th St	212-755-1464
Roos, Gilla Ltd/555 Madison Ave	212-758-5480
Rubenstein, Bernard/215 Park Ave So	212-460-9800
Ryan, Charles Agency/200 W 57th St	212-245-2225
Sanders, Honey Agency Ltd/229 W 42nd St	212-947-5555
Schuller, William Agency/1276 Fifth Ave	212-532-6005
Silver, Monty Agency/200 W 57th St	212-765-4040
Smith, Friedman/850 Seventh Ave	212-581-4490
The Starkman Agency/1501 Broadway	212-921-9191
Stars/360 E 65th St #17H	212-988-1400
STE Representation/888 Seventh Ave	212-246-1030
Stein, Lillian/1501 Broadway	212-840-8299
Stewart Artists Corp/215 E 81st St	212-249-5540
Stroud Management/119 W 57th St	212-688-0226
Summa/38 W 32nd St	212-947-6155
Szold Models/644 Broadway	212-777-4998
Talent Reps Inc/20 E 53rd St	212-752-1835
Tatinas Models & Fitters Assoc/1328 Broadway	212-947-5797
Theater Now Inc/1515 Broadway	212-840-4400
Thomas, Michael Agency/305 Madison #4419	212-867-0303
Total Look/404 Riverside Dr	212-662-1029
Tranum Robertson Hughes Inc/2 Dag Hammarskjold Plaza	212-371-7500
Triad Artists/888 Seventh Ave	212-489-8100
Troy, Gloria/1790 Broadway	212-582-0260
Universal Attractions/218 W 57th St	212-582-7575
Universal Talent/505 5th Ave	212-661-3896
Van Der Veer People Inc/225 E 59th St #A	212-688-2880
Waters, Bob Agency/510 Madison Ave	212-593-0543
Wilhelmina Models/9 E 37th St	212-532-6800
Witt, Peter Assoc Inc/215 E 79th St	212-861-3120
Wright, Ann Assoc/136 E 57th St	212-832-0110
Zoli/146 E 56th St	212-758-5959

Northeast

Cameo Models/392 Boylston St, Boston, MA	617-536-6004
Carnegie Talent Agency/300 Northern Blvd, Great Neck, NY	516-487-2260
Conover, Joyce Agency/33 Gallowae, Westfield, NJ	201-232-0908
Copley 7 Models & Talent/29 Newbury St, Boston, MA	617-267-4444
The Ford Model Shop/176 Newbury St, Boston, MA	617-266-6939
Hart Model Agency/137 Newbury St, Boston, MA	617-262-1740
Johnston Model Agency/32 Field Point Rd, Greenwich, CT	203-622-1137
National Talent Assoc/40 Railroad Ave, Valley Stream, NY	516-825-8707
Rocco, Joseph Agency/Public Ledger Bldg, Philadelphia, PA	215-923-8790
Somers, Jo/29 Newbury St, Boston, MA	617-267-4444
Trone, Larry/19-A Dean St, New Castle, DE	302-328-8399

Southeast

Act 1 Casting Agency/1460 Brickell Ave, Miami, FL	305-371-1371
The Agency South/1501 Sunset Dr, Coral Gables, FL	305-667-6746
Amaro Agency/1617 Smith St, Orange Park, FL	904-264-0771
Artists Representatives of New Orleans/1012 Philip, New Orleans, LA	504-524-4683
Atlanta Models & Talent Inc/3030 Peachtree Rd NW, Atlanta, GA	404-261-9627
Birmingham Models & Talent/1023 20th St, Birmingham, AL	205-252-8533
Brown, Bob Marionettes/1415 S Queen St, Arlington, VA	703-920-1040
Brown, Jay Theatrical Agency Inc/221 W Waters Ave, Tampa, FL	813-933-2456
Bruce Enterprises/1022 16th Ave S, Nashville, TN	615-255-5711
Burns, Dot Model & Talent Agcy/478 Severn St, Tampa, FL	813-251-5882
Byrd, Russ Assoc/9450 Koger Blvd, St Petersburg, FL	813-586-1504
Carolina Talent/1347 Harding Pl, Charlotte, NC	704-332-3218
Cassandra Models Agency/635 N Hyer St, Orlando, FL	305-423-7872
The Casting Directors Inc/1524 NE 147th St, North Miami, FL	305-944-8559
Central Casting of FL/PO Box 7154, Ft Lauderdale, FL	305-379-7526
Chez Agency/922 W Peachtree St, Atlanta, GA	404-873-1215

Dassinger, Peter International Modeling/1018 Royal, New Orleans, LA	504-525-8382
A del Corral Model & Talent Agency/5830 Argonne Blvd, New Orleans, LA	504-482-8963
Directions Talent Agency/400-C State St Station, Greensboro, NC	919-373-0955
Dodd, Barbara Studios/3508 Central Ave, Nashville, TN	615-385-0740
Faces, Ltd/2915 Frankfort Ave, Louisville, KY	502-893-8840
Falcon, Travis Modeling Agency/17070 Collins Ave, Miami, FL	305-947-7957
Flair Models/PO Box 373, Nashville, TN	615-361-3737
Florida Talent Agency/2631 E Oakland Pk, Ft Lauderdale, FL	305-565-3552
House of Talent of Cain & Sons/996 Lindridge Dr NE, Atlanta, GA	404-261-5543
Irene Marie Models/3212 S Federal Hwy, Ft Lauderdale, FL	305-522-3262
Jo-Susan Modeling & Finishing School/3415 West End Ave, Nashville, TN	615-383-5850
Lewis, Millie Modeling School/10 Calendar Ct #A, Forest Acres, SC	803-782-7338
Lewis, Millie Modeling School/880 S Pleasantburg Dr, Greenville, SC	803-271-4402
Mar Bea Talent Agency/923 Crandon Blvd, Key Biscayne, FL	305-361-1144
Marilyns Modeling Agency/3800 W Wendover, Greensboro, NC	919-292-5950
McQuerter, James/4518 S Cortez, Tampa, FL	813-839-8335
Parker, Sarah/425 S Olive Ave, West Palm Beach, FL	305-659-2833
Polan, Marian Talent Agency/PO Box 7154, Ft Lauderdale, FL	305-525-8351
Pommier, Michele/7520 Red Rd, Miami, FL	305-667-8710
Powers, John Robert School/828 SE 4th St, Fort Lauderdale, FL	305-467-2838
Professional Models Guild & Workshop/210 Providence Rd, Charlotte, NC	704-377-9299
Remington Models & Talent/2480 E Commercial Blvd PH, Ft Lauderdale, FL	305-944-6608
Rose, Sheila/8218 NW 8th St, Plantation, FL	305-473-9747
Serendipity/3130 Maples Dr NE #19, Atlanta, GA	404-237-4040
Signature Talent Inc/PO Box 221086, Charlotte, NC	704-542-0034
Sovereign Model & Talent/11111 Biscayne Blvd, Miami, FL	305-899-0280
Spivia, Ed/PO Box 38097, Atlanta, GA	404-292-6240
Stevens, Patricia Modeling Agency/3312 Piedmont Rd, Atlanta, GA	404-261-3330
Talent & Model Land, Inc/1501 12th Ave S, Nashville, TN	615-385-2723
Talent Enterprises Inc/3338 N Federal Way, Ft Lauderdale, FL	305-949-6099
Talent Management of VA/2940 N Lynnhaven Rd, Virginia Beach, VA	804-486-5550
The Talent Shop Inc/3210 Peachtree Rd NE, Atlanta, GA	404-261-0770
Theatrics Etcetera/PO Box 11862, Memphis, TN	901-278-7454
Thompson, Jan Agency/1708 Scott Ave, Charlotte, NC	704-377-5987
Top Billing Inc/PO Box 121089, Nashville, TN	615-327-1133
Tracey Agency Inc/PO Box 12405, Richmond, VA	804-358-4004

Midwest

A-Plus Talent Agency Corp/666 N Lakeshore Dr, Chicago, IL	312-642-8151
Advertisers Casting Service/15 Kercheval Ave, Grosse Point Farms, MI	313-881-1135
Affiliated Talent & Casting Service/28860 Southfield Rd #100, Southfield, MI	313-559-3110
Arlene Willson Agency/9205 W Center St, Milwaukee, WI	414-259-1611
Creative Casting Inc/430 Oak Grove, Minneapolis, MN	612-871-7866
David & Lee Model Management/70 W Hubbard, Chicago, IL	312-661-0500
Gem Enterprises/5100 Eden Ave, Minneapolis, MN	612-927-8000
Hamilton, Shirley Inc/620 N Michigan Ave, Chicago, IL	312-644-0300
Lee, David Models/70 W Hubbard, Chicago, IL	312-661-0500
Limelight Assoc Inc/3460 Davis Lane, Cincinnati, OH	513-631-8276
Marx, Dick & Assoc Inc/101 E Ontario St, Chicago, IL	312-440-7300
The Model Shop/415 N State St, Chicago, IL	312-822-9663
Monza Talent Agency/1001 Westport Rd, Kansas City, MO	816-931-0222
Moore, Eleanor Agency/1610 W Lake St, Minneapolis, MN	612-827-3823
National Talent Assoc/3525 Patterson Ave, Chicago, IL	312-539-8575
New Faces Models & Talent Inc/310 Groveland Ave, Minneapolis, MN	612-871-6000
Pastiche Models Inc/161 Ottawa NW #300K, Grand Rapids,	

MI	616-451-2181
Powers, John Robert/5900 Roche Dr, Columbus, OH	614-846-1047
Schucart, Norman Ent/1417 Green Bay Rd, Highland Park, IL	312-433-1113
Sharkey Career Schools Inc/1299-H Lyons Rd Governours Sq, Centerville, OH	513-434-4461
SR Talent Pool/206 S 44th St, Omaha, NE	402-553-1164
Station 12-Producers Express/1759 Woodgrove Ln, Bloomfield Hills, MI	313-855-1188
Talent & Residuals Inc/303 E Ohio St, Chicago, IL	312-943-7500
Talent Phone Productions/612 N Michagan Ave, Chicago, IL	312-664-5757
Verblen, Carol Casting Svc/2408 N Burling, Chicago, IL	312-348-0047
White House Studios/9167 Robinson, Kansas City, MO	913-341-8036

Southwest

Aaron, Vicki/2017 Butterfield, Grand Prairie, TX	214-641-8539
Accent Inc/6051 N Brookline, Oklahoma City, OK	405-843-1303
Actors Clearinghouse/501 N IH 35, Austin, TX	512-476-3412
ARCA/ Freelance Talent/PO Box 5686, Little Rock, AR	501-224-1111
Ball, Bobby Agency/808 E Osborn, Phoenix, AZ	602-264-5007
Barbizon School & Agency/1647-A W Bethany Home Rd, Phoenix, AZ	602-249-2950
Bennett, Don Agency/4630 Deepdale, Corpus Christi, TX	512-854-4871
Blair, Tanya Agency/3000 Carlisle St, Dallas, TX	214-748-8353
Creme de la Creme/5643 N Pennsylvania, Oklahoma City, OK	405-721-5316
Dawson, Kim Agency/PO Box 585060, Dallas, TX	214-638-2414
Ferguson Modeling Agency/1100 W 34th St, Little Rock, AR	501-375-3519
Flair-Career Fashion & Modeling/11200 Menaul Rd, Albuquerque, NM	505-296-5571
Fosi's Talent Agency/2777 N Campbell Ave #209, Tucson, AZ	602-795-3534
Fullerton, Jo Ann/923 W Britton Rd, Oklahoma City, OK	405-848-4839
Hall, K Agency/503 W 15th St, Austin, TX	512-476-7523
Harrison-Gers Modeling Agency/1707 Wilshire Blvd NW, Oklahoma City, OK	405-840-4515
Kyle & Mathews/5250 Gulfton #3-A, Houston, TX	
Layman, Linda Agency/3546 E 51st St, Tulsa, OK	918-744-0888
The Mad Hatter/7349 Ashcroft Rd, Houston, TX	713-995-9090
Mannequin Modeling Agency/204 E Oakview, San Antonio, TX	512-231-4540
Melancon, Joseph Studios/2934 Elm, Dallas, TX	214-742-2982
Models and Talent of Tulsa/4528 S Sheridan Rd, Tulsa, OK	918-664-5340
Models of Houston Placement Agency/7676 Woodway, Houston, TX	713-789-4973
New Faces Inc/5108-B N 7th St, Phoenix, AZ	602-279-3200
Norton Agency/3900 Lemon Ave, Dallas, TX	214-528-9960
Plaza Three Talent Agency/4343 N 16th St, Phoenix, AZ	602-264-9703
Powers, John Robert Agency/3005 S University Dr, Fort Worth, TX	817-923-7305
Shaw, Ben Modeling Studios/4801 Woodway, Houston, TX	713-850-0413
Southern Arizona Casting Co/2777 N Campbell Ave #209, Tucson, AZ	602-795-3534
Strawn, Libby/3612 Foxcroft Rd, Little Rock, AR	501-227-5874
The Texas Cowgirls Inc/4300 N Central #109C, Dallas, TX	214-696-4176
Wyse, Joy Agency/2600 Stemmons, Dallas, TX	214-638-8999

Rocky Mountain

Aspen/Vannoy Talent/PO Box 8124, Aspen, CO	303-771-7500
Colorado Springs/Vannoy Talent/223 N Wahsatch, Colorado Springs, CO	303-636-2400
Denver/ Vannoy Talent/7400 E Caley Ave, Engelwood, CO	303-771-6555
Illinois Talent/2664 S Krameria, Denver, CO	303-757-8675
Mack, Jess Agency/111 Las Vegas Blvd S, Las Vegas, NV	702-382-2193
Morris, Bobby Agency/1629 E Sahara Ave, Las Vegas, NV	702-733-7575
Universal Models/953 E Sahara, Las Vegas, NV	702-732-2499

West Coast

Adrian, William Agency/520 S Lake Ave, Pasadena, CA	213-681-5750
Anthony's , Tom Precision Driving/1231 N Harper, Hollywood, CA	213-462-2301
Artists Management Agency/2232 Fifth Ave, San Diego, CA	619-233-6655

Barbizon Modeling & Talent Agy/15477 Ventura Blvd, Sherman Oaks, CA	213-995-8238
Barbizon School of Modeling/452 Fashion Valley East, San Diego, CA	714-296-6366
Blanchard, Nina/1717 N Highland Ave, Hollywood, CA	213-462-7274
Brebner Agency/185 Berry St, San Francisco, CA	415-495-6700
Celebrity Look-Alikes/9000 Sunset Blvd #407, W Hollywood, CA	213-273-5566
Character Actors/935 NW 19th Ave, Portland, OR	503-223-1931
Commercials Unlimited/7461 Beverly Blvd, Los Angeles, CA	213-937-2220
Crosby, Mary Talent Agency/2130 Fourth Ave, San Diego, CA	714-234-7911
Cunningham, William D/261 S Robertson, Beverly Hills, CA	213-855-0200
Demeter and Reed Ltd/70 Zoe #200, San Francisco, CA	415-777-1337
Drake, Bob/3878-A Fredonia Dr, Hollywood, CA	213-851-4404
Franklin, Bob Broadcast Talent/10325 NE Hancock, Portland, OR	503-253-1655
Frazer-Nicklin Agency/4300 Stevens Creek Blvd, San Jose, CA	408-554-1055
Garrick, Dale Intern'l Agency/8831 Sunset Blvd, Los Angeles, CA	213-657-2661
Grimme Agency/207 Powell St, San Francisco, CA	415-392-9175
Hansen, Carolyn Agency/1516 6th Ave, Seattle, WA	206-622-4700
International Creative Management/8899 Beverly Blvd, Los Angeles, CA	213-550-4000
Kelman, Toni Agency/8961 Sunset Blvd, Los Angeles, CA	213-851-8822
L'Agence Models/100 N Winchester Blvd #370, San Jose, CA	408-985-2993
Leonetti, Ltd/6526 Sunset Blvd, Los Angeles, CA	213-462-2345
Liebes School of Modeling Inc/45 Willow Lane, Sausalito, CA	415-331-5383
Longenecker, Robert Agency/11500 Olympic Blvd, Los Angeles, CA	213-477-0039
Media Talent Center/4315 NE Tillamook, Portland, OR	503-281-2020
Model Management Inc/1400 Castro St, San Francisco, CA	415-282-8855
Neuman, Allan/825 W 16th St, Newport Beach, CA	714-548-8800
Pacific Artists, Ltd/515 N La Cienaga, Los Angeles, CA	213-657-5990
Playboy Model Agency/8560 Sunset Blvd, Los Angeles, CA	213-659-4080
Powers, John Robert/1610 6th Ave, Seattle, WA	206-624-2495
Remington Models & Talent/924 Westwood Blvd #545, Los Angeles, CA	213-552-3012
Schwartz, Don Agency/8721 Sunset Blvd, Los Angeles, CA	213-657-8910
Seattle Models Guild/1610 6th Ave, Seattle, WA	206-622-1406
Shaw, Glen Agency/3330 Barham Blvd, Los Angeles, CA	213-851-6262
Smith, Ron's Celebrity Look-Alikes/9000 Sunset Blvd, Hollywood, CA	213-273-5566
Sohbi's Talent Agency/1750 Kalakaua Ave #116, Honolulu, HI	808-946-6614
Stern, Charles Agency/9220 Sunset Blvd, Los Angeles, CA	213-273-6890
Studio Seven/261 E Rowland Ave, Covina, CA	213-331-6351
Stunts Unlimited/3518 Cahuenga Blvd W, Los Angeles, CA	213-874-0050
Tanner, Herb & Assoc/6640 W Sunset Blvd, Los Angeles, CA	213-466-6191
TOPS Talent Agency/404 Piikoi St, Honolulu, HI	808-537-6647
Wormser Heldford & Joseph/1717 N Highland #414, Los Angeles, CA	213-466-9111

Casting

New York City

BCI Casting/1500 Broadway	212-221-1583
Brinker, Jane/51 W 16th St	212-924-3322
Brown, Deborah Casting/250 W 57th St	212-581-0404
Burton, Kate/271 Madison Ave	212-243-6114
C & C Productions/445 E 80th St	212-472-3700
Carter, Kit & Assoc/160 W 95th St	212-864-3147
Cast Away Casting Service/14 Sutton Pl S	212-755-0960
Central Casting Corp of NY/200 W 54th St	212-582-4933
Cereghetti Casting/119 W 57th St	212-307-6081
Claire Casting/118 E 28th St	212-889-8844
Complete Casting/240 W 44th St	212-382-3835
Contemporary Casting Ltd/41 E 57th St	212-838-1818
Davidson/Frank Photo-Stylists/209 W 86th St #701	212-799-2651

Production/Support Services

Continued

Please send us your additions and updates.

Deron, Johnny/30-63 32nd St	718-728-5326
DeSeta, Donna Casting/424 W 33rd St	212-239-0988
Digiaimo, Lou/513 W 54th St	212-713-1884
Fay, Sylvia/71 Park Ave	212-889-2626
Feuer & Ritzer Casting Assoc/1650 Broadway	212-765-5580
Greco, Maria Casting/1261 Broadway	212-213-5500
Herman & Lipson Casting, Inc/114 E 25th St	212-777-7070
Howard, Stewart Assoc/215 Park Ave So	212-477-2323
Hughes/Moss Assoc/311 W 42nd St	212-307-6690
Iredale/ Burton Ltd/271 Madison Ave	212-889-7722
Jacobs, Judith/336 E 81st St	212-744-3758
Johnson/Liff/1501 Broadway	212-391-2680
Kressel, Lynn Casting/111 W 57th St	212-581-6990
L 2 Casting, Inc/4 W 83rd St	212-496-9444
McCorkle Casting Ltd/264 W 40th St	212-840-0992
Navarro-Bertoni Casting Ltd/25 Central Park West	212-765-4251
Reed/Sweeney/Reed Inc/1780 Broadway	212-265-8541
Reiner, Mark Contemporary Casting/16 W 46th St	212-838-1818
Schneider Studio/119 W 57th St	212-265-1223
Shapiro, Barbara Casting/111 W 57th St	212-582-8228
Shulman/Pasciuto, Inc/1457 Broadway #308	212-944-6420
Silver, Stan/108 E 16th St	212-477-5900
Todd, Joy/2 W 32nd St	212-239-4469
Weber, Joy Casting/250 W 57th St #1925	212-245-5220
Wollin, Marji/233 E 69th St	212-472-2528
Woodman, Elizabeth Roberts/222 E 44th St	212-972-1900

Northeast

Baker, Ann Casting/6 Wheeler Rd, Newton, MA	617-964-3038
Booking Agent Lic/860 Floral Ave, Union, NJ	201-353-1595
Central Casting/623 Pennsylvania Ave SE, Washington, DC	202-547-6300
Dilworth, Francis/496 Kinderkamack Rd, Oradell, NJ	201-265-4020
Holt/Belajac & Assoc Inc/The Bigelow #1924, Pittsburgh, PA	412-391-1005
Lawrence, Joanna Agency/82 Patrick Rd, Westport, CT	203-226-7239
Panache/3214 N St NW, Washington, DC	202-333-4240

Southeast

Central Casting/PO Box 7154, Ft Lauderdale, FL	305-379-7526
DiPrima, Barbara Casting/2951 So Bayshore Dr, Coconut Grove, FL	305-445-7630
Elite Artists, Inc/785 Crossover, Memphis, TN	901-761-1046
Manning, Maureen/1283 Cedar Hts Dr, Stone Mt, GA	404-296-1520
Taylor Royal Casting/2308 South Rd, Baltimore, MD	301-466-5959

Midwest

Station 12 Producers Express Inc/1759 Woodgrove Ln, Bloomfield Hills, MI	313-855-1188

Southwest

Abramson, Shirley/321 Valley Cove, Garland, TX	214-272-3400
Austin Actors Clearinghouse/501 North 1H 35, Austin, TX	512-476-3412
Blair, Tanya Agency/Artists Managers/3000 Carlisle #101, Dallas, TX	214-748-8353
Chason, Gary & Assoc/5645 Hillcroft St, Houston, TX	713-789-4003
Greer, Lucy & Assoc Casting/600 Shadywood Ln, Richardson, TX	214-231-2086
Jr Black Acad of Arts & Letters/723 S Peak St, Dallas, Tx	214-526-1237
KD Studio/2600 Stemons #147, Dallas, TX	214-638-0484
Kegley, Liz/Shari Rhodes/2021 Southgate, Houston, TX	713-522-5066
Kegley, Liz/Shari Rhodes/5737 Everglade, Dallas, TX	214-475-2353
Kent, Rody/5338 Vanderbilt Ave, Dallas, TX	214-827-3418
New Visions/Box 14 Whipple Station, Prescott, AZ	602-445-3382
Schermerhorn, Jo Ann/PO Box 2672, Conroe, TX	409-273-2569

Rocky Mountain

Aspen/Vannoy Talent/PO Box 8124, Aspen, CO	303-771-7500
Colorado Springs/Vannoy Talent/223 N Wahsatch, Colorado Springs, CO	303-636-2400
Denver/ Vannoy Talent/7400 E Caley Ave, Engelwood, CO	303-771-6555

West Coast

Abrams-Rubaloff & Associates/9012 Beverly Blvd, Los Angeles, CA	213-273-5711
Associated Talent International/9744 Wilshire Blvd, Los Angeles, CA	213-271-4662
BCI Casting/5134 Valley, Los Angeles, CA	213-222-0366
C H N International/7428 Santa Monica Blvd, Los Angeles, CA	213-874-8252
Celebrity Look-Alikes/9000 Sunset Blvd #407, West Hollywood, CA	213-273-5566
Commercials Unlimited/7461 Beverly Blvd, Los Angeles, CA	213-937-2220
Creative Artists Agency Inc/1888 Century Park E, Los Angeles, CA	213-277-4545
Cunningham, William & Assocs/261 S Robertson Blvd, Beverly Hills, CA	213-855-0200
Davis, Mary Webb/515 N LaCienega, Los Angeles, CA	213-652-6850
Garrick, Dale Internat'l Agency/8831 Sunset Blvd #402, Los Angeles, CA	213-657-2661
Hecht, Beverly Agency/8949 Sunset Blvd #203, Los Angeles, CA	213-278-3544
Kelman, Toni Agency/8961 Sunset Blvd, Los Angeles, CA	213-851-8822
Leonetti, Caroline Ltd/6526 Sunset Blvd, Los Angeles, CA	213-462-2345
Lien, Michael Casting/7461 Beverly Blvd, Los Angeles, CA	213-550-7381
Loo, Bessi Agency/8235 Santa Monica, W Hollywood, CA	213-650-1300
Mangum, John Agency/8831 Sunset Blvd, Los Angeles, CA	213-659-7230
Morris, William Agency/151 El Camino Dr, Beverly Hills, CA	213-274-7451
Pacific Artists Limited/515 N LaCienega Blvd, Los Angeles, CA	213-657-5990
REB-Sunset International/6912 Hollywood Blvd, Hollywood, CA	213-464-4440
Rose, Jack/6430 Sunset Blvd #1203, Los Angeles, CA	213-463-7300
Schaeffer, Peggy Agency/10850 Riverside Dr, North Hollywood, CA	818-985-5547
Schwartz, Don & Assoc/8721 Sunset Blvd, Los Angeles, CA	213-657-8910
Stern, Charles H Agency/9220 Sunset Blvd, Los Angeles, CA	213-273-6890
Sutton Barth & Venari/8322 Beverly Blvd, Los Angeles, CA	213-653-8322
Tannen, Herb & Assoc/6640 Sunset Blvd #203, Los Angeles, CA	213-466-6191
Wilhelmina/West/1800 Centyry Park E #504, Century City, CA	213-553-9525
Wormser Heldford & Joseph/1717 N Highland #414, Hollywood, CA	213-466-9111
Wright, Ann Assoc/8422 Melrose Place, Los Angeles, CA	213-655-5040

Animals

New York City

All Tame Animals/37 W 57th St	212-752-5885
Animals for Advertising/310 W 55th St	212-245-2590
Berloni Theatrical Animals/314 W 57th St Box 37	212-974-0922
Canine Academy of Ivan Kovach/3725 Lyme Ave	718-682-6770
Captain Haggertys Theatrical Dogs/1748 First Ave	212-410-7400
Chateau Theatrical Animals/608 W 48th St	212-246-0520
Claremont Riding Academy/175 W 89th St	212-724-5100
Dawn Animal Agency/160 W 46th St	212-575-9396
Mr Lucky Dog Training School Inc/27 Crescent St	718-827-2792

Northeast

American Driving Society/PO Box 1852, Lakeville, CT	203-435-0307
Animal Actors Inc/Box 221, RD 3, Washington, NJ	201-689-7539
Davis, Greg/Box 159T, RD 2, Greenville, NY	518-966-8229
Long Island Game Farm & Zoo/Chapman Blvd, Manorville, NY	516-727-7443
Parrots of the World/239 Sunrise Hwy, Rockville Center, NY	212-343-4141

Production/Support Services

Continued

Please send us your additions and updates.

Southeast

Dog Training by Bob Maida/7605 Old Centerville Rd,
   Manassas, VA 713-631-2125
Studio Animal Rentals/170 W 64th St, Hialeah, FL 305-558-4160

Midwest

Plainsmen Zoo/Rt 4, Box 151, Elgin, IL 312-697-0062

Southwest

Bettis, Ann J/Rt 1-A Box 21-B, Dripping Springs, TX 512-264-1952
Dallas Zoo in Marsalis Park/621 E Clarendon, Dallas, TX 214-946-5155
Estes, Bob Rodeos/PO Box 962, Baird, TX 915-854-1037
Fort Worth Zoological Park/2727 Zoological Park Dr., Fort
   Worth, TX 817-870-7050
International Wildlife Park/601 Wildlife Parkway, Grand Prairie,
   TX 214-263-2203
Newsom's Varmints N' Things/13015 Kaltenbrun, Houston, TX
   713-931-0676
Scott, Kelly Buggy & Wagon Rentals/Box 442, Bandera, TX 512-796-3737
Taylor, Peggy Talent Inc/6311 N O'Connor 3 Dallas Comm,
   Irving, TX 214-869-1515
Y O Ranch/Dept AS, Mountain Home, TX 512-640-3222

Rocky Mountain

Denver/Vannoy Talent/7400 E Caley Ave, Engelwood, CO 303-771-6555

West Coast

American Animal Enterprises/PO Box 337, Littlerock, CA 805-944-3011
The American Mongrel/PO Box 2406, Lancaster, CA 805-942-7550
Animal Action/PO Box 824, Arleta, CA 818-767-3003
Animal Actors of Hollywood/864 Carlisle Rd, Thousand Oaks,
   CA 805-495-2122
Birds and Animals/25191 Riverdell Dr, El Toro, CA 714-830-7845
The Blair Bunch/7561 Woodman Pl, Van Nuys, CA 213-994-1136
Casa De Pets/11814 Ventura Blvd, Studio City, CA 818-761-3651
Di Sesso's, Moe Trained Wildlife/24233 Old Road, Newhall, CA
   805-255-7969
Frank Inn Inc/12265 Branford St, Sun Valley, CA 818-896-8188
Gentle Jungle/3815 W Olive Ave, Burbank, CA 818-841-5300
Griffin, Gus/11281 Sheldon St, Sun Valley, CA 818-767-6647
Martin, Steve Working Wildlife/PO Box 65, Acton, CA 805-268-0788
Pyramid Bird/1407 W Magnolia, Burbank, CA 818-843-5505
Schumacher Animal Rentals/14453 Cavette Pl, Baldwin Park,
   CA 818-338-4614
The Stansbury Company/9304 Santa Monica Blvd, Beverly
   Hills, CA 213-273-1138
Weatherwax, Robert/16133 Soledad Canyon Rd, Canyon
   Country, CA 805-252-6907

Hair & Make-Up

New York City

Abrams, Ron/126 W 75th St 212-580-0705
Baeder, D & Sehven, A/135 E 26th St 212-532-4571
Barba, Olga/201 E 16th St 212-420-8611
Barron, Lynn/135 E 26th St 212-532-4571
Beauty Booking/130 W 57th St 212-977-7157
Blake, Marion/130 W 57th St 212-977-7157
Boles, Brad/ 212-724-2800
Boushelle/444 E 82nd St 212-861-7225
Braithwaite, Jordan/130 W 57th St 212-977-7157
Hammond, Claire/440 E 57th St 212-838-0712
Imre, Edith Beauty Salon/8 W 56th St 212-758-0233

Jenrette, Pamela/300 Mercer St 212-673-4748
Keller, Bruce Clyde/422 E 58th St 212-593-3816
Lane, Judy/444 E 82nd St 212-861-7225
Multiple Artists/42 E 23 St 212-473-8020
Narvaez, Robin/360 E 55th St 212-371-6378
Richardson, John Ltd/119 E 64th St 212-772-1874
Stessin, Warren Scott/ 212-243-3319
Tamblyn, Thom Inc/240 E 27th St 212-683-4514
Weithorn, Rochelle/431 E 73rd St 212-472-8668

Northeast

E-Fex/623 Pennsylvania Ave SE, Washington, DC 202-543-1241

Southeast

Irene Marie Models/3212 S Federal Hwy, Ft Lauderdale, FL 305-522-3262
Parker, Julie Hill/PO Box 19033, Jacksonville, FL 904-724-8483

Midwest

Adams, Jerry Hair Salon/1123 W Webster, Chicago, IL 312-327-1130
Alderman, Frederic/Rt 2 Box 205, Mundelein, IL 312-438-2925
Bobak, Ilona/300 N State, Chicago, IL 312-321-1679
Camylle/112 E Oak, Chicago, IL 312-943-1120
Cheveux/908 W Armitage, Chicago, IL 312-935-5212
Collins Chicago, Inc/67 E Oak, Chicago, IL 312-266-6662
Emerich, Bill/PO Box 14523, Chicago, IL 312-871-4659
International Guild of Make-Up/6970 N Sheridan, Chicago, IL 312-761-8500
Okains Costume & Theater/2713 W Jefferson, Joliet, IL 815-741-9303
Simmons, Sid Inc/2 E Oak, Chicago, IL 312-943-2333

Southwest

Dawson, Kim Agency/PO Box 585060, Dallas, TX 214-638-2414

Rocky Mountain

DeRose, Mary Fran/7350 Grant Pl, Arvada, CO 303-422-2152

West Coast

Andre, Maurice/9426 Santa Monica Blvd, Beverly Hills, CA 213-274-4562
Antovniov/11908 Ventura Blvd, Studio City, CA 818-763-0671
Armando's/607 No Huntley Dr, W Hollywood, CA 213-657-5160
Bourget, Lorraine/559 Muskingum Pl, Pacific Palisades, CA 213-454-3739
Cassandre 2000/18386 Ventura Blvd, Tarzana, CA 818-881-8400
Cloutier Inc/704 N Gardner, Los Angeles, CA 213-655-1263
Craig, Kenneth/13211 Ventura Blvd, Studio City, CA 818-995-8717
Design Pool/11936 Darlington Ave #303, Los Angeles, CA 213-826-1551
Francisco/PO Box 49995, Los Angeles, CA 213-826-3591
Frier, George/, , CA 213-393-0576
Gavilan/139 S Kings Rd, Los Angeles, CA 213-655-4452
Geiger, Pamela/, , CA 213-274-5737
Hamilton, Bryan J/909 N Westbourne Dr, Los Angeles, CA 213-654-9006
Hirst, William/15130 Ventura Blvd, Sherman Oaks, CA 818-501-0993
HMS/1541 Harvard St #A, Santa Monica, CA 213-828-2080
Johns, Arthur/8661 Sunset Blvd, Hollywood, CA 213-855-9306
Ray, David Frank/15 Wave Crest, Venice, CA 213-392-5640
Samuel, Martin/6138 W 6th, Los Angeles, CA 213-930-0794
Serena, Eric/840 N Larabee, Bldg 4, W Hollywood, CA 213-652-4267
Studio Seven/261 E Rowland Ave, Covina, CA 213-331-6351
Total You Salon/1647 Los Angeles Ave, Simi, CA 805-526-4189
Towsend, Jeanne/433 N Camden Dr, Beverly Hills, CA 213-851-7044
Welsh, Franklyn/704 N LaCienega Blvd, Los Angeles, CA 213-656-8195

Hair

New York City

Albert-Carter/Hotel St Moritz	212-688-2045
Benjamin Salon/104 Washington Pl	212-255-3330
Caruso, Julius/22 E 62nd St	212-751-6240
Daines, David Salon Hair Styling/833 Madison Ave	212-535-1563
George V Hair Stylist/501 Fifth Ave	212-687-9097
Moda 700/700 Madison Ave	212-935-9188
Monsieur Marc Inc/22 E 65th St	212-861-0700
Peter's Beauty Home/149 W 57th St	212-247-2934
Pierro, John/130 W 57th St	212-977-7157

Northeast

Brocklebank, Tom/249 Emily Ave, Elmont, NY	516-775-5356

Southeast

Yellow Strawberry/107 E Las Olas Blvd, Ft Lauderdale, FL	305-463-4343

Midwest

Rodriguez, Ann/1123 W Webster, Chicago, IL	312-327-1130

Southwest

Southern Hair Designs/3563 Far West Blvd, Austin, TX	512-346-1734

Rocky Mountain

City Lights Hair Designs/2845 Wyandote, Denver, CO	303-458-0131
Zee for Hair/316 E Hopkins, Aspen, CO	303-925-4434

West Coast

Anatra, M Haircutters/530 No LaCienega, Los Angeles, CA	213-657-1495
Barronson Hair/11908 Ventura, Studio City, CA	818-763-4337
Beck, Shirley/ CA	213-763-2930
Edwards, Allen/455 N Rodeo Dr, Beverly Hills, CA	213-274-8575
Ely, Shannon/616 Victoria, Venice, CA	213-392-5832
Fisher, Jim/c/o Rumours, 9014 Melrose, Los Angeles, CA	213-550-5946
Francisco/PO Box 49995, Los Angeles, CA	213-826-3591
Grieve, Ginger/ CA	818-347-2947
Gurasich, Lynda/ CA	818-981-6719
The Hair Conspiracy/11923 Ventura Blvd, Studio City, CA	818-985-1126
Hjerpe, Warren/9018 Beverly Blvd, Los Angeles, CA	213-550-5946
HMS/1541 Harvard St #A, Santa Monica, CA	213-828-2080
Iverson, Betty/ CA	213-462-2301
John, Michael Salon/414 N Camden Dr, Beverly Hills, CA	213-278-8333
Kemp, Lola/ CA	213-293-8710
Lorenz, Barbara/ CA	213-657-0028
Malone, John/ CA	213-246-1649
Menage a Trois/8822 Burton Way, Beverly Hills, CA	213-278-4431
Miller, Patty/ CA	818-843-5208
Morrissey, Jimie/ CA	213-657-4318
Payne, Allen/ CA	213-395-5259
Phillips, Marilyn/ CA	213-923-6996
Sami/1230 N Horn Ave #525, Los Angeles, CA	213-652-5816
Sassoon, Vidal Inc/2049 Century Park E #3800, Los Angeles, CA	213-553-6100
Trainoff, Linda/ CA	818-769-0373
Vecchio, Faith/ CA	818-345-6152

Make-Up

New York City

Adams, Richard/130 W 57th St	212-977-7157
Armand/147 W 35th St	212-947-2186
Bertoli, Michele/264 Fifth Ave	212-684-2480
Bonzignor's Cosmetics/110 Fulton	212-267-1108
Lawrence, Rose/444 E 82nd St	212-861-7225
Make-Up Center Ltd/150 W 55th St	212-977-9494
Oakley, Sara/	212-749-5912
Richardson, John Ltd/119 E 64th St	212-772-1874
Ross, Rose Cosmetics/16 W 55th St	212-586-2590
Sartin, Janet of Park Ave Ltd/480 Park Ave	212-751-5858
Stage Light Cosmetics Ltd/630 Ninth Ave	212-757-4851
Suzanne de Paris/509 Madison Ave	212-838-4024

Northeast

Damaskos-Zilber, Zoe/78 Waltham St #4, Boston, MA	617-628-6583
Douglas, Rodney N/473 Avon Ave #3, Newark, NJ	201-375-2979
Fiorina, Frank/2400 Hudson Terr #5A, Fort Lee, NJ	212-242-3900
Gilmore, Robert Assoc Inc/990 Washington St, Dedham, MA	617-329-6633
Meth, Miriam/96 Greenwood Ln, White Plains, NY	212-787-5400
Minassian, Amie/62-75 Austin St, Rego Park, NY	212-446-8048
Phillipe, Louise Miller/22 Chestnut Pl, Brookline, MA	617-566-3608
Phillipe, Robert/22 Chestnut Pl, Brookline, MA	617-566-3608
Rothman, Ginger/1915 Lyttonsville Rd, Silver Spring, MD	703-241-4556
Something Special/1601 Walter Reed Dr S, Arlington, VA	703-892-0551
Zack, Sandra/94 Orient Ave, East Boston, MA	617-567-7581

Southeast

Star Styled of Miami/475 NW 42nd Ave, Miami, FL	305-541-2424
Star Styled of Tampa/4235 Henderson Blvd, Tampa, FL	813-872-8706

Southwest

ABC Theatrical Rental & Sales/825 N 7th St, Phoenix, AZ	602-258-5265
Chelsea Cutters/One Chelsea Pl, Houston, TX	713-529-4813
Copeland, Tom/502 West Grady, Austin, TX	512-835-0208
Corey, Irene/4147 Herschel Ave, Dallas, TX	214-528-4836
Dobes, Pat/1826 Nocturne, Houston, TX	713-465-8102
Ingram, Marilyn Wyrick/10545 Chesterton Drive, Dallas, TX	214-349-2113
Stamm, Louis M/721 Edgehill Dr, Hurst, TX	817-268-5037

Rocky Mountain

Moen, Brenda/ CO	303-871-9506
Moon Sun Emporium/2019 Broadway, Boulder, CO	303-443-6851

West Coast

Astier, Guy/11936 Darlington Ave #303, Los Angeles, CA	213-826-1551
Blackman, Charles F/12751 Addison, N Hollwyood, CA	818-761-2177
Blackman, Gloria/12751 Addison, N Hollwyood, CA	818-761-2177
Case, Tom/5150 Woodley, Encino, CA	818-788-5268
Cooper, David/3616 Effie, Los Angeles, CA	213-660-7326
Cosmetic Connection/9484 Dayton Way, Beverly Hills, CA	213-550-6242
D'Ifray, T J/468 N Bedford Dr, Beverly Hills, CA	213-274-6776
Dawn, Wes/11113 Hortense St, N Hollywood, CA	818-761-7517
Fradkin, Joanne c/o Pigments/8822 Burton Way, Beverly Hills, CA	213-858-7038
Francisco/PO Box 49995, Los Angeles, CA	213-826-3591
Freed, Gordon/ CA	818-360-9473
Geike, Ziggy/ CA	818-789-1465
Henrriksen, Ole/8601 W Sunset Blvd, Los Angeles, CA	213-854-7700
Howell, Deborah/291 S Martel Ave, Los Angeles, CA	213-655-1263
Koelle, c/o Pigments/8822 Burton Way, Beverly Hills, CA	213-668-1690

Production/Support Services

Please send us your additions and updates.

Kruse, Lee C/ CA	818-894-5408
Laurent, c/o Menage a Trois/8822 Burton Way, Beverly Hills, CA	213-278-4430
Logan, Kathryn/ CA	818-988-7038
Malone, John E/ CA	818-247-5160
Manges, Delanie (Dee)/ CA	818-763-3311
Maniscalco, Ann S/ CA	818-894-5408
Menage a Trois/8822 Burton Way, Beverly Hills, CA	213-278-4431
Minch, Michelle/339 S Detroit St, Los Angeles, CA	213-484-9648
Natasha/4221 1/2 Avocado St, Los Angeles, CA	213-663-1477
Nielsen, Jim/ CA	213-461-2168
Nye, Dana/ CA	213-477-0443
Odessa/1448 1/2 N Fuller Ave, W Hollywood, CA	213-876-5779
Palmieri, Dante/ CA	213-396-6020
Penelope/	213-654-6747
Pigments/8822 Burton Way, Beverly Hills, CA	213-858-7038
Romero, Bob/5030 Stern Ave, Sherman Oaks, CA	818-891-3338
Rumours/9014 Melrose, W Hollywood, CA	213-550-5946
Sanders, Nadia/ CA	213-465-2009
Shulman, Sheryl Leigh/ CA	818-760-0101
Sidell, Bob/	818-360-0794
Striepke, Danny/4800 #C Villa Marina, Marina Del Rey, CA	213-823-5957
Tuttle, William/	213-454-2355
Tyler, Diane/	415-381-5067
Warren, Dodie/	818-763-3172
Westmore, Michael/	818-763-3158
Westmore, Monty/	818-762-2094
Winston, Stan/	818-886-0630
Wolf, Barbara/ CA	213-466-4660

Stylists

New York City

Baldassano, Irene/16 W 16th St	212-255-8567
Bandiero, Paul/PO Box 121 FDR Station	212-586-3700
Barritt, Randi/240 W 15th St	212-255-5333
Batteau, Sharon/130 W 57th St	212-977-7157
Benner, Dyne (Food)/311 E 60th St	212-688-7571
Berman, Benicia/399 E 72nd St	212-737-9627
Bromberg, Florence/350 Third Ave	212-255-4033
Cheverton, Linda/150 9th Avenue	212-691-0881
Chin, Fay/67 Vestry St	212-219-8770
Cohen, Susan/233 E 54th St	212-755-3157
D'Arcy, Timothy/43 W 85th St	212-580-8804
Davidson/Frank Photo-Stylists/209 W 86th St #701	212-799-2651
DeJesu, Joanna (Food)/101 W 23rd St	212-255-3895
Eller, Ann/7816 Third Ave	718-238-5454
Final Touch/55-11 13th Ave	718-435-6800
Galante, Kathy/9 W 31st St	212-239-0412
George, Georgia A/404 E 55th St	212-759-4131
Goldberg, Hal/11 Fifth Ave	212-982-7588
Greene, Jan/200 E 17th St	212-233-8989
Herman, Joan/15 W 84th St	212-724-3287
Joffe, Carole Reiff/233 E 34th St	212-725-4928
Klein, Mary Ellen/330 E 33rd St	212-683-6351
Lakin, Gaye/345 E 81st St	212-861-1892
Levin, Laurie/55 Perry St	212-242-2611
Lopes, Sandra/444 E 82nd St	212-249-8706
Magidson, Peggy/182 Amity St	212-508-7604
Manetti, Palmer/336 E 53rd St	212-758-3859
McCabe, Christine/200 W 79th St	212-799-4121
Meshejian, Zabel/125 Washington Pl	212-242-2459
Meyers, Pat/436 W 20th St	212-620-0069
Minch, Deborah Lee/175 W 87th St	212-873-7915
Nagle, Patsy/242 E 38th St	212-682-0364
Orefice, Jeanette/	718-643-8266
Ouellette, Dawn/336 E 30th St	212-799-9190
Peacock, Linda/118 W 88th St	212-580-1422

Reilly, Veronica/60 Gramercy Park N	212-840-1234
Sampson, Linda/431 W Broadway	212-925-6821
Scherman, Joan/450 W 24th St	212-620-0475
Schoenberg, Marv/878 West End Ave #10A	212-663-1418
Seymour, Celeste/130 E 75th St	212-744-3545
Sheffy, Nina/838 West End Ave	212-662-0709
Slote, Ina/7 Park Ave	212-679-4584
Smith, Rose/400 E 56th St #19D	212-758-8711
Specht, Meredith/166 E 61st St	212-832-0750
Weithorn, Rochelle/431 E 73rd St	212-472-8668
West, Susan/59 E 7th St	212-982-8228

Northeast

Bailey Designs/110 Williams St, Malden, MA	617-321-4448
Baldwin, Katherine/109 Commonwealth Ave, Boston, MA	617-267-0508
Carafoli, John (Food)/1 Hawes Rd, Sagamore Beach, MA	617-888-1557
E-Fex/623 Pennsylvania Ave SE, Washington, DC	202-543-1241
Gold, Judy/40 Sulgrave Rd, Scarsdale, NY	914-723-5036
Maggio, Marlene - Aura Prdtns/Brook Hill Ln Ste 5E, Rochester, NY	716-381-8053
Rosemary's Cakes Inc/299 Rutland Ave, Teaneck, NJ	201-833-2417
Rothman, Ginger/1915 Lyttonsville Rd, Silver Spring, MD	703-241-4556
Rubin, L A/359 Harvard St #2, Cambridge, MA	617-576-1808

Southeast

Foodworks/1541 Colonial Ter, Arlington, VA	703-524-2606
Gaffney, Janet D/464 W Wesley N W, Atlanta, GA	404-355-7556
Kupersmith, Tony/320 N Highland Ave NE, Atlanta, GA	404-577-5319
Parker, Julie Hill/PO Box 19033, Jacksonville, FL	904-724-8483
Polvay, Marina Assoc/9250 NE 10th Ct, Miami Shores, FL	305-759-4375
Torres, Martha/927 Third St, New Orleans, LA	504-895-6570

Midwest

Alan, Jean/1032 W Altgeld, Chicago, IL	312-929-9768
Carlson, Susan/255 Linden Park Pl, Highland Park, IL	312-433-2466
Carter, Karen/3323 N Kenmore, Chicago, IL	312-935-2901
Chevaux Ltd/908 W Armitage, Chicago, IL	312-935-5212
Ellison, Faye/3406 Harriet Ave S, Minneapolis, MN	612-822-7954
Emruh Style Design/714 W Fullerton, Chicago, IL	312-871-4659
Erickson, Emily/2954 No Racine, Chicago, IL	312-281-4899
Heller, Nancy/1142 W Diversey, Chicago, IL	312-549-4486
Lapin, Kathy Santis/925 Spring Hill Dr, Northbrook, IL	312-272-7487
Mary, Wendy/719 W Wrightwood, Chicago, IL	312-871-5476
Pace, Leslie/6342 N Sheridan, Chicago, IL	312-761-2480
Perry, Lee Ann/1615 No Clybourne, Chicago, IL	312-649-1815
Pohn, Carol/2259 N Wayne, Chicago, IL	312-348-0751
Rabert, Bonnie/2230 W Pratt, Chicago, IL	312-743-7755
Sager, Sue/875 N Michigan, Chicago, IL	312-642-3789
Seeker, Christopher/100 E Walton #21D, Chicago, IL	312-944-4311
Shaver, Betsy/3714 N Racine, Chicago, IL	312-327-5615
Style Vasilak and Nebel/314 W Institute Pl, Chicago, IL	312-280-8516
Weber-Mack, Kathleen/2119 Lincoln, Evanston, IL	312-869-7794

Southwest

Bishop, Cindy/6101 Charlotte, Houston, TX	713-666-7224
Janet-Nelson/PO Box 143, Tempe, AZ	602-968-3771
Taylor, John Michael/2 Dallas Commun Complex # Irving, TX	214-823-1333
Thomas, Jan/5651 East Side Ave, Dallas, TX	214-823-1955

Rocky Mountain

DeRose, Mary Fran/7350 Grant Pl, Arvada, CO	303-422-2152

West Coast

Akimbo Prod/801 Westbourne, W Hollywood, CA	213-657-4657
Alaimo, Doris/8800 Wonderland Ave, Los Angeles, CA	213-851-7044
Allen, Jamie R/, Los Angeles, CA	213-655-9351

Continued

Please send us your additions and updates.

Altbaum, Patti/244-CS Lasky Dr, Beverly Hills, CA	213-553-6269
Azzara, Marilyn/3165 Ellington Drive, Los Angeles, CA	213-851-0531
Castaldi, Debbie/10518 Wilshire Blvd #25, Los Angeles, CA	213-475-4312
Chinamoon/642 S Burnside Ave #6, Los Angeles, CA	213-937-8251
Corwin-Hankin, Aleka/1936 Cerro Gordo, Los Angeles, CA	213-665-7953
Craig, Kenneth/13211 Ventura Blvd, Studio City, CA	818-995-8717
Davis, Rommie/4414 La Venta Dr, West Lake Village, CA	818-906-1455
Design Pool/11936 Darlington Ave #303, Los Angeles, CA	213-826-1551
Evonne/ CA	213-275-1658
Flating, Janice/8113 1/2 Melrose Ave, Los Angeles, CA	213-653-1800
Frank, Tobi/1269 N Hayworth, Los Angeles, CA	213-552-7921
Gaffin, Lauri/1123-12th St, Santa Monica, CA	213-451-2045
Governor, Judy/963 North Point, San Francisco, CA	415-861-5733
Graham, Victory/24 Ave 26, Venice, CA	213-934-0990
Granas, Marilyn/200 N Almont Dr, Beverly Hills, CA	213-278-3773
Griswald, Sandra/963 North Point, San Francisco, CA	415-775-4272
Hamilton, Bryan J/1269 N Hayworth, Los Angeles, CA	213-654-9006
Hewett, Julie/7551 Melrose Ave, Los Angeles, CA	213-651-5172
Hirsch, Lauren/858 Devon, Los Angeles, CA	213-271-7052
HMS/1541 Harvard St #A, Santa Monica, CA	213-828-2080
Howell, Deborah/219 S Martel Ave, Los Angeles, CA	213-655-1263
James, Elizabeth/5320 Bellingham Ave, N Hollywood, CA	213-761-5718
Kimball, Lynnda/133 S Peck Dr, Beverly Hills, CA	213-461-6303
King, Max/308 N Sycamore Ave, Los Angeles, CA	213-938-0108
Lawson, Karen/6836 Lexington Ave, Hollywood, CA	213-464-5770
Lynch, Jody/19130 Pacific Coast Hwy, Malibu, CA	213-456-2383
Material Eyes/501 Pacific Ave, San Francisco, CA	415-362-8143
Miller, Freyda/1412 Warner Ave, Los Angeles, CA	213-474-5034
Minot, Abby/53 Canyon Rd, Berkeley, CA	415-841-9600
Moore, Francie/842 1/2 N Orange Dr, Los Angeles, CA	213-462-5404
Morrow, Suzanne/26333 Silver Spur, Palos Verdes, CA	213-378-2909
Neal, Robin Lynn/3105 Durand, Hollywood, CA	213-465-6037
Olsen, Eileen/1619 N Beverly Dr, Beverly Hills, CA	213-273-4496
Parshall, Mary Ann/19850 Pacific Coast Hwy, Malibu, CA	213-456-8303
Prindle, Judy Peck/6057 Melrose Ave, Los Angeles, CA	213-650-0962
Russo, Leslie/377 10th, Santa Monica, CA	213-395-8461
Shatsy/9008 Harratt St, Hollywood, CA	213-275-2413
Skinner, Jeanette/1622 Moulton Pkwy #A, Tustin, CA	714-730-5793
Skinner, Randy/920 S Wooster St, Los Angeles, CA	213-659-2936
Skuro, Bryna/134-B San Vicente Blvd, Santa Monica, CA	213-394-2430
Sloane, Hilary/6351 Ranchito, Van Nuys, CA	213-855-1010
Surkin, Helen/2100 N Beachwood Dr, Los Angeles, CA	213-464-6847
Thomas, Lisa/9029 Rangely Ave, W Hollywood, CA	213-858-6903
Townsend, Jeanne/433 N Camden Dr, Beverly Hills, CA	213-851-7044
Tucker, Joan/1402 N Fuller St, Los Angeles, CA	213-876-3417
Tyre, Susan/ CA	213-877-3884
Valade/ CA	213-659-7621
Weinberg & James Foodstyle/3888 Woodcliff Rd, Sherman Oaks, CA	213-274-2383
Weiss, Sheri/2170 N Beverly Glen, Los Angeles, CA	213-470-1650

Costumes

New York City

Academy Clothes Inc/1703 Broadway	212-765-1440
AM Costume Wear/135-18 Northern Blvd	718-358-8108
Austin Ltd/140 E 55th St	212-752-7903
Capezio Dance Theater Shop/755 Seventh Ave	212-245-2130
Chenko Studio/167 W 46th St	212-944-0215
David's Outfitters Inc/36 W 20th St	212-691-7388
Eaves-Brookes Costume/21-07 41st Ave	718-729-1010
G Bank's Theatrical & Custom/320 W 48th St	212-586-6476
Grace Costumes Inc/254 W 54th St	212-586-0260
Herbert Danceware Co/902 Broadway	212-677-7606
Ian's Boutique Inc/1151-A Second Ave	212-838-3969
Karinska/16 W 61st St	212-247-3341
Kulyk/72 E 7th St	212-674-0414
Lane Costume Co/234 Fifth Ave	212-684-4721

Martin, Alice Manougian/239 E 58th St	212-688-0117
Meyer, Jimmy & Co/428 W 44th St	212-765-8079
Michael-Jon Costumes Inc/39 W 19th St	212-741-3440
Mincou, Christine/405 E 63rd St	212-838-3881
Purcell, Elizabeth/105 Sullivan St	212-925-1962
Rubie's Costume Co/1 Rubie Plaza	718-846-1008
Sampler Vintage Clothes/455 W 43rd St	212-757-8168
Stivanello Costume Co Inc/66-38 Clinton Ave	718-651-7715
Tint, Francine/1 University Pl	212-475-3366
Universal Costume Co Inc/1540 Broadway	212-575-8570
Weiss & Mahoney Inc/142 Fifth Ave	212-675-1915
Winston, Mary Ellen/11 E 68th St	212-879-0766
Ynocencio, Jo/302 E 88th St	212-348-5332

Northeast

At-A-Glance Rentals/712 Main, Boonton, NJ	201-335-1488
Baldwin, Katharine/109 Commonwealth Ave, Boston, MA	617-267-0508
Barris, Alfred Wig Maker/10 E Sirtsink Dr, Pt Washington, NY	516-883-9061
Costume Armour Inc/Shore Rd Box 325, Cornwall on Hudson, NY	914-534-9120
Douglas, Rodney N/473 Avon Ave #3, Newark, NJ	201-375-2979
House of Costumes Ltd/166 Jericho Tpk, Mineola, NY	516-294-0170
Penrose Productions/4 Sandalwood Dr, Livingston, NJ	201-992-4264
Strutters/11 Paul Sullivan Way, Boston, MA	617-423-9299
Westchester Costume Rentals/540 Nepperhan Ave, Yonkers, NY	914-963-1333

Southeast

ABC Costume/185 NE 59th St, Miami, FL	305-757-3492
Atlantic Costume Co/2089 Monroe Dr, Atlanta, GA	404-874-7511
Carol, Lee Inc/2145 NW 2nd Ave, Miami, FL	305-573-1759
Fun Stop Shop/1601 Biscyne Blvd Omni Int F27, Miami, FL	305-358-2003
Goddard, Lynn Prod Svcs/712 Pelican Ave, New Orleans, LA	504-367-0348
Poinciana Sales/2252 W Flagler St, Miami, FL	305-642-3441
Star Styled/475 NW 42nd Ave, Miami, FL	305-649-3030

Midwest

Advance Theatrical Co/1900 N Narragansett, Chicago, IL	312-889-7700
Backstage Enterprises/1525 Ellinwood, Des Plaines, IL	312-692-6159
Be Something Studio/5533 N Forest Glen, Chicago, IL	312-685-6717
Broadway Costumes Inc/932 W Washington, Chicago, IL	312-829-6400
Brune, Paul/6330 N Indian Rd, Chicago, IL	312-763-1117
Center Stage/Fox Valley Shopping Cntr, Aurora, IL	312-851-9191
Chicago Costume Co Inc/1120 W Fullerton, Chicago, IL	312-528-1264
Ennis, Susan/2961 N Lincoln Ave, Chicago, IL	312-525-7483
Kaufman Costumes/5117 N Western, Chicago, IL	312-561-7529
Magical Mystery Tour, Ltd/6010 Dempster, Morton Grove, IL	312-966-5090
Okains Costume & Theater/2713 W Jefferson, Joliet, IL	815-741-9303
Stechman's Creations/1920 Koehler, Des Plaines, IL	312-827-9045
Taylor, Corinna/1700B W Granville, Chicago, IL	312-472-6550
Toy Gallery/1640 N Wells, Chicago, IL	312-944-4323

Southwest

A & J Costume Rental, Dsgn & Const/304 White Oaks Dr, Austin, TX	512-836-2733
ABC Theatrical Rental & Sales/825 N 7th St, Phoenix, AZ	602-258-5265
Abel, Joyce/Rt 1 Box 165, San Marcos, TX	512-392-5659
Campioni, Frederick/1920 Broken Oak, San Antonio, TX	512-342-7780
Corey, Irene/4147 Herschel Ave, Dallas, TX	214-528-4836
Incredible Productions/3327 Wylie Dr, Dallas, TX	214-350-3633
Lucy Greer & Assoc. Casting/600 Shadywood Ln, Richardson, TX	214-231-2086
Moreau, Suzanne/1007-B West 22nd St, Austin, TX	512-477-1532
Nicholson, Christine/c/o Lola Sprouse, Carrollton, TX	214-245-0926
Old Time Teenies Vintage Clothing/1126 W 6th St, Austin, TX	512-477-2022
Second Childhood/900 W 18th St, Austin, TX	512-472-9696
Starline Costume Products/1286 Bandera Rd, San Antonio, TX	512-435-3535

Production/Support Services

Continued

Please send us your additions and updates.

Thomas, Joan S/6904 Spanky Branch Court, Dallas, TX   214-931-1900
Welch, Virginia/3707 Manchaca Rd #138, Austin, TX   512-447-1240

Rocky Mountain

And Sew On-Jila/2017 Broadway, Boulder, CO   303-442-0130
Raggedy Ann Clothing & Costume/1213 E Evans Ave, Denver,
  CO   303-733-7937

West Coast

Aardvark/7579 Melrose Ave, Los Angeles, CA   213-655-6769
Adele's of Hollywood/5059 Hollywood Blvd, Hollywood, CA   213-663-2231
American Costume Corp/12980 Raymer, N Hollywood, CA   818-764-2239
Auntie Mame/1102 S La Cienaga Blvd, Los Angeles, CA   213-652-8430
Boserup House of Canes/1636 Westwood Blvd, W Los
  Angeles, CA   213-474-2577
The Burbank Studios Wardrobe Dept/4000 Warner Blvd,
  Burbank, CA   818-954-1218
California Surplus Mart/6263 Santa Monica Blvd, Los
  Angeles, CA   213-465-5525
Capezio Dancewear/1777 Vine St, Hollywood, CA   213-465-3744
CBS Wardrobe Dept/7800 Beverly Blvd, Los Angeles, CA   213-852-2345
Courtney, Elizabeth/8636 Melrose Ave, Los Angeles, CA   213-657-4361
Crystal Palace (Sales)/8457 Melrose Ave, Hollywood, CA   818-761-1870
Design Studio/6685-7 Sunset Blvd, Hollywood, CA   213-469-3661
E C 2 Costumes/431 S Fairfax, Los Angeles, CA   213-934-1131
Fantasy Costume/4310 San Fernando Rd, Glendale, CA   213-245-7367
International Costume Co/1269 Sartori, Torrance, CA   213-320-6392
Kings Western Wear/6455 Van Nuys Blvd, Van Nuys, CA   818-785-2586
Krofft Entertainment/7200 Vineland Ave, Sun Valley, CA   213-875-0324
LA Uniform Exchange/5239 Melrose Ave, Los Angeles, CA   213-469-3965
MGM/UA Studios Wardrobe Dept/10202 W Washington Blvd,
  Culver City, CA   213-558-5600
Military Antiques & War Museum/208 Santa Monica Ave,
  Santa Monica, CA   213-393-1180
Minot, Abby/53 Canyon Rd, Berkeley, CA   415-841-9600
Nudies Rodeo Tailor/5015 Lanskershim Blvd, N Hollywood,
  CA   818-762-3105
Palace Costume/835 N Fairfax, Los Angeles, CA   213-651-5458
Paramount Studios Wardrobe Dept/5555 Melrose Ave,
  Hollywood, CA   213-468-5288
Peabodys/1102 1/2 S La Cienega Blvd, Los Angeles, CA   213-352-3810
Piller's, Jerry/8163 Santa Monica Blvd, Hollywood, CA   213-654-3038
Tuxedo Center/7360 Sunset Blvd, Los Angeles, CA   213-874-4200
Valu Shoe Mart/5637 Santa Monica Blvd, Los Angeles, CA   213-469-8560
Western Costume Co/5335 Melrose Ave, Los Angeles, CA   213-469-1451

Props

New York City

Abet Rent-A-Fur/307 Seventh Ave   212-989-5757
Abstracta Structures Inc/347 Fifth Ave   212-532-3710
Ace Galleries/91 University Pl   212-991-4536
Adirondack Direct/219 E 42nd St   212-687-8555
Alice's Antiques/552 Columbus Ave   212-874-3400
Alpha-Pavia Bookbinding Co Inc/55 W 21st St   212-929-5430
Archer Surgical Supplies Inc/544 W 27th St   212-695-5553
Artisan's Studio/232 Atlantic Ave   718-855-2796
Artistic Neon by Gasper/75-49 61st St   718-821-1550
Arts & Crafters/175 Johnson St   718-875-8151
Arts & Flowers/234 W 56th St   212-247-7610
Associated Theatrical Designer/220 W 71st St   212-362-2648
Austin Display/139 W 19th St   212-924-6261
Baird, Bill Marionettes/41 Union Square   212-989-9840
Baker, Alex/30 W 69th St   212-799-2069
Bill's Flower Mart/816 Ave of the Americas   212-889-8154
Brandon Memorabilia/222 E 51st St   212-691-9776

Breitrose, Mark/156 Fifth Ave   212-242-7825
Brooklyn Model Works/60 Washington Ave   718-834-1944
California Artificial Flower Co/225 Fifth Ave   212-679-7774
Carroll Musical Instrument Svc/351 W 41st St   212-868-4120
Chateau Stables Inc/608 W 48th St   212-246-0520
Churchill/Winchester Furn Rental/44 E 32nd St   212-535-3400
Constructive Display/142 W 26th St   212-675-7320
Cooper Film Cars/132 Perry St   212-929-3909
Cycle Service Center Inc/74 Sixth Ave   212-925-5900
Doherty Studios/252 W 46th St   212-840-6219
Eclectic Properties Inc/204 W 84th St   212-799-8963
Encore Studio/410 W 47th St   212-246-5237
Florenco Foliage Systems Inc/30-28 Starr Ave   718-729-6600
Furs, Valerie/150 W 30th St   212-947-2020
Golden Equipment Co Inc/422 Madison Ave   212-838-3776
Gordon Novelty Co/933 Broadway   212-254-8616
Gossard & Assocs Inc/801 E 134th St   212-665-9194
Gothic Color Co Inc/727 Washington St   212-929-7493
Guccione/333 W 39th St   212-279-3602
Harra, John Wood & Supply Co/39 W 19th St, 11th Fl   212-741-0290
Harrison/Erickson/95 Fifth Ave   212-929-5700
Jeffers, Kathy-Modelmaking/106 E 19th St 12th Fl   212-475-1756
Joyce, Robert Studio Ltd/321 W 44th St #404   212-586-5041
Kaplan, Howard/35 E 10th St   212-674-1000
Karpen, Ben/212 E 51st St   212-755-3450
Kempler, George J/160 Fifth Ave   212-989-1180
Kenmore Furniture Co Inc/156 E 33rd St   212-683-1888
Mallie, Dale & Co/35-30 38th St   718-706-1234
The Manhattan Model Shop/40 Great Jones St   212-473-6312
Manhattan Model Shop/40 Great Jones St   212-473-6312
Maniatis, Michael Inc/48 W 22nd St   212-620-0398
Manwaring Studio/232 Atlantic Ave   718-855-2796
Marc Modell Associates/430 W 54th St   212-541-9676
Mason's Tennis Mart/911 Seventh Ave   212-757-5374
Matty's Studio Sales/543 W 35th St   212-757-6246
McConnell & Borow Inc/10 E 23rd St   212-254-1486
Mendez, Raymond A/220 W 98th St #12B   212-864-4689
Messmore & Damon Inc/530 W 28th St   212-594-8070
Metro Scenery Studio Inc/215-31 99th Ave   718-464-6328
Modern Miltex Corp/280 E 134th St   212-585-6000
Morozko, Bruce/41 White St   212-226-8832
Movie Cars/825 Madison Ave   212-288-6000
Newell Art Galleries Inc/425 E 53rd St   212-758-1970
Nostalgia Alley Antiques/547 W 27th St   212-695-6578
Novel Pinball Co/593 Tenth Ave   212-736-3868
The Place for Antiques/993 Second Ave   212-475-6596
Plant Specialists Inc/524 W 34th St   212-279-1500
Plastic Works*/2107 Broadway @ 73rd   212-362-1000
Plexability Ltd/200 Lexington Ave   212-679-7826
Porter-Rayvid/155 Attorney   212-460-5050
Portobello Road Antiques Ltd/370 Columbus Ave   212-724-2300
The Prop House Inc/76 Ninth Ave   212-691-9099
The Prop Shop/26 College Pl   718-522-4606
Props and Displays/132 W 18th St   212-620-3840
Props for Today/15 W 20th St   212-206-0330
Ray Beauty Supply Co Inc/721 Eighth Ave   212-757-0175
Ridge, John Russell/531 Hudson St   212-929-3410
Say It In Neon/434 Hudson St   212-691-7977
Simon's Dir of Theatrical Mat/27 W 24th St   212-255-2872
Smith & Watson/305 E 63rd St   212-355-5615
Smith, David/   212-730-1188
Solco Plumbing Suplies & Bathtubs/209 W 18th St   212-243-2569
Special Effects/40 W 39th St   212-869-8636
Starbuck Studio - Acrylic props/162 W 21st St   212-807-7299
State Supply Equipment Co Inc/68 Thomas St   212-233-0474
Theater Technology Inc/37 W 20th St   212-929-5380
Times Square Theatrical & Studio/318 W 47th St   212-245-4155
Uncle Sam's Umbrella/161 W 57th St   212-582-1976
Whole Art Inc/259 W 30th St   212-868-0978
Wizardworks/67 Atlantic Ave   718-349-5252
Zakarian, Robert Prop Shop Inc/26 College Pl   718-522-4606
Zeller, Gary & Assoc/Special Effects/40 W 39th St   212-869-8636

Production/Support Services

Continued

Please send us your additions and updates.

Northeast

Antique Bicycle Props Service/113 Woodland Ave, Montvale, NJ	201-391-8780
Atlas Scenic Studios Ltd/46 Brokfield Ave, Bridgeport, CT	203-334-2130
Baily Designs/110 Williams St, Malden, MA	617-321-4448
Baldwin, Katherine/109 Commonwealth Ave, Boston, MA	617-267-0508
Bestek Theatrical Productions/218 Hoffman, Babylon, NY	516-225-0707
Cadillac Convertible Owners/, Thiells, NY	914-947-1109
Dewart, Tim Assoc/83 Old Standley St, Beverly, MA	617-922-9229
Geiger, Ed/12 Church St, Middletown, NJ	201-671-1707
Hart Scenic Studio/35-41 Dempsey Ave, Edgewater, NJ	212-947-7264
L I Auto Museum/Museum Square, South Hampton, NY	516-283-1880
Master & Talent Inc/1139 Foam Place, Far Rockaway, NY	516-239-7719
Model Sonics/272 Ave F, Bayonne, NJ	201-436-6721
Newbery, Tomas/Ridge Rd, Glen Cove, NY	516-759-0880
Pennington Inc/72 Edmund St, Edison, NJ	201-985-9090
Rindner, Jack N Assoc/112 Water St, Tinton Falls, NJ	201-542-3548
Stewart, Chas H Co/6 Clarendon Ave, Sommerville, MA	617-625-2407
Strutters/11 Paul Sullivan Way, Boston, MA	617-423-9299

Southeast

Alderman Company/325 Model Farm Rd, High Point, NC	919-889-6121
Arawak Marine/PO Box 7362, St Thomas, VI	809-775-1858
Charisma Prod Services/PO Box 19033, Jacksonville, FL	904-724-8483
Crigler, MB/Smooth As Glass Prod Svcs/607 Bass St, Nashville, TN	615-254-6061
Dangar, Jack/3640 Ridge Rd, Smyrna, GA	404-434-3640
Dunwright Productions/15281 NE 21st Ave, N Miami Beach, FL	305-944-2464
Enter Space/20 14th St NW, Atlanta, GA	404-885-1139
Kupersmith, Tony/320 N Highland Ave NE, Atlanta, GA	404-577-5319
Manning, Maureen/1283 Cedar Heights Dr, Stone Mountain, GA	404-296-1520
Miller, Lee/Rte 1, Box 98, Lumpkin, GA	912-838-4959
Player, Joanne/3403 Orchard St, Hapeville, GA	404-767-5542
S C Educational TV/2712 Millwood Ave, Columbia, SC	803-758-7284
Smith, Roscoe/15 Baltimore Pl NW, Atlanta, GA	404-252-3540
Sugar Creek Studio Inc/16 Young St, Atlanta, GA	404-522-3270
Sunshine Scenic Studios/1370 4th St, Sarasota, FL	813-366-8848
Winslow, Geoffrey C/1027 North Ave, Atlanta, GA	404-522-1669

Midwest

Advance Theatrical/125 N Wabash, Chicago, IL	312-889-7700
Becker Studios Inc/2824 W Taylor, Chicago, IL	312-722-4040
Bregstone Assoc/440 S Wabash, Chicago, IL	312-939-5130
Cadillac Plastic/1924 N Paulina, Chicago, IL	312-342-9200
Carpenter, Brent Studio/314 W Institute Pl, Chicago, IL	312-787-1774
Center Stage/Fox Valley Shopping Cntr, Aurora, IL	312-851-9191
Chanco Ltd/3131 West Grand Ave, Chicago, IL	312-638-0363
Chicago Scenic Studios Inc/2217 W Belmont Ave, Chicago, IL	312-477-8362
The Emporium/1551 N Wells, Chicago, IL	312-337-7126
Hartman Furniture & Carpet Co/220 W Kinzie, Chicago, IL	312-664-2800
Hollywood Stage Lighting/5850 N Broadway, Chicago, IL	312-869-3340
House of Drane/410 N Ashland Ave, Chicago, IL	312-829-8686
Merrick Models Ltd/1426 W Fullerton, Chicago, IL	312-281-7787
The Model Shop/415 N State St, Chicago, IL	312-822-9663
Okains Costume & Theater/2713 W Jefferson, Joliet, IL	815-741-9303
Scroungers Inc/351 Lyndale Ave S, Minneapolis, MN	612-823-2340
Starr, Steve Studios/2654 N Clark St, Chicago, IL	312-525-6530
Studio Specialties/409 W Huron, Chicago, IL	312-337-5131
White House Studios/9167 Robinson, Kansas City, MO	913-341-8036

Southwest

Creative Video Productions/5933 Bellaire Blvd #110, Houston, TX	713-661-0478
Desert Wren Designs, Inc/7340 Scottsdale Mall, Scottsdale, AZ	602-941-5056
Doerr, Dean/11321 Greystone, Oklahoma City, OK	405-751-0313
Eats/PO Box 52, Tempe, AZ	602-966-7459
Janet-Nelson/PO Box 143, Tempe, AZ	602-968-3771
Marty, Jack/2225 South First, Garland, TX	214-840-8708
Melancon, Joseph Studios/2934 Elm, Dallas, TX	214-742-2982
Southern Importers/4825 San Jacinto, Houston, TX	713-524-8236
Young Film Productions/PO Box 50105, Tucson, AZ	602-623-5961

West Coast

A & A Special Effects/7021 Havenhurst St, Van Nuys, CA	818-782-6558
Abbe Rents/600 S Normandie, Los Angeles, CA	213-384-5292
Aldik Artificial Flowers Co/7651 Sepulveda Blvd, Van Nuys, CA	213-988-5970
Allen, Walter Plant Rentals/5500 Melrose Ave, Hollywood, CA	213-469-3621
Altbaum, Patti/244-CS Lasky Dr, Beverly Hills, CA	213-553-6269
Anabel's Diversified Services/PO Box 532, Pacific Palisades, CA	213-454-1566
Antiquarian Traders/8483 Melrose Ave, Los Angeles, CA	213-658-6394
Arnelle Sales Co Prop House/7926 Beverly Blvd, Los Angeles, CA	213-930-2900
Asia Plant Rentals/1215 225th St, Torrance, CA	818-775-1811
Astrovision, Inc/7240 Valjean Ave, Van Nuys, CA	818-989-5222
Backings, c/o 20th Century Fox/10201 W Pico Blvd, Los Angeles, CA	213-277-0522
Baronian Manufacturing Co/1865 Farm Bureau Rd, Concord, CA	415-671-7199
Barris Kustom Inc/10811 Riverside Dr, N Hollywood, CA	213-877-2352
Barton Surrey Svc/518 Fairview Ave, Arcadia, CA	818-447-6693
Bischoff's/449 S San Fernando Blvd, Burbank, CA	213-843-7561
Boserup House of Canes/1636 Westwood Blvd, W Los Angeles, CA	213-474-2577
Brown, Mel Furniture/5840 S Figueroa St, Los Angeles, CA	213-778-4444
Buccaneer Cruises/Berth 76W-33 Ports O'Call, San Pedro, CA	213-548-1085
The Burbank Studios Prop Dept/4000 Warner Blvd, Burbank, CA	818-954-6000
Cinema Float/447 N Newport Blvd, Newport Beach, CA	714-675-8888
Cinema Mercantile Co/5857 Santa Monica Blvd, Hollywood, CA	213-466-8201
Cinema Props Co/5840 Santa Monica Blvd, Hollywood, CA	213-466-8201
City Lights/404 S Figueroa, Los Angeles, CA	213-680-9876
Colors of the Wind/2900 Main St, Santa Monica, CA	213-399-8044
Corham Artifical Flowers/11800 Olympic Blvd, Los Angeles, CA	213-479-1166
Custom Neon/3804 Beverly Blvd, Los Angeles, CA	213-386-7945
D'Andrea Glass Etchings/3671 Tacoma Ave, Los Angeles, CA	213-223-7940
Decorative Paper Productions/1818 W 6th St, Los Angeles, CA	213-484-1080
Deutsch Inc/426 S Robertson Blvd, Los Angeles, CA	213-273-4949
Ellis Mercantile Co/169 N LaBrea Ave, Los Angeles, CA	213-933-7334
Featherock Inc/20219 Bohama St, Chatsworth, CA	818-882-3888
First Street Furniture Store/1123 N Bronson Ave, Los Angeles, CA	213-462-6306
Flower Fashions/9960 Santa Monica Blvd, Beverly Hills, CA	213-272-6063
Games Unlimited/8924 Lindblade, Los Angeles, CA	213-836-8920
Golden West Billiard Supply/21260 Deering Court, Canoga Park, CA	213-877-4100
Grand American Fare/3008 Main St, Santa Monica, CA	213-450-4900
Haltzman Office Furniture/1417 S Figueroa, Los Angeles, CA	213-749-7021
The Hand Prop Room/5700 Venice Blvd, Los Angeles, CA	213-931-1534
Hawaii Design Create/1750 Kalakaua Ave #116, Honolulu, HI	808-235-2262
The High Wheelers Inc/109 S Hidalgo, Alhambra, CA	213-576-8648
Hollywood Toys/6562 Hollywood Blvd, Los Angeles, CA	213-465-3119
House of Props Inc/1117 N Gower St, Hollywood, CA	213-463-3166
Hume, Alex R/1527 W Magnolia, Burbank, CA	213-849-1614
Independent Studio Svcs/11907 Wicks St, Sun Valley, CA	213-764-0840
Iwasaki Images/19330 Van Ness Ave, Torrance, CA	213-533-5986
Jackson Shrub Supply/9500 Columbus Ave, Sepulveda, CA	213-893-6939
Johnson, Ray M Studio/5555 Sunset Blvd, Hollywood, CA	213-465-4108
Krofft Enterprise/1040 Las Palmas, Hollywood, CA	213-467-3125
Laughing Cat Design Co/723 1/2 N La Cienega Blvd, Los Angeles, CA	213-854-0135

Production/Support Services

Continued

Please send us your additions and updates.

Living Interiors/7273 Santa Monica Blvd, Los Angeles, CA	213-874-7815
Macduff Flying Circus/5527 Saigon St, Lancaster, CA	805-942-5406
Malibu Florists/21337 Pacific Coast Hwy, Malibu, CA	213-456-2014
Marvin, Lennie Entrprs Ltd/1105 N Hollywood Way, Burbank, CA	818-841-5882
McDermott, Kate/1114 S Point View, Los Angeles, CA	213-935-4101
MGM Studios Prop Dept/10202 W Washington Blvd, Culver City, CA	213-836-3000
Modelmakers/216 Townsend St, San Francisco, CA	415-495-5111
Mole-Richardson/937 N Sycamore Ave, Hollywood, CA	213-851-0111
Moskatels/733 S San Julian St, Los Angeles, CA	213-627-1631
Motion Picture Marine/616 Venice Blvd, Marina del Rey, CA	213-822-1100
Music Center/5616 Santa Monica Blvd, Hollywood, CA	213-469-8143
Omega Cinema Props/5857 Santa Monica Blvd, Los Angeles, CA	213-466-8201
Omega Studio Rentals/5757 Santa Monica Blvd, Hollywood, CA	213-466-8201
Pacific Palisades Florists/15244 Sunset Blvd, Pacific Palisades, CA	213-454-0337
Paramount Studios Prop Dept/5555 Melrose Ave, Los Angeles, CA	213-468-5000
Photo Productions/400 Montgomery St, San Francisco, CA	415-392-5985
The Plantation/38 Arena St, El Segundo, CA	213-322-7877
Post, Don Studios/8211 Lankershim Blvd, N Hollywood, CA	818-768-0811
Producers Studio/650 N Bronson Ave, Los Angeles, CA	213-466-7778
Professional Scenery Inc/7311 Radford Ave, N Hollywood, CA	213-875-1910
Prop City/9336 W Washington, Culver City, CA	213-559-7022
Prop Service West/918 N Orange Dr, Los Angeles, CA	213-461-3371
Rent-A-Mink/6738 Sunset Blvd, Hollywood, CA	213-467-7879
Roschu/6514 Santa Monica Blvd, Hollywood, CA	213-469-2749
Rouzer, Danny Studio/7022 Melrose Ave, Hollywood, CA	213-936-2494
Scale Model Co/4613 W Rosecrans Ave, Los Angeles, CA	213-679-1436
School Days Equipment Co/973 N Main St, Los Angeles, CA	213-223-3474
Silvestri Studios/1733 W Cordova St, Los Angeles, CA	213-735-1481
Snakes/6100 Laurel Canyon Blvd, North Hollywood, CA	213-985-7777
Special Effects Unlimited/752 N Cahuenga Blvd, Hollywood, CA	213-466-3361
Spellman Desk Co/6159 Santa Monica Blvd, Hollywood, CA	213-467-0628
Stage Right/Box 2265, Canyon Country, CA	805-251-4342
Star Sporting Goods/1645 N Highland Ave, Hollywood, CA	213-469-3531
Stembridge Gun Rentals/431 Magnolia, Glendale, CA	818-246-4833
Studio Specialties/3013 Gilroy St, Los Angeles, CA	213-480-3101
Stunts Unlimited/3518 Cahuenga Blvd W, Los Angeles, CA	213-874-0050
Surf, Val/4807 Whitsett, N Hollywood, CA	818-769-6977
Transparent Productions/3410 S Lacienaga Blvd, Los Angeles, CA	213-938-3821
Tri-Tronex Inc/2921 W Alameda Ave, Burbank, CA	213-849-6115
Tropizon Plant Rentals/1401 Pebble Vale, Monterey Park, CA	213-269-2010
UPA Pictures/4440 Lakeside Dr, Burbank, CA	213-556-3800

Locations

New York City

Act Travel/310 Madison Ave	212-697-9550
Ayoub, Jimmy/132 E 16th St	212-598-4467
C & C Productions/445 E 80th St	212-472-3700
Carmichael-Moore, Bob Inc/PO Box 5	212-255-0465
Dancerschool/400 Lafayette St	212-260-0453
Davidson/Frank Photo-Stylists/209 W 86th St #701	212-799-2651
Howell, T J Interiors/301 E 38th St	212-532-6267
Juckes, Geoff/295 Bennett Ave	212-567-5676
Kopro, Ken/206 E 6th St	212-677-1798
Leach, Ed Inc/160 Fifth Ave	212-691-3450
Location Connection/31 E 31st St	212-684-1888
Location Locators/225 E 63rd St	212-832-1866
Loft Locations/50 White St	212-966-6408
Marks, Arthur/140 E 40th St	212-685-2761
Myriad Communications, Inc/208 W 30th St	212-564-4340

NY State Film Commission/230 Park Ave #834	212-309-0540
The Perfect Place Ltd/182 Amity St	718-570-6252
Ruekberg, Brad/3211 Ave I #5H	718-377-3506
Terrestris/409 E 60th St	212-758-8181
This Must Be The Place/2119 Albermarle Terrace	718-282-3454
Unger, Captain Howard/80 Beach Rd	718-639-3578
Wolfson, Paula/227 W 10th St	212-741-3048

Northeast

C-M Associates/268 New Mark, Rockville, MD	301-340-7070
Cinemagraphics/100 Massachusetts Ave, Boston, MA	617-266-2200
Connecticut State Travel Office/210 Washington St, Hartford, CT	203-566-3383
Cooper Productions/175 Walnut St, Brookline, MA	617-738-7278
Delaware State Travel Service/99 Kings Highway, Dover, DE	302-736-4254
Dobush, Jim/148 W Mountain, Ridgefield, CT	203-431-3718
E-Fex/623 Pennsylvania Ave SE, Washington, DC	202-543-1241
Film Services of WV Library Comm/1900 Washington St E, Charleston, WV	304-348-3977
Florentine Films, Inc/25 Main St, Northampton, MA	413-584-0816
Forma, Belle/433 Claflin Ave, Mamaroneck, NY	914-698-2598
Gilmore, Robert Assoc Inc/990 Washington St, Dedham, MA	617-329-6633
Girl/Scout Locations/One Hillside Ave, Port Washington, NY	516-883-8409
Great Locations/97 Windsor Road, Tenafly, NJ	201-567-1455
Hackerman, Nancy Prod Inc/6 East Eager St, Baltimore, MD	301-685-2727
Hampton Locations/109 Hill Street, South Hampton, NY	516-283-2160
The Hermitage/PO Box 4, Yorktown Heights, NY	914-632-5315
Jurgielewicz, Annie/PO Box 422, Cambridge, MA	617-628-1141
Krause, Janet L/43 Linnaean St #26, Cambridge, MA	617-492-3223
Lewis, Jay/87 Ripley St, Newton Center, MA	617-332-1516
The Location Hunter/16 Iselin Terr, Larchmont, NY	914-834-2181
Location Scouting Service/153 Sidney St, Oyster Bay, NY	516-922-1759
Location Services/30 Rockledge Rd, W Redding !, CT	203-938-3227
Location Unlimited/24 Briarcliff, Tenafly, NJ	201-567-2809
Maine State Development Office/193 State St, Augusta, ME	207-289-2656
Maryland Film Commission/45 Talvert, Annapolis, MD	301-269-3577
Massachusetts State Film Bureau/100 Cambridge St, Boston, MA	617-727-3330
McGlynn, Jack/34 Buffum St, Salem, MA	617-745-8764
Nassau Farmer's Market/600 Hicksville Rd, Bethpage, NY	516-931-2046
New Hampshire Vacation Travel/PO Box 856, Concord, NH	603-271-2666
NJ State Motion Pic Dev/Gateway One, Newark, NJ	201-648-6279
Nozik, Michael/9 Cutler Ave, Cambridge, MA	617-783-4315
Pennington Inc/72 Edmund St, Edison, NJ	201-985-9090
Pennsylvania Film Bureau/461 Forum Bldg, Harrisburg, PA	717-787-5333
Penrose Productions/4 Sandalwood Dr, Livingston, NJ	201-992-4264
PhotoSonics/1116 N Hudson St, Arlington, VA	703-522-1116
Proteus Location Services/9217 Baltimore Blvd, College Park, MD	301-441-2928
RenRose Locations, Ltd/4 Sandalwood Dr, Livingston, NJ	201-992-4264
Rhode Island State Tourist Division/7 Jackson Walkway, Providence, RI	401-277-2601
Strawberries Finders Service/Buck County, Reigelsville, PA	215-346-8000
Terry, Karen/131 Boxwood Dr, Kings Park, NY	516-724-3964
Upstate Production Services, Inc/277 Alexander St #510, Rochester, NY	716-546-5417
Verange, Joe - Century III/545 Boylston St, Boston, MA	617-267-9800
Vermont State Travel Division/134 State, Montpelier, VT	802-828-3236
Washington DC Public Space Committee/415 12th St, N W Washington, DC	202-629-4084

Southeast

Alabama State Film Commission/340 North Hull St, Montgomery, AL	800-633-5898
Baker, Sherry/1823 Indiana Ave, Atlanta, GA	404-373-6666
Bruns, Ken & Gayle/7810 SW 48th Court, Miami, FL	305-666-2928
Charisma Prod Services/PO Box 19033, Jacksonville, FL	904-724-8483
Crigler, MB/Smooth As Glass Prod Svcs/607 Bass St, Nashville, TN	615-254-6061
Dangar, Jack/3640 Ridge Rd, Smyrna, GA	404-434-3640

Darracott, David/1324 Briarcliff Rd #5, Atlanta, GA	404-872-0219
Fl State Motion Picture/TV Svcs/107 W Gaines St, Tallahassee, FL	904-487-1100
Georgia State Film Office/PO Box 1776, Atlanta, GA	404-656-3591
Harris, George/2875 Mabry Lane NE, Atlanta, GA	404-231-0116
Irene Marie/3212 S Federal Hwy, Ft Lauderdale, FL	305-522-3262
Kentucky Film Comm/Berry Hill Mansion/Louisville, Frankfort, KY	502-564-3456
Kupersmith, Tony/320 N Highland Ave NE, Atlanta, GA	404-577-5319
McDonald, Stew/6905 N Coolidge Ave, Tampa, FL	813-886-3773
Miller, Lee/Rte 1, Box 98, Lumpkin, GA	912-838-4959
Mississippi State Film Commission/PO Box 849, Jackson, MS	601-359-3449
Natchez Film Comm/Liberty Pk Hwy, Hwy 16, Natchez, MS	601-446-6345
North Carolina Film Comm/430 N Salisbury St, Raleigh, NC	919-733-9900
Player, Joanne/3403 Orchard St, Hapeville, GA	404-767-5542
Reel Wheels/2267 NE 164th St, Miami, FL	305-947-9304
Remington Models & Talent/2480 E Commercial Blvd PH, Ft Lauderdale, FL	305-566-5420
Rose, Sheila/8218 NW 8th St, Plantation, FL	305-473-9747
South Florida Location Finders/7621 SW 59th Court, S Miami, FL	305-445-0739
Tennessee Film Comm/James Polk Off Bldg, Nashville, TN	615-741-3456
TN State Econ & Comm Dev/1007 Andrew Jackson Bldg, Nashville, TN	615-741-1888
USVI Film Promotion Office/, St Thomas, VI	809-774-1331
Virginia Division of Tourism/202 North 9th St, Richmond, VA	804-786-2051

Midwest

A-Stock Photo Finder/1030 N State St, Chicago, IL	312-645-0611
Illinois State Film Office/100 W Randolph #3-400, Chicago, IL	312-793-3600
Indiana State Tourism Development/1 N Capital, Indianapolis, IN	317-232-8860
Iowa State Development Commission/600 E Court Ave #A, Des Moines, IA	515-281-3251
Kansas State Dept-Econ Div/503 Kansas Ave, Topeka, KS	913-296-3481
Location Services Film & Video/417 S 3rd St, Minneapolis, MN	612-338-3359
Manya Nogg Co/9773 Lafayette Plaza, Omaha, NB	402-397-8887
Michigan State Travel Bureau/PO Box 30226, Lansing, MI	517-373-0670
Minnesota State Tourism Division/419 N Robert, St Paul, MN	612-296-5029
Missouri State Tourism Commission/301 W High St, Jefferson City, MO	314-751-3051
ND State Business & Industrial/Liberty Memorial Bldg, Bismarck, ND	701-224-2810
Ohio Film Bureau/30 E Broad St, Columbus, OH	614-466-2284
Station 12 Producers Express/1759 Woodgrove Ln, Southfield, MI	313-569-7707
Stock Market/4211 Flora Place, St Louis, MO	314-773-2298

Southwest

Alamo Village/PO Box 528, Brackettville, TX	512-563-2580
Arkansas State Dept of Economics/#1 Capital Mall, Little Rock, AR	501-371-1121
Blair, Tanya Agency/3000 Carlisle, Dallas, TX	214-748-8353
Cinema America/Box 56566, Houston, TX	713-780-8819
Dawson, Kim Agency/PO Box 585060, Dallas, TX	214-638-2414
Duncan, S Wade/PO Box 140273, Dallas, TX	214-828-1367
El Paso Film Liaison/5 Civic Center Plaza, El Paso, TX	915-544-3650
Epic Film Productions/1203 W 44th St, Austin, TX	512-452-9461
Fashion Consultants/262 Camelot Center, Richardson, TX	214-234-4006
Flach, Bob/3513 Norma, Garland, TX	214-272-8431
Fowlkes, Rebecca W/412 Canterbury Hill, San Antonio, TX	512-826-4142
Grapevine Productions/3214-A Hemlock Avenue, Austin, TX	512-472-0894
Greenblatt, Linda/6722 Waggoner, Dallas, TX	214-691-6552
Griffin, Gary Productions/12667 Memorial Dr #4, Houston, TX	713-465-9017
Kessel, Mark/3631 Granada, Dallas, TX	214-526-0415
MacLean, John/10017 Woodgrove, Dallas, TX	214-343-0181
Maloy, Buz/Rt 1 Box 155, Kyle, TX	512-398-3148

Maloy, John W/718 W 35th St, Austin, TX	512-453-9660
McLaughlin, Ed M/3512 Rashti Court, Ft Worth, TX	817-927-2310
Murray Getz Commer & Indust Phot/2310 Genessee, Houston, TX	713-526-4451
Nichols, Beverly & Skipper Richardson/6043 Vanderbilt Ave, Dallas, TX	214-349-3171
OK State Tourism-Rec Dept/500 Will Rogers Bldg, Oklahoma City, OK	405-521-3981
Oklahoma Film Comm/500 Will Rogers Bldg, Oklahoma City, OK	405-521-3525
Putman, Eva M/202 Dover, Richardson, TX	214-783-9616
Ranchland - Circle R/Rt 3, Box 229, Roanoke, TX	817-430-1561
Ray, Al/2304 Houston Street, San Angelo, TX	915-949-2716
Ray, Rudolph/2231 Freeland Avenue, San Angelo, TX	915-949-6784
Reinninger, Laurence H/501 North IH 35, Austin, TX	512-478-8593
San Antonio Zoo & Aquar/3903 N St Marys, San Antonio, TX	512-734-7184
Senn, Loyd C/PO Box 6060, Lubbock, TX	806-792-2000
Summers, Judy/1504 Harvard, Houston, TX	713-661-1440
Taylor, Peggy Talent/6311 N O'Connor 3 Dallas Comm, Irving, TX	214-869-1515
TBK Talent Enterprises/5255 McCullough, San Antonio, TX	512-822-0508
Texas Film Commission/PO Box 12428 Capitol Station, Austin, TX	512-475-3785
Texas Pacific Film Video, Inc/501 North IH 35, Austin, TX	512-478-8585
Texas World Entrtnmnt/8133 Chadbourne Road, Dallas, TX	214-358-0857
Tucson Film Comm/Ofc of Mayor Box 27370, Tucson, AZ	602-791-4000
Wild West Stunt Company/Box T-789, Stephenville, TX	817-965-4342
Young Film Productions/PO Box 50105, Tucson, AZ	602-623-5961
Zimmerman and Associates, Inc/411 Bonham, San Antonio, TX	512-225-6708
Zuniga, Tony/2616 North Flores #2, San Antonio, TX	512-227-9660

Rocky Mountain

Montana Film Office/1424 Ninth Ave, Helena, MT	406-449-2654
Wyoming Film Comm/IH 25 & College Dr #51, Cheyenne, WY	307-777-7851

West Coast

California Film Office/6922 Hollywood Blvd, Hollywood, CA	213-736-2465
Daniels, Karil, Point of View Prod/2477 Folsom St, San Francisco, CA	415-821-0435
Design Art Studios/1128 N Las Palmas, Hollywood, CA	213-464-9118
Excor Travel/1750 Kalakaua Ave #116, Honolulu, HI	808-946-6614
Film Permits Unlimited/8058 Allott Ave, Van Nuys, CA	213-997-6197
Herod, Thomas Jr/PO Box 2534, Hollywood, CA	213-353-0911
Juckes, Geoff/3185 Durand Dr, Hollywood, CA	213-465-6604
Location Enterprises Inc/6725 Sunset Blvd, Los Angeles, CA	213-469-3141
The Location Co/8646 Wilshire Blvd, Beverly Hills, CA	213-855-7075
Mindseye/767 Northpoint, San Francisco, CA	415-441-4578
Minot, Abby/53 Canyon Rd, Berkeley, CA	415-841-9600
Newhall Ranch/23823 Valencia, Valencia, CA	818-362-1515
Pacific Production & Location Svc/424 Nahua St, Honolulu, HI	808-926-6188
San Francisco Conv/Visitors Bur/1390 Market St #260, San Francisco, CA	415-626-5500

Sets

New York City

Abstracta Structures/347 Fifth Ave	212-532-3710
Alcamo Marble Works/541 W 22nd St	212-255-5224
Baker, Alex/30 W 69th St	212-799-2069
Coulson, Len/717 Lexington Ave	212-688-5155
Dynamic Interiors/760 McDonald Ave	718-435-6326
Golden Office Interiors/574 Fifth Ave	212-719-5150
LaFerla, Sandro/108 W 25th St	212-620-0693
Lincoln Scenic Studio/560 W 34th St	212-244-2700
Moroxko, Bruce/41 White St	212-226-8832

Production/Support Services

Continued

Please send us your additions and updates.

Oliphant, Sarah/38 Cooper Square	212-741-1233
Plexability Ltd/200 Lexington Ave	212-679-7826
Set Shop/3 W 20 St	212-929-4845
Siciliano, Frank/125 Fifth Ave	212-620-4075
Stage Scenery/155 Attorney St	212-460-5050
Theater Technology Inc/37 W 20th St	212-929-5380
Variety Scenic Studio/25-19 Borden Ave	718-392-4747
Yurkiw, Mark/568 Broadway	212-243-0928

Northeast

The Focarino Studio/31 Deep Six Dr, East Hampton, NY	516-324-7637
Foothills Theater Company/PO Box 236, Worcester, MA	617-754-0546
Penrose Productions/4 Sandalwood Dr, Livingston, NJ	201-992-4264
Trapp, Patricia/42 Stanton Rd, Brookline, MA	617-734-9321
Videocom, Inc/502 Sprague St, Dedham, MA	617-329-4080
White Oak Design/PO Box 1164, Marblehead, MA	617-426-7171

Southeast

Crigler, MB/Smooth As Glass Prod Svcs/607 Bass St, Nashville, TN	615-254-6061
Enter Space/20 14th St NW, Atlanta, GA	404-885-1139
The Great Southern Stage/15221 NE 21 Ave, N Miami Beach, FL	305-947-0430
Kupersmith, Tony/320 N Highland Ave NE, Atlanta, GA	404-577-5319
Sugar Creek Scenic Studio, Inc/465 Bishop St, Atlanta, GA	404-351-9404

Midwest

Becker Studio/2824 W Taylor, Chicago, IL	312-722-4040
Centerwood Cabinets/3700 Main St NE, Blaine, MN	612-786-2094
Chicago Scenic Studios Inc/213 N Morgan, Chicago, IL	312-942-1483
Dimension Works/4130 W Belmont, Chicago, IL	312-545-2233
Douglas Design/2165 Lakeside Ave, Cleveland, OH	216-621-2558
Grand Stage Lighting Co/630 W Lake, Chicago, IL	312-332-5611
Morrison, Tamara/1225 Morse, Chicago, IL	312-864-0954

Southwest

Country Roads/701 Ave B, Del Rio, TX	512-775-7991
Crabb, Ken/3066 Ponder Pl, Dallas, TX	214-352-0581
Dallas Stage Lighting & Equipment/1818 Chestnut, Dallas, TX	214-428-1818
Dallas Stage Scenery Co, Inc/3917 Willow St, Dallas, TX	214-821-0002
Dunn, Glenn E/7412 Sherwood Rd, Austin, TX	512-441-0377
Edleson, Louis/6568 Lake Circle, Dallas, TX	214-823-7180
Eschberger, Jerry/6401 South Meadows, Austin, TX	512-447-4795
Freeman Design & Display Co/2233 Irving Blvd, Dallas, TX	214-638-8800
H & H Special Effects/2919 Chisholm Trail, San Antonio, TX	512-826-8214
Houston Stage Equipment/2301 Dumble, Houston, TX	713-926-4441
O'Dell, Dale/2040 Bissonet, Houston, TX	713-521-2611
Reed, Bill Decorations/333 First Ave, Dallas, TX	214-823-3154
Texas Scenic Co Inc/5423 Jackwood Dr, San Antonio, TX	512-684-0091
Texas Set Design/3103 Oak Lane, Dallas, TX	214-426-5511

Rocky Mountain

Love, Elisa/1035 Walnut, Boulder, CO	303-442-4877

West Coast

Grosh, R L & Sons Scenic Studio/4144 Sunset Blvd, Los Angeles, CA	213-662-1134
Act Design & Execution/PO Box 5054, Sherman Oaks, CA	818-788-4219
American Scenery/18555 Eddy St, Northridge, CA	818-886-1585
Backings, J C/10201 W Pico Blvd, Los Angeles, CA	213-277-0522
Carthay Set Services/5176 Santa Monica Blvd, Hollywood, CA	213-469-5618
Carthay Studio/5907 W Pico, Los Angeles, CA	213-938-2101
CBS Special Effects/7800 Beverly Blvd, Los Angeles, CA	213-852-2345
Cloutier Inc/704 N Gardner, Los Angeles, CA	213-655-1263
Erecter Set Inc/1150 S LaBrea, Hollywood, CA	213-938-4762
Grosh, RL & Sons/4144 Sunset Blvd, Los Angeles, CA	213-662-1134
Hawaii Design Create/1750 Kalakaua Ave #116, Honolulu, HI	808-235-2262
Hollywood Scenery/6605 Elenor Ave, Hollywood, CA	213-467-6272
Hollywood Stage/6650 Santa Monica Blvd, Los Angeles, CA	213-466-4393
Krofft Entrprs/1040 Las Palmas, Hollywood, CA	213-467-3125
Pacific Studios/8315 Melrose Ave, Los Angeles, CA	213-653-3093
Producers Studio/650 N Bronson Ave, Los Angeles, CA	213-466-3111
RJ Show Time/1011 Gower St, Hollywood, CA	213-467-2127
Shafton Inc/5500 Cleon Ave, N Hollywood, CA	818-985-5025
Superstage/5724 Santa Monica Blvd, Los Angeles, CA	213-464-0296
Triangle Scenery/1215 Bates Ave, Los Angeles, CA	213-661-1262

IndexIllustrators, Photographers & Graphic Designers